BRITISH
DESTROYERS
& FRIGATES

BRITISH DESTROYERS & FRIGATES

THE SECOND WORLD WAR AND AFTER

NORMAN FRIEDMAN

SHIP PLANS BY A D BAKER III
With additional drawings by Alan Raven

CHATHAM PUBLISHING

LONDON

MBI PUBLISHING, MINNESOTA

Frontispiece
HMS *Dunkirk*, the last of the unconverted 1943 'Battle' class to remain in service.
All uncredited photographs from the collection of A D Baker III

Copyright © Norman Friedman 2006
Ship plans © A D Baker III
Additional drawings © Alan Raven

First published in Great Britain in 2006 by Chatham Publishing,
Park House, 1 Russell Gardens, London NW11 9NN

Chatham Publishing is an imprint of Lionel Leventhal Ltd

Distributed in the United States of America by
MBI Publishing Company, Suite 200, 380 Jackson Street,
St Paul, MN 55101-3885, USA

British Library Cataloguing in Publication Data
Friedman, Norman, 1946-
British destroyers and frigates, the Second World War and after
1. Great Britain. Royal Navy – History – 20th century
2. Destroyers (Warships – Great Britain – History
3. Destroyer escorts – Great Britain – History
4. Frigates) – Great Britain – History – 20th century
I. Title
623.8'254' 0941

ISBN-10: 1861761376
ISBN-13: 19781861761378

A Library of Congress Catalog Card No. is available on request

ISBN 1 86176 137 6

Designed by Roger Daniels
Printed and bound in Singapore by Kyodo Printing Company

Contents

To absent friends:
David Lyon and Antony Preston

A/A	anti-aircraft		FADE	Fleet Aircraft Direction Escort
ABCD	atomic, bacteriological, chemical defence		FBC	Future Building Committee
ADR	Aircraft Direction Room		FKC	Fuse Keeping Clock
A/D	aircraft direction		ft	feet
A/S	anti-submarine		ft/sec	feet per second
AAW	anti-aircraft warfare		GAP	Guided Anti-air Projectile (missile)
ACNS	Assistant Chief of the Naval Staff		GDS	gunnery direction system
ACNS(H)	Assistant Chief of the Naval Staff (Home Waters)		GIUK	Greenland-Iceland-UK (gap)
ACNS(W)	Assistant Chief of the Naval Staff (Weapons)		GM	metacentric height
ACNS(T)	Assistant Chief of the Naval Staff (Training)		GNAT	German Naval Acoustic Torpedo
ADAWS	Action Data Automation Weapon System		GRU	Gyro Rate Unit
ADR	aircraft direction room		GRUB	Gyro Rate Unit Box
AEW	airborne early warning		GZ	Righting Lever (of stability)
AFCB	Admiralty Fire Control Box		HA	high angle
AFCC	Admiralty Fire Control Clock		HE	high explosive
AIC	Action Information Centre		HF/DF	High Frequency Direction Finding
AIO	Action Information Organisation		HMAS	His/Her Majesty's Australian Ship
ASE	Admiralty Signals Establishment		HMCS	His/Her Majesty's Canadian Ship
ASP	Automatic Surface Plot		HMNZS	His/Her Majesty's New Zealand Ship
ASW	anti-submarine warfare		HMS	His/Her Majesty's Ship
BAD	British Admiralty Delegation		HP	horsepower
BHP	brake horsepower		HSMS	High Speed Mine Sweep
BUSTER	Bofors Universal Stabilized Tachymetric Electric Radar		HTP	high test peroxide
CAAIS	Computer-Assisted Action Information System		ICS	Integrated Communication System
CACS	Computer-Assisted Combat System		IFF	Identification, Friend or Foe
CDS	Comprehensive Display System		IHP	indicated horsepower
CID	Committee on Imperial Defence		in	inches
CIWS	Close-In Weapons System		kHz	kilohertz
C-in-C	Commander-in-Chief		kts	knots
CNS	Chief of the Naval Staff		kW	kilowatts
CO	commanding officer		LA	low angle
CPO	Chief Petty Officer		LWL	length on waterline
CRBF	Close Range Barrage Fire		m	metres
DACR	Direct Action Close Range		MCMV	mine countermeasures vessel
DASW	Director of Anti-Submarine Warfare		MCRS	Medium Range, Constant Speed
DAWT	Director of Air Warfare and Training		MDAP	Mutual Defence Assistance Program
DCNS	Deputy Chief of the Naval Staff		MFAR	Multi Function Array Radar
DCT	director control tower		MHz	megahertz
DEE	Director of Electrical Engineering		MoD	Ministry of Defence
DGD	Director of Gunnery Division		MTB	motor torpedo boat
DGS	Director General Ships		NID	Naval Intelligence Division
DME	Director of Mechanical Engineering		OA	overall
DNAD	Director of Naval Air Division		OPV	Offshore Patrol Vessel
DNAW	Director of Naval Air Warfare		PAC	Parachute and Cable (rockets)
DNC	Director of Naval Construction		PO	Petty Officer
DND	Department of Navigation and Direction		psi	pounds per square inch
DNO	Director of Naval Ordnance		RA(D)	Rear Admiral (Destroyers)
DNOR	Director of Naval Operational Requirements		RAM	Rolling Airframe Missile
DNOT	Division of Naval Operations and Training		RCNC	Royal Corps of Naval Constructors
DNSD	Division of Naval Staff Duties		RFA	Royal Fleet Auxiliary
DNW	Division of Naval Warfare		rpb	rounds per barrel
DOAE	Defence Operational Analysis Establishment		RPC	remote power control
DoD	Director of Dockyards		rpg	rounds per gun
DOD	Director of Operations Division		RPM	revolutions per minute
DoD(H)	Director of Dockyards (Home Waters)		SCC	Ship Characteristics Committee
DPT	Digital Plot Transmitter		SDPC	Ship Design Policy Committee
DRE	Department of Radio Equipment		SHP	shaft horsepower
DRW	Department of Radio Warfare		SNO	senior naval officer
DTAS	Department of Torpedoes and A/S		SSGW	Small Ship Guided Weapon
DTASW	Department of Torpedoes, A/S and Weapons		STAAG	Stabilised Tachymetric AA Gun
DTD	Director of Tactical Division		SULE	Superintendent of Underwater Launching Equipment
DTM	Director of Torpedoes and Mines		SYMES	Systematic Machinery Programme
DTSD	Director of Tactical and Staff Duties Division		TIU	target indication unit
DUW	Department of Undersea Warfare		tons/sq in	tons per square inch
DUM	Director of Underwater Weapons Materiel		TSDS	Two Speed Destroyer Sweep
E-in-C	Engineer-in-Chief		UNDEX	Underwater Experiment Establishment
ECM	electronic counter-measures		UP	Unrotated Projectile (rocket)
ECCM	electronic counter-counter-measures		USS	United States' Ship
ERA	Engine Room Artificer		VCNS	Vice Chief of the Naval Staff
ESM	electronic surveillance measures		VDS	variable-depth sonar
EW	electronic warfare		yds	yards

CHAPTER 1

Introduction

The destroyer began with the torpedo, the first capital-ship killing weapon a small ship could carry. Just before the First World War the Royal Navy learned, for the first time in the world, how to wield its fleet's destroyers both to defend against enemy torpedo attacks and to deliver attacks of its own. The great surprise of the First World War was that the fast heavily-armed ship designed to fight a torpedo war was at least as useful in many other roles, both with the fleet and outside it. Here a First World War 'V&W' class destroyer fires a torpedo. (Royal Naval Museum, Portsmouth)

This book tells the story of British destroyers and escorts (sloops, later frigates) from the slide towards the Second World War to the present. It therefore begins in the mid-1930s. A later volume will, it is hoped, carry the story back to the first destroyers and also to the first ships intended to screen the battle fleet against torpedo attack. Throughout the period covered by this book the Royal Navy was under terrible financial strain as it tried to contend with rapidly-changing technology and also with a rapidly-changing strategic situation. Often its approach was extremely creative, for example blending nominally different types of ships together so that an affordable force could cover the full range of roles. Examples include the 'Tribal' class destroyers, the 'Hunt' class destroyer/fast escorts, the abortive post-war cruiser/destroyer, and the *Leander* class frigates.

Throughout, Britain had to balance home or European defence against the defence of overseas interests, which included the Empire both formal and informal. The two roles were connected. The two Empires provided much of Britain's economic muscle, and the raw materials needed to produce whatever would be used for home defence. Conversely, a Britain weak at home could not afford sufficient forces to protect distant possessions. Home and Empire were bound together by the sea lanes. Access to the resources of Empire certainly encouraged Winston Churchill to hold out against the Germans

in 1940. Conversely Churchill saw the Battle of the Atlantic, the battle to retain access to overseas resources, as crucial. In peacetime the Royal Navy, as Britain's only fully mobile force, was key to protecting the Empire against subversion and against local aggression.

After the Second World War the same sorts of threat surfaced in the form of regular Soviet forces in Europe threatening Britain while revolutionaries (and local armies) threatened the Commonwealth and the remaining informal Empire in the Middle and Far East. The latter threat was greater after 1945 than it had been before 1939. Against this rising threat Britain had much-reduced resources, about a quarter of national wealth having been expended to win the war. To some extent that was made up for by US support: in 1949 First Sea Lord had to admit that the Royal Navy alone could no longer protect British sea lanes.[1]

In 1948 the British Government designated 1957 as the 'year of maximum danger', the target for fleet modernisation.[2] In what amounted to an inversion of the pre-war Ten Year Rule, it was accepted that the Soviets would probably fight, but that they would be restrained until 1957 both by wartime devastation and by a lack of nuclear weapons (assuming that they would not have their first atomic bomb until 1952). Given the 1957 horizon, the British could concentrate on developing new weapons and systems until the mid-1950s. The outbreak of war in Korea in 1950 (following the Soviet bomb test in 1949) was a terrifying surprise: it was taken throughout the West as a precursor of the Third World War. For Britain, preparation for such a war meant creating an army to help block a Soviet advance into Western Europe, and creating a fleet to fight a new version of the Battle of the Atlantic. The emphasis was on frigates and on minesweepers.

As their attempt to rearm failed, the British found them-

FOOTNOTES: Notebooks are the constructor's notebooks held by the Brass Foundry station of the National Maritime Museum. ADM, PREM and T225 references are to files at the Public Record Office of The National Archives (TNA).
[1] ADM 205/83. The three 'pillars' of British strategy were the defence of the United Kingdom itself, of sea communications, and of the Middle East. Hence the need for a balanced fleet, rather than one specialising in ASW or in mine countermeasures, the two chief elements of trade protection. In May 1949 the First Sea Lord wrote that the affordable 'Restricted Revised' fleet could be cut back from the wartime fleet proposed the previous September (reductions including eight FADE and forty-eight frigates) 'by relying on the American Navy for ... half the Naval Forces required for the control of the sea communications in the North Atlantic and the Mediterranean, and for all the forces required for the control of sea communications in the South Atlantic and Pacific'. In the same file ACNS wrote that 'It is politically impossible for this country, whose very life depends on secure sea communications, to [surrender] some part of its essential sea security ... wholly to the safe keeping of another power, however friendly. [That] would mean accepting complete domination of our policy in peace and war by another country'.
[2] In 1934 the year 1939 was designated the year of maximum danger, presumably as a way of dramatising the reversal of the earlier Ten Year Rule. The 1939 date did not, it appears, become a formal target for rearmament in the way that the 1957 date was treated.
[3] ADM 167/144. A review of naval policy, as part of the Chiefs of Staff Radical Review, began in 1954. Its Steering Committee consisted of Controller, VCNS, the Secretary of the Board and a representative of the Second Sea Lord (responsible for personnel). A December 1954 revision of the initial June 1954 naval policy paper argued that both sides would probably avoid risking uncontrollable escalation because all-out war was increasingly unfightable. Also, the Soviets believed that the West was doomed, and thus that their main task was to deter a Western attack against themselves. Cold War tensions would most likely be released in local (Third World) wars. As reflected in internal studies completed in 1955–6, contemporary US Navy long-range planners reached very similar conclusions. The first version of the Admiralty paper argued that in the H-bomb era a reserve fleet could survive only by being dispersed to commercial ports too minor to be nuclear targets. The necessary additional manpower was not available; the reserve fleet would have to be cut. ADM 167/150 includes a June 1957 study of naval measures applicable only to Global War, hence probably to be cut.

selves rethinking their strategy. They began to see nuclear war as unfightable; deterrence might preclude a Third World War. Soviet aggression would make itself felt in 'warm' rather than 'hot' wars in the Third World. For the Royal Navy, the shift became explicit as a result of the 1957 Defence Review.[3] Examples of such 'warm war' involvement were the 1956 Suez attack, the 1961 Kuwait crisis, the 1964 confrontation with Indonesia, the Rhodesian blockade, the Falklands War of 1982, and the Armilla Patrol in the Gulf from 1980 onwards. Now attention was concentrated on amphibious and carrier-centred strike forces rather than on the convoy escorts of the first post-war decade. Initially the shift away from the 'hot war' mission promised considerable savings, as the number of frigates and destroyers could be cut drastically, and the reserve fleet pruned.

However, it was understood that NATO, which was concerned entirely with the 'hot' war, was a major element in the deterrence which had made the shift possible. A considerable British commitment to NATO remained, mainly in the form of substantial ground and air forces, which by the 1960s were increasingly expensive because the Soviet forces they faced were more and more capable. Meanwhile defence, including naval, resources declined.[4] A crisis came in 1966: the new Labour government decided that it could not afford to replace the ageing carriers, the core of the 'warm war' capability. For a short time the Royal Navy argued that it still needed a very numerous fleet of escorts to handle global commitments, but the government soon announced withdrawal from East of Suez – from what was left, it seemed, of the Empires.[5] NATO became the Royal Navy's priority. The naval power-projection role was justified by the need to reinforce northern Norway in wartime. The last pre-Falklands defence review, in 1981, would have lopped off this capability as unaffordable, reducing the Royal Navy to an ASW force useful only in conjunction with other NATO navies. However, the Falklands War, in 1982, showed that the overseas role could not be avoided; flexible naval forces were essential insurance against strategic surprise. Even before the Falklands, the 'Cod War' with Iceland had demanded considerable naval forces to protect a vital British interest. Beginning in November 1975 three and later five frigates had to be kept constantly on patrol; ultimately twenty-one frigates were involved. With the

end of the Cold War the strategic situation reversed itself, the overseas role now being dominant. This shift is visible in the decision to build the Type 45 destroyer to screen new carriers and to dispose of modern but specialised Type 23 frigates.

Close co-operation between the United States and Britain, at least on an informal level, seems to have survived the Second World War. The US Navy supplied equipment for British trials, and the British were kept well aware of the early post-war US naval building programme. More generally, knowledge of US building programmes seems to have had considerable influence on the Royal Navy. Co-operation in ASW and in intelligence seems to have been particularly close. Later there was crucial material assistance. During the very difficult early post-war period, the British seem to have assumed that, should the Third World War break out, the United States would once again be the arsenal of democracy. They therefore adopted US calibres (as in the 5in Medium Calibre Gun which figured in the abortive cruiser/destroyer) and gun barrels (the elements of guns which wear out most quickly), if not US gun mounts. The British bought US lightweight torpedoes for escorts and for their helicopters. Under the Mutual Defense Assistance Programme (MDAP) of the early 1950s the US Navy supplied some key equipment. Examples were the 3in/50 gun and the SPS-6 destroyer radar.

The Role of the Destroyer

The role of the destroyer, which was usually integral to the fleet, changed radically over the period this book covers. Perhaps the most important development after the First World War was that the fleet was likely to steam a considerable distance before engaging an enemy fleet, at least in the favoured case of the Far East. Thus destroyers would have both a main battle role and a screening role *en route* to battle, in the latter case against submarine, air and mine threats. None of these threats would apply during a battle, because enemy aviators and submariners would find it too difficult to distinguish friend from foe, and because it would be too easy for a fleet to accidentally run over a minefield laid for its own benefit.

For all navies, the destroyer mattered because she carried the ship-killing torpedo. Mass torpedo attacks could be worthwhile even if they were not pressed home. For example, the enemy fleet commander might feel compelled to turn, as at Jutland, to avoid their torpedoes. That torpedo attack saved the German fleet from destruction, although it made no hits. In the Battle of the Barents Sea in the Second World War, destroyers covering a convoy deterred German heavy units from attacking by threatening torpedo attacks. Similar tactics proved effective in the Mediterranean against Italian heavy units. Torpedoes were also used as intended: for example, in 1945 a British destroyer flotilla sank the large Japanese cruiser *Haguro* with a perfectly-executed torpedo attack.

The British hoped for more. Beginning about 1913 they

[4] Keith Speed, who was Navy Minister in the early Thatcher Government, explained that about 1980 inflation in defence goods was running about 5 per cent above other forms of inflation, so that a pledge within NATO to increase spending by 3 per cent a year above inflation actually bought less each year. Speed, *Sea Change* (Ashgrove Press, Bath: 1982), p 86.

[5] Withdrawal from Aden was announced in February 1966 as one consequence of the Defence Review that eliminated the British carriers (Aden was evacuated in November 1967). In July 1967 withdrawal from Singapore and Malaysia was announced. However, the British would retain capability in the region. Under continuing economic pressure the British government announced in January 1968 that it would withdraw completely from East of Suez, and that the carriers would be retired in 1972 rather than in 1975, as originally planned. Bahrain, the last British naval base in the Gulf, was closed on 15 July 1971. The Singapore naval base was handed over to the Singapore government on 1 November 1971. A residual British/Australian/New Zealand presence ended in 1974. Without the need to protect the route to the East, the Mediterranean was no longer a vital area. Withdrawal from Malta (by 31 March 1979) was announced in the 1975 Defence White Paper, and on 1 April 1976 the British ended their continuous naval presence in the Mediterranean.

sought to use their own destroyers both to break up enemy destroyer attacks and to attack the enemy battle fleet. There was a major problem. Battleships all had anti-destroyer guns. It was extremely difficult for gunners to distinguish friendly from enemy destroyers in the heat of battle. There was no equivalent to what we call IFF – Identification, Friend or Foe. Any destroyer which came close enough to be dangerous was fair game. The British solution was for the fleet commander to keep track of the destroyer force as it manoeuvred relative to the battle line, *ie* to maintain a tactical plot. To avoid overloading this manual plot, the British had to treat destroyer flotillas as units, each controlled by its own flagship: a flotilla leader. That is why the Royal Navy insisted, up until the end of the Second World War, on building such special flotilla leaders (a pre-war flotilla comprised a leader and two four-ship divisions or squadrons). The British knew that this was hardly universal practice. In 1936, for example, in a discussion of destroyer construction, a British officer remarked casually that only certain navies – the US and Japanese – would fight the way the British hoped to. Only they would use their destroyers against British destroyers, in a kind of dogfight preceding a fleet action.

Given the *en route* screening role, the Royal Navy began to install Asdic (sonar) on all new-construction destroyers in 1931. On 17 June 1932 the Admiralty ordered all destroyers

fitted with Asdic. The number of destroyers assigned to a fleet was set by the number of battleships, *ie* by the length of the line of ships to be screened, using a vee formation (bent screen) extending far enough back that a submarine could not sneak around.[6] Based on such reasoning, in 1919 the Admiralty decided that the two main fleets, Home and Mediterranean, would need a total of nine destroyer flotillas (a figure which could be cut back if the submarine threat were somehow eliminated).

As for mines, British practice was to equip many destroyers with the Two-Speed Destroyer Sweep (TSDS). That in turn required winches and fittings on the quarterdeck. TSDS was conceived as a search rather than a clearance sweep, *ie* a means of protecting the fleet (or at least detecting minefields) while on passage; hence its presence on board destroyers. It was expected to cut all unprotected moored mines, as well as a proportion of moored mines with anti-sweep devices; the percentage would increase with sweep speed and depth. Unlike all other sweeps, TSDS could be used at up to 25kts. However, at speeds above 12kts the swept swath was narrow. Doctrine called for four destroyers steaming and sweeping abreast of a column of battleships.[7] Fitting TSDS was by no means equivalent to the US destroyer minesweeper conversion. It did not,

[6] George Franklin, *Britain's Anti-Submarine Capability 1919-1939* (Frank Cass, London: 2003), p 138, shows a screen used in a 1933 fleet exercise. The Royal Navy also tried circular screens.
[7] In a crosstide of more than one knot the third and later ships would probably be endangered.

British destroyers were conceived primarily for their fleet support role, operating in flotillas integrated with the fleet's capital ships and cruisers. Ships from the Home and Mediterranean Fleets are shown at Gibraltar in the late 1930s for the annual combined exercise, the Home Fleet battleship and cruisers distinguishable by their dark grey paint. Destroyers show their pennant numbers and funnel bands indicating their flotillas. Note the Spanish Civil War recognition markings on cruisers' B turrets. (Royal Naval Museum, Portsmouth)

for example, provide any means of sweeping non-contact mines, such as magnetic mines. An attempt early in the war to develop a destroyer magnetic sweep, which like TSDS could be installed as needed, appears not to have come to fruition.[8] Note that a destroyer which could be fitted with TSDS normally was not rigged for sweeping and thus functioned as a standard destroyer. The main impact of the anti-submarine screening and TSDS requirements was to add equipment to a destroyer's quarterdeck and thus to require a larger hull. Whether to provide for TSDS became an important wartime design issue.

The pre-war attempt to use destroyers to augment fleet anti-aircraft firepower were less successful, partly because the British considered high-angle fire incompatible with the high muzzle velocity needed for good surface (anti-destroyer) shooting. This idea did have considerable impact on the designs of the 'Tribal', 'J' and 'L' classes. During the Second World War a solution was found in the dual-purpose main battery of the 'Battle' class.

The Admiralty's ideal pre-war destroyer force included seven

[8] ML 139/40 of 25 February 1940, in the 'J' Class Cover, approves in principle fitting a destroyer LL (magnetic) sweep, already well into development, to units of the 'J', 'K' and 'Tribal' classes. To make it usable by the widest range of ships, the sweep would have an independent source of electric power. Trials had been run at 12kts using the old destroyer HMS *Skate*. A 'Tribal' would land No. 4 twin 4.7in to provide space for the winch. 'J' and 'K' class destroyers would land their TSDS and their depth charge trap. Production of six 22-knot LL sweeps was approved in March 1940. They were never used.

flotillas for duties outside the battle fleet, including local ASW defence. One key role was trade protection, often meaning convoy escort. Because they were armed with torpedoes, destroyers were a potent counter to individual heavy surface raiders (cruisers were never available in sufficient numbers). The surface raider problem was most prominent for convoys to Russia. Successful attacks (or even threats, in the case of the battleship *Tirpitz* against Convoy PQ 17) seem to have demonstrated to Stalin the potential of such ships, and this experience may explain his post-war fascination with large cruisers, most of which his successors cancelled.

During the First World War, destroyers provided the overwhelming majority of convoy escorts, because they were fast and numerous and had sufficient range. In November 1918 the Royal Navy operated 412 of them, largely against U-boats. Many were worn out by wartime usage, but even in 1930 the Royal Navy destroyer force considerably exceeded the sixteen flotillas (144 ships) deemed necessary. That year, however, the London Naval Treaty limited British destroyer tonnage. The Royal Navy needed some destroyer substitute for convoy warfare. It adopted what would now be called a high-low mix policy, the low (or less capable) end being the convoy sloop. Such ships were not limited by treaty: they had neither torpedoes nor destroyer speed (which was not needed for convoy work). Even at this low end, numbers did not approach what was

Destroyers were also valued for many duties outside the battle fleet. HMS *Melbreak*, a 'Hunt' class destroyer photographed in October 1942, symbolised that role. The small cross-shaped antennas on her yardarm are for the British Type 86M ship-to-ship and ship-to-air VHF voice radio.

needed, and the Second World War frigate programme produced numerous lower-end ships. The problem was partly one of geography. At the outset U-boats had to transit considerable distances before they could attack shipping. Minefields off the British East Coast and between Scotland and Norway could help confine them (the British attack on Norway in 1940 was partly intended to extend mining to the coastal Leads in Norwegian territorial waters, which the Germans were using). Once war broke out, however, U-boats appeared much farther afield than expected, and it became clear that convoys would have to be escorted to Halifax, to Gibraltar, to Sierra Leone, and to Jamaica – which added a requirement for another 100 escorts. The situation worsened enormously after the Germans gained bases on the Atlantic by conquering France and Norway in 1940, in effect multiplying the size of their force. Matters worsened when the Italians entered the war. Now shipping had to take the long route around the Cape, and that route became more important as a means of supplying the army protecting the Middle East, with its vital oil.

The other key role was the fight for the narrow seas, particularly between Britain and the Continent. They included the approaches to the Port of London via the Channel. As the Second World War approached, this problem of securing coastal shipping became more and more important. It explains, for example, the anti-aircraft armament of late-1930s escorts. The 'Hunt' class was built largely to deal with this problem, their creators recalling the First World War struggle for the narrow seas, fought by surface striking forces based at places like Harwich. The Second World War echo of the North

Sea battles was the lengthy battle in the Channel, often against German motor torpedo boats. British destroyers in the Mediterranean fought the offensive end of a similar battle. More generally, destroyers were valued because of their speed. Hence the development of destroyer minelayers, which were used in both World Wars.

With the end of the Second World War, classic fleet-on-fleet engagements seemed most unlikely. The new kind of fleet, built around a carrier, would still face the kinds of *en route* threats which had become prominent after the First World War. The destroyer's screening role now dominated, her torpedo attack role surviving mainly because the Soviets began building large cruisers, like the *Sverdlovs*, which might attack convoys. Much later the surface attack role returned to some extent when the Soviets built major surface combatants with anti-ship missiles. Truly affordable low-end escorts became much more difficult to build with the advent of higher-performance submarines and therefore of new ASW sensors and weapons. It was no longer clear that sufficient numbers could be built. Would there ever be a role for a Third World War corvette? The perception that this was so changed British (and allied) naval strategy and in turn changed the requirements levied on frigates. Ultimately the distinction between destroyer and frigate changed. A Type 22 Batch III frigate is larger and more expensive than a Type 42 Batch III destroyer. The difference is that one is specialised in ASW and the other in area AAW. The frigate actually has much more anti-ship firepower than the destroyer, which in a way places it closer to a classical destroyer. The low end is no longer low. This melding may be traced back to 1960, when *Leander* class

frigates were bought as fleet escorts instead of modernising *Daring* class destroyers.

Creating Ships

For most of the period covered by this book British warship designs were produced by the Admiralty technical or materiel departments, led by the Department of Naval Construction, whose Director (DNC) signed each design (later, as noted below, Director General Ships, DGS, superseded DNC). The process was a spiral, DNC's constructors producing a sketch to fulfil draft Staff Requirements (and to see whether they were practicable). Sometimes the staff did not realise the implications of its requirements (*eg* in ship size) until the sketch had been created. The requirements were then revised, and the process continued. Revision also took into account the views of other departments, such as those involved in ordnance.

The parties to this process were the seagoing fleet, the staff, and the Admiralty materiel departments. Generally the seagoing fleet demanded maximum performance, often (in the case of destroyers and frigates) in a minimum platform. Because the fleet had direct experience of recent designs, its views tended to reflect operating experience. Staff officers had recent seagoing experience, but they were more aware of new technical possibilities. They had to balance individual performance against numbers. DNC and the other technical departments presented technical realities which often went counter to what the fleet and the Staff thought could be achieved. There was thus an inevitable feeling that the designers could have done better. Particularly during the Second World War, British seagoing officers complained that foreign, especially US, de-

signers seemed to be producing more heavily-armed ships than theirs, and DNC periodically found himself defending his products. For the staff, particularly after the Second World War as resources became tighter, the complaint was typically that ships were far too expensive, the suspicion being that private designers were doing better for foreign clients.

This triangle is neither unique nor new. For example, early in the twentieth century Royal Navy cruisers were often compared, to their disadvantage, with Elswick cruisers built for export. The defence was generally that the export ships lacked crucial but subtle qualities, such as magazine capacity, which usually did not appear in published data. Until the early 1950s the Thornycroft yard often offered its designs to the Royal Navy. The Royal Navy rejected many of them, accepting only what became the 'Hunt' Type IV (*Brecon* and *Brissenden*). The main ground for rejection was that Thornycroft did not understand modern weapon and sensor requirements; the builder tended to emphasise the features foreign buyers found most attractive, speed and armament per ton. In this book the only other private design bought for the Royal Navy was the Type 21 frigate.

However, by the late 1980s there was a pervasive perception within the British government that private defence contractors were more effective than their in-house (civil service) equivalents. By that time the Royal Navy had long abandoned attempts to develop its own weapons and electronic systems. DGS was the last hold-out of in-house development. Now the Royal Navy (like the US Navy) assigns the entire design task to a private contractor, such as BAE in the case of the Type 45 destroyer. The in-house organisation survives in a

By 1930, destroyer roles included many non-traditional ones, such as convoy escort. The London Naval Treaty signed that year drastically reduced the British destroyer fleet, just as the Royal Navy saw an increased need for shipping protection. It developed sloops as slow substitutes (*ie* not limited by treaty) for destroyers in that role. Their ultimate development was the *Black Swan* class. HMS *Snipe* is shown post-war.

The Royal Navy thought of the Commonwealth navies as an integrated fleet. For example, Commonwealth and Royal Navy ships all shared a common series of pennant numbers. As war came to seem imminent, the Australians chose a design for emergency production. They considered and rejected the *Black Swan* and *Kingfisher* class sloops and the *Halcyon* class minesweepers. Instead, the design of a small sloop was developed by Australian naval constructors and submitted to their Navy Board (equivalent to the Admiralty) on 3 February 1939. It was smaller than a 'Flower' class corvette: 680 tons, 180ft on the waterline (186ft overall) x 31ft x 10ft, and was expected to make 15.5kts on the output of two triple-expansion engines, which could be built in railway workshops. Projected armament was two 4in guns, depth charges (with Asdic), and minesweeping equipment. Projected endurance was 2,850nm at 12kts. Although officially a minesweeper, the resulting *Bathurst* class was called a corvette by the RAN, and it often functioned as one. The first four were ordered in December 1939, followed by thirty-two more RAN ships. The Royal Navy ordered ten in January 1940, and then another ten; these ships were lent to the RAN during the war. Of these ships, thirteen served under British operational control, two beginning their war service in the Mediterranean. In addition, the Royal Indian Navy ordered four for construction in Australia (another three, ordered from Indian yards, were cancelled in March 1945). Wartime armament was a 4in gun forward and a 20mm gun or 12pdr aft; by the end of the war most had a single Bofors aft. HMAS *Mildura* is shown at Sydney. Completed in July 1941, she served as both an escort and a sweeper. (RAN via John Mortimer)

managerial role, monitoring the process. Maintaining separate monitoring and design agencies may be substantially less flexible than the previous DNC/DGS organisation. On the other hand, it can be argued that weapons and related systems are now so deeply enmeshed in a ship design that the classical constructors are not nearly as important as in the past; better to contract a ship to an integrated systems house. Yet without its in-house, hence disinterested, designers, the staff may no longer be able to understand the consequences of its choices, particularly at the critical earliest stages of a project. It will probably be unable to judge technical issues. A set of requirements for which no sketch has been made may have surprising consequences (such as huge size to maintain a stealthy shape) – which may be impossible to correct without major and expensive contract changes. To some extent the Royal Navy has tried to solve the problem by writing more flexible contracts and by forming joint teams of naval officers and contractors.

As the Royal Navy shrank in the 1970s, so did the naval staff and the Admiralty departmental structure. There seems no longer to be anything resembling the permanent structure which produced the Staff Requirements prominent in this book. Instead, *ad hoc* groups are formed. Their advantage – and disadvantage – is that they begin with a clean sheet of paper. Although members are aware of their own experience, they are unlikely to be aware of the many policy issues which had shaped previous ships. The problem is aggravated by the lengthening interval between ship designs. For both the Royal Navy and the US Navy, very long design periods are now tolerated. A constructor may work on very few separate designs throughout a career, hence gain very little experience to apply to subsequent ships. There seem to be more and more layers of review between initial concept and approval for construction. To a cynic, the purpose of the extra studies is to delay actually spending money on construction – ultimately at a high cost. The same cynic might suggest that delay was entirely acceptable during a Cold War when nuclear deterrence made war quite unlikely. With the

end of the Cold War, the situation seems to have changed.

The lengthening interval between separate designs reflects a reduction in the number of ships bought each year. One explanation is that ships themselves are growing considerably more expensive, due partly to the rising cost of their weapon systems. The same annual appropriation buys fewer. As the numbers fall, shipyards find themselves compelled to raise costs in order to pay their overheads. The only way to maintain even a shrunken force is to extend individual ship lifetime and so to increase the interval between classes. That is possible because, despite many claims to the contrary, weapons technology has largely stabilised after violent changes between 1940 and, say, 1965. That probably exemplifies the S-shaped curve which technology so often follows: very slow at first, then more and more rapid, and then slow again as the potential of a given technology is wrung out.

Until well after the Second World War, the Admiralty was largely independent of other British defence decision-making, the Cabinet often limiting itself largely to splitting overall resources between the services. The Admiralty felt only a limited need to explain its reasoning to outsiders. Ship requirements and designs were almost completely an internal matter, although there was sporadic interference from above (as is evident, for example, in wartime Minutes from Prime Minister Winston Churchill).

The civilian head of the Board of Admiralty was the First Lord, who was responsible to Parliament. The professional members were five Sea Lords plus the Vice and Assistant Chiefs of the Naval Staff. The First Sea Lord (roughly equivalent to the US Chief of Naval Operations) was also Chief of the Naval Staff (CNS). The Third Sea Lord was also Controller, responsible for naval materiel and the materiel departments (Fifth Sea Lord, however, was responsible for naval aircraft). Second Sea Lord was responsible for personnel, Fourth for dockyards and bases.

Unlike the contemporary US Navy, the Royal Navy did not form large units into which new technologies could be slotted, like the US Bureau of Ordnance. Instead, the Royal Navy added a Gunnery Department for fire control, when such devices first became important, retaining the earlier Department of Naval Ordnance, which provided guns. Torpedoes and Mines were, however, lumped together. The effect of this organic process was to create much more varied opinion at the level at which Staff Requirements and designs were debated, but it was also somewhat more cumbersome, and after the Second World War the different units were gradually amalgamated.

Perhaps the greatest lesson of the Battle of the Atlantic was how difficult it was to extemporise the large ASW fleet required. Yet ships simple enough to be mass-produced were not very useful in peacetime. One solution, adopted by the Royal Navy, was to convert existing destroyers into fast ASW frigates and then to place most of them in reserve, against the threat of a war considered quite possible from 1957 onwards. HMS *Undine* is shown in February 1954. As it happened, the advent of H-bombs made it much likelier that World War III could be averted by deterrence, and that the main threat would be limited war in the Third World. The reserve fleet was abandoned.

The most important material departments frequently appear in this book in the form of their directors: DNC (naval construction: DNC was Chief Constructor and Principal Professional Advisor to the Board); Engineer-in-Chief (E-in-C, the only department not denoted by the initial letter D); DEE (electrical engineering, not to be confused with radio and radar); DNO (naval ordnance); DGD (gunnery division: fire control, later gunnery and anti-air warfare, though still abbreviated DGD); DTM (torpedoes and mines); DAS (anti-submarine, often A/S, initially mainly concerned with Asdic); DSD (signals); DND (navigation and direction), DOD (Operations Division), DoD (dockyards). During the run-up to the Second World War DTM and DAS merged to become DTAS (Torpedoes and A/S) and later DTASW (adding weapons). During the war a new Department of Radio Warfare (DRW) was created. There was also, for a time a Department of Radio Equipment (DRE).

Until 1939 DNC and his department were located at the Admiralty in London, making it relatively simple for the Board and the Staff to interact with DNC and senior constructors. At the approach of war, the bulk of the organisation was evacuated a considerable distance to Bath, leaving DNC a small London section for urgent studies in response to Staff requests. This section was responsible for initial sketches made during the development of a Staff Requirement. With the entire organisation badly overloaded in the early 1950s, the London section was assigned detailed development of the third-rate ASW frigate (Type 17) and of its lineal successors, which became the Type 81 'Tribal' class frigate. Rivalry between the London section and the main DNC organisation at Bath may have affected the development of the *Leander* class.[9] Separate Sections at Bath were responsible for different types of ships.[10] The post-war 'County' class missile destroyers were probably a unique case of carry-over from one section (5, developing missile ships) to another (7, for destroyers). The section organisation may have slowed the amalgamation of destroyers and frigates in the late 1950s.

DNC headed the Royal Corps of Naval Constructors (RCNC).[11] Their lengthy training included a period of sea time to give them a feeling for the fleet's needs and for the realities of ships. Such men could not be trained rapidly in an emergency. Shortages of experienced constructors plagued the Royal Navy both during the run-up to the Second World War and during the Korean War mobilisation. In both cases overworked constructors made errors with serious design consequences. DNC both designed the ships and monitored their construc-

[9] D K Brown, the historian of British warship design, was a member of the London section, and was responsible for the basic Type 81 design.
[10] In November 1946, the DNC Department included a production organisation at its headquarters. It had overseas outposts in the United States and in Canada. Bath was presided over by a Deputy DNC (DDNC) with ten assistants, each supervising a group of Sections, forty-eight in all. Constructors' notebooks suggest how rarely any one Constructor shifted from one type of ship to another.
[11] The history of the Royal Corps is D K Brown, *A Century of Naval Construction: The History of the Royal Corps of Naval Constructors* (Conway Maritime Press, London: 1983).

After 1948 the Royal Navy formally acknowledged that only within an alliance could it guarantee the security of Britain's global sea lines of communication. That position was formalised in 1949 with the formation of NATO, and the Royal Navy now frequently operated in company with allied fleets. This photograph of Malta in the 1960s shows a mixed NATO fleet including a British *Tiger* class cruiser and Dutch, French and Italian cruisers and destroyers. Another feature of the post-war period was the blurring of the distinction between different categories of surface combatants, particularly after missiles provided destroyers with cruiser-level firepower, and armour ceased to be significant. One irony was that in the late 1970s the Royal Navy could plausibly argue that, with allied forces either depleted or tied up elsewhere (as in the Mediterranean), it would have to fight largely alone to guarantee access to the Eastern Atlantic and the Channel. (Royal Naval Museum, Portsmouth)

After the Second World War the different categories of surface combatants began to merge. Big destroyers like HMS *Diana*, shown on 18 September 1954, came close to being small cruisers, although they lacked the self-supporting features of such ships. Later large destroyers, the 'Counties' and HMS *Bristol*, were sometimes called cruisers, although they lacked important cruiser features including protection. (A&J Pavia via John Mortimer)

tion. Thus his department included superintendents at the yards and constructors at dockyards throughout the Empire and with the fleets. There was a separate Director of Dockyards (DoD, not to be confused with the Director of the Operations Division, DOD).

Many departments had their own laboratories and schools, the latter often responsible for development work. Examples included the DNC test tank at Haslar, HMS *Excellent* for DGD, HMS *Vernon* for DTM, and HMS *Osprey* for DND. Asdics were developed by the A/S Experimental Establishment at Fairlie. British naval radars and post-war command systems were developed by the Admiralty Signals Establishment, ASE. Overall, the experimental establishments expanded considerably in wartime, one of the most important being the Underwater Experimental Establishment, UNDEX, which figures in this book in decisions on the *Daring* class hull structure, and which conducted many early post-war tests of ships to destruction. Note that DNO relied on industry for gun mounting designs; Vickers seems to have had a monopoly.

Some of the Departments represented branches of the service; officers chose their specialities, attended special schools, and carried those specialities forward through their careers. The branches competed but apparently did not exchange much information. It is inherent in such a system that claims by any one branch are accepted by the others. Before the Second World War the two major weapons specialities were gunnery and torpedoes (ASW was an outgrowth of the torpedo branch). A gunner was Director of Plans and a torpedo expert was

Director of Tactics. Thus Director of Plans was unlikely to know much about underwater warfare. This organisational accident may explain why pre-war British officers so overrated the effectiveness of Asdic and ASW tactics.[12]

The Naval Staff began as a war planning and intelligence organisation, hence the natural forum to decide what sort of materiel the navy needed. First Sea Lord was both operational head of the Royal Navy and Chief of the Naval Staff (CNS), with a Deputy (later Vice) Chief (DCNS or VCNS) under him. In the wartime and early post-war organisation, VCNS was responsible for policy. Under him were the Naval Intelligence Department and the Directorate of Plans (Operations). At the next level down the Assistant Chief of the Naval Staff (ACNS), under Controller, supervised the Tactical Division (director, DTD) later the Tactical and Staff Duties Division (director, DTSD), which prepared and circulated draft Staff Requirements. In theory, writing a Staff Requirement was the first step in a design, although in practice sketch designs might be developed informally in advance of actual staff requirements. Typically Controller asked for a draft Staff Requirement for circulation for comment among the Staff Divisions. Controller and the Sea Lords (ultimately First Sea Lord) adjudicated disputes among them. Requirements were also sent to DNC so that a draft sketch design could be produced as a test of feasibility. During and after the war ACNS was also in charge of operational research (Directorate of Operational Research, DOR), and other ACNS

[12] Franklin, *Britain's Anti-Submarine Capability 1919-1939*, pp 30–1.

positions, such as ACNS(T) for trade protection (mainly the Battle of the Atlantic), were created during the war. ACNS(W), for weapons, was responsible for Staff Requirements.

Discussion of design proposals by the full Board became difficult during the war. In 1942 a Future Building Committee (FBC) chaired by ACNS(W) was formed. Considering both the overall shape of the fleet and particular ship choices, it was important for wartime destroyer development. The FBC may have been formed largely in response to various disasters in 1940 and 1941 at the hands of Axis aircraft. Although it lapsed at the end of the war, the idea of a co-ordinating committee outside the Board was attractive. The Ship Design Policy Committee (SDPC) was formed in 1947 as, in effect, a filter between design studies and the Board: it had to endorse a proposed design before it could be presented to the Board.[13] It seems to have been considered unwieldy; in 1959 a new Ship Characteristics Committee (SCC) was formed. The post-war successor to the FBC was the Fleet Requirements Committee, formed in the late 1950s.

After the war the ultimate size and shape of the fleet was very much a Cabinet-level issue and the subject of Defence Reviews. Until about 1956 such reviews might be led by a Minister of Defence, but he had little or no staff supporting him, hence had to accept Service views. In October 1955 Prime Minister Anthony Eden was surprised to learn that defence

plans called for spending an unaffordable £2 billion in 1959. In response he expanded the role of the previously powerless Ministry of Defence to ensure that the composition and balance of each service corresponded to overall Cabinet policy, *ie* that spending was reined in. Its civilian chief would have power over the service heads. A separate Chairman of the Chiefs of Staff Committee would be created. In tandem with these changes Eden ordered a Long Term Defence Review. It was completed late in 1956, coinciding with the débâcle at Suez which seemed to illustrate the bankruptcy of current policy. The review announced drastic cuts in keeping with the largely unannounced but seismic change in British national strategy towards nuclear deterrence and a capability to fight only limited wars. At much the same time similar financial pressure created the modern US Defense Department. In both cases the determining factor was probably the exploding cost of new technology.

In January 1957 it was announced that all proposals from the individual services would go through the Ministry of Defence. The Chairman of the Chiefs of Staff Committee became Chief of Staff to the Ministry of Defence, or Chief of the Defence Staff (the first was former First Sea Lord Admiral Lord Louis Mountbatten). Now a Minister of Defence, answerable to the Cabinet, could bypass the service chiefs altogether in allocating resources. By 1962 new projects had to be endorsed first by the Defence Research Policy Committee (or Defence Research Committee), and then by the Operational Requirements Committee, both staffed from all the services

At the other end of the scale, frigates grew in sophistication to the point where they were fleet escorts operating with destroyers. Ultimately the main distinction was that destroyers offered area air defence, whereas frigates offered superior ASW capability; ships of both categories were of about the same size, and frigates were sometimes considerably more expensive than destroyers. HMS *Rhyl*, shown in 1982, was built just as this shift was occurring. The dark patch at her bow was probably due to heat generated by her diesel generators. She is shown as modernised, with Seacat and a helicopter deck aft, and with a towed (variable-depth) sonar at her stern.

[13] Ordered set up by Board Minute 4185, 30 October 1947 (ADM 167/129), with Controller in the chair, other members to be DCNS (Air; Fifth Sea Lord), ACNS, DTSD, Deputy Controller, DNE, Vice Controller (Air), Deputy Controller (R&D), DNC, and E-in-C.

As the home market for destroyers and frigates contracted, British firms became more dependent on exports. Perhaps the most successful deal of all was the sale of six frigates to Brazil. They were loosely related to Type 21, with much the same weapon system. The first two, *Niteroi* and *Defensora*, are seen in the Channel *en route* to Brazil. (Vosper Thornycroft)

in hopes of making them more objective. They were then passed to a separate Weapons Production Committee before being submitted to the Cabinet Defence Committee for final approval. A project began as a Staff Target which evolved into a Staff Requirement and was approved as an Operational Requirement. The first ship project subject to such review was the Type 82 (*Bristol*) guided missile destroyer.

As in the United States in the 1960s, the key to controlling the services was operations analysis, comparing different forces which seemed to be directed at similar goals, conducted at the Ministry rather than at the service level. By the late 1960s the services had largely been shorn of their own operational research organisations, so they had little means of resisting MoD analyses on their own terms. In the navy's case the new kind of analysis had particularly bad consequences. The contributions of various platforms and forces could be compared only in discrete, well-defined roles. That is very useful when weapons or forces are designed to deal with a single scenario, such as an armoured force to deal with a Soviet attack on the Central Front; it is far less useful for general-purpose forces whose great strength is in their flexibility. Furthermore, this type of analysis is essentially static: it does not take account of an enemy's reactions to what friendly

forces do. However, much of what navies do with their mobility is exactly that: they change the enemy's perceptions and even the terms of the problem. That is why navies exercise great influence even though they may rarely fight. For example, in the 1970s it was common in the United States to divide up the fleet into special-purpose arms, distinguishing sea control from power-projection forces, and to evaluate each on its own terms. The US Maritime Strategy of the 1980s, a classical large-navy concept (applicable to the Royal Navy as to the US Navy) aimed to seize sea control by using forces usually designated for power projection. It may be that the effect of sea power often can be appreciated only in a dynamic war game, in which the enemy's behaviour changes over time. This is why, during the 1980s, the US Navy invested so heavily in its wargaming facilities.

The Ministry of Defence Operational Analysis Establishment (DOAE), began a major study of maritime warfare in 1973. The Ministry of Defence was under intense pressure to cut naval spending, both because of British economic problems and because it was considered vital to spend more on the Central Front in Germany. DOAE studies apparently helped justify the sort of cuts which were wanted. Forces were evaluated in a narrowly-defined NATO war. Naval roles such as

pre-hostilities marking and trailing and attacks on Soviet surface combatants at the outbreak of war were listed. On these terms the surface force was compared with submarines and with land-based aircraft. Inevitably there were gross simplifications. Aircraft generally seemed to be a better and more economical choice. They offered great mobility; once they had attacked, they could quickly return to base, reload and attack again. At least in theory, their airborne radars could detect even relatively small targets at long range. It was not in DOAE's remit to point out that the aircraft were tied to British bases, or that weather might well prohibit their use. By 1974 DOAE was recommending aircraft for surface strike missions, pointing out the limitations of the Exocet then being deployed. It appears that DOAE analysis justified killing the big Type 43 destroyer and then justified the 1981 naval cuts (the relevant papers have not yet been released). For the researcher, the shift towards centralised authority and the DOAE is evident in the decline of Admiralty policy papers in The National Archive (formerly the Public Record Office) in favour of Ministry of Defence papers, often produced by the Royal Navy.

The Treasury became more and more involved in the details of British naval forces. As the agency responsible for controlling spending (since it has to raise the funds), the Treasury in effect functioned as a balance wheel to the services. Beginning in the late 1960s, Treasury documents show considerable scepticism about new naval programmes. The Royal Navy found that the explanations it produced were often used as a basis for further protests. That was particularly evident in the case of the Type 22 frigate, whose mission changed quite radically without any formal statement of what was happening.

Through and beyond the 1970s the Admiralty and its staff were severely cut and the Staff Divisions amalgamated. DTSD became as Director of Tactics and Staff Duties, and much later DTWP (Tactics, Weapons, and Policy). Ultimately he became Director of Operational Requirements (Navy), DOR(N), sometimes styled DNOR. There were periodic reorganisations. In 1954 TASW became the Department of Undersea Warfare (DUW). There was considerable amalgamation in the late 1950s as the Admiralty tried to avoid drastic cuts in front-line forces due to a severe budget squeeze. In 1984 CNS, with ACNS below him, directed four major divisions: DNW (Naval Warfare), DNOT (Operations and Training), DNSD (Naval Staff Duties), and a Secretarial division.

Probably the most striking change was the creation of super-departments. In February 1956 the Nihill Committee was created to consider reorganisation of design, taking into account complaints from sea that US ships had better layouts and used lighter and more compact equipment. On the recommendation of its 1958 report, the DNC, E-in-C (as DME, Director of Mechanical Engineering), DEE, DNE (Naval Equipment), and a new DNP (naval production) departments were all combined in a new Director General, Ships organisation in new buildings at Foxhill in Bath. DNC left Whitehall for Bath. DNO, DGD and DUW (among others) merged under a new Director General Weapons (Naval), DGW(N). The same reorganisation created the Ship Characteristics Committee and established a five-year term of office for Controller. About two decades later the ship organisation moved to Abbey Wood in Bristol. As noted, DGS is now a monitoring rather than a design organisation. At least for the moment, the Type 23 frigate seems to have been the swan-song of the Royal Navy's own warship designers.

Acknowledgements

First and foremost I would like to thank my wife Rhea, who so often and so lovingly encouraged and assisted me in this lengthy project. For my birthday very early in our marriage she bought me Edgar March's *British Destroyers*, which first awed me and then made me realise how much more was to be learned and said. I particularly thank Rhea for helping me find a way to photograph Ship's Covers at the National Maritime Museum and thus to assemble key material for the early chapters of this book. The late David Lyon, king of the Museum's Draught Room, introduced me to the Covers, and shared his enormous knowledge of, and enthusiasm for, British torpedo craft. The late David R Topliss, of the Brass Foundry station of the Museum, introduced me to the constructors' notebooks, which have proved so valuable a source. My good friend A D Baker III largely illustrated this book, read an earlier draft, and provided much excellent advice. His drawings are based partly on originals held by the National Maritime Museum at the Brass Foundry. D K Brown illuminated the logic of British ship design, as seen from the inside. I am grateful to both the late J David Brown and Captain Chris Page RN, successive heads of the Royal Navy Historical Branch. Their staffs were also extremely kind to me. I am particularly grateful to Jock Gardner and to Malcolm Llewellyn-Jones. Dr David Stevens and Josef Straczek of the Royal Australian Navy Historical Branch were also very helpful. I am also very grateful to my friends the late Antony Preston, Alan Raven, Dr Eric Grove, John Mortimer, David Andrews RCNC, and Chuck Haberlein of the US Naval Historical Center. I would like to thank the staffs of the Brass Foundry, past and present, of the Public Record Office (now part of The National Archives), and of the US Navy Operational Archives, on all of whom I depended heavily. I am grateful to the staffs of the libraries of the Imperial War Museum and of the Science Museum. Special thanks go to the Freedom of Information staff of The National Archive and also to the Defence Logistics Organisation Frigate Integrated Project Team, for the latter's response to a Freedom of Information request. Although I benefited from much help, I alone am responsible for the views in this book and for any errors it contains.

CHAPTER 2
Beginning the Slide Towards War

HMS *Nubian* is shown at Malta before the Second World War, with Spanish Civil War recognition markings on B gun mount, and with all four 4.7in mounts. Her quadruple pompom occupies Q position, and the two gun tubs (zarebas) between her funnels are occupied by quadruple 0.5in machine guns. Note that the battleship in the background also has the air recognition stripes on her B turret. (A&J Pavia via John Mortimer)

For the Royal Navy, the slide towards the Second World War began with the failure of naval arms limitation treaties in the early 1930s. The failures of the treaties, as well as Japanese aggression in Asia, showed that war was once again entirely thinkable. New threats, particularly air and submarine threats, were suddenly far more urgent. Among the results were a new kind of large destroyer, the 'Tribal' class, and a new kind of small escort, the sloop.

In a world exhausted by the First World War, naval arms limitation was a way of avoiding a pointless, and quite possibly dangerous, Pacific naval arms race. The Washington Treaty limited new battleship construction, but it did not eliminate the underlying tensions which had caused the battleship-building race. Instead, attention turned to the largest warships which could be built in unlimited numbers, 10,000-ton cruisers armed with 8in guns. The British government was particularly concerned to end the nascent building race in such ships because the Royal Navy needed large numbers of cruisers, the figure typically being set at seventy. Of the seventy, forty-five were needed to protect the sea lines of communication which tied together the Empire and fed Britain. This figure, set in 1919, was based on geography, hence could not be reduced on the basis of cuts in foreign cruiser forces (their ships might still strike anywhere). Since any potential enemy might well use large cruisers to raid that commerce, at least the trade pro-

tection ships should have been 10,000-tonners. Such a programme would have been ruinously expensive. At the same time, the fleet needed its own cruisers, to act as its scouts and to back up its destroyer force. These ships would generally be smaller than the trade-protection cruisers.

Beginning with an abortive conference at Geneva in 1927, the British tried to convince the other maritime powers to stop building large cruisers. In the British view, it was time to limit all major warship construction by limiting ships in the different categories and then limiting the totals in each category. For example, an upper limit had to be set on destroyers so that no country would get around the cruiser limit simply by building large destroyers (as the French, and to a lesser extent the Italians, were beginning to do). The Geneva conference collapsed largely because the United States refused to accept the British argument that the Royal Navy needed a more numerous cruiser force because, unlike the United States, it had a much larger trade-protection role.

By 1929, faced with the continuing construction of large cruisers, the British government was willing to make a much greater concession, cutting its own cruiser force to fifty ships in order to gain American agreement. This concession was potentially so damaging to the Empire that the First Sea Lord felt compelled to make a special statement demanding that it be considered no more than a temporary step, and to circulate the statement to the Dominion governments.[1] Signed on 22 April 1930, the new treaty was to run up to 31 December 1936. As of that date, the signatories were to have scrapped enough ships to meet the new lower limits. It barred further construction of 8in gun cruisers in return for limits on overall cruiser tonnage in each fleet. Neither the French nor the Italians signed. To induce them to abide by treaty limits, the treaty included an 'escalator' clause (Article 21): if a treaty power (Britain, the United States, Japan) decided that its national security was materially affected by construction by a non-signatory, it could increase its own tonnage, notifying the others of that increase. They could then make proportionate increases of their own. The French and the Italians did stop building 8in gun cruisers. The Japanese increased their treaty quota from the 67 per cent of the Washington Treaty to 70 per cent, but they wanted parity (they would abandon the treaty system in 1934 on the grounds that to deny them parity was intolerable).

The Admiralty seems to have assumed that cruiser size (hence cost) was tied directly to the use of 8in guns. That may have been wishful thinking tied to British distaste for triple gun mounts. If no more than four multiple mounts could usefully to placed on board a cruiser, then the largest ship would have eight guns, and 7,000 tons (as in a *Leander*) was perfectly adequate. Unfortunately neither the Americans nor the

---

[1] CNS Admiral of the Fleet Sir Charles Madden told the Cabinet on 17 January 1930 that the cut was acceptable only for a 'strictly limited period' under *current* international conditions, in a statement widely circulated through the Navy.

Japanese agreed. By early 1933, both were building 10,000-ton cruisers armed with five triple 6in (the US *Brooklyn*s and the Japanese *Mogami*s). Since Japan was the most likely future enemy, the advent of its ships was particularly disastrous. They had to be matched, ship for ship, or they could freely raid British trade in wartime. Particularly unfortunately, the 1930 treaty was framed in terms of total tonnage, the fifty-ship figure being no more than an estimate based on small cruisers the British hoped to build. Building larger cruisers would limit the British to far fewer.

For the moment these limits were no problem, as overage ships could be retained until 1936. However, it would soon be time to replace the First World War 'C' and 'D' class fleet cruisers. The treaty precluded much new cruiser construction. Small as they might be, destroyers were the only surface combatants which could make up for the loss of cruiser numbers within the fleet. The Royal Navy was being forced to adopt exactly the strategy which the treaty-framers were trying to prevent.

Given their experience in the First World War, the British badly wanted to resolve the submarine threat by treaty. U-boats had nearly defeated Britain. However, it was also clear that unrestricted German submarine warfare had drawn the United States into the war on the Allied side, with decisive effects. Thus US submarine officers who initially advocated unrestricted submarine warfare against Japan in a future war drew back. If American submarines sank numerous neutral – British – ships, would Britain be drawn into the war on Japan's side? Submarines survived because they had other

virtues. Their stealth made them ideal scouts in enemy-held waters – a consideration as significant for the British (contemplating war with Japan) as for the Americans (with the same war in view). The French argued that submarines were the only sort of coast defence they could afford. No submarine ban was enacted, and the Admiralty had to face the possibility of a new submarine war.

In order to sell a ban, the Admiralty had offered to cut the British destroyer force – their main ocean ASW force – by 50,000 tons, from an initial target of 200,000 tons. To the Admiralty's horror, the British Cabinet, intent on cutting naval costs, adopted the 150,000-ton limit on underage destroyer tonnage, even though the ban was not adopted. As they had proposed at Geneva, the British sold a 1,500-ton limit on destroyer tonnage, with the exception that 16 per cent of ships could displace up to 1,850 tons. The exception to the 1,500-ton limit was vital, because it allowed for the flotilla leaders essential to Royal Navy tactical policy. Destroyer lifetime was set as sixteen years for ships laid down after 31 December 1920, and as twelve years for ships laid down before 1 January 1921. Thus wartime British destroyers were all eligible for replacement by the early 1930s.

The 150,000-ton limit amounted to about ten flotillas of maximum-size ships (each comprising a leader and eight destroyers). Even at 1,400 tons per ship (as in the early units of the 'A' through 'I' series), the sixteen flotillas would have required 201,600 tons. That proved irrelevant only because, with their very large force of First World War ships, the British had not begun building new destroyers until well into the 1920s.

HMS *Eskimo* shows typical wartime modifications. X twin 4.7in mount has been replaced by a twin 4in anti-aircraft gun. The after funnel has been cut down and the mainmast landed. The weapons in the gun tubs are not very visible, and it is not clear whether she has Oerlikons in her bridge wings, as would become standard. She carries the fixed frame of a Type 286 air-search radar at her masthead, and Type 285 fire-control radar atop her director. The ship's mainmast has been replaced by a low frame carrying radio antennas, less likely to interfere with anti-aircraft fire. Note also the bulwarks built up around the gun mounts. By this time the ship's pennant number had been changed from F75 to G75.

By 1934 they had only ordered seven and a half flotillas of modern destroyers. In the event, by the time all overage destroyers were to have been scrapped, war was clearly coming, and the British invoked the escalator clause to save many of them.

Maximum destroyer gun calibre was initially set at 5in, the maximum in the US Navy, and then at 5.1in (130mm) to accommodate the French. DNO built and tested a 130mm gun to see whether the Royal Navy should adopt the new maximum calibre, but experiments on board the leader HMS *Kempenfelt* showed that the ammunition for this gun was too heavy for easy handling on board a destroyer.[2] The existing 4.7in destroyer gun fired a 50lb shell, which was comparable to those fired by foreign destroyers with somewhat larger-calibre guns (*eg* the Japanese 5in/50, which fired a 50.7lb shell, albeit at a higher muzzle velocity, about 3,000ft/sec vs 2,650ft/sec for the British). The treaty established two new unlimited categories: torpedo boats (up to 600 tons) and sloops or small gunboats. The Royal Navy used the latter to make up for the loss of trade-protection destroyers (see Chapter 4).

The British negotiated the London Naval Treaty in the peacetime context of the 'Ten Year Rule', the annually-renewed assumption that war would not break out for a decade. On this basis the Admiralty's fears of an insufficient cruiser force could be dismissed. Annual renewal of the Rule had begun when the Foreign Office specifically rejected the Admiralty warnings of Japanese aggressiveness. The Rule in turn justified drastic cuts not so much in shipbuilding as in buying expendables such as ammunition and fuel for war stocks. As early as May 1930, however, Lord Vansittart, Permanent Secretary of the Foreign Office, wrote privately that although Britain had to uphold the hopes of the League of Nations, Europe was 'riddled with pre-war thought', presumably a reference both to Mussolini and to growing nationalist spirit in pre-Nazi Germany. Then Japan began to move in the Far East, endangering the British formal and informal empires there. In June 1931 the Admiralty set up a Naval Planning Committee chaired by the First Sea Lord (other members were DCNS, ACNS and Director of Plans). Although its first product was a 'Naval Appreciation of War with Russia', it soon turned to the problems of the Far East. In 1932 the committee reviewed the problems of a 'Locarno War' in which Britain's guarantee of the post-First World War settlement might have to be made good (probably as a way around Foreign Office refusal to face Japanese realities). It became clear that the limits accepted in the London Treaty were too low. Japanese aggression in the Far East showed that the League of Nations, on which the British Government relied, was impotent. All of this did not even take into account potential threats in Europe.

On 15 July 1931 the British Cabinet formally decided to re-examine the Ten Year Rule in view of likely developments in 1932, although it wanted to delay to see whether a new Disarmament Conference at Geneva might be successful. Once it was clear that the conference was stalemated, the Cabinet approved the Chiefs of Staff recommendation that the Rule be dropped. A new Defence Requirements Committee met beginning on 15 November 1933 to identify the worst deficiencies in readiness.

HMS *Ashanti* shows typical early war modifications.

[2] The trials were announced in the 1930 edition of *Progress in Gunnery*, ADM 186/304. The gun used a 70lb shell, which proved too heavy for easy handling in a seaway (ADM 186/323). Trials were conducted on board HMS *Acheron* in 1931 to decide the heaviest usable destroyer shell (ADM 186/309).

It was time to rethink ship characteristics. Towards the end of 1933 the fleet commanders and their destroyer commanders replied to an Admiralty request ('Strategical Problem "F"') for advice as to the characteristics of future ships.[3] The commanders wanted something more powerful. Trials showed that a 62lb shell was the heaviest that could easily be handled on a destroyer.[4] The 62pdr (4.7in/50) became an important factor in pre-war destroyer designs, although it appeared on board only one class ('L'/'M'). The alternative was a twin power-operated version of the existing standard 4.7in/45 (50pdr). Power operation would make it viable even on board a lively destroyer.

Given the new American and particularly the new Japanese cruisers, the British felt compelled to design a similar large new cruiser (the 'M' class, later to become the 'Town' class). Its considerable displacement ate into the limited cruiser tonnage available under the 1930 Treaty, at just about the time that the small First World War cruisers of the 'C' and 'D' used for fleet work had to be replaced. Any new fleet cruiser built using available tonnage would have to be quite small.[5] Some fleet cruiser roles, such as countering enemy reconnaissance, general command of the van and the rear (to beat off enemy torpedo attacks), and to support destroyer flotillas against enemy cruisers, required fairly large ships. Others, such as

searching, shadowing and screening, might be carried out by smaller ships.

Given the limited available tonnage the Naval Staff envisaged a new Scout Cruiser. To indicate available options, in August 1934 DNC produced a series of cruiser sketch designs designated P through U.[6] The Royal Navy was already buying the 5,200-ton *Arethusa* class, with three twin 6in turrets and a speed of 32.25kts, with 3in side and 2in deck protection over her magazines and 2¼in side and 1in deck over her machinery. The question was how much displacement could be saved by sacrificing the turrets for single weather-deck mountings. The Staff asked for a 4,500 to 5,000-ton ship with similar armament. Design P showed that six single 6in and four 4in HA guns could be accommodated on 4,500 tons, with good protection (corresponding to that then planned for the 'Town' class), but at lower speed (30.75kts). To increase speed to 33kts (Design Q) required 5,000 tons. Even then turrets had to be abandoned in favour of open mounts. Setting displacement at 4,500 tons and speed at 33kts (Design R) required magazine side protection be cut from 3in–4in to 3in; but machinery protection, covering a larger area, had to be cut much more drastically (from 3in side and 1in deck to 1¾in side and ⅜in deck or ¾in side and 1in deck). Thus Design R showed that a 6in-gun ship on 4,500 tons could not have satisfactory protection over her machinery. Retaining the earlier level of protection and the desired 33kt speed (Design S) cost half the gun battery. Adopting triple 6in mounts would not solve the problem (Design T), because a six-gun ship with proper protection and speed would displace 5,600 tons. Design Q was con-

[3] The letter has not been found. The Admiralty reply (A.L. M/TD 91/33 of 27 March 1934) indicated to what extent the requests were being met. 'J' Class Ship's Cover.
[4] ADM 186/328, Progress in Gunnery for 1935.
[5] In 1935 Director of Plans pointed out that of 86,500 tons of cruisers which might be laid down in 1934–6, the 1934 and 1935 Programmes (five 'Towns', two *Arethusas*: 59,550 tons) left only 26,800 tons for the 1936 Programme, barely enough for the three 'Towns' squeezed into it. Adding two more ships, *Belfast* and *Edinburgh*, using the escalator clause left another 8,000 tons. Were the 'V Leader' allowed to grow into the cruiser category (at 2,000 tons), one of the two last 'Town' class cruisers would have to be deferred to 1940, leaving only enough for a 5,000-tonner. The 'V Leader' thus had to be held down to the 1,850-ton destroyer limit.

[6] ADM 1/8828, 'New Construction Cruisers 1935', gives the cruiser and 'V Leader' data.

At Malta, HMS *Tartar* shows the most prominent late-war modification, the lattice foremast carrying Type 276 (half-cheese antenna) radar, with Type 291 on a topmast. The stub mainmast, typically mounted by 1942, carries the standard British 'bird cage' HF/DF antenna. The gun tubs amidships and the bridge wings carry Oerlikons, the latter in twin power mounts. Another pair of twin power Oerlikons is just visible abaft the searchlight platform, which seems to be empty. (A&J Pavia via John Mortimer)

sidered the best of the lot, but reverting to open mounts would take up deck space and might sacrifice important fighting advantages. Overall, none of these designs could be considered well-balanced.

Another possibility was to move towards a destroyer. At 3,500 tons, Design U offered five single 6in guns and a speed of 38kts, but no magazine protection at all (1in side and ⅜in deck over machinery). This design offered good seakeeping, but she would be vulnerable to destroyer fire, and she would be expensive at about £900,000. She would offer a large target. The new Controller, Rear Admiral Reginald Henderson, realised that a large destroyer might be equivalent to a small cruiser in terms of firepower. The fleet cruiser deficit might then come off destroyer rather than cruiser tonnage. Henderson was very innovative; he was later responsible for the armoured carriers, the *Black Swan*s and the 'Hunts'. He understood that a twin mount could very nearly replace the usual destroyer single mount, doubling the firepower available in a hull of acceptable length (length was important because it determined manoeuvrability). Even a ship of twice the displacement – a small cruiser – would not be so much longer that she would carry very many more mounts, single or twin. The effect of either a 4.7in or a 6in shell on an unarmoured ship would be not too much less than that of the single 6in gun which might arm a very small cruiser.[7] The new heavy 4.7in shell was nearly two-thirds the weight of a cruiser shell, and the new twin mounting could take either the existing 50pdr or the new gun. A big destroyer armed with twin 4.7in guns might be a match for a small cruiser.

The destroyer might also carry equivalent communications gear. The major difference would be that she would be entirely unarmoured. A 'V Leader' was appended to cruiser Designs P through U. The name indicated only that she was alternative 'V' and that she was built to destroyer leader standards, not that she had any functional connection to the destroyer leaders. This ship would cost about half as much as the smallest conventional cruiser, 'U'. The cruiser would enjoy some advantages in sea-keeping, but it was questionable that she could fight her guns in weather worse than that in which the 'V Leader' could fight. The 'V Leader' was conceived as the best gun ship possible within leader (1,850 tons) tonnage, to oppose the best foreign destroyers, the Japanese *Fubuki* and the French *Fantasque*. With her ten twin mountings, she clearly outgunned the former. The latter was clearly more powerful (2,570 tons, five 5.5in guns, about £700,000), but the 'V Leader' offered a greater volume of fire and the unarmoured French ship offered a larger target. Ideally the 'V Leader' would have displaced 2,000 tons, but that was prohibited by treaty.[8]

Had the extra tonnage been available, it would have gone into better scantlings rather than into anything offering better sea-keeping. To get the maximum armament on minimum length, the sketch showed three twin mounts superimposed forward and a single funnel rather than two uptakes. The ship would be 365ft long. The most obvious cost of the extra guns was a reduction to one quintuple torpedo tube mount.

The Naval Staff found the 'V Leader' very attractive. She could make up for the lack of fleet cruisers due to Treaty limits – and to the need to concentrate on big cruisers to deal with the large new Japanese *Mogami*s. Late in 1934 an Admiralty memorandum on the small cruiser question concluded that 'a force of ['V Leaders'] should engage with confidence any other force of unprotected ships at present built or building at the same cost'. Late in September 1934 the Staff circulated DNC's sketches and a paper explaining the concept to the Home and Mediterranean Fleet commanders (they returned their comments in November and December 1934). Overall, the Home Fleet commander approved the new design, but the Mediterranean Fleet commander disagreed: the design was a poor compromise between destroyer and cruiser; such hybrids had never been worthwhile. Buying 'V Leaders' would cut the number of destroyers and the number of torpedoes. In good weather the ship would offer no marked superiority over destroyers for reconnaissance. In bad, speed and fighting ability would fall off more markedly than in Design U. The main threats to the fleet were air and submarine attack by day and, to a lesser extent, destroyer attack at night. The only antidote to the submarine was Asdic-equipped destroyers; for the other threats a small cruiser would do. For the Mediterranean he wanted anti-aircraft firepower in a real cruiser. He thought that on 3,500 tons he could get twelve dual-purpose 4.7in guns by accepting much lower speed (26kts); he also hoped for armour and for some destroyer features (a heavy torpedo battery, Asdic, depth charges). The Naval Staff and the Board of Admiralty rejected this specialised type. The 'V Leader' was armed somewhat like the proposed cruiser (at the time, 40° elevation was considered useful against aircraft), and the proposed cruiser was too slow to evade larger cruisers. Later the Board approved a small anti-aircraft cruiser somewhat like the Mediterranean commander wanted, the *Dido* class. Second in command in the Mediterranean was, if anything, even more negative.

Rear Admiral (Destroyers) (RA(D)), the Mediterranean destroyer commander, liked the 'V Leader' because it would release his destroyers for their legitimate roles. At present they were often detached for cruiser duties. A flotilla of 'V Leaders' would help attacking destroyers beat off opposition, particularly since they would not have to concentrate on themselves joining in the torpedo attack. On flying days the 'V Leaders'

---

[7] Doubling the number of guns (ten × 4.7in vs five × 6in) doubled the chance of hitting within a salvo, but the greater rate of fire of the 4.7in gun more than doubled the rate of hitting. Although a 6in shell had twice the explosive power of a 4.7in, trials showed that either would be adequate against a small unprotected ship. The 6in gun was clearly superior against any armoured ship: 2in side armour could keep out 4.7in shell beyond 7,000 yds, but it could be penetrated by 6in fire beyond 17,000 yds. 1934 memorandum on small cruisers in ADM 1/8828.

[8] In the draft of a memorandum describing the ship the word 'existing' is written in pencil before Treaty; presumably the Admiralty hoped to increase maximum destroyer size in the next treaty.

HMAS *Arunta*, 4 April 1949, in wartime configuration except that she has a US SC-2 air-search radar and six single Bofors guns instead of the wartime Oerlikons. Note that she lacks the bulwarks added to British ships of this type.

would operate with the destroyer flotillas; on non-flying days they would relieve the destroyers of scouting duties. RA(D) was also aware of a study of a conventional destroyer armed with the new gun mounting: on 2 November 1934 Controller had asked DNC whether it would be possible to use the new gun in future destroyer flotillas. He wanted to compare the firepower of a flotilla so armed with that of a flotilla of six 'V Leaders.' DNC replied that he could mount such weapons in A, B and X positions, allowing sufficient weight for the more powerful (62pdr) gun DNO then envisaged. Compared to the latest standard destroyer ('H' class) the ship would have to be lengthened 6ft (to 'E' class length) and beam increased by 3in. Displacement would increase 80 tons, and the total extra cost for the flotilla and leader would amount to £225,000, about two-thirds of the cost of a destroyer.[9] RA(D) pointed out that eighteen six-gun ships, which he preferred, could be had for the same price as fourteen 'V Leaders'. Director of Plans agreed. The most pressing issue was flotilla gunpower, not the cruiser problem. The original Admiralty letter to the fleet commanders was sent before the six-gun alternative had been worked out. Somewhat later the paper was also sent to the China Fleet commander, who alone was familiar with conditions in the most likely war then contemplated, against Japan. Like the Home Fleet commander, he liked the new concept.

The 'V Leader' concept was explained to the Board at its meeting on 25 October 1934. ACNS called for six ships, equivalent in cost to a conventional flotilla. Recalculation suggested that seven would cost about as much as the usual nine destroyers of a flotilla. DCNS pointed out that under the London Treaty the 16 per cent of destroyers which could be

1,850-tonners equated to just under thirteen ships: seven in 1935 and then six or seven in 1936. The figure seven was attractive partly because it was thought that the tactical unit would be the senior officer's ship plus a pair of three-ship divisions. On 20 February 1935 the First Sea Lord formally recommended to the Board that seven 'V Leaders' be included in the 1935 Programme. The implication was that another seven would be ordered in 1936, each flotilla going to one of the two main fleets. The Board approved the seven ships, which might have eight or ten 4.7in guns (Controller favoured eight). At this stage they were to be built instead of the usual annual nine-ship flotilla.

Meanwhile the situation was changing. Japan had withdrawn from the Washington Conference structure in March 1934, claiming that nothing short of parity with the other sea powers would satisfy her. Parity was unacceptable to them, because each of them had responsibilities both in the Atlantic and in the Pacific. Giving Japan parity would make it impossible to meet her fleet on equal terms in the Pacific. Early in 1935 a new naval arms limitation conference convened in London in hopes of salvaging some sort of naval arms control. The British position on destroyers was to continue the 150,000-ton limit, though presumably on underage ships rather than on the force as a whole. A few weeks after the conference opened, the Japanese walked out, their demand for parity having been rejected. Without Japanese agreement to some form of ratio, there was no further point in maintaining overall limits to fleets.

Thus Director of Plans pointed out early in February 1935 that ships in the 1936 Programme could be laid down in the unrestricted year (1937) following the end of the 1930 treaty limits. However, any ships bought under the 1935 Programme (laid down early in 1936) would still come under the 1930 limit

[9] Controller, Rear Admiral Henderson, to First Sea Lord, 12 November 1934, enclosing DNC's outline tracing of the ship. On about 1,400 tons a destroyer could have a single mount in A position and twins in B and X. DNC (F Bryant) estimated that the ship would be 326ft long on the waterline (as in the 'E' class) and 33ft 6in beam, and would displace 1,430 tons standard (55 tons more than an 'E').

HMAS *Bataan* is shown post-war, her searchlight platform cut down completely and a twin Mk V Bofors mounted in her pompom position. All of her Oerlikons have been replaced by single Bofors. When D numbers replaced the original I series pennant numbers, the ship's original 191 was replaced by D191 because the number D91 had already been assigned.

on overall British destroyer tonnage. Placing ships in the 1936 Programme to avoid the limits violated the spirit, but not the letter, of the 1930 London Treaty. It followed that the 1935 Programme should be limited to the usual annual flotilla, preferably the six-gun design; the 'V Leader' should be deferred to 1936.[10] Since by that time there would no longer be a limit on cruiser tonnage, the implication was that this special design might not be needed at all. On the other hand, there was hardly time to design a new small fleet cruiser. Presumably because the new ships really were not conventional destroyers, ultimately they were included in the 1935 programme *in addition to* the usual destroyer flotilla (which became the 'I' class, the last of the cycle begun in the 1920s). The idea of the six-gun destroyer was dropped without comment, presumably because the design effort required to produce the 'V Leader' precluded it. The tonnage problem was solved because the British government invoked the 'escalator clause' in the 1930 Treaty, to retain overage ships which otherwise would have been scrapped as new ones were completed.

The idea of operating the ships in flotillas was soon dropped. If the ship's main weapon was the gun, then a seven-ship tactical organisation would be too cramped. A cruiser-like squadron of four would be far more attractive. Unfortunately the decision to build eight came on 4 October 1935, the day after the Treasury was told that there would be seven ships

[10] Director of Plans memo 4 February 1935, in ADM 1/8828.

in the 1935 Programme. It had also been told that they would be additional to the usual annual flotilla. Thus the Board had to provide nine in 1936 to achieve the desired total of sixteen (a flotilla of eight for each of the two main fleets).

There was considerable debate over what to call the ship. 'V Leader' was inappropriate, as she was not a leader in any sense. There was some interest in reviving the old frigate or corvette designation, much as after the Second World War the US Navy called its super-destroyers frigates; the Admiralty Librarian was asked to describe the lineage of these names, and the reasons they had been dropped. Other rejected alternatives were:

> Scout (preferred by Director of Tactical Division), rejected for emphasising scouting over fighting.
> Scout Destroyer (rejected as it would provoke the French, the implication being that their *Fantasques* were 'scouts' to be destroyed).
> Destroyer Scout.
> Patrol Destroyer (rejected as too defensive; Support Destroyer was preferred).
> Cruiser Destroyer (rejected because it implied attack on cruisers).
> Heavy, Large, or Super Destroyer.

In the end (June 1935) the choice fell on 'Tribal' Class

Destroyer, 'Tribal' being a good name in the Royal Navy and avoiding any definition of the type. However, the Support Destroyer designation survived in many documents.

The first Staff Requirements were circulated in March 1935.[11] Primary characteristics were good gun armament and good communications and plotting arrangements, suitable for production in sufficient numbers. At the least the 'V Leader' would have roughly the radio (W/T) capabilities of a destroyer leader, but with the sets arranged more like those of a cruiser, for general fleet work. The ship had to be small enough to avoid becoming too attractive a target, but large enough to be a good gun platform with sufficient firepower, and to have good seakeeping. Maximum speed was set at 36kts. Endurance would be about 5,500nm at 15kts, and displacement would be within the 1,850-ton treaty limit. At this stage specified armament was five twin 4.7in and torpedoes. Three of the twin mounts would be forward and two aft, for the best possible arcs, despite the enlarged silhouette that would entail. They would be controlled from a Director Control Tower (DCT), as such ships would probably engage targets that would be difficult to select, and hence would need the comfort and facilities of a cruiser-type DCT. Ammunition supply would be 200 rounds of low-angle per gun, plus fifty for high-angle fire (mounts were provided with twenty ready-use rounds per barrel).

The ship's functions included contribution to the anti-aircraft defence of the fleet, convoys and harbours. A Naval Anti-Aircraft Gunnery Committee was convened in 1931. In 1932 it specifically recommended against developing a dual-purpose destroyer gun: 1929 trials of a 60° mounting in HMS *Bulldog* had been unsuccessful.[12] The key assumption was that any destroyer gun had to be served from the deck of the ship. The higher the elevation of the gun, the higher the trunnions, because they had to lift the gun high enough to allow it to recoil (at maximum elevation) without hitting the deck. Higher-powered guns required more trunnion height because they recoiled further. Above a certain trunnion height, it would be impossible for a man standing on the deck of the ship to feed the gun. The solutions were either to provide a pit under the gun mount (reducing the ship's deck strength) or to place the crew on a platform above the deck, revolving with the gun, as in the contemporary US 5in/38. That in turn required more complex arrangements (such as ammunition hoists revolving with the gun mount), which the Royal Navy rejected. As for the new heavy shell, trials showed that for elevations above 50°, power ramming was necessary. Insisting on 60° or 70° elevation for a 4.7in mounting would require full power operation for training and loading. DNO considered such a mounting, with its complexity and size (silhouette) entirely

unsuited to a small ship such as a destroyer.[13] DNO argued that trials showed that the maximum size of gun which could be successfully hand-loaded at all elevations, and which was really suited to anti-aircraft use from a destroyer, was the 4in (35lb shell), whose twin mounting weighed 14 tons, somewhat more than a 40°-elevation single 4.7in (62pdr). According to a 1936 Admiralty memorandum on destroyer characteristics, 'no considerations of HA fire can be countenanced which might prejudice LA fire until such time as aircraft threaten the successful accomplishment of the destroyer's main object – which is delivery of a torpedo attack'.[14] The 4in gun offered a good chance of stopping an enemy destroyer, but a destroyer stopped without being sunk could still fire torpedoes; sinking the destroyer required the most powerful gun a British destroyer could mount, the 4.7in.[15] Moreover, it seemed unlikely that bombers would attack destroyers; surely they would concentrate on the battleships. Given the entirely practicable elevation of 40°, a destroyer could engage bombers for some time as they approached.[16] She might well help break-up formations and thus prevent the bombers from attacking effectively. Thus the 1931 Committee recommended that that all destroyer guns be capable of 40° elevation, which it expected would offer a significant contribution to fleet air defence. Ideally the guns should also be available to help defend the fleet in harbour, when it would be particularly vulnerable to bombers. The first ships affected were the 'E' class of the 1931 Programme. It was accepted that a ship operating independently (for trade protection) or as a convoy escort might well be the bombers' objective, which is why sloops were armed with 4in anti-aircraft guns in the mid-1930s.

Short-range anti-aircraft weapons, which could be improvised in an emergency, were considered less urgent, probably largely because it was not yet understood that they would be the main defence against the most potent means of attacking individual ships, dive-bombing. Unfortunately for the Royal Navy, the 1931 committee reported just before dive-bombing was accepted as a successful tactic, although by 1935, with a British dive bomber (the Skua) entering service, this view had been reversed. The most powerful short-range weapon was the 2pdr pompom, the eight-barrel version of which was first proposed in a fleet anti-aircraft study in 1921. It ran successful trials in 1927 and entered service in 1930 as

---

[11] TD 43/35, with functions given in AL. 0345/34 of 28 November 1934, in Cover 541 ('Tribal' Class).
[12] The report of the 1931 Committee, essentially descriptions of air threats to ships, is ADM 186/317. The high-angle destroyer mount had been proposed in 1926, the initial goal being 70° elevation. This CP Mk XIII mounting was hand-trained and elevated but used power ramming for high angles.

[13] C E B Simeon, DNO, 8 May 1936, quoted in Folio 1 of the 'J' Class Cover.
[14] In the 'J' Class Cover.
[15] A 1936 calculation, made early in the 'J' class design, compared the four 4.7in of a conventional destroyer to three twin 4in (both 42 tons of gun mountings). Broadsides would be, respectively, 248lbs and 210lbs, but the 4in fired more rapidly (totals forty and ninety shells per minute, so the 4in ship would make about twice as many hits per minute at 7,000 yds).
[16] Minute Sheet M.209/35 in ADM 1/8828. Analysis of the 4.7in battery in connection with the 'Tribals' showed that a bomber flying level at 5,000ft would be under fire at ranges from 13,000 yds down to 2,500 yds (2 minutes at 160kts, at the time a reasonable figure). The higher the bomber the more limiting the 40° elevation limit: at 12,000ft only between 11,000 and 7,000 yds (0.75 minutes). However, flying higher would reduce bombing accuracy. The destroyer would probably be attacked directly only when operating independently, in which case her freedom of manoeuvre would make her too difficult a target for anything but a dive bomber. Such aircraft were considered very difficult targets because as they dove their rates of change of bearing and elevation would be too high for effective fire control, except in the line of attack and very close to the target. The pompom was *not* considered a solution to this problem.

HMCS *Haida*, September 1948, before reconstruction. (Canadian Dept of National Defence)

a battleship weapon. However, it was too massive for a cruiser or a destroyer. The 1931 Naval Anti-Aircraft Gunnery Committee recommended development of a quadruple version (Mk VII, sometimes called Mk M in design documents), which became the standard Second World War destroyer weapon. It was tested in 1935–6 on board HMS *Crusader*, by which time it had already been incorporated into many ship designs. Although initially considered an anti-aircraft weapon, by 1937 tests had shown that it had considerable potential against a new threat, the motor torpedo boat (MTB), which had become much more prominent during the Abyssinian crisis in the Mediterranean. The pompom remained in service throughout the Second World War, supplemented but not replaced by various 40mm Bofors mounts. It was far more successful than the broadly equivalent US quadruple 1.1in gun. The gun was a 40mm/39, and should not be confused with the wartime Bofors 40mm/60, which had a much higher muzzle velocity (typically 2,890ft/sec vs. 2,040ft/sec in the original weapon and later 2,400ft/sec using a lighter projectile, 1.7lbs rather than 2lbs). The mount could fire up to 115 rounds per gun per minute. A typical Mk VII* weighed 8.6 tons, compared to 8.8 tons for the single 4.7in (50pdr) CP Mk XVII in an 'G' class destroyer. Pre-war faith in the pompom was limited. During the discussions leading up to the construction of the 'Tribal' class, it was argued that the value of the pompom might lie more in the enemy's fear of it than in its chance of actually shooting down aircraft.[17] Without a director, and with a low muzzle velocity, the pompom was considered unlikely to get many hits at over 1,000 yds range. Trials on board the ex-battleship *Centurion* suggested not more than 5 per cent hits, and the pompom would have only ten seconds of firing time before bomb release by a dive bomber.

The pompom was supplemented by a hand-operated quadruple 0.5in machine gun introduced in 1932, its four barrels mounted one above the other. Unlike the pompom, this weapon was of little significance during the war, having been overtaken (like the 0.5in in the US Navy) by the 20mm Oerlikon.[18] The fleet response to the 1933 letter asked for a multi-barrel anti-aircraft gun between 2pdr and 0.5in calibre, to replace both. That seems to have been the origin of a sextuple 0.661in gun, a prototype of which was ordered from Vickers in 1935. Expected rate of fire was 300 rounds per gun per minute, each shell weighing 3oz. Thus the 0.661in fired 1,800 rounds per minute, compared to about 460 for the pompom; but each of its shells weighed less than 10 per cent as much, so the weight of fire was only about 37 per cent that of the pompom (though far more than that of the 0.5in). Thus, properly aimed, the 0.661in would get many more hits than an equally-well aimed pompom; but each hit would be far less effective and its aiming apparatus was considered much inferior to that of the pompom. The 0.661in was cancelled in 1938, partly because its fire control was inferior to that of the 2pdr, and partly because it was considered much less effective against MTBs. For the new ship, possible short-range batteries, in order of preference, were two pompoms, one each side, plus multiple 0.5in machine guns if possible; or one pompom on the centreline with two multiple machine guns, one each side; or the maximum possible number of multiple machine guns.

Ideally the DCT would have been used for both high- and

[17] ADM 167/93.
[18] The quadruple mount was Mk III. In November 1940 MTB-type power-operated twin Mk Vs were ordered mounted on board all 4.7in 'L' class destroyers and all 'M' class destroyers. Later the project was expanded, on the grounds that it would save manufacturing effort and personnel. Ships involved were *Lookout* and *Loyal*, the 'M' class, *Noble*, *Nonpareil*, *Norseman*, *Onslow*, *Opportune*, *Obdurate*, *Onslaught*, *Orwell*, *Obedient*, *Pakenham*, and probably other 'P' class destroyers (they were also planned at that time for the 'Q' and 'R' classes).

HMCS *Haida*, taken from the carrier HMCS *Magnificent*, June 1949, before reconstruction. (Canadian Dept of National Defence)

low-angle fire, but at a meeting on 1 March 1935 DNO estimated that a dual-purpose tower would be too heavy. Moreover, no existing combined tower could provide gyro firing. The choice was to keep the range finder and the DCT (low angle, as in existing destroyer leaders) separate. The separate rangefinder could, it was hoped, be replaced by a combination anti-aircraft director and rangefinder then being fitted to a sloop for trials. The reference to reasonably calm weather set the rate of power train and elevation, which determined how much roll and pitch the fire control system could handle (10°/sec was selected, which was not enough for bad weather). Limiting some of the mounts to low-angle fire would save some weight, but the idea was soon rejected: more, not less, anti-aircraft capability was wanted.

The torpedoes were wanted for night and poor weather, so they should be ready on either side. Alternatives were a triple mounting on each side; or fixed tubes on each side (if possible three, in nests or singles as convenient); or a quintuple mounting arranged with three tubes firing one way and two the other; or a conventional quintuple mount with power train controlled from the bridge, so that it could be trained very quickly. The ship would have Asdic for ASW, as in recent destroyers.

DNC developed five designs and reported two to Controller on 19 March: one with five and one with four twin mounts.[19]

[19] The designs were designated A through E. A was the five-mount design; B was A with speed reduced to 35.5kts (41,500 SHP, 1,830 tons); C was the same ship with speed reduced to 35kts (40,000 SHP, 1,810 tons). D was the four-mount design for 37kts (48,000 SHP, 1,830 tons), and E was the five-mount design with Q gun replaced by a quadruple pompom (45,000 SHP, 36kts, 1,845 tons). Of these designs, A through C were 370ft × 36ft, D was 360ft × 36ft, and E was 366ft × 36ft. ACNS proposed omitting A mount in the five-mount design, raising the forecastle 2½ft. This idea was not pursued.

The five-mount design had one mounting amidships between the funnels, capable of training 20° forward of the centreline on either side. Superimposing three mounts forward was rejected, possibly because the estimated weight of a mounting had increased 4 to 5 tons since the original sketch. In both designs the aftermost 4.7in mount could train 32° off the centreline on forward bearings; X gun could train from 7° (level) to 154° at all elevation angles. Each also had a pair of quadruple 0.5in machine guns on the bridge. Standard displacement of the five-gun version was 1,870 tons with 240 rounds per 4.7in gun (cutting to 190 per gun would bring it to 1,850 tons). Asdic and depth charges were omitted (adding them would cost 10 tons). The four-gun version had four quadruple 0.5in machine guns, two on the bridge and two in the waist. Replacing the two in the waist with a four-barrel pompom between the funnels would increase displacement from 1,832 tons to 1,845 tons. Both versions had quadruple torpedo tubes (quintuple would cost another 5 tons). Each design offered 2½ft more freeboard forward than earlier destroyers and leaders, to add an extra deck (with more accommodation) forward.

Several of the alternatives were developed to test the effects of reducing maximum speed to 35kts or increasing it to 37kts. In the five-mount version, cutting power from the original 45,000 SHP (for 36kts) to 41,500 SHP (35.5kts) would reduce displacement to 1,828 tons; cutting to 40,000 SHP (35kts) would bring displacement down again, to 1,812 tons. This version was 370ft long. Endurance was greater than required, at about 6,000nm at 15kts clean (5,250nm when six months out of dock).

The four-mount version was 360ft long, and it was rated at 37kts (48,000 SHP). The version with the pompom had 45,000 SHP engines for 36kts. It later turned out that new boilers could give another 2,000 HP on about the same length and weight needed to provide 35.5kts, for the required 36kts.

British cruisers were being designed with alternating engine and boiler rooms, so that no single hit would immobilise them. The Naval Attaches reported that large foreign destroyers were being similarly designed: the Italian *Navigatori*s had a single engine room between their boiler rooms, and the French *Fantasque*s had alternating engine and boiler rooms. Could that be done in the new super-destroyer? The machinery in the 35.5kt design, was 131ft long; alternating spaces would require 165ft. That in turn would stretch the ship to 420ft (2,100 tons), increasing target size by about 11 per cent, and another fifteen ratings would be required. Control would be made more difficult (by splitting up the engines), and any advantage in protection would be illusory in an unarmoured ship. This was exactly opposite to the conclusion reached about the same time by the US Navy. By adopting higher steam conditions, the US Navy had made its machinery much more compact, so that it did not have to pay anything like the penalty envisaged by the E-in-C.

ACNS observed that the treaty limits were sure to end very soon. Could a markedly superior ship not be had on 2,000 tons? DNC and the E-in-C thought that 150 tons more would buy a bit better seakeeping, but that advantage would be difficult to quantify. The 1,850-ton standard displacement might be confusing because it did not correspond to the earlier Navy List (normal) measurement. ACNS might well be thinking of earlier small cruisers rated at 2,000 tons – which was equivalent to 1,850 tons standard.

From a visual point of view, the most striking feature of the design was a new type of bridge, which met demands for a lower silhouette. As it was expected that destroyers would often attack at night, the height and bulk of their silhouettes might well decide the range at which they would be spotted in a pre-radar age. In British destroyers the helmsman stood on the deck below the open bridge. Combining his position with the bridge would save a deck level, 6 or 7ft. Another way to save height would be to limit the helmsman to an indirect view. The British adopted a compromise. The helmsman was moved ahead of the bridge, so that it did not have to be a full deck-height above him. The roof above this forward position was sloped up. Because the helmsman stood alone, he did not need

HMS *Eskimo* as completed, 5 March 1939, with the original four twin 4.7in mounts. Atop her bridge is a 12ft rangefinder director Mk II overlooking the standard director control tower (DCT) for her 4.7in guns. This was the first class in which a 12ft instrument replaced the earlier 9ft rangefinder. For surface fire Mk II functioned purely as a rangefinder, its crew using 'follow-the-pointer' equipment to stay with the target under fire by the DCT. However, it could function as an anti-aircraft director in its own right. The below-decks calculators were the Admiralty Fire Control Clock (AFCC) Mk I for surface fire and the Fuse-Keeping Clock (FKC) Mk I (so-called because it had to calculate fuse settings) for anti-aircraft fire. The hand-trained DCT contained a gyro-stabilised sight for surface action. It was operated by the trainer and layer who aimed it and by the cross-level operator who compensated for the angle at which the DCT was tilted around the line of sight. Targets were designated by the Control Officer. The Spotting Officer estimated errors in range and the Rate Officer errors in line (associated with errors in estimating target speed and course). Both layer and trainer had gyro-stabilised binoculars, to acquire a target, and gyro-stabilised sights. A layer (elevation operator) was needed to compensate for the ship's motion (in effect, to measure the apparent up- and down-motion of the line of sight to the target, even though in fact the target was fixed on the surface of the sea). (A D Baker III)

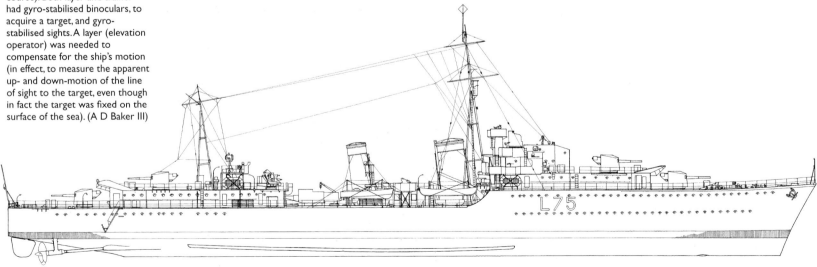

a full deck width, so the sides of his space were angled back to the full width of the open bridge above. The new type of bridge was characteristic of British destroyers up to the end of the Second World War. It was tested in two 1934 destroyers (*Hero* and *Hereward*) and it was fitted to the 1935 destroyers ('I' class) built in parallel with the 'V Leaders'. The net effect of the change was to reduce bridge height from 36ft to 32ft, bringing it back to about the same level as in the 'V' class of the First World War. For the 'Tribals', the new bridge was described as a way of holding down superstructure height while keeping the open bridge clear of the taller gun mounts; but it was also described as a way of reducing bridge height in destroyers with single 4.7in guns, a response to fleet pressure for lower silhouettes. The new bridge shape was tested extensively in a wind tunnel. It was designed to deflect wind, but it could not deflect spray or rain. Hence a partial roof was fitted, with two Kent clear-view screens on the front windscreens.

As presented to the Board, the sketch design offered a maximum speed (at standard displacement) of 36kts (32.5kts fully loaded) on 44,000 SHP. Although engine and boiler rooms did not alternate, the engine room was divided by a transverse bulkhead, which would make it more difficult to put out of action with a single shell hit, and the three boilers were in three separate rooms. The sketch design, approved on 1 August, showed five twin 4.7in mounts, of which X mount was raised above the quarterdeck (to cover its ammunition supply), with Y superimposed above it. There was no space for a pompom, but the ship had two of the standard quadruple 0.5in machine guns, on either side of the bridge. However, in July DNC had written that ammunition supply to Q (No. 3) gun was unsatisfactory, the shell rooms being some distance away (shells would have to be carried along the forecastle deck), and its arcs were limited; it might be better to replace it with pompoms on either side. The Board approved this change on 20 September 1935. DNC then proposed substituting a single eight-barrel pompom, which could be located clear of gun blast, on the after superstructure. By November, the design had been changed again, this time to place one four-barrel pompom forward of the mainmast, on the after superstructure, and one between the funnels. Ultimately the pompom between the funnels was eliminated in favour of a pair of quadruple 0.5in machine guns. In this form the Legend and drawings were approved by the Board on 28 November 1935. The only major change after that was a more sharply raked ('French') bow, which it was hoped would keep A gun mount drier.

HMS *Ashanti* as in late 1941 or early 1942, refitted with a twin 4in gun in X position and Type 286 radar (with fixed 'bedstead' array) forward. She shows 'Headache' on her foremast, having been one of the first ships so fitted. Note that she retained her original quadruple 0.5in machine guns between her funnels, but also had Oerlikons on the signal deck and aft. (Alan Raven)

HMCS *Athabaskan* as refitted late in 1943, with a lattice foremast and twin Oerlikons. The Canadian 'Tribals' had extra beam and therefore could have their quadruple 2pdrs raised a deck level to the position occupied in British ships by the searchlight aft. The lattice mast overcame vibration problems experienced with the earlier tripods. As here, the lattice could also carry a topmast with HF/DF, whereas ships with tripods generally carried their HF/DF arrays on a stub mainmast (some ships with lattice masts also carried them that way). (Alan Raven)

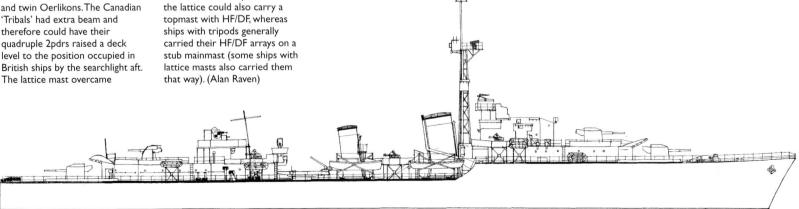

Two flotillas (sixteen ships) were built for the Royal Navy. These 'Tribals' were certainly the most famous of all British destroyers, and probably the best-looking. They were certainly well-liked, the only apparent defect being some structural weakness (which was corrected) which can probably be traced to a willingness to increase hull stresses so as to stay within the Treaty displacement limit. On the other hand, their considerable size made wartime modification relatively easy. The sixteen ships saw intense action, so that by 1945 only four of them survived. Unlike other pre-war ships, they were not immediately discarded, which says something for their continuing perceived value (they were, however, stricken in 1948).

Once war broke out, it became painfully obvious that the 40° 4.7in gun was an inadequate anti-aircraft weapon. In May 1940 (see Chapter 5) DNC held an emergency meeting to improve destroyer anti-aircraft armament. For the 'Tribals', Controller proposed to replace No. 2 or No. 3 mount with a twin 4in. No.2 was rejected because that would so greatly reduce ahead fire and also because it would cause considerable blast on the bridge. The twin 4in gun in No. 3 position was controlled by a high-angle DCT (with Type 285 radar) which replaced the earlier three-man rangefinder.

As in other destroyers, these ships suffered considerable wartime weight growth. By 1942 they typically displaced 117 tons more than when completed, of which only 45 tons could definitely be identified. Stability suffered: metacentric height fell from 2.67ft to 2.09ft, based on inclining experiments on *Eskimo* and *Bedouin* in August 1941. Typical additions, by 1942, were radar (Type 286PQ for air search and Type 285 for 4.7in fire control), MF/DF, HF/DF (FH 3 aft), the two 4in guns, four single and then twin Oerlikons (wings of signal deck and after deckhouse), two single Oerlikons (between the funnels), additional depth charges (for a total of forty-six, soon exceeded), and protective plating on the searchlight platform, in way of the main guns, and mattresses (for splinter protection) at the anti-aircraft guns and at the transmitting station. Gun shields were stiffened. Lookout positions were added. Permanent degaussing and SA equipment (against acoustic mines) were installed. The ship was fitted for Arctic operations, and 35 tons of permanent ballast added. Against that, the No. 3 4.7in gun and 0.5in guns had been removed, the mainmast had been replaced by a pole, the depth charge throwers and eight depth charges lowered from the after deck house to the upper deck, the after funnel cut down by 4ft, and a 25ft gasoline-powered motor boat landed. Ultimately ships were fitted with air search and target indication radar (Types 291 and 293), the latter on a lattice foremast. A short pole aft carried HF/DF.

The two largest Commonwealth navies chose to build versions of this class. The Australians expected to have to deal with raiders in any future war, and their cruiser fleet was limited, and so they may well have emphasised the quasi-

cruiser role. In February 1936 the Admiralty advised the RAN to build a unit of four large destroyers, and in June the Australian Naval Staff chose the 'Tribal' class. The Government postponed any decision, but in October 1938, with war clearly imminent, it approved a programme including three 'Tribals' (later reduced to two) plus twelve MTBs. The MTBs were later eliminated in favour of two more 'Tribals', only one of which, *Bataan*, was built. Larger numbers may have been planned. A May 1939 report by the Australian Chiefs of Staff proposed further naval expansion including, among other ships, four more 'Tribals' (its report also called for a capital ship with a screen of four more destroyers, presumably not 'Tribals'). While under construction the three Australian ships were modified to match the British 'Tribals', with the twin 4in gun in X position.

The Canadians also wanted 'Tribals' for their cruiser-like qualities. By November 1936 the RCN force goal was a total of eighteen modern destroyers, but until January 1939 the Canadian government agreed only to buy six. At that time, with war clearly imminent, the government proposed to lay down two 'Tribals' in Canada in each of the next six years, as well as numerous smaller units. The first major Canadian building programme was approved on 19 September, soon after Canada entered the war. A three-year programme approved in October 1939 called for completion of the first two years' worth of ships, including four destroyers, during the first year and a half. Two more destroyers would be ordered in each of the following two years, for a total of eight.

It was soon clear that the destroyers could not be built in Canada; the Canadians hoped to barter ASW ships (initially to have been *Black Swans*) for British-built destroyers. The British initially refused, because so much of the equipment of the sloops involved would have come from British production and so would have competed with British construction of the same type of ship. On 25 October 1939, however, with Canadian Cabinet approval, the Canadian Chief of Naval Staff revived the barter idea, this time offering corvettes, which would be built entirely in Canada. He estimated that five corvettes should be exchanged for one British-built 'Tribal'. The Admiralty agreed in principle, but ultimately it was impossible to equate costs in the two countries. The decision was therefore for the Royal Navy to order ten corvettes in Canada while the Canadians ordered two 'Tribals' in the UK (on 11 April 1940), each country paying for the ships. The Canadians ordered a second pair of 'Tribals' on 1 March 1941.

Compared to the British ships, they had another foot of beam, and their hulls were specially stiffened to reduce stresses (which had proven excessive in the British ships; this was not ice stiffening). There was an auxiliary boiler in the forward boiler room to heat living and machinery spaces. Gravity tanks were also heated, as they might freeze. A 44in searchlight with stabilised sights replaced the 24in hand-operated

searchlights of the standard 'Tribal', and generator capacity was increased to suit it. The ships were modified to reflect British war experience, *eg* getting a 4in gun in No. 3 position. Depth charge stowage on each rail was increased from three to six. The bridge was modified to take lookouts and radar. Due to their larger beam, these ships could mount more light anti-aircraft guns, *eg* six Oerlikons rather than the four of the British ships. The second pair of ships received new dual-purpose directors.

The Canadians were still interested in building 'Tribals' at home, at least partly to develop their warship-building industry. In June 1941 their Privy Council agreed to order two ships in Halifax. The Canadian E-in-C feared they were too complex, and would have preferred *Black Swans*. British yards could build the ships much more quickly. DNC had already suggested that a smaller destroyer might be easier to build, perhaps the pre-war 'F' class or the Intermediate (see Chapter 3) modified with conventional transverse rather than longitudinal framing. DNO wondered whether he could supply sufficient gun mountings by the time the hulls and machinery were ready. The Canadian Navy Minister and the Chief of Naval Staff disagreed, arguing that there was no point in wasting time on less complex types. Initially machinery and other components would have been ordered in Britain, but when

The big Polish destroyer *Blyskawica* (Lightning) was the closest British export equivalent to a 'Tribal'. Two such ships were built, and the Polish Navy planned to build two more in home yards. Probably the most important difference from the 'Tribals' was the least visible: these ships were large fast destroyers, without the command and control arrangements otherwise associated with cruisers. Nor were they subject to treaty limitation. The ships were somewhat larger than 'Tribals' (2,011 tons standard) with much more powerful machinery (54,500 SHP), for a rated speed of 39kts, which they slightly exceeded on trials. When they escaped to Britain in 1939, it was found that they were top-heavy, suited to the

relatively calm Baltic but not to the North Atlantic. Both had to be cut down, and the surviving unit, *Blyskawica*, was rearmed with four twin 4in guns and four Oerlikons. She survives as a museum ship. J S White won a 1934 design competition, defeating Swan Hunter in the UK. White's successful design showed two superimposed mounts forward, but A mount was a single, as in some later Royal Navy destroyer proposals. The Swan Hunter design showed only the twin mount forward. Thornycroft, Vickers, and Yarrow all decided not to bid. The competition was opened because a design offered in 1933 by the main French destroyer builder, Ateliers et Chantiers de la Loire, was rejected (this yard had recently

built the previous pair of Polish destroyers, the *Burza* class). The French design was broadly similar to that of the slightly earlier *Le Fantasque*, except that it had two triple torpedo tubes on the centreline. Its gun armament was the five 130mm of the French ship. Both British designs showed standard British weapons, 4.7in guns. However, when they were designed pompoms were not available for export, so *Blyskawica* had foreign-made weapons: two twin Bofors guns in Dutch stabilised mountings (the Swan Hunter design showed a pair of single 40mm guns). Fire controls were supplied by Sperry in the United States. Torpedo tubes were the French 550mm type, for standardisation with the earlier destroyers.

two more 'Tribals' were included in the 1942/43 programme it became worth while to manufacture them in Canada. The last two Canadian-built ships, *Cayuga* and the second *Athabaskan*, were completed with four twin 4in anti-aircraft guns, four Bofors (one twin, two singles), and two twin Oerlikons. They had the late-war Mk VI director, with Type 275 radar. Post-war modifications to the Australian and Canadian ships are described in Chapter 11.

CHAPTER 3
What Sort of Destroyer?

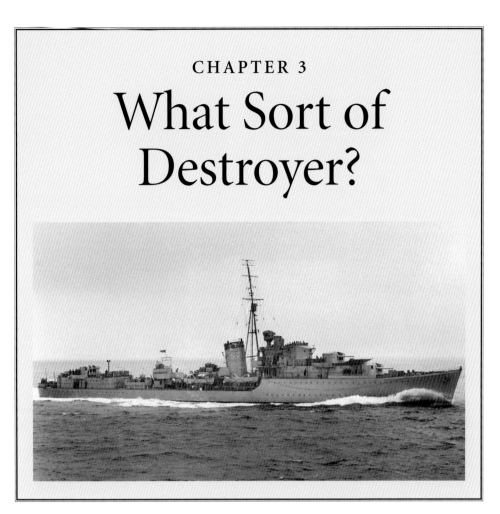

The 'Tribals' were not really destroyers. What sort of true destroyers, if any, should succeed them? If the destroyer was mainly a large torpedo boat, her guns were intended only to help her fight through cruisers or destroyers screening the enemy capital ships, her targets. However, if her main role was to protect the battleships from the enemy's torpedo force, then guns became far more important. Would a fleet action begin with a mêlée in which the destroyers on both sides simply destroyed each other?

In 1936 DTSD considered the fleet defence and torpedo attack roles so contradictory that he suggested building two different types, attackers (A) and counter-attackers (B). A would be small ships comparable to the old Admiralty 'S' class, armed primarily with torpedoes, while B would be large gun ships (perhaps 'Tribals') intended mainly to clear the way for the attackers. Director of Navigation W G Benn argued that it was only because of the shortage of cruisers that British destroyers were being so heavily armed with guns; given enough cruisers, perhaps the counter-attack destroyer would be unnecessary. This contradiction was never resolved. The British found themselves building larger and larger destroyers offering both heavier gun batteries and powerful torpedo batteries, while looking back fondly at the 'purer' destroyers built prior to the 'Tribals'.

A new tactical factor in 1936 was the possibility of war against Italy, which had a massive fleet of MTBs effective in the relatively calm Mediterranean. This was when the new *King George V* class battleships were given very low sheer so that their main battery guns could engage MTBs right ahead (at a considerable cost in seakeeping). Destroyers screening the fleet would have to deal with them just as with submarines and aircraft. The main destroyer weapon against such craft was the multiple pompom.

For a time it seemed that there would be two parallel lines of development, 'Tribals' and true destroyers with heavy torpedo batteries. That had happened in 1935 with the 'Tribal' and 'I' classes, and plans called for doing much the same thing in 1936 (the torpedo destroyers were sometimes called Supplementary Destroyers). Much the same thing was expected for the 1937 and 1938 Programmes, the 'Tribals' being superseded by a new 'Super Tribal' design. Under the usual alphabetical naming sequence, the 1936 destroyers would be the 'J' class, the 1937 ships the 'K' class, and the 1938 ships the 'L' class. The 62pdr gun would be introduced in the 1937 'Super Tribals' and in the 1938 'L' class.[1]

The treaty system was changing radically. In March 1934 the Japanese had announced their withdrawal from the treaty system, effectively ensuring that whatever replaced the Washington Treaty and the 1930 London Treaty would not limit total destroyer or cruiser tonnage. Distinctions between destroyers and cruisers would become meaningless. There would still, of course, be a need to hold down unit destroyer tonnage in the interest of building sufficient numbers at a reasonable price. The new treaty worked out at the 1935 London Naval Conference incorporated a last attempt to hold back

---

[1] Folio 3 of 1936 Programme (Support) destroyers, signed 25 August 1936. It was assumed that each destroyer flotilla would be nine ships, each 'Tribal' or 'Super Tribal' flotilla eight ships.

qualitative races in ship design. Each party undertook to publish details of new ships four months before they were laid down. The hope was that no party could spring a surprise, leaving others so far behind that they would feel compelled to race to catch up, as happened in 1906 with HMS *Dreadnought*. The 1930 Treaty had included a publication requirement (displacement, principal dimensions, calibre of largest gun), but the new treaty, which came into force on 31 December 1936, demanded far more details. It affected the next destroyer class ('J'). Later the publication requirement made it impossible to lay down 'Hunt' class destroyers before sufficient time had elapsed, despite the sense that war was rapidly approaching.

In effect the 1936 destroyer began with the Admiralty's 1933 letter (Strategic Problem F) on destroyer design issues. It responded to general dissatisfaction with the standard destroyers which had evolved since the late 1920s, which could be seen as improved versions of the First World War 'V & W' class. Given treaty limits on total destroyer tonnage, they had been built to minimum displacement and to minimum length. High-power machinery filling the area amidships pushed the guns and bridges towards the bows, the after guns and superstructure towards the stern. The ships were criticised as wet forward and as crowded aft. Hulls were considered too weak, presumably because of weight-saving measures. This policy was reversed in the 'G' and later classes, the spacing between their hull frames being restored to that standard until the end of the First World War.

To get more firepower on forward bearings, the fleet asked for larger forward arcs for the after guns. Leaders should have the fifth gun, dropped to cut their displacement (so as to stay within treaty limits), restored. This was done in HMS *Exmouth*

and later leaders. All guns should have 40° elevation, so that the separate 3in anti-aircraft gun could be eliminated. Quintuple (pentad) torpedo tubes should replace the earlier quadruples, a step approved for the 1935 'I' class. All new destroyer designs should have Asdic and fittings for TSDS, and they should be arranged for easy and rapid conversion to minelaying. The fleet was satisfied with the legend (standard displacement) speed of 35kts, which equated to about 31kts in deep condition.

The Admiralty was particularly interested in reducing destroyer silhouette. RA(D), the Mediterranean destroyer commander (Rear Admiral A B Cunningham), considered gun arrangement the key factor.[2] With a twin mount forward instead of two singles, the bridge could be lowered about 4ft. However, Cunningham doubted that the twin was the equal of a single mount. Later the idea of replacing both forward mounts with one twin was rejected on the ground that a separate mounting was needed to fire starshell for illumination at night.

The new twin mount could drastically reduce congestion aft by replacing X and Y mounts. Mounted atop the after superstructure, it would enjoy better forward arcs. The ship could be made shorter, with three rather than four gun mountings (a twin occupied much the same length as a single). Eliminating X gun would make it possible to enlarge the after superstructure. The larger deckhouse could accommodate the staff of a flotilla leader within the same dimensions as the destroyers of the flotilla (at the cost of quarterdeck space otherwise used for TSDS or for minelaying). Many advantages were seen in giving the leader the same silhouette and size as the ships

---

[2] Cunningham's proposals are in the 'Tribal' cover (540), but the Admiralty analysis is in the 'J' Class Cover.

HMS *Jervis* is shown at Malta, 27 December 1945. Her 4in gun has been landed and her after torpedo tubes restored. She has twin power Oerlikons abeam her bridge and singles in the former searchlight position between the torpedo tubes. The lattice foremast carries a Type 276 radar and HF/DF on a topmast. The short tripod aft carries Type 291 air-search radar. Note that X gun trains aft instead of forward. The new masts were fitted during a May 1945 refit. (A&J Pavia via John Mortimer)

of her flotilla. The leader's fifth gun could be provided in a somewhat larger ship by making the forward superimposed gun a twin mount.

It might be possible to eliminate the after boiler room and its funnel by using two rather than three boilers. The desired pompom could then replace the after funnel, without lengthening the ship. A single-funnelled ship would also have the desired smaller silhouette. It was also argued that using a single funnel would make it more difficult for a submarine officer to estimate the ship's path. The single funnel idea had already been rejected in 1929. E-in-C had argued that it would be more difficult to turn up the output of a larger boiler, so that a two-boiler ship would accelerate more slowly, an important tactical consideration. Boiler cleaning (necessary every twenty-one days of steaming and/or once each quarter) would be complicated. The crew of a three-boiler ship could clean one at a time, having two available. However, a two-boiler ship would be shut down completely. Because both boilers would be secured when in harbour, she would need a second diesel and a small low-pressure boiler for harbour services, adding weight and complexity and violating standard policy against providing equipment not essential for combat. E-in-C wanted any two-boiler design limited to a single flotilla pending service experience.[3] DNC later argued that larger boiler rooms would make the ship more survivable, because a typical torpedo would flood only one boiler room rather than two.

A meeting of the Tactical Division on 9 July 1936 proposed characteristics similar to those of earlier destroyers, except for additional anti-aircraft armament (a quadruple pompom and

two quadruple 0.5in machine guns) and the quintuple torpedo tubes introduced in the 'I' class. The guns would be 62pdrs, and all mounts would have ammunition hoists and shell rooms (adding 4ft to length). It seems not to have been obvious to those involved that the added pompom was about the size and weight of a single 4.7in gun mount. Speed (32kts deep) and endurance (5,300nm at 15kts) were those of the earlier ships. A P Cole, the constructor responsible for the new design, said that this combination would require a 1,560-ton ship, about 100 tons larger than the last pre-'Tribal', 335ft long on the waterline (beam 34ft 6in, hull depth 19ft 6in).[4] The most economical arrangement would be with one funnel (two rather than three boilers), with a twin mounting aft and two singles forward. Eliminating the pompom would reduce length by 5ft and beam by 3in.

The basic two-boiler design had two single mounts forward and a twin aft. A preliminary calculation showed that using single mounts aft would add 40 tons (1,600 tons standard) and 9ft of length. Alternatives were a larger leader with one of the forward singles replaced by a twin, and versions with three boilers. DNC reported these alternatives on 26 August, arguing that decisions were urgent if orders were to be placed in January 1937. Another possibility raised at this time was a destroyer with three twin 4in, but Cole said that if the ships were to be ordered towards the end of the year, there was not enough time to develop two completely different designs. That killed the 4in concept, at least for the moment. There was also interest in a larger ship with the twin mounts superimposed forward. Cole pointed out that the upper deck armament weight of such a ship, including pentad tubes, would

HMS *Norseman* shows a typical wartime arrangement, with a 4in anti-aircraft gun in place of her after torpedo tubes.

[3] This memorandum dated 12 August 1936 is in the 'J' Class Cover.

[4] Folio 5 of 'J' Class Cover, memo by the constructor.

G 97

be only about 10 tons less than that of a 'Tribal', and hence the dimensions would be similar.

DTSD considered these ships too large. He wanted the two foremost destroyer experts, Rear Admiral Cunningham and Commodore H Pridham-Whipple (Cdre(D), the Atlantic Fleet destroyer commander) brought together and informed that either requirements had to be cut or a larger ship accepted. Later this idea morphed into a call for a conference on destroyer size, to be held by Cdre(D) and six officers. Controller opted for the larger ships. On 6 September he decided that the ship would have a twin gun aft and that the leader and destroyer would have the same dimensions. Controller wanted to trade off torpedo tubes for more guns: could a twin mount be fitted forward (total five guns) if the tubes were made quadruple? What would the displacement be if the tubes were quadruple and all the guns twins?[5] On 11 September a new series of sketch designs was begun, with three twin mounts and two or three boilers.

Nothing had really been settled. On 17 September Captain Bellairs, responsible for Staff Requirements, asked the constructor for the effect of omitting the pompom: the answer was 100 tons. He thought the Staff was about to revert to a conventional design with four 4.7in, no pompom, two 0.5in machine guns, and two sets of quintuple torpedo tubes, with three boilers. The Staff wanted some more alternatives from DNC before convening the planned conference. They included three single 4.7in or twin 4in and eight tubes. Other possibilities were all-gun ships ('Tribals') and ships with very weak gun armament but heavy torpedo batteries (the attackers). Cole pointed out that there was very little time for additional studies; the ships had been approved by Parliament and an immediate decision would be needed if the specifications and drawings were to be ready in time.

Bellairs had prepared a chart showing how destroyers had grown since the 'S' class of the First World War; would the six officers continue to ask for large destroyers, or would they simplify requirements? Cole stopped him: would endurance

be reduced? He considered endurance, hence oil fuel capacity, the deciding factor in destroyer size. The Captain doubted that it would be cut.

On 24 September Controller held a meeting to decide the characteristics of the 'J' Class. Present were ACNS (incoming and outgoing: Admirals Kennedy-Purvis and Cunningham, the latter formerly RA(D)), DNC, E-in-C, DTM and Cole.[6] Controller rejected the single 4.7in solution as a large but lightly-armed ship comparing unfavourably with foreign destroyers. At first uncertain, ACNS ultimately agreed. DNO strongly urged that destroyers have power-worked mountings, reversing a position of a few months earlier. Controller decided, and ACNS agreed, that the design should be for three twin 4.7in. The pompom was clearly essential. Controller wanted to cut back to quadruple tubes, but both current and past ACNS rejected that, and the quintuples stayed. E-in-C was forced very reluctantly to accept the two-boiler plant. Given production problems, ships would probably be completed with one twin mount and two singles, the singles being replaced in about the first year of their life.

Because these decisions were not final without Board approval, Controller ordered small drawings prepared showing several versions: ships with three twin 4.7in and two or three boilers; and with four single 4.7in and two or three boilers. However, only one design would be worked out in detail: three twin 4.7in and two boilers. It was 348ft long and would displace 1,700 tons. Refined estimates now showed that using single mounts would have carried no length penalty and might even save a few tons. It seems not to have mattered that the Naval Staff still backed the version with two single 4.7in forward; they felt that they might as well go back to the 'Tribal' class if the ship was to have three twins. For the next destroyers, the Staff would ask for four high-angle (70°) mountings.[7]

On 5 October the design, then rated at 1,650 tons standard, was circulated to the two main fleet commanders. If adopted, it would probably become the standard type, replacing the 'A'

HMS *Napier* as completed, April 1941, was typical of the 'J'/'K'/'N' series. Overlooking the ship's director control tower (DCT) is a three-man rangefinder. In this class the DCT was intended to control both surface and anti-aircraft fire. The rangefinder could therefore transmit both range and elevation to the DCT. This arrangement proved unsatisfactory (presumably because inherent delays were too great for anti-aircraft fire) and was completely revised in mid-1941. The DCT was now limited to surface fire and the rangefinder modified to function as an anti-aircraft director. The visible sign of the change was the addition of a shield revolving with the rangefinder. The modified unit was fitted for installation of Type 285 range-only radar, and had angle of presentation binoculars for the Control Officer. In accordance with decisions taken in 1940, she has a 4in anti-aircraft gun in place of her after torpedo tubes, but its utility was limited partly because it could not be controlled very effectively by the fire control system. At this time the ship had no Oerlikons and no radar; she had the pre-war quadruple 0.5in machine gun in the two platforms alongside her bridge. These weapons survived well into the Second World War, and were still mounted in numbers as late as 1942. To supplement them *Napier*, *Nestor*, *Nizam*, *Norman*, and the Dutch *Tjerk Hiddes* and *Van Galen* all had paired MTB-style power twin 0.5in machine guns on the quarterdeck between the TSDS winches (some may have had only a single such mounting). (A D Baker III)

[5] Folio 8, 'J' Class Cover.

[6] Folio 15, 'J' Class Cover, memo by DNC.
[7] Memo of conversation with Captain Bellairs by Mr Cole, 29 September 1936, in Folio 16 of 'J' Class Cover.

HMS *Jupiter* is shown late in 1940 or early in 1941, as initially refitted (with the 4in anti-aircraft gun), with the distinctive diamond of her pre-war HF/DF antenna on her foremast. This equipment was ineffective against short signals of the type used by the Germans in wartime. The antenna is sometimes identified as MF/DF, but the standard wartime MF/DF was a rectangular coil, not this diamond, and the standard wartime HF/DF 'birdcage' was built up of diamond-shaped arrays plus compensating elements. Note the prominent galley exhaust on the after side of her funnel. In later ships this pipe was buried in the funnel, visible only in that it extended above the top of the funnel. (Alan Raven)

HMS *Nepal* is shown as completed in 1942, with air-search (Type 291) and main battery fire-control (Type 285) radar, and with six Oerlikons. (Alan Raven)

HMS *Javelin* is shown in February 1944, after a refit, with her after torpedo tubes restored, 'birdcage' HF/DF on a stub mainmast, and four twin 20mm guns. The wartime 'birdcage,' which was identified with electronic systems suited to short signals, was introduced in 1941. The same array was used with both wartime outfits, FH3 and FH4, which differed considerably electronically. (Alan Raven)

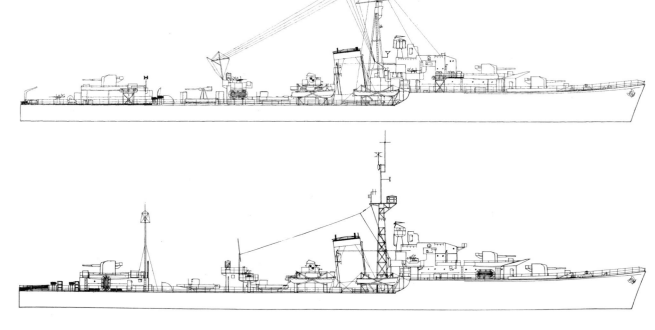

through 'I' series. Given its firepower, it would be unnecessary to repeat the 'Tribals', so that the 1937 and later annual programmes would each consist of two flotillas of 1,650-ton ships.

Both commanders supported the new design. C-in-C Mediterranean considered it necessary to match foreign types, despite the consequent reduction in numbers and in handiness. He particularly liked the increased gun armament, especially for forward fire. He proposed stiffening the ship so that ultimately X mounting could be replaced with a 70° mounting (no such mounting could have been installed forward without increasing deck heights). C-in-C Home Fleet wanted deep speed increased to 33kts, but the 3,000 SHP required could not be provided by two boilers.

Both commanders wanted X gun to bear closer to dead ahead. Because it used hydraulic power, the mounting could not freely rotate through 360°; it had to bear either dead ahead or dead astern, turning to either side of this bearing. Only a gun capable of bearing dead ahead could follow a target crossing the bow (otherwise, to go from one side to the other the gun would have to train all the way around), but it could not follow one crossing the stern. The design initially showed it bearing dead astern. First Sea Lord Admiral Chatfield argued that ahead fire in destroyers was the most important consideration, as 'it is more important that destroyers should be able to fight their way against opposition when advancing to the attack than after the attack, when their own smoke-screens are, in themselves, not only offensive, but would interfere with gunfire'. However, the 4.7in guns were considered anti-aircraft weapons, despite their limited elevation of 40°. Not only the Mediterranean crisis, but now the early part of the Spanish Civil War emphasised the air threat to the fleet, and in the Spanish case to individual destroyers on patrol. The most likely directions for air attack were from right ahead or dead astern, to provide the bomber with the largest possible target. A blind arc aft would deprive a destroyer of any anti-aircraft fire right aft. Yet the directors on the bridge also had significant aft blind arcs. By this time C-in-C Mediterranean was much concerned with the threat of MTBs. His planned tactic was to turn away, in which case astern fire might be particularly important. Ultimately the matter had to be decided by the First Sea Lord (CNS), who agreed with Controller that the blind arc should be right aft. An

important factor for Controller was that this arrangement made possible a rig offering better radio reception (main aerials carried to the ensign staff).

The ship had to be able to use her 4.7in guns in harbour, with her boilers (hence her hydraulic power) shut down. Diesels would provide electric power in harbour, and the solution was electric pumps at the gun mountings (electro-hydraulic power). That required two 150 kW turbo-generators in the engine room, rather than the earlier standard two 100 kW. Largely to enable the ships to drill and to fight in harbour, they were given two 50 kW diesel generators in the forward boiler room. There was no emergency generator outside the machinery spaces, that not being standard Royal Navy practice.

Since the new twin mount was power-operated, the fleet wanted it to be fully enclosed, with substantial advantages for weather and blast protection. Ammunition supply would be simplified, saving personnel (twenty-four men per ship, as a rough estimate). Fully-enclosed mountings forward could be placed closer together. The fleet noted such mountings in the US destroyer *Porter* and in recent Japanese ships (the *Fubuki* and *Shiryatsuyu* classes). DNO estimated that adopting turret mountings would increase weight per mounting from 23¼ tons to 50 tons, adding about 75 tons to the ship. Probably some of that would be compensated for by reducing hull weight, but DTSD was not sure that any advantages would be commensurate with the loss of all-round view and accessibility within a cramped mounting. The Director of Plans (Admiral T V Philips, who would be lost on *Prince of Wales* due to failure of anti-aircraft fire) strongly favoured development of a true high/low angle mounting. That 'none of the eight post-war destroyer flotillas can at present produce any effective fire against aircraft is [a situation] which it is difficult to contemplate with equanimity'. He also looked forward to the saving of personnel promised by enclosed mountings. Enclosed mountings were not available for the 'J' class, but they were adopted in the next design, the 'L' class (see below).

The fleet wanted increased endurance, as the nominal 5,300nm at 15kts did not correspond to realistic conditions. DNC estimated that actual endurance would be 5,650nm at 15kts, compared to 5,700nm for the 'Tribals' and 5,300nm for the 'G' class, assuming that ammunition per gun was held down to 200 rounds, as approved at a Sea Lords' conference. It was argued that improved fire control made it unnecessary to fire as many rounds per hit. Adopting the fleet's preferred 250 rounds per gun would cost a reduction in fuel and hence of endurance (to 5,400nm). On 2 December Controller ordered the design developed on the basis of 250 rounds per gun.

The Mediterranean Fleet commander was particularly concerned that the ships had large stabilised searchlights (to follow targets despite a destroyer's lively motion), preferably 44in diameter in place of the previous 24in. They were intended not so much to illuminate targets for the destroyer herself but to serve accompanying battleships, so that the latter would not light up to become targets.[8] This capability was demonstrated at Matapan in 1941, when, on command, destroyers illuminated Italian cruisers for the battleship *Warspite* to sink. New binoculars offered greater night vision range which in itself made it possible to fight at longer ranges, for which more powerful searchlights were needed. In addition, in January 1936 C-in-C Mediterranean endorsed the use of destroyer searchlights to help defend a fleet in harbour against air attack.

DNC recognised that these large destroyers would not be as handy as their smaller predecessors, and he hoped to solve the problem by improving their hull form. Twin rudders were considered but not adopted. For the first time in British practice, the ships were longitudinally framed. DNC claimed that this type of construction, with welding, would make it easier to reinforce the side plating. Existing destroyers had been criticised as too flimsy, too easily damaged when coming alongside each other (which was normally how they were moored at bases).

C-in-C Home Fleet Admiral Roger Backhouse, who was later briefly First Sea Lord, suggested that the ships be organised like 'Tribals', in two divisions. He considered a flotilla of eight handier than one of nine, and also better for peacetime training (in two divisions). Presumably that helped justify cancellation of a ninth ship, which was to have been the flotilla leader (HMS *Jubilant*). With only eight ships in a flotilla, C-in-C Mediterranean wanted to reduce the loss in torpedo fire by adopting quintuple tubes. All subsequent destroyers were built in flotillas of eight, the leader identical to the others in dimensions if not quite in configuration.[9]

The sketch design was submitted for Board approval on 28 November 1936; estimated displacement was 1,660 tons for the destroyer and 1,665 tons for the leader. Waterline length was 348ft. A Legend showed an endurance of 5,650nm at 15kts. DNC Stanley V Goodall submitted detailed drawings for Board approval on 22 March 1937. The only remaining issues were structural arrangements to allow installation of pompom directors (when developed) and the blind arcs of the low-angle director.

The 1936 London Treaty applied to these ships. As supplied to the other parties to the treaty standard displacement for the destroyer and the leader was as above but detailed changes brought them up to 1,690 tons and 1,695 tons in the final Legend and then as high as 1,705 tons and 1,707 tons. Fortunately the treaty had not yet been ratified when the figures were supplied, so they were not set in print. However, in September 1937 Goodall was very concerned that the official armament had been four 4.7in guns, the expected battery on completion. The British press would criticise their weak

---

[8] Folio 55, 'J' Class Cover. C-in-C Mediterranean (18 August 1936). The 44in searchlight was formally approved in February 1937. In the 'J' class they were only rod-controlled (*ie* in train but not in elevation). Full stabilisation was only in the experimental stage. Existing searchlights were considered inadequate both in accuracy of control and in illuminating power.
[9] On 9 December 1936 Henderson formally ordered that the 'J' class flotilla consist of eight rather than nine ships; this would also apply to the two repeat 'J' flotillas in the 1937 and later programmes. The ninth ship, HMS *Jubilant*, was cancelled on 18 January 1937. Folio 33, 'J' Class Cover.

HMS *Laforey* at speed off Pantellaria, June 1943. She has fire-control and air-search radar, but no surface-search set. The 4in gun which replaced her forward torpedo tubes is barely visible.

HMS *Loyal* is shown in October 1942. She retained both sets of torpedo tubes because her enclosed Mk XX 4.7in gun mounts offered higher elevation, 50°, and thus were sometimes considered dual-purpose (they actually were not). Note that her wheelhouse was raised (and her bridge roof flattened) to clear the higher 4.7in mounts. She shows Oerlikons alongside her bridge. By November there were also Oerlikons alongside the searchlight platform. The single director atop the bridge was Rangefinder Director Mk IV, Type TP, the P indicating a type of gyro-stabilised sight. It was effective in surface control but less so in anti-aircraft operation. This device incorporated a stabilised 12ft rangefinder. The director was power-trained except originally in *Laforey*, *Lookout* and *Marne*. Shown atop the director is a Type 285 range-only radar.

armament. As soon as ships were armed with all six guns the British would be charged with breach of faith, particularly if any were completed with all six. In what might now seem a ludicrous burst of legalism, he pointed out that in the latter case 'we might be told that in accordance with Article 16 laying of keel should have been deferred to at least 4 months after we had informed other High Contracting Parties that it was six 4.7in.' His solution was simply to inform them that although the intention was to complete with four guns they had been designed for six. As it happened, all were completed with the full planned battery.

In service the ships offered better performance in rough weather (much less bumping) but they were considered wet. Wetness was attributed to the relatively bluff fore end and low silhouette of the design. It would also be characteristic of the War Emergency destroyers built with 'J' class hulls. In January 1940 the CO of HMS *Jackal* wrote that wetness from spray on the bridge and on No. 2 gun mounting was very much worse than in earlier classes. 'At any speed over 19kts, if there

is a wind of anything above force 2 on the bow, you get a lot of spray; with a wind and sea of 4–5 on the bow fighting efficiency would be impaired at 20kts or above. This serious defect is the only criticism I have to make of the seagoing qualities of these excellent ships.'

The 'L' Class

The 1937 Programme envisaged two more destroyer classes, 'K' and 'L', of which the 'K' class would be repeat 'Js'. The 'L' class, to be ordered later, would have the enclosed twin 4.7in mounting DNO was developing in response to fleet reactions to the 'J' design. A and B guns could be closer together, as the crew of A mount would be shielded from the blast from B. The new mount would train over 360°, so there would be no dispute over ahead vs astern fire for X mounting. The added weight of the new mounting might be balanced by reductions in complement. Due to delays in the mounting design, design of the ships to be ordered in August 1937 had not yet begun in the spring of that year.

Destroyer tactics assumed a 10-knot margin over the battle line, but the new battleships would make 27kts. Enemy ships would have similar speeds. The speed margin seemed particularly vital for day torpedo attack. Would only torpedo bombers and MTBs be fast enough in future? Late in June 1937 Controller asked for a 40-knot destroyer. Cole tried four alternatives: 44,000 SHP, as in a 'J'; 56,000 SHP; 60,000 SHP; and 72,000 SHP (L.44, L.56, L.60, and L.72). The 72,000 SHP plant required staggered turbines, which increased length. E-in-C could place 70,000 SHP turbines side by side in a ship designated L.70: 2,500 tons (3,265 tons deep load; 410ft on the waterline × 40ft beam). Its most unusual feature was after torpedo tubes placed on the quarterdeck. It would make 40kts at standard displacement and 35.5kts fully loaded. Equivalent figures for L.44 were 36kts and 32kts. Both designs showed three twin 4.7in in weatherproof mountings, a quadruple 2pdr pompom, and quadruple rather than quintuple torpedo tubes (to reduce topweight). Using weatherproof mountings would save seventeen men. Estimated costs were £905,000 for L.70 and £683,000 for L.44, compared to £590,000 for a 'J'. These designs were submitted on 4 August 1937.

Was so fast a destroyer justified? Controller (Admiral Henderson) considered it a much better bargain than the new *Dido* class cruiser, just approved. He repeated his argument for the 'Tribals' almost three years earlier: the cruiser and destroyer categories were in effect merging. The new 4.7in mounting did offer better anti-aircraft performance than the earlier one, but not as good as the 5.25in gun in a *Dido*. Thus the ideal might be an intermediate ship with three 5.25in (*Dido*-type) mounts; a minimum might be four twin 4.7in weatherproof, two quadruple torpedo tubes, two quadruple pompoms and two of the new multiple machine guns

(0.661in). This armament would broadly correspond to that of the French *Mogador* class super-destroyer, which was larger than L.70. If such a ship could be had for £1 million, then ten would be cheaper than the planned three *Dido* and eight 'J'-class destroyers of the 1938 Programme.

On 7 September DNC offered Controller two super-destroyers, which he called L.72 and L.90. Each had the minimum gun and torpedo armament above, without TSDS or normal depth charges or minelaying equipment. Only the longer L.90 could accommodate pompoms. L.72 was 2,745 tons standard, 420ft long, and would make 39.3kts at standard displacement (35kts deep load). L.90, 475ft long (3,205 tons) would make the desired 40kts at standard displacement (36.5kts deep load). These ships would have seakeeping qualities comparable to the small fleet cruisers of the *Arethusa* class. Controller pointed out that the 1937 Programme allowed for destroyers (treaty category C) rather than cruisers (category B), which in his mind ruled out L.90. Both Fourth Sea Lord and ACNS (Cdre Holland) were generally favourable. L.72 would cost about £1.5 million – half as much as a *Dido*, but twice as much as an improved 'J' class destroyer. Complement would be 234.

On 27 September 1937 ACNS polled the senior fleet commanders.[10] C-in-C Mediterranean pointed out that the Royal Navy was no longer suffering the effects of the 1930 London Treaty; why continue to build hybrids? During the Abyssinian crisis just ended he had never had enough destroyers, and his war plans showed serious shortages. Adopting the 2,750-tonner would just compound the problem. If foreign navies followed the British lead, it would become the standard type, and it would be even more difficult to obtain enough ships

[10] MFO 1953/37, in the 'L' Class Cover.

HMS *Matchless* shows standard wartime modifications, including the substitution of a 4in anti-aircraft gun for the after torpedo tubes.

(at present only the French were building *Mogador*s). As for speed, experience with battlecruisers (in effect, fast battleships) showed that conventional destroyers could work quite effectively with them. Tactics could be modified. C-in-C Home Fleet agreed; it would be best to keep building 1,650-tonners.

On 13 October Chatfield met with DCNS, Controller, ACNS, DNC and DNO to discuss the destroyer situation. Royal Navy policy was still to maintain sixteen modern destroyer flotillas; recent programmes (up to the 'K' class) had produced twelve. What should the remaining four be? At present the greatest need was for the powerful gun type, both to meet foreign destroyers and to deal with air and MTB attack. However, the same flotillas which in the Mediterranean would have to face air and MTB threats would accompany the fleet to the Far East, the most likely venue for a fleet action – when torpedoes would be vital. It was therefore generally agreed that the 'gun type' should be limited to four flotillas – which would mean the two 'Tribals' and perhaps two more flotillas armed with the new 62pdr gun in enclosed turrets. The 'L' class destroyer could be imagined either as a modified 'K', *ie* a torpedo-attack destroyer of more or less classical type, or as a gun-attack ship. As offered to Controller, she had three turrets and the two torpedo tubes of the 'J' and 'K' (but quadruple rather than quintuple, to limit weight). The design showed a pompom (as in a 'J' or 'K') and a sextuple 0.661in, but ACNS preferred two pompoms. DNC said that would mean a longer, less handy ship, requiring so much redesign that construction might be unacceptably delayed. Controller thought of the new ship as a conventional torpedo-attack destroyer with two sets of tubes. However, First Sea Lord, DCNS and ACNS all focussed on gun attack and thus were willing to sacrifice a set of torpedo tubes to gain a second pompom. DNC solved the problem: the ship would be arranged so that the after torpedo tubes could quickly be replaced by a pompom.

DNC undertook to complete the design quickly enough to lay down the first of class before the end of the 1937 financial year. The ship was given more powerful machinery (48,000 SHP rather than 44,000 SHP) to offset the topweight associated with the new weatherproof gun mounting; it would about 1 knot to maximum speed. The design showed a pompom and a 0.661in with one bank of quadruple torpedo tubes. A legend dated 20 October 1937 showed a standard displacement of 1,815 tons, but length was the same as that of a 'J'-class destroyer (348ft on the waterline); speed would be 37.5kts at standard displacement and 33kts deeply loaded.

The Naval Staff was told to give further consideration to whether the last two flotillas (to make up the sixteen) should revert to the earlier standard type (effectively repeat 'I' class) or should be repeat 'Js'. The consensus at this time was that these flotillas, which would not be laid down before 1939, should be mainly torpedo craft.[11]

[11] Memo by First Sea Lord Admiral Chatfield, 14 October 1937, in 'L' Class Cover.

Unfortunately the weight of the enclosed 4.7in mounting began to grow far beyond DNO's estimates. Guns were on individual trunnions, hand- rather than power-elevated, perhaps to save weight. As of late 1937, maximum elevation, which would determine trunnion height, had not been fixed (it would be set at 50°). Each 'J' class mount weighed about 29 tons. In February 1937 the estimated weight of the new mount was 38 tons 2 cwt and 2 quarters, but in an April 1937 drawing it was 40.8 tons. In October, there were still no official weights. In November DNO said that the mount was only at the sketch design stage. All DNC could do late in 1937 was order Cole to examine how the ship's dimensions would have to be changed should the weight *per mounting* be 10 tons more than DNO had promised. As late as May 1939, DNO admitted that he could not give final weights until the mount was completed the following year. Cole hoped that it would be within 50 tons (DNO thought 42½ tons). Because the pilot mounting could not be sent to sea for trials (it could not fit any ship without the appropriate structure), there had to be some doubt as to whether it was really suitable to a ship with such light structure. To make matters worse, the estimated centre of gravity of the machinery was higher than had been expected, so the 'J' class hull form had to be abandoned.

The only acceptable solution was a larger hull, roughly the size of a 'Tribal'. In December 1937 the Board was offered a new design with standard displacement given as 1,925 tons (2,576 tons deep load). Expected speed was 36kts at standard displacement (32.4kts deeply loaded). The hope that the new gun mountings could be provided in 'J' dimensions had failed, although the new ships did require a substantially smaller crew (a reduction of forty men was claimed). Each would be £100,000 (about a sixth) more expensive than a 'J', although less expensive to run (by about £7,000 per year) due to the smaller crew.

Delays in pompom production precluded the desired two-pompom anti-aircraft battery, so the design showed two sets of torpedo tubes with provision for replacing the forward set with a second pompom. Unlike the 'J' series, these ships were given power-operated torpedo tubes on the theory that, with only one set of tubes, they would have to be able to shift rapidly from beam to beam. This one would also have a combined high- and low-angle DCT incorporating the rangefinder. Electric power grew again, to two 200 kW turbo-generators and two 60 kW diesel generators (the earlier 50 kW type running at higher speed to generate more power). The Board approved the legend and drawings on 7 April 1938, one flotilla being ordered as the second of the 1937 Programme.

Admiral Chatfield noted that probably not more than half the destroyers would serve with the battle fleet; the others would be use for anti-submarine and other escort and patrol duties. It was important to bear this in mind when considering the sheer cost of the destroyer force. Admiral

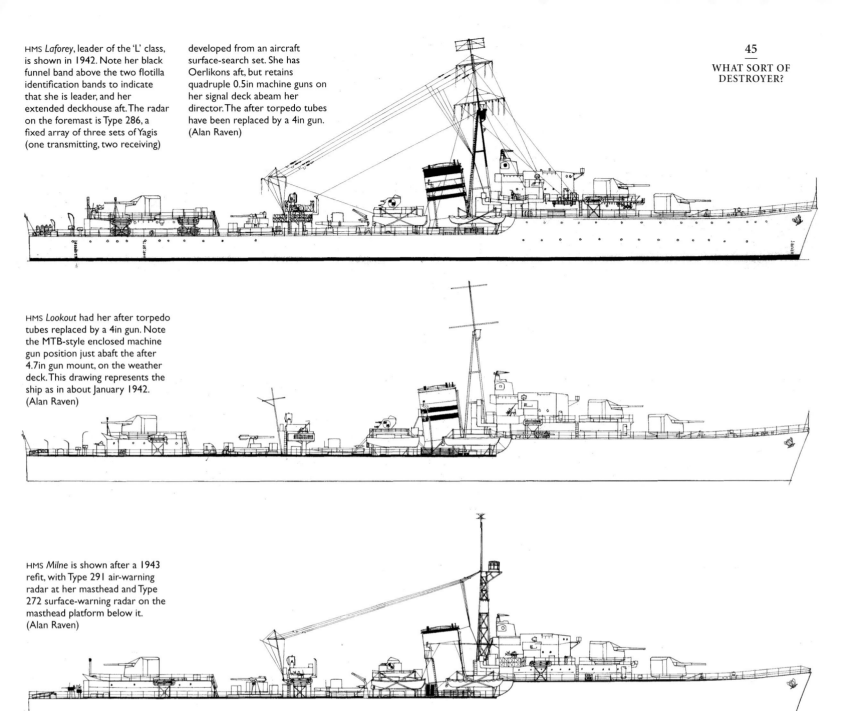

HMS *Laforey*, leader of the 'L' class, is shown in 1942. Note her black funnel band above the two flotilla identification bands to indicate that she is leader, and her extended deckhouse aft. The radar on the foremast is Type 286, a fixed array of three sets of Yagis (one transmitting, two receiving) developed from an aircraft surface-search set. She has Oerlikons aft, but retains quadruple 0.5in machine guns on her signal deck abeam her director. The after torpedo tubes have been replaced by a 4in gun. (Alan Raven)

HMS *Lookout* had her after torpedo tubes replaced by a 4in gun. Note the MTB-style enclosed machine gun position just abaft the after 4.7in gun mount, on the weather deck. This drawing represents the ship as in about January 1942. (Alan Raven)

HMS *Milne* is shown after a 1943 refit, with Type 291 air-warning radar at her masthead and Type 272 surface-warning radar on the masthead platform below it. (Alan Raven)

Backhouse suggested a way out: to produce a smaller type of destroyer suitable for some of the special duties, perhaps even fleet minesweeping, but not for fleet torpedo attack or for defence against enemy destroyers. This was not a new idea; in the past the fleet role had been emphasised because new fleet destroyers were so badly needed. Now, with the fleet flotillas reasonably well filled out, there was still an enormous need for ships for the other roles. The contrast was particularly obvious if all new destroyers were the large type. This comment seems to have been the origin of the 'Hunt' class.

For the moment, Chatfield hoped that the 1938 Programme ('M' and 'N' classes) could revert to a smaller design. Unfortunately changing to an entirely new destroyer design would take time. The Sea Lords met on 10 October 1938 to consider the future destroyer programme. One flotilla was planned for each of 1939, 1940 and 1941.[12] Should they all be repeat 'Ls'? ACNS preferred a repeat 'Tribal', which offered a much superior gun battery as well as better speed and endurance, and saved £800,000 in the 1939 Programme. He focussed on the decision to buy the 'L' class before testing its mounting; surely it was better, as in the 'Tribals', to send a new mounting to sea before ordering ships armed with it. Controller said that had not been the case: the 'Tribals' and their mountings were ordered together, one mounting being completed early to test for teething problems. Many in the fleet had considered it a mistake to order the ships before the mounting had been tested. Had that been done the class would not yet have

[12] TD 499/38 in Folio 6D of the 'M' Class Cover.

been in service. Doing the same for the 'L' class would entail a delay of about five years. The Japanese were already using a mounting like that planned for the 'L' class. Controller won this fight, but unhappiness with the 'L' class mounting may explain why pilot versions of both wartime dual-purpose 4.5in twin mounts went to sea, even though in one case (the between-decks Mk IV) the destroyer mount was a slightly modified version of one already in service on board larger ships.

DCNS (Cunningham) wanted to revert to the small type of the past, with an armament of two twin 4.7in and eight torpedo tubes. Like DTSD in 1936, he wanted to split the destroyer force into gun and torpedo ships, this time with one flotilla of large destroyers to two of small ones. DCNS considered the 'L' class neither a gun nor a fleet destroyer (he had similar but less vehement objections to the 'K' class). He and others wanted a repeat 'Tribal'. First Sea Lord (Backhouse) favoured the 'L' class because he liked their heavy torpedo battery and because he considered six guns sufficient for general work. Initially he was willing to substitute a third (modified) flotilla of 'Tribals' for a repeat 'L' class in 1939, preferably with six rather than four torpedo tubes, and with somewhat greater endurance (3,500nm at 20kts). DNC rejected any repeat 'Tribal', because that design did not incorporate the considerable advances in design in the 'J' class: a better hull form (better cross-section) for sea-keeping, longitudinal framing for sturdiness, and the more compact and less expensive two-boiler powerplant. To incorporate these advances in something like a 'Tribal' would take six months of design work, and that would entail too great a delay. The alternative that some favoured, a repeat 'Tribal' with a second set of torpedo tubes, would take about as long, and would be a very long, unmanoeuvrable

ship, displacing about 2,000 tons and costing about £680,000. It would be impossible, as some hoped, simply to replace the pompom in a 'Tribal' with a second set of tubes.

Controller argued that the fifty-four existing smaller destroyers were enough for a fleet of seventeen capital ships; at Jutland eighty-one destroyers sufficed for thirty-eight capital ships. Surely heavily-gunned destroyers were also needed – in the last war the gun had been the main weapon of the ships on the Harwich and Dover patrols. Given the larger number of mountings involved, repeat 'Tribals' would be available no sooner than repeat 'Ks' or repeat 'Ls'. Both the fleet commanders complained that the 'L' was too big and too expensive, preferring to repeat the 'J'/'K' class.

A meeting on 22 November 1938 (First, Second, and Third Sea Lords, DCNS, ACNS, DNC and E-in-C) decided that the 1938 Programme ships ('M' class) would be repeat 'Ls' but with more oil fuel stowage, hence only one pompom. The 'L' class ships already building would be similarly altered. Fuel was needed because of increased emphasis on endurance to work with the Fleet. As of January 1939 estimated endurance was 5,500nm at 15kts (4,000nm at 20kts, 2,250nm at 25kts). Controller again beat back the key objection that repeating the 'L' class should await sea experience with its complex new mounting. Since the first 'Ls' would not be at sea until 1940, waiting for experience would delay a repeat class to the 1941 Estimates (1942 orders); probably they would not be built at all. That would leave one class of destroyers with a unique type of gun and mounting, 'in effect a freak type'. It would be better to cancel the 'L' class mountings (not the ships) altogether and continue to use the 'J' type. DNC calculated that a 'J' class armament in the big 'L' class hull would be unac-

HMS *Milne* is shown on 16 December 1944, recently refitted with Type 276 radar atop her new lattice foremast, the topmast carrying HF/DF. The pole aft carries the standard destroyer air-search radar, Type 291. The director carries Type 285 radar. The coloured funnel bands indicate the flotilla. Flotilla bands were standard before the war, but were largely abolished in the Home Fleet after Dunkirk. They persisted in the Mediterranean through 1942, gradually dying off after that (but were revived in 1945 in the British Pacific Fleet). Ships had one, two, or three bands, which in pre-war practice could be red, white, or black (in 1939 two flotillas had no bands). From 1946 on the bands were eliminated, and ships carried their flotilla numbers on their funnels.

ceptable: it would have excessive metacentric height making it too lively a gun platform.

First Sea Lord called a meeting on 4 January 1939 to reconsider his decision. He wanted quick Treasury approval for the gun mountings of the two flotillas to be ordered in 1939. With the international situation visibly deteriorating, he wanted numbers, which meant repeating an existing design. Controller told him that he would gain little time by switching from 'L' to 'K' class ships. For ships ordered in May 1939, it would take twenty-four to twenty-seven months to complete a flotilla of 'Ks', twenty-four and twenty-nine months for 'Ls'. DNO said that to produce an 'L'-class mounting took 1.8 times as much work as to produce a 'K'-class mounting: shops that could turn out two flotillas' worth of K-class mountings in a year could produce only one flotilla's worth of 'L' mountings in sixteen months. Nothing could be done about the other bottleneck, fire control. The first 1939 flotilla could receive repeat 'K' mountings between May and October 1941 or repeat

'L' mountings between May and December. The second flotilla could get 'K'-type mountings between November 1941 and April 1942, or 'L' mountings between January and August 1942. These facts 'filled [First Sea Lord] . . . with despair.'

ACNS considered the 'L' class superior as gun boats to the 'Tribals' thanks to their weatherproof mountings and heavier shells, and Second Sea Lord said that for the sake of morale British destroyers should be as powerfully armed as their foreign counterparts. Fourth Sea Lord pointed out that the only way to obtain destroyers quickly was to return to single mountings, but no appropriate ship design existed. Except for ACNS, those present agreed to repeat the 'L' class, for its better armament and its reduced crew.

Once it had been decided not to fit the second pompom, the torpedo armament was reconsidered. Since power training had been chosen only because it seemed the ships would end up with a single set of tubes, it could be dropped now that they were expected to keep both sets permanently. It turned

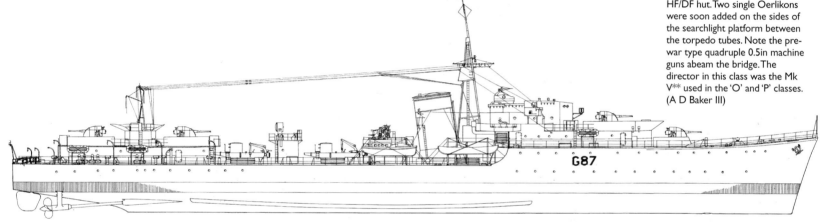

HMS *Lance*, shown in June 1941, was one of four 'L' class destroyers completed with four twin 4in guns because of delays in producing the enclosed twin 4.7in mount. The device on her foremast is an HF/DF coil of pre-war type. Below the yardarm on her foremast is the HF/DF hut. Two single Oerlikons were soon added on the sides of the searchlight platform between the torpedo tubes. Note the pre-war type quadruple 0.5in machine guns abeam the bridge. The director in this class was the Mk V** used in the 'O' and 'P' classes. (A D Baker III)

HMS *Lance* was completed with twin 4in rather than 4.7in guns. The pilothouse in this class was raised (the bridge structure had a nearly flat roof) to clear the big twin enclosed Mk XX 4.7in mounting; the change is particularly visible in ships completed with much smaller gun mounts. Note the change from an F to a G pennant number in this 1942 photograph, taken shortly before the ship was bombed to the point of becoming a constructive total loss.

out that a hand-trained pentad mount would weigh about as much as a power-trained quadruple mount, so in April 1939 DTM and DTSD argued that such mounts should be used, to gain two torpedoes without any weight penalty. The extra torpedoes offered a reserve against further growth of the 4.7in gun mount. After some debate, the decision was made in June that the 'M' class would have pentads. However, by April 1940 this decision was being reconsidered. Quadruple hand-worked tubes were formally approved at a Controller's Meeting on 13 August 1940.

By the time the 'L'-class ships were approaching completion there were only enough gun mounts to provide two for each. Instead of completing eight half-armed ships (A and X mountings only), four were modified and armed with four twin 4in each, the other four having the full 4.7in battery. Proposals for this rearmament were in hand by 12 March 1940. A plan to use only three mounts, which would not have involved much structural alteration, was also considered. Yet another alternative was to provide a fifth twin 4in in place of the after torpedo tubes. The four-mount scheme was approved at a Controller's meeting on 16 April 1940. All eight 'M'-class destroyers received their full batteries. DNC Goodall later remarked that the saving in time was disappointing, and

that mountings could be provided only at the expense of other ships; even then major alterations were required, which took considerable time.[13] All of this left open the design of the second 1938 flotilla, the 'N' class, which was essentially a repeat 'J' (see below).

The AA improvement ordered in 1940 (see Chapter 5) for the 'J' through 'N' classes was a 4in gun replacing the after set of torpedo tubes. Many ships were fitted with a pair of MTB-style twin 0.5in machine guns on the quarterdeck. Most surviving ships (at least *Jervis*, *Javelin*, *Kelvin*, *Kimberley*, *Nepal*, *Nizam*, *Norman* and the Dutch ships) had their second bank of torpedo tubes restored beginning in 1942. Initially two 20mm guns replaced the earlier quadruple 0.5in guns in the bridge wings and another pair were added abeam the searchlights (of the 'N' class, only *Norman* ever had 0.5in guns). When the 4in guns were landed, all of these mounts were replaced by twins. The twin 0.5in guns on the quarterdeck were replaced by single 20mm. Late in the war *Norman* was fitted with a lattice mast carrying a US SG-1 surface search radar, which replaced the Type 271 'lantern' previous carried on her searchlight platform. It in turn was replaced by a single 40mm gun.

Of the eight 'N' class, only *Nepal* served in the Royal Navy during the Second World War, although the others were generally under British operational control and were subject to standard British modifications. *Noble* and *Nonpareil* were sold to the Dutch and modified for East Indies service. In April 1940 Rear Admiral John Tovey, destroyer commander in the Mediterranean, proposed that four new 'N' class destroyers replace the four First World War RAN destroyers under his command. In the event the Australians received all four ships (*Napier*, *Nestor*, *Nizam* and *Norman*) but retained the older units as well. *Nerissa* served (as *Piorun*) with the wartime Polish Navy. Late in the war the Australian ships (except *Norman*, apparently) received single Bofors guns in place of their after torpedo tubes, the maximum being one on the searchlight platform and two on deck (*Nepal* had one gun, on the starboard side of the main deck just abaft the searchlight, and *Nizam* had one to port, later moved to the searchlight platform). *Kimberley* also had a single Bofors.

With the end of the Second World War, several South American navies approached British builders for destroyers. The results can be compared with the wartime 'L' class. This large destroyer was designed by Yarrow early in 1947 for Argentina; it was marketed by a consortium consisting of Thornycroft, White, and Yarrow (the original drawing is in the Thornycroft collection of the National Maritime Museum).

This was probably the only attempt to export the enclosed Mk XX 4.7in mount designed for the 'L' class. Dimensions: 398ft (wl), 414ft (oa) x 42½ft x 23ft (hull depth), standard displacement 2,705 tons. Beside the three twin 4.7in, armament was two twin Bofors, four Oerlikons, and one pentad torpedo tube, plus depth charges. The ship would have made 35kts on 58,000 SHP. This design featured unit machinery,

which probably explains the considerable growth over the 'L' class. It also offered exceptionally good accommodations, an important sales advantage for an export ship. The Argentines did not buy any destroyers at this time.

13 Remarks dated 10 September 1940 in the 'L' Class Cover. The ships involved were *Lance*, *Larne*, *Legion* and *Lively*.

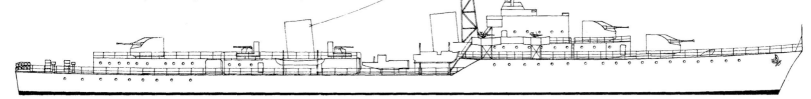

The New Intermediate Class

By late 1938 war seemed close. It is clear that to the Admiralty, and probably to the British government as a whole, the British climb-down at Munich in November 1938 was not a way of ensuring Prime Minister Chamberlain's guarantee of 'peace in our time', but rather an attempt to buy a short breathing space.[14]

On 23 November 1938 First Sea Lord Admiral Backhouse asked the Staff to propose requirements for an intermediate (between 'J' and 'I' classes) destroyer, which he envisaged as a 1,400–1,500-ton ship, effectively a modernised 'I' class fleet (torpedo) destroyer with a different gun armament emphasising anti-aircraft capability. It was assumed that the 4.7in gun would be the new 62pdr instead of the earlier 50pdr, so mounts had to be somewhat more widely spaced. Armament options included the 'J' class twin 4.7in gun, but not the heavier weatherproof weapon in the 'L' class. Fleet commanders' comments on the repeat 'L' class showed that they wanted the new ship to have five guns rather than four (as in the 'I' class), and that they wanted greater endurance. ACNS wanted at least five guns, on the ground that the tendency abroad (*ie* in Germany, Japan and the United States) was to mount five guns on about 1,620 tons. It would probably be more economical to mount six, in which case the ship would be a repeat 'J'. Fleet opinion also seemed to favour a pompom and eight torpedo tubes. Favoured endurance was at least that of the 'F' class, 3,150nm at 20.5kts. A ship with such characteristics would be about the size of one of the large destroyer leaders, such as HMS *Inglefield*. To First Sea Lord, anything much over 1,500 tons was so close to a 'J' that there was little point in not simply reproducing the larger ship.

Backhouse clearly envisaged a dual-purpose main gun, but no such weapon existed. Director of the Naval Air Division (DNAD) very reasonably dismissed high-altitude bombing as a minor threat. Torpedo bombers, which could be engaged by conventional low-angle guns, were the most serious air threat to destroyers. Six might have a 90 per cent chance of sinking an 'F' class destroyer steaming at 25kts. A combination of main battery barrage fire and close-range automatic fire could destroy at least two of the six before they reached dropping range (500 yds). DNAD considered that measures against torpedo bombing would also protect against dive bombing, in retrospect a somewhat odd conclusion.

Initially the 'J'-class twin mount was favoured because it was lighter than two singles. Director of Plans wanted both twins forward, for maximum fire with minimum end-on silhouette. That, however, would make the ship vulnerable and would give her a high silhouette. When firing on after bearings A mount would suffer because the open part of its shield would be open to the wind from ahead. It was already known that such a ship would be bow heavy. If there was only one twin mount, DTSD wanted it forward, with single mounts fore and aft. Since the single gun would be used to fire starshell, there were objections to placing it aft. DTSD therefore preferred five guns: a twin in A with a single superimposed in B position, and a twin mount aft as in the 'J' and 'K' classes.

On 19 December 1938 ACNS asked for two designs, A and B, based on 'J'-class hulls, each with twin mounts fore and aft. A (310ft long) had the twins in A and Q positions and a pompom in X position. B (352ft) substituted a twin mount for the pompom in X, and moved the pompom to a structure abaft the funnel. By way of comparison, a 'J'-class destroyer was 356ft long. Two days later DCNS called for three more alternatives. X (315ft) was essentially A with the positions of the pompom and the after twin mount interchanged atop the after deckhouse. Y (330ft) added a single 4.7in gun in B position, to fire starshell. To compensate for the additional topweight, the pompom was moved from the after deckhouse and down onto the weather deck. In Z (330ft) the starshell gun was moved aft to X position, the after twin 4.7in being moved down onto

HMS *Oribi* was an Intermediate destroyer conceived as an alternative to large ships like the 'Js' and 'Ls'. She was built under the first War Emergency Programme but had not been conceived as a mass production destroyer. She is shown in December 1941. Atop the ship's bridge is a Mk V** director characteristic of the class. It was set very low on the bridge because data were transmitted by a turning shaft, and the longer the shaft the greater the distortion due to twisting. Thus the Transmitting Station (calculator space, with the FKC) was directly underneath in the bridge structure. In the designation, the first star indicated that a rangefinder cover was fitted, the second that the director had a Type 285 radar. In the Transmitting Station were an Admiralty Fire Control Box (AFCB), an FKC and a Gyro Level Calculator. The AFCB was the surface fire calculator, and it had a switch to select the FKC for anti-aircraft fire. This was the same arrangement as in an anti-aircraft sloop, which had a Mk III director transmitting data electrically. The radar had an Auto Barrage Unit. When all the guns were loaded with shells timed for a particular range, they could be fired automatically when the radar registered the appropriate range. (A D Baker III)

---

[14] In September 1938, before Munich, war had seemed so close that on the 30th DNC wrote a memo on which armament would be fitted if Brazilian and Greek destroyers then building in British yards were taken over on the outbreak of war. The Greek ships were armed with German 5in guns, so DNO would have to find surplus 4.7in guns for them. They were delivered before war broke out in 1939, but the Royal Navy took over the Brazilian ships.

the weather deck. In all three designs, the guns on the forecastle and weather decks were atop bandstands. In both Y and Z the forward torpedo tubes were set under a boat deck extending the forecastle aft, an attempt to save length. Length was initially underestimated because no provision had been made for boiler and engine room vents or for blast: more realistic figures were 335ft for X (1,550 tons) and 340ft for Y (1,630 tons).

None of these designs was acceptable. DNC pointed out that cutting armament saved little length, because the main factors were the positions of the funnel(s), the boiler room intakes, access to the machinery spaces and to the lower deck compartments aft (otherwise cut off from the fore part of the ship by the machinery spaces), and the vents to the engine and gearing rooms. Other factors were blast interference between the 4.7in guns and the searchlights and pompoms, and ammunition supply to the guns. Previous attempts to find a better arrangement of guns and torpedo tubes had all failed.

On 6 January First Sea Lord asked Controller to arrange for the first formal sketch designs of the emergency destroyer. A would be similar to pre-'J' class destroyers but with a four-barrel pompom and two smaller anti-aircraft guns. Alternatives would be a twin mount aft or twin mounts fore and aft. B would be on the same general lines but with five guns (two twins and one single, the single preferably in A position). Displacement should be held below 1,500 tons. If B exceeded it, DNC should calculate the effect of eliminating one set of torpedo tubes (perhaps using a quintuple for the remaining

one). For ease of production, fire controls would duplicate those in the earlier ships (with provision to fit a Fuse Keeping Clock (FKC – see Chapter 5) later for high-angle fire), speed (standard displacement) would be 36kts, and endurance with a clean bottom would be 3,500nm at 20kts. In each case, First Sea Lord wanted an estimate of building time (from date of ordering): war was imminent. DNO rejected mounting a fifth 4.7in in place of the pompom due to ammunition supply problems. As for fire control, he much preferred separate DCT and rangefinder, as in the 'J' class, to the dual-purpose director of the 'L' class.

On 23 January 1939 First Sea Lord asked DNC to confirm that building Intermediates rather than the 'L' class would save £100,000 per ship. DNC said they would probably cost no more than £600,000, and First Sea Lord said he would tell the First Lord that building the smaller ships would save £800,000 to £1 million on the whole flotilla. Given the details of the alternative designs, First Sea Lord said that it was not as important to work out designs as to provide a basis for an initial decision. He was quite willing to accept one set of torpedo tubes, and to get sufficient endurance he would go as high as 1,500 tons. The ships should be as simple as possible so that they could be produced rapidly in case of war. If war did not break out he would build Intermediate flotillas in 1940 and 1941, then return to large destroyers.

First Sea Lord suggested arming the ships with four single 20mm Oerlikons, a weapon just becoming available, instead of one quadruple pompom, an idea DNO later rejected. DNC

later pointed out that a quadruple pompom with its ammunition was heavier than a single 4.7in 50pdr gun, so the ship would be more nearly comparable to a five-gun leader than to the four-gun standard ('A' through 'I' class) destroyer.

Given First Sea Lord's sense of urgency, DNC was able to submit sketches on 1 February 1939. Because it appeared that the new design might be built as the 'N' class, design options were designated in an N series (design A was also NA, etc). These designs used the same two-boiler arrangement as the 'J' and 'L' classes. A (NA) had four single 62pdr guns, a quadruple pompom, two smaller machine guns, and two sets of quadruple torpedo tubes (1,513 tons, 334ft). To fit the ship as a leader would cost one bank of tubes. Eliminating one bank of torpedo tubes would save 10ft and 98 tons. Adopting the twin 4.7in would add 2 tons (beam would have to be increased). Eliminating the pompom would save about 8½ tons. DNO considered the Royal Navy committed to the 62pdr, which would shoot better than the 50pdr. Adopting it added 2 tons per single mounting (adopting 50pdrs would save 10 tons). DNC estimated that NA could be completed about 2½ years after gun mountings (the controlling item) were ordered, say in September 1939.

B, the five-gun alternative (two twins, one single), was rejected as much too large (1,655 tons, 345ft). Omitting a set of torpedo tubes did not save the design because it would cut only 10 feet and 65 tons.

On 23 February First Sea Lord ordered a separate study of a destroyer for emergency construction. DNO having pointed out that the only gun mounting easy to supply in an emergency was the twin 4in already adopted for many classes, including the various escorts, First Sea Lord asked for a destroyer so armed. This design was designated NC1, so clearly it was also considered an alternative Intermediate design. It had three twin 4in, a quadruple 2pdr, the usual pair of quadruple 0.5in machine guns, and two sets of torpedo tubes as well as TSDS. It came out at 1,520 tons (333ft on the waterline), with an endurance of 3,750nm at 20kts and a speed of 36.5kts in standard condition and 32kts at deep load.

The DCNS (Cunningham) and his ACNS considered that NA offered little advantage over the earlier standard type. She would be larger, with an excessive complement; her cost would be staggering, yet she would have less gunpower than foreign designs. Cunningham welcomed the decision to develop a single 62pdr, although he wanted greater elevation. However, he did not like the decision to retain the simple form of fire control in which the rangefinder was separate from the director proper. As a former destroyer officer he argued that range-finding was one of the major problems of destroyer gunnery, caused largely by the difficulty of operating a separate rangefinder in a lively ship. Better to mount it in the director, which should be dual-purpose. Nor was he so sure that it would be wise to eliminate the pompom director, because it

removed layers and trainers from the blast and flash of firing. The pompom should be moved aft to between the sets of torpedo tubes.

DNC considered some more radical ways to hold down destroyer size. Loading problems ruled out fixed athwartships torpedo tubes; the MTB type at an angle to the centreline consumed too much space; and torpedo tubes could not be mounted atop the boiler uptakes because the downtakes could not be lowered. Nor could DNC accept the contemporary American practice of carrying oil tanks up to the upper deck. Only tanks underwater should be used in wartime. DNC admitted that the American practice would reduce the length of the ship, but then argued (in contradiction to all his attempts to reduce length) that a shorter ship would have less space available for accommodation, and would be more difficult to drive. Using American-style tanks in NA would save 10ft and 58 tons, and speed in deep condition would fall a knot. E-in-C claimed that the Americans overcame this problem by driving their machinery much harder, but he reported that they had considerable problems (which had already been largely overcome). He was apparently unaware of the very successful US move to much higher steam conditions. Fuel consumption (hence load) might be reduced by using cruising turbines, but in 1933 that idea had been rejected because of unacceptable weight and complication.

Controller called a conference on 7 March to discuss the critiques. DNO pointed out that if an emergency arose or if First Sea Lord wanted the destroyers earlier, 50pdr guns would have to be accepted. Twin 50pdrs could be produced before single 62pdrs, but the quickest option would be the existing single 50pdr. To Controller's question whether that would only further complicate ammunition supply, DNO pointed out that reserves built up for earlier classes would still be in place. He gave DNC the impression that, as in the earlier mountings, the single 62pdr would exceed its estimated weight. Since DNO claimed that with 4.7in guns arranged for high-angle fire (if 40° could be considered high-angle) and control, the pompom was not needed, Controller asked for a sketch of an Intermediate without a pompom. DNC estimated that this new design (ND) would displace 1,400 tons (318ft on the waterline) at a cost of £500,000, compared to £480,000 for an 'H' class destroyer. NA would have cost £580,000. The 'H' class leader, *Hardy*, which was probably most comparable to NA, actually cost £540,000; a 'J' class destroyer cost £635,000.

Wisely unwilling to jettison the pompom, Controller found a repeat 'J' class destroyer a better bargain than the expensive Intermediate. First Sea Lord agreed. For the second 1938 flotilla, then, the question was whether to persist with the 'L' class or to revert to a repeat 'J' class. Gun mount production was the key. DNO said that the first set of mountings for the repeat 'L' class ('M' class) would not be delivered until January 1942. If the second flotilla were also to be a repeat 'L', its guns could not

begin delivery until February 1942. This was far too late. When DNO said that he could provide mountings for a repeat 'J' class destroyer in about June 1941, that decided First Sea Lord: the 'N' class would be a repeat 'J'. On 21 March 1939 Controller ordered that the 'N' class would be a repeat 'K' ('J') class.

A few detail questions remained: quintuple vs. quadruple torpedo tubes, provision of a pompom director, TSDS, and depth charge arrangement. The 'J' class had been designed for quintuple tubes, although First Sea Lord thought quadruple sufficient. Ultimately he agreed to keep the extra tubes as a way of carrying additional torpedoes. First Sea Lord accepted DNO's argument that a pompom director would add too many men and too much complexity without offering much greater effectiveness. He did decide to provide both TSDS and depth charges.

With the 'N' class, the sixteen modern flotillas desired by the Royal Navy were complete, so no destroyers at all were included in the 1939 Programme. The Admiralty now proposed a new standard of strength, to meet the simultaneous threats of the three Axis powers. It would have entailed up to twenty-two flotillas, but it had not been approved by the Cabinet by

the time war broke out in September 1939. By this time DNO was not too intent on keeping the 62pdr. He now found questionable the trials which had led to its adoption. The effect of a 62pdr hit might really not be too different from that of a 50pdr. He feared that men drafted into new destroyers in wartime would be unable to handle 62pdr ammunition. Moreover, if only two flotillas got the 62pdr, only a small reserve of such ammunition would be built up. DCNS agreed. However, Second Sea Lord, in charge of personnel, thought that having the 62pdr would improve morale, as crews would not feel so undergunned facing German destroyers armed with five 5in guns.

While work proceeded on the Intermediate, on 28 January 1939 First Sea Lord ordered work begun on a destroyer suitable for rapid wartime construction. Very large numbers would be needed to fight the prolonged war he expected. Those involved in the Intermediate Destroyer project were also thinking about the emergency design, requirements for which were quite similar. At this time the Naval Hypothesis (the planned initial war programme) showed a flotilla of repeat standard

Photographed on 23 March 1945, HMS *Offa* shows some typical wartime modifications: Type 293 radar atop a lattice foremast, HF/DF on a topmast, and Type 291 aft. She retained the 4in anti-aircraft gun. The searchlight was replaced by Oerlikons.

destroyers. That they were the 'G' class suggests that the Hypothesis had been drawn up about 1934; later the 'H' and 'I' classes would have been substituted. DNO favoured a combination of Fast Escorts and repeat standard destroyers. The 'G' (or later) class destroyers could not be substituted for Fast Escorts because they were more complex. However, substituting Gs for the 1939 destroyers ('M' and 'N' class) would considerably accelerate production.

However, a repeat 'G' (or other standard) destroyer was unacceptable because she lacked a multiple pompom. 'Hunts', which had been designed for mass production (see Chapter 4) were not destroyers. Something new was needed. First Sea Lord concluded from DNO's comments that it would have to be armed either with single 4.7in 50pdr guns or with twin 4in anti-aircraft weapons. On 23 February he asked DNC to develop two alternatives: one with four 4.7in, one with three twin 4in. Each would also have a quadruple pompom and two quadruple torpedo tubes. Neither would have TSDS. Both would have the 38,000 SHP plant of the earlier Intermediate design. The 4in version was the Design NC already described. Construction would take about two years. There the matter rested for a time.

First Sea Lord was still interested in the Intermediate destroyer for the 1940 Programme, which he apparently did not consider equivalent to the emergency mass production type. On 20 March 1939 he ordered a sketch design, which DNC produced in May. By this time the first 'J' class destroyers were at sea, showing that their new longitudinal construction was successful. It was therefore adopted for the new ship. The design was a modified NA, still with its 62pdr guns. Asdic and depth charges (two rails with six charges each and two throwers) were added. Estimated endurance was 3,600nm at 20kts. There was enough weight to accommodate quintuple tubes, but warhead rooms would have to be enlarged at the expense of oil fuel, and endurance would fall to 3,500nm. Whether the leader could be of the same size depended on complement (officers could easily be accommodated, but the necessary ratings might need more deck space). The main uncertainty in the design was the weight of the single 62pdr, which had not

yet been designed. Unexpected weight growth, the bane of the 'Tribal' and 'L' classes, would require more beam.

DNC pointed out that the new Intermediate might also be suitable as the Quick Production Destroyer First Sea Lord wanted. The 50pdr gun could simply be substituted for the planned 62pdr. Otherwise requirements for the two types matched. With 62pdrs the Intermediate would cost £585,000, compared to £635,000 for a 'J' with six 50pdrs. To make her required speed, the ship needed 38,000 SHP, which in turn would entail a new machinery plant. To save production time DNC therefore offered (to E-in-C) to accept the more powerful repeat 'J' class machinery for easier production. DNC told his designer to try a 'J'-class hull form, deviating only if forced to do so to accommodate the machinery.

Compared to a repeat 'K'-class destroyer ('N' class), the new design could much more easily be manned. However, the ships were more lightly armed (even with the heavier gun, they would have about 83 per cent of the broadside of the ship with six 50pdrs), they would cost nearly as much, and if they had to be armed with a new gun mount (single 62pdr) they might not be completed any more quickly.

The principal remaining issue was endurance. The 470 tons of oil provided in this design would give 3,650nm at 20kts if the ship started at deep displacement with a clean bottom. That had been accepted by CNS. However, in a memo dated 6 June Director of Plans asked instead for the practical ability to operate for a day 1,000nm from a fleet base, reserving 33 per cent of fuel for action and maintaining a continuous sea speed of 20kts. That was considered equivalent to 3,700nm starting deep and clean. However, the tables of standard ship characteristics (CB 1815), which might be considered indications of what ships could actually do, were based on a ship six months out of dock, with 5 per cent allowance for weather. In that case DNC estimated that the ship would grow to 1,710 tons (standard).[15] The increased speed and endurance of the

HMS *Orwell*, shown as completed in 1942, had four 4in guns and both sets of torpedo tubes. She was fitted for quick conversion to a minelayer (the associated sponsons at the stern are not shown here). The four 'O' class minelayers were not used as such until April 1945, when *Obedient*, *Opportune* and *Orwell* and the fast minelayer *Apollo* laid a deep ASW minefield in the Polyarnoe Inlet, the approach to Murmansk, between Syet Novolok and Kildin Island. The fourth 'O' class destroyer, *Obdurate*, did not take part because she had been mined in 1944 and was still under repair. The three destroyers had practised the previous month by filling gaps in existing deep ASW fields around the British Isles. The object on the searchlight platform is a twin power-operated MTB-type 0.5in machine gun, two of which were fitted to all four ships, in addition to their four Oerlikons (two in *Obdurate*). These weapons were not mounted in the 4.7in non-minelaying ships of this class. Pairs of these power mountings were also mounted on board earlier large destroyers: at least on board HMS *Lookout*, *Martin*, *Napier* and *Nizam*. They were first listed in the October 1941 book of British warship particulars, and they were still listed as late as April 1943. (Alan Raven)

---

[15] At 20kts the ship would steam 480nm on the full day 1,000nm (each way) from base, so she would steam 2,480nm at 20kts on 67 per cent of her fuel (leaving 33 per cent for action), giving the 3,700nm. DNC's estimate was based on the assumption that the result would be somewhere between a 'Tribal' and the original Intermediate. The new ship would be about the size of *Hardy*, which had a theoretical endurance of 3,500nm but a practical one (CB 1815) of only 2,800nm.

new battleships would probably worsen the situation; good endurance would become more important than ever. It might be more important than in the past to have destroyers work with the battleships, given the advent of long-range torpedo attack from bombers.[16] Director of Plans was willing to accept a larger ship; she would have better seakeeping. He considered (in July 1939!) that with the advent of radar the tactical disadvantage due to larger size would not much matter. DNC observed that, from the point of view of production, it would be simplest just to repeat the 'J' class, as all the drawings, moulds, and patterns already existed.

On 21 July Controller reviewed the emergency programme. The Intermediate design was scheduled for completion in August. Controller asked that it be accelerated, modified to use repeat 'J' class machinery and 50pdr rather than 62pdr guns (but with provision to take the latter if they became available).[17] DNO said that the director control tower and fire control clock would not be ready in time, so Controller ordered the ships designed to be fitted with them later. At least initially they would receive 'Hunt' class fire control systems. DNC

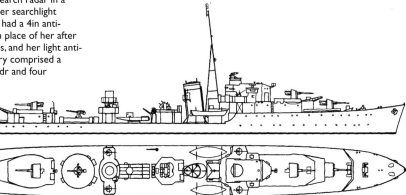

HMS *Oribi* was transferred to Turkey in June 1946 to replace a ship taken over by the Royal Navy in 1939 and lost. The Royal Navy rightly saw the large British export warship industry as a valuable mobilisation resource, since ships under construction could be taken over at the outbreak of war. As the Turkish *Gayret*, *Oribi* was in a typical wartime configuration, with Type 271 surface-search radar in a 'lantern' on her searchlight platform. She had a 4in anti-aircraft gun in place of her after torpedo tubes, and her light anti-aircraft battery comprised a quadruple 2pdr and four Oerlikons.

was to report whether the design could be completed sufficiently so that if war broke out tomorrow ships could be completed between March and June 1941. Representatives of the Naval Staff asked if another flotilla could be laid down at the same time. Although guns, mountings, and fire control might not be ready in time, the resulting hulls could take them from damaged destroyers (Controller doubted this could be done). DNC considered the design mature enough for the first ships to emerge in April 1941 (later the earliest completion date was moved up to May 1941). Given special arrangements to prepare and approve drawings in stages, shipbuilders could make an early start.

The Admiralty asked the builders to produce the drawings,

agreeing to pay them back if war did not break out and ships therefore were not ordered. Hawthorn Leslie laid off the destroyer and the leader and also produced plans for the upper and forecastle decks of the leader. This yard argued that a new knuckled bow form was needed to make the ship drier than the notoriously wet 'J' class. The constructor at the firm supported the idea, but it was not adopted, probably to avoid delays in construction. Fairfield produced the preliminary shell expansion and drawings for the vertical and flat keels. Denny did the framing and the upper and forecastle deck drawings for the destroyer. All three yards received the sketch designs by 2 September, and rough plate lines, body plan, and constructional sections went out by 9 September.

The first flotilla ('O' class) was ordered on 3 September, the second ('P' class) on 2 October, for completion between March 1941 and February 1942. The design was not submitted for Board approval until 8 December (the Board formally approved the Legend and drawings on 21 December 1939). There were some changes to the 'J' class machinery. With hand-powered main armament the ships needed less electrical power, so they had two 80 kW turbo-generators and two 50 kW diesel generators. To accommodate 'J' class machinery, beam had to be increased from 34ft 6in to 35ft and hull depth from 19ft 6in to 20ft 6in. Initially the design had slightly more tankage than the Intermediate design, 500 tons, for 3,850nm at 20kts (clean). The Controller was told that ships would make 3,900nm at 20kts using 505 tons of oil. Provision for the 62pdr required considerable rearrangement aft, because the gun was 2ft longer than the 50pdr. The guns were brought forward, and their relocated magazines cut into oil stowage aft. To avoid an 8in trim by the bow in deep condition, the hull was lengthened forward by 3ft (to 340ft on the waterline) and tankage forward reduced by 20 tons (another 15 tons had already been lost aft), leaving an estimated capacity of 470 tons (3,650nm). Remarkably, more detailed calculations showed 496 tons without any trim (3,800nm, equivalent to 3,100nm on CB 1815 basis). Figures quoted at the end of October 1939 were 3,850nm clean and deep and 3,150nm on the CB 1815 basis. As the design proceeded, the ship was cut back to 337ft (1,530 tons, then 1,540 tons standard).

It was already clear that existing destroyers were too short-ranged. A division of destroyers had been sent to the South Atlantic to deal with U-boats operating there. Their supply was a matter of concern; their passage overseas would have been materially simpler had they had the greater endurance the Staff now wanted. Another unexpected wartime development was the formation of hunting groups to deal with surface raiders like *Graf Spee*. It had been reported, falsely, that the raider was working with submarines. Even if that did not prove true, the hunting groups might have to deal with U-boats already overseas, so it would be desirable to have destroyers working with them – if the destroyers had sufficient

---

[16] Probably Japanese torpedo bombers – the ones which later sank *Prince of Wales* and *Repulse* – were meant, but this may refer to the Italians.
[17] To push the project ahead, Cole asked permission to stop summer leave in his section. He estimated that the sketch design could be completed within a month. In another two months structural sections and Part 1A specifications could be ready, and ships laid down. Building drawings and Part 1B specifications would take another 3½ months. Some of this work could be telescoped, design proceeding as ships were built and drawings approved at the builders as soon as they were ready. Construction would take eighteen months (total twenty from zero), so if work began in July 1939 the first ships could be completed in May 1941. Under more normal procedures the second design stage would take three months and the third five months.

HMS *Penn*, armed with 4in guns, is shown operating with the British Pacific Fleet in 1946. Instead of Type 276 or Type 293, she has a US-supplied SG-1 surface-search radar just below her crow's nest. Type 291 is at the masthead. The gun visible abeam the bridge is a single 40mm 'Boffin'. (RAN via John Mortimer)

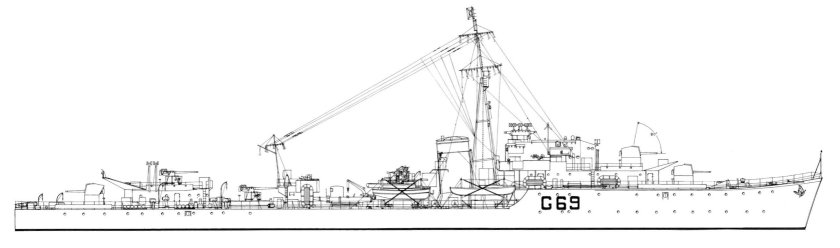

endurance. The Staff noted that new First Lord Winston Churchill had recently raised the question of adding destroyers to the hunting groups.

To provide greater potential endurance, early in November DNC ordered some spaces made oil-tight so that they could be filled with fuel if need be: 34 tons under the forward magazine and shell room (250nm); 135 tons (1,000nm) in and under the forward magazine and shell room (two forward 4.7in mountings landed); 18 tons (30nm) in the torpedo warhead room; 126 tons (950nm) in way of the after magazine and shell rooms, with compartments filled to the lower deck and the two after 4.7in mountings landed. Strength would prohibit all of this being carried simultaneously. Similar modifications were proposed for the 'J' class.[18] DNC was able to resist a proposal to revive peace tanks (above-water fuel stowage) on the ground that they were dangerous and prone to leakage.

[18] Landing one twin 4.7in and carrying oil in its magazine and shell room would gain 50 tons (370nm at 20kts); modification would take about a month. Landing one set of torpedo tubes and carrying oil in the warhead room would buy 20 tons (120nm), but alternative stowage would be needed for depth charges and other items carried there in wartime.

Unlike the 'J' class, this ship had a small mainmast between X and Y mountings (it was placed abaft X to give the latter better forward arcs). Space was provided to stow up to forty-four depth charges, although the design showed the usual peacetime outfit of thirty. There was no provision for TSDS. A 44in searchlight was mounted atop the engine room ventilator, with two stabilised sights on the bridge.

During construction estimated displacement grew from 1,540 tons to 1,555 tons. Additions included de-gaussing equipment (4 tons), a bridge shelter (1 ton), fourteen additional depth charges to bring the total to forty-four (3 tons), and steel instead of copper piping (2 tons). Deep displacement increased from 2,140 tons to 2,161 tons. Some weights were cut. For example, the funnel was shortened by 4ft and the after deckhouse by 4in (by 3in in the leader, which had a slightly lower but larger deckhouse). Structure in way of the magazines and shell rooms was made oil-tight (for emergency use as tankage), but that was not officially reported. Ships were completed with a 4in anti-aircraft gun in place of their after

HMS *Paladin*, shown in December 1941, was completed with an all-4in anti-aircraft armament (her gun shields differed from those of 'O' class destroyers with 4in guns). (A D Baker III)

HMS *Obdurate* as a minelayer, 17 September 1952. The two Oerlikons abeam the bridge have been replaced by single Bofors guns, but the searchlight platform amidships is empty. Her original pennant number was G39; NATO required D numbers for destroyers.

HMS *Obedient* rigged for minelaying, 13 November 1952, showing a single Bofors abeam her bridge. Note the D pennant number replacing her original number, G48. This stern view shows the mine rails.

torpedo tubes. The 'P' class had improved pumping arrangements. Bombing damage delayed construction of *Onslow* by about a month.

The light anti-aircraft battery originally planned, in addition to the pompom, was two quadruple Mk IV machine guns (0.5in) in the bridge wings. It was decided to replace all of them with Oerlikons and to add two Oerlikons abeam the searchlight. Only *Oribi* and *Offa* ever had the quad 0.5in guns. However, *Petard* and possibly *Porcupine* had twin MTB-type 0.5in machine guns abreast the searchlight as a temporary replacement for the planned single Oerlikons (*Onslow* had these mounts in the bridge wings).

While the ships were under construction, it was decided (in January 1941) to rearm eight of them with five single 4in anti-aircraft guns and one set of torpedo tubes.[19] That could be done without delaying completion, except for *Pakenham* (five weeks) and *Pathfinder* (four weeks). Ships so armed were all given P names so that they could form a homogenous flotilla: *Onslow* (renamed *Pakenham*), *Onslaught* (renamed *Pathfinder*), *Paladin*, *Penn*, *Persistent*, *Porcupine*, *Petard* and *Partridge*. In 1942 Q 4in gun was ordered replaced by a second bank of torpedo tubes. *Petard* and *Pathfinder* were completed in this form. *Paladin* and *Penn* may never have been modified. Twins later replaced the bridge wing Oerlikons in *Pathfinder* and *Penn*, and the searchlight weapons in *Paladin*.

In December 1942 it was proposed to arm *Pakenham* and *Paladin* with three twin 4in guns. A quick investigation showed

---

[19] The proposal was formally approved in mid-May 1941 and given the Board stamp on 12 June 1941. Initially 4in guns were simply substituted for the original 4.7in, after which a fifth was approved as an alternative to the after torpedo tubes, as in 4.7in destroyers.

that if the guns were mounted in A, B and X positions (Y gun being landed), the two forward mountings would have half the usual allowance of 4in shells, and the torpedo tubes would have to be landed as weight compensation. Early in 1945 *Petard* was refitted with two twin 4in guns in B and X positions, apparently as part of a more general project to rearm the class. She also had two Oerlikons on the bridge wings and four amidships.

Obdurate, *Obedient*, *Opportune* and *Orwell* were ordered completed as minelayers, carrying sixty mines and armed with three 4in anti-aircraft guns. They could be converted back into destroyers, armed with five 4in guns, within 48 hours. This change delayed the completion of *Obdurate* and *Obedient*. Minelaying equipment came from the 'G', 'H' and 'I' classes. As in the 'P' class, ships all had their fifth 4in gun replaced by a second bank of torpedo tubes. The other four retained their 4.7in guns, with a single 4in anti-aircraft weapon replacing the after tubes. About May 1942 C-in-C Home Fleet asked that the remaining 'O' class destroyers be completed with four 4.7in guns, both sets of torpedo tubes, two Oerlikons (in addition to their pompoms), and no mines. That came too late. Apparently only *Onslow* later had her 4in gun landed and the second bank of tubes installed. Ships were completed with four single Oerlikons, two replacing the planned 0.5in guns in the bridge wings and two abreast the searchlight. Twins replaced the bridge wing single Oerlikons in the minelayers in 1943–4. In at least some ships, the twins in the bridge wings were later replaced by single Bofors (visible on board *Obedient* in 1953). After April 1943 twins replaced the amidships Oerlikons in *Offa*, *Onslaught* and *Onslow*.

HMS *Obdurate* was an Intermediate destroyer completed as a minelayer (note the mine chutes at the stern), seen in December 1946. The lattice foremast carried a Type 293 radar and an IFF interrogator; the pole mainmast carried Type 291. Oerlikons had replaced the searchlight between the two sets of torpedo tubes.

CHAPTER 4
Defending Trade

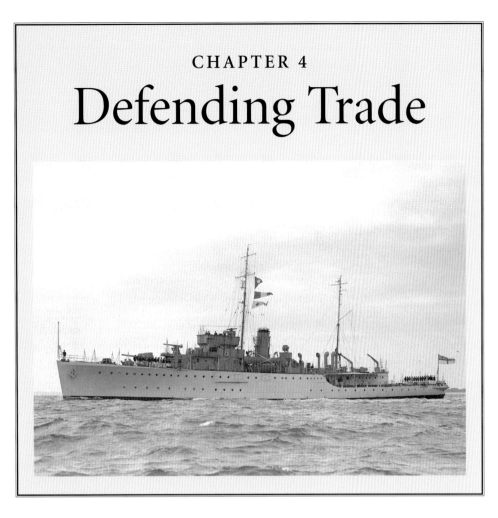

Destroyers had provided the bulk of the Royal Navy's ocean convoy escorts against submarines in the First World War, but the sixteen-flotilla force accepted in the inter-war years was not nearly large enough to screen both fleet and convoys. With the destruction of surplus destroyers and the low destroyer tonnage limit imposed by the 1930 London Naval Conference, the prospective gap worsened dramatically. The Conference also made it clear that foreign powers were unwilling to join the British in banning submarines. In sloops, which were not limited by treaty, the British found a substitute for destroyers escorting convoys. Prior to 1930 they had been built for wartime minesweeping and for peacetime Imperial policing, in effect as midget cruisers, with a single 4in gun and a landing party, but they were not intended as convoy escorts. So many ports and fleet bases would have to be swept at the outbreak of war that there was a standing requirement for fifty-three sloops, the assumption being that many more would be built during the run-up to war.

Before the abortive 1927 Geneva disarmament conference, the British proposed limits on the exempt class (sloops): guns of no more that 5in calibre and a speed of up to 18kts. Maximum tonnage would be 2,000 tons, and the ships could not carry torpedo tubes. Conversations with the Americans and the Japanese (the 'Coolidge Negotiations') pushed the maximum calibre up to 6.1in and added a proviso that such

ships could not carry more than four guns greater than 4in calibre (reduced to 3in calibre in the 1930 treaty).[1] At London in 1930 the Japanese proposed, and the other parties accepted, that given the trend towards higher speeds the maximum should be raised to 20kts. These limitations shaped the designs of the sloops the Royal Navy built after 1930, which became the high end of a high-low escort mix during the Second World War.

The failure of the 1930 naval arms treaty focussed attention on ASW. During the First World War the British had detected many U-boats at long range, either by radio direction-finding or by code-breaking. Given approximate U-boat positions, convoys or very important individual ships could be ordered to take evasive action.[2] U-boats thus found the ocean nearly empty. When they did encounter a convoy, they could not fire torpedoes fast enough to sink many of its ships. Escorts would be unable to prevent a submarine from attacking (as the screens around fast warships were expected to do), but would run down and kill submarines which had attacked. Plans called for assigning two sloops equipped with Asdic (see below) to each convoy, down from the five escorts planned in 1924. Asdic was expected to give each escort a much better chance of gaining and maintaining contact with an attacking submarine. In the face of convoy tactics, the U-boats of the future would surely concentrate on coastal waters near the ends of convoy routes, where they would inevitably find targets. That conclusion was widely understood; for example, the US Navy instructed its own submarines to concentrate on just such areas.

Unknown to the British, the Germans developed a countermeasure. Evasive action by convoys required radio communication. Captain (later Admiral) Karl Dönitz, in charge of the U-boat arm, thought that German code-breakers could read evasion instructions to convoys, providing him with their approximate locations in the open ocean. He would place patrol lines of U-boats ('wolf packs') athwart those tracks, giving a reasonable chance of engaging convoys in the open ocean. Concentrated against a convoy, the wolf pack could, he hoped, destroy it; it could certainly overwhelm a light escort. Dönitz was aware that wolf-pack operations entailed considerable communication, and thus the possibility that boats would be detected. To that end he sought systems which would be difficult to detect, culminating in the wartime 'squash' or burst transmitter, Kurier.

The situation for the battle fleet was quite different than that of one of numerous convoys, because an enemy could probably afford to concentrate enough resources to establish its location, and would cue submarines to attack it. The fleet therefore needed a solid screen of destroyers, with positions calculated to assure submarine detection.

[1] Position going into the 1930 Treaty, and the attribution of the increased speed to the Japanese are from ADM 116/2742.
[2] Franklin, *Britain's Anti-Submarine Capability*, p 145, quotes the 1932 edition of the handbook of ASW tactics, CB 3002. Convoys would be protected mainly by evasion.

Asdic and Weapons

The pre-war Admiralty often stated that Asdic (sonar) had solved the submarine problem, by enabling escorts to detect submerged U-boats. The term was a made-up word to incorporate the letters A/S, for anti-submarine; the Asdic development station was the A/S Experimental Establishment at Airlie.[3] Pre-war and wartime sets were later described as searchlights. They sent out a single ping in a conical beam (about 16–20° wide). The operator pinged and then waited for an echo. Only when he was sure that no echo had been returned from that direction did he turn his set to ping in a new direction. An operator typically searched in steps of 5°. While he did so, the ship moved, so that nominally adjacent beams really had considerable gaps between them. If there was an echo, the operator swung his beam back and forth over the target to find the direction more precisely. This 'cut-on, cut-off' technique was much the same procedure then used in radio direction-finders, finding direction by seeing where the signal seemed to vanish. It took time, during which the submarine had a chance to evade by manoeuvring violently enough. Actually localising a contact would take several pings and several steps. Sonars with a limited effective search arc were justified by analysis indicating that a submerged, *ie* very slow, submarine could attack only from ahead, in a narrow sector defined by 'limit-

---

[3] The often-repeated story that Asdic stood for Anti-Submarine Detection Investigation Committee is apparently false.

ing lines of approach'. There was no means of changing beam elevation angle to measure target depth; the rule of thumb (which could be 200ft off) was that depth was a third of the range at which the target left the sonar beam. Ultimately it was clear that searchlight sonar was much more a means of gaining and maintaining contact with a submarine which had revealed itself in some other way, *eg* by firing a torpedo. Note that these and other British surface ship sets through the 1960s had retractable transducers.

Beyond Asdic itself, the key pre-war development was the chemical recorder, work on which began in 1928. Asdic range was proportional to the time delay between ping and echo. The chemical recorder was based on the electrochemical paper technology then being used to receive photographs by fax. The amplified return signal was fed through a stylus moving across the paper. When it was activated by the signal, it marked the paper; because the stylus was moving at constant speed, the point at which it marked the paper indicated the range. The paper itself moved along at a constant speed, so that each ping left a distinctive mark. A faired line drawn down the paper indicated the range rate. If that was constant, the point at which the ship would pass over the submarine, provided she was headed directly for the target, could be predicted. At that point depth charges could be dropped. Development of a production version began in 1932, and it was ready in 1934. Typically there were two settings. For search the stylus could be set for a full

HMS *Erne* was a *Black Swan* class frigate. She was conceived as an A/A and A/S escort, the former role being reflected in her heavy anti-aircraft battery and the director (with Type 285 radar) atop her bridge. The lattice structure aft carries the 'lantern' of a Type 271 surface-search radar (some ships apparently had Type 272). The topmast carries an important A/S sensor, HF/DF.

travel of 2,500 yds; for attack, 1,000 yds. The range recorder triggered a ping when it began each sweep across the paper, so the ping rate increased for the 1000-yard setting. In the summer of 1939 there was an abortive attempt to use a standard range recorder to fire an ahead-thrown weapon, but this did not become feasible until later in the war.[4] During the Second World War a second recorder, of bearing, was added, so that a target's bearing rate could be measured.

The recorder changed ASW tactics. Without a recorder, a ship could detect a submarine but not estimate its course and speed. She therefore had to rush so as to arrive at the last known submarine location in time to pepper the area with depth charges, thus making ASW ship speed vital. This tactic was not too different from the pre-Asdic practice of rushing to the location indicated by the origin of a torpedo track or by a periscope. The final rush of course alerted the submarine, so a two-ship attack was devised: one ship steamed slowly so as not to alarm the submarine, to be coached by the other (holding contact) into attacking position. This idea may account for pre-war plans to provide each convoy with two Asdic escorts. With the recorder, the ship could project ahead the submarine's motion. The initial application seems to have been the Medium Range Constant Speed (MRCS) attack, in which the ship steamed at maximum Asdic speed (typically 18kts) beginning about 900 yds from the target in hopes of limiting the blind time during which the submarine could evade. Ultimately the recorder made it possible to attack without pouncing, hence using much slower, hence much more affordable, craft. This change justified the adoption of the wartime corvette instead of the expensive pre-war fast coastal escort. After war broke out, it became clear that U-boat commanders knew that an attack was imminent when the attacker, losing contact, accelerated to drop charges over the spot at which the U-boat had last been detected by her Asdic. The countermeasure was to revive the two-ship attack, which was called a 'creeping' attack (ie without final acceleration).

In theory, moreover, the recorder offered the sort of data which could have been used to aim an ahead-thrown weapon, which could be fired before contact was lost. Work on a 3.5in stick-bomb thrower began in 1924. It was tested on board the destroyer *Torrid* in 1930, and it figured in early designs for Convoy Sloops (see below), but by 1934 it had been abandoned. Asdic was not nearly precise enough to aim a single projectile at a submerged submarine (wartime ahead-thrown weapons used multiple projectiles to cover the area of uncertainty of an Asdic contact). Thus the Royal Navy relied on a pattern of five Mk 7 charges forming a diamond shape in the water, with one in the centre (three from the stern rail, two from throwers).[5] Charges carried 290lbs of explosive and had six settings, down to a maximum of 500ft. Based on model

experiments, the charge was assumed lethal within 40ft of a submarine. Depth settings were based on range when contact was lost (three to six times depth, typically assuming a maximum U-boat depth of 300ft). The standard pre-war outfit of two throwers plus rails (thirty depth charges) proved quite inadequate. In practice about one attack in twenty was lethal, partly because placement errors were about four times those of pre-war exercises. U-boat hunts were prolonged, with numerous re-attacks requiring unexpectedly large numbers of charges. Re-attacks were complicated because the sound of each temporarily swamped the ship's Asdic. Pre-war interest in heavier patterns was revived in wartime. The wartime standard ten-charge pattern comprised two superimposed diamonds 100ft apart in depth, to produce a sandwich effect. A fourteen-charge pattern added an intermediate layer of four heavy charges. It was abolished in April 1943 because trials showed that there was sometimes mutual interference between heavy charges from the quarter throwers and from the rails resulting in failures. The theoretical chance of success was no greater than that of a ten-charge pattern. Eliminating the fourteen-charge pattern saved space and weight (four throwers and racks), men (sixteen to twenty), and industrial effort.

Late in 1940 a new Mk 7 heavy depth charge (with a weight, to make it sink at 16½ft/sec rather than 10ft/sec) was introduced, with a maximum setting of 550ft. Furthermore, during the war the more powerful explosive Amatol replaced Minol as the filling of depth charges, increasing lethal range to 52ft. Another wartime development was a 1-ton (Mk X) depth charge considered equivalent to a ten-charge pattern by itself. Raised in 1938, the idea was abandoned, but then revived in January 1941 (as an initiative by C-in-C Western Approaches) as a torpedo tube weapon. Entering service in March 1942, it was initially disliked by COs who feared that its shock effect would destroy their ships. However, in July 1942, modified to sink much more rapidly, it emerged as a possible solution to deep-diving U-boats. Mk 10*, which would explode at greater depth, was introduced in April 1943. Destroyers converted to escorts typically carried two Mk 10 and two deeper-set Mk 10* in their quadruple tubes. Mk X was also dropped from special stern racks in 'Captain' class frigates. It also figured in early versions of the post-war frigate design.

The first standard destroyer Asdic, Type 119, first installed in the 'B' class, was optimised for Mediterranean conditions and for a maximum search speed of 18–20kts. It introduced the bridge loudspeaker standard in later sets. Listening to it, those in command could sense the way the situation was developing. Type 121 ('D' through 'G' classes) introduced a gyro-stabilised transducer. Type 124 ('C' and 'H' classes) had the first chemical range recorder; it was controlled from a 'silent' cabinet on the lower deck, with secondary control on the bridge. Type 127, conceived for convoy sloops, was the first set with a bearing plotter (using the bearing of the trans-

---

[4] Willem Hackmann, *Seek and Strike* (HMSO, London: 1984), pp 180–7.
[5] ADM 189/175, a technical history of Second World War ASW weapons prepared late in 1945 (date based on internal evidence).

ducer) to assist the CO during an attack. Instruments were in the direction-gear compartment. Type 128 (1937, initially for the 'L' class), the last pre-war set, had a range recorder and a new amplifier. It was mechanically trained, controlled from a hut on the bridge. Types 122 and 123 were simpler sets for trawlers with portable domes, the latter very widely used during the Second World War. The transducer was trained mechanically by a flexible shaft with a relative-bearing indicator.

Associated with Asdic was a large-scale (*ie* short range) plot used to visualise the tactical situation. In the *Black Swans* and contemporary destroyers the navigational plot was used alternatively for A/S (by switching to a larger scale). The plot was on the level below the bridge, visible (through glass, a view plot) from above. In the 'L' class and earlier ships the plot was in a combined plotting and signal office, but in the *Black Swans* it was in the wheelhouse. In these ships and in the 'Hunts' (in effect fast *Black Swans*) the view plot was separate from the A/S (Asdic) hut, whereas in earlier destroyers it had been part of the A/S table, presumably adjacent to the range recorder.

Just as Dönitz developed a counter to convoy tactics, he developed one to Asdic, although he had less idea of exactly what Asdic could and could not do. That the British had not changed their surface weaponry when they adopted it indicated to him that it could not detect a surfaced submarine. He therefore trained his submariners to attack at night on the surface. They could run much faster than the convoy and thus would not be limited to the forward sector. Many more escorts would thus be needed for each convoy. The pre-war Royal Navy seems to have been aware of this kind of threat, but it had no effective means of detecting surfaced U-boats at night. All that it could do was add escorts in the rear of the convoy. The ultimate solution was radar.

ASW Policy

Initially (in 1931), plans called for four A/S escorts for a convoy of up to sixteen to twenty merchant ships. That was deemed unaffordable, so the number was halved.[6] Given limited numbers, the escort was to deal with a submarine after it attacked, rather than to screen the convoy from attack. It was apparently not imagined that submarines had to be hunted to destruction, which might require detaching the sloop for hours, or even for days. For a European war, based on the expected number of convoys, 102 A/S ships were needed (a similar number would be needed for a Far Eastern war).[7] Thirty might be old destroyers (seventeen of which would have Asdic by the end of 1936, the rest by 1941) and fifteen more would be existing sloops not originally designed to be fitted with Asdic. These sloops would begin a war as

minesweepers, and then shift to convoy escort work. These figures left a shortage of fifty-seven convoy escorts for a war in either Europe or the Far East.

Local defence, which had a higher priority, was more daunting. It entailed escorting convoys through coastal waters to reach defended ports, and also prosecuting an offensive against submarines off the coast (*ie* patrolling and hunting). In the opening Phase I, a European war would require 308 local

defence units (an Eastern war, 109). In Phase II (first year) these numbers would rise to, respectively, 518 and 342; in Phase III (war fully-developed), 638 and 412. For Phase I, 291 trawlers had been earmarked. Due to their low speed, trawlers could hunt, but they could not pounce on a submarine reported at any distance. One hundred British trawlers would be fitted out at the outbreak of war and another 100 in the first few months. Another ninety-one more-or-less suitable vessels had been earmarked on foreign stations.

There was no hope of building enough inshore ASW ships in peacetime. The Royal Navy adopted a high-low policy, in which the bulk of such craft would be requisitioned fishing trawlers (the numbers of which were huge) equipped with stockpiled Asdics. At the high end, surviving First World War coastal ASW units (P-boats and PC-boats: *Spey, Dart, P.40, P.59* and *P.74*) serving as tenders to various schools and for

HMS *Enchantress* is shown on 12 April 1945. The prominent object above her bridge is the 'lantern' of her Type 271 surface-search radar, with its office directly below, to minimise signal loss in waveguides. *Enchantress* was built with three 4.7in guns, but landed Q gun shortly after completion to leave space for additional accommodation aft in her pre-war role as Admiralty yacht. In wartime Q gun was replaced by a single shielded 12pdr. She also had two quadruple 0.5in machine guns, which were later replaced by four single Oerlikons. A Hedgehog was added in April 1942. A sister-ship, *Bittern*, had twin 4in dual-purpose guns instead of 4.7in. The third ship, *Stork*, was completed as an unarmed survey ship but then armed like *Bittern* just before the war.

[6] Reference in the 1932 memorandum to M.01487/31.
[7] The terminal ports were Lough Swilly, Rosyth, Milford Haven, Sierra Leone, Malta, Port Said, Halifax and Kingston (Jamaica). Some routes were assigned only single escorts. Numbers also depended on whether local refit facilities were available, since otherwise allowance would have to be made for the period steaming back and forth to the refitting port.

fishery protection would need replacement as their hull lives expired in 1935–6.

Urgent measures taken in 1932 included buying quartz for Asdic transducers, increasing depth charge production (to overcome gross deficiencies due to the just-abandoned Ten Year Rule), and trial and immediate production of the set planned for trawlers (to be followed by trials of the similar set for sloops). All new sloops would be fitted so that Asdic could be installed on short notice. The number of trawlers to be taken up initially in an emergency was to be increased from 100 to 135. The urgency of the problem is indicated by another step: ASW was to be made the subject of annual meetings in June or July, to keep the Naval Staff informed of progress.

Sloops

In the wake of the London Conference, Director of Tactical Division (DTD) stated that sloops would have to replace destroyers as convoy escorts. For Controller (Rear Admiral Backhouse), the new convoy role required seakeeping and endurance to keep up with a fast (12-knot) convoy; a gun primarily to deal with an enemy submarine but also powerful enough to deal with an armed merchant raider or a light warship (hence perhaps more powerful than that of existing sloops); a means of detecting and destroying submerged submarines; and tropical habitability (for the many Empire convoy routes passing through tropical waters). Both a reasonable gun armament and tropical habitability were already required for the peacetime sloop role. The peacetime role required light draft and comparatively high endurance, but also comfortable accommodation for senior diplomatic officials. The minesweeper role also required tropical habitability. For minesweeping, it was already accepted that the ship had to be able to defend herself against submarines and possibly air attacks, but no effort had been made to fit Asdic or depth charges. To meet the growing threat of air attack, the ships should have at least one anti-aircraft gun, plus Lewis (machine) guns. The latter would be needed for peacetime policing, and it would also protect against low-flying aircraft. Ultimately the choice was two low-angle guns (4in at least, preferably 4.7in) plus one high-angle gun, and eight Lewis guns. Initially plans called for alternative peacetime (two 4in) and wartime gun batteries, but the idea was rejected on the ground that ships had to be designed always for wartime operation. One key difference between the minesweeper and escort requirements was the need for shallow draft in a minesweeper; for an escort there had to be sufficient draft for good Asdic performance. Minesweepers were already required to have an endurance of 5,000nm at 10kts, with a maximum speed of 16–17kts and a continuous sea speed of 12kts (the ships were to sweep at or above 10kts).

The current standard ASW battery for self-protection was four depth charges in two hydraulically-operated chutes,

but clearly an escort would need more. An ahead-throwing weapon, the Stick Bomb Thrower, was under development, as was an explosive paravane (both ultimately abortive). Space would be provided for emergency installation of Asdic. The bridge would have to be enlarged to accommodate instruments and a plotting table, in a space about 5ft × 2.5ft. Controller (Rear Admiral Backhouse) was worried that if Asdic were not fitted in peacetime, in an emergency there might not be time to do so. The sloop would have an HF radio to communicate with the Fleet and at long range. She had to be able to communicate with aircraft.

A May 1931 Controller's conference decided to split sloops off from the smaller minesweepers. The 1931 Programme was the first to be affected: it included both two sloops (*Grimsby* class) and two specialised minesweepers (*Halcyon* class). Staff requirements were circulated by DTD on 8 June 1931.

DNC's sketch design (December 1931) showed a slightly beamier version of the previous *Shoreham* class. For Controller its most important improvement was substituting two 4.7in guns and one 3in anti-aircraft gun for the 4in guns of earlier sloops.[8] The forward 4.7in gun was moved 10ft forward of the position of the earlier 4in, and the after 4.7in was moved 4ft further aft. Despite the split in roles, the ship was still intended for wartime minesweeping: the after 4.7in could be removed to reduce draft for sweeping. In wartime two depth charge throwers could also replace her minesweeping winch. Compared to *Shoreham*, the design offered reduced draft (by 8in). Rearrangement of compartments (moving the diesel generator from the centreline to the wings alongside the engine room) made it possible to reduce length by 15ft. Similar machinery was used (2,000 SHP twin-screw geared turbines), and estimated speed was 16kts deep (16.5kts at standard displacement, 1,060 tons). Extending the superstructure to accommodate the 3in gun made it possible to improve the CO's accommodation, providing him with a separate sleeping cabin. The large spare cabin for the distinguished passengers (an important peacetime feature) was moved from the lower to the upper deck, displacing the wardroom (which was moved to the lower deck). A new compartment was provided for the Asdic. One question, which had not been resolved as of mid-1932, was whether Asdic use would be intermittent or nearly constant. That would decide the number of operators to be carried. The Board approved the design on 14 January 1932. Eight *Grimsby* class sloops were built. An A/S sloop was planned for the 1933 Programme (see below), but the design was not yet ready, so the *Grimsby* class was repeated that year. That happened again in 1934 with the last pair, *Aberdeen* and *Fleetwood*. The RAN expressed interest. The four *Yarra* class were built in Australia to plans furnished by the Royal Navy.

[8] According to a penned note dated 18 April 1931 in the *Grimsby* Cover, Controller had just ordered the standard combination of one high-angle and one low-angle 4in, which he considered too weak, replaced by one dual-purpose and one low-angle 4.7in. The former would have been the 60° mounting then being tested (unsuccessfully) on board the destroyer *Beagle*.

By 1934 the threat of air attack against merchant shipping seemed much more significant, so in May substitution of twin dual-purpose 4in guns for the 4.7in was proposed. Note that this came before the threat of war against Italy over Abyssinia, which is often said to have motivated intense British interest in anti-aircraft firepower. In July DNO proposed testing a new 4in dual-purpose control system in one of the 1934 sloops (which would be completed in 1936). A new house would have to be added at the after end of the bridge to accommodate it. The test batteries actually planned were three single 4in (replacing both the 4.7in and the 3in anti-aircraft), in *Aberdeen*, or two twin 4in, in *Fleetwood*. The number of 4in guns was set, not by space or weight, but by the London Treaty restriction to no more than four guns larger than 3in. The Board chose the three-gun battery for future sloops 'for the time being', presumably hoping to replace single with twin mounts once the Treaty limit lapsed; twins were used for trials. At the same time the Board decided that the 4in gun in the coastal sloops (see below) should be dual-purpose.

Aberdeen was dropped from the test programme because the equipment might not be ready in time for her: she replaced the earlier sloop *Bryony* (First World War 'Flower' class) as the yacht of C-in-C Mediterranean, with accommodation similar to that arranged in the post-war sloop *Falmouth* (*Shoreham* class) for C-in-C China. Such ships had their after 4in replaced by temporary accommodations. No. 3 gun was not fitted, but the ship was stiffened to take it. *Fleetwood* became the anti-aircraft test ship. Fitting her and testing her left the fleet short a sloop, which would have served on the Africa Station. Given the importance of the anti-aircraft battery, that was accepted. Aside from the new armament, the ships were also slightly re-arranged internally to reduce wardroom noise, which had caused complaints in HMS *Lowestoft* (the diesel and steam generator rooms were interchanged). As an expression of the air attack problem, in June 1938 doctrine called for each coastal convoy (*ie* within range of aircraft) to have two A/A as well as two A/S escorts, one escort at each corner of the convoy.[9]

Convoy Sloops

As of 1932 plans called for one convoy sloop each year for the next fifteen years, to form a nucleus force; eight would be complete by 1942. At a meeting on A/S sloops on 2 February 1932 Controller asked. DNC to sketch both an ocean escort and a local defence ship on the lines of the First World War PC-boat (about 600 tons). These requirements were considered so urgent that, even though they had not yet been approved by First Sea Lord, DCNS quickly agreed that the ships might be included in the 1933 Programme. Although they did not approach what turned out to be necessary, the Admiralty's analysis and its actions went far beyond those of any other navy of the time.

ACNS initially suggested arming the ocean escort with three 6in guns, as in the new French sloops (*Bougainville* class, with three 5.5in guns), but DCNS argued that a ship so armed would be something between a weak surface escort and an overly complex and expensive ASW ship. CNS (First Sea Lord) stressed the need for simplicity. Director of Plans wanted speed, on the ground that a sloop leaving a fast (12-knot) convoy for a two-hour submarine hunt needed enough speed to return promptly. She would also have to deal with submarines capable of up to 19kts on the surface (only a few were faster). Controller wanted a design for rapid cheap production (he and E-in-C hoped for as little as six to seven months wartime building time, though that proved wildly optimistic). Director of Plans agreed that quick wartime construction was absolutely

[9] CAB 102/535, a post-war history of warship requirements, 1934–9.

HMS *Lark* was a Modified *Black Swan* class frigate. Note that all the light anti-aircraft guns visible are twin power and single hand-operated Oerlikons, the latter abeam the bridge. The radar on the masthead platform is Type 276 for surface search; Type 291 is at the masthead. Note the absence of HF/DF.

essential. He pointed out that old destroyers offered the necessary speed, though they might not be able to maintain even convoy speed in bad weather.

DNC was asked for at least three 4.7in and one 3in anti-aircraft gun, for good sea-keeping qualities, and for a speed of 18kts deeply loaded. His April 1932 sketch design showed a 1,700-ton sloop (275ft [289ft overall] × 36ft 6in × 11ft), with a standard displacement of 1,220 tons. She could carry the required guns plus the new ahead-throwing ASW weapon (a 3.5in stick-bomb thrower with fifty bombs) and forty depth charges (two throwers). The estimated weight of the stick-bomb thrower was based on that of the trials installation in the destroyer *Torrid*. Power had to be increased to 3,300 SHP to get the required speed at deep displacement. Endurance was 7,500nm at 12kts (DOD wanted 7,000nm, and the conference wanted 3,400nm). Estimated cost was £180,000. The ship could be used for minesweeping. The 3.5in stick-bomb thrower could be replaced by a fourth 4.7in gun, in which case the ship would match a destroyer's gun armament (Controller considered three such guns inadequate). An alternative with 6in guns would displace 1,400 tons (standard) and would cost £210,000, but destroyer experience strongly suggested that a 6in gun could not be fought in a seaway. There was some question as to whether a ship capable of 18kts deeply loaded, hence of over 20kts at standard displacement, would be outside the sloop category, and would therefore count as a destroyer under the London Naval Treaty. In June 1932 DNC was told to replace the bomb thrower with a fourth 4.7in gun, and to omit the 3in anti-aircraft weapon (the London Treaty allowed only four guns of 3in or larger calibre).

The Board approved the design on 22 June 1933 for the 1933 Programme. Laid down as *Bittern*, the prototype convoy sloop was completed as the Admiralty yacht *Enchantress*, with only three (later two) of her four 4.7in guns. The design

provided for two depth charge chutes (twelve charges each) and two throwers, for the total of forty charges. Compared to DNC's proposal, she was somewhat shorter (266ft [282ft overall] × 37ft × 8ft [9ft aft], 1,190 tons standard). No more convoy escorts were included in the 1934 Programme, but a repeat *Bittern* was included in the 1935 Programme, with another ship (*Stork*) in 1936. Plans at this time also showed a second ship in the 1936 Programme.

By late 1935 a new policy required all-dual-purpose armament in small ships. As of mid-November Controller (Rear Admiral Henderson) hoped to shift to an all-anti-aircraft battery for sloops in 1936. The only immediately viable choice was the twin 4in tested on board *Fleetwood*. Three twin 4in weighed about as much as four low-angle 4.7in, the proposal being to use A, B and Y positions (X was over the boiler room, and was not considered very good for a gun mounting). However, *Fleetwood*, which was to test the gun and the associated fire controls, would not be ready until November 1936. Should the ships be delayed to await the results of trials? A single 4.7in was suggested, a 70° mounting being under development (with tests planned for late 1936). The single 4.7in dual-purpose gun on board the *Nelson* class battleships, which was considered as an alternative, was obsolete, was long out of production, and was far too heavy.

Because the London Treaty was still in force, the proposed battery could not be mounted in any ship ordered during the 1935 financial year: requests for bids sent out in December 1935 specified four low-angle (destroyer-type 40°) 4.7in guns. ACNS suggested moving the ship to the 1936 Programme, which would place them outside the treaty. She could be enlarged and given higher speed. *Bittern* stayed in the 1935 Programme. The ships were considered too urgent to delay them any further. As of February 1936, DNC expected to order the two 1936 sloops near the end of the financial year, about March 1937. They could not be re-ordered to reflect trials.

HMS *Enchantress* was an Admiralty Yacht converted from the sloop HMS *Bittern*. She is shown as completed in April 1935; the 4.7in gun amidships was replaced by a small deckhouse shortly after. Sloops like this one were conceived because the 1930 London Naval Treaty limited British destroyer strength and thus eliminated destroyers which would otherwise have performed non-fleet duty such as convoy escort. In effect a large sloop was a slow destroyer without torpedo tubes. (A D Baker III)

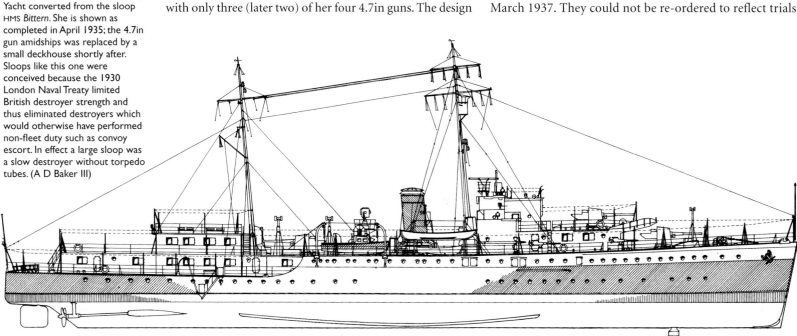

That proved to be a good decision, because by May the dual-purpose 4.7in was dead.

Now the question was whether to arm the ships with three or four twin 4in. Henderson asked verbally for three, which presented no problem at all. Four would need a somewhat larger ship, probably 10ft longer and 6in beamier, about 1,200 tons, with somewhat deeper draft (8ft 3in mean). No. 4 gun would be mounted on the upper deck, for stability, with No. 3 superfiring over it. Henderson proposed arming the 1935 ship (*Bittern*) with three twin 4in and the two 1936 ships with four. There was now interest in adding one or more pompoms – each of which weighed about as much as a twin 4in gun.

Controller strongly favoured the four-gun ship, and ACNS and DCNS both liked it. Director of Plans wanted to replace one twin mount with a pompom. The Staff (as well as DTSD and D of TD) preferred three twins and two pompoms. First Sea Lord approved the 4in guns but wanted to reflect further on close-range armament. A decision was urgent because information had to be produced for the builders. It seemed that the 1935 ship, *Bittern*, would have three mounts. For quicker production, the same battery was installed on board the first 1936 ship, *Stork*.

Bittern was fitted with experimental Denny-Brown stabilisers, which seemed key to using so small and lively a ship as an anti-aircraft platform. The stabiliser could both reduce roll and also induce a roll in calm weather to simulate heavy weather. It turned out that *Bittern* could fire effectively even with a roll of 10–15°.

Two more ships included in the 1936 Programme, *Egret* and *Auckland* (ex-*Heron*), got the four 4in mountings. If for some reason the twin 4in proved unsuccessful, they could have single 4in instead. The extra guns, and 250 rounds per gun, cost about 80 tons more displacement. Beam was increased to 37ft 6in to maintain stability. These ships also had a new Asdic (Type 127), replacing the earlier Type 124.

Re-evaluation

By this time the international situation was becoming much grimmer. In 1935 Britain signed a naval agreement under which the Germans limited themselves to 35 per cent of British naval strength, including submarines (previously denied them altogether under the Versailles Treaty). Upon announcing the desire to do so, they could demand parity in submarines. The British hoped that they could at least delay the growth of the U-boat arm. Early in the spring of 1939 the Germans announced that they wanted parity, and that summer they denounced the treaty altogether. However, they went to war with the treaty-limited force. In 1935 it was estimated that 105 escorts would be needed to fight a European war, a figure reduced to ninety (with an increase to 114 as early as possible) when more detailed plans were drawn up in 1937.[10] Another forty patrol vessels were needed. The escort estimate for the Far East was eighty-eight, because its much larger sea areas favoured evasive routeing, and it was thought that ships could sail independently except in the North Pacific, near Japan. It was thought that, at least at first, the main air threat to shipping would be in port.

From a programme point of view, escorts competed with minesweepers. At the outbreak of war a total of sixty-eight minesweepers would be needed (forty-seven in the Far East and twenty-one in European waters), up from an earlier estimate of fifty-one.[11] Initially it was hoped that sloops might initially be assigned to sweep ports and then shifted to ASW, but DTM pointed out that the initial mining threat would be exactly the enemy submarines against which ASW ships would fight. Ultimately all minesweepers were fitted with Asdic so

[10] CAB 102/535.
[11] Required numbers were: twenty-one in home waters (all minesweepers), fourteen in the Mediterranean (four of which could be sloops), seventeen in the East Indies (which could include four Indian sloops and three British sloops), twelve in China (which could include five sloops), two in Australia, and two in South Africa (which could both be sloops). The earlier figure of fifty-one required construction of thirty sloop minesweepers in the alternating three-and two-ship annual programmes approved by the Defence Requirements Committee in 1937.

HMS *Egret* as fitted, November 1938. The very heavy anti-aircraft battery reflects the view that aircraft would probably be the main threat to trade in coastal waters. That is also why the 'Hunt' class had an all-anti-aircraft battery. Atop the ship's bridge is the new Mk III rangefinder director, a modified version of the Mk II in a 'Tribal,' transmitting its data electrically to a Transmitting Station (calculation space). Because it was to be used for both surface and anti-aircraft fire, this director accommodated a separate Rate Officer, who estimated the speed and course of a surface target. (A D Baker III)

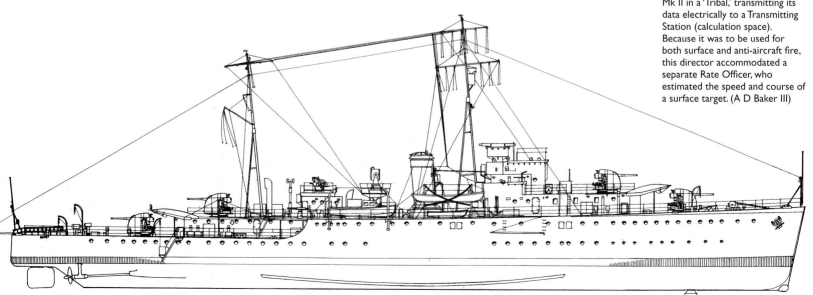

that they could function as escorts (the RAN's wartime *Bathurst* class was used mainly as escorts). As a stop-gap, Director of Plans proposed rearming thirty-six old 'V & W' class destroyers as convoy escorts, beginning with two each in 1937, 1938 and 1939, and then reviewing.[12]

Plans as of 22 April 1936 called for one convoy, two minesweeping, and two coastal sloops in 1937; one convoy, three minesweeping, and two coastal in 1938; and two convoy, two sweeping, and two coastal in 1939. This was quite inadequate, so in September an increase was suggested: two convoy, five sweeping, and three coastal sloops each year, for totals of six convoy sloops, fifteen sweepers, and nine coastal sloops – at a cost of something over £2 million. ACNS cut the number of sweepers per year to four, on the grounds that the First World War ships, which had seen little service in recent years, might have more life left in them. The ASW ships could not be similarly cut.

Could the different categories be re-merged? In August 1936 DNC pointed out that the 1936 Convoy Escort could be converted to minesweeping by removing the after 4in mount, although she did draw considerably more water than *Fleetwood* (10ft 3in to 10ft 6in as opposed to 9ft 3in). Given an early decision, the ships could be completed with minesweeping gear aft, and provided with portable rails and depth charge throwers as in *Fleetwood* (if the full outfit could not be carried without interfering with her minesweeping capability). The sloop minesweepers, though smaller than patrol sloops, could be used for ordinary sloop duties (HMS *Harrier* and *Hussar* had already made experimental tropical cruises to test this idea).

To meet criticism that sloops drew too much water for minesweeping, DNC proposed ballast tanks to adjust draft. When empty, they would reduce draft to an appropriate minesweeping figure (8ft 6in); full, they would give 11ft for A/S. Filled with fuel, the tanks would increase endurance to 10,000nm. With present sloops, maximum fuel load for sweeping was about 150 tons (compared to 600 tons for other sloop duties). A sketch design was offered in December 1936. Engineroom length fixed the length of the ship at 260ft (1,110 tons). That was enough for two twin 4in and one pompom. The 4in gun aft would be in X position, the sweep winch below it in Y, with the minesweeping store below it. The forward gun would be in A, the pompom in B. Length could be cut to 250ft (1,070 tons standard) by rearranging the machinery, placing the boilers side by side (which E-in-C found acceptable). Speed (with the same power) would fall to 19.75kts at standard displacement (19kts deep). This ship would cost £330,000, compared to £192,000 for *Grimsby* a few years earlier. Most of the increase was due to armament (£43,000 vs £5,000 for gun mountings, £24,000 vs £6,000 for guns, £54,000 vs £9,000 for ammunition).

This was not much of a bargain. By the time it had been submitted attention had shifted back to a more conventional design with heavier anti-aircraft armament. The designers were already working on a revised *Egret*, omitting sweep gear and supporting structure. A quadruple pompom replaced one of the twin 4in guns. Because she would be slightly longer, the new ship would also be slightly faster. A comment that bow protection 'may be needed, should be in design' suggests that ramming was being envisaged as an emergency ASW measure. As only one ship in six would have to be fitted for sweeping, that version could probably be deferred to the 1938 Programme.[13]

Black Swan

Controller (Henderson) decided that he wanted a general-purpose sloop, convertible for sweeping, despite the contradiction between the A/S and sweeping roles. He asked DNC for a combination of the three types: convoy escort, sloop and coastal. DNC replied that meeting the maximum requirements of all three would require a 1,250–1,300-ton ship, and even then she could not carry both full armament and sweep gear. However, a ship based on *Fleetwood* could be built in two-thirds the time as one designed to the full Staff Requirement.[14] The main new development was the stabiliser, as tested on board *Bittern*. The designers provided the necessary space (about 7ft long) and weight.[15] Because the sloop had a real peacetime role, she had to be arranged for peacetime cruising. For example, she needed a large spare cabin (which could be the officers' smoking room). Operating abroad, a separate natives' mess would be required.

The Convoy Escort was the largest sloop yet, mainly due to an attempt to increase speed (though not to the desired figure, 20kts when pursuing a submarine). She would displace 1,225 tons standard (288ft 6in) and 1,650 tons deep. The same 4,300 SHP powerplant used in previous large sloops would propel her at 19.75kts (standard) or 19kts (deep). Standard displacement included the minesweeping gear, but not all the depth charges (she would carry rails). If required as an escort, she would land her minesweeping fittings and pick up depth charges at a base. The ship could not meet the minesweeping requirement, because she drew 10ft 6in deep (9ft 3in with 150 tons of fuel). This design was submitted in January 1937.

Formal Staff Requirements (TD 40/37) were issued on 24 March 1937. Long-range anti-aircraft armament, all on the centreline, would be at least four 4in (six preferred). As the design developed, the 4in magazines were ordered enlarged

12 After scrappings, fifty-three 'V & W' class destroyers were left for this purpose.

13 Notes dated 5 November 1936 in *Black Swan* Cover.
14 DNC based the design on displacement limited to about 1,000 tons. She would displace 1,075 tons standard (267ft); on 3,600 SHP she would make 19.5kts at standard load and 18.5kts at deep load. Endurance would be 6,300nm at 12kts. Armament would be two twin 4in and one quadruple pompom. Minesweeping equipment other than the winch would be removed for escort operations. When oil fuel was cut to 125 tons, draft would be 8ft 6in. The estimated cost of the Convoy Escort was £330,000; this ship could be built, to commercial (Lloyd's or British Corporation) specifications for £270,000.
15 There was some question as to whether Denny-Brown stabilisers should be specified; the decision was to leave that out and let the Admiralty buy the stabilisers separately (which would be best, the constructor involved said, in view of the secrecy involved).

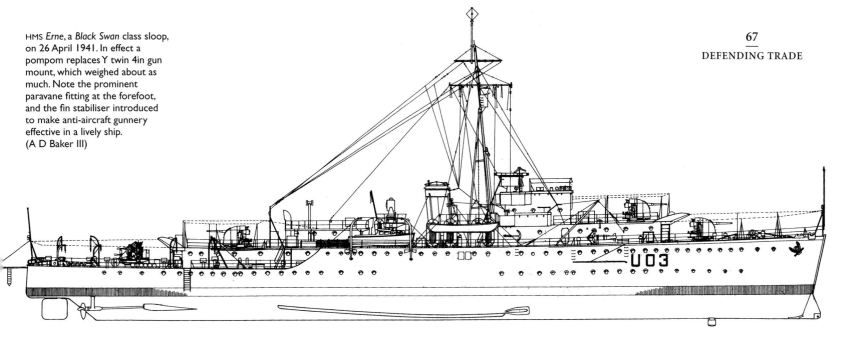

HMS *Erne*, a *Black Swan* class sloop, on 26 April 1941. In effect a pompom replaces Y twin 4in gun mount, which weighed about as much. Note the prominent paravane fitting at the forefoot, and the fin stabiliser introduced to make anti-aircraft gunnery effective in a lively ship. (A D Baker III)

to take up to 400 rounds per gun, rather than the 250 of earlier designs (this was impractical: there was not enough volume below decks). A good close-range weapon (the pompom) was very desirable. Asdic was clearly essential, and the desired depth charge battery was forty charges (five-pattern: two throwers plus stern rails capable of laying three charges consecutively, all controlled from the bridge). A new requirement (first raised late in the *Egret* design) was HF/DF.

Minimum performance was 7,500nm at 12kts with four months' stores, with an ideal speed of 20kts when operating against a submarine. The ship had to be able to maintain steam for not less than 17kts for long periods, to give her a dash capability against a submarine. For good manoeuvrability the ship needed twin screws. Captain Bellars of the Naval Staff objected to the low speed; he wanted more than 20kts (but the designer taking notes observed that such speeds were 'definitely undesirable in view of possible limitations in future', presumably a reference to a possible future treaty). Bellars' suggestion of internal combustion engines with electric drive was rejected. It was, however, clear that for ASW the ship might have to accelerate very quickly, and it was conceded that quickly working up from 500 HP to 1,800 HP might be a problem. Besides her minesweeping role, the ship was arranged so that she could lay mines. When not sweeping, the ship would have to use paravanes to pass through a minefield.

This 1937 Convoy Escort became the *Black Swan* class, the most successful British wartime escort. Four were built under the pre-war 1937 and 1938 Programmes. Two more were included in the 1939 Programme presented to the Cabinet in February 1939, but they were cancelled before being ordered. Once war broke out, a modified version was ordered. The series began with ten under the 1940 Programme and two more under the 1940 Supplemental (plus four for the Royal Indian Navy).[16] Further orders were fourteen under the 1941

Programme (two transferred to India, total of three cancelled 1945), and two in 1942 (not ordered). Another two planned for the 1944 Programme (to replace 1941 and 1942 ships not ordered), were dropped in 1945. The first four Indian ships may have been modified versions of the *Bittern* class. As First Sea Lord, Admiral Chatfield reportedly tried to interest the Royal Canadian Navy in this type.

Ten modified ships were ordered in March 1940. Minesweeping capacity, which had been re-introduced into the *Black Swan* class after having been omitted from the previous two, was eliminated. DASW wanted the weight thus freed to go into four more depth charge throwers and two more traps, and a total of up to 120 depth charges.[17] DoD(H) saw the very heavy depth-charge battery as valuable in an A/S Striking Force, but not in the usual convoy role. He argued that weight should go instead into anti-aircraft weapons, such as an additional quadruple pompom. At the beginning of April, Controller ruled in favour of the extra pompom, additional splinter protection to bridges, directors and guns, and the maximum number of depth charges (but no more than 100). In fact the ships were modified to carry 110 charges (eight rather than two throwers, three rather than two stern rails).

The next step, taken slightly later in April, was to add a foot of beam to the 1940 ships. That restored the original metacentric height (2.5ft) and provided the necessary margin against expected further additions. Speed fell slightly, the estimate being 19.2kts rather than 19.4kts deep (20.08kts vs 20.14kts light) at 1,270 tons vs 1,204 tons; deep displacement would be 1,855 tons rather than 1,766 tons. Bridge protection increased from quarter-inch magnetic steel and ³⁄₁₆in and ³⁄₈in non-magnetic to half-inch magnetic steel and ⅝in non-magnetic. Originally there had been no splinter protection at all over the guns; now it was ½in D1HT steel. As modified, the

---

[16] Based on a list dated 27 January 1942 in the Modified *Black Swan* Cover.

[17] This was early in March 1940. DMS agreed to eliminate the sweep gear, but found it difficult to imagine why 100 or more depth charges were needed; he could not believe Asdic was so ineffective.

HMS *Lapwing* on 17 March 1944. Note the unusual double-letter pennant number.

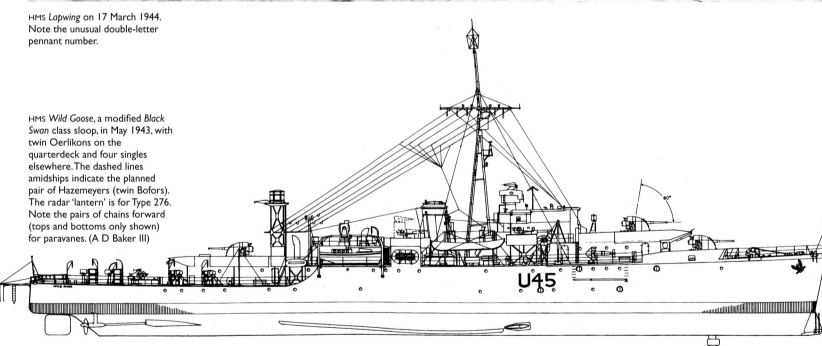

HMS *Wild Goose*, a modified *Black Swan* class sloop, in May 1943, with twin Oerlikons on the quarterdeck and four singles elsewhere. The dashed lines amidships indicate the planned pair of Hazemeyers (twin Bofors). The radar 'lantern' is for Type 276. Note the pairs of chains forward (tops and bottoms only shown) for paravanes. (A D Baker III)

ships kept the same upper deck, the additional beam at the waterline (actually at 8ft 3in draft) causing tumblehome. Yarrow, which was responsible for the detailed plans, complained that new hull drawings were needed, but that it could not produce them quickly enough because of the pressure of work.[18] Yarrow argued that metacentric height was already sufficient to accommodate the extra 2pdr, six more depth charge throwers, and thirty-four more depth charges. DNC was unmoved; the firm had understated the problem.

[18] Projects included eight 'Hunts', four of them with increased beam, and two 'L' class destroyers, one with 4in guns and the other with 4.7in.

In October 1940, DTM had second thoughts about eliminating minesweeping capacity. Initially the second pompom had been placed on the quarterdeck, but now it was raised, the two pompoms being placed side by side near the break of the forecastle. That made for better arcs (the single pompom originally on the centreline had been blocked fore and aft). Ammunition supply would not be so direct as previously for the second gun, but was better for the first. Given the cleared quarterdeck, a minesweeping winch could be installed if the ship went back to four depth charge throwers, two rails, and forty charges. Director of Plans, however, felt

that it would be wasteful to equip a ship with heavy anti-aircraft armament as a minesweeper, given the great demand for convoy protection against air attacks.

The 1941 series had further changes. Twin Bofors guns with radar (Type 282) directors replaced the pompoms (the 1940 ships retained pompoms because a change would have delayed delivery). A new Asdic (Type 144) was fitted. Generating capacity was increased (turbo-generators to 100 kW each, diesels to 70 kW each). SA gear, for self-protection against acoustic mines using flat plates in the bow to transmit underwater noise, was also installed. The mainmast was eliminated. Automatic electric emergency lanterns replaced oil lighting.[19] The 1942 ships were to have had a single Stabilised Tachimetric AA Gun (STAAG – twin Bofors) instead of the two Bofors of the earlier units.

For the 1944 Programme, beam was increased to 39ft 6in at the 10ft 6in waterline and the forecastle deck widened 2ft to restore the original form (no tumblehome), except for increased beam. The new form was developed in detail by Denny. Simply repeating the 1940 design was rejected because the reserve of stability had been exhausted (ships had to flood some oil tanks to maintain stability when lightly loaded); there was no longer any Board Margin; the ships were cramped (ideally they would have been lengthened 20ft); they were trimming by the bow because the weight aft for minesweeping had long gone (the complaint was when ships had expended their depth charges); they needed rearrangement; and they could not easily accommodate some important new equipment (Squid, Hedgehog and the Type 650 missile jammer). They needed a larger bridge and better grouping of their officers (much of the problem would be solved by bringing the officers under the bridge as in the *Algerines*). The Modified *Black Swan* was already 200 tons heavier than a *Black Swan*. To improve trim, the centre of buoyancy was moved about a foot forward. Scantlings were increased, and the structure in way of the break of the forecastle and the after end of the deck-house improved for greater strength.[20] Longitudinal bulkheads were kept in the same places to increase fuel and fresh water stowage. As in the latest modified *Black Swan*s, armament was three twin 4in, two twin US-type Bofors, two twin power 20mm, two single 20mm, four depth charge throwers and two rails (twelve charges each).

Construction had run so slowly that the two supplemental 1940 ships (*Snipe* and *Sparrow*) were not to be laid down until October and September 1944. Thornycroft's *Actaeon* had largely been prefabricated, but as of March 1944 it had not yet been laid down. One question was whether these ships should be built to the new beamier design, in addition to the five 1944 ships.

The 'Hunts'

In 1937, C-in-C Home Fleet Admiral Roger Backhouse suggested building a new type of small destroyer to supplement the very large ones. It was painfully clear that the Royal Navy needed numbers, and that large destroyers could not be built quickly enough. When he became First Sea Lord in 1938 Backhouse revived the idea. On 30 August 1938 he asked the Staff to evaluate a destroyer significantly less expensive than the new fleet type, for quick construction. Cost was to be given full weight. In his letter Admiral Backhouse noted that 'to some extent we already have these qualities in the Escort Vessels, but they are too slow and the latest is too expensive'.[21] The immediate result was the Intermediate destroyer, which emerged as the 'O' class in 1939.

However, Backhouse was also interested in something smaller. On 5 September 1938 he asked DNC to sketch a small destroyer, for all the numerous destroyer duties outside the fleet: escort, patrol, etc. He also wondered whether the new

[19] Two 1940 Supplemental ships, built at Denny (transferred from Devonport), replaced two cancelled at John Brown (*Snipe* and *Sparrow*). Two ordered from White under the 1940 Supplemental were replaced by 'Hunt' class destroyers. Two from Thornycroft were replaced by the 'Hunt' class destroyers *Brecon* and *Brissenden*, and two more from Swan Hunter were replaced by other 'Hunt' class destroyers. Other ships were transferred among the Royal Dockyards. Notes based in part on George Moore, *Building for Victory* (World Ship Society: n.d.).

[20] Ships were showing structural weaknesses because their longitudinal bulkheads had been scaled up from those of *Egret*. There was also trouble on the upper deck in way of the superstructure.
[21] Intermediate Destroyer Cover, Folio 6C. Backhouse referred to a paper in which his predecessor, Admiral Chatfield, remarked that two types of destroyer would be needed in future, undoubtedly because the big fleet destroyers were becoming far too expensive.

HMS *Lark* as in April 1944, with Type 293 radar at her foretop. Her light anti-aircraft battery is four twin and two single Oerlikons. The topmast carries Type 291. Halfway up the topmast is the 'egg timer' IFF transponder, Type 253. Below Type 293 is the IFF interrogator. (Alan Raven)

HMS *Amethyst*, 1950, repaired after her famous dash past Communist Chinese shore batteries in 1949. Her new lattice foremast carries a Type 293 target-indication radar. The hooded object in the gun tub is a Mk V twin Bofors. The two single Oerlikons below the bridge have been retained; in some ships they were later replaced by single Bofors guns on open platforms. This configuration was typical of late-war ships of this type.

large destroyers were really suitable for massed operations. In either case it was essential to reduce neither sea-keeping nor endurance. Cuts might fall on guns and torpedo tubes. Backhouse said there was no special urgency in the matter, but in September 1938 it seemed that war was imminent. A new Fast Escort might be the only destroyer-like ship which could be produced in a hurry. Without one, the only alternatives were destroyers (thirty months' building time) and escorts (sloops: twenty-one months).

DNC Sir Stanley Goodall had written to Controller on 2 September that 'it will be seen that there is very little time for discussion of new types'. However, given Backhouse's interest, on 22 September he asked his designers for two sketch designs of Destroyer Escorts, to follow destroyer practice generally but with a 'very open mind' as to arrangements. One was to have two twin 4in dual-purpose guns, one forward and one aft (200 rounds per gun, as in the destroyers converted to escorts), plus two quadruple 0.5in machine guns and two twin or one quadruple 21in torpedo tube. The ship would have Asdic and depth charges, and was to be capable of minesweeping (TSDS, HSMS [High Speed Mine Sweep] and the low-speed sweep for the *Black Swan* class were to be considered). She was not to be a minelayer, but the effects of providing

minelaying capacity were to be investigated. Speed was to be 28–31kts depending on load. Endurance was to be 3,500nm at 15kts. The ship would be stabilised. As in destroyers, boilers would be in two separate rooms. Scantlings, particularly at the waterline, would be slightly heavier than in destroyers. A second sketch design was to be developed for a 25-knot ship, as above but without torpedo tubes, and with a speed of 20–26kts depending on load.

By 26 September Goodall had the two sketch designs. Estimated costs were £375,000 and £310,000, and the ship was now described as an Escort Vessel (Destroyer Lines). The 30-knot ship would displace 810 tons standard (265ft × 27ft × 17ft depth), and was expected to make 31kts standard (28kts deep) on 17,000 SHP. She would have one quadruple torpedo tube. There was no provision for minelaying. The 25-knot alternative would attain 26kts in standard condition (24kts deep). In its case the boiler room was too short (40ft) to be worth subdividing. With the stabiliser fitted, the ship could carry enough oil only for 3,000nm at 15kts. The designers listed a long series of amenities that would have to be omitted, and noted that deck area per man would be about 80 per cent of that in recent destroyers. This ship would displace 640 tons standard with a stabiliser (232ft × 25ft 5in × 7ft).

The designs were presented to CNS, Controller and Admiral Cunningham on 28 September. They asked for a new Escort Vessel capable of 29–32kts, armed with three twin 4in (one forward, two aft), without any torpedo tubes or TSDS, but with Asdic and depth charges and with stabilisers for effective anti-aircraft fire. Its essential feature would be seaworthiness, which would mean good freeboard, a flared bow (as in the 'J' class), a bridge well abaft the bow, and strong sides. Displacement could be as much as 100 tons greater than in the initial 30-knot design. An alternative design would have two twin 4in and one triple torpedo tube (or the ship could be designed so that one twin 4in could be replaced by a triple torpedo tube). In effect this was a fast *Black Swan* in which endurance and the 2pdr pompom were traded for much higher speed. Because the *Black Swan* machinery was relatively heavy for its output, that was not outlandish (the new ship was, however, much smaller than a *Black Swan*, too).

By October 1938 the 1939 Programme showed twenty of the new Fast Escorts – and none of the earlier slow Convoy Escorts (*Black Swan*s). The tentative 1939 Programme was one destroyer flotilla, five escorts, and five patrol vessels, but CNS (First Sea Lord) decided to replace both the escorts and the patrol vessels would with the new fast escort.[22] He explained the policy to the Board at a meeting on 10 October 1938. The Cabinet Committee on Defence Programmes and Acceleration soon recommended building ten fast escorts at once. About a month later First Sea Lord explained that the First World War had shown that the destroyer was 'the most useful we possessed for all manner of services, and that it was in fact indispensable'. However good they might be, the *Black Swan*s could not fully substitute for them, *eg* in protecting fast (troop) convoys, patrolling off harbours and bases, screening warships, and offensive patrols such as the Dover Patrol, which helped secure the North Sea in the last war. Yet modern destroyers were too slow to build. Earlier smaller types lacked sufficient anti-aircraft armament 'and it has been well shewn that an HA armament is necessary in Destroyers in future in order

that they may be suitable for employment in areas liable to air attack'.[23]

Not everyone agreed. ACNS observed that two patrol vessels could be bought for the price of one 'Hunt' or *Bittern*. He preferred two patrol ships and one sloop to two Fast Escorts. The chemical recorder, moreover, made high speed less essential. Slower and much less expensive ships, such as trawlers (about a tenth the cost of a fast escort or sloop) might be effective. Cunningham (DCNS) argued that speed was still quite important: the faster the hunter could reach the quarry the smaller the area to be searched or depth-charged. He therefore wanted all effort concentrated on the new Fast Escorts, which could maintain their speed in rough weather. First Sea Lord agreed.

Given the new requirement for two A/A escorts per convoy, in June 1938 the Committee on Imperial Defence (CID) concluded that forty ships were needed. The Munich crisis that autumn revealed the desperate need for smaller warships. In November the Cabinet approved the first ten 'Hunts' as a supplement to the 1938 Programme, and added another ten in the 1939 Programme. All twenty were ordered in March 1939. However, they could not be laid down until June 1939 because under the 1936 London Naval Treaty a set interval had to elapse between notification (to the other signatories) that ships were being ordered and when they could be laid down. All that could be done was to assemble material so that construction could be speeded up. On 21 July 1939 Controller chaired a meeting on the emergency programme to be ordered in the event of war, which seemed imminent. Among its decisions was to include twenty repeat escorts. Another sixteen were ordered in December 1939. Initial plans for the 1940 Programme called for thirty-four more 'Hunts', but four were ordered instead as *Black Swan*s.

To meet the schedule, the basic design had to be complete by the end of the year, less than three months away. DNC's designers moved very quickly. By 10 October DNC was inspect-

[22] As described by Director of Plans in Folio 6B, Intermediate Destroyer Cover.

[23] Statement dated 5 November 1938 in Intermediate Destroyer Cover, in connection with future escort construction.

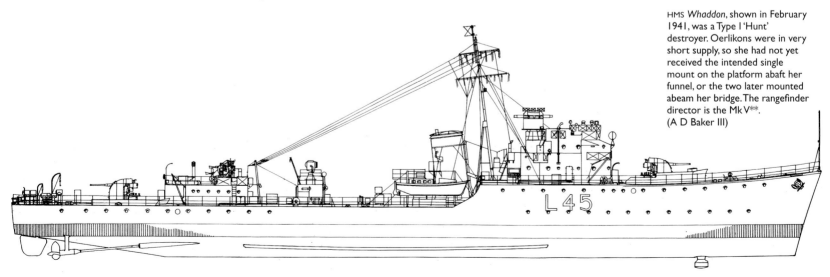

HMS *Whaddon*, shown in February 1941, was a Type I 'Hunt' destroyer. Oerlikons were in very short supply, so she had not yet received the intended single mount on the platform abaft her funnel, or the two later mounted abeam her bridge. The rangefinder director is the Mk V**. (A D Baker III)

ing design drawings. E-in-C saw the outlines of the machinery spaces on 12 October; he was asked for an 18,000 SHP plant, with two boilers in separate boiler rooms. Endurance was set at 3,000nm at 15kts. At the same time DNO was given the provisional armament: three twin 4in (200 rounds per gun plus fifty ready-use), two quadruple 0.5in machine guns, four Lewis guns, two depth charge throwers and one rail (twenty depth charges, with ten more in wartime).

The 265ft × 28ft 3in × 16ft 6in hull initially envisaged could accommodate seven officers and 113 ratings. However, the minimum complement needed to fight the ship was seven officers and 143 ratings. Comparison with existing ships showed that this figure was, if anything, conservative. For example, an 'R' class destroyer needed 147 men. Another thirty men would require 20ft more of ship; in view of the desire to hold down size, the designers pressed the various departments on their estimates. They allowed the ship to grow to 272ft (875 tons rather than 850 tons). Examining the drawings, Goodall remarked that the extra 7ft of length would also improve trim and provide a margin for contingencies, such as the need for more oil or for more refrigerated space. He asked his designers to investigate the effect of reducing speed from 29–32kts to 27–30kts, of cutting armament down to four 4in (with the original speed), or increasing endurance to 4,000nm. Because machinery might be shrunk by raising propeller revs, he asked for the effect on propulsive coefficient (propeller efficiency) of increasing to 400 RPM.

The final version was 272ft × 28ft 3in × 18ft 6in (875 tons), armed with the three twin 4in (250 rounds per gun deep load), two quadruple 0.5in machine guns, and depth charges. For seakeeping, No.1 gun was placed on a platform 18in above the forecastle proper. As promised, speed was 29–32kts. At First Sea Lord's instance, endurance was changed to 2,500nm at 20kts, which required more fuel oil (DNC ordered machinery spaces compressed to provide the necessary volume). Total complement was five officers and 142 ratings. Deck space forward would allow for a crew of 126. The necessary extra space was provided aft for the CPOs, POs and ERAs. Officers lived and messed forward in accordance with Controller's instructions (First Sea Lord had remarked that in an anti-aircraft ship of this type it would be most desirable for the crew of the guns aft to live near them). Estimated cost was £390,000.

Inspecting the drawings in December 1938, DNO remarked that after the first fifteen old destroyers were converted to escorts, the stream of twin 4in mountings would be shifted to the projected twenty Fast Escorts before destroyer conversions resumed. Asked how far design and construction could be simplified, Yarrow replied that it would be best simply to repeat an existing ship, such as the smaller pre-'Tribal' destroyer (*eg Bulldog*) or *Black Swan*. A new special design would be far less useful, even if it were particularly adapted to quick production. Goodall rejected this advice. The new escort design

would completely replace the old slow one. There was no point in repeating the *Black Swan* class. However, as a way of simplifying construction, the ship was designed with transverse framing rather than the new longitudinal type DNC was then applying to destroyers. The structure was designed to use as much mild steel as possible, and design stresses were reduced to 7.5 tons/sq in in tension and 6.0 tons/sq in in compression. Aware of the project, Thornycroft offered its own 1,000-ton destroyer (four twin 4in guns), which was rejected. It lacked crucial facilities such as a large enough radio room and Asdic. It was much likelier to capsize than comparable Royal Navy designs, and it would probably be considerably weaker.

DNC submitted the design to the Board on 29 November, about six weeks after work began. Thanks partly to E-in-C's efforts in improving fuel consumption at 20kts, he could promise the desired 2,500nm at that speed (and 3,500nm at 15kts, more than originally expected). To maintain the required 29kts in deep condition with increased displacement, SHP had been increased to 19,000, so expected speed at standard load was now 32.5kts. Perhaps most importantly, detailed investigation of hull strength showed that the ship could be built of ungalvanised scantlings, which would save time and money. Although complement was larger than initially envisaged, it could be fitted into the hull with accommodation on standard destroyer scale. That crewmen serving the guns were aft, near them, was still a major design feature. As in other British destroyers, seakeeping was a key consideration. DNC pointed out that the ship had greater freeboard than destroyers of similar size, the forward gun mounting being protected by a breakwater and raised on a bandstand.[24] A stabiliser was provided for better anti-aircraft fire in a seaway. It became a somewhat controversial feature. In wartime it proved ineffective below 12kts, and over 15kts it gave the ships a jerky motion which made gun-laying difficult. However, in bad weather it improved steering in a stern sea, because it reduced the roll up to 10 per cent.[25] Estimated cost was £397,000. There was some difficulty over electrical generating capacity, the designers arguing that DEE's demands could not be met within the limited machinery space and the weight. They offered two 50 kW (later 60 kW, with 25 per cent overload) turbo-generators and two 20 kW diesel generators. DEE argued that the later could not meet the normal harbour load. For example, running both diesels the ship could either be heated or she could run her radio or her signalling light, but not all three. This was accepted by Controller. The ships were 'required to

---

[24] The use of the bandstand was based on a report from HMS *Whitley*, an early 'V & W' escort conversion (November 1938). Raising the mounting above the deck would greatly reduce spray interference when steaming into a head sea, although it would increase blast effects on the bridge.
[25] 'Battle' Class Cover, in connection with fitting stabilisers in that class. In a letter dated 1 May 1942, Vice Admiral A H Taylor, C-in-C The Nore, argued that on the basis of East Coast experience stabilisers could be omitted to gain extra fuel tankage; his 'Hunts' seldom used them. According to T D Manning, *The British Destroyer* (Putnam, London: 1961), p 118, captains disliked the stabilisers because they were useful only in a beam sea or in a sea on the bow. Fins on a ship heading into a head sea would break the surface, straining the ship. In a quartering sea there was an alarming tendency to broach-to. The system's great electric consumption affected radars, and the spaces involved reduced watertight integrity.

HMS *Liddesdale*, shown on 21 May 1942, was a 'Hunt' class destroyer completed to the original (Group I) design. She was fitted with a 2pdr bow chaser for coastal convoy work. As yet she had no surface-search radar (Type 291 is at her masthead).

perform the work of a modern escort, and at the same time be capable of carrying out the manifold duties hitherto done by destroyers, except attendance on a fleet.' They had the Asdic and depth charges of the usual fleet destroyer (with forty rather than thirty depth charges, as in *Black Swan*) plus 'special provision for visual signalling and night look-out positions to meet requirements of a ship escorting a convoy.' They were therefore called Fast Escorts. The new ships all received the names of foxhunts, so they became the 'Hunt' class.

While the design was being worked out, DNC was asked whether a quadruple pompom could be added. This weapon was increasingly important, both to deal with close-in aircraft and, probably, a perceived MTB threat. In submitting the design, DNC said that it could (and later would) replace the two quadruple 0.5in machine guns over the engineers' stores, the ammunition displacing some 4in ammunition aft. The director would replace the secondary steering position. There was certainly space, and enough structure could be worked in at that point in the ship. However, the quadruple pompom weighed about as much as a twin 4in mount, whereas the 0.5in machine gun was quite light. In effect DNC was agreeing to increase armament weight by about a third without much compensation. He was installing approximately the armament of a *Black Swan* on about a quarter less displacement, and the increase was largely in topweight. This was far too good to be true.

Apparently the intent had been to replace one of the twin 4in with the pompom of similar weight. For example in November, DTSD commented in passing that although the ships had been designed with three twin 4in, they would prob-ably end up with two such mounts and the pompom. Asked to estimate the change in complement when the pompom was added, DNO wrote about the saving due to eliminating one 4in mount – only to be told that the pompom was *in addition* to the three twin 4in. According to a June 1939 DNC paper in the Ship's Cover, the cost of the pompom would be about 16 tons more standard displacement and half a knot in speed in deep condition. Given the considerable weight of the pompom, it would seem in retrospect that there was a problem. Either the ship without the pompom was far too stiff (with too great a metacentric height) or the pompom would have more than consumed whatever margin had been designed in.

The pompom issue was a symptom of a serious problem, that the ship's stability had been grossly overestimated. Given the urgency of various design programmes at this point, it is surprising that the new Fast Escort was the only disaster. Probably everyone in the DNC design branch was badly over-taxed. In this case it appears that the basic stability calculation, which should have been done independently by two constructors, was actually done by one and then copied. The figures seem to have been worked with reference to the wrong baseline, well above the keel, producing an illusory degree of stability. DNC did not notice, nor did he heed the implicit warning DNO gave him.

It is striking in retrospect how urgent the project was. In November 1938 Prime Minister Neville Chamberlain returned from Munich waving his piece of paper and saying that his agreement to let Hitler take Czechoslovakia had guaranteed 'peace in our time,' but privately he said that he had found

Hitler was the nastiest human specimen he had ever met. Those in the Admiralty, and probably those in the government as a whole, understood that war had been deferred, not avoided. The pace of British rearmament accelerated; Chamberlain almost certainly understood that he had bought only a few months. Quite possibly the few months were needed to bring the nascent British national air-defence system, using radar and new fighters, into service. The building programme shifted towards those types which were always described as having no peacetime role. The urgency of the programme seems

to have been due to the Chiefs of Staff view that the Germans would seek a quick knock-out blow, using all their U-boats and minelaying capacity at the outset.

The post-Munich atmosphere is evident in projects like the new Fast Escort. This design had no peacetime role; it was manifestly not a sloop. Numerous typical amenities had been eliminated at the design stage.[26] It was the escort needed in very large numbers early in a war, when there would not be enough convoy escorts. Alternatively, it might be considered a new-construction equivalent to the 'V & W' class destroyers then

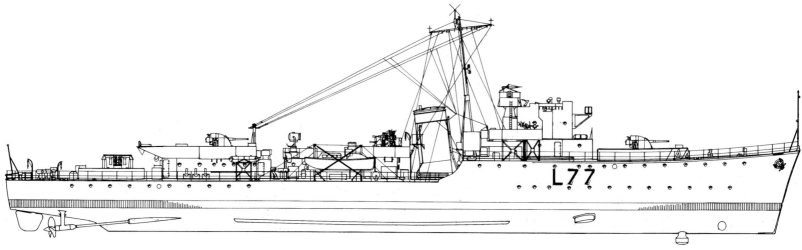

ABOVE: HMS *Grove*, shown in February 1942, was a Type II 'Hunt' class destroyer, her hull 'kippered' to accept the original planned gun armament of three twin 4in and a quadruple pompom. Note also her reduced

bridge structure, as compared to a Type I ship. The fin visible under the second 7 in her pennant number is for her stabiliser, intended, as in a *Black Swan*, to make her an effective anti-aircraft gun platform. Seagoing opinion

was divided as to its value. In a few ships, such as HMS *Eridge*, single Oerlikons were mounted at forecastle deck level, at the break of the forecastle, rather than in the bridge wings. Ships refitted for Pacific service in 1945 received

two single Mk III hand-worked Bofors (one forward of the bridge, one on the quarterdeck) instead of their Oerlikons. Ships so fitted were HMS *Avon Vale*, *Beaufort*, *Exmoor*, *Ledbury*, *Tetcott* and *Zetland*. (A D Baker III)

BELOW: HMS *Farndale*, a Group II 'Hunt', is shown on 26 February 1947. The small radar at her masthead is a Type 268 developed for motor torpedo boats. The weapon in the bridge wing is a twin power Oerlikon.

being urgently converted into specialised escorts, to make up the numbers desperately needed. Tenders for construction of the first ten, to be built under the 1939 Programme, were invited on 20 December 1938, when specifications were complete but building drawings were only at the pencil stage (the design was not formally submitted until 23 January 1939). The Board approved the Legend and Drawings on 2 February 1939.

When the firms received the tenders, they independently calculated hull and machinery weights. Their figures exceeded DNC's, who had to accept that the ships would be heavier than expected. He had to accept higher-quality steel (D steel) instead of mild steel and also fill out the hull form to maintain buoyancy. Estimated standard displacement rose from 890 tons to 925 tons and beam was increased. Filling out the form also added fuel oil stowage, which made it possible to maintain the required endurance despite increased resistance. The increased displacement would reduce speed at deep load from 29kts to 28kts.

This class introduced a disguised square-cut stern (in effect a transom stern), which cut resistance by 0.5 per cent at full speed (32kts) and by 1.5 per cent at cruising speed (20kts) at standard displacement. At deep load, with the stern more fully immersed, the effect was far greater: 3 per cent at full speed (29kts) and 4.5 per cent at 20kts. At the load at which endurance was measured, with half oil, saving was about 3 per cent. The waterline forward was also fined. At full speed that had no effect, but at 20kts it gave another 2 per cent.[27] After tenders had been invited, it was formally approved to fit the pompom, at the cost of 200 rounds of 4in ammunition per ship.[28] At some point in 1939 the depth charge allowance was increased to fifty.

CNS asked for an alternative design for the second batch of ten ships with four guns and a triple or quadruple torpedo tube. In February 1939 DNC offered a pompom in place of X gun, with one triple tube, to hold down displacement. The design had to be considerably modified, the break of the forecastle being moved 14ft forward and the after superstructure shortened by 4ft. A warhead room displaced some of the after 4in magazine. Although the result was similar to the original design, the resulting armament was not at all interchangeable. Moreover, so great a change would inevitably badly slow production, since fresh drawings would be needed.

The Staff was sceptical about the torpedo. Director of Plans saw two possible reasons: to give the ships a means of self-defence against superior enemy ships, and to enable them to be used as escorts against enemy light cruisers and destroy-

ers. He doubted that the first was worth giving up a third of their long-range anti-aircraft battery. As for the second, the Royal Navy was already retaining a flotilla of old destroyers armed with torpedoes and 4.7in guns, which would last until 1943–4 – at which time they would be replaced by 'A' and 'B'

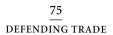

HMS *Avon Vale* is shown on 19 May 1944, with a 2pdr bow chaser and Type 271 radar (in the lantern, with IFF interrogator on top) and HF/DF (on the stub mainmast) aft.

class destroyers released from main fleet duty. If escorts did need torpedo tubes, it would be easiest to retain one set of tubes in the five 'V & W' leaders being converted to escorts.[29] ACNS agreed, and he also referred to the production issue. First Sea Lord came around to this view when reminded that during the First World War none of the destroyers outside the Grand Fleet (*eg* in the Harwich Force, the Dover Patrol and the convoys) ever fired torpedoes.[30] The second series of ten ships ordered in 1939 would repeat the first ones, except for installation of the pompom.

The first ship, HMS *Atherstone*, was inclined at the builder, Cammell Laird, as yet unarmed, on 4 February 1940.[31] The result was shocking. DNC must have been uneasy, because he immediately recognised a serious problem. He asked for curves of the ship's righting arm (GZ) with 100 tons ballast in light condition, for the extra light condition, and for the deep condition. At once the effect of removing No. 2 (X) gun and adding

[26] DNC's October 1938 list included a wooden deck covering, a refrigerator, hot and cold running water for the officers and running water for the washbasins (reverting to pre-1937 practice for destroyers), pantries for the CPOs and ERAs, hot cupboards outside the galleys, a water purifier, nickel silver fittings, and double awnings and a canvas room. However, CNS did require good headroom in living spaces and good messing and sleeping accommodation.
[27] From notes (October 1939) on a proposal to use a similar stern in the Third Emergency Flotilla, in that Cover.
[28] Originally only the second ten ships were to have the pompom. However, in December 1939 it was decided to fit it to all but the first five ships to complete, *Atherstone, Berkeley, Fernie, Garth* and *Hambleton*.

[29] Stability would make it impossible to retain tubes in other 'V & W' class destroyers being converted.
[30] At the end of a conference on 14 March 1939, First Sea Lord said that, having thought about the issue at length, he wanted repeats, *ie* no new design for the second ten ships.
[31] Report of Inclining Experiment (and account of follow-up) in Notebook 499/1 (F W Matthews). As inclined, the ship weighed 735 tons. To complete she would add 130 tons of armament, 90 tons of equipment, 78 tons of hull, and 50 tons of machinery; 12.5 tons on board would come off. Calculated deep displacement was 1,342.5 tons (1,018.9 tons light). Calculated metacentric height (GM) deep was 1.03ft (0.65ft light). Maximum righting arm (GZ) would be 0.669ft at an unacceptable 40° (and -0.825ft at 67°, ensuring that the ship would roll over in a heavy sea). Thus it is not true, as sometimes claimed, that the stability problem was discovered when a gun mount was lowered onto the ship in dock, and she began to roll over because she had zero or negative metacentric height.

HMS *Derwent*, a Group III 'Hunt', leaves HMS *Illustrious* after oiling.

100 tons of ballast was calculated.[32] A comparison between the design and reality showed relatively small differences. The error had been in the design, not in any weight growth during construction.[33]

'HUNT' CLASS: DESIGN AND REALITY

	Legend	Modified	Realised	Proposed
LBP	264ft 3in	264ft 3in	264ft 2in	264ft 3in
LWL	272ft	272ft	272ft	272ft
Beam	28ft 3in	29ft	29ft	29ft
Displacement	890 tons	925 tons	1,022 tons	1,010 tons
Draft	7ft 11in	8ft 0in	8ft 7in	8ft 6in
Draft Deep	9ft 8in	9ft 9in	10ft 5in	10ft 4in
Speed (std)	32.5kts	32kts	30.25kts	30.5kts
Speed (deep)	29kts	28.25kts	26.5kts	26.75kts
Oil fuel	235 tons	242 tons	247 tons	247 tons
Endurance	3,700nm @ 15kts	2,500nm @ 20kts	2,500nm @ 20kts	2,325nm @ 20kts
Complement	142–144	142–144	159	130
4in (200 rpg)	6	6	6	4
capacity (rpg)			217	250
Pompom	–	–	1 (1,800 rpb)	1 (1,800 rpb)
0.5in MG	2 (10,000 rpb)	2 (10,000 rpb)	–	–
Equipment	58 tons	58 tons	65 tons	57 tons
Machinery	270 tons	285 tons	295 tons	295 tons
Armament	87 tons	88 tons	116 tons	88 tons
Hull	450 tons	469 tons	521 tons	495 tons
Stabilisers	25 tons	25 tons	25 tons	25 tons
Ballast	–	–	–	50 tons
Standard	890 tons	925 tons	1,022 tons	1,010 tons

The 'realised' column is the ship as inclined at Cammell

Laird and found not stable enough for sea. The 'proposed' column is the proposed solution, in which X gun is eliminated and the after deck house cut down. The director was lowered 2ft, and the funnel cut down by 2ft. Other cuts were removal of the 16ft planing dinghy with its trolley and gasoline stowage, reduction of deck covering to 3/16in steel in mess spaces (with Bostic adhesive), fitting of Semptex walkways on the weather decks, and elimination of awning stanchions. Except in *Atherstone*, the bandstand under A gun was eliminated. It appeared that a 320ft ship (1,360 tons) would have been required to carry the full projected armament (three twin 4in, a pompom and fifty depth charges).

As modified, *Atherstone* was again inclined on 25 March. Now there was enough margin of stability to increase 4in ready-use ammunition to thirty-six rounds per gun, and to retain the fifty depth charges. Ships affected were the first twenty plus the first three of the War Programme (*Blencathra* and *Brocklesby* at Cammell Laird and *Liddesdale* at Vickers on Tyne). These

---

[32] Calculations in Notebook 499/1, dated 4 February 1940. The change would also cut about ten men from the ship's complement. In this case, with 100 tons of ballast, GM (deep) would be 1.68ft, and GZ (max) would be 1.23ft at 40°, stability vanishing at just under 67°. In light condition GM would be 1.79ft, and range of stability would be similar. Another calculation removed X gun and placed the pompom atop a reduced after deckhouse; 75 tons of ballast would be added. In that case GM (deep) would be 1.8ft. The designer proposed omitting both No. 2 gun and the pompom, reducing the after superstructure, limiting depth charges to thirty, limiting ready-use ammunition to forty-eight rounds per gun, eliminating deck covering, removing a diesel generator, and adding 50 tons of ballast (p 181 of the notebook). GM (deep) would rise to 1.89ft (1,301 tons). Other variations included adding more ballast and allowing for fifty depth charges and the pompom (with 60 tons of ballast).

[33] Table from Notebook 499/1, p 211.

twenty-three ships were later designated Type I. Swan Hunter developed a solution: 'pulling out' the hull lines to increase beam to 31ft 6in, a practice later called 'kippering'.[34] The ships so modified could carry the original armament, with all three twin 4in. They became Type II. Thirty-three were built. In April 1940 a revised Staff Requirement added a twin torpedo tube (a quadruple mount with the two inner tubes removed). The new version would use the same machinery.[35] A first estimate showed a considerably larger hull, 282ft × 32ft 6in (1,475 tons deep). Instead the ship was redesigned using the Type II hull. The resulting Type III was not too different from that First Sea Lord had asked for in 1939, albeit with fewer torpedoes. This variant had a vertical funnel (like contemporary cruisers of the *Fiji* and Improved *Dido* classes) to make it more difficult for an observer to judge their course. Twenty-eight were built. The other two ships (Type IV) were a separate Thornycroft design, to an order originally let for two *Black Swans*.[36]

Before the disastrous *Atherstone* inclining experiment, the 'Hunts', like the destroyers, were considered for inclusion in A/S Striking Forces, for which purpose they would need much heavier depth-charge armament. Controller suggested two alternatives. One was a full depth-charge battery as in the destroyer *Havelock*, with four throwers on each side and three chutes, and if possible 100 charges (as many as possible on the upper deck). The two after twin mounts would have to be landed. The second was simply to remove Y gun, adding as many charges as possible.[37]

Various weights were added in wartime. Oerlikons and platforms were added on either side of the bridge. Ships were initially fitted with Type 286 radar, its office being on the forecastle deck abaft the bridge to port. Later the director was fitted with Type 285 (range-only) radar. Short-range VHF radio was installed. Bow 'chasers' (single 2pdrs) were added to deal with German small combatants (E-boats) in the Channel on board eighteen Type I ships, seven Type II ships (*Avon Vale*, *Bedale*, *Calpe*, *Cowdray*, *Krakowiak* [ex-*Silverton*], *Lamerton* and *Lauderdale*) and six Type IIIs (*Albrighton*, *Bleasdale*, *Eskdale*, *Glaisdale*, *Stevenstone* and *La Combattante* [transferred to the Free French]). Initial weight compensation for the chaser and Oerlikons was removal of twenty depth charges (CAFO 2234/41), but these were reshipped in June 1943. Ships with the bow chasers trimmed by the bow and tended to be wet forward.

By the end of the war, two Type II (*Beaufort* and *Exmoor*) and three Type III (*Belvoir*, *Easton* and *Melbeak*) had two single 40mm. *Brecon* had two single 40mm, and *Brissenden* two single 2pdrs. At least one Type I (*Mynell*) had her quadruple pompom replaced by a twin 40mm gun, a change which would have been made in others had the war continued. The typical Oerlikon battery was two guns in a Type I, up to four in a Type II, and up to six in a Type III. Other typical additions were an auto-barrage unit for the Transmitting Station (with associated equipment in the director), SA gear for self-protection against acoustic mines, steam and electric heating for the pompom. The pompom itself was provided with 10lb protection in the form of a zareba (gun tub).

The Thornycroft design owed nothing to the Admiralty type described above. It had a long forecastle for greater

[34] The Cover gives no date for this change, but Notebook 499/1 mentions a visit to Swan Hunter on 6 March 1940 to examine their method of 'pulling out' the lines, adding plating to the keel and to all decks, with a width of about 2ft 11in. Hydrostatic calculations were ready by 8 March.
[35] Recounted in Notebook 499/1. The Cover gives no information.
[36] Of the thirty-four escorts included in the 1940 Programme, at one point ten were to have been *Black Swans*, but six were re-ordered as 'Hunts': two Swan Hunter (*Bolebroke* and *Border*), two White (*Easton* and *Eggesford*), and two Thornycroft (*Brecon* and *Brissenden*).
[37] Notebook 499/1, describing a visit by DASW and DEM officers on 17 February 1940.

HMS *Bleasdale*, shown early in the summer of 1945, was a Group III 'Hunt' assigned to East Coast convoys, as indicated by her 2pdr bow chaser (ships converted as small headquarters ships for the Normandy landing also had bow chasers). The long vertical dipole standing out forward of her mast is her Headache (voice radio intercept) antenna, used to pick up German coastal forces transmissions. Her Type 271 surface-search antenna is in the 'lantern' aft. Less visible are the masthead Type 291 radar and the two small voice radio antennas (Type 86M) at the ends of her yardarms, used both to control friendly coastal forces and to communicate with aircraft.

HMS *Aldenham* was a Type III 'Hunt' class destroyer with torpedo tubes instead of the third twin 4in gun. Note the absence of surface-search radar. Some ships received three twin Oerlikons in place of the three singles shown. In a few ships refitted for Pacific service, the Oerlikons were replaced by single hand-worked Mk III Bofors guns, one on a platform forward of the bridge and one right aft. Ships so modified were HMS *Belvoir, Easton, Haydon, Melbreak* and *Talybont*. (A D Baker III)

strength (and for covered access above the machinery spaces) and a sharply knuckled bow (for seakeeping). These features were of special interest to those designing the post-war long-forecastle escorts. A special 'wind trap' on the fore side of the bridge structure was intended to keep the bridge dry. The pear-shaped funnel incorporated a spiral central division plate to hide the glow of the ship's furnaces from aircraft.[38]

The CO of *Brecon* considered the extension aft of the forecastle a great step forward, because it made for safe access in all weathers. The ship's double flare allowed the forward 4in gun to be fought in almost any weather. However, due to the extra lift given by the wide bows, she began to 'bump' before other 'Hunts'. At speed in moderate weather the low flare turned the bow wave over very sharply instead of the usual big sweep,

which made considerable spray. The flare also made the forward mess decks very roomy. High freeboard made for extra seaworthiness (presumably for a much wider range of stability), but it also acted as a large sail area in bad weather. The ship was not handy in wind. In a Force 4 or higher she took a permanent list and tended to turn into the wind. When going very slowly, stopped, or with stern way on, the bows flew off very quickly, so manoeuvring in narrow waters could be difficult. The ship rolled a lot, and very quickly, but that was acceptable because with the high freeboard even the largest rolls felt safe. The ship steered badly in a following sea, yawing widely. Decking over the space over the machinery made the engine and boiler rooms very hot in hot weather. Taking the boiler room draught from inside did not help, and wind-sails (for ventilation) could not be rigged. The special Thornycroft funnel was a success, as very little smoke came onto the bridge in a following wind. On the other hand, the wind trap on the fore side of the bridge structure was effective only when the wind was right ahead, otherwise not being worth its extra weight. The CO of *Brissenden* considered the high, dry foredeck a great advantage; other 'Hunts' would be hampered by seas washing over their forecastles. He also noted the tendency to bump. The shelter deck gave safe access but compartments in it could be quite hot, and ventilation was poor (he wanted fans); even the machinery spaces, which had increased numbers of fans, were too hot. At speeds above 10kts the ship had an excessive tendency to turn into the wind due to her heel; at low speed or stopped she tended to turn away from the wind on the bow due to the sheer of the fore-

---

[38] Thornycroft was apparently aware quite early of Admiralty interest in light destroyers. Sir John Thornycroft offered designs T1267 and T1268 to Controller on 24 October 1938, each with two twin 4in and quadruple torpedo tubes, but with speeds of 35kts and 30kts, respectively. They incorporated the extended forecastle deck, but in these designs it extended over the torpedo tubes, holes being cut in the ship's sides for them. The designs were rejected for, among other things, insufficient endurance and poor survivability. When a new Controller, Rear Admiral Bruce Fraser, visited Thornycroft in March 1940, the designs were revived. This time the firm offered two or three twin 4in guns and a quadruple 2pdr, plus four depth charge throwers (eighty charges). The four alternatives were 260ft to 280ft long, displaced 915 tons to 1,115 tons, and were rated at 27kts to 32.5kts in light condition. The designs were again rejected, among other things because the ships were expected to roll heavily (*ie* were top-heavy). In April 1940 Thornycroft offered three more alternatives (T1306–1308), of which the last had three twin 4in guns and was 280ft x 32.75ft x 15.5ft (depth), displacing 1,475 tons fully loaded, with a rated speed of 30.75kts (25,000 SHP). The side openings for the torpedo tubes were again criticised (as a discontinuity in the ship's structure, hence a weak point), the ships were considered top-heavy, and fuel tankage was too limited. Thornycroft must have considered that it still had a good chance of selling the design, however, because a further version, T1309P, was submitted on 31 May 1940 (280ft, 1,460 tons fully loaded), and then T1310. It finally eliminated the side openings, it had a partially enclosed bridge, and its 2pdr was moved further from No. 2 gun to improve the latter's forward arcs. Power was reduced to the 19,500 SHP of other 'Hunt' class destroyers. This design was accepted with some modification, such as substitution of triple for the proposed quadruple torpedo tubes. The revised version of October 1940 was 283ft long, displacing 1,170 tons standard and 1,515 tons fully loaded. Expected speed was 28kts in standard condition. Claimed endurance was 2,350nm at 20kts, compared to 2,750nm in T1310 (with 285 tons rather than 300 tons of oil). Details are taken from John English, *The Hunts* (World Ship Society, London: 1987).

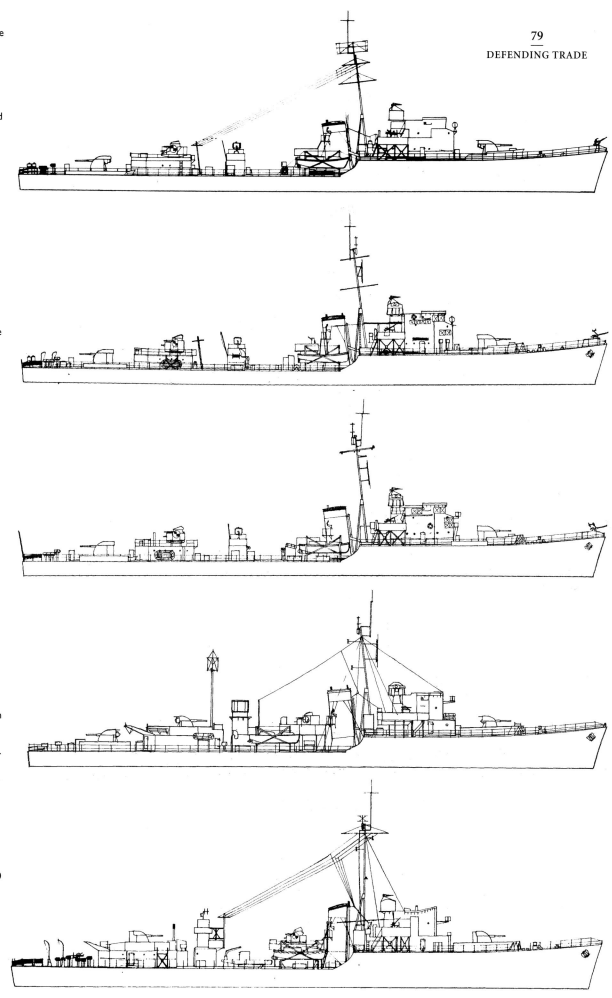

HMS *Lamerton* is shown late in 1941, with Type 286 radar at her foretop, and with a 2pdr chaser in her bows. The latter was typically mounted on board ships expected to engage enemy coastal forces, *eg* in the Channel. The cross at her foretop represents Type 86 VHF radio, which was fitted on board 'Hunts' operating in coastal waters so that they could communicate with friendly aircraft and with British coastal forces in direct support. Ships fitted with Type 291, which needed a masthead position, had the smaller paired Type 86M antennas at the ends of their yardarms. (Alan Raven)

HMS *Liddesdale* is shown in 1942, with typical coastal electronics, Headache and Type 86 radio, and with a 2pdr bow chaser. As yet, however, she had no surface-search radar. The radar at the masthead is presumably the rotating version of Type 286. Note the shielded Lewis gun on the platform abaft the funnel. (Alan Raven)

HMS *Fernie* is shown as in January 1943, with Headache and Type 86 radar, and with a typical coastal operations bow chaser. (Alan Raven)

HMS *Avon Vale* in 1944, with the standard Type 271 surface-search radar 'lantern' just forward of X twin 4in mount, with Headache and Type 87 radio on her foremast, and with HF/DF on her mainmast. She had just been rebuilt at Chatham after having been torpedoed in the Mediterranean on 29 January 1943, the hull forward of the bridge being blown away. Repairs were completed on 24 April 1944, having begun on 12 July 1943. Not shown in this drawing is the IFF interrogator atop the Type 271 radar 'lantern'. (Alan Raven)

HMS *Easton* is shown as in 1944, with Type 650 anti-missile jamming gear aft, next to the Type 271 radar 'lantern.' The antenna atop the 'lantern' is an IFF interrogator. In 1945 she had single Bofors guns forward and aft, having been refitted for Pacific service between May and August 1945. During this refit her Type 271 surface-search radar was replaced by a small Type 268 atop her foremast. (Alan Raven)

castle, and with the slightest stern way her stern tried to go straight into the wind. The ship could not be steered accurately (*eg* for oiling at sea) at less than 10kts in a wind of more than Force 4. In a wind of Force 3 or more she was difficult to manoeuvre in harbour. He doubted that the elaborate bridge structure was worth while, but he did appreciate the more spacious arrangements, such as separate piloting and signal offices. Both ships were laid up at the end of the war.

To some extent the 'Hunts' seem to have inspired the US destroyer escorts, some of which the Royal Navy operated as 'Captain' class frigates, but this was a conceptual, not a design relationship. A proposal in June 1939 for a US second-line mass-production destroyer died in January 1940, probably mainly because the naval leadership knew that Congress tended to authorise the same number of destroyers, whether they were large or small. However, in the summer of 1940 President Roosevelt apparently personally asked for a design for an austere destroyer. He seems to have been well aware of what the British were building; at about the same time he asked for a small fast attack transport roughly similar to ships the British were then converting. The President went so far as to order the Navy to buy four such ships, to two different designs which roughly corresponded to the early proposals for what became the 'Hunt' class. One was a 1,050-tonner with two 5in guns and two quadruple torpedo tubes, with a speed of 35kts; the other was a 750-tonner with two 3in or 4in guns and triple torpedo tubes. In November 1940 the order was changed to a 1,175-ton BuShips design, armed with two 5in guns. A 12,000 SHP powerplant would have driven such a ship at 24.5kts. The logic which had prevailed the previous January almost killed this project, too, but by January 1941 the United States was very nearly at war, and a supplemental 1941 Programme called

for fifty escorts – exactly the designation then being applied to the 'Hunts'. This time Characteristics (the US equivalent of British Staff Requirements) more nearly resembled those of the corvettes and the new frigates, with a speed of 17kts, and the ships were intended for the Western Atlantic.

In the autumn of 1940 BuShips had placed an attaché, Captain E L Cochrane, in London, where he was much impressed by the 'Hunts', although he found them wet in a seaway and too narrow-beamed. He had also become impressed with the British open bridge, which he considered ideal for convoy watch-keeping. In 1941 Cochrane was head of the BuShips Preliminary Design section, responsible for the new design. Cochrane chose to develop the 1,175-tonner as the basis for the new convoy escort. Given his British experience, Cochrane insisted on dual-purpose guns (although in theory the ships were to operate in an area without air opposition), and on triple torpedo tubes to deal with surface raiders (he specifically cited the British choice of twin tubes for the 'Hunt' Type III). Again, because conventional destroyers seemed a far better proposition, the escorts were cancelled in May 1941.

By this time, however, President Roosevelt had signed the Lend-Lease Bill, under which materiel could be lent to the British. Cochrane himself persisted with the design despite cancellation of the escorts. On 17 June the CNO asked for a comparison between the new design and the British 'Hunt' and 'River' classes. Not long afterwards, on 23 June, the British Supply Council in North America asked the Secretary of the Navy for 100 escort destroyers, the existence of which was clearly already known. The main change was an armament of three 3in/50 instead of the 5in guns, and the torpedo tubes were foregone. The ships were given a high British-style bridge (requested in February 1942). President Roosevelt approved

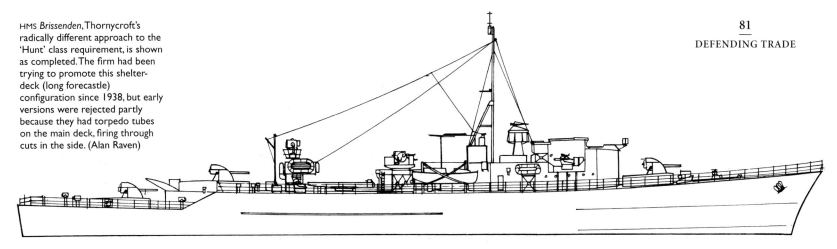

HMS *Brissenden*, Thornycroft's radically different approach to the 'Hunt' class requirement, is shown as completed. The firm had been trying to promote this shelter-deck (long forecastle) configuration since 1938, but early versions were rejected partly because they had torpedo tubes on the main deck, firing through cuts in the side. (Alan Raven)

The 'Hunt' class made a considerable impression on a US special attaché, Captain E C Cochrane, who spent part of 1940 in London. Later head of the Bureau of Ships, Cochrane was probably instrumental in beginning a somewhat similar US programme. It faltered – the US Navy preferred full-size destroyers – but was saved by a British request for 100 ships. Some of the resulting destroyer escorts were transferred to the Royal Navy under the Lend-Lease programme to become the British 'Captain' class. HMS *Holmes* was a *Buckley* class frigate. Initially the ships were disliked for their quick rolls and unpleasant motion, but they were successfully modified for British service. They were valued for the PPI displays of their SL surface-search radars, which specially fitted them to control coastal forces in night actions. *Holmes* displays the bow 2pdr chaser which armed many ships working with Coastal Forces. Note also the masthead HF/DF which replaced her air-search radar. Unlike her US sisters, *Holmes* had no multiple 1.1in anti-aircraft gun, only Oerlikons to supplement her 3in/50s. The latter were criticised as insufficient to deal with surfaced submarines. Unlike *Holmes*, many 'Captain' class frigates were given gun shields.

the first fifty on 15 August 1941. With the United States soon at war, powerplants were a major bottleneck. The initial problem was gearing, so one solution was diesels: four driving through submarine-type generators and motors, and four more through gearing. Because diesels were in short supply, ships received only the first four, so they were half-powered. Others were lengthened to accommodate turbo-electric plants of the original output (the extra length reduced resistance, so they did not lose speed due to their extra displacement). The Royal Navy received seventy-eight 'Captain' class frigates: thirty-two slow diesel-electric *Evarts* class and 46 fast turbo-electric *Buckley* class. Another twenty-one similarly-armed 'Colony' class frigates received from the United States were derived from the British 'River' class (see Chapter 7).

Early British reports from sea (in the 'Captain' Class Cover) reflected differences between British and US design practices.

The 'Captain' class was criticised as having little or no capacity for damage control, *ie* for having been conceived as expendable. Their natural period of roll unfortunately coincided with the period of a typical North Atlantic wave, so rolling was spectacularly bad. The CO of HMS *Duckworth* reported that his ship was 'agreeably dry in most weather, and after riding out a short Atlantic gale I can report that there seems to be small risk of weather damage ... the ships behave like corks'. However, they could not be driven anywhere within four points of the sea above 10kts in prevailing short steep North Atlantic seas. In a long swell, they rode very well but seemed ill-suited to close-in operations with other ships. As for rolling, 'since this is being written at sea it is difficult to describe with reticence the nauseating movements of these vessels in the open sea'. The worst complaint was of a violent lurching which made the ships poor gun (or Hedgehog) platforms in anything

The US Navy built a variety of different destroyer escorts, due to difficulties in providing sufficient machinery. HMS *Blackwood* (K313) had the short hull of the original design, which was intended to make a 'Hunt'-like 26kts using 12,000 SHP geared turbines. With gearing in short supply, ships were powered instead by submarine-type diesels with half the power; they were therefore limited to a speed of 20kts. The later *Buckley* class did have turbines, but had electric drive. That took up more space, so they had to be lengthened, and the greater hull length compensated for their extra displacement, so speed was roughly as originally envisaged (the Royal Navy rated these ships at 24kts, the US Navy at 23kts). *Blackwood* shows some typical British modifications in this November 1943 photo: a shield for A mount, removal of the air-search radar, increased depth charge stowage aft. She has a twin Bofors forward of her No. 3 3in gun and five Oerlikons, the standard battery for her class.

but a following sea. There was some speculation that they suffered because they had originally been designed to carry two enclosed 5in/38 guns instead of the three open 3in/50s, as well as a triple torpedo tube (which the British ships lacked). US ships also had much heavier anti-aircraft batteries (the British ships generally had no 40mm guns). The cure was to reduce their stiffness (excessive metacentric height). Depth charges were moved up to deck stowage and special rails were laid for Mk X charges. After that the ships seem to have been considered quite satisfactory.

Coastal Sloops (Patrol Vessels)

A series of coastal sloops, later described as corvettes, was developed in parallel with the large convoy sloops, the initial Staff Requirement being issued in 1932. No peacetime programme to produce the numbers needed for war could have been justified, given the fleet's urgent need for larger and more complex ships. The first six coastal or patrol sloops were direct replacement for existing ships which had survived from the First World War, and which performed necessary peacetime tasks. Two relieved the fishery protection craft *Dart* and *Spey*, while he other four replaced the units of the 1st A/S Flotilla, which were used for essential Asdic training. It was tacitly assumed that the sloops would operate in groups of five (a division of four plus a spare). In 1935, when the Royal Navy was being rebuilt to face a Far Eastern war, the goal was three such divisions. Two years later, when it was clear that the threat might include the Germans, the goal was eight

such divisions at the outbreak of war (in the First World War the Royal Navy built fifty-three P-boats and PC-boats). Presumably the basis was the number of areas which would have to be patrolled. The programme proposed in 1932 called for a nucleus force of seventeen specialised coastal escorts (coastal sloops), of which nine would be built by 1942. As of 1933, the wartime requirement was estimated as forty such craft, to supplement the eighty ocean convoy sloops and about thirty older destroyers released from fleet duty.

The 1933 to 1936 Programmes each included a single coastal sloop. In 1937, however, two were ordered, and policy changed to envisage two per year. That year's version of the British rearmament programme, DRC 37, envisaged continuing the policy, so that by 1942 there would be a total of sixteen, of which fourteen would have been completed. It was argued that since the craft were designed for rapid wartime production, it might be safe to put off completing the projected nucleus. In April 1937 ACNS pointed out that even with her limited U-boat fleet Germany, as aggressor, could maintain a submarine campaign as intense as that of the First World War for short periods. Hence the decision to accelerate to three patrol vessels per year in 1938. At that rate there would be twenty-four by 1943, after which the building rate could be reduced again to two per year. In fact 1938 was the last year of orders, because in 1939 the effort shifted to the 'Hunt' class and, for coastal work, to the 'Flower' class. The first six ships (1933 through 1937 Programmes) were the *Kingfisher* class. The three 1938 ships were the follow-on *Guillemot*s. Although they

were specifically conceived for mass production, when the emergency came the 'Flower' class was built instead, to an entirely different concept.

The 1933 coastal sloop was based on the First World War PC design, itself derived from a sub-chaser or patrol boat. As conceived, the ships had machinery identical to that of the PC, with two boilers in separate boiler rooms and twin-screw geared turbines (3,500 SHP, 20kts). Estimated endurance was 3,500nm at 12kts or 3,000nm at 14kts. Armament was one 4in gun, eight Lewis guns, and a heavy depth charge battery (two twelve-charge chutes and two throwers with eight charges each, a total of forty depth charges). The Asdic was a destroyer type with a hoisting dome.[39] Compared to the PC, the ship was slightly longer (234ft rather than 230ft on the waterline, lengthened to 240ft in the course of design) and slightly heavier at the initial design stage (570 tons rather than 524 tons), with the same draft (8ft) and slightly less speed on slightly less power (3,500 SHP for 20kts compared to 4,000 SHP for 20.5kts). The most striking differences were Asdic and the as-

[39] Data from ADM 167/89, a series of descriptions of ships sought under the 1933 Estimates.

sociated much larger depth charge load. Because prototypes had to be built in peacetime, it was vital to keep them in the exempt category. Hence the limitation to 20kts (though displacement under 600 tons would also have done so). Also, engines of higher power would be difficult to produce in quantity in wartime. Captain A/S, in charge of Asdic development, considered 20kts sufficient to find and hunt submarines.

Compared to the First World War P-boat, *Kingfisher* was likely to be drier, with its destroyer-like forecastle hull. The result was less than happy, however, because effective Asdic operation required a deeper draft (ideally 10ft rather than the 7ft 3in the ships actually drew, which was less than expected [the ships came out underweight]). There was also speculation (in 1935) that Asdic performance was disappointing in part because of the shape of the forefoot. *Kingfisher* proved too lightly built. Moreover, her seakeeping qualities, which were key to her role, came under criticism when she was used to hunt for the disabled trawler *Amethyst* in 1937.

An updated Staff Requirement, TD 173/35 of 6 September 1935, applied to the later units of the class (from *Kittiwake*

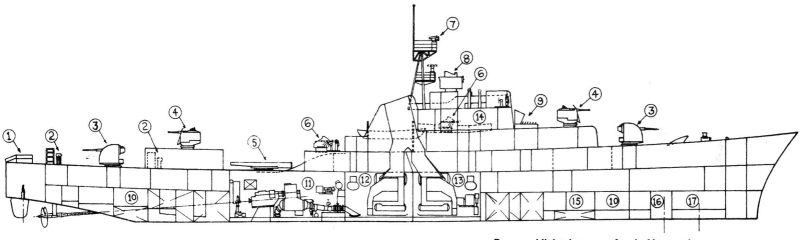

Several navies approached British builders after the war for light destroyers, in effect updated equivalents to the 'Hunt' class. TWY 1725 was a joint proposal by Thornycroft, White, and Yarrow for six Venezuelan ships. The initial and much smaller version of this design (TWY 1686) was completed in 1951 (986 tons, 273ft (wl) x 31ft x 16¾ft (hull depth)ft, one 105mm Bofors DP gun, two Bofors, three or four quad Oerlikons, with depth charge throwers aft, 32kts half-loaded; Venezuela would supply the 105mm gun and some of the Bofors). Thornycroft also developed a version, presumably for offer to the Royal Navy, with the armament of a Type 14 frigate (two Limbo, three Bofors). The version shown here was formally offered to Venezuela on 10 October 1952, at a unit price of £1.79 million. Competitors were Dutch, German, and Italian yards.

An Italian yard, Ansaldo, won this competition, apparently because it could deliver six months earlier. The Italian design in turn made a considerable impression on the US Navy (and thus inspired adoption of an Italian design for the NATO second-class frigates bought for Denmark and Portugal a few years later; Type 14 losing that competition). Indonesia bought two sister-ships. In January 1954 Israel approached Yarrow to buy two destroyers for delivery in 27 and 33 months. The competitors were the Dutch, the French, and the Italians. Yarrow proposed to use Y.100 machinery and the new Vickers 4in gun. Characteristics: 284ft LOA x 32ft mld x 17ft 3in (hull depth) x 9ft 6in (loaded), displacement 1,200 tons trial (half load)/1,350 tons full load, 30,000 SHP for 34kts, estimated endurance 2,600nm at 17kts (220 tons of oil fuel, 10 tons of diesel oil), complement

120. Armament: three single 4in Mk N, three Bofors L70, two twin Oerlikon, one triple torpedo tube. At about the same time the Egyptians also requested destroyers. Ultimately the British decided to sell each country two reconditioned 'Z' class destroyers, which presumably became surplus as the frigate reconstruction programme ran down. Ecuador opted to buy two 'Hunt' class destroyers instead of building new ones. Peru approached British builders for two destroyers better than those supplied to Ecuador, but ended up getting two surplus US *Fletchers*. One important factor in the export market of the early 1950s was that Britain had very few surplus war-built ships; most were retained as a war reserve. That changed dramatically in 1957, when British strategy shifted to emphasise current Third World operations. (A D Baker III)

Proposed light destroyer for the Venezuelan government

Length: 295ft 0in waterline
Breadth: 33ft 0in moulded
Depth: 18ft 0in moulded
SHP: 25,000 (twin screw, twin rudder)
Speed at half load: 32kts

1. Depth charge racks (P&S)
2. Depth charge mortars and reload racks (P&S)
3. Twin 4in Mk XIX mount
4. Twin 40mm Mk V (centreline)
5. Triple 21in torpedo tube mount
6. Twin 20mm Mk V Oerlikon mount (P&S)
7. Type 293 radar
8. 4in gun director, with radar
9. Split Hedgehog A/S spigot mortar (P&S)
10. 4in magazine
11. Engine room
12. Boiler room No. 2
13. Boiler room No. 1
14. Operations room
15. 40mm, 20mm, and Hedgehog magazine
16. Scanning sonar transducer compartment
17. Naval stores and depth-determining sonar compartment

onwards). A proposal for a heavier gun armament was rejected on the grounds that a small ship armed with a single 4in gun, and with rapid acceleration and good manoeuvrability would be a formidable enemy for a surfaced submarine. There was some interest in changing to a dual-purpose 4in gun, and four twin Lewis guns were provided to defend against low-flying aircraft. There was a desire for twenty more depth charges and two more throwers (the appropriate depth charge pattern was being investigated). Speed was set at 20kts. Because the ships might supplement ocean escorts, endurance was set at 3,400nm at 14kts or 5,000nm at 10kts, considerable distances determined by the longest Empire convoy run, from London to Sierra Leone.[40] On this basis *Kittiwake* and later units had their draft increased to 8ft.

There was also interest in an auxiliary A/S type for port protection, to search and hunt inshore. It would make 18–19kts, and might have to cruise for four days at 10kts with a margin for a burst of speed when dealing with a submarine. That might equate to an endurance of 1,600nm at 10kts. This ship would need a single 4in gun to deal with surfaced submarines, plus twenty-five depth charges (five-charge pattern). Draft would have to be enough for good Asdic performance. Maximum displacement would be 600 tons, to avoid treaty limitations. As in the case of the convoy sloop, a natural question was whether such a ship could also work as a minesweeper and, for that matter, could also provide a coastal convoy with anti-aircraft protection. DNC doubted it. In February 1937 he remarked that the ships were too lively to be valuable for anti-aircraft. Above Sea State 4 they would pitch so badly that their propellers would come out of the water and race; speed would be reduced to about 7kts, too slow for effective sweeping.

A new design (the *Guillemot* class) was prepared in 1937 to a new Staff Requirement (TD 39/36). It used a new hull form tested at Haslar. It was intended to offer better sea-keeping and deeper draft. The new form was expected to be better (*ie* requiring less power) than *Kittiwake* at maximum speed, though slightly inferior at low speed, and about as good as a cruiser form in general. The First World War P-boat form, which was superior at speeds under 20.5kts, was rejected because its beam:draft ratio was too low for adequate stability. The ship could not be shortened forward (as suggested by Haslar) because internal space was already critical due to the reduction from 240ft to 230ft. Standard displacement increased from the 498 tons of *Kittiwake* to 570 tons (full load was 725 tons in *Kittiwake*, and in the new design was 710 tons). Minimum deep draft was 8ft under the Asdic dome.

Unlike the earlier class, this one would have a high-angle 4in gun. It had the same forty depth charges, but with four throwers (the Staff Requirement called for an eight-charge pattern and between forty and sixty charges). This requirement had shifted back and forth. After *Kingfisher* was built with two throwers, experiments were made with the next two ships, *Mallard* and *Puffin*, equipped with four throwers and sixty charges, and *Widgeon*, the next ship, was assigned four throwers and forty charges – which is what the writers of the 1936 Staff Requirement initially intended. Then Commander Cooper of the Tactical Division pointed out that the throwers could be reloaded rapidly enough for the original pair of throwers to suffice. Experiments showed that it would take five minutes to reload, and a five-charge pattern was standard. The outcome was that four were retained in the *Kingfisher*s so fitted (*Mallard*, *Puffin*, *Kittiwake* and *Sheldrake*); their depth charge allowances were cut to forty. *Widgeon* and later units (of the new class) would get two throwers and forty charges as standard (TD 267/37). Each of two rails carried twelve charges, and each thrower had another six charges (including one in the thrower). Another four charges were stowed against the bulkhead near the throwers. Machinery repeated that of the previous class. The Staff Requirement emphasised very quick acceleration from 6kts to 18kts. Estimated endurance was 3,200nm at 12kts under trial conditions. An unusual requirement was to be able to trim by the bow under light load condition, specifically to place the Asdic deep enough to be effective. The Board approved the new design on 3 February 1938.

A/S Trawlers were in effect the low-end supplement to the patrol vessel. They could be obtained in vast numbers, they were good sea boats, and they could be manned and worked by their own peacetime fisherman crews. However, they were no more than substitutes for properly-designed ASW ships. In 1934 an Admiralty trawler, primarily for auxiliary ASW service, was designed in outline form for emergency construction. It could also be used for minesweeping. She displaced 480 tons and carried twenty-five depth charges (five-pattern). An 850 IHP reciprocating steam engine would drive her at 12kts, and her boiler would be coal-fired. The design emphasised good manoeuvrability, with a balanced rudder. As of 1936, the planned armament was one 4in low-angle gun, one 3in anti-aircraft gun, Asdic and two depth charge throwers. The ship's role (anti-submarine or minesweeping) would be chosen when she was built.

The contract for an emergency design was let to Smith's Dock on 22 April 1938, based on their *Mastiff* and *Bassett* (ordered 27 November 1934 and 27 January 1937, respectively). The Royal Canadian Navy built four similar ships. DNC signed the design on 23 January 1939. As the situation worsened, twenty of this 'Tree' class were ordered (5 and 8 June 1939). The projected war emergency programme included another twenty; in an emergency, 100 would be built. They were part of a prearranged emergency programme for 703 auxiliary A/S and minesweeping units to be ordered on the

---

[40] A 1938 table of distances between bases, to estimate required escort endurance, showed 1,144nm between Portsmouth and Gibraltar, 1,805nm between Gibraltar and Alexandria, 1,394nm between Port Said and Aden, 2,107nm from Aden to Colombo, 1,567nm from Colombo to Singapore, and 1,459nm from Singapore to Hong Kong. The table did not show the run across the Atlantic.

HMS *Guillemot* was a coastal sloop, designed for mass production but ultimately unsuited to it. She is shown in May 1942.

outbreak of war. As of late 1938 it was understood that most new-construction trawlers would be used for A/S, since they were the largest and fastest available. Most trawlers taken up from trade would be used for minesweeping.

When the Board met during the Czech crisis to consider emergency measures, one of them was to buy between eight and ten laid-up commercial trawlers for immediate conversion to minesweepers. It was accepted that many more would be taken up from trade on mobilisation, but that would take time; and some craft would be needed at the outbreak of a war which might break out by surprise. In fact five trawlers were bought in January 1939 and another ten in February. The Royal Navy had already bought twenty-one trawlers in November 1935, during the Abyssinian crisis.

When war broke out, the emergency programme was executed, another twenty trawlers being ordered as the Dance class on 9 September 1939. The modified *Basset* design formed the basis for the wartime 'Shakespearian' (repeat *Mastiff* with more powerful machinery: twelve units, ordered 12 December 1939) and 'Isles' (repeat *Basset*: 128 units, ordered from 6 April 1940 on; nineteen completed as danlayers, four as controlled minelayers) classes. Three similar ships (designed by Robb, ordered 26 September 1939) were built in the United Kingdom for New Zealand (which considered them *Kiwi* class corvettes).

*Basset*s were also ordered in Burma (four, all lost when the country was overrun by the Japanese) and India (forty-four, of which twenty-three were cancelled in February 1945), and the 'Isles' class was ordered in Canada (sixteen built, of which seven were retained by the RCN). These ships resembled short-forecastle corvettes rather than commercial trawlers, with their superstructures amidships rather than well aft. The *Kiwi*s were unique in having their forecastles extended to amidships and their forecastle decks extended to abeam the boiler casing. The 1916 'Castle' design was ordered built in New Zealand (fourteen units). Commercial designs were ordered in the UK ('Military' [nine units], 'Hills' [ten, including two controlled minelayers], 'Round Table' [eight], and 'Fish' [ten]), in Brazil (six units, all turned over to the Brazilian Navy), and in Portugal (sixteen units, four cancelled).

For the purposes of this book, the most significant thing about the trawler was that the corvette began life as a somewhat better alternative to it (see Chapter 6). Six Smith's Dock whalers were taken over while under construction to become the 'Lake' class. They were thus closest to the corvettes, which were derived from whalers. Trawlers were typically armed with 12pdrs (the 'Dance' class had 4in guns) and with light machine guns and depth charges. Some were used as convoy rescue ships.

CHAPTER 5

The War Emergency Destroyers

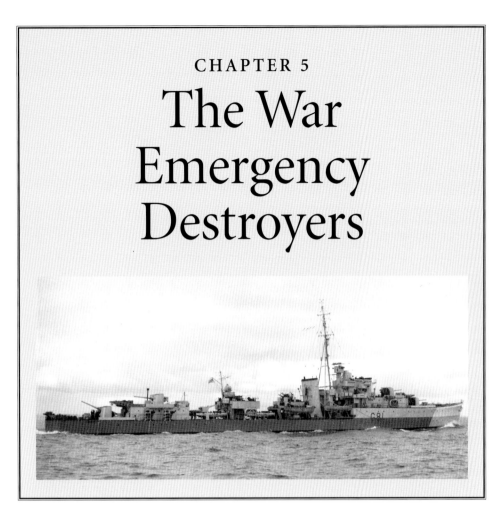

HMAS *Quiberon*, one of the first series of War Emergency destroyers, at sea during the Second World War. Note the absence of any surface-search radar. Also notable is the pennant number, in the same series as that used by Royal Navy destroyers: before and for some years after the war the Royal Navy and the Commonwealth Navies were considered a single unified entity. (John Mortimer)

Although they were ordered under the War Emergency programmes, the 'O' and 'P' classes reflected neither new wartime requirements nor the overriding need for mass production. The original design requirement, that they be limited to 1,500 tons, badly limited their endurance. A new design developed late in 1939 was the basis of twelve wartime flotillas, ninety-six ships, forming the 'Q' through 'Z' and 'C' series, progressively improved during the Second World War. The 'Q' class, the first of the flotillas (initially code-named 'Cubs') was ordered at the expense of delaying the first two *Lion* class battleships by a year. Initially the choice for the 'Cubs' seemed to be between another repeat 'K' class and repeat Intermediates, as for quick production they would have to be a repeat design. Moreover, they would have to use repeat equipment, such as the existing 50pdr gun (on 3 October DNO said that to be completed in 1941 and early 1942 any War Programme destroyers would have to be armed with the existing gun). The 62pdr was still seen as the destroyer gun of the future, to the point that DNO hoped to develop a twin open mount like the 50pdr twin of the 'Tribal' class. There was a tacit assumption that any design selected for continuous wartime production had to be adapted to later rearmament with 62pdr guns, and DNC pointed out that, with modified magazines and shell rooms, the Intermediates could be adapted.

The basis of the new design was DCN's proposal to get the required fuel capacity by modifying the existing 'K' class hull to take the armament of an Intermediate destroyer. By late November the Staff still had not formally chosen characteristics for the design, but it was clearly on the point of adoption: on 30 November Controller asked for an estimate of the delay it would entail. He would ask the Naval Staff whether they could accept such a delay if that bought something like what they wanted. By 6 December Cole had a second sketch design, based as required on the 'J' class hull, 348ft long (1,635 tons standard compared to 1,772 tons for the 'J' class). The only modification to the hull was a square-cut stern, as in the 'Hunt' class, to improve performance at cruising speed. It was initially expected to add about 100nm of endurance. Model tests at Haslar suggested that in half-oil condition the improvement would be 3 per cent at 35kts and 1.5 per cent at 20kts, so the ship would gain 70nm at 20kts.[1]

Nos. 1 and 2 twin 4.7in were both replaced by single mounts in the same positions; a new superstructure was built aft for Nos. 3 and 4 guns, and the bulkheads adjusted below it. The deck atop the after deckhouse was extended slightly to keep depth charges clear of the blast of No. 4 gun. With only half as many 4.7in guns forward, the ship needed only half the magazine space; No. 2 magazine (of the 'J' class) was used instead to stow extra oil. Because this was a 'J' class hull, it could relatively easily be rearmed with twin 4.7in guns (though that was never done). Given the simplified armament, DNO considered fire control rather than gun mountings the main production bottleneck. At a meeting on 9 January Controller formally ordered that the class use the 50pdr gun. The design offered normal depth charge stowage (thirty charges), with one thrower on each side and two traps aft. An increase to forty-five (fifteen stowed below) had recently been approved for the 'J' and 'K' classes; in the new design it was soon done, at a cost of 2 tons. TSDS had been eliminated in favour of additional oil fuel.

As in the Intermediates, the powerplant was a version of that in the 'J' class. Fitting the large turbo-generators (155 kW) of the 'J' class provided enough power to heat the mess decks electrically (as had recently been approved for the 'L' and 'M' classes). The usual auxiliary boiler and its steam heating system could therefore be omitted. When the ships were being built the machinery was further modified for survivability. The first ships, the 'Q' class (3rd Flotilla), got an additional standby diesel generator (10 kW) in the gearing room. Beginning with the 'R' class the two main diesel generators were separated, so that a single hit could not knock both of them out. In both classes, cable runs were placed lower in the hull to make them less vulnerable (a change made about April 1941). Telemotor leads had already been lowered.

The 'J' class hull could be loaded to a deep displacement of

---

[1] When laying off the 'R' class, the John Brown shipyard resisted the change in the 'J' class hull form, because the new stern, with its hard knuckle, was more difficult to build. The yard relented when told that it offered a gain of about 0.5 per cent at 20kts.

about 2,380 tons. The lighter armament left more weight to be added as fuel. By this time the Staff requirement was a day operating 1,000nm from base with 35 per cent allowance for combat, equivalent to 3,815nm at 20kts. The 615 tons of oil were expected to give much greater endurance than in the past, 3,750nm on the basis used in the official fleet handbook, CB 1815 (4,680nm clean). Later the ships were credited with 25 per cent greater endurance than the Intermediates. Even this might be insufficient, and it was suggested that ships be fitted with above-water ('peace') tanks to increase endurance, on the understanding that they would be filled last and emptied first, and that adding them would not delay completion. DNC rejected the idea on the grounds that such tanks would increase hull stresses beyond current limits, and Controller concurred. First Sea Lord was not so sure. Ships with peace tanks full might be damaged in bad weather, but in fine weather they might be quite valuable. DNC's clinching argument was that destroyers would often operate in unexpectedly bad weather. Would any fleet commander delay an operation because they were overloaded with oil?

Even with the extra oil, the ship would be considerably stiffer than a 'J' (estimated GM was 3.25ft rather than 2.48ft). This stiffness equated to a margin of stability which Cole thought could probably accept any reasonable topweight which might be added in wartime, without recourse to the ballasting already evident in the 'J' and 'K' classes. He expected that the new ship would have quintuple tubes rather than the quadruples of the Intermediates, extra depth charges, 62pdr guns,

and splinter protection for their bridges and searchlight platforms. Estimated speed was 36.75kts at standard displacement and 31.5kts deeply loaded.

The 'J' class bridge would be modified on the lines of those of the Intermediates to accommodate similar fire control systems. The after superstructure was modified to meet a new requirement that men be able to go aft from the machinery spaces under cover. To do that, the switchboard was placed in a new watertight compartment abaft the gearing room, from which a passage led to an upper deck scuttle inside the after superstructure. Enclosing the switchboard met another new requirement, now approved for the 'J' and 'K' classes. Presumably both new requirements reflected war experience operating in heavy weather.

Even though the ships had not yet been ordered, Controller decided in mid-December to order the machinery that month (he originally wanted to order only six sets, pending a decision as to whether to build a 15in gun battleship, which became *Vanguard*, and two 'Tribals' for Canada). At a meeting on 3 January 1940 the Sea Lords decided to order the 3rd Emergency Flotilla ('Q' class) to the proposed design.

Given the variety of potential destroyer roles, the ships were designed to accept three alternative (and easily interchanged) armament fits, an idea proposed by DCNS at a meeting on 7 February 1940 chaired by First Sea Lord (Admiral Pound). Such alternatives became standard in later Emergency Destroyer designs. By April 1940, three configurations had been chosen:

HMS *Scourge* in August 1943. The most visible change from the first series of War Emergency ships is that her heavy anti-aircraft gun (in this case a Hazemeyer twin Bofors) has been interchanged with her searchlight, the latter now being abaft the funnel. Twin Oerlikons are visible abeam the searchlight platform. There is no surface-search radar, only Type 291 on a topmast.

A. Four guns, forty-five depth charges (two throwers, two traps), no TSDS. By March 1941 an increase to seventy depth charges (thirty Mk VII heavy, forty Mk VII) had been approved pending initial inclining experiments to show that it could be accommodated. With two additional throwers, ships could fire ten-charge patterns (two per thrower, two from the stern rails). This battery was first installed in the 'R' class. These and the later Emergency Destroyers had a new type of thrower, which did not eject the depth charge carrier; each thrower had five charges in a ready-use rack in addition to the one on the carrier. No gun had to be sacrificed.

B. Maximum ASW configuration: three guns, eight throwers, two traps, 120 charges, fourteen-charge pattern. This was similar to the configuration recently approved for the ex-Brazilian destroyers (*Havant* class). The limit on the number of throwers was upper deck space, which was constricted by the size of the after superstructure. With a larger after superstructure, the leader could accommodate only four throwers (ten-charge pattern), with 100 rather than 120 depth charges (sixty-three Mk VII heavy and fifty-seven Mk VII).

C. Three guns, TSDS, forty-five depth charges. The fourth gun had to be landed because during the design TSDS had already been surrendered for additional fuel oil. Initially leaders had after superstructures so much larger than those of destroyers that they could not have been fitted with TSDS, but from the 'R' class onwards officers were moved forward, and the deckhouse reduced to destroyer size. In 1942 DOD (Home) observed that TSDS had rarely if ever been used since the outbreak of war, but he agreed to building half of new destroyers with the necessary steam pipes, bed plates, etc. The other half were convertible to heavier depth charge batteries (Scheme B). The first eight Emergency destroyers assigned to the Far East were fitted with TSDS.

As First Lord, Winston Churchill reviewed the design – and hated it: 1,650-ton destroyers were so large that U-boat com-

manders would find them worth sinking. DCNS replied that those at sea with the fleet or in the rough Western Approaches preferred larger, not smaller, ships for their endurance and sea-keeping. For other places the older smaller destroyers and the new 'Hunts' would do. Moreover, the two large destroyers torpedoed or mined to date, *Kelly* and *Jersey*, had survived, where earlier leaders (*Grenville* and *Exmouth*) had not. In any case, to meet requirements now being raised, such as TSDS and extra endurance, the ship would need an extra 100 tons. By the end of the war the main criticism of these ships would be not that they were too large but rather that they were too small to be fitted with what had become absolutely essential. Their successors of the 'Weapon' and 'G' classes would be the low-end companions to the much larger 'Battles' and *Daring*s.

Although the design and legend were submitted on 20 January, the Board requested more material, which it received on 4 March. On 27 March 1940 Controller ordered that the 3rd and 4th Emergency Flotillas ('Q' and 'R' classes) be built to the same design. The design having been approved, hulls were ordered on 2 April 1940. As the ships were largely repeat 'Js', building drawings were not issued. As work began on the ships, France collapsed; the invasion of Britain seemed imminent. At a meeting in Bath on 20 May, Assistant Controller announced that ships which could not be completed that year would be suspended to accelerate work on those, particularly 'Hunts', that could be. Orders for equipment, such as gun mountings, which could be used elsewhere, *eg* on board damaged ships being repaired, would not be suspended. Controller was particularly anxious not to disrupt the skilled labour essential to recovery once the crisis passed. For the moment, the 4th Flotilla ('R' class) and ten *Black Swan*s (ordered 15 April 1940) were suspended, the former on 28 May. Once the crisis of the Battle of Britain had passed, work resumed on longer-term programmes. On 9 September the suspension order on the 4th Flotilla ('R' class) was lifted.

The design was modified during construction. For the first time in current British destroyers, aluminium was eliminated wherever possible, to release it to the aircraft industry (that

HMS *Quality*, shown as completed, was typical of the first series of War Emergency destroyers. Note the separate high- and low-angle directors atop her bridge. Atop her foremast is the antenna of a Type 291 air-search radar, and atop her high-angle director is the 'fishbone' of Type 285. Note the boxy shields of the 4.7in guns, limited to 40° elevation. The searchlight platform amidships is the emergency conn. With minor changes, this design was retained for ninety-six ships of twelve war-built flotillas. (Alan Raven)

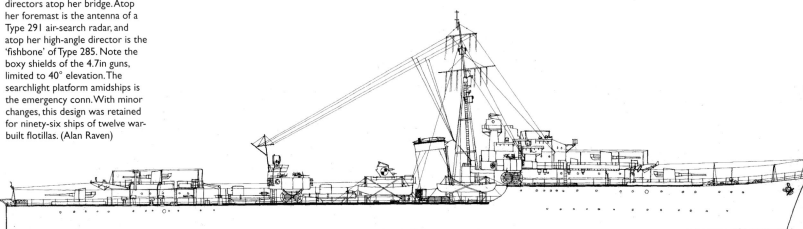

was impossible for stability reasons in earlier ships). The 'J' class hull was stiffened to reduce stresses in the upper deck. Pumping arrangements were improved. The 'R' class were fitted out for tropical service.

With no covered access between the forward and after parts of the ship the two ends were in effect isolated; machinery spaces extended up to the weather deck. The 'V' class introduced a gangway between the forecastle and the after deckhouse, but it hardly offered protected access. With the support of Deputy Controller (as stated in November 1940), in the 'Q' class and later Emergency Flotillas some officers and about half the crewmen were moved aft to quarters near the after battery. At the same time accommodations were rearranged for quicker access to action stations. Reportedly these changes were also intended to preclude the loss of all officers from a hit aft. VCNS objected to mixing officers and enlisted men, and particularly wanted it avoided in ships which would probably remain in commission after the war.

RA(D) proposed fitting two (rather than one) ships in each flotilla as leaders, to make up for the loss or disablement of so many of the pre-war leaders. That was practical because in the newer destroyers the leader was not too different from the other ships in the flotilla, the main difference being extra accommodations. The solution was to fit all ships with the necessary cabin space. When a ship operated as leader, nine officers (including the CO) were forward and four aft; as a destroyer she would have five officers forward and two aft.

Quentin was the first Emergency Destroyer to complete, in March 1941. As might have been expected, she was criticised for her limited armament. Answering the Senior Executive Officer in June 1942, DNC compared a 'Q'-class destroyer with *Veteran*, her First World War equivalent:

COMPARISON OF 'Q'-CLASS DESTROYER AND HMS *VETERAN*

	'Q'	*Veteran*
Generators	2 × 155 kW TG, 2 × 50 KW DG, 1 × 10 kW DG	2 × 26.25 KW TG
Radio	Type 49, 533, 534, 60 (Leader only), FM 7, VC-VP, HF/DF	Type 4, Type 15
W/T Space total	190 sq ft (208 sq ft in Leader)	65 sq ft
LP Room	215 sq ft	49 sq ft
Gyrocompass Rm	25 sq ft	—
Control	120 sq ft	56 sq ft
SLs	1 × 44in stabilised, 2 × 20in SP, 2 × 6in signalling	1 × 20in, 2 × 10in SP
Steering Gear	Electro Hydraulic	Steam
Ventilation	1 × 20in, 2 × 17¼in, 6 × 12½in, 1 × 10in, 3 × 7½in, 6 × 5in	3 × 12½in , 2 × 7½in
Radiators and fires	40	6
S/A Gear	Fitted	—
DC	Fitted	—
A/S	Fitted	—
Echo-sounding	Fitted	—
Rnds/4.7in	250	140
Ammo Supply	Bollard hoists and ammo quadruple carriers	Hand
Comms	Voicepipes and telephones, sound reproducers	Voicepipes
RDF	Types 285, 290	—
Protection	Zarebas to main and CRAA, bridge protection	—

As the alliance with the United States developed during 1941, British officers came into contact with US warships, and the *Benson* class was naturally compared with the new Emergency Destroyers. The Naval Intelligence Division (NID) circulated a comparison between the new 'S' class and USS

HMS *Swift* shows the lattice foremast fitted to many ships during the war, initially to support a Type 272 surface-search radar in a shallow 'lantern'. The topmast carries Type 291 air-search radar. *Swift* was mined off Sword Beach at Normandy on 24 June 1944.

HMS *Rocket*, in August 1943, shows early war modifications, particularly installation of a Type 272 surface-search radar on the stub mast on her searchlight platform. She was later one of two prototype Type 15 frigate conversions. Note the reversion to separate high- and low-angle directors, the rangefinder (for both roles) being carried in the high-angle Rangefinder Director Mk II(W), together with its radar equivalent, Type 285. The (W) in the designation indicated a windshield. Note also the galley exhaust at the fore end of the after deckhouse, needed because so much accommodation was moved aft. (Alan Raven)

Wilkes (DD 441).[2] Both ships were of comparable displacement (1,650 tons standard and 2,383 tons in service for the US destroyer, 1,650 tons and 2,430 tons estimated for the British), the US ship being slightly shorter (341ft vs 348ft on the waterline) and beamier (36ft vs 35ft 8in), riding slightly deeper (13ft 4in vs 12ft). NID described the US ship as wet along the upper deck in poor weather. Each ship had four main guns (dual-purpose in the US case). The British incorrectly thought that the US four-gun ship had a lighter anti-aircraft battery (ten single 0.5in machine guns compared to the stabilised twin Bofors and the Oerlikons of the British ship). Actually the US ships were built either with five guns (and machine guns) or with four guns and multiple Bofors and Oerlikons. The two sets of quintuple torpedo tubes of the US ship were compared to a single set of quadruple tubes in the British, but in fact 'S' class destroyers were generally completed with all eight tubes. The US ship carried twenty-five depth charges (600lbs) compared to the sixty-five (originally seventy) of the British destroyer. At this stage the US ship had only a single Y-gun; the British had two throwers (which might be equated to the Y-gun). The US ship had more powerful engines (50,000 SHP at 370 RPM vs 40,000 SHP at 340 RPM) and was slightly faster (35kts rated, 33.8kts in service). She carried less oil (456 tons vs 615 tons) and NID reported that she had less endurance (3,430nm vs 4,700nm at 20kts). However, British endurance was quoted for clean condition, and US machinery was substantially more efficient. Such comparisons were often raised as the war brought the two navies together, and British officers tended to be impressed with US warships.

As for seagoing qualities, the carrier *Victorious* was accompanied across the North Atlantic at the end of 1942 by three ships of this type, *Racehorse*, *Redoubt* and *Quickmatch*. The CO of *Victorious* was 'much impressed' by their seakeeping qualities. The CO of *Racehorse* said that his ship was always quite comfortable even in a 50-knot gale, except when steer-ing directly into the sea and the swell. He did find the bridge wet and A gun unusable; there was no up-draft to blow wind and spray up and over the heads of those on the bridge. CO of *Redoubt* was impressed that A gun and the forecastle in general emerged undamaged; the ship was dry below decks. As in *Racehorse*, the bridge and the flag decks shipped considerable water during the worst weather.[3] After tests with an early 'R' class unit, the 'S' class and later Emergency Flotillas were modified with a new bow based on that of the 'Tribals'.

Destroyers in the Eastern Fleet encountered some problems, such as deck cracking. Some of this could be attributed to quick construction, builders not always following instructions to make sure that corners of all openings were carefully rounded. Unlike their sister-ships in the other fleets, the first few Emergency Destroyers in the Eastern Fleet also suffered from some stern cracks. Ventilation was a more pressing issue. Although the new ships were ventilated on much the same scale as their predecessors, by 1944 DNC Department wanted more ventilation for ships steaming hard blacked-out in the tropics. Unfortunately production of fans could not keep up with new construction, so ships already in service were sometimes very uncomfortable. Even so, DNC found it reassuring (and even surprising) that the constructor assigned to the Eastern Fleet, Pengelly, wrote that 'apart from sick bay . . . there is not much wrong with the ventilation of these ships. I think it can be stated that Destroyers are more comfortable to live in on this station than most other ships, apart of course from their behaviour in bad weather when I prefer something bigger.'[4] *Quality*, *Quentin* and *Quickmatch* were manned by the Royal Australian Navy instead of the three 'M' class destroyers originally planned.

The 5th and 6th Emergency Flotillas ('S' and 'T' classes), the rest of the 1940 War Programme, were ordered in the spring of 1941 (9 January and 14 March) as repeat 'Rs'. They were to have the new 55° mounting (with the existing 40° mounting as a fall-back if it was not ready in time). By February 1941

[2] NID 2596/41, quoted in the Emergency Destroyer Cover. It is undated, but the designation indicates 1941. A reference to war damage to USS *Kearny* suggests late 1941.

[3] Despatches summarised in the Emergency Destroyer Cover.
[4] Correspondence between Pengelly and DNC in Emergency Destroyer Cover.

HMS *Wizard*, on 27 March 1944, shows the 'cheese' of Type 276 atop her lattice foremast, with an HF/DF array atop her topmast.

plans called for ordering another five Flotillas (7th through 11th, 'U', 'V', 'W', 'Z' and 'Ca' classes) under the 1941 War Programme, beginning with the 7th Flotilla in June 1941.[5]

From flotilla to flotilla the ships were gradually improved and their displacement increased, so that in January 1944 the Ship's Book of the 'V' class showed 1,808 tons standard, the heaviest yet (the leader displaced 1,830 tons). Deep load was given as 2,530 tons with full fuel or 2,222 tons with half fuel. *Volage* ran trials on 25 May 1944 at 2,477 tons, making 30.25kts at full power. An inclining experiment in January 1945 showed that in her short life *Virago* had already gained about 64 tons. Additions included Arctic fittings, such as steam coils, lagging, and heating for numerous outside positions including those of the main and secondary armament, as well as gilled tube heaters in the ship's ventilation system. In February 1945 they were stripped from *Saumarez* and all 'V' class ships in view of their planned tropical service.

The 1941 Emergency Destroyers were to have been the last with low-angle guns; plans called for ordering the new 'Battle' class, with an all-high-angle armament, in 1942. As the design evolved, it became clear that a 'Battle' would be far larger than an Emergency Destroyer. Initial proposals for the 1942 Programme were simply for two flotillas of such ships, because they could not be built in anything like the same numbers as the Emergency Destroyer (forty ships – five flotillas – per year in 1940 and in 1941). Given the rate at which destroyers were being sunk, even at this rate the force would grow by only about twenty by the end of 1944. Slowing production would not help. Late in 1941 it was estimated that ten

Emergency Destroyers (a modified design designated Q.1) could be built for every eight 'Battles'. A third alternative was a modified 'L' class destroyer armed with 4in guns (L.1). Both the 'Battle' and L.1 had all-high-angle batteries, but L.1 lacked anti-destroyer firepower. Director of Plans asked what the proper proportions should be in the 1942 Programme. DOD(H) and (F) wanted an all-high-angle programme split evenly between 'Battles' and L.1; Q.1 was ruled out for its lack of high-angle guns. Moreover, DGD said, building L.1 would insure against teething trouble with the 'Battle' class gun. However, it seemed that buying the L.1 design would add very few ships. In January 1942 DNC estimated that British yards could produce about thirty 'Battles' and ten L.1 or Q.1.

C-in-C Home Fleet emphasised the need for numbers. The new destroyer was too large and expensive for A/S screens or for action in confined waters, as in Norway, and it did not meet the requirement for a small destroyer to be produced in numbers. He was quite willing to accept Q.1 to get them. His officers agreed, but differed as to whether they preferred L.1, Q.1, or a repeat 'Tribal' or 'J' class destroyer. C-in-C Home Fleet proposed building two flotillas of 'Battles', which were good anti-aircraft ships, and as many Q.1s as possible to get the necessary numbers. VCNS also wanted two flotillas of 'Battles' plus as many Q.1s as Controller could lay down. He did want the anti-aircraft firepower of the Q.1 design improved, perhaps by trading one set of torpedo tubes (making the other set quintuple) for another anti-aircraft gun. Ultimately it was decided that the 1942 Programme would consist of the two flotillas of 'Battles' plus as many of 'Q' size as possible, though DNC warned that building time for a 'Q' class destroyer would not be much less than that for the

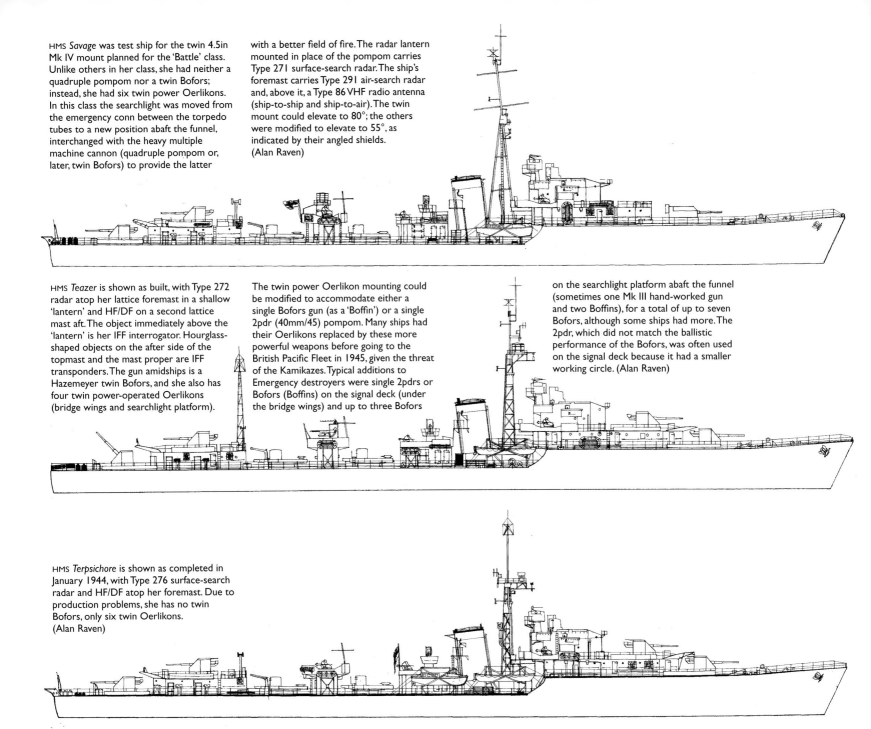

HMS *Savage* was test ship for the twin 4.5in Mk IV mount planned for the 'Battle' class. Unlike others in her class, she had neither a quadruple pompom nor a twin Bofors; instead, she had six twin power Oerlikons. In this class the searchlight was moved from the emergency conn between the torpedo tubes to a new position abaft the funnel, interchanged with the heavy multiple machine cannon (quadruple pompom or, later, twin Bofors) to provide the latter with a better field of fire. The radar lantern mounted in place of the pompom carries Type 271 surface-search radar. The ship's foremast carries Type 291 air-search radar and, above it, a Type 86 VHF radio antenna (ship-to-ship and ship-to-air). The twin mount could elevate to 80°; the others were modified to elevate to 55°, as indicated by their angled shields. (Alan Raven)

HMS *Teazer* is shown as built, with Type 272 radar atop her lattice foremast in a shallow 'lantern' and HF/DF on a second lattice mast aft. The object immediately above the 'lantern' is her IFF interrogator. Hourglass-shaped objects on the after side of the topmast and the mast proper are IFF transponders. The gun amidships is a Hazemeyer twin Bofors, and she also has four twin power-operated Oerlikons (bridge wings and searchlight platform). The twin power Oerlikon mounting could be modified to accommodate either a single Bofors gun (as a 'Boffin') or a single 2pdr (40mm/45) pompom. Many ships had their Oerlikons replaced by these more powerful weapons before going to the British Pacific Fleet in 1945, given the threat of the Kamikazes. Typical additions to Emergency destroyers were single 2pdrs or Bofors (Boffins) on the signal deck (under the bridge wings) and up to three Bofors on the searchlight platform abaft the funnel (sometimes one Mk III hand-worked gun and two Boffins), for a total of up to seven Bofors, although some ships had more. The 2pdr, which did not match the ballistic performance of the Bofors, was often used on the signal deck because it had a smaller working circle. (Alan Raven)

HMS *Terpsichore* is shown as completed in January 1944, with Type 276 surface-search radar and HF/DF atop her foremast. Due to production problems, she has no twin Bofors, only six twin Oerlikons. (Alan Raven)

big new ship.

The 'Battles' would have 4.5in guns, and in February Controller agreed that all the 1942 destroyers (and later ones) would be so armed. The 4.5in gun offered better ballistics than the 4.7in as well as a heavier (55lb) shell than any 4.7in but those on the 'L' and M classes. Moreover, ammunition could be standardised with battleships and aircraft carriers by modifying their mountings to take the separate ammunition which destroyers would have to use. The gun was placed on the existing 55° 4.7in mounting. Rejected alternatives were an 80° mounting based on one used by the British army, the use of three twin 4in guns, and a modified 'M' class with a single 80° 4.7in mounting replacing one twin 4.7in gun (the ship would also have had three twin Bofors, four Oerlikons, two sets of quadruple torpedo tubes, and forty-two depth charges). The 80° alternative was rejected out of hand because it would have required a hull of roughly 'L' size (1,900–1,950 tons, compared to 1,710 tons for 'Q'). The modified 'M' would have been the size of a 'Battle' but with the lower endurance of the 'L' class. The choice of the 55° 4.5in gun was made retroactive to the 10th and 11th Emergency Flotillas ('Z' and 'Ca' classes). For 1942, then, the full forty-destroyer programme consisted of two flotillas of the new large destroyers and three modified Emergency Destroyers ('Ch', 'Co' and 'Cr' classes). In effect the 'Weapon' class of the 1943 Programme was an outgrowth of the proposal to arm the 1942 Emergency destroyer with three twin 4in guns, but it was different enough to be an entirely new class, described in the next chapter. Like the 1942 Fleet

HMS *Grenville* was leader of the 'U' class, with a lengthened after deckhouse to accommodate the necessary extra quarters and offices. She and *Ulster* were the only two of the class completed with tripods rather than with the new short lattice masts, which they later received. Note the Hazemeyer twin Bofors in the position between the torpedo tubes, which in earlier versions of this design was occupied by the searchlight. *Grenville* shows the angled gun shield faces associated with the 55° mounting adopted as a stop-gap while true dual-purpose weapons were produced. (A D Baker III)

Destroyers, the 1942 Emergency class ('Ch', 'Co' and 'Cr' classes) was equipped with the Mk VI Director Control Tower, the first in British service with full dual-purpose capability (see below). As weight compensation for the new director and for the associated remote power control equipment for the 4.5in guns, these ships had one rather than two sets of torpedo tubes, the after position remaining empty.

Crown was completed in 1947 as the last of the Emergency Destroyers. By the time they were built, the Emergency Destroyers were clearly obsolescent. They lacked useful anti-aircraft firepower, but given the lack of appropriate weapons there was no easy remedy. They would not have been effective against the fast submarines the Germans introduced at the end of the war, which the Soviets were expected to du-plicate. However, they offered a key virtue: they required much smaller complements than the big 'Battles', and were thus particularly attractive for foreign stations. Some of them therefore remained active while 'Battles' were laid up. In April 1947, for example, plans called for keeping sixteen 'Battles' and the four 'Weapons' in the Home Fleet; the Mediterranean Fleet would have no 'Battles' at all, but rather the eight 'Ch' class and up to eight other Emergency Destroyers (at the time it had one 'T' class and three 'V' class). The British Pacific Fleet would have the eight 'Co' class. Controller told department heads that owing to the manning situation 'Battles' and 'Weapons' could not be sent abroad for the foreseeable future. About half the Emergency Destroyers in British hands were active at this time.

Photographed in the early 1950s, HMS *Ulysses* had Type 293, recognisable by its upward tilt angle, atop her lattice foremast. Note the rails for illuminating rockets on B gun shield, and the empty searchlight platform amidships.

Guns

Experience in 1940 in Norway and then at Dunkirk clearly showed that pre-war ideas about destroyer anti-aircraft fire had been very wrong. VCNS later observed that the fleet (and many in the Staff) had begun to demand higher-angle destroyer guns during the Spanish Civil War, which he saw as the beginning of modern sea-air warfare. Plans to fit all destroyers with large anti-aircraft guns were drawn up at a meeting at Bath on 17 May 1940. Given the threat of German invasion, it was essential that ships be out of action for the minimum time. Weapons could be improved later.

From an anti-aircraft fire control point of view, the three Emergency Flotillas were equivalent to the old standard destroyers, the main difference being that they could take much more additional weight. Pre-'Tribal' destroyers from the 'E' class on would be fitted with a new three-man rangefinder for anti-aircraft control. One heavy anti-aircraft gun would be installed. In the first two Emergency Flotillas, a 4in gun replaced one set of torpedo tubes. In the new ships the four single 4.7in could be replaced by two twin 4in, but that seemed a poor armament for such large ships unless they were to be used for inshore work. As in the first two Emergency Flotillas, a 4in anti-aircraft gun was chosen to replace one set of torpedo tubes. In this form the Legend and drawings were approved by the Board on 21 May 1940.

The British were experimenting with multiple rocket launchers, which they called Unrotated Projectiles (UPs). Multiple fixed mountings at different elevations and angles of training could be fired remotely individually or in banks of five. The meeting proposed crash development of a mounting to replace an after set of torpedo tubes. An alternative, fitting rocket rails to the 4.7in gun shields, was dropped due to technical problems and because a mount so fitted could not be used as a gun (note that later in the war rails for rocket flares were often mounted on gun shields). Other rejected proposals were to replace 0.5in machine guns with rockets and to fit rocket rails to the remotely-controlled searchlight mountings.

Controller was asked whether the elevation of the 4.7in gun could be increased, to make it a more useful dual-purpose weapon. DNO's solution, offered in September, was a 55° mounting, the most that could be achieved without drastic modification. It would be ready for the 5th and 6th Flotillas ('S' and 'T' classes). Because the ships had been designed to take more powerful weapons, such as 'J'-type twin mounts, they could easily accept heavier guns (in January 1941 DNC said that even a 25 per cent increase on DNO's estimated weight could be accepted). DNO asked whether, if the 5th and later Flotillas were to have the new semi-anti-aircraft gun, they still needed the 4in in place of their torpedo tubes. Thanks to the delay in building them (see below), the 'R' class (4th Flotilla) were arranged to take the 55° mounting, although it was accepted that they would initially be armed with the earlier lower-angle guns.

The request to Controller began the movement towards a destroyer with dual-purpose guns, which culminated in the 'Battle' class. DTSD rejected the 55° mounting as a poor compromise.[6] He was willing to accept the only available high-angle gun, the twin 4in. It was admittedly much inferior to the 4.7in, but it offered a higher rate of fire. However, ACNS(H) considered anti-aircraft firepower overrated: destroyer guns were primarily to engage other destroyers, and their anti-aircraft batteries were mainly to ensure that they survived to carry out torpedo attacks. He revived the argument that no sufficiently high-powered gun could elevate high enough, yet fire at surface targets. Moreover, dive bombers, the main air threat, often attacked in groups: so the ship had to be able to split her fire. A quadruple pompom could engage only a single target, while on much the same weight each of four to six Oerlikons could engage its own target. Conventional low-angle guns could handle torpedo bombers. However, VCNS trumped ACNS(H)'s argument: for each day the destroyer was likely to engage another destroyer, there were probably fifty on which she had to engage aircraft. Admiral Pound was aware that the new US destroyers, whose gunnery practices British officers had recently witnessed, had 'a most efficient' High Angle/Low Angle mounting. He claimed, wrongly, that German destroyer guns could elevate to 80–90°, hence that the British could do just as well. On 17 October VCNS ordered that in principle future destroyer guns should be true dual-purpose weapons elevating to 70° or 80° or more. DNO began preliminary work. For the moment, the Emergency destroyers would get 55° guns (if possible elevation would be increased to 60°).

The US 5in/38 was the only possible near-term solution. Given its lower muzzle velocity, it lacked the hitting power of the 4.7in, but that was acceptable. The only question was whether it could be obtained almost as quickly as the 55° mounting. Thus on 16 November 1940 a message was sent to the Naval Mission in Ottawa, responsible for procurement from North America. The British were also very interested in the associated US Mk 37 fire control system. Definite requirements were five guns with two sets of control for a 'D'-class cruiser, one director, one computer and one set of power controls for one British mounting, and twelve sets of long-range control gear with power controls to fit British mountings (for delivery between early 1944 and 1946 for the planned battleships *Vanguard*, *Lion* and *Temeraire*). Possible requirements were guns and fire controls for sixteen destroyers completing in 1942–3 and another twenty sets of long-range fire controls for delivery between early 1943 and the end of that year (one new carrier and four new cruisers). It seemed likely that the 5th and 6th Flotillas ('S' and 'T' classes) would ultimately get the US guns.

DNC considered it impossible to design a structure capa-

---

[6] DTSD comment 24 September 1940 in the Emergency Destroyer Cover; this seems to have been the origin of the 'Battle' class.

HMS *Volage* was one of the few later War Emergency destroyers to be armed with pompoms rather than Hazemeyers.

ble of taking both the British 55° gun and the US 5in/38. The most significant difference from British practice was the requirement to provide a handling room under each mount. Modified internally, the existing hull could carry three 5in (one forward), but DNC rejected that as a weak battery. A definite decision as to armament would have to be taken by late 1941, before ships had been launched, so they could still be rearranged at reasonable cost. However, when armed with the 5in/38 the existing hull would trim by the bow and hence would be wet; it would also suffer excessive stress. A hull redesigned for the 5in/38, but armed with the lighter British 55° mounting, would be too lively. To take two American guns forward the hull would have to be stiffened and given 6in more beam to maintain freeboard and improve stability. In this case the forward magazine and shell room would both be enlarged and subdivided, and No. 2 mounting moved 5ft forward to suit the new magazine arrangements. The bridge would be raised 2ft so that the helmsman could see over No. 2 mounting. Greater displacement would probably cost half a knot in speed.

At the end of December DNO was no nearer to getting the American guns. He had not even received general arrangement drawings on which a new hull design could be based. The 5th and 6th Flotillas would therefore have the 55° gun, no matter how unsatisfactory. The possibility that American guns might still arm the 7th Flotilla ('U' class) was real enough that in January 1941 DNC ordered Haslar to test the modified hull form. To deal with expected trim by the bow, the model tank compressed the fore body and stretched the after

body, retaining the after cut-up for manoeuvrability. Beam was 36ft 2in (35ft 8in in the earlier flotillas). VCNS was impossibly optimistic. The definite British requirements were embodied in early Lend-Lease agreements, and the cruiser *Delhi* refitted in the United States to serve as test ship. Directors planned for the battleships equipped *Vanguard* and the carriers *Ark Royal* and *Eagle*. Other Mk 37 directors equipped the second group of 'Battle' class destroyers. However, no more 5in guns were provided.

Given delays with the US guns, a First Sea Lord meeting (21 February 1941) decided that all forty of the 1941 ships (7th through 11th Flotillas) would be armed with 55° mountings and with two sets of torpedo tubes (see below), plus one heavy close-range weapon and four Oerlikons. Given the 55° gun, ACNS argued successfully that the 4in gun was no longer needed as alternative to one set of tubes. Director of Plans' proposal that at least one flotilla have six guns was turned down on the ground that the 4.7in twin had inadequate elevation; better to wait for the new high-angle mount in a new hull.

Both existing secondary weapons, the pompom (40mm/39) and the 0.5in machine gun, were inadequate. Their wartime replacements were the Bofors 40mm/60 and the 20mm Oerlikon, the latter already known and of considerable interest before the outbreak of war. The pompom lacked range due to its low muzzle velocity and its lack of any predictor (fire control computer). A Dutch ship fleeing the Nazis, *Willem van der Zaan*, carried a gun mount that seemed to solve the problem: a twin power-operated triaxially stabilised Bofors carrying a predictor sight, called the Hazemeyer (an early prod-

uct of the company later known as Signaal). Fire control was fully tachymetric, far in advance of anything available in the United Kingdom at the time. The mounting incorporated a small rangefinder, and was considered (accurately) suitable for installation of the Type 282 radar then being developed to control close-range anti-aircraft weapons. Overall size and weight approximated that of the Mk VII quadruple pompom installed in destroyers. The Bofors gun itself was already being made for the army. DNO and representatives of DTSD inspected the ship on arrival in Britain. British naval officers who witnessed tests were so impressed that, with Dutch agreement, first one and then both mountings on board the ship were removed for further tests and to enable manufacturing drawings to be made. DNO expected that the Hazemeyer would prove superior to the director-controlled pompom then being installed in cruisers. In November 1940 he proposed fitting it even at the expense of Oerlikons. In December DNO proposed buying fifty mountings initially (the Free Dutch wanted eight sets for their own ships). The Hazemeyer was placed in production as Mk IV. Initially the main significance of the Hazemeyer was that it might be so effective than the single 4in anti-aircraft gun was no longer needed; ships could have both sets of torpedo tubes.

The Hazemeyer was far heavier (and more temperamental) than the US twin Bofors, which relied on a separate simple Mk 51 director (the US Navy bought the Bofors on the basis of tests using the same ship, but it did not want the mounting). Ultimately it was fitted with its own Type 282

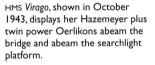

HMS *Virago*, shown in October 1943, displays her Hazemeyer plus twin power Oerlikons abeam the bridge and abeam the searchlight platform.

radar. Development of a follow-on twin triaxially-stabilised BUSTER (Bofors Universal Stabilized Tachymetric Electric Radar) was abandoned late in the war, but the twin biaxially-stabilised Stabilised Tachymetric AA Gun (STAAG) saw considerable post-war service (a single version was cancelled). STAAG initially carried both an on-mount radar (like the roughly contemporary US GUNAR) and its own diesel generator. The generator, rangefinder and ammunition hoists were all eliminated in an attempt to keep weight *down* to 15 tons.[7] The lighter alternative, Utility Mk V, was equivalent to the wartime US twin Mk 1. Both used an external director. Beginning in 1945, Mk V was installed on board many destroyers and some sloops and frigates. The Royal Navy also used a single Mk III army mount (equivalent to the US Mk 3), superseded in wartime by the navalised Mk VII. Both replaced Oerlikons at the end of the war on board ships bound for the Pacific, and post-war. The first single Bofors were mounted on board some large British warships in 1941. At

---

[7] STAAG had much the same sad story as the weatherproof 4.7in 62pdr. In 1942 estimated weight was 8.5 tons, rising to 9 tons and then in 1943 to 11 tons. Planned installations were based on this last weight, but as of 4 January 1945 the figure was 17.5 tons. Drastic simplification was ordered to reduce that to 15 tons. This weight growth ruled out plans for STAAGs to replace the Hazemeyers in the 10th and 11th Emergency Flotillas. By way of comparison, a US twin Bofors with Mk 49 director (more elaborate than the Mk 51 actually used) weighed 8.3 tons, and the US *quadruple* Bofors with Mk 49 weighed 11.8 tons. STAAG's only advantages were stabilisation, on-mount radar, and, initially, a small diesel generator. The British Utility Mk V (6 tons) was roughly equivalent to the US twin Bofors. The British equivalent to the US Mk 51 director was the Simple Tachymetric Director ('Austerity'), which weighed 11½ cwt (1,288lbs, something over half a ton). In March 1944 DNC estimated that a single BUSTER could replace a set of torpedo tubes in any of the 'Tribal', 'J', 'K', 'N' or Emergency classes, or the pompom in a 'Tribal' through 'P' class (if ballast were added). It could not replace the pompom in an Emergency destroyer because the extended platform it required would foul boat stowage on the starboard side. Ships with Mk VI directors could not take the added topweight. All of this was before the immense weight of the BUSTER mounting had been appreciated.

the end of the war many ships had single Bofors guns replacing twin power-operated Oerlikons, the resulting mount being called a 'Boffin'.

The Oerlikon was very well liked for its light weight. Until about 1942 it was the main close-range weapon installed on board British ships. The Royal Navy continued to emphasise the Oerlikon well after the US Navy had concluded that it was a secondary weapon, to the point that in 1945 the British Pacific Fleet command had to recommend its elimination in favour of Bofors guns because it had proven so ineffective against Kamikaze attacks. A twin power-operated Mk V mount, with joystick control and, in later versions, a gyro sight, was introduced in 1942. Because this mount depended on a ship's electric power, which could be disabled, policy was set at 50

per cent hand-worked guns (or at least two such mounts). The British hoped ultimately to adopt the unpowered US twin Oerlikon in place of their unpowered single mount, but none seems to have been supplied in wartime. Thus an approved armament of four twin Mk V in a 1942 'Battle' class destroyer was changed to two twin Mk V and two hand-worked singles. As of January 1944 the approved battery of the Emergency

HMS *Whelp* was among the few late War Emergency destroyers completed with a pompom, seen between her torpedo tubes, rather than a twin Bofors. Note also the absence of a searchlight in the position abaft the funnel. This class introduced a single dual-purpose Rangefinder Director Mk III(W). It had electrical data transmission (note the tall stalk). Mk III(W) differed from Mk II(W) mainly in that it had a position for the Rate Officer, responsible for estimating surface target course and speed. He had formerly been accommodated in the separate DCT. The vertical bar on her funnel indicated her role as a division (half-flotilla) leader. Destroyer flotillas were organised in two four-ship divisions. After the war, flotillas were ultimately cut to four ships each, and the divisions eliminated. (Alan Raven)

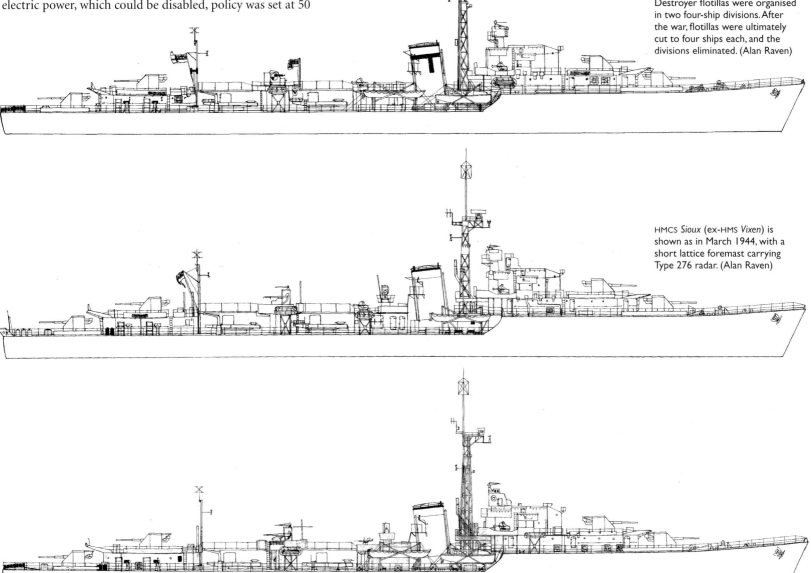

HMCS *Sioux* (ex-HMS *Vixen*) is shown as in March 1944, with a short lattice foremast carrying Type 276 radar. (Alan Raven)

HMS *Caesar* was a unit of the initial flotilla of the 'C' class, which had two sets of torpedo tubes and a lightweight director on the bridge. The 'Z' and 'Ca' classes, which had the new 4.5in gun, were to have been equipped with Mk 6 directors, but they were not ready in time. Instead of the Mk III(W) of

the 'Z' class, they were fitted with K Director Mk I (the 'K Tower'), the K referring to a gyro-stabilised surface sight. There was a separate anti-aircraft sight. Due to production delays, some 'Z' and 'Ca' class destroyers had to go to sea without their directors. Initially the K Tower was hand-trained, its

operators following pointers set from below decks. By late in the war, however, the tower was power-trained and hence could be remotely power-controlled from the Transmitting Station below decks. Either arrangement made it possible to slew the director onto targets indicated by the Gun

Direction System using Radar Type 293. The system's Type 285M or 285P used beam-switching to stay locked onto a surface target (but not an air target, as there was no beam-switching in elevation). Using radar data displayed in the Transmitting Station, the Below Layer and Below Trainer there

could remotely control the director to stay on target. Because Type 285 could not track an air target, the director could control blind anti-aircraft fire. Because of production problems, some ships were completed without the K Mk I director. *Caesar* is shown as completed. (Alan Raven)

HMS *Savage* tested the between-decks dual-purpose twin 4.5in gun planned for the 'Battle' class. Note the 'lantern' of the Type 271 surface-search radar between the two banks of torpedo tubes.

Flotillas and the 'J', 'K' and 'N' classes was four twin Mk V ('O', 'Q' and 'R' classes had two twins and two singles).

In December 1940 DNC offered alternative armaments for the Emergency Destroyers. A was the ACNS(H) proposal: six Oerlikons in place of both the pompom and the 0.5in. Oerlikons on a platform abaft the funnel would be staggered so they could fire across the ship. B replaced the after pair of Oerlikons with a Hazemeyer. In C the Hazemeyer was amidships. DTSD selected B. This battery (with 55° guns, and without a 4in gun) was adopted in January 1941 for the 5th and 6th Emergency Flotillas ('S' and 'T' classes). On 21 February the First Sea Lord's meeting on the subject decided that the 7th ('U' class) and later Flotillas would have two sets of tubes, although there might not be enough torpedoes to fill them. Policy adopted in June 1941 called for one Hazemeyer and four to six Oerlikons. DGD studies showed that against a dive bomber an Oerlikon was likely to be more effective than a single predictor-controlled 4in gun up to 3,000ft, and that up to 10,000ft a pompom was much more effective. Even so, the 4in gun was retained as an alternative to one set of tubes. The 3rd and 4th Flotillas ('Q' and 'R' classes), which had been allocated 4in guns, were completed instead with quadruple pompoms, six Oerlikons and two sets of torpedo tubes. They still had provision for the 4in gun. DTSD having remarked in June 1941 that it might be needed in some areas. By that time it would be useful mainly to fire starshell.

Reviewing the issue in March 1942, DTSD distinguished ships operating in the Home, Mediterranean and Far Eastern theatres. In both of the latter they would be subject to intense air attack, but would have to attack enemy heavy ships:

they should retain both sets of tubes. Ships facing heavy air attack should have a director-controlled pompom, a Hazemeyer or a US twin Bofors with director in place of the 4in. Without the 4in gun one of the three or four 4.7in would have to be reserved for starshell. To resolve the question, on 22 April DTSD asked the Home, Mediterranean, and Eastern Fleet commanders about DGD's options. In June C-in-C Mediterranean added another possibility. The best German pilots were pressing home their attacks despite Oerlikon fire, or were bombing accurately from outside Oerlikon range. There was little point either in retaining the 4in gun or replacing it with more Oerlikons. He favoured a pair of director-controlled 12pdr (3in/45) with shells fused to burst between 1,500 and 850 yds. Neither quadruple pompoms nor twin Bofors were immediately available, and replacing a set of torpedo tubes with either would involve about two months of work. It would be somewhat easier to install either twin Oerlikon or two single 12pdrs. However, 12pdrs were not immediately available, and DGD rejected this weapon altogether: by the end of 1942 torpedo tubes could be replaced by paired twin Oerlikons and, later, by predictor-controlled Bofors (presumably Hazemeyers). The other C-in-Cs preferred to retain both sets of tubes, and the conclusion (in June) was that all ships would be completed with normal armament. The main outcome seems to have been a decision to replace the single Oerlikons with four power-operated twins. In fact the 'Q' class was refitted with twins in the bridge wings (this definitely applied to *Quail* and *Queensborough*). They retained their four amidships singles. Of the 'R' class, *Roebuck* and *Rocket* were completed with

twins in the bridge wings. The others were refitted this way.

Beginning with the 'S' class the searchlight, formerly between the torpedo tubes, was moved to the platform abaft the funnel, the multiple heavy machine cannon replacing it. In effect this was a declaration that clear arcs of anti-aircraft fire were more important than illumination for night action (*Savage*, which had the prototype twin dual-purpose 4.5in gun, had the 'lanterns' of Type 271 radars on her searchlight platform). This class also replaced the pompom with a Hazemeyer, although slow production precluded installation in some cases (*Scorpion* alone had a quad pompom). All but *Swift* and *Savage* had four twin Oerlikons. The latter two had an extra pair on the 40mm platform (in 1944 *Savage* added two singles on the shelter deck forward).

The 'T' class were assigned a twin Bofors and four twin Oerlikons. However, instead of the twin Bofors *Troubridge*, *Tumult*, *Tuscan* and *Tyrian* had two single Oerlikons, and *Terpsichore* had two twins (all later received the twin Bofors). In March 1944 the Mediterranean Fleet ordered pairs of single Army-type Bofors guns fitted to the 'T' class. *Tumult*, *Tyrian*, *Terpsichore* and *Troubridge* were all modified at Malta. *Tuscan* was to be taken in hand on arrival at Alexandria (she might have received only one Bofors, replacing one of the two Oerlikons on the Bofors gun deck). The others would be taken in hand upon arrival in Malta for reboilering. *Termagant* received only a single Bofors. Similarly, *Undine* and *Urchin* were completed with two twin Oerlikons in place of their twin Bofors. Of the 'V' and 'W' classes, *Volage*, *Wessex* and *Whelp*

were completed with a pompom instead of the planned twin Bofors. *Verulam*, *Wakeful* and *Wizard* also received two single Bofors in place of the twin Oerlikons on their Bofors platforms. The Oerlikon was still popular, and on 17 November 1944 DNC approved fitting a single Oerlikon on the searchlight platform (this was not done, however).

By spring 1944 plans were in hand to build up a British Pacific Fleet. Eastern Fleet drew up plans to rearm ships at Durban and Simonstown in South Africa and Bombay in India as they steamed East to join the new fleet. DNC approved a mid-April 1945 a proposal by C-in-C East Indies to replace the four single Oerlikons on the searchlight platform with four single Army Bofors. To avoid excess topweight, ready-use ammunition stowage had to be halved and the height of the zareba (gun tub) around each weapon strictly limited. DNC offered an alternative in which single Bofors or single 2pdrs replaced twin Oerlikons on the searchlight platform and the flag deck. The four Mk III Bofors were fitted to *Rapid*, *Rocket* and possibly other 'Q' and 'R' class destroyers and to *Saumarez*.

Of the 'T' class, *Tyrian* was not further refitted. *Tumult* had a third Mk III abaft her funnel, and single 2pdr pompoms in place of her bridge wing Oerlikons (all Oerlikons were landed). *Troubridge*, *Termagant* and *Tuscan* all received an additional single 40mm gun in the searchlight position, their four single Oerlikons all being replaced by Boffins. *Grenville*, *Ulysses*, *Ursa*, *Undine* and *Urchin* were all similarly modified. *Urania*, *Venus* and *Vigilant* had single Mk III Bofors in place of all four Oerlikons. *Verulam* received two Mk III Bofors on her upper

HMS *Kempenfelt*, leader of the 'V' class, displays the squared-off stern characteristic of the War Emergency destroyers.

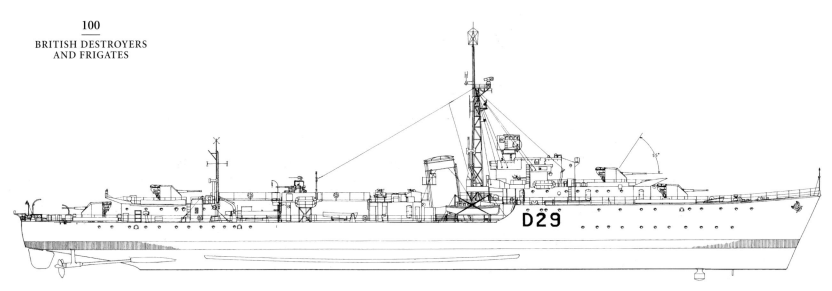

HMS *Charity*, shown in April 1946, was the ultimate development of the War Emergency class, with a Mk 6 HA/LA Director and the associated remote power control (RPC) for her 4.5in guns. The director carried the twin antennas of the Type 275 radar. Unlike Type 285, Type 275 could track a target in bearing and elevation, and thus could be used for blind anti-aircraft fire. Note that the director was designated in a series of HA/LA directors otherwise used for cruisers and capital ships; it was a different series from the Rangefinder Directors on board destroyers, sloops, and anti-aircraft frigates. Initially the director fed a wartime-type FKC, which limited the system's anti-aircraft capability. Post-war versions had the Flyplane calculator (computer) instead, and were considered far more effective at long range (Flyplane was later much disliked for its complexity and unreliability). The typical destroyer system was designated F.P.S. 5. Later systems which eliminated this computer but retained director and radar were MRS 6 and MRS 7. As weight compensation for the director and RPC, the ship had one rather than two sets of torpedo tubes. In addition to the twin Bofors (Hazemeyer) between the two torpedo tube positions (the forward being unoccupied), HMS *Charity* had two single Oerlikons (in the bridge wings) and two single Vickers 2pdrs (on the former searchlight position abaft the funnel). Her foremast carried her Type 293M target indication radar and her HF/DF; the stub mainmast carried her Type 291 air search set, with IFF transponders on short yards fore and aft. The object just abaft Type 293M is the ship's IFF interrogator (Type 244). ASW armament is two throwers and two six-charge racks. (A D Baker III)

Fire Control

As the Emergency Destroyers developed, they were fitted with a wide variety of fire-control systems. At the outset the Royal

deck abeam her mainmast. *Volage* received four single Mk III Bofors instead of her pompom; all her Oerlikons were landed. *Vigilant* reportedly had two single Bofors on her forecastle (plus the two replacing the two twin power Oerlikons on her searchlight position). One ship, probably *Venus*, had a very heavy battery of ten Bofors: two on the signal deck (under the bridge wings), four on the searchlight platform, the usual twin Hazemeyer between the torpedo tubes, and a very unusual two single mounts on the weather (upper) deck aft, just forward of the after deckhouse, clearing the after torpedo tubes. After the war, however, this battery was soon cut to one twin Bofors and four twin power Oerlikons (others in the class had six twin power Oerlikons). *Wager* had four Boffins in place of her Oerlikons, and a single Mk III in place of her searchlight. *Kempenfelt*, *Whelp* and *Wessex* all just had their searchlights replaced by single Mk III Bofors. *Wakeful* had three (rather than two) Mk III in the position abaft the funnel. Of the 'Z' class, *Myngs* received single 2pdrs in place of twin Oerlikons in her bridge wings and one Mk III Bofors in place of her searchlight. *Zephyr* had single 2pdrs in place of the Oerlikons on her Bofors deck. *Zenith* had her Oerlikons replaced by single 2pdrs. *Zebra* had two, and *Zealous* four, single power 2pdrs.

Of the 'Ca' class, only *Caprice* had a quadruple pompom. All but *Cassandra* had single 2pdrs (three in *Cavendish*, four in the others); *Cavendish* had two single Oerlikons instead. Of the 'Ch' class, *Chieftain*, *Chivalrous* and *Childers* all had two single Bofors; *Comet* had two twin Oerlikons, and the others all had two single power 2pdrs. *Childers* and *Comet* each had two single Oerlikons. Of the 'Co' class, *Concord*, *Comus* and *Consort* each had two single Bofors; the others had two single 2pdrs. All had two single Oerlikons, as did the remaining 'Cr' class.

Navy had effective surface (low-angle) systems but lacked any effective high-angle or dual-purpose system; this gap was filled only at the end of the war with the Mk VI system. As in the contemporary US Mk 37 system, the British used an aloft director control tower (DCT) feeding data to a below-decks computer in what they called a Transmitting Station. Those in the DCT tracked the target. The DCT also included the spotter observing the fall of shot and sending down appropriate corrections, to bring guns on target.

The first destroyer DCTs, introduced in the 1920s, had no integral rangefinders. Range was periodically measured by a separate rangefinder. That was sufficient in a simple engagement, but there was always a possibility that the rangefinder would be trained on the wrong target. The earliest ships described in this book (the 'Tribal' class) had a hand-trained director with three operators: a trainer, a layer, and a cross-level operator (the latter typically below the other two, and to one side).[8] Above and behind were three officers, each with his own large sighting port: a control officer flanked by a spotting officer and a rate officer. The trainer and layer had binocular sights and telescopes, both connected to the same gyro-stabiliser. The layer and the cross-level operator tracked the horizon (in two directions at right angles), in effect sensing the ship's pitch and roll so that the system could compensate (in battleships a gyro was usually used for this purpose). A three-man range finder was mounted above and abaft the director control tower. The 'Tribals' were the first British class to have 12-foot rather than 9-foot directors.

The Transmitting Station contained a computer, the Admiralty Fire Control Clock (AFCC). Given data from the DCT, it projected ahead target position, and this projection was displayed in the DCT as feedback, allowing those inside to correct AFCC projections. Unlike a surface ship fire control system, the destroyer system did not maintain a plot of

---

[8] This type of director was first installed on board 'C' and 'D' class destroyers and their leaders (*Duncan* and *Kempenfelt*) in 1932 (ADM 186/309). In 1935 it was decided that on refitting 'A' and 'B' classes would receive similar directors. All had separate 9ft rangefinders intended only for surface use. The below-decks computer was the AFCC.

target position based on DCT and range-finder observation, presumably on the theory that no such plot was worthwhile at short range. Sloops had the simpler Admiralty Fire Control Box (AFCB). Given data from the AFCC or AFCB, the Transmitting Station fed bearing and elevation orders to the guns, whose layers and trainers 'followed the pointer' on their indicators. They could respond quickly enough to handle surface targets, but for effective anti-aircraft fire remote power control (RPC) was necessary. It was introduced late in the war.

The anti-aircraft calculator was the Fuse Keeping Clock (FKC), first tested on board HMS *Fleetwood*.[9] The Royal Navy relied on its fire control officers to estimate target speed, using a slightly more sophisticated equivalent to a ring sight (actually an image of a ring) projected on a screen. As aircraft speeds increased, such estimation became less and less precise. In addition, the systems assumed that the target was moving at a constant altitude, which made sense for level and torpedo bombers, but not at all for dive bombers. As in the surface system, there was feedback. The control officer tracked the aircraft in his Angle of Presentation (A/P) binoculars, which sent elevation and bearing to the FKC; the FKC in turn could drive the binoculars so that the officer could check the accuracy of the solution.

The alternative to estimating target speed, which was known to DGD before the war – and which the US Navy used – was

to measure target speed using gyros. Such speed measurement was termed tachymetric. The Royal Navy rejected it as too complex and unreliable, but by 1938 opinion had reversed. In 1938 DGD announced that it was 'urgently desired' to add a tachymetric (deflection-measuring) capability.[10] In 1939 trials were proceeding on board the converted anti-aircraft cruiser HMS *Coventry*, and all ships were expected to have fully-stabilised gyro trackers by 1942–3, but the outbreak of war ended the programme. It has often been said that the choice against a tachymetric system crippled British heavy anti-aircraft gunnery throughout the Second World War. The wartime attempt to solve the problem was installing Gyro Rate Units (GRUs) to measure target angular speed. The GRU transmitted the vertical and horizontal rates it measured to the Gyro Rate Unit Box (GRUB) in the Transmitting Station. GRU was most accurate at high angular rates, which meant at short ranges. Using GRUB, the rates could be inserted into the calculator. Because the basic system had not been designed to use tachymetric inputs, the GRU and GRUB were only stopgaps. Like much of the rest of the British system, GRUB was designed to deal with targets flying straight and level, projecting ahead their angular positions; but GRU could measure rates for a manoeuvring or diving target.

In the 'Tribals' the rangefinder was incorporated in a rangefinder director Mk II used for anti-aircraft fire (at lim-

HMS *Zest*, photographed on 28 April 1952, displays her Mk III(W) director. Her sole close-range weapon is the cocooned Hazemeyer amidships; the postwar Royal Navy cocooned many such weapons in order to save scarce manpower while retaining capacity in the event of war. Note also that her Y 4.5in gun has been landed.

[9] See *Progress in Gunnery* for 1938, ADM 186/349. The first installations were in the 'Tribals' and the *Bittern* class, but plans called for installation on board all destroyers, escorts, large minesweepers, armed merchant cruisers, etc.

[10] ADM 186/349. The installation programme is in *Progress in Gunnery* for 1939, ADM 239/137.

The 'Ca' class was effectively a repeat 'Z' class; HMS *Caesar* is shown in 1945. She has not yet been fitted with her Hazemeyer twin Bofors amidships. Thus her close-range battery is apparently limited to single Bofors abeam the bridge and on the searchlight platform abaft the funnel.

ited angles), feeding an FKC (Mk III was the corresponding dual-purpose sloop director). In the 'J' class the DCT was modified to provide anti-aircraft capability, a simple three-man rangefinder replacing the rangefinder director of the 'Tribals'. This arrangement proved impractical, and was completely revised in 1941. The DCT was modified to limit it to surface fire. The rangefinder was modified to function as a rangefinder director. That entailed adding a control officer's seat, with angle of presentation binoculars and means of transmitting data to the Transmitting Station below decks. A windshield was added to protect the operators as they turned the director, and a Type 285 radar mounted on top. The layer had a director firing pistol. These arrangements were repeated in the 'K' and 'N' classes, which were repeat 'Js'. This was also the arrangement in the later 'E' through 'I' class destroyers as modified in wartime.

The 'L' and 'M' classes had a new dual-purpose power-trained Director Mk IV Type TP, which may have been related to the combined DCT/rangefinders which were being installed on board export destroyers for Brazil and Turkey.[11] It was turret-shaped rather than cylindrical, with its rangefinder near its after side. The P indicated the P-type gyro-stabilised sight, employing a master gyro to stabilise the layer's, trainer's, and control and rate officers' binocular sights and the rangefinder, but not the associated Type 285 radar, which was added after the units had been designed. Reportedly it was unsuccessful against aircraft. The anti-aircraft version of the 'L' class had a modified rangefinder director of quite different design.

The 'O' and 'P' class destroyers had rangefinder directors in the same series as the 'Tribals', except that, as in sloops, they lacked separate surface directors. In this series Mks IV and V were mechanically linked to the Transmitting Station by shafts replacing the earlier wiring with its synchros. Presumably the shift away from electrical transmission reflected a known shortage of precision electrical manufacturing capacity.[12] The shafts had to be kept relatively short, so the directors in these ships were set low and their Transmitting Stations were immediately below in the superstructure. The 'O' and 'P' classes had Mk V**, the first star indicating a windscreen and the second a radar (Type 285). This version had a specially strengthened rangefinder mounting to overcome the vibration of a ship running at high speed. The Transmitting Station contained an FKC and a sloop-type Fire Control Box (FCB) rather than a Clock. 'Hunts' had much the same system (Mk V or V*, FKC Mk III, FCB Mk II).

In effect the 'Q' through 'V' class destroyers reverted to the 'Tribal'-class system, comprising a surface DCT and a rangefinder director Mk II(W) for anti-aircraft fire (the W indicated a windscreen). Data was electrically transmitted, but the director was not power-stabilised. The 'W' class introduced a dual-purpose rangefinder director, Mk III(W), originally planned (by August 1941) for the 'U' and later classes. In April 1942 a dual-purpose director was ordered fitted to the 9th–11th Emergency Flotillas ('W', 'Z' and 'Ca' classes), to the 1942 Fleet Destroyers, and to the third and fourth Canadian 'Tribals'.

[11] Much of the destroyer fire control material in this chapter is from Peter Hodges in P Hodges and N Friedman, *Destroyer Weapons of World War II* (Conway Maritime Press, London: 1978).

[12] According to the 1938 *Progress in Gunnery*, destroyers and larger escorts used electrical transmission; smaller escorts used mechanical.

These ships received Mk III(W) directors. To accommodate the new director, the after end of the bridge had to be widened and extended and fittings rearranged. This alteration was approved for the 'O' and 'P' classes. The 'Z' and 'Ca' classes were to have had the new Mk VI dual-purpose director (see below), but it was not ready in time. Instead they were fitted with a HA/LA director Mk I Type K, the K referring to a gyro-stabilised surface sight. There was a separate anti-aircraft sight. This director resembled that in the 'L' and 'M' classes, with its self-contained dual-purpose rangefinder and a Type 285 radar on the roof. As in pre-war practice, it had separate ports for level and cross-level (sightings of the horizon).

Late in the war destroyers were divided into four groups according to their fire control capability, each being given a priority for fire control modernisation. Group D was the later Emergency Destroyers, which already had a modern director system. Replacing their K towers with Mk VI was therefore a low priority, although installing remote power control (RPC) was vital. Group C were the earlier Emergency Destroyers. As Priority 1 they were get new directors and to have their 4.7in guns replaced by 4.5in. That would bring them into line with the Battles and the latest Emergency Destroyers. Group B, earlier ships, were to be rearmed as in Group C. Group A had 40° guns. They might be rearmed as Group D or possibly with twin 4in guns, which were in good supply. Using those guns, more than one flotilla at a time could be rearmed. It had already been proposed to arm the last two Canadian 'Tribals' with 4in RPC twin mounts controlled by Mk VI directors. The third through sixth ships had

Mk III(W) directors, three twin 4.7in, and one twin 4in.

The wartime failure of conventional heavy anti-aircraft fire control systems led to the development of barrage directors designed to fire guns automatically, their shells set to burst at a selected range between 1,000 and 5,000 yds. Relatively simple barrage directors were developed. In destroyers they were sometimes used to provide an alternative channel of fire control. The major wartime medium-calibre fire control development was the Mk VI director and its associated Flyplane computing system (for anti-aircraft fire; for surface fire there was a version of the AFCC). At least in its initial form, Mk VI had an integral rangefinder and a pair of nacelles for its Type 275 radar (lightweight post-war versions often dispensed with the rangefinder). Unlike previous destroyer directors, Mk VI had a freely-trainable selector sight permitting the control officer to seek further targets while the director tracked a chosen one. The director was gyro-stabilised and could be controlled from the Tallboy (radar) console. It fed both a surface fire computer (the AFCC Mk XII) and a high-angle computer (Flyplane). Both were essential. For example, without the AFCC the system could not accept spotting corrections for range and line, or settings for target inclination and speed.

Another important wartime development was electric (remote) fuse-setting, which greatly reduced the system 'dead' time between calculation and fuse-setting at the gun. On the other hand, the proximity fuse, so important for the wartime US Navy, seems not to have been very successful in wartime British service. In 1945 the British Pacific Fleet commander reported that proximity fuses had shot down only

HMCS *Crusader*, little modified in Canadian service, photographed on 26 August 1954. The most obvious changes were the addition of the funnel cap and of the Canadian Sperry Mk II navigational radar (on the foremast platform, below Type 293). She shows single Bofors guns abeam the bridge and on the searchlight platform, and a twin mount on the platform amidships. The forward torpedo tubes were suppressed as weight compensation for the Mk VI director and RPC. Note the pennant number without any Flag Superior, a practice adopted by the Royal Canadian Navy in 1949.

one aircraft – one of his own Seafires.

Radar

Radar, initially called RDF (radio direction-finding, a cover designation), was the most radical wartime destroyer development. It revolutionised air defence, and eliminated the cloak of darkness which protected German U-boats – and which made classical destroyer torpedo attacks possible. The initial metric-wave technology provided valuable air warning, but the broad beams produced by British sets could not be used

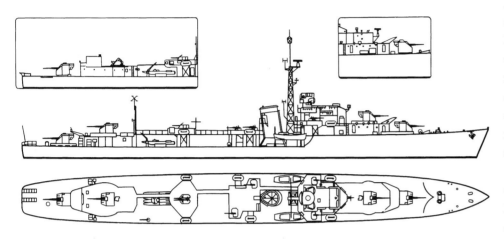

The basic 'C' class arrangement, with details of the stern of *Consort* ('Co' Class) and forward superstructure of *Creole* ('Cr' class) as insets.

to cue anti-aircraft guns. For British destroyers microwave radar (centimetric rather than metric wavelength) was more valuable because its shorter waves could come closer to the surface of the water. Thus it could detect surfaced submarines at useful ranges. Because it had a narrow beam, it could be used to designate air targets to guns (and, in other forms, as a fire-control radar).

By July 1940 DNC was considering proposals for destroyer installation. The first destroyer set was the metric-wave Type 286, developed soon after Dunkirk from the Coastal Command ASV Mk I.[13] As in aircraft, it used fixed antennas: one to transmit, two (on either side) to receive. The ship scanned by turning; a target could be located within about 10°. Type 286P (February 1941) was a rotating version. Type 290 was an unsuccessful improved version; ultimately the related Type 291 was adopted. Typically it could detect an aircraft flying at 10,000ft at about 30nm, and a destroyer at 6–6.5nm. It could not detect a surfaced submarine beyond about 2,000 yds. Types 286P, 290 and 291 all used the same X-shaped antenna, and thus cannot be distinguished in photographs.

Centrimetric radar became practicable just as U-boats began attacking on the surface at night, where they were immune to Asdic. The key, the magnetron, was first tested in February 1940. Trials in November and December 1940 showed that centimetric radar could detect surfaced submarines. A prototype Type 271X was ready for trials on board the corvette

Orchis in February 1941; by that time 150 had already been ordered. In March, *Orchis* detected a surfaced submarine at 5,000 yds and a periscope at 1,500 yds. The much more powerful Type 271Q gained about 40 per cent in range. The radar was given a 'cheese' antenna with a relatively broad beam so that it would not be much affected by the ship's motion. Its protective 'lantern ' became typical of corvettes, frigates, and destroyers (the Type 272 destroyer version proved unsatisfactory). Type 273 was a large-ship version. Type 276 for destroyers had a more powerful magnetron (500 kW rather than 100 kW) and a single- rather than double-cheese antenna. None of these radars had an automatically-rotating antenna, so none had the PPI (map-like) display now typical of radars. At least as late as 1944, PPIs were associated with US-produced surface-search radars such as the SL on board Lend-Lease 'Captain' class frigates. The PPI offered sufficient definition to allow the ship to distinguish between several ships and craft operating in close proximity, which was why these ships were assigned to control coastal forces in the Channel.[14]

A 1943 radar generation shared transmitters (500 kW), receivers and displays (PPIs) but had different antennas: Types 293 and 277 (originally Type 273 Mk V). The former was in effect a Type 276 with its half-cheese tilted up at a 15° angle (to keep the beam clear of the water) and enlarged to give a narrower beam (4° rather than 6° wide). The beam, broad in elevation (35°), gave maximum probability of detecting an aircraft. This was a short-range high-definition air search set for target indication (mainly of air targets) to fire control. Range sufficed to give anti-aircraft guns time to react. Type 293M, which appeared in the Pacific in 1945, used a larger 'cheese' to form a narrower beam (3° wide in the horizontal), which in turn increased range; the post-war 293Q had a still narrower beam (2°). Under an April 1943 plan all fleet destroyers and all ships with primary anti-aircraft functions, such as the 'Hunts' and *Black Swans*, would receive Type 293 in place of Type 271 or 272. As of mid-1943 planned interim equipment was Type 272 Mk III and Type 291; once the new sets entered production (planned for January 1944), Type 291 would be eliminated because Type 293 offered sufficient air-search capacity. This was not actually done, but it shows what was wanted. As of the autumn of 1944, ships not to be modernised with Type 293 (*eg* destroyers prior to the 'S' class) were to have their Type 272s modified with power drives for continuous rotation and with PPIs, to become Type 272Ps. This version offered about 40 per cent more surface coverage than Type 293, but weighed about 70lbs more.

The wartime Target Indication Unit (TIU) Mk 2 was associated with the new generation of narrow-beam gunnery

13 For wartime radar development, see F A Kingsley (ed), *Radar and other Electronic Systems in the Royal Navy in World War 2* (Macmillan, London: 1995) and D Howse, *Radar At Sea: The Royal Navy in World War 2* (Macmillan, London: 1993).

14 The ships used were *Duff, Retalick, Stayner, Thornburgh, Torrington* and *Trollope. Byard, Duckworth, Essington* and *Calder* were under conversion to Coastal Forces Control Ships at the end of the war. For this purpose they were armed with three 3in/50, one twin 40mm (from the 'Colony' class), seven single 40mm, and ninety depth charges instead of the usual 110 (with four throwers). Work was ordered stopped on 23 August 1945.

radars, Types 275 and 262. It projected three bearing lines (strobes) on the PPI of a Type 293 radar. When one was positioned over a blip on the PPI, that bearing was sent automatically to the appropriate weapon. Similar devices could transmit two ranges from the unit's ranging element. Because targets were often designated visually, the TIU could also accept inputs from Visual Target Indication sights. Emergency destroyers completing after June 1944 got the TIU. By 1943, with TIU 2 only beginning development, it was already being criticised for its slow data rate (4 to 8 seconds), due to the slow rotation of the Type 293 radar. A contract was therefore let in October 1943 for a new Target Indication radar, which became the post-war Type 992. It was to have a data rate of no more than 1 second (*ie* 60 RPM rotation rate), to be able to handle eight targets (eight channels), and to be able to detect a small aircraft flying at 30,000ft at 30,000 yds with accuracy and resolution better than that of Type 293. A great post-war question was whether Type 992 and the associated TIU 3 should be fitted to all new ships. A radar, visual sights and a TIU constituted a Gunnery Direction System (GDS). Type 293 and TIU 2 were parts of GDS 2; the later GDS 2* used Type 293Q radar. Installation of GDS 2* and successors became a major part of post-war modernisation programmes.

The tall narrow antenna of Type 277 produced a slender beam less affected by reflection off the water, hence better for surface search. Because the antenna could be tilted up and down, Type 277 could also be used for height-finding, for gun fire-control and also for aircraft direction. Type 277 was expected to be so effective against surfaced U-boats that in 1942 DASW was willing to cut depth charge numbers by up to 20 per cent to compensate for its additional weight. The April 1943 plan assigned it to ships requiring better surface-search capability (A/S destroyers, sloops, frigates, and corvettes). In May 1943 Type 277 was ordered installed in all ASW ships (but this order was cancelled a year later for the 'Flower' class). Because Type 277 had only limited air-search capability, ships would retain Type 291 wherever possible. Later in the war, however, it was pointed out that German radars operating in the same (metric) band could pick up Type 291 transmissions, so that it might be quite dangerous to use. By January 1945 DSD was proposing that it *not* be fitted alongside Type 293. Because they were quite heavy, the new radars required lattice masts (ordered, for example, for fleet destroyers late in May 1943). However, many ships still had pole or tripod masts at the end of the war. Note that early radar installations often had the radar office near the antenna, to minimise signal loss in the cable or waveguide between antenna and office. All of these radars operated at S-band (10cm wavelength). Wavelength limited their ability to detect really small targets – like the snorkels the Germans introduced in 1944. By the

HMCS *Crescent* is shown in January 1952, essentially unchanged since completion. She was later rebuilt similarly to the British Type 15s. In January 1945 the Admiralty offered Canada a full destroyer flotilla for the Pacific War; the Canadian War Committee accepted the following month. Only two ships had been transferred by the end of the war. These were in addition to the two 'V' class destroyers transferred in 1944 as a result of an agreement reached at the 1943 Quebec conference (Quadrant). The Admiralty had offered *Eskimo* and *Tartar*, but the Canadians held out for more modern ships.

end of the war the British were developing Type 972, a shorter-wavelength set (X-band, 3cm), a modified Type 268 MTB radar with a new antenna.[15] The initial set of this type was the post-war Type 974, characterised as a high-definition surface-search radar.

By itself, search radar had limited value. At best a radar scope might offer a snapshot of the situation. What a tactical officer needed was a sense of what was happening, of where the objects seen on a screen were going. He needed a plot of successive radar observations. The idea of plotting was not at all new, but the idea that each ship had to maintain a running plot of observed targets was quite new. This running plot was also the obvious place to concentrate all other information on the tactical situation, both to make sense of the radar picture and to give the best possible basis for decision-making. The Royal Navy developed what it called an Action Information Organisation (AIO); the space in which the plot was maintained was alternatively called an Action Information Centre (AIC), an AIO, or an Operations Room (OR). The latter term predominates in this book. To some extent the AIO corresponded to the Filter Centre the RAF developed to use radar data for land-based air defence, an important function being to deduce what was actually happening from fragmented and intermittent radar and other data. In modern parlance the filter centre or the AIO was a tactical fusion centre. Because the AIO concentrated all available shipboard tactical information, ships were sometimes experimentally fought from it. However, officers preferred to be able to see the ships and aircraft around them. That was hardly irrational, since even the best radar could not adequately show quick manoeuvres.

Ships devised their own plotting techniques. However, the AIO concept envisaged the exchange of data between ships, so techniques in each fleet were standardised. Because ships were often transferred from fleet to fleet, in June 1943 the Admiralty set up a committee to standardise AIO practice. On 22 September Cdre(D) called a meeting of Home Fleet Staff Officers to decide AIO layouts for destroyers. Those from *Sioux* (Canadian 'V' class) and *Myngs* ('Z' class) produced layouts in which space was made by extending the existing Chart House/Plotting Office (to starboard abaft the pilothouse, alongside the Asdic office) to starboard to the side of B gun deck. This modification had recently been approved and carried out in *Kempenfelt* ('W' class leader) and was about to be done in *Vigilant*. Some ships were fitted while building. For the rest, the approved scheme promulgated in January 1945 envisaged an Operations Room (including the charthouse extended to starboard); a Target Indicating Room (with TIU), a device

allowing those on the open bridge (compass platform) to view the PPI and the plot in the Operations Room; and a 'Y' (radio/radar intercept) room (QD space). In leaders the Operations Room was a separate space; in destroyers it was combined with the HF/DF office. Radar pickets (not produced in wartime) would have an additional Aircraft Direction Room. Overall, the AIO demanded more space adjacent to, or more likely immediately under, the compass platform/bridge. The most extreme wartime solution to this problem was the redesigned bridge structure in the *Daring* class.

The 'Battles', 'Weapons', Canadian 'Tribals' and the later 'C' class had the full scheme (OR, TIR, QD). The 'Ca' class received the full scheme except for *Cambrian*, *Caprice* and *Cassandra*, completing in May and June 1944, which received only ORs. Of the 10th Emergency Flotilla, only *Zest*, *Zodiac*, *Zambesi* and *Zealous* received ORs, to suit their structures. Earlier ships of the 'A' and later classes were ordered fitted as convenient. As of the spring of 1944, a few ships were already being fitted: *Nubian* (full scheme but no TIU), *Kelvin* (full scheme, but no TIU), *Tartar* (OR only), *Obdurate* (full scheme, but no TIU), *Musketeer* (OR only), *Savage* (OR only), *Scourge* (OR plus QD but no 'Y' receiver), *Escapade* (OR only), *Derwent* (OR and QD), *Holderness* (OR and QD) and *Badworth* (OR and QD). That this list was so short illustrates just how hard-pressed British shipbuilders were in the spring of 1944, and also why the 'C' class was in such greater demand than earlier destroyer classes immediately after the war, before much could be done in the way of structural modification to existing ships.

Paralleling these search sets were fire-control sets. By 1940 the British had 50cm gunnery sets. These range-only sets were, in effect, electronic equivalents to optical range-finders. Type 285 was used for destroyer main batteries. Beam-switching, introduced in Type 285M/P (1942), made automatic tracking possible, including measurement of bearing rate. The radar produced two overlapping beams (left/right). Switching between them, the radar could tell whether it was centred on the target. Because the beam did not give elevation data, blind anti-aircraft fire was still impossible. A parallel set for heavy automatic guns was Type 282 (beam-switching version Type 282M).

The S-band replacement for Type 285 was Type 275, used in the late-war Mk VI director and also in the British version of the US Mk 37 director. Its pair of antennas (transmission and reception) could scan their beams conically, in effect beam-switching both vertically and horizontally. However, at least the original version did not track fully automatically. Instead, an operator below decks manually corrected for the beam position error measured by the radar. Once the Type 275 radar, with full blind-fire capacity, appeared, systems were designed to function in either aloft (director) or below-decks (radar) mode. The Tallboy radar console in the Transmitting Station could control the director remotely, and its integral

---

[15] Existing ship radars found it difficult to detect the snorkels first encountered during the Normandy landings. A meeting of the U-boat Warfare Committee on 7 December 1944 chose Type 972, a modified MTB radar (Type 268), as the best option. Thirty developmental radars were ordered at once, but pressure was relaxed after Germany surrendered (DA/SW argued that the Japanese would surely adopt the snorkel). Mass production was cancelled in favour of developing a successor which it was hoped would be superior to Type 277 as a general surface search set, and also as an anti-snorkel set.

barrage unit could be set for four separate barrage salvoes. Instead of S-band, the Type 262 successor to Type 282 operated at X-band.

Air-search radars competed for masthead space with HF/DF, which intercepted German U-boat radio signals and indicated their direction. Because such direction-finding was limited to the HF surface wave, detection generally indicated that the U-boat was within about 30nm, and a fast ship could be assigned to run down the line of bearing to deal with the U-boat. The main British set was FH 4. Late in 1940 installation of HF/DF in the main wireless office (*ie* on the foremast) was suspended to allow installation of Type 286. In November 1941 a stub pole mast for HF/DF was approved at the fore end of the after superstructure for the 'Q' and later classes.[16]

'Headache' (communications intercept) was another important passive sensor. Initially it referred to German voice radio, as used by E-boats (MTBs). *Ashanti* and *Matabele* had the first installations, late in 1941, at which time they were on Russian convoy runs. The next installations were on 'Hunt' class destroyers assigned to East Coast convoys, some fleet destroyers receiving 'Headache' late in 1942. 'Headache' was a form of 'Y' (electronic intercept). By 1945 there were four standard outfits: QC (30 kHz–30 MHz), QD (28–143 MHz), QN (130–210 MHz) and QP (300–650 MHz). Most fleet destroyers were scheduled to receive QC and QD; some would also have QN and QP.

By the end of the war some destroyers were being fitted with intercept and direction-finding sets intended to deal with enemy radar emissions (RU1 through RU4). Policy adopted in January 1945 was to fit RU1 and RU4 (when produced) aft as they were too heavy to replace HF/DF on the foremast.[17] Since HF/DF had to be removed from the foremast in any case, to clear arcs for Type 293, it was suggested that all intercept gear would be moved aft. The only problem was that offices had to be found close to the antennas, to limit the length of waveguides, and space aft was limited. In addition, space had to be found for the 'Y' (radio intercept) search equipment (Outfit QD) and the related antenna. Note that at least in post-war British warships 'Y' and radio warfare were always associated with the Third Wireless Office, which was always close to the Operations Room.

A tentative programme for escorts was to fit one-third of the 'Bay' class with HF/DF, one-third with RU1 and one-third with RU4. Others probably could not take the weight of the new radar intercept sets, and thus would get only HF/DF. Sloops, corvettes and 'Hunts' could take HF/DF or radar, not both. Since it would be a considerable time before direction-finders covering enemy radars became available for escorts, the issue was deferred.

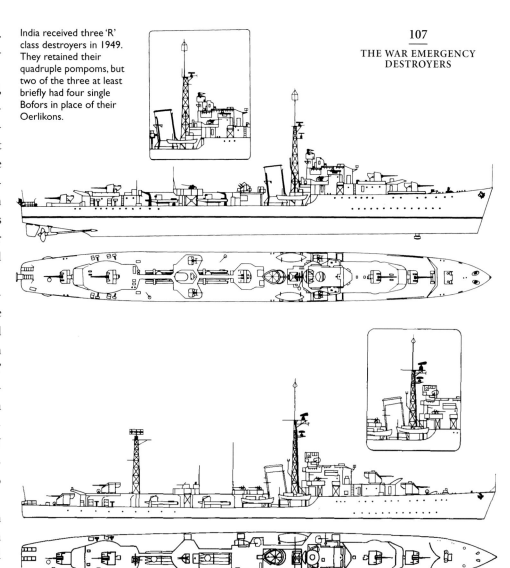

India received three 'R' class destroyers in 1949. They retained their quadruple pompoms, but two of the three at least briefly had four single Bofors in place of their Oerlikons.

A 'Z' class destroyer as modernised for Egypt by J. Samuel White between May 1963 and July 1964. Major changes were installation of a Mk 6 director on the bridge (presumably with Remote Power Control for the 4.7in guns) and fitting of a lattice mainmast carrying a Marconi AWS-10 air-search radar. The earlier Type 293 target-indication radar was retained (presumably upgraded to serve the new director and the associated TIU) and a new surface-search set (presumably Type 978) was installed. The HF/DF formerly carried at the masthead was removed. Light anti-aircraft armament was six Bofors. The ships retained their eight torpedo tubes and their depth charges; Squid was not installed. Both ships had been refitted, with few or no changes from their Royal Navy configuration, before transfer in 1955–6. Two sisters were transferred at the same time to Israel; they were not modernised in the 1960s. Unlike the Egyptians, the Israelis were interested in fitting Squid, but it seems that was not done. Of these four ships, the Israeli *Eilat* had the misfortune of being the first surface combatant in the world to be sunk by an anti-ship missile. In 2006 the Egyptian *El Fateh* survives as a museum ship, her sister-ship having been sunk in 1970. Despite her modifications, she is the closest surviving ship in the world to a Second World War Emergency destroyer.

[16] In July 1941 *Gurkha* and *Lance* received HF/DF forward (instead of Type 286M radar) specifically for accurate location of submarines in a special position. *Legion* and *Lively* received similar gear aft, so that they could retain ASV radars forward. Somewhat later all destroyers were ordered fitted with HF/DF.

[17] A distinction was drawn between 'Y' (communications intercept and exploitation) and 'U' (radar intercept and exploitation). 'Y' included HF/DF (FH 4) and VHF/DF (FV 5) and search facilities. Presumably 'U' was chosen because UHF was the earliest radar band. Q was radio intercept equipment, which was part of 'Y' ('Headache'). Both systems were in the 'Third Wireless Office', so designated to distinguish it from the main office and from the second (emergency) office. Different Q systems were designated by letter, eg QD, which was the standard set fitted in 1945. The standard systems of the 1940s and 1950s were QP (HF), QD (VHF), and QN (UHF); they were succeeded in the 1960s by QR (VHF) and QS (UHF). Post-war V/UHF radio-intercept antennas were the 'sword' (Outfit ACH) and 'derby' (Outfit AQA) for, respectively, VHF and UHF. QS also used the 'candlesticks' otherwise used for UHF communication. Radar intercept and DF systems were RU1 (100–500 MHz, metric radars), RU2 (500–1,000 MHz), RU3 (1,000–3,000 MHz), and RU4 (2,000–6,000 MHz). RU4 was tested on board the ex-minesweeper *Saltburn* in February–March 1945. At this stage it used a vertical part-cylindrical reflector with a pole carrying a receiver at its focus. Some ships on coastal escort duty used their HF/DF frame coils with VHF receivers as VHF direction-finders (FV3, a rush job operating at 41–46 MHz). Other FV sets used for radio warfare were FV4, a modified carrier homing set, and the late-war FV7 (30–100 MHz). A crash pre-production programme was to yield twelve each of RU1 and RU4 in July 1945, production sets following in October. These sets were installed in very limited numbers post-war. RU1 used a servoed vertical 6ft square grid (6ft×6ft×1ft, about 500lbs), turning between brackets on its vertical axis. RU3 and RU4 used cheese antennas like that of the Type 293 radar (36in wide×30in high×9in deep and 20in×15in×9in, respectively). Each destroyer flotilla would have three RU1, three HF/DF, and two RU4 ships. Later an RV series, presumably related to the RU series, was developed; RV2 was a special system developed for the D-Day landings. Some data are taken from ADM 239/604, a 1949 official history of wartime naval radio warfare, including the Type 650 and 651 sets developed to jam German air-to-surface guided missiles. Post-war radar receivers were designated in a U series, eg UA-3 or UAA-1 or UAT. Note that with the advent of UAA-1, ESM was moved into the Operations Room.

CHAPTER 6
New Destroyer Classes

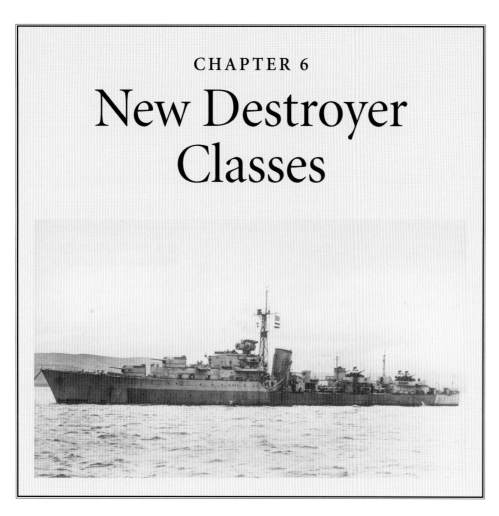

HMS *Lagos*, photographed as completed, shows the 4in gun just abaft her funnel.

The 1942 Fleet Destroyer ('Battle' Class)

DNO's initial answer to the mid-1940 question of providing a dual-purpose gun for destroyers was quite unsatisfactory: as recounted in Chapter 5, he could increase the elevation of the usual single mount only to 55°. Unfortunately dive bombers typically dropped their bombs at just such an angle; to hit them the gun needed at least another 20° of deflection angle, for a minimum acceptable elevation limit of 75°. Periodically the possibility of the army's 85° single mounting was raised, but it was always rejected as unsuited to a lively ship. The largest destroyer gun which could easily elevate to near-vertical angles was the 4in gun. It later became clear that DNO could modify the one truly dual-purpose mount firing a shell of roughly destroyer calibre, the twin between-decks 4.5in in an enclosed pillbox shield, which currently armed the new fleet carriers, the battlecruiser *Renown* and three rebuilt *Queen Elizabeth* class battleships. In these ships it fired fixed ammunition, while a destroyer would use separate shells and cartridge cases. The more serious problem was that the mount was quite heavy – which had not really mattered in the capital ships then carrying it.

From the Norwegian campaign (April–June 1940) on there was considerable interest in an all-dual-purpose destroyer battery. DTSD formalised it by stating, on 21 October, that Staff Requirements should require that all future long-range guns for destroyers and smaller ships be dual-purpose. He noted that all modern US destroyers had fully dual-purpose main batteries (their British detractors claimed that they were top-heavy). War experience showed that four guns should fire ahead, and also that the very expensive 62pdr was not really needed (the extreme range it offered could not really be exploited). DTSD was therefore willing to accept even the 4in gun. He wanted at least two such weapons, with 85° elevation, effective fire control, and ship stabilisation (as in a 'Hunt' or a converted anti-aircraft destroyer). In addition DTSD wanted two heavy close-range mountings (pompoms or twin Hazemeyer Bofors) and four Oerlikons; to get so much he was willing to surrender remote power control of the main battery (but without such control, the heavier weapons would be far less effective). ACNS(W) rejected the 4in as not 'man enough' for a destroyer; he wanted a dual-purpose 4.7in gun elevating to 85°. Deputy Controller urged a decision soon enough for a new gun mounting to be available in time for the next new construction programme (1942).

As a preliminary to writing a Staff Requirement for the 1942 destroyer, the idea was discussed at a 9 April 1941 Deputy Controller's meeting. Opinion did not unanimously favour the dual-purpose gun. DNC and DNO both advocated something like the 'Tribal', as it was then being rearmed, with six 4.7in and a twin 4in anti-aircraft gun. Director of Plans offered two possibilities, one with four single 62pdrs (one elevating to 85°, the others to 40°), and one with two twin low-angle 4.7in (50lbs) and one single high-angle gun. DTSD preferred the 4in 'L' class (four twin 4in). DTSD asked for sketches of all four alternatives, in each case with the two sets of quadruple torpedo tubes considered the minimum to have a good chance of hitting a fast freely-manoeuvring target (experience had also shown the value of having one mount trained on each beam at night). ACNS(H) rejected both Director of Plans' concepts, one because it offered too little ahead fire ('we always chase and seldom stop our enemy') and the other as overgunned. He thought that the greatest threat to destroyers and to the ships they escorted would be low-level air attack. He therefore preferred three twin 4.7in (40°) and four-cornered anti-aircraft fire (four twin Bofors), the extra light AA being paid for by eliminating one set of torpedo tubes.

Anti-aircraft fire was not the only controversial issue: ACNS(W) objected that too much was being sacrificed for a large torpedo battery, which would probably never be used, since with the advent of radar, surely classical night torpedo attacks were no longer possible. Furthermore, the rigid line of battle was obsolete; in future ships would fight in small flexible groups with greater freedom of manoeuvre, hence being bad torpedo targets. All of this proved quite premature. Moreover, like the US Navy, the British were apparently entirely unaware of Japanese torpedo tactics and capabilities, which would be demonstrated so dramatically in the South

HMS *Barfleur* is shown as completed. Note the 4in gun abaft the funnel, intended solely to fire starshell. It was necessary because otherwise one of the 4.5in mounts would have been dedicated to this purpose. The 4in was selected after several alternative flare projectors had been rejected. This gun had no associated director, hence was not considered useful for any other purpose. This class introduced the Mk VI director, with its Type 275 radar capable of blind anti-aircraft fire. *Barfleur* has the standard late-war destroyer rig, with Type 293 on the lattice foremast and Type 291 (air warning) on a stub mainmast aft. The topmast carries her HF/DF array. (A D Baker III)

Pacific. As for the British, not long after ACNS(W) spoke, Home Fleet destroyers made night attacks on the German battleship *Bismarck* on 26 May 1941. The effort to drive them off, inescapable in view of the threat they represented, kept her fire-control crews awake and may have contributed substantially to their failure to deal with the heavy ships which sank her the next day. Other British destroyer torpedo attacks contributed substantially to sinking the *Scharnhorst* in 1943. The threat of torpedo attacks helped protect convoys both in the Mediterranean and in the Arctic from major enemy surface attackers, and near the end of the war a British destroyer flotilla torpedo attack sank the Japanese heavy cruiser *Haguro*. Postwar, the potential anti-raider role of the torpedo kept this weapon on board British destroyers.

As in the Emergency programme, operational endurance would drive up the size of the ship. DTSD wanted 4,000nm at 12–14kts. He suspected that alone would require something like a 'J'-class hull. VCNS supported DTSD: for every day a destroyer fired at another ship she fired twenty times at aircraft. The existing 4in gun was not enough. He agreed with the ACNS(H) proposal for a four-cornered close-range anti-aircraft battery, using twin Bofors rather than pompoms, but also wanted at least six, and probably eight, Oerlikons. VCNS agreed with ACNS(W) that opinion was so divided that it would take a conference or perhaps a committee to decide the issue. Even so, on 14 May 1941 Controller felt comfortable asking DNC to sketch the ship VCNS implicitly supported, armed with four dual-purpose 4.7in guns (four twin 4in as alternative) and four-cornered close-range anti-aircraft weapons. This was the beginning of the 'Battle' design.

To DNC, the only dual-purpose 4.7in gun on the table was a notional single 80° mounting, which weighed about as much as a twin 4in. Unfortunately each of the four Hazemeyers (twin Bofors) weighed about as much as a single 4.7in 40° mount-

HMS *Lagos*, photographed on 28 December 1945, was a 1942 'Battle' whose 4in gun had been replaced by two single Bofors abreast. Twin Bofors are visible on the amidships platform and on the after superstructure; the single mounts elsewhere are less visible. (A&J Pavia via John Mortimer)

ing. DNC's initial approach would have displaced 2,250 tons, which was too large for yards which typically built destroyers side by side. It was also too large for Controller. Cutting two of the twin Bofors and using more compact (modified 'Tribal' rather than 'L' class) machinery made it possible to reduce standard displacement to 2,000 tons, but that still seemed a bad bargain. DNC then suggested using a notional twin between-decks mounting whose weight he estimated on the basis of the twin 4.5in. He argued that to be practicable any high-angle destroyer mounting had to use a between-decks design, the crew and ammunition supply parties working under cover and the disability of very high trunnions being markedly reduced. DNC offered three gun mounts (one aft), fearing criticism that a ship at least as large as a 'Tribal' would have only half the battery. The three designs were submitted on 22 June 1941. Controller was impressed by the extent to which the Bofors mounts forced up the size of the ship, so he asked whether destroyers might be limited to Oerlikons only. Eliminating the Bofors in DNC's six-gun ship would cut tonnage by 75 tons and increase speed by a knot.

Only DNC's six-gun option approached what was wanted. Canvassing destroyer officers, Controller concluded that all of them wanted four main battery guns firing forward, at least some heavy HA guns, and plenty of Oerlikons. If 4.7in guns were wanted the ship would be expensive, with twins forward. The only acceptable cheap destroyer would be a super Emergency type with three twin 4in. A meeting on 11 July 1941 produced a set of draft Staff Requirements. Speed would not be less than 32kts deeply loaded, and endurance would be 7,000nm at 12kts 'clean' (as in an Intermediate); it was not clear that the 4,000nm at 20kts quoted by DNC would meet this requirement. For good seakeeping the ship would have 'Tribal' class bows and the 'J' class bridge, which had proven quite satisfactory. She would be stabilised for long-range anti-aircraft accuracy. The main battery would be two twin dual-purpose 4.7in. Controller asked for a sketch of a ship with the desirable close-range battery (four twin Bofors, six Oerlikons), but for comparison he soon also asked for a version with a twin 4in gun in place of two of the Bofors, and for one with eight Oerlikons but no Bofors at all. The ship would also have a depth-charge battery capable of firing ten-charge patterns (*ie* four throwers).[1]

A sketch design was submitted to the Board in September. Not only did the destroyer officers prefer having both twin mounts forward, that was also the only way to accommodate the very heavy close-range battery.[2] The two mounts were unusually widely spaced (and widely spaced from the bridge) to give generous after arcs. It was unacceptable to devote one of the mounts to fire starshell, so the sketch design showed two starshell mortars (and two Oerlikons) on a midships platform. Alternatives were to modify some of the Bofors guns to fire starshell, or to place a single 4in gun on the platform (as was actually done). Diesel generator capacity was increased so that the ship could fire her power-operated guns even in harbour, with boilers cold.[3] Compared to DNC's most recent sketch design, this one was somewhat larger (2,280 tons vs 2,250 tons) with a more powerful modified 'L'-class plant producing 50,000 SHP rather than 48,000 SHP (for 31.5kts deep, half a knot less than Controller had wanted). She would have 20 per cent better endurance than the 'J' and 'K' class (but 5 per cent less than the 'Q' class): 4,400nm at 20kts (clean) or 7,700nm at 12kts. As in the recent past, above-water 'peace tanks' were rejected as a way of providing the desired endurance.

The Board approved the sketch and the Staff Requirements on 9 October, but the design was still controversial. First Sea Lord accepted it 'in deference to professional opinion' but feared that so large a ship could not be built in sufficient numbers. Ultimately the Royal Navy found itself adopting a high-low mix approach, in which big fleet destroyers were built alongside ships of about Emergency size. The 1942 Programme thus included three flotillas of Emergency Destroyers (see Chapter 5). DNC was surprised that, after all the destroyer officers had favoured concentrating the armament forward, DOD(H) argued for guns firing aft. Two sketch designs showed that any other gun arrangement would require an unacceptably larger ship.

DNO developed a new between-decks mounting, firing 4.5in rather than 4.7in shells (the 4.5in shell was actually heavier, at 55lbs). Mock-ups were inspected at Barrow on 28 August and 20 October 1941. Progress was quick because this was a version of an existing mounting: the prototype tested on board HMS *Savage* was modified from a spare made for the carrier *Illustrious*. The guns were to be controlled by a new Mk VI director using a new anti-aircraft computer (Flyplane). The new computer system and its radar (Type 275) in turn demanded more space. Plans called for installing stabilisers, but internal space was very tight. Instead of stabilisers the ships could stow more oil (up to 135 tons, to supplement the usual supply of 700 tons) or the 100 kW diesel generator otherwise located in the engine room. The Transmitting Station (fire control computer space) could be lowered to protect it. Ultimately the stabiliser was omitted from all but two ships, *Camperdown* and *Finisterre*. There was some fear that, because she was so much larger than earlier destroyers, the new one would be far less manoeuvrable, but trials at Haslar suggested that she would turn faster and tighter than any previous destroyer except the

---

[1] As of January 1942 the approved depth charge battery was four throwers and two rails, with sixty depth charges. When fitted with TSDS the ship would land her after set of torpedo tubes and her port depth charge rail.
[2] As expressed in a signal of 6 April 1942 to British Admiralty Delegation in Washington, presumably for the benefit of the US Navy. 'Battle' Class Cover.

[3] Each turbo-generator was rated at 200 kW rather than the 155 kW of the Emergency Destroyer. The harbour fighting load was 200 kW. Typically one diesel was placed in each machinery space. In 1941 the most powerful diesel-generator was 75 kW, so a third was needed. Given a damage report on HMS *Janus*, it had to be in a compartment without steam lines. Initially it was to have been forward of the machinery, but by February 1942 it had been placed in the gearing room (and all were 100 kW units). There was insufficient space for a proposed fourth generator.

small 'Hunt'. DNC found the results very reassuring, showing that the conscious effort to hold down length had been well justified. As of April 1942 design displacement was 2,285 tons, the growth of 35 tons being accounted for by increased electric power, the use of a 4in starshell gun (immediately abaft the funnel), and provision for Arctic operations. The sixteen large 1942 Fleet Destroyers all received 'Battle' names.

The new destroyer, so much larger than earlier ones, attracted strong criticism from the fleet, even from the commander of the Home Fleet destroyers. Many argued that the ships were defensively armed, and that they were too weak compared to US destroyers of similar size. Given this sentiment, in mid-1942 the Future Building Committee decided that in future ships of this type the 4in starshell gun would be replaced with a standard 55° 4.5in gun, which could be considered part of the primary armament as well as a starshell gun.[4] Weight compensation would be the removal of one twin Bofors and one Oerlikon. This change was incorporated in the 1943 'Battle' class.

By the time the ships were being completed more powerful close-range anti-aircraft guns were badly wanted. In April 1945 the Oerlikons on the wings of the deck below the bridge wings were ordered replaced by single power-worked 2pdr Mk XVI* (single power-worked 40mm Mk VII were rejected as causing too much congestion). In June 1945 C-in-C Pacific Fleet asked that the 4in gun be replaced by two single

[4] From a history of the 'Battle' class compiled by DTSD for the Future Building Committee as TSD 3005/44, in ADM 116/5151.

As flagship of Reserve Forces, HMS *Trafalgar* shows her full battery of four (albeit cocooned) Hazemeyer Bofors guns, as well as cocooned depth charge throwers, on 21 March 1952.

RIGHT: HMS *Sluys*, photographed in 1949, has already lost her two amidships twin Bofors. She retained six single mounts (one right aft is not visible) and two twins.

BELOW: HMS *Hogue*, photographed on 7 March 1957, illustrates the modernised version of the 1942 'Battle' class, in which a single Squid replaced the single 40mm gun right aft. The radar is Type 293. Some modernised ships, such as HMS *Vigo*, retained only one twin Bofors aft.

Bofors. Initially ships received hand-worked Army-type Bofors (Mk III LS); plans called for providing gyro gunsights (equivalent to the US Mk 14) for ships completing after September 1945, and power-worked Mk VII mounts for ships completing after December 1945. The typical early post-war battery included six single Bofors: one forward of the bridge on B gun deck, two in the bridge wings, two replacing the 4in gun, and one on the quarterdeck (replaced on modernisation by a single Squid). This was in addition to four twin Bofors: two on the structure between the two sets of torpedo tubes and two on the after deckhouse, for a total of fourteen 40mm guns (the two midships twins were removed on modernisation). Only five ships (*Armada*, *Barfleur*, *Camperdown*, *Hogue* and *Trafalgar*) ever had the 4in gun. As flares were still desirable for precise night firing, ships eventually had a medium-range rocket flare launcher which could be mounted on the side of a gun mount.

The 1943 Fleet Destroyer (Repeat 'Battle' Class)

Work on choices for the 1943 Programme began in the spring of 1942, and it was by no means obvious that the big 'Battles' would be repeated.[5] Six years of Staff discussion of destroyer priorities had produced no real agreement as to roles, types and the characteristics of Fleet and Intermediate destroyers. DGD upset the logic of the 'Battle' class by telling the Future Building Committee that in the face of the worst air threat, the dive bomber, one twin predictor-controlled twin Bofors gun (such as a Hazemeyer) was roughly equivalent to the pair of high-angle 4.5in. He conceded that the heavier gun was much more valuable against torpedo bombers, but for that role it did not have to elevate to 80°. In the 'Battle' class the price of elevating beyond 55° was about 300 tons. The heavy elaborate between-decks mounting could be abandoned. For DNC, the weight saved could buy a third twin 4.5in (all having 55° elevation) and pentad rather than quadruple tubes, while still re-

ducing displacement. Probably mainly because arranging the three mounts required greater length (382ft), he found that the ship would displace 2,445 tons (standard), more than a 'Battle', rather than the 2,000 tons he had hoped for.[6]

Given DGD's views, would it be better to arm a ship entirely with close-range weapons? It was now estimated that a predictor-controlled twin Bofors would be effective out to about 1,600 yds, giving it a 20 per cent chance of bringing down an aircraft with six seconds' fire. That was too little to make such a ship an attractive proposition as an escort. Even so, the idea was pursued to some extent.

On 1 August 1942 a frustrated Churchill told the War Cabinet that he was inclined to cancel the big destroyers altogether in favour of more numerous smaller ones, to be completed in one rather than two years.[7] To outflank the Admiralty, the War Cabinet ordered the issue investigated by the Secretary of State for Dominion Affairs, the Foreign Secretary and the Minister of Production, in conjunction with the Board. Controller pointed out that building times for large and small destroyers were not really so different. The main differences would be in cost (£250,000) and in complement (44 per cent more in the larger ship). There was, moreover, a critical displacement, about 1,700 tons. Some yards could not build anything much larger. Because the notional single 4.5in high-angle gun probably could not be built, the all-anti-aircraft battery for a 1,700-ton destroyer would have to be three twin 4in. Churchill was right: it was impossible to use the 'Battle' design for all of the 1943 ships. On the other hand, DNC's idea of high-angle Hazemeyers complementing a low-angle main battery was rejected. In mid-August DTSD laid out the only two realistic choices: the big destroyer with four dual-purpose guns, all forward; and the Intermediate, for which he favoured the current four 55° single 4.5in guns. What had to be decided was the proper proportion between them.

Impressed by both the dual-purpose logic and by the fleet's distaste for the unbalanced main battery arrangement, on 4 September DNC proposed a larger ship armed with three twin

---

[5] The Board was particularly impressed by a letter dated 18 April 1942 from an experienced destroyer officer, Captain P J Mack, rejecting the ship with all four guns forward. He would much prefer a 'J'-class configuration with guns capable of 55° or 60° elevation, plus a twin Bofors or quadruple 2pdr in the same position as in a 'J', five or more Oerlikons, and eight or ten torpedo tubes.

[6] Particulars from Notebook 608/1, p 217.
[7] Minutes of 3rd Future Building Committee meeting, 1942, in ADM 116/5150.

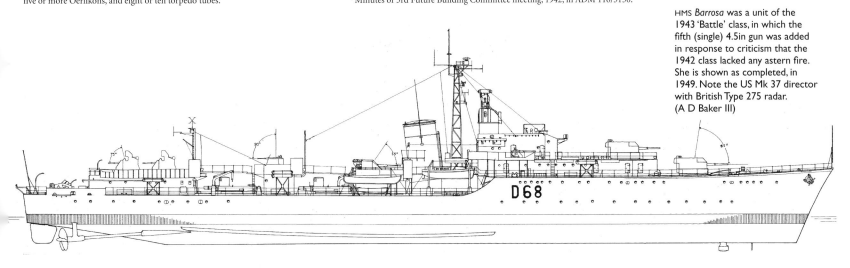

HMS *Barrosa* was a unit of the 1943 'Battle' class, in which the fifth (single) 4.5in gun was added in response to criticism that the 1942 class lacked any astern fire. She is shown as completed, in 1949. Note the US Mk 37 director with British Type 275 radar. (A D Baker III)

The newly-completed 1943 'Battle' class destroyer HMS *Agincourt*, in July 1947. Her distinguishing features are the US Mk 37 director and the fifth 4.5in gun, abaft the funnel.

4.5in mounts, all the between-decks type. His exercise designing the ship with three twin 55° mounts seems to have inspired him to eliminate two twin Bofors as weight compensation. DNC that the ship would displace 2,500 tons. Probably because the three 4.5in mounts effectively set the ship's length, it came out to the same 382ft as the ship with three 55° mounts.[8] The number of torpedo tubes would be set by the ship's length. The design was soon modified to show four or more fixed torpedo tubes firing 15° off the bow, fleet sentiment (as reflected by the Future Building Committee) favouring salvoes which could be fired nearly dead ahead. This design was not pursued further; it was significant mainly for showing how easily destroyer size could jump up.

Attempts to develop a new large-destroyer design were derailed because by late in 1942 DNO was offering a lighter-weight twin high-angle 4.5in mounting better adapted to destroyer installation, the upper deck Mk VI.[9] It was expect-

ed to weigh only two-thirds as much as the between-decks Mk IV. There was no point in a new 1943 design because the new mounting would not be ready in time. Critics of the 'Battle' class were compelled to agree that it was the best available compromise. The big jump in capability would come in 1944. An agreement was very nearly reached to abandon the designation 'destroyer' altogether.[10]

The 1943 ships did show two important improvements: a new US-supplied Mk 37 fire control system, and the single 4.5in gun. DNO described the Mk 37 as considerably in advance of anything likely to be available from British sources for some time. The Royal Navy had been trying to buy it in quantity since 1941. It could be adapted to the British 5.25in, 4.5in and 4in guns, but each version required considerable effort to adapt it to the required set of ballistics. The US Navy chose 5.25in and 4.5in. It offered forty-two fire control systems, of which four were assigned to the battleship *Vanguard*. Of the other thirty-eight, with 4.5in ballistics, twelve were needed for the three *Ark Royal* class carriers, so the twenty-six remaining set the maximum number of 1943 'Battle' class destroyers, but there was considerable confusion as to how many would be built to a repeat 1942 design and how many to a new design (see below). Building capacity set the entire 1943 Programme at forty destroyers, as in 1942. Initial plans (October 1942) called for four flotillas of large and one of smaller destroyers, but Mk 37 supplies limited the large de-

[8] Future Building Committee minutes show DNC designs BA and BC. BA was 2,750 tons standard (400ft long) with three twin (notional) 55° upper deck mounts, four twin Bofors, eight Oerlikons, two pentad torpedo tubes and seventy depth charges. BC was 3,250 tons (410ft), with three 80° between-decks mounts, two twin Bofors, eight Oerlikons, two pentads, and seventy depth charges. Each version had a 60,000 SHP powerplant, compared to 50,000 SHP in the 1942 'Battle'. Speeds (deep load) were, respectively, 32kts and 30.5kts. A somewhat later Design BD had three twin upper deck mounts, with two fixed twin torpedo tubes or two twin Oerlikons. Design QA showed that a fresh design for what amounted to a standard War Emergency destroyer ('Q') with a second twin Bofors and RPC would increase standard displacement to 2,000 tons (360ft).
[9] This expectation proved exaggerated. In 1942 it was hoped that Mk VI would not exceed 40 tons. As built, typical revolving mass weight was 44 tons. Unlike previous mountings, Mk IV was lighter than expected (or perhaps DNC and DNO made more pessimistic early estimates). Although weight per mounting was taken as 60 tons, typical revolving weight was 46.05 tons plus 4.7 tons for hoists and 5 tons for gun units, a total of 50.75 tons. In April 1943 the required rate of fire for Mk VI was increased from 14 to 18 rpg/minute, compared to about 12 rpg/minute for Mk IV. That cut the hoped-for reduction of complement compared with Mk IV to no more than one or two per mounting. Moreover, because all of the mechanism was above decks, the gunhouse was considerably taller than that of Mk IV.

[10] Minutes of 3rd and 7th Future Building Committee meetings, 1943, cited in TSD 3005/44, above.

stroyers to slightly over three flotillas, the remaining two being Intermediates.

A third possible improvement could not be carried out in this class. Much impressed by the survival of uss *Kearny* after she was torpedoed off Iceland in 1941, the British became interested in her type of alternating engine and boiler rooms (an idea raised and rejected for the 'Tribal' class). DNC doubted that this arrangement would really improve survivability. He feared that a change in machinery arrangement would jeopardise production; the Emergency Destroyer programme had been successful because it changed so little from year to year. New machinery would be justifiable only if it were kept in production for at least three years' worth of large destroyers. Given strong interest in the alternating arrangement, DNC used it in a series of designs he prepared in October 1942 as alternatives to a repeat 1942 destroyer. Despite her more compact turbines and boilers, *Kearny* required 127ft to house the 50,000 SHP which took up 121ft in the 1942 Destroyer. In August 1942 E-in-C reported that a 50,000 SHP plant with alternating engine and boiler rooms would be 122ft long (680 tons), compared to 118½ft (655 tons) for the plant already designed into the ship. The new plant might also need wider beam and a special hull shape. A few days later DNC asked for a 60,000 SHP version, presumably for the 1943 Fleet Destroyer. In September E-in-C offered a 54,000 SHP plant (130ft, 845 tons, with four boilers), but said that he would prefer to hold to the current 50,000 SHP (he could use the existing turbines and boilers). For production reasons he preferred to hold to the existing 50,000 SHP plant.

The great question was how many 1943 ships could benefit from the lighter-weight Mk VI mounting. In April 1943 Controller decided to limit the 1943 'Battle' class to two flotillas (sixteen ships), the next one (eight ships, or ten including the last of the twenty-six) receiving the new mountings. Their beam would increase from 40ft 3in to 41ft. DNO hoped to deliver between three and four Mk VI mountings per month beginning in December 1944, which could arm twenty-one repeat 'Battles' or fourteen three-mount ships of a new design. The likely timing of construction led to plans, as of August 1943, to build twenty-one ships to a slightly modified 1942 design, the last five being ordered to a new and perhaps larger design, which would probably have three Mk VI. The first of these would complete about February–March 1946. However, as of November 1943 plans called for arming the last two flotillas (actually ten ships) with Mk VI (two, not three, mounts). These ships would have the 4in starshell gun. Displacement would be 2,327 (rather than 2,292) tons standard and 3,229 (rather than 3,185) tons fully loaded. Ultimately only the last five 1943 ships were ordered built with Mk VI instead of Mk IV mounts. They were cancelled at the end of the war; only the first 1943 'Battle' class flotilla, with its between-decks mounts, was completed.

As the 1943 'Battle' design was completed, the new STAAG twin Bofors was being designed. Plans for the first two 1943 flotillas called for three STAAGs (in place of the four Hazemeyers in the 1942 ships), but given the shortage of mountings the ships were completed with two STAAGs and a Mk V. As in the 1942 ships, single Mk VII Bofors were mounted on B gun deck under the bridge wings (despite the fact that the bridge was a foot wider than in the 1942 ships). The planned centreline mounting on B gun deck forward of the bridge was eliminated. Because their 4.5in Mk VI mountings were expected to be lighter, the last two 1943 flotillas were initially assigned four STAAGs (plus four power-operated twin Oerlikons). As STAAG weight continued to grow, this battery was cut back to that of the other 1943 ships. However, the Australian 'Battles', which had had the new Mk VI mount and the British Mk VI director, and were slightly beamier (41ft), had three STAAGs (one between the tubes, two further aft), plus six single Mk VII Bofors (one before and two abeam the bridge, two abaft the funnel, one on the quarterdeck alongside the Squid) and two pentad torpedo tubes. They had a single Squid aft. To clear the higher B mount, the bridge was raised, and to keep it clear of smoke the funnel was given a

prominent cap. This design, rather than the larger *Daring*, was the post-war mobilisation prototype, to have been put into production in the event of an emergency.

By the time the 1942 'Battle' design was complete, British officers were well acquainted with contemporary US destroyers, which many of them considered superior to DNC's products. Again and again during the war DNC and DNO took

The Mk VI 4.5in gun, shown here on board HMAS *Anzac*, was the key to placing more guns on board a ship of acceptable size. This photograph was taken in Sasebo Harbour, Japan, on 18 August 1951.

pains to point out that US hulls and weapons did not meet British criteria. However, after wartime visit to the United States Captain Bellars of DTSD branch observed that, despite supposed deficiencies, 'their ships do not sink any more easily than ours'. DNC's earliest defense, in December 1943, was based on a comparison between the 'Battle' class and the US *Sumner* (DD 692) class, which seems particularly to have impressed British naval officers. He attacked the idea that the ship was the same size as a 1942 'Battle'. Although the US Navy rated *Sumner* as 2,200 tons standard, under British rules her standard displacement would be 2,412 tons as designed, and probably closer to 2,512 tons as completed. Based on the inclining experiment for HMS *Barfleur*, the standard displacement of a 1943 'Battle' would be 2,397 tons. A 1942 'Battle' devoted 14.2 per cent of her standard displacement to armament, compared to 14.1 per cent for the *Sumner* as designed. DNC estimated that the considerable increase in anti-aircraft weapons in ships as completed would increase the proportion of standard displacement devoted to armament in *Sumner* to 15.6 per cent, which was not too impressive. He did admit that the US Navy got much more for its money. Virtually all British mountings were considerably heavier than their US counterparts. DNC estimated that the US twin Bofors weighed half as much as a STAAG: even the quadruple weighed only 75 per cent as much as the STAAG. These were probably understatements.

US hulls were substantially lighter. The British had much

higher freeboard forward, which they (probably correctly) considered essential for sea-keeping; overall, British destroyers performed far better in rough weather. They also had more deck covering, which DNC considered the minimum acceptable for reasonable living conditions (he later admitted that he could save 10 tons by adopting the US practice of painting decks instead of covering them with linoleum). The US Navy also accepted a shallow-plate bilge keel in place of the deep-vee type the British favoured, which DNC considered essential to good seakeeping. Weight devoted to protection in the 'Battle' seemed to be about twice that in a *Sumner*. The US Navy saved hull weight by cutting superstructure volume: it provided half as much living space for officers and about two-thirds as much for enlisted men. British destroyers were burdened by heavy electric equipment and wiring. *Sumner* had about half the electrical weight of the comparable 1943 'Battle'. A 1944 'Battle' (*ie Daring* class) required 40 tons for two 300 kW turbo-generators and three 100 kW diesels; the US Navy needed 24 tons for two 300 kW turbo-generators and one 100 kW diesel.

DNC claimed that the 1943 'Battle' had 10 per cent better endurance. The US Navy agreed: it stretched most of the *Sumner*s (to become the *Gearing* class) specifically to add tankage. Because it was willing to replenish ships at sea, the US Navy could make do with a much smaller stores and provisions load; DNC thought that applying this approach to British destroyers would save 15 tons. American ship's boats were

The Royal Australian Navy version of the 'Battle' class: HMAS *Anzac*, 1954.

about 5 tons lighter, but it seemed unlikely that the Royal Navy would adopt that approach (moreover, British wartime practice was to carry three boats, where the US Navy found one or two sufficient).

Compared to a *Sumner*, a 'Battle' hull was 90 tons heavier, of which 30 tons of the savings in the US ship could be attributed to higher stress in the keel, 5 tons to a shallower bilge keel, and 5 tons to a lighter forecastle deck. On the basis of his analysis, DNC proposed to save hull weight and thus to increase the proportion available for armament. Adopting a higher keel stress would save 25 tons, and another 25 tons could be saved on framing by welding and using special steel shapes. The thickness of the exposed part of the forecastle deck was excessive. American ships lacked the breakwater typical of British designs, but that was really not needed given the sturdy structure of the new 4.5in mounting. Using aluminium for superstructures, as in the United States, could save 10 tons, but that might not be practicable in wartime.

Criticism by British naval officers persisted through the war, as they came into contact with heavily-armed foreign destroyers (and other classes of warships). For example, in 1944 HMS *Vernon*, the torpedo development establishment, reported both Japanese and German destroyers greatly superior to in their torpedo batteries, in features such as power training and re-load gear. Surely DNC's attitude towards topweight was unduly conservative? Told that British destroyers could not af-

HMS *Battleaxe*, shown on 16 January 1948, was one of four large Intermediate destroyers intended as successors to the Emergency class. She was completed with double Squid in place of B twin 4in gun. The array of four short dipoles atop her foremast is for VHF/DF; the short pole mast aft carries Type 291. Secondary weapons are two STAAGs aft and two single Bofors abeam the bridge.

ford more torpedoes because that would cost vital gun power, *Vernon* replied that ' British ships are also inferior in gunpower and indeed compensating superiority in any salient feature is hard to find . . .'. Director of Plans, who generally agreed, suggested that the Staff conduct a wider analysis, to be co-ordinated by DTSD, which was responsible for the basic characteristics of British destroyers. DTSD strongly disagreed that British destroyers were inferior in gun power or in any other basic characteristic to foreign contemporaries of similar displacement. However, because so many officers at sea had views similar to *Vernon*'s, DTSD agreed that it was time for an analysis. DTSD suggested using the 1943 'Battle' rather than the familiar Emergency Destroyer as the British example. Director of Plans pointed out that serious limitations had been accepted in order to produce the latter quickly enough, reflecting British unpreparedness in 1939 rather than DNC's competence. The foreign ships were the US *Sumner*, the German 'Narvik' series and the Japanese *Asahio* (their last pre-war class). No copy of the resulting February 1945 paper, TSD 737/44, has been found, but the Covers include DNC's comments. Given limited information about the German and Japanese ships, DNC seems to have concentrated on the *Sumner*.

The 1943 Intermediate Destroyer ('Weapon' Class)

By the spring of 1942, when the 1943 Programme was being formulated, it was clear that the Emergency type was obsolete. In March 1942 DNC was told that the ship would have four or five single dual-purpose mountings. The decision having been taken to standardise on 4.5in guns, it seemed that the choice lay between the existing 55° mounting (producing, in effect, a War Emergency destroyer), the undesirable army mounting, or something new. There was hardly time to produce a new single mounting. DGD's preference for predictor-controlled Bofors guns seemed to offer a way out. A battery limited to three sextuple predictor-controlled Bofors, four twin Oerlikons, and depth charges (seventy charges) was proposed.[11] DGD claimed that this battery offered at least three times the value (albeit at short ranges) of the new fleet destroyer, and six times the value of a War Emergency destroyer against torpedo bombers. DTSD was skeptical; surely such firepower was not worth the loss of other destroyer capability (he suggested building carriers instead). Director of Plans formally rejected the idea altogether in mid-May, on the ground that a more conventional destroyer was a better compromise. A meeting on 17 July 1942 called by ACNS(W) agreed that there did exist a requirement for special AAW and ASW screening vessels for carriers (one likely role of the all-close-range ship), but that such escorts probably should not be built at the expensive of fleet destroyers. If they were built, the main requirements would be seakeeping and endurance comparable to that of the carri-er they would screen. DTSD and DNC were therefore to produce outline Staff Requirements for two alternative types, one with the all-close range armament. The other would have 4in, 4.5in or 5in guns, so that if the proximity fuse then under development were successful, it could be used in such a ship (such fuses could not be used with smaller guns). The sextuple mounts were so massive that they made the ship far too large. After a Future Building Committee meeting in October 1942 she was cut down to two twin Bofors, two twin Oerlikons, three or four fixed torpedo tubes on each side, and seventy depth charges (ten-pattern). All of this was much lighter than a more conventional armament (166 tons of armament at deep load, compared to 204 tons for a typical 4.5in ship), but it also made it clear that she was not worth the trouble.

DGD's emphasis on the Bofors seemed to justify a reversion to the 55° gun. For the initial designs, the minimum close-range battery was two twin predictor-controlled Bofors. This was effectively an 'S' class destroyer with armament weight increased by 26 tons (16 tons of it in the Bofors). In June 1942 the designers were asked for 1,800-ton ships with beam limited to 36ft 6in to fit all available building slips, particularly John Brown's two covered slips. Endurance would be 4,000nm at 20kts (as in a 'Tribal').[12] This was a bit larger than an Emergency destroyer. To achieve the desired 32kts the ship would need 42,000 SHP (speed fell to 31.5kts when the 40,000 SHP Emergency powerplant was used).

Given increasing interest in alternating boiler and engine rooms, on 12 August Director of Plans asked for such a plant. He also wanted greater endurance at higher speed (20–25kts) for Pacific operations. E-in-C considered the existing Emergency Destroyer too small to accommodate alternating plants. To accommodate the desired machinery, the beam limit was relaxed to 36ft 10in. Because it was longer than conventional machinery, it was difficult to accommodate four separate main battery mounts. Instead, in September DNC offered two twin 55° 4.5in guns (redesigned 'J' class mounts), one twin Bofors (probably in B position), two quadruple torpedo tubes (one twin Bofors as alternative to the after torpedo tubes), four twin Oerlikons, and ten-pattern depth charges, with greater endurance (4,700nm at 20kts) and a speed (deep) of 31.5kts. This ship would have displaced about 1,870 tons.

Now DGD reversed himself. He admitted that heavier guns would gain enormously in effectiveness as soon as improvements already in train were made, such as remote power control (RPC) and electric (remote) fuse-setting. The proximity fuse promised even better results. The 4in gun was once again worth examining: compared to a single 4.5in it offered a higher rate of fire which more than made up for its lighter shell.

The low-end destroyer was growing too large for its intended role, which was quantity production on available slips. About

---

[11] Details in Notebook 608/1, dated 27 July 1942. Armament weight would have been 184 tons, the three Bofors amounting to 60 tons without their ammunition (which came to 17.3 tons of ready-use ammunition and another 69 tons in magazines).

[12] Notebook 608/1 (W G Warren).

October 1942 the designers were told to cut back, to the earlier maximum beam of 36ft 6in and to a displacement of 1,700 tons. Close-range armament would include one or two twin Bofors, and the ships would have one torpedo tube (or none). Endurance would be 4,700nm at 20kts. Speed (deep) had to be at least 30.5kts. A new round of designs was ordered: one with four single 55° RPC 4.5in guns, lone with three twin 4in RPC guns (the dual-purpose battery), and one with three single 80° RPC 4.5in guns. DGD quickly killed the last as unrealistic, as similar designs had been killed in the past.

The only really attractive option was the design with three twin 4in. Eliminating one mount made it possible to envisage a shorter hull, which in turn might accommodate a smaller powerplant. Thus the initial sketch showed a 340ft × 36ft 6in hull (2,450 tons deep), with a 37,000 SHP powerplant (35,900 SHP would give the required 30.5kts). By this time (October 1942), the Future Building Committee was interested in fixed torpedo tubes, which could reduce the length the torpedo battery took up. DTSD visited Bath on 20 October 1942 to see the design alternatives. He ordered a fresh design with three twin 4in guns, two twin Bofors, two twin Oerlikons, eight fixed torpedo tubes, and five-pattern depth charges (seventy charges). At this stage the ship was 345ft long. It was lengthened another 5ft to 350ft (QJ). Standard displacement was 1,825 tons (2,575 tons deep load). At a Future Building Committee meeting Deputy First Sea Lord asked the effect of increasing the depth-charge pattern to ten charges. He accepted the stated cost, 25 tons and a quarter-knot of speed. The resulting ten-charge design had beam increased to 37ft and displacement to 1,865 tons.

The model was shown to the Future Building Committee on 26 October. Given the large number of 1943 'Battles' armed with 4.5in guns, there was little opposition to the 4in design. The ship could engage five air targets simultaneously (one with the 4in, two with the Bofors, two with Oerlikons). DTSD stressed the need for eight torpedoes, the minimum effective number. The powerplant was that of the Emergency Destroyer ('J'-class type), producing 40,000 SHP. Endurance (clean) was 4,700nm at 20kts. Then the new alternating machinery was added, and displacement (standard) rose to 1,920 tons. This was despite E-in-C's reluctance to install it in an enlarged Emergency hull (in this case, with 38ft beam). Length devoted to machinery was determined both by internal volume (which E-in-C's figures emphasised) and by topside arrangement; an alternating power plant required two funnels. In these ships the lattice foremast was built around the forefunnel, much as in the later US 'mack'. A similar arrangement was adopted for the 1944 Fleet and Intermediate destroyers. Beam increased to 37ft 6in. The new small destroyers were now the largest in the fleet except for the 'Battles'. At this stage their lines were based on those of the 'Battle' class, and, like them, they were scheduled to get US Mk 37 fire control systems (ultimately they received the British Mk 6/Flyplane combination instead).

By this time the best ASW weapon was Squid, so it figured in the usual set of alternative armaments. Five alternative batteries were offered:

A: Heavy depth charges: fourteen-pattern (eight throwers, two rails, 100 charges) at the cost of four fixed tubes.
B: TSDS: five-charge pattern (two throwers, one rail, fifty charges).
C: A/S: split Hedgehog or alternative (Squid), five-

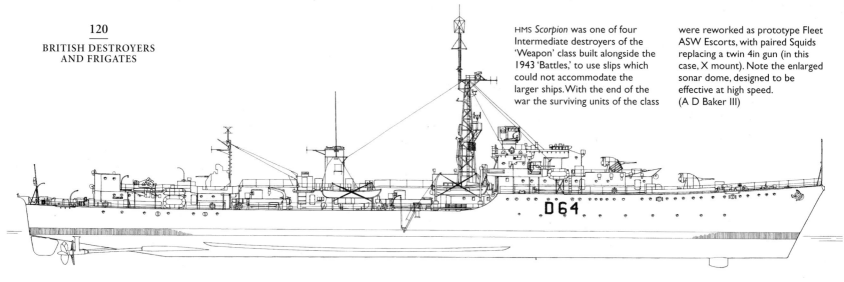

HMS *Scorpion* was one of four Intermediate destroyers of the 'Weapon' class built alongside the 1943 'Battles,' to use slips which could not accommodate the larger ships. With the end of the war the surviving units of the class were reworked as prototype Fleet ASW Escorts, with paired Squids replacing a twin 4in gun (in this case, X mount). Note the enlarged sonar dome, designed to be effective at high speed. (A D Baker III)

charge patterns, may land four fixed torpedo tubes.

D: Modified torpedo tubes: one pentad instead of fixed tubes.

E: Improved close-range AA: add four twin power Oerlikons, land torpedo tubes as necessary.

At its meeting on 1 March 1943 the Future Building Committee decided to abandon the fixed torpedo tubes in favour of two revolving quadruple tubes, to solve problems in torpedo control (ultimately pentad tubes were chosen). As compensation it had to accept a normal five-charge rather than ten-charge pattern (making provision to trade one set of tubes for a ten-charge pattern), and only fifty depth charges. Standard displacement was now 1,955 tons, far beyond what anyone might consider acceptable.

Alternative batteries then became:

A: Normal armament: six 4in, two twin Bofors with predictors, two twin power Oerlikon, eight torpedo tubes, five-charge pattern (two throwers, two tracks, fifty charges).

B: Heavy depth charge battery: ten-pattern (four throwers), 100 charges, land one set of tubes (soon abandoned).

C: As A but land second set of tubes to provide a total of seventy charges (alternatively, land one set of tubes in favour of TSDS).

D: Land both sets of tubes in favour of an ahead-throwing ASW weapon (Hedgehog or Double Squid).

E: Land one set of tubes in favour of six rather than two twin Oerlikons.

In 1945, with the new STAAG in sight, the projected armament was revised to show two STAAGs, which greatly exceeded the allowable close-range armament topweight of 22 tons. Deputy Controller offered one set of torpedo tubes as compensation, but that was only 4 tons. There was also interest in adding single Bofors guns. As in the 1943 'Battles', there was

some question of whether placing them in the bridge wings would make for excessive congestion. These ships were also to have four Oerlikons.

The first two ships were the last two of twenty-six Intermediates in the 1942 Programme, ordered as units of an abortive 13th ('Ce') Emergency Flotilla (*Centaur* and *Celt*, renamed *Scorpion* [ex-*Tomahawk*] and *Sword*). The forty-ship 1943 Programme included another fourteen Intermediates, but in all nineteen of these ships were ordered. Three ordered from Scotts had to be cancelled (23 December 1944) when the design grew to the point that they could not easily be built on those slips, leaving two full flotillas. There seems to have been some confusion at the end of the war as to whether plans actually called for nineteen ships (counting the Scotts order). Thus initial discussions of the results of cancelling one flotilla included references both to eleven and to eight remaining ships. By December 1945 it seemed likely (as actually happened) that another four ships would be cancelled, leaving only half a flotilla of ships roughly comparable to the Emergency Destroyers, but very differently armed. Of these ships, seven had been launched.

There was some question as to what to do with the class. DTASW wanted six completed as experimental fast escorts. DAWT proposed completing eight as radar pickets and 'pylons' (reference ships for fleet air defense). DGD considered the ships' armament too weak, and commented that if weight was needed for better ASW weapons all torpedoes (except the future Bidder) should be given up, as well as, if need be, one 4in mounting. Director of Plans seems to have been alone in thinking that eleven, rather than eight, ships were left. He proposed to complete the first ones to the original design and the others without their after gun mountings so that they could be completed as experimental fast escorts. Deputy Controller proposed an ASW conversion. Technology was changing very rapidly, so it might be necessary to lay up the ships until ASW policy was clear. In the end, four ships were completed as prototype fleet ASW escorts (see Chapter 8). All the others were cancelled.

The *Daring* class was the ultimate expression of classic British destroyer design; HMS *Daring* herself is shown in August 1952, as completed. (A D Baker III)

The 1944 Fleet Destroyer (*Daring* Class)

Like the 1942 and 1943 Programmes, the 1944 Programme, which turned out to be the last wartime one including destroyers, envisaged a mix of large (Fleet) destroyers and smaller Emergency-size ones. Ultimately that meant two flotillas of *Daring*s, two of smaller destroyers (the abortive *Gallant* class). The *Daring*s were the largest conventional British destroyers and, as it happened, a bridge to the next stage of development, the 'County' class. They were sometimes referred to as 1944 'Battles'. Immediately after completion the Royal Navy tried to avoid calling them destroyers at all, terming them '*Daring* class ships' and using them almost as small cruisers (albeit without a cruiser's ability to operate without tender or base support). Note that, although the Royal Navy considered the ships extraordinarily large, in fact they were only slightly larger than the contemporary US *Gearing* class, and much smaller than the destroyers the US Navy was contemplating in 1944–5. The smaller companion 'G' class became a post-war yardstick for destroyer design.

In both cases the two major design factors were the new lightweight twin 4.5in Mk VI or upper deck (as opposed to between-decks) gun mount and the demand for unit machinery (in effect, alternating engine and boiler rooms). In February 1943 DNO suggested that given savings both in weight and in crew in the new mounting, a third might be placed on board a 1943 'Battle'. DNC found the idea practicable, and prepared a sketch design (which was not submitted to the Future Building Committee).[13] In May 1943 the Future Building Committee considered but abandoned this idea. That it seemed that three mounts could be incorporated in a 1943 'Battle' hull

helps explain the surprise at how large the *Daring*, in effect the three-mount 'Battle', was. Since the main defect of the 'Battle' was its lack of an aft gun mount, these developments probably explain the Naval Staff request for a six-gun ship as the 1944 follow-on to the 'Battle' class, which became the *Daring*. Early in 1943 DNO thought that a mounting might be available as early as March/April 1943, to be placed on board HMS *Cossack* (13th Emergency Flotilla) just as the Mk IV prototype went on board the earlier *Savage*. That proved hopelessly optimistic. The prototype Mk VI mount was installed post-war on board HMS *Saintes*, but removed after trials.[14]

Given the problems with the 'Battle' class, the Future Building Committee decided to write a Staff Requirement for a three-mount ship, without reference to the size of the ship. It was shocked at what it got. On 2 August 1943 it asked DNC for a rough sketch design. He offered a 3,500-ton ship (4,500 tons fully loaded), which Controller promptly rejected.[15] DNC complained privately that he was being asked to add more armament without designing a much larger ship, but that was unfair: the whole point of the design was that the new gun mount was so much lighter. Deputy First Sea Lord would accept no more than 2,750 tons. His order of priorities was three twin mounts; two quadruple torpedo tubes; Bofors (one forward on the centreline); speed; and a Squid. One possibility was to use increased beam to carry a Bofors on each side abeam the bridge, to provide forward fire. Cutting one set of torpedo tubes might save some weight. The Staff was prepared to mount the after 4.5in on the upper (weather) deck rather than on the after superstructure, but ultimately that proved impossible because it left too little space below the mount. Controller also wanted DNC to sketch a ship with two 4.5in, fore and aft; it became the 1944 Intermediate Destroyer ('G' class).

Unhappily aware that it would be difficult to provide three

[13] From the point of view of weight, the cost of the third mounting would be two of the four twin Bofors, the after set of torpedo tubes, and the stabiliser. The 4in starshell gun would be eliminated, its platform extended to take the remaining pair of twin Bofors. The desired four-cornered coverage would be lost. The bridge would be raised to clear No. 2 mount. The compartment abaft the gearing room would become the after 4.5in magazine. Oil tanks would be rearranged to provide space, and the diesel generator aft resited. DNC expected little effect on displacement, stability, strength, or trim. Adopting unit machinery would present no great difficulty. A design on these lines showed three Mk VI mounts, two twin Bofors, twelve Oerlikons, two twin fixed torpedo tubes, and fifty depth charges (five-charge pattern), with a stabiliser on 2,450 tons standard (375ft waterline length, compared to 364ft for a 'Battle'). The existing 50,000 SHP plant would drive it at 35.25kts (standard) or 30.5kts (full load), and on 740 tons of oil fuel it could make 4,400nm at 20kts (clean). The Future Building Committee found the cost of the third mount too steep.

[14] The cruiser *Cumberland*, earmarked for ordnance tests, would not be ready in time.
[15] The design was based on a proposed Staff Requirement (TSD 2628/43) dated 19 June 1943. DNC pointed out that he could save 400 tons (from 3,500 tons standard) if a speed (deep) of 31kts could be accepted. On 7 July DTM remarked that the projected ships were closer to the old *Comus* class light cruisers than to 'Battles'. He considered them more heavily armed than half the British light cruisers in service in 1914. *Daring* Class Cover.

The big *Darings* were the 1944 version of the 'Battle' series. HMS *Diamond* is shown, on 24 April 1952. Through the early 1950s the *Darings* were the baseline against which larger destroyers were conceived.

gun mounts on the desired tonnage, in mid-August DNC offered a repeat 'Battle' with upper deck mounts fore and aft, plus four twin BUSTERs (predecessors of the STAAG), and nine twin power Oerlikons. DNO killed it: four guns should fire forward. Deputy Controller then demanded the three-mount ship he had wanted in the first place. DNC offered a 2,750-tonner (the limit previously proposed), but Controller now said that he might not be able to get the Cabinet to approve anything larger that a 'Battle'. Moreover, it seemed odd that a six-gun ship using lighter gun mounts would be so much larger than the five-gun ship with heavy between-deck mounts. The important differences may have been the new machinery arrangement and the extra hull length entailed by the third twin mount. Controller therefore asked whether the fifth (55° single) mount could somehow be given the same rate of fire as the twin mounts. DNO told him that would require a new mounting, which would weigh about 28 tons (roughly twice as much); the ship would have to be redesigned. He considered two twin upper-deck mounts superior to five guns including two between-decks mounts.

Controller and his deputy were not convinced that the greater rate of fire would offset the fifth gun or, for that matter, whether the new mount was worthwhile. Only pilot mounts would be built in 1943. It was no longer possible to equip five of the 1943 ships with two Mk VI each, and to build the last six 1943 ships to an entirely new design using the new mount. Given his skepticism, Controller also said that, if a new design were not approved, the 1944 'Battles' would be repeat 1943

ships with between-decks mounts, which had just proven successful in HMS *Savage*. DNO argued that since the upper-deck mount intended to replace it was already in production, it was important to place two mounts in a prototype ship.

Work now began on the three-mount design. The Staff Requirement called for three upper-deck mounts, four BUSTERs, six twin Oerlikons, two pentad torpedo tubes, Squid plus five-pattern depth charges (fifteen charges), HA/LA fire control and two barrage directors. DNC saw a rough 374ft version on 25 September 1943. All of the armament high in the ship made for stability problems, so the constructor developing the design suggested balancing it with more machinery weight. The most E-in-C could offer using two boilers (for a conventional arrangement) was 54,000 SHP, which would increase machinery weight from 635 tons to 735 tons. The resulting 2,707-ton ship was at roughly the limit Deputy First Sea Lord had offered. DNC approved the idea, and sketches were begun for Controller, together with explicit comparisons with the US *Sumner* (DD 692) class. As submitted, the ship would have displaced 2,720 tons (length 377ft). An alternative and less satisfactory 50,000 SHP ship would have been slightly smaller (2,685 tons, 374ft). The designs did not quite meet the Staff Requirement, as they showed three BUSTERs and four Oerlikons and quadruple torpedo tubes, with depth charges but without the desired Squid. They showed the US Mk 37 fire control system and one barrage director (a second could be provided at the cost of a BUSTER). The sketches showed 12.1 per cent of deep displacement devoted to arma-

ment, which DNC could compare to 11.35 per cent in the supposedly better-armed US ship, and 12.0 per cent in a 1942 'Battle' (9.05 per cent in a 'Weapon', and only 8.64 per cent in an 'S'-class Emergency Destroyer). As noted, British weights did not match perceptions because British mountings, particularly for the Bofors guns, were far heavier than their US equivalents. Too, the comparison used the *Sumner* as designed, with the original two twin Bofors and six 20mm, and with six depth charge throwers and two rails, but only fourteen heavy (600lb) charges and twenty-four light (300lb) ones. The ships were completed with, among other things, two quadruple Bofors and five more 20mm in addition to the original weapons. Additional length made it possible to fit a new high-speed (above 20kts) sonar dome. E-in-C offered more efficient machinery, approaching wartime US standards. Through 1942, he had resisted any attempt to switch from existing reliable, if heavy and massive, machinery. By April 1943 he had reversed himself, promising 12 per cent better fuel economy in the 1944 'Battles' without increasing machinery weight, based on practices to be tested in the 'Weapon' class.

The Future Building Committee recommended adopting the 54,000 SHP design, but asked for more torpedo tubes, searchlights and ASW weapons. There was strong Staff support for more torpedoes, but not for searchlights, which seemed less valuable as radar was developed. DASW wanted depth charges replaced with the new Squid. A majority of the Staff considered Squid too large for a destroyer. DASW argued that depth charges would be obsolescent by the time the ships entered service. Squid was probably the only effective means of attacking a submarine which penetrated the screen. Destroyers screening fleet units had to be able to deter submarine attacks. Without Squid, the ship would be a small cruiser with defensive Asdics and depth charges (to embarrass any trailing submarine). Like the *Scylla* class cruisers, she would

augment an ASW screen, but she would never be considered an ASW combatant. For the moment, his argument won the day.

So large a ship presented some problems. Could it be made as manoeuvrable as smaller destroyers? DNC thought that a long after cut-up and a new bow form should help. The original Staff Requirement included a clause emphasising the need for maneuverability to protect against torpedo attack (this clause was later omitted, possibly in error). The 'Battle' and 'Weapon' classes had already been given a long cut-up and specially-shaped stern and rudder. By March 1945 DNC had chosen to use twin rudders, based on US tank tests which suggested that at maximum speed (in a *Sumner*) they would reduce tactical diameter by 70 yds and time to swing 90° from 55 to 47 seconds, both very desirable.

The ship would be beamier (in relation to her depth) than previous ships, so structural design had to be revised. An alternative long-forecastle design was rejected because it would have to be beamier to retain its stability. A deeper hull could be built of lighter material (stresses would be reduced), but that in turn would reduce protection to the machinery. DNC argued that extra covered space would invite weight additions after the ships entered service, that placing the torpedo tubes higher in the ship was probably unsatisfactory , and that the boats would lose the protection of the break of the forecastle. Hull weight was clearly an issue. DNC could not be sure of how much he could save pending underwater explosive trials. Nor was it clear how far welding could be used, partly because that in turn would require that steel sections be specially adapted to such construction.

The ship was too large. Proposed weight-reduction measures included reducing deck heights, lowering the magazines, eliminating the forward barrage director, and stowing liquids and provisions in spaces under the hold flats. Adding Squid

HMS *Daring* shows her short-lived raked funnel, on 29 July 1953. The raked funnel casing soon had to be landed to reduce topweight. The ship's forefunnel is just visible inside her lattice foremast.

HMS *Defender*, on 12 March 1953, with the stubby after funnel.

dition of about 31.5kts (at 3,260 tons).

The ship still seemed too large, so on 19 February 1944 a new design limit of 2,500 tons was imposed. The most important change was elimination of Squid in favour of ten-pattern depth charges. Expected dimensions were 370ft × 42ft × 22.5ft (standard displacement, as calculated in March 1944, was 2,498 tons). Controller then decided that he wanted to retain the usual 1 per cent Board Margin. That brought expected standard displacement up to 2,598 tons. By May the design had been further slightly modified, two twin Oerlikons being replaced by a third twin Bofors. Expected standard displacement was 2,631 tons (3,358 tons deep). This was the sort of figure which had been rejected in the past, but the design was now mature enough that there was little fear of further growth. At 2,630 tons the design was submitted for Board approval. There was a further proposal to change the diesel generator requirement to sufficient power to provide emergency power at sea in the event of complete immobilisation due to loss of steam. On 19 August 1944 Controller formally decided to proceed with these ships.

The depth charge was still obsolescent, so in October 1944 the Squid requirement was revived (it was also wanted for the 1944 Intermediate design). Without the space previously allocated forward, it had to be on the quarterdeck. A single Squid there (thirty projectiles) weighed 16 tons; eliminating depth charges (22.4 tons) more than made up for it. Installing Squid also cleared space which might be wanted for an after director. In December 1946 DUSW pressed for provision to replace Squid with the newer Limbo, which he considered the only weapon which might become available within the next five years capable of coping with the new fast submarines. That was approved, but no *Daring* class ship was ever fitted with the weapon.

With attention turning to Japan, the destroyer torpedo suddenly seemed far more significant. Reports from the Pacific described striking Japanese successes, and also mentioned that their destroyers carried reloads with special fast-reloading equipment. The British had never really considered withholding torpedoes to get a second chance at a target; they thought that only a full broadside had much of a chance of making hits. *Vernon* argued that conditions had changed. Radar made it possible to fire from much greater ranges, but the greater running time would give an enemy more time to evade; therefore the more torpedoes that could be fired, the better the chance of a hit. Some US destroyers had twelve or even sixteen tubes, compared to the four or eight of British ships. Heavy torpedo batteries had shown what they could do in the Solomons, whereas the British failure when the German *Scharnhorst* and *Gneisenau* ran up the Channel (February 1942) could be ascribed to the lack of numbers of torpedoes (six per ship).[16] In April 1944 *Vernon* therefore advocated arming new destroyers with three centreline pentads. DTSD agreed,

forward (twenty-five salvoes) and an extra set of quadruple torpedo tubes aft in place of its depth charges increased the ship 15ft in length (12ft forward for the Squid, 3ft aft for the torpedo tubes). Space in the bridge structure was already too tight. Moving the two forward BUSTERs outboard would make it possible to enlarge the operations room, extend the bridge, and enlarge the A/S control room, as well as the CO's living spaces. The wider forward superstructure below the wider bridge would add accommodations, freeing space below for a POs' mess and for increased crew space. The main constraint on the position of the BUSTERs had been the need to give them the best possible arcs across the bow, so that they would be able to fire at aircraft crossing ahead of the ship. To preserve those arcs, the guns would need sponsons projecting outboard of the ship, with hinged sections so that the ships could come alongside. A similar expedient – which had proven quite unpopular – had been tried in the 'Tribals'. Thus modified, the ship would displace 2,568 tons (3,706 tons deep load). It was clear that she would grow considerably during detailed design.

The designer recalled that in the contemporary *Gallant* design 60 tons had been saved by welding and by using aluminium. Such practices could save 80 tons in a modified design. Other cuts were substitution of two pentad for the three quadruple tubes, one twin Bofors, and two-thirds of the planned Board Margin. Standard displacement (at a more detailed stage in the design) would be about 2,590 tons. Reducing endurance from 5,000nm to 4,400nm would cut 84 tons of oil fuel (7ft of length), leaving a 375ft ship displacing about 2,560 tons in standard condition, with a speed in deep con-

citing prisoner-of-war evidence that the latest Japanese destroyer (*Shimakaze*) had three centreline pentads. DNC said he could not add another centreline mount on the available tonnage. It had been decided to arm the 1943 'Battle' and 'Weapon' classes with pentad rather than quadruple torpedo tubes. That would also be done in the two 1944 classes. The possibility of providing Japanese-style reloads was raised but dropped. After the design had been approved, the pentad mountings were modified for power operation. That was also done in the 1944 'Weapons' ('G' class), but it could not be done in the 1943 ships, because there was not enough weight margin (2.5 tons was involved).

Unitised, or staggered, machinery was requested on 10 August 1944 by the Future Building Committee. Each of two machinery spaces held a boiler and a turbine; the spaces were separated by an empty space so that no single hit could disable the ship. The space was important because a hit near the place where the boiler room of one set of machinery adjoined the engine room of the other could disable a ship with alternating engine and boiler rooms. The arrangement was called 'staggered' because the turbines were no longer side by side, as in earlier British designs. Staggering would add slightly to the ship's length (3ft 6in) and to her tonnage (20 tons directly) and would require six more ratings. This practice, proposed and rejected in the past, seems to have been acceptable partly because higher-performance turbines and boilers were more compact. A staggered plant required a second funnel, since with a single funnel it would be impossible to provide the desired gap between the units.

In October 1944 E-in-C produced estimates for both 50,000 SHP and 54,000 SHP high-efficiency plants, respectively 122ft

and 124ft long, weighing 680 tons and 735 tons (DNC's suggestion that three or four boilers be used to produce the 60,000 SHP of modern US destroyers was rejected). The blade rate was slightly reduced (from 320 RPM in the 'Battles' to 300 RPM) for better efficiency and also for the better sonar performance (self-noise) requested by the Staff. Partly because the new destroyer required far more electronics, she had more than 60 per cent more electrical output than any previous British destroyer. Ultimately half the class used new AC electrical systems (the others had the previously universal DC systems), the hope being that once AC had been proven, future installations could be lighter. Initially, only the two building at Yarrow were to have AC power, but in November 1946 Controller announced that he would approve DEE's proposal to do two more, and that was formally approved the following October.

While the *Daring* design was being prepared, the Royal Navy became interested in converting destroyers into radar pickets (fighter directors). Although ultimately the new ships were not fitted for this role, the attempt to provide the necessary space explains their unusual bridge form. At first the least capable wartime destroyers, the 'Os' and 'Ps', were nominated for conversion. That entailed both added internal spaces and

[16] Folio 21, 'Weapons' Class Cover. Captured Japanese documents (apparently ADM1/12647) dated December 1943 showed that they considered reloads absolutely necessary. On 12–13 July 1943 they '. . . engaged an enemy surface force consisting primarily of Cruisers; and in two attacks succeeded in sinking three . . . and setting one on fire. But they ran out of torpedoes and were unable to drive home their success'. According to the same Japanese document, 'in view of the development of Radar and of the special characteristics of night fighting, it is most likely that future torpedo warfare will become close-in assault following medium range torpedo attack . . . continuous firing is increasingly important . . . the present re-loading device needs still more improvement in speed and certainty'. During the night action of 5–6 July 1943 two Japanese destroyers took 1 hour and 14 minutes to reload, and never found the enemy on returning to action. However, other Japanese destroyers completed a reload (eight tubes each) in 20 minutes on 12–13 July 1943. The British wondered whether the additional set of tubes in *Shimakaze* represented a change of policy, as she seemed to have no reloads.

HMS *Diamond* is shown on 18 March 1961 as refitted, with one bank of torpedo tubes replaced by a deckhouse and with the modern MRS 3 director in place of the earlier Mk VI. The topmast carries HF/DF above three sets of UA 3/4 ESM antennas. The close-range battery has been reduced to a pair of single Bofors, but the director aft is retained to provide a second channel of 4.5in fire.

a US-supplied SP pencil-beam radar (as in the contemporary US *Gearing* conversion). The new spaces were an Aircraft Direction Room (ADR) and the SP radar office. The air-conditioned ADR presented particular difficulties. The ships also needed an enlarged Operations Room accommodating, among other things, improved displays such as a Skiatron projection screen. There would also be additional radar power rooms and maintenance and store rooms. Suddenly volume (in this case, represented by deck space) was a critical issue. Other requirements were two voice radios (radio telephones, or R/T, Type 87M) to communicate with aircraft, and VHF/DF, used to identify particular aircraft and to home them onto the ship. Without the latter there could be no assurance that fighter patrols could rendezvous with the ships to which they were assigned. In this design the SP radar would have been accommodated on a short lattice mast amidships. It is unclear whether any of the 'O' and 'P' class began conversion.

The new *Daring*s were natural candidates for fighter direction, ACNS(W) wanting them so fitted in view of their size and value. At first the expected price was only one twin Bofors. However, a designer estimated that if fighter direction was a firm requirement, and no reduction in close-range armament could be accepted (a prudent reaction, given what would happen to US Navy radar pickets off Okinawa the next year), the ship would have to be redesigned, gaining about 12ft in length and 50 tons in displacement. However, the ships were already considered too large. A sketch showed the SP radar on the midships Bofors platform. The ship lacked a US-style long-range precision air-search set, and the existing Type 281 was too heavy. The ships were therefore allocated the usual destroyer combination of Type 291 (air search, broad beam) and Type 293 (gun target indication). A long-range Type 992 target-indication set was under development, and when it was ready it would replace Type 293 atop the lattice foremast.

The real problem was space. There was very little within the hull. That left the bridge structure, but it could not be extended aft because of the positions of the Bofors guns there. Initially it seemed that it could be extended forward only by eliminating the wheelhouse, placing the steering position deep in the ship. However, both DND and DNE had recently emphasised the need for the helmsman to see forward over the gun mountings. Since the Mk VI 4.5in mounting was considerably higher than the earlier Mk IV, the helm actually had to be raised from its position in earlier 'Battle' class destroyers. If no extra space were available, perhaps the Operations Room could be designed so that it could be converted into an ADR when needed. That would be acceptable only if ships could work in pairs, one with an Operations Room and one with an ADR. Splitting the ADR into an Operations Room forward and an ADR aft was rejected because the ship would not have enough officers to supervise both.

Ultimately the part of the bridge structure on 01 deck was enlarged by extending it forward and outward. Instead of moving the helmsman out of the bridge structure, he was moved up to compass platform level, a departure from earlier British practice. That transformed the bridge structure into the shape characteristic of the *Daring* class. Plotting facilities and a PPI were installed on the bridge, and a second automatic plot (to control an ASW force, for example) installed.

Finding space did not solve the weight problem presented by new equipment including SP. Advocates of the fighter director role argued that the ability to control fighters would more than make up for the loss of one of three twin Bofors. Director of Plans doubted that destroyers would need such facilities, because friendly fighters would be present only with larger formations, including cruisers better suited to aircraft control. DAWT thought that unlikely, given his sea experience during the first three years of the war. Fighters would normally be present, and destroyers unable to control them effectively would be sunk. At least one-third of ships (and preferably 40 to 50 per cent) should be so fitted. DTSD wanted at least one ship in any force capable of directing aircraft. On that basis he and DGD proposed 25 per cent. Controller, who knew how little yard capacity there was, was willing to fit two or three ships with fighter direction at the expense of one Bofors mount at one yard. In December 1944 it was decided that ships would be completed without fighter-direction facilities, but suited for later installation at the expense of the midships Bofors mount. ACNS(W) pointed out that the *Daring*s would not be completed until 1948–50 (which was grossly optimistic), and by then experience in the Pacific would have clarified the need for fighter direction. New radars might be light enough not to cost a Bofors gun, or the gun itself might be superseded by first-generation guided missiles. The issue was postponed to the beginning of 1946 (see Chapter 8).

Habitability became a special concern because, without any real change in Staff Requirements, complement grew from 260 in the sketch design to 345 in the final version, operating as a leader. After the war, DNE argued that it was time to take a firm stand on living space, which until then had been the only 'compressible' factor in a design increasingly governed by the need for internal space. In wartime COs tended to accept additional men without paying much attention to their accommodation. Ships overcrowded in peacetime would probably be intolerably crowded in wartime, when they would have to remain at sea for longer and longer (as demonstrated in the Pacific War). DNC claimed that, even so, the *Daring*s had more deck area per man than in the past. Habitability improvements included features such as a laundry, stainless steel basins in the washplaces, and all-electric cooking with centralised food preparation. Most of these features were added after the design had been completed.

At the end of the war one of the two projected flotillas was cancelled, but the other was completed. Construction was badly

slowed because builders concentrated on more lucrative merchant ship work (which the British government considered more important, as it would contribute to national recovery). Electrical auxiliaries were a particular bottleneck, because their manufacturers were concentrating on export orders.

Partly because construction was so protracted, there were considerable changes after the design had been approved. DGD wanted a second 4.5in fire control channel, because without one ships might find it difficult to engage targets on bearings near dead astern. Thus plans originally called for an MRS 1 barrage director, with a below-decks computer, aft. It in turn was replaced by a Close Range Barrage Fire (CRBF) Director, partly because its below-decks space and weight demands were unacceptable. The planned Buster twin Bofors mountings were replaced by STAAGs, and ultimately the centreline STAAG was replaced by a Utility Bofors, its director also serving as the after control channel (with very limited capacity) for the 4.5in guns.

Under attack for the sheer size of the *Daring*, DNC Department could take comfort in the much greater size of the destroyer then being designed by the US Navy: SCB 2 or DD 927, ultimately built to a rather different design as USS *Mitscher*. At the time the US ship would have displaced 3,200 tons standard and 4,400 tons fully loaded. Each design showed three main battery gun mounts (twin 5in/54 in the US ship as then conceived, 4.5in Mk VI for the British). Each also had two quintuple torpedo tubes and an ASW weapon (the US design specified only that it be within 16½ tons). The British ship had three STAAGs, each of which might be considered roughly comparable to one of the four US twin 3in/50s. Both ships had free-swinging anti-aircraft guns. It seemed that the

Royal Navy was getting more for its money, as the US ship was far larger (length 450ft, later increased to 476ft, on the waterline, compared to 390ft for a *Daring*). The difference in complement was smaller, the US ship requiring thirty officers and 328 enlisted, compared to fourteen and 305 for the British.

The RAN ordered four ships in 1946 (of which HMAS *Waterhen* was cancelled and scrapped on the slip in 1954). They were completed with single Limbo rather than Squid, and with one set of torpedo tubes rather than two. The anti-aircraft battery was two Mk V twins and two single Bofors.

The 1944 'Weapon' Class ('G' Class)

The 4in main armament accepted in the 1943 'Weapons' was not altogether popular. At a Future Building Committee meeting on 28 January 1944, First Sea Lord proposed rearming the 'Weapons' with four single 55° 4.5in guns and, if practicable, two pentad torpedo tubes. Clearly there would be little problem from the weight point of view. The arrangement would be a problem, because the bridge would have to be moved bodily back to due to the longer barrel of the 4.7in gun in B position. That would probably be possible if the combined mast-funnel, already under consideration, was adopted. The fatal objection was the extent to which the ships would have to be redesigned and drawings redone. The suggestion did point to a need for something heavier in the 1944 'Weapons' just then being designed.

On 11 February DNC was instructed to produce a new 'Weapon' class sketch design with two twin 4.5in Mk VI guns, using the maximum amount of welding. DNC opposed the idea on the grounds that DNO probably could not produce enough mountings for both the 1944 'Battles' and the 1944

The *Gallant* class would have been the Intermediate companions to the *Darings*. As in the War Emergency ships, they were designed for several alternative armaments. B position could accommodate either two twin Oerlikons or two Squids. In the latter case the compartment below would have been the Squid handling room, projectiles passing up through a trunk in the deck. Dashed lines at the stern show where minesweeping gear (TSDS) would have been installed as an alternative to depth charges. Note the US-type Mk 37 director, as in the 1943 'Battle' class. Note also that the forward gunwale is offset to port. (A D Baker III)

British destroyers were often compared to their export equivalents, like the Venezuelan *Aragua*, shown in 1956. DNC was obliged to explain why ships which seemed to carry more weapons on about the same displacement as their British contemporaries were actually often inferior. British officers who saw the foreign ships did not always agree.

'Weapons'. The 44in searchlight could be eliminated, but a barrage director, to provide a second channel of fire, was essential. Beam could be increased by 6in compared to the 1943 ships. Although lighter than the mountings in the 'Battle' class, the upper deck 4.5in mountings were appreciably heavier than 55° RPC mountings. A rough estimate showed that 4.5in mountings and ammunition would weigh about twice as much as the 4in guns of the 1943 design. Proposed compensation was one of the two sets of torpedo tubes, one twin Bofors, the barrage director, and the 44in searchlight; the 18-ton Board Margin would also be absorbed.

The new design went ahead because it was more attractive than a repeat 1943 'Weapon'. The basic requirement was to carry the two twin 4.5in in a hull which could be built on the same slip as a 1943 'Weapon', which meant limiting standard displacement to 2,000 tons. To retain all 'Weapon' features seemed to require at least 2,100 tons. The new ship retained the same machinery but had to be made somewhat beamier (39ft 6in vs 38ft) and heavier (1,995 tons vs 1,945 tons standard, 2,740 tons vs 2,702 tons deep load). Note that 1,995 tons was 10 tons over the legend originally approved. The after mounting had to be atop the after deckhouse. There was insufficient support further aft, where the cut-up reduced buoyancy, and there was insufficient space for the large gun-bay used by the 4.5in mount. The deckhouse was needed to accommodate galleys, washrooms, etc., as well as some of the officers. Compared to the 1943 design, this one had the same long cut-up aft. It added a modified stern contour for good turning qualities.

The Board approved the sketch design in March 1944, with quadruple torpedo tubes rather than the pentads ultimately chosen. To deal with the substantial increase in tonnage over the 1943 'Weapon', beam had to be increased by 18in, which added hull weight (ships could still be built on the same slips).

There was also added weight to deal with the concentration of armament weight at the ends of the ship, in the form of the two big 4.5in. Weight growth was restrained by surrendering the Board Margin (0.66 per cent); by liberal use of aluminium alloy, as in the *Darings*; by widespread use of welding; by lowering the bridge a foot, by reducing the length of the forward superstructure; and by using American-style braided cable rather than British-style lead-covered cable. All of this would save about 65 tons. As in some earlier ships, designers considered and rejected the US practice of carrying fuel tanks up to the upper deck. Cutting endurance to 4,400nm at 20kts, as in the *Darings*, would require a complete redesign.

As in earlier designs, several alternative armaments were offered:

A: Two twin 4.5in, two twin Bofors, two twin Oerlikons, two pentad torpedo tubes, two depth charge throwers and one track (50 depth charges); sonars would be Types 144 and 147. The twin Bofors were STAAGs rather than the earlier BUSTERs.
B: Land one set of torpedo tubes, add depth charges to provide a pattern of ten (four throwers, two rails, 100 depth charges).
C: Land both torpedo tubes, ten-pattern, 145 depth charges.
D: Land one set of tubes and fit TSDS.
E: Land both sets of tubes and fit Squid.
F. Land one set of tubes and fit four twin power Oerlikons and two twin hand-operated Oerlikons.

For a time alternative E was dropped (June 1944), but it was then revived. Two flotillas were planned. The one ordered was cancelled in 1945, but the G design became the basis for post-war studies of minimum destroyer size.

Post-war Exports

The big wartime destroyers formed the basis for the most successful early post-war export designs, produced by Vickers. The company sold three large destroyers to Venezuela and then two to Chile. DNC compared these heavily-armed export designs with their British counterparts. Vickers offered a wide range of designs to Venezuela, including a large destroyer (Design 1126) armed with the Mk IV gun mountings of the 'Battle' class and a medium ship. The Venezuelans bought the larger one, which DNC considered roughly comparable to a *Daring*. He compared the medium destroyer (which the Venezuelans did not buy) to the 'Battle' and 'Weapon' classes. Because the Venezuelan ship carried the same gun mounts as the 'Battle' class, it is sometimes used as an illustration of what could have been done with that hull; but it was a much larger ship.

Comparative details, as collected in 1949 in by DNC were:

	Large Venezuelan	*Daring*	Medium Venezuelan	'Battle'	'Weapon'
Length OA	402ft	390ft	378ft	379ft	365ft
Length PP	374ft 6in	366ft	351ft 6in	355ft	341ft 6in
Beam	42ft	43ft	40ft 6in	40ft 3in	38ft
Depth	22ft 9in	22ft	21ft 6in	22ft	20ft 6in
Std/Deep	2,600/3,300 tons	2,610/3,352 tons	2,180/2,700 tons	2,315/3,153 tons	1,965/2,700 tons
Std, mean	—	—	9ft 9in	10ft 4in	9ft 8in
Deep	—	—	11ft 6in	12ft 11in private ship	12ft 2in
At Std	50,000 SHP = 34.5kts	54,000 SHP = 34.75kts	40,000 SHP = 34kts	50,000 SHP = 35.75kts	40,000 SHP = 34kts
Turbo generators	2 × 200 turbo-alt	2 × 350 TG	2 × 200 turbo-alt	2 × 200	2 × 200 TG
Diesel generators	2 × 100 D-alt	3 × 150 DG	2 × 100 D-alt	3 × 100	2 × 100 DG
Radius	4,000nm @ 17kts	4,400nm @ 20kts	4,000nm @ 17kts	4,400nm @ 20kts	5,000nm @ 20kts
Complement	254	341 (leader)	219	236	260 (leader)
		313 (private ship)			230 (private ship)
4.5in (rpg)	6 (600)	6 (2,250)	4 (400)	4 (1,500)	6 × 4 (2,400)
40mm (rpg)	16 (8,000)	2 × STAAG, 1 × Mk V (8,640)	10	4 (5,670)	4 (5,670)
				4 × 20 (9,600)	4 × 20 (9,600)
Torpedo tubes (torpedoes)	3 (3)	10 (10)	3 (3)	8 (8)	8 (8)
DC	30	—	30	60	50
Squid	—	30 rounds	—	—	—
4in Star shell	—	—	—	60	—
Hull	1,397 tons	1,312 tons	1,185 tons	1,204 tons	1,039 tons
Machinery	675 tons	705 tons	560 tons	655 tons	570 tons
Armament	353 tons	435 tons	235 tons	350 tons	258 tons
Equipment	200 tons	224 tons	160 tons	178 tons	163 tons
Oil fuel	600 tons	598 tons	500 tons	699 tons	620 tons
Reserve feed water	45 tons	43 tons	40 tons	45½ tons	39 tons
Margin	30 tons	26 tons	20 tons	21 tons (protection)	13 tons (protection)

The bridge of the Venezuelan ship looked much better than that in a *Daring*, but DNC suspected it would suffer from high wind velocity over its top, so that the compass platform would be useless. Accommodation in the large Venezuelan destroyer was more lavish than in a *Daring*, and was available partly because a large deckhouse had replaced the forward torpedo tubes. The ship had less radar (and no radar-controlled close-range armament), less ammunition, and less stores (about half or less of what *Daring* carried, which was surprising in view of the large fuel capacity). Although she had unitised machinery (despite her single stack), she had old-style 400 psi boilers. The heavier hull of the Venezuelan ship suggested that lower hull stresses had been specified, so that it was more like a 'Battle'. No aluminium had been used in deckhouses and other structures. The blast of the after 4.5in mount would likely make the numerous after Bofors guns useless. The Venezuelan order coincided with the British rearmament programme, and by 1952 the Venezuelans were complaining that the programme was delaying their ships (they may have wanted access to new British weapons in return).

Vickers went on to sell two more destroyers to Chile. Ordered about November 1953, they were initially offered as a *Daring* class hull with 'Battle' arrangement (about 3,300 tons deep). Later a 2,600-ton destroyer was offered with a 4.7in main battery and 4in anti-aircraft guns. Ultimately they became a kind of showcase of Vickers and Marconi equipment, such as the new single automatic 4in gun and Marconi radars. Laid down in 1956/7, the ships were delivered in 1960. Chile returned for more destroyers in 1965; presumably these negotiations ultimately led to the purchase of a pair of *Leanders* about five years later (from Yarrow, not Vickers).

A later attempted destroyer sale to Colombia was aborted by the Foreign Office. At the same time Sweden was about to sell destroyers to Indonesia. Apparently to preclude this sale, the Foreign Office arranged for Vickers to withdraw its offer in favour of the Swedes.[17] Another aborted sale was part of a package requested by Brazil in 1952; it was rejected because it would have interfered with the ongoing British rearmament programme (which was already being delayed) and because Brazil would have paid in sterling, in effect using wartime British payments, rather than in the dollars the British economy badly needed. Foreign Office files do not show any other serious approaches for destroyers, although Thornycroft files show sketch designs offered to Argentina (1947, in combination with White and Yarrow) and Peru. Several countries were interested in light destroyers, and in one case (Ecuador) an approach ended in the sale of 'Hunts'.

[17] This sequence is suggested by the sequence of papers listed in the Foreign Office index, but the papers themselves were not found. Of the other major South American countries, in the late 1940s Argentina seems to have sought cruisers (the Vickers papers at the Brass Foundry show several drawings) but not destroyers. A Brazilian approach to buy a fleet in Britain failed because they would have been paid for in Sterling rather than in dollars, in effect out of British debts to Brazil. There was considerable interest in surplus British war-built destroyers; for example in 1964 the Egyptians sought a 'Battle'.

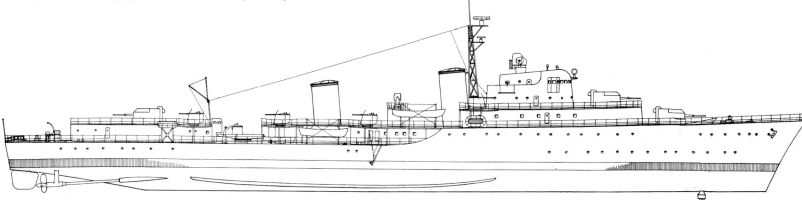

Proposed post-war export destroyers might be considered broad equivalents to the *Darings* and 'Battles'. TWY 1737 was proposed to Brazil by a consortium consisting of Thornycroft, White, and Yarrow. In addition to the data on the drawing, overall length was 400ft and displacement was 2,750 tons standard and 3,500 tons fully loaded, slightly larger than a *Daring*. The 60,000 SHP powerplant envisaged (with three boilers; it was not unitised as in a *Daring*) would have driven the ship at 35kts. Special attention was paid to ventilation. Vickers-Armstrong would have provided armament, which was the subject of considerable debate (about April 1953 the Brazilians decided that they wanted the *Daring*-type main battery director. The first two

Mk 6 mount shown here instead of the 'Battle'-type Mk 4). Further versions offered in February 1954 showed either a mixed battery (twin 4.5in in A, single 4in in B plus two more abaft the funnel), two twin 4.5in in A and B positions, two single 4in aft, and two twin Bofors 120mm guns in A and B, with another on the shelter deck amidships and another in Y position aft. Presumably the single 4in were Vickers' new Mk N, which ended up on board the Chilean *Almirante Williams* class (it was rejected by the Royal Navy). In March, Vickers proposed an all-4in armament, with eight guns: one in A position, two offset in B, one on either side of the after funnel, one on either side of the after superstructure, and one on the centreline aft. In April Thornycroft

and White admitted that combining 4.5in and 4in guns would present serious problems. At least one version of the design apparently used US 5in guns. This project was part of a larger Brazilian programme offered to various British shipyards. The yards approached the British government for financial backing. They were refused both because the Royal Navy was already experiencing serious delays in its rearmament programme (and Brazilian construction would worsen the situation) and because the Brazilians wanted to pay in sterling, which would not have helped Britain's serious dollar indebtedness. (A D Baker III)

Design for a large destroyer for the Brazilian Goverment

Length: 389ft 0in waterline
Breadth: 43ft 0in moulded
Depth: 22ft 9in moulded

1. Squid A/S mortar
2. Squid projectile room (to port)
3. Twin 4.5in Mk VI mountings
4. Quintuple 21in torpedo tube mount
5. Single 40mm Bofors (P&S)
6. Simple Tachymetric Directors (P&S)
7. Mk VI gun director
8. 40mm magazine and provisions room
9. 4.5in magazine and shell room
10. Engine room
11. Boiler room No 2
12. Boiler room No 1
13. Diesel alternator compartment
14. 4.5in magazine
15. 4.5in shell room
16. Sonar transducer compartment

Vickers-Armstrong offered this large destroyer to Venezuela in 1949; there was also a companion medium destroyer. Three *Nueva Esparta* class ships were built to a modified design with a single trunked funnel, a rather different streamlined bridge, and a Mark 6 main battery director. The first two units were ordered in 1950. British destroyer files show a ship somewhat larger than a *Daring*, 374ft 6in (pp) compared to 366ft for a *Daring*; 402ft overall compared to 390ft for a *Daring*. Beam was 42ft (43ft for *Daring*), and hull depth was 22ft 9in (*Daring* was 22ft). Displacement was similar, 2,600 tons standard and 3,300 tons deep load. A 50,000 SHP powerplant, somewhat less powerful than that of a *Daring*,

would have driven the ship at 34.5kts. Armament seemed impressive, with six 4.5in guns in Mk IV mountings (the Mk VI mountings of the *Daring* class had not been released for export) and a remarkable sixteen Bofors guns, plus a triple torpedo tube. The difference was a much smaller ammunition supply: 600 rather than 2,250 rounds of 4.5in, 8,000 rounds of 40mm for sixteen barrels rather than 8,640 rounds for six barrels in a *Daring* – and a much lighter torpedo battery. *Daring* had a Squid, but that had not been cleared for export, so the Venezuelan ship had thirty depth charges. The Venezuelan ship also had much less electric power, two 200 kW (rather than 350 kW) turbo-generators and two 100 kW

diesels rather than the three 150 kW units of the Royal Navy ship. The less efficient powerplant made for shorter range: 4,000nm at 17kts (600 tons of oil) compared to 4,400nm at 20kts on 590 tons for a *Daring*. Complement would have been 254, compared to 313 (341 for a leader) in the Royal Navy ship. A weight breakdown showed that the Venezuelan ship devoted less tonnage to armament (353 tons vice 435 tons) and to machinery (675 tons vice 705 tons). The use of the Mk IV mounts made the Venezuelan ship seem comparable to a 'Battle' rather than, as was the case, to the much larger *Daring*. The medium destroyer, which was about 'Battle' size (378ft overall x 40ft 6in, 2,180 tons standard, 2,700 tons fully

loaded), had a similar armament: two twin 4.5in, ten Bofors guns, and the one triple torpedo tube. DNC commented that the bridge looked good (much better, certainly, than the one in a *Daring*), but he suspected it would suffer from high wind velocity over its top, so that the compass platform would be useless. As in many export designs, accommodation (more for officers than for ratings) was far more lavish than in British warships, partly because the design provided much more space in a large deckhouse replacing the forward torpedo tubes. The ship also had less radar (and no radar-controlled close-range armament), ammunition, and stores (about half or less of what *Daring* carried, which was surprising in view of the

large fuel capacity). Although she had unitised machinery, she had old-style 400 psi boilers. The heavier hull of the Venezuelan ship suggested that lower hull stresses had been specified, so that it was more like a 'Battle'. No aluminium had been used in deck houses and other structures. As for the massive anti-aircraft battery, the blast of the after 4.5in mount would likely make the after Bofors useless. The Venezuelan order coincided with the British rearmament programme, and by 1952 the Venezuelans were complaining that the programme was delaying their ships (their demand for access to new British weapons in return may explain release of the modern Mk 6 director). (A D Baker III)

Vickers-Armstrong sold Chile two large destroyers of the *Almirante Williams* class. The initial offer seems to have been for the Venezuelan design, described as a *Daring* class hull with 'Battle' arrangement (about 3,300 tons deep load). This project sketch still shows considerable similarity to the large Venezuelan destroyers (hull dimensions and hull sections are the same). Initial negotiations were completed about November 1953, the order being announced in January 1954 and then signed in May 1955. This design was the one shown in the official sketch released in 1958. By 1955 Vickers was allowed to sell its new automatic Mk (N) single 4in gun, shown here. Note also the Squid aft, and the quadruple (rather than triple) torpedo tube. The six single Bofors are probably the new L70s. At this stage the design showed

standard British destroyer radars, Type 291 and Type 293. As actually delivered in 1960, the ships had plated-in foremasts carrying new Marconi export radars: SNW-10 for air search, SNW-20 for surface search, and SNG-20 for gun fire control. Their Bofors guns were controlled by Dutch (Signaal) M44 radars in the waist, and they had quintuple torpedo tubes. Chile returned for more destroyers in 1965; presumably these negotiations ultimately led to the purchase of a pair of *Leander*s about five years later (from Yarrow, not Vickers). The British

Foreign Office aborted an attempted Vickers destroyer sale to Colombia, presumably involving similar ships (no designs seem to survive in Vickers files at the National Maritime Museum), apparently in a complicated attempt to convince Swedish builders not to sell such ships to Indonesia (they were sold instead to Colombia). (A D Baker III)

Dimensions:
374ft 9in between perpendiculars,
384ft waterline (at 10 ft draft)
402ft overall x 43ft;
Hull depth 23ft 6in to upper deck amidships (14ft 3in to lower deck).
Armament:
Four single Vickers 4in Mk (N)R
Six single 40mm 70-cal Bofors L/70
One triple Squid A/S mortar
One quadruple 21in torpedo tube mounting

T1784 was Thornycroft's unsuccessful bid for the Chilean destroyer contract won by Vickers, for the *Almirante Williams* class. It shows the company's typical long-forecastle hull, first adopted in wartime for the two Type IV 'Hunts' (the company described this ship as having a

Brecon hull). Despite having only a single funnel, this design offered unitised machinery. The 4in guns were the Mk N adopted for the Chilean ships. (A D Baker III)

Proposed Chilian (*sic*) destroyers outside profile

Length: 375ft 0in waterline
Breadth: 43ft 0in moulded
Depth: 22ft 6in to main deck; 30ft 0in to forecastle deck
Standard displacement: 2,700 tons approx.
SHP: 54,000 (echelon machinery); 60,000 (non echelon)

Speed (half fuel condition): 33.25kts (33.5kts 60,000 SHP)
Armament:
Four single 4in Mk (N)R
Four single 40mm Bofors
One triple Squid A/S mortar
One quadruple 21in torpedo tube mounting
Two 4in directors
Four Simple Tachymetric Directors (not shown on drawing)

TWY 1888 Proposed destroyers for the Brazilian Government

Length: 352ft 0in waterline
Breadth: 37ft 3in moulded
Depth moulded: 20ft 0in to main deck
Armament:
Four single 4in L/62 guns with Mk (N)R mountings
Five single L/70 40mm Bofors MTE
One triple Squid A/S mortar

1. Squid A/S mortar
2. Single 4in L/62 gun
3. Simple Tachymetric Directors (P&S)
4. Single 40mm L/70 Bofors (P&S)
5. Mk VI gun director
6. Single 40mm L/70 Bofors (C/L)
7. Bridge
8. Radar room
9. Operations room
10. Squid projectile stowage
11. 4in magazine
12. 40mm magazine
13. Engine room
14. Auxiliary room
15. Boiler room No 2
16. Boiler room No 1
17. Sonar gear compartments

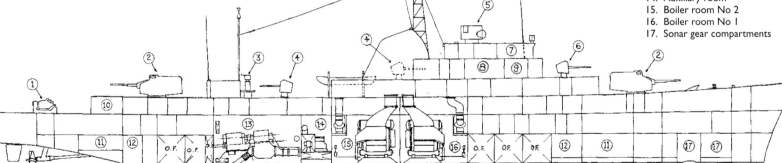

This destroyer (TWY 1888) was proposed to Brazil by a consortium of Thornycroft, White, and Yarrow. Its hull lines harked back to a 1944 proposal for an alternative to the 'Weapon' class (T1347, modified as T1351) using *Brecon* lines. That was a 370-footer

(2,200 tons standard) using a typical wartime powerplant (40,000 or 45,000 SHP). The advantage of the *Brecon* hull was that it allowed for much more topweight, so Thornycroft could offer the same gun armament but three pentad tubes – nearly three

times the torpedo battery – and 50 per cent more light anti-aircraft weapons (three twin Hazemeyer Bofors), plus more fuel in a fuller hull. As in *Brecon*, the firm claimed better ventilation of 'tween decks and a less windy bridge. T1351 was a shortened

version (350ft, 2,705 tons deep load). The version shown here was much more lightly armed, with Vickers' automatic 4in guns. Secondary armament was two twin or five single L70 Bofors; there were apparently no torpedo tubes. Displacement was given as

2,122½ tons normal (not a condition usually used) and 2,490 tons fully loaded. This ship was probably offered as a less expensive alternative to the large Brazilian destroyer shown above. (A D Baker III)

CHAPTER 7
Wartime Ocean Escorts

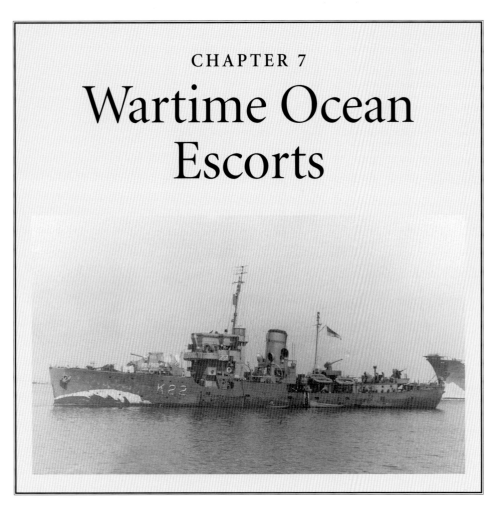

HMS *Gloxinia* was an early 'Flower' class corvette, with a short forecastle reminiscent of her whaler/trawler design origin. She shows a 4in gun forward, a 12pdr abaft her mainmast, and a single 2pdr right aft. Radars are Type 271, in a 'lantern' just abaft the bridge, and Type 286 at the masthead.

Numbers

Throughout the Second World War, the demand was first for large numbers of escorts and then for escorts suited to long runs. At the outset it was imagined that ASW escorts would be needed mainly near shore, but the German wolf-pack tactics made mid-ocean convoying essential. The pre-war level of four escorts per convoy proved insufficient in the face of wolf packs. By 1943 policy called for a close convoy escort of two large escorts (frigates or converted destroyers) and four to six corvettes (some of which might be replaced by large trawlers). Close escorts were supplemented by separate Support Groups, which could pursue and kill U-boats without exposing a convoy. They could also reinforce a convoy under particularly heavy attack. A typical support group consisted of four or five large escorts, which might be destroyers, sloops, or 'River' class frigates (however, one consisted of a 'River' leading ten 'Flower' class corvettes). By late in the war the accepted number of escorts per convoy had grown to eight or twelve. Support groups (Escort Groups) were slightly smaller. Against this need for many more escorts, wartime operational analysis showed that very large (hence fewer) convoys were preferable to small ones. They were not appreciably easier for U-boats to detect, and they did not occupy a significantly larger area of ocean. At least in theory escorts covered the convoy's perimeter, and the perimeter increased far more slowly than the number of ships being protected.

As of the summer of 1940 a total of 336 A/S ships were built and building, including 146 corvettes (nine later cancelled), and ninety 'Hunts' and sloops. With the German victories in France and Norway, so many more were needed that in July the Admiralty merged the minesweeper and ASW categories. By the autumn of 1941 troop convoys to the Middle East were being convoyed around the Cape and convoys were being escorted all the way across the Atlantic.

Estimated 1940 and 1941 requirements were:

	Summer 1940		Autumn 1941	
	Required	Built/Building	Required	Built/Building
Escorts	436	400	720	476
Fast Sweepers	245	100	184	153
Trawlers	1,900	600	1,100	650
Magnetic Sweepers	500	450	708	695

The British could not hope to build enough escorts; US and Canadian production was vital. Estimated British capacity in 1939 was forty 'Hunts' and seventy corvettes, in addition to an annual programme of two destroyer flotillas and thirty minesweepers. An annual programme suggested in 1941 was thirty sloops, eighty corvettes, forty fast minesweepers and thirty trawlers. The Admiralty took over merchant-ship slips at Harland & Wolff in Belfast to obtain another twenty corvettes (nine were later cancelled in favour of LSTs). Wartime expansion made it possible to order more destroyers in later programmes: two flotillas in 1940 plus two more in the supplemental programme, and then forty (five flotillas) in 1941 and later years.

There was also a crucial distinction between short- and long-range escorts. In the autumn of 1941 escorts had to make much longer runs. In the worst case as then understood, the Germans would seize Dakar and Madagascar, which would make the Cape route far more dangerous. Figures below were prepared in 1941 and projected to 1943 (endurances were at 12kts):

	Available	Required	Worst Case
Up to 3,500nm	322	48	72
3,500 to 6,000nm	236	451	440
Over 6,000nm	0	0	108

This explains why in 1941 the British so badly wanted 100 long-range US destroyer escorts.

Once the United States entered the war, it was clear that the Battle of the Atlantic could be won only by pooling building capacity on both sides of the Atlantic. Allocation and overall building policy thus were subject to the Combined (*ie* British and US) Chiefs of Staff. At a conference in Washington in June 1942 they drew up planning guidelines as their CCS 80/2. At this time the British, who had primary responsibility for Atlantic convoys, estimated that they needed a total of 1,044 escorts for all theatres under their operational control.[1] Given

numerous demands on shipbuilding, a compromise figure of 725 was accepted. It was assumed that, although the requirements of particular theatres might change, overall figures could be set. The initial estimate was:

	Atlantic	Pacific	Mediterranean	Indian Ocean	Total
British	550	—	10	165	725
US	380	210	—	—	590

On this basis the British were allocated 100 US-built destroyer escorts (they received seventy-eight 'Captain' class destroyer escorts and twenty-one 'Colony' class frigates).

In the spring of 1943 the British projected the situation to 1945, assuming that all ships of existing programmes were completed, that the US would allocate about 100 more ships to them (which did not happen), and that casualties would be 8 per cent a year. They omitted large fleet minesweepers from their totals.

	As of 1 June 1943	From New Construction		Losses Casualty	Overage	Net at end of programme
		British	US			
British	477	450	200	118	87	922
US	110	—	652	70	53	639

The surpluses of 197 for the British and forty-nine for the US Navy suggested that escort building could be curtailed. The British also estimated that 922 ships were about all the Empire could man.

Not long afterwards the Battle of the Atlantic began to turn in the Allies' favour. The Quadrant summit conference (Quebec, August 1943) reviewed escort shipbuilding. The First Sea Lord wanted to maintain the priority for escort building for at least another year, but the US Navy wanted to increase amphibious production at the expense of cargo ships and possibly escorts. Director of Plans concluded that no more escorts would be included in the 1944/5 Programme. The Admiralty finally cancelled fifty-two frigates and fifty corvettes on 30 October 1943. By this time the British were finding it difficult to man all the ships they had. Shortly after the mass cancellation First Sea Lord (Admiral Cunningham) asked for Canadian help to man ten frigates (seven 'Rivers' and three 'Lochs'), among other ships. They were transferred in 1944. The Admiralty was deeply interested in alternative roles for the escorts it had already laid down or completed, as discussed below.

Corvettes

As war approached, the coastal patrol role was considered more important than that of the ocean escort. However, the new small coastal escorts seemed ineffective. In January 1939 CNS (First Sea Lord) requested a survey of potential ASW ships. Alternatives were trawlers (either commercial vessels or specially-built to Admiralty specifications), whalecatchers (converted or newly built to Admiralty specifications), an adapted minesweeper, a coastal patrol ship modified for quick production, and a 'Hunt'. Conventional warships were far too expensive, could be built by only a few yards, and would take too long to build. Their machinery, whether geared turbines or diesels, would be in short supply in wartime. Only the reciprocating engines used by trawlers and whalecatchers would be easy to obtain. Such craft would be much cheaper to operate, partly because they needed much smaller crews: typically twenty-four for a trawler or thirty for the whalecatcher being considered (*Southern Pride*), but 144 for a 'Hunt' and sixty-three for the *Guillemot* class coastal patrol craft. It had to be accepted that these craft would lack the desired speed, 20–22kts, to run down fast submarines on the surface, which proved unfortunate when the Germans unexpectedly operated their U-boats on the surface at night when attacking convoys. It also had to be accepted that the commercial craft would not approach naval standards of survivability.

While DNC (Sir Stanley Goodall) was completing this survey, on 8 February he was visited by Edward Reed, the Smith's Dock designer. Having recently designed the Admiralty trawler, Reed was promoting his new, somewhat faster *Imperialist*.[2] DNC considered it little better than the Admiralty design. He was more interested in Reed's new whalecatcher *Southern Pride* and in the steam whaler *Sondra*.[3] There was a real operational difference between the 15kts of the whalecatcher and the 11kts of the trawler. The whalecatcher had been earmarked for wartime ASW conversion in 1935, but its unusual layout made it more expensive than in a trawler, and it was not considered at all survivable. Its bar keel precluded installation of a retractable Asdic. Reed offered to develop a ship which would combine the advantages of the whalecatcher and the trawler and would make 15–16kts. He estimated that the first ship could be built in six months, after which ships could be delivered at three-week intervals. Key to this building rate was the use of existing machinery and merchant-type Scotch boilers (DNC wanted warship-type water tube boilers to attain somewhat higher speed). Given Reed's proposal, on 20 March Controller proposed to build whalecatchers in the 1940 Programme (1939–40 Estimates), if a suitable design could be produced. Goodall submitted the design to the Board on 3 April 1939: 900 tons (standard), 16kts, 4,000nm at 12kts, with a complement of about thirty-five men. A somewhat larger al-

---

[1] ADM 1/13688, New Construction Escort Vessels (to be) Laid Down in 1944, file dated 1943.

[2] In a written contribution to a discussion at the Institution of Naval Architects, Reed recalled having designed the First World War 'Z' whalers, which might be considered predecessors to the 'Flowers', and then the 'Kil' class; he described the 'Flowers' as the ships proposed for construction at the end of the First World War. A W Watson, 'Corvettes and Frigates', in *Selected Papers on British Warship Design in World War II* (Conway Maritime Press, London:1983), papers presented to the Institution of Naval Architects in 1947.

[3] *Sondra* was 148ft 6in × 27ft 6in × 15ft 6ft × 8ft 10½in (fwd)/ 12ft 8in (aft), with one water tube boiler for 2,080 IHP at 153 RPM (15.178kts). *Southern Pride* was slightly larger: 160ft 9in × 31ft × 18ft × 11ft 9in (fwd)/15ft 7in (aft), with two boilers (one water tube) for 2,300 IHP at 166 RPM (16kts estimated). The standard Admiralty trawler was 150ft × 27ft 6in × 15ft 9in × 8ft 5⅜in (fwd)/ 12ft 1⅞in (aft), 683¼ tons deep, with 850 IHP at 150 RPM. (estimated 12.28kts). *Imperialist* was larger: 171ft 3in × 28ft 6in × 16ft × 12ft 4in (fwd)/17ft 11in (aft), using a 1,026 IHP triple-expansion engine at 137 RPM (12.903kts on trial).

ternative design using coal-burning machinery was rejected.

The whalecatcher was initially treated as a fast trawler, with the same Admiralty equipment, including a trawler Asdic (Type 123), a 4in gun, a Lewis gun either side of the bridge (later replaced by an Oerlikon) and a trawler depth charge battery (two throwers, twenty-five charges). Controller wanted the supports for the 4in gun to be able to take either a low-angle or an anti-aircraft weapon. By May a better Asdic (Type 128) had been chosen, and the outfit of 4in rounds was 100 rather than the fifty-two of the trawler. Complement was twenty-nine, including two officers (to provide three watches in the engine room). Ships would be built at trawler yards. Like the trawler, the whalecatcher could be used either for ASW or for minesweeping; in July 1939 Controller specifically decided against choosing one role or the other (many were fitted for sweeping, and late in 1939 some were towing magnetic [LL] sweeps).

Compared to *Southern Pride*, the new ship had a much longer forecastle, to accommodate the 4in gun, but it still stopped short of the bridge. The gun was raised on a bandstand (as in the contemporary Fast Escort ['Hunt']) to keep it dry. The rather tall bridge structure comprised an enclosed compass house over a wheelhouse slightly above forecastle deck level, the compass house being raised to give a good view over the bows. Asdic instruments were in the wheelhouse. As in a whalecatcher, the mast was stepped forward of the bridge, somewhat obscuring the view (in the whaler, it carried the lookout, who had to be as far forward as possible). Manoeuvrability was extremely important. The design originally showed a square stern post and rudder, Reed offering

instead a balanced spade rudder with deadwood cut away. DNC observed that retaining the deadwood would give the ship a quick rate of turn but a larger tactical diameter. The last major pre-war addition to the design was a single 2pdr on the centreline abaft the funnel (July 1939, in connection with the emergency building programme). Plans called for ultimately replacing it with a quadruple pompom, for which there was certainly space and weight, but that was never done. Compared to the faster *Guillemot*, the whalecatcher was less manoeuvrable and had less acceleration. While the whaler design went ahead, DNC had J S White revise the *Guillemot* design for quicker and cheaper production. Nothing seems to have come of this effort.

With war close in April 1939, the Committee on Imperial Defence (CID) asked for proposals which could be implemented in less than a year. Both the London Naval Treaty and the time limit ruled out more 'Hunts', so the Admiralty asked, among other units, for ten patrol vessels. They were the whalers, in the emergency building programme laid out in July 1939. By that time the whaler was the 1939 A/S Patrol Vessel, making it a clear replacement for the *Guillemot*. Reed's design became the first major Second World War escort, the 'Flower' class. The ships were initially called A/S Whalers. However, on 3 January 1941 they were renamed corvettes, and they are remembered as such. Ultimately the corvette designation came to indicate a second-rate or mass-production ASW craft, to be compared to the more capable but more expensive frigate.

By July further CID studies had brought the desired total to forty, another sixteen being added in August 1939. The first twenty-six ships (plus four for France, three of which being

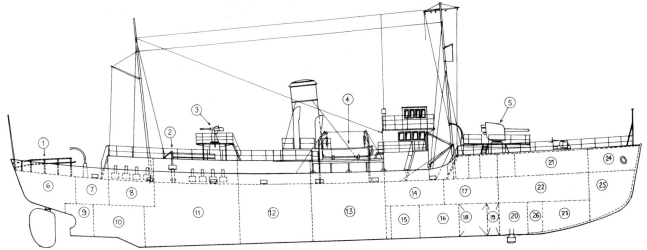

The 'Flower' class design as of February 1940. The main mast was later deleted and the radio aerials carried to spreaders on the funnel. (A D Baker III)

Patrol vessels of whaler type
('Flower' class corvette)
Concept as of February 1940

1. Two twelve-charge DC racks
2. DC thrower (P&S with DC davit above; sixteen DCs deck-stowed)
3. 2pdr Mk VIII pom-pom AA
4. 16ft dinghy (P&S)
5. 4in Mk IX gun on CPI mounting
6. Steering gear compartment
7. Provisions (Port); No 1 stores room

8. Petty Officers' Mess (Port); P.O. cabins (Starboard)
9. After peak
10. Engineers' stores
11. Engine room
12. Boiler room No 2, flanked by oil fuel tanks
13. Boiler room No 1, flanked by oil fuel tanks
14. Stores, pantry, wardroom (Port); officers' cabins (Starboard)
15. 2pdr magazine, flanked by oil fuel tanks
16. Spirit room (Port); lobby (Centreline); 4in

(Starboard)

shell room and magazine
17. Crew space
18. Reserve feed water
19. Fresh (potable) water
20. ASDIC (sonar) compartment
21. Crew space
22. Crew space
23. Chain locker
24. Main naval stores
25. Fore peak
26. No 4 naval stores

later taken over by the Royal Navy) were ordered on 25 July 1939 under the final peacetime programme, the 1939/40 Estimates (1940 Programme). Another thirty were ordered (1940 Supplemental Programme) on 31 August, including six for France, which were taken over on 6 July 1940.[4] The emergency programme called for fifty more: twenty were ordered (from a single yard, Harland & Wolff, the only contract given to a major builder) on 19 September, and another ten (from various yards) on 21 September 1939. Of another twenty planned in December 1939, only eighteen could be ordered immediately, the last two being subject to negotiations with the Ministry of Shipping, which was using the same yards for commercial production.[5] A further twenty were ordered from Harland & Wolff on 8 April 1940, of which six were for the French Navy (taken over by the Royal Navy in July 1940) and six were cancelled on 23 January 1941 (to make way for steam LSTs). Thus British orders to mid-1940 amounted to 114 ships in six groups. Another thirty projected ships were re-ordered late in 1940 as 'River' class frigates (see below), but three were later re-ordered as 'Flowers'.

The 1941 British programme (1940/1 Estimates) was twenty-one ships. British orders amounted to twelve ships.[6] Another three planned units were cancelled in favour of steam LSTs. Of two ships ordered late in 1941, one was reordered as a 'Castle' class corvette. The other was transferred to Canada upon completion. The 1942 Programme (1942/3 Estimates) was six more ships, two of which were cancelled (one after being ordered). Ten ships were ordered during the 1942/3 financial year, of which one was cancelled and three were transferred to Canada upon completion.[7]

Once war broke out, it became clear that convoys would have to be escorted over much greater distances. Thus in January 1940 the estimated requirement was 436 ocean escorts and 1,100 A/S ships. The corvettes could no longer be limited to coastal waters; they would have to stay at sea much longer.[8] For that they a much larger complement. The original plan (May 1939) was for two officers (a retired lieutenant commander or reservist in command plus a reserve sub-lieutenant or a Royal Navy Warrant Officer), three petty officers and twenty-four ratings. This small complement had been one of the attractions of the design in the first place. In September 1939 it was increased to thirty-two with the notation that four more would have to be borne for the engine room if the ship were to spend long periods at sea. In October

there was a further increase to forty-five: four officers, six petty officers, twenty-five seamen and ten stokers. Adding a steward and a leading cook brought the total to forty-seven. The seamen included a torpedoman to handle the depth charges, a Higher Submarine Detector (HSD – see below), and two Submarine Detectors for the Asdic. By mid-1940 ships were having their forecastles extended aft, to about abeam the funnel, to provide more accommodation and also to make them drier. Many were modified during refits. The depth charge load was increased to forty in November 1939, and by April 1941 ships typically had an additional pair of throwers and a total of sixty depth charges.

The first ships entered service in the autumn of 1940. In fair weather there was little difference in Asdic performance between a whalecatcher and a destroyer, and the catcher was little worse than a destroyer while steaming into the sea or in a following sea. However, in a head sea she was very wet, to the point that poor living conditions were clearly affecting personnel. In a beam sea (State 3 or 4) the ships rolled very heavily, up to 40° each way, and their Asdics were practically useless, many personnel being out of action due to sea sickness. The situation naturally worsened as fuel was expended.[9] The CO of *Hibiscus* reported in October 1940 that his ship rolled up to 50° each way, the roll being very short and sharp. He wanted larger bilge keels and the mainmast (which contributed inertia, keeping the ship rolling) removed. The larger bilge keels were duly fitted, but the more basic problem was that the ships were much shorter than the typical winter North Atlantic wave, so that they pitched badly. Ships also yawed badly, that being the price of their excellent manoeuvrability. The corvettes were also criticised for their congestion, their poor ventilation and their lack of electric power.

Given these problems, DNC decided to provide increased sheer and flare to new ships. On 1 November 1940 Controller asked Reed to prepare working plans for a 'modified "Flower" class'.[10] Ships not yet far advanced in mid-1941 were taken in hand. These ships had their 4in guns on a taller bandstand so that they could still fire down over their bows at surfaced submarines at close range. Ships already in service would be ballasted to reduce their metacentric height and thus to slow

[4] On 22 March 1940 it was decided to transfer to France *Snowdrop*, *Tulip*, *Verbena*, *Veronica*, *Wallflower* and *Zinnia*, all ordered for the Royal Navy on 31 August 1939. This order was reversed after France fell.
[5] Ten were ordered on 12 December, and another ten on 15 December.
[6] Two on 28 June, six on 3 August, one on 24 August, one on 24 August, one on 24 October, and one on 29 October.
[7] The 1941 ships were ordered on 24 October and 8 December. The 1942 ships were ordered on 26 February (one), 15 May (two), 22 July (three), 25 July (two), 28 July (one), and 30 July (one, cancelled, not laid down).
[8] There was some hope that corvettes could replace armed merchant cruisers used in the Northern Patrol blocking shipping *en route* to Germany via the North Sea. To this end six early ships were fitted with longer-range radio sets and with a tall mainmast to raise their aerials: *Gladiolus*, *Arabis*, *Clarkia*, *Calendula*, *Gardenia* and *Periwinkle*, but they lacked the necessary rough water endurance.

[9] Report by C-in-C Western Approaches, 20 September 1940, in the 'Flower' Class Cover (No. 611A). Discussing the Watson paper, W J Holt RCNC, who had been involved in wartime coastal craft design, remarked that liveliness was a function of ship size. The 'Flower' was small for the winter North Atlantic and relatively fast for her size; 'inevitably crews experienced a rough time'. As unpleasant as the ride in a 'Flower' might have been, Holt reminded his audience that a smaller faster ship was far worse: '... from personal experience ... the motion of a corvette ... is positively stately in comparison with the motion of a coastal forces craft in the same seaway'. D K Brown has pointed out that accounts of very rough North Atlantic weather date mainly from when corvettes were the dominant ocean escorts. Such anecdotes are extremely rare for the larger 'River' class, but it is unlikely that the ocean became markedly calmer. Brown sees the anecdotes as evidence of the connection between escort size and seakeeping.
[10] Notes in the 'River' rather than the 'Flower' Class Cover. *Samphire* (Smith's Dock) was prototype. *Stonecrop*, *Sweetbriar* and *Vetch*, also at Smith's, were also modified. A mid-1941 discussion made specific reference to two ships then building at Alexander Hall, *Hyderabad* (ex-*Nettle*) and *Poppy*. Another ship at this yard was *Coriander*, which became the Free French *Commandante Detroyat*. At least one ship completed in 1940, *Bluebell*, seems to have been modernised. Others modified on the slip included *Lotus* (ii) and *Meadowsweet* building at Hill under 12 December 1939 orders; *Pink* in the same series; *Potentilla*, *Thyme*, and *Snowflake* of the 8 August 1940 series, *Godetia* ordered on 24 August 1940, *Tamarisk* ordered on 24 October 1940, *Balsam* ordered on 29 October 1940, and the ships ordered in 1941–2.

their roll. As for yawing, one ship (*Snowdrop*, the next to complete) would have her deadwood filled-in for tests. Other improvements were also considered at about this time. A sketch prepared before the meeting showed a twin 4in anti-aircraft gun forward in a zareba and superfiring quadruple 0.5in machine guns aft. The front of the bridge was curved, presumably to deflect seas coming aboard, and above it was a radar antenna. Four depth charge throwers were arranged on each side of the quarterdeck, reloaded via a gantry above them, with the charges stowed below decks. On the centreline were three lines of charges, discharging via stern ports.

Initially some ships had separate air lookout platforms built atop their compass houses, raising their superstructures. Bridge wings at wheelhouse level were extended to accommodate machine guns (initially 0.303in, later Oerlikons). Ships refitted or completed with long forecastles had the compass house removed, so that the bridge structure was lowered, the wings remaining at the same height. The Royal Navy much preferred a clear view across the bridge, which in this case was obstructed by the wheelhouse. The next stage, then, was to eliminate the wheelhouse, the wheel being moved down a deck. In this naval-style bridge the Asdic hut was moved to a position overhanging the fore end, the charthouse being alongside. It then matched the bridge recently designed for the 'River' class (see below). Ships with increased sheer had their bridges raised a level so that the wheelhouse below the bridge still had a clear view over the bows, at that time a definite requirement.

For all corvettes, radar was generally the Type 271 'lantern', initially directly abaft the pilothouse and later offset to port or starboard. The most important wartime advance in weaponry was addition of a Hedgehog spigot mortar (see below) either in a 'split' version, with twelve rounds on each side of the superstructure, or more often simply offset from the centreline.

The corvettes had two crucial limitations. Firstly, U-boats attacking at night on the surface could outrun a corvette, so Controller asked Reed for higher speed. In 1940 Reed promised to investigate a 20-knot design. The second issue, not raised at this time at least in the context of the corvettes, was range. Because they had been designed for coastal work, the corvettes lacked the endurance to cross the Atlantic with a convoy. Convoys were therefore run in stages, escorts changing in Iceland. The need to pick up new escorts near Iceland created a choke point near Iceland, which U-boats could exploit despite British attempts to route convoys evasively (later the need to remain within range of very long-range ASW aircraft had similar consequences).[11] Hence the need for much greater range in the next class, the 'River' class frigate.

Canada was the other major corvette builder. To get around the limits of British yards, the Admiralty initially proposed ordering ships in the United States and Canada. A plan to buy seventy ships had to be scaled down drastically because it

[11] Commander Ken P Hansen, RCN, gained this insight in his study of Second World War naval logistics. In 1941 US Atlantic Fleet commander Admiral E J King pointed out the problem and offered to provide US escorts all the way across; US destroyers had the necessary range. In Hansen's view the Royal Navy rejected King's proposal because it would have placed US officers in tactical command of convoy escort groups.

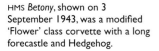

HMS *Betony*, shown on 3 September 1943, was a modified 'Flower' class corvette with a long forecastle and Hedgehog.

involved scarce foreign exchange; it soon became entangled with the Canadian 'Tribal' class destroyer programme (see Chapter 2). The pre-war Canadian expansion programme included eight anti-submarine ships (four for each coast), expanded to forty (eight groups of five) by October 1939. Including projected replacements, the Canadians wanted sixty escorts and forty-eight minesweepers (the two had to be traded off, because a minesweeper required about the same industrial effort as an escort). Initially the planned escort was the *Bramble* class, which the Royal Navy used as a minesweeping sloop (the minesweeper was the smaller *Bangor*). Then the Canadians learned, almost accidentally, of the 'Flower' design. At its spring 1939 meeting the Canadian Manufacturers' Association decided to send a delegation to the United Kingdom to study war production. It sailed on 27 July and returned at the end of August. A shipbuilding subcommittee returned with 'Flower' class plans, brought to the Canadian National Research Council by a member attached to the mission. The Canadian naval staff preferred the 'Flower' to the *Bramble* because it was simpler, hence easier to build. Its reduced endurance was considered acceptable for ships which would operate only in coastal waters.

By December 1939 it seemed that thirty ships could be built in 1940 and sixty in 1941. When the two-year programme was approved by the Canadian Privy Council in February 1940, it seemed likely that corvettes would be bartered for 'Tribal' class destroyers. Thus the four destroyers in the programme (see Chapter 2) required that at least twenty corvettes be ordered. Canadian requirements accounted for another forty-four ships, for a total of sixty-four corvettes under the 1939/40 and 1940/1 Programmes. In addition, another six were ordered in December 1940, and another ten in March 1941. It turned out, however, that the British lacked sufficient foreign exchange to buy all twenty, but when the United States passed the Lend Lease Act in March 1941, that financial problem was solved. The ten ships ordered for the Royal Navy were in effect replaced by ten more ordered to US account (for ultimate transfer to the British), and the US Navy ordered another five (October–December 1941). The total of early 'Flowers' built in Canada was thus ninety-five, far more than the Canadians imagined they could build in 1940–1. Of the fifteen Lend-Lease ships, the US Navy retained eight, the other seven being turned over, as planned, to the Royal Navy. The Royal Navy transferred another ten British-built corvettes to the US Navy under reverse Lend-Lease.

When the barter agreement collapsed in March 1940, the Canadians were left with fifty-four corvettes, more than they had planned (which was a bare minimum in any case), and fewer minesweepers than they wanted (ultimately twenty-eight were ordered). They therefore modified their version of the 'Flower' design for better sweeping capacity. The galley was moved to just forward of the engine room to clear space on the quarterdeck for a steam winch, the stern was widened and squared off to provide space for sweeping fairleads as well as depth charge tracks, and special sweeping davits were fitted. The extra weight aft, which might have raised the bow and thus affected sonar performance, was accepted (in fact 'Flowers' tended to be bow-heavy, so the modification was successful). Because Canada lacked industrial capacity, these ships had magnetic rather than gyro compasses, and so had to make do with trawler (Type 123) rather than sloop Asdics. Similarly, Canada did not produce the 2pdr pompom mounted aft in British 'Flowers', so they generally had two twin 0.5in machine guns aft, with Lewis guns on the bridge. Minesweeping gear was ordered landed in May 1942. From hull 61 on, Canadian corvettes had their forecastles extended. The sixteen repeat 'Flowers' of 1940–1 were built without minesweeping fittings (they could be distinguished by the lack of davits), and they had water tube rather than Scotch boilers.

By early 1941 the Canadian Naval Staff wanted to buy only 'River' class frigates in future (and *Algerine* rather than *Bangor* class minesweepers), but the Canadian Great Lakes shipyards could not build them (they could not pass through the locks to the St Lawrence River). Nor were there resources to design a new frigate with 'River' performance but short enough (255ft). The Canadians therefore ordered more corvettes, modified with extended forecastles and increased sheer and flare. The foremast was finally moved abaft the bridge structure, for better visibility. The superstructure was redesigned, as in the British Modified 'Flower' class, the 4in gun being placed on a bandstand to clear spray, with a wide platform connecting it to the wheelhouse (the Hedgehog was on this platform). These ships were armed with the new Mk XIX semi-automatic 4in gun, using fixed rather than separate ammunition, elevating to 60°. Their funnels were vertical rather than raked, to make it more difficult for a U-boat commander to judge their course through his periscope. Boilers had forced draught, so there were no ventilators. The bow was noticeably more raked (length overall was 208ft 4in instead of the earlier 205ft 1in). These ships had additional fuel tanks, for an endurance of 7,400nm at 10kts (the Canadians originally rated the ships at 3,450nm at 12kts), and were described as the IE (Increased Endurance) type. This series amounted to thirty-eight ships (twenty-seven completed): eight in February 1942, eight (one cancelled) in April 1942, seventeen (five cancelled) at the end of June 1942, and five (all cancelled) in June 1943. Note that the June 1942 ships are associated with the Canadian 1943/4 Programme. This programme lagged badly, so seven corvettes were switched to the later 'Castle' design in 1943 (they were cancelled before they could be ordered). The *Algerine* class minesweepers, which replaced the smaller *Bangors*, could be built on the Lakes, and the Canadians planned to use them as follow-on corvettes. The Royal Navy strongly disagreed. Since the Canadians had little need for new

minesweepers, they willingly traded *Algerines* for British-built corvettes: four 'Flowers' (see above) and twelve 'Castles'. The French planned to order twenty-three ships, including six from French yards. Of these the Royal Navy took over sixteen. Four French-built ships were completed for the Germans and two were cancelled. Totals built amounted to 145 British, 122 Canadian, and four French.

Plans called for building further units in Australia and in Hong Kong, but that was not done. The closest Australian equivalent was the smaller *Bathurst* class minesweeper, which was often used as (and called) a corvette. The Royal New Zealand Navy called some large trawlers corvettes.

This very large programme was dwarfed by wartime requirements. In July 1939 the estimated requirement for home waters was 236 A/S and A/A escorts, of which 172 had been provided. The latter figure comprised the thirty-six 'V' and 'W' class destroyers scheduled for escort conversion and the eleven old 'R' and 'S' class destroyers, forty-nine sloops (including RAN), twenty 'Hunts' and fifty-six corvettes.[12]

There was no Lend-Lease equivalent to the 'Flower' class. The closest was the US PCE, derived from the 180ft *Admirable* class ocean minesweeper designed for the Royal Navy in 1940. Although 150 such ships were included in the original 1941 Lend-Lease programme, ultimately only fifteen were transferred, as the 'Kil' class. They operated in A/S Groups at Gibraltar and Freetown, showing they were considered too small for the North Atlantic. The larger ex-US *Auk* class minesweepers (British *Catherine* class) were only rarely used as escorts.

With the Battle of the Atlantic turning in the Allies' favour by mid-1943 these small escorts were no longer so badly needed. Given their very low speed, they were never considered for

---

[12] CAB 102/536.

The sketch on which the 'River' class was based shows its *Black Swan* ancestry. In effect a very heavy depth charge battery largely replaced the heavy anti-aircraft battery of the *Black Swan*, and commercial rather than naval construction standards also ate up weight. This is the version with a triple-expansion powerplant. (A D Baker III)

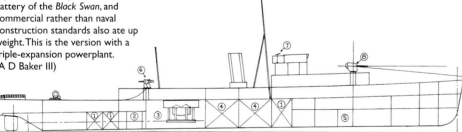

Corvette of 20 knots speed

Admiralty DNC 30/B 9 0
Nov. 1940
Proposal 'A'
Approx dimensions:
283ft 0in bp x 36ft 0in x 17ft 6in depth moulded x 10ft 6in mean draft x 1,600 tons.
Trim about 4ft 0in by the stern
Machinery:
Two sets reciprocating; total IHP 5,500. Two watertube boilers

Armament:
One 4in Mk IX gun on CP1 mounting
Two 2pdr Mk VIII on Mk VIII mountings
Two Lewis guns
Arrangements for combined A/S and M/S equipments with a total of fifty depth charges and Mk 2 Orepesa sweep
Proposal 'B'
Approx dimensions:
283ft 0in bp x 34ft 6in x 17ft 6in depth moulded x 10ft 0in mean draft x 1,360 tons.

Machinery:
Two sets of geared turbines and two watertube boilers; total SHP 4,300.
Armament:
As for Proposal 'A'
1. Oil fuel tank
2. 2pdr magazine
3. Engine room
4. Boiler room, flanked by oil fuel tanks
5. 4in magazine
6. 2pdr (P&S, staggered)
7. Lewis MG (P&S)
8. 4in BL gun

post-war modernisation. Modification as small monitors for the D-Day landings was rejected in favour of modified landing craft. After the war, their excellent sea-keeping qualities made 'Flowers' useful as ocean weather ships.

Ahead-Throwing Weapons

While the 'Flowers' were being built, work proceeded on a variety of ahead-thrown anti-submarine weapons. Their potential was appreciated pre-war, at least by the ASW (Asdic) research group at Fairlie. In 1939 it reported research beginning to compare the effects of a single massive depth charge (1,600lbs) with numerous 25lb contact charges. In January 1940 Fairlie was given permission to design a multiple depth charge mortar in co-operation with Vickers-Armstrong.[13] It employed a line of barrels on a fore-and-aft axis which could swing both to stabilise them against roll and to move the point of impact from port to starboard. About the same time Thornycroft offered a five-barrel version of its First World War depth charge mortar, later called the 'Five Wide Virgins'. Fixed in the deck, it was neither stabilised nor aimable. Among others proposing alternative weapons, the new Miscellaneous Weapons Department proposed to adapt the army's spigot mortar as a lighter alternative to a conventional mortar. With Fairlie's roll stabilisation, a 24-spigot version became Hedgehog (wartime Hedgehogs were manually stabilised). Only Hedgehog and the 'Five Wide Virgins' reached the trial stage. They represented two very different approaches. Hedgehog made up for Asdic imprecision by firing a large number of bombs, which fell in a 120ft circle (which could be moved within about 20° port or starboard by tilting the spigots). The bombs therefore had to be quite small, but it turned out that each was still large enough to penetrate a submarine's pressure hull if it hit. Bombs which did not hit did not explode, so they did not roil the water like a failed depth-charge attack. In theory, Hedgehog did not need any estimate of U-boat depth, although in practice an indication of depth made it far more accurate. Without a depth-finder, the usual assumption was 175ft. In theory the Thornycroft mortar made up for imprecision by using large depth charges which should be lethal if they fell near the submarine (in effect it produced an aimed depth charge attack), but in the absence of stabilisation it was difficult to aim.

Hedgehog won out over the Thornycroft mortar because its estimated kill probability (based on simulator runs) was 50 to 60 per cent, compared to an estimated 20 per cent for depth charges (6 per cent in reality). Sea trials were conducted on board HMS *Westcott*, the weapon replacing A gun. In early 1942 tests five out of eight salvoes hit the target, and

---

[13] Hackmann, *Seek and Strike*, p 365. By mid-1939 the Fairlie A/S establishment was interested in using multiple small projectiles. By 1940 it envisaged a pair of ten-barrel mortars, one on each side of the forecastle, producing a circular pattern in the water. DNO ordered explosive content increased from 20lbs to 30lbs. That required redesign of the Fairlie mortar, but had little effect on Hedgehog, which had no barrel within which the projectile travelled. By June 1941 Hedgehog was clearly the favoured choice, although work on the Thornycroft mortar continued.

HMS *Helmsdale* shows a typical wartime 'River' class configuration, with a Type 271 radar 'lantern' at the after end of her bridge and HF/DF on her topmast. Her Hedgehog is barely visible at the base of her forward superstructure. Note the long open quarterdeck, adopted originally for minesweeping. *Helmsdale* became A/S experimental ship in 1945, replacing HMS *Kingfisher*; she was fitted with double Squid in B position.

by the end of the year Hedgehog had been installed on board over 100 ships. By June 1943, about forty of sixty 'River' class frigates had Hedgehog on board, together with about seventy-two of 120 'Flowers', two of thirty *Black Swans*, and fourteen of thirty 'A' through 'I' class escort destroyers.

Hedgehog proved unexpectedly unpopular: those firing it gained no reinforcement in the form of an explosion to indicate that something had happened. Thus it lacked the 'moral effect' of depth charges. Moreover, unlike their experience with depth charges, crews attacking with Hedgehog never saw a U-boat forced to the surface: it either sank the U-boat or had no effect at all. Without such visual evidence of success, real kills tended to be scored only as 'probables'. Hedgehog sank its first submarine only in November 1942, and until the end of 1943 its success rate was only about 10 per cent, comparable to that in a depth charge attack. Only in early 1944 did a special group at the Londonderry ASW base find out why. New instructions prevented use in unfavourable conditions but required it in favourable ones. In shallow water in the Channel during the Normandy landings it achieved better than 40 per cent success. By that time its perceived ineffectiveness had led to the development of the non-contact Squid which in effect superseded it (see below).

The 'River' Class

Adapting the 'Flowers' to open-ocean escorts was never seen as more than a stopgap. German occupation of France and Norway in the spring of 1940 provided bases on the Atlantic coast, greatly enlarging U-boat operating areas. To catch a surfaced U-boat, an escort needed a sea speed of about 20kts.[14] Given the major deficiencies in the 'Flower' class, on 27 November 1940 First Sea Lord convened a conference to de-

cide what sort of ship should be built. It was understood that the desirable escort speed was 22kts in half-oil condition.

Preparing for the meeting, DNC rejected the desired speed: he and E-in-C argued jointly that to be that fast a ship would have to be 350ft long (later he said 300–320ft), displacing about 1,500 tons simply to maintain her speed in the Atlantic. She would need a 12,000 SHP powerplant, which would have to be steam turbines (in short supply): diesels were not powerful enough, and a reciprocating plant would be too massive and would not provide enough acceleration. Many corvette builders had no experience with turbines, and their building berths were not long enough for such a ship. DNC developed two alternative designs, both with long forecastles (as in the modified corvettes) for good sea-keeping, both capable of either ASW or minesweeping, and both with armament which would also be offered for a converted ex-US flush-deck ('Town' class) destroyer. Proposal A used two sets of 'Flower' class reciprocating machinery and water tube boilers to generate 5,500 IHP, which would give 20kts in half-oil condition. Dimensions were 283ft × 36ft × 17ft 6in × 10ft 6in (1,270 tons standard). Proposal B used a repeat *Black Swan* powerplant (4,300 SHP geared turbines) and would displace 1,030 tons standard; it too would make about 20kts in half-oil condition. DNC and E-in-C much preferred the somewhat slower Proposal A.

Chairing, ACNS(T) Rear Admiral H R Moore laid out Staff Requirements for an 'ideal convoy escort': good seakeeping, a speed of at least 20kts (ideally 22kts in half-oil condition), and an endurance at economical speed of 3,500–4,000nm. The gun battery could be limited to one dual-purpose 4in gun with the 'simplest fire control', two single 2pdrs and two Oerlikons. The important armament would be 100 depth charges with enough throwers (four each side) to provide a pattern of fourteen. The ship would need a bow reinforced

---

[14] Explaining the logic of the new design in a despatch dated 16 February 1941, the US Naval Attaché mentioned speed rather than range.

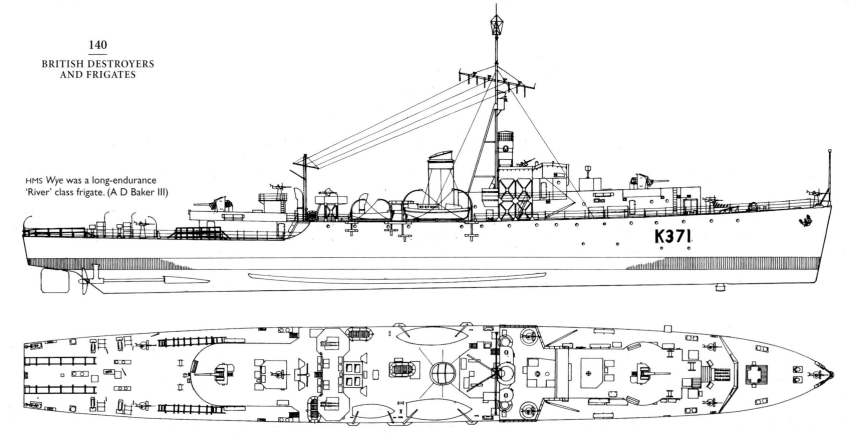

HMS *Wye* was a long-endurance 'River' class frigate. (A D Baker III)

for possible ramming (and for ice), and she would have to be handy, to manoeuvre against a submerged submarine, with considerable astern power and with machinery simple enough for an inexperienced crew. DNC offered the new fast corvette already sketched (the term had already been adopted, at least unofficially).

DNC suggested rebuilding the 'Town' class destroyers supplied by the United States. To get enough ships, he proposed lobbying the Americans (he said the US Navy still had 120 such ships on hand). Ships might even be fitted out in the United States. With forward boilers removed (to provide more oil fuel) the ship would still produce 13,000 SHP, sufficient for 22kts, with short bursts at 25kts. Endurance under war conditions would be 3,800nm at 15kts. There were clear disadvantages, such as the lack of a forecastle, hence poorer seakeeping than might be desired. However, the bridge could be moved aft to be clearer of seas coming aboard and modified to resist weather better. All the torpedo tubes would be removed. Gun armament would be reduced to one US-type low-angle 4in gun and one British-type dual-purpose 4in gun (which could fire starshell), plus two single 2pdr pompoms and two Oerlikons. The main armament would be the desired heavy battery of eight throwers and three depth charge traps. DNC admitted that her turning performance would not be very good. Deputy Controller was less than impressed. The only ships suitable for conversion were sixteen 1,190-ton ships transferred to Britain (other flush-deckers were not considered suitable). Given the pressing need for escorts, he was willing to modify only ships out of action for more than eight weeks for defects and repairs. In fact only three ships were en-

tirely rebuilt, their two forward funnels being removed to convert them into long-range escorts.

New construction was the only realistic solution. DNC pointed out that Design A met all the requirements except the 22kts speed. Controller agreed, and orders to develop Design A were placed on 28 November. A few days later VCNS formally agreed that the speed was acceptable. Design A was sent to the Board late in January 1941. DNC said that seven firms which had built 'Flower' class corvettes could build the new ships, and that they had already been sent particulars of the design. The Board approved the Legend and drawings on 7 March 1941. The project was so urgent that formal Staff Requirements had never been written, though drafts were circulated in January through March 1941. Controller formally approved the Staff Requirement on 1 June 1941. DNC's fast corvette became the 'River' class frigate.

It was decided at the outset that the ship's amenities would be to warship standard; the merchant ship standard had been criticised in the 'Flower' class. She would be ventilated to warship standard, and officers would live forward. She would have awnings for tropical service. Given the much greater electrical load than that in a 'Flower', the ship would have two 60 kW reciprocating steam generators and a 60 kW diesel generator. The ship used the *Black Swan* hull structure, with some additional material to reduce stresses and thus to allow for construction by non-naval builders. She followed merchant ship practice in some details, for quicker production. Scantlings were reviewed by Lloyd's Register and the British Corporation (in current terms, these were non-MilSpec ships).

The requirement was urgent: DNC's designers worked very

fast. Within two weeks they had a sketch design available for inspection. It was 295ft 6in long on the waterline (283ft between perpendiculars, 301ft 4in overall) trimmed 4ft by the stern to give the propellers sufficient immersion. Form and dimensions were set by the desire to sustain 20kts under Atlantic conditions. The ships were given considerable flare and sheer forward for dryness in heavy weather. To limit rolling, they had a square midships section and deep bilge keels. For dryness, the forecastle extended right aft. For good turning the ship had a large rudder and the deadwood was cut away aft. The hull was modelled on those of the *Black Swan* and the *Halcyon* class ocean minesweeper. The new ship was described as much like a *Black Swan*, but with far less armament (in effect, but never described as, a second-rate sloop).

At a conference in Bath on 10 December 1940, E-in-C suggested that some ships might have to have turbines after all; even reciprocating engine capacity was limited. He proposed a souped-up *Black Swan* powerplant (5,000 SHP, 20.25kts in half-oil condition), turning smaller propellers at higher RPM, hence no longer needing the large trim by the stern. The required redesign was clearly undesirable, but heavier (and higher-powered, 6,500 SHP) turbines were fitted to five ships: *Cam, Chelmer, Ettrick, Halladale* and *Helmdale*. They were not redesigned, and they had the same boilers as the reciprocating ships. Because the installation was quite inefficient (it was chosen by necessity, not any desire for better speed) the extra power added only 0.6kts.

From an Asdic point of view, the new design was attractive because of its deeper draft and reduced tendency to roll. Corvettes suffered from quenching (the sonar coming out of the water or at least rising to too shallow a depth), probably due to their very quick, deep roll. The ex-US destroyers also quenched badly due to their shallow draft. The ship would have Type 128 Asdic because she would have the necessary gyro-compass and because the directing gear could be only 35ft from the forepeak. The original design showed a hut at the after end of the bridge to contain both Asdic controls and radar (ASV) gear. However, by late January 1941 there was a definite preference for moving the A/S controls to the fore end of the bridge, with the roof of the structure sloped forward and glass shield atop it. This arrangement would soon also be adopted in the 'Flower' class (see above). The Staff Requirement called for Asdic to be operable in any conditions under which a destroyer could operate hers. While this design was being developed, Reed had produced his own design for a 20-knot corvette, resembling a stretched 'Flower', powered by two sets of corvette engines. It was rejected.[15]

Initially the ASW armament was limited to depth charges; only later was an ahead-throwing weapon added. By December 1940 the battery was set at eight throwers (thirty-two depth charges), thirty charges on rails, and at least thirty-eight charges

---

[15] The design showed a long forecastle covering the engine room. Armament and fittings would be as in a 'Flower'. Reed submitted weights on 26 November and a preliminary design on 6 December 1940, for a 320ft (between perpendiculars) × 39ft × 19ft × 11ft 6in ship, 2,095 tons fully loaded (1,545 tons light).

HMS *Tay*, shown on 1 April 1950, was one of the few 'Rivers' updated late in the Second World War. A Type 277 radar replaced her Type 271 'lantern,' and the Oerlikons at the break of the forecastle were replaced by single Bofors. She retained three single Oerlikons on her foredeck, one in her eyes and two abeam her Hedgehog.

K235

in a magazine, for a total of 100. This very heavy depth-charge battery could deliver a double-layer pattern, which was considered essential. Ultimately the after decks were strong enough for 100 depth charges, 50 per cent of them heavy (600lbs rather than 300lbs). The first twenty-four ships had the 100 depth charges; later units had 120. All had eight throwers and two stern tracks, for a fourteen-charge pattern. Originally three depth-charge rails were wanted, but it was clearly difficult to combine them with the desired minesweeping capability. DTASW wanted depth-charge rails covered in so that charges could not be stuck in place by dried salt spray, but that could not be done. While the ship was being designed, an ahead-throwing weapon, an abortive 13.5in depth-charge thrower, was being developed. In mid-January 1941 DNC confirmed that the forecastle and the upper deck forward could be adapted to either this thrower or to a multiple depth-bomb gun.

Hedgehog was adopted, with sufficient ammunition for six salvoes. An important issue was whether fitting a Hedgehog would limit the depression of the 4in gun, necessary to engage a surfaced U-boat at short range. Late in the war there was interest in re-siting Hedgehog to the signal deck (B position), as in the projected Squid conversion described below. *Monnow* seems to have been unique in being refitted with a split Hedgehog abeam her 4in gun, to reduce sea damage. A new power-stabilised Hedgehog became available in 1945. The first ship to receive it was *Tay*. *Ness* was taken in hand on the Tyne in July 1945 before being fitted with Bofors guns. As of 1 August it was scheduled for *Aire, Inver, Dart, Evenlode* and any other ships scheduled for service in the Far East. Ships which had already had their tropical refits would be fitted abroad. However, this programme ended with the Japanese surrender.

Ships had sufficient space for a magnetic (LL) sweep, but only at the expense of their wire sweep gear. They were also fitted for acoustic sweeping. As a sweeper the ship could carry fifty depth charges. Designing the ships so that they could operate as sweepers had a consequence: upper deck width had to be maintained right aft. That in turn provided a reserve of

buoyancy at the stern. On the other hand, the quarterdeck was quite low, and in April 1943 there were complaints of local structural damage there aboard HMS *Waveney* due to bad weather. Some strengthening was needed. For sweeping, the ship would carry only the forward 4in gun, plus three multiple close-range guns (two to fire forward, two on the beam, and three astern). Endurance would be 2,000nm at 18kts.

The initially-approved gun battery was two 4in (single mounts fore and aft); four sided close-range anti-aircraft guns (single 2pdrs or Oerlikons: only *Rother* and *Spey* had 2pdrs), two firing ahead and two astern (two in the bridge wings, two at the break of the forecastle); and four light machine guns. These weapons would be supplemented by a single illuminant projector (such as the Holman Projector). In addition to these anti-aircraft weapons, in 1943 some ships (including *Deveron, Mourne, Tweedy* and *Tavy*) received a pair of 6pdrs on the forecastle abeam the Hedgehog, to engage surfaced submarines. Beginning in 1942, ships had their single Oerlikons replaced by twins. In August Director of Plans urged DTSD and DGD to provide corvettes (*ie* the new frigates) with more powerful anti-aircraft armament, as they might be used on convoys to Russia and to Malta; however, he would not accept any great increase in building time nor any loss of endurance. Subject to avoiding any delay in completion, ships were ordered fitted with positions for six more Oerlikons (total ten), which were not to be fitted without instructions (to limit additional topweight). The six guns were ordered fitted to *Rother, Spey, Tay* and *Exe*. *Test* received five guns. A month later three more ships were ordered fitted: *Wear, Kale* and *Jed*. In October 1942 *Wear* showed one mount right forward, and one on each side abeam her Hedgehog, for a total of seven Oerlikons. By 1945 some ships, such as *Helford*, had ten single Oerlikons (no twins). Extra Oerlikons were considered temporary. By this time DGD was pressing for one 4in mounting (preferably a twin) with a barrage director (using radar and an auto barrage control unit), plus two twin Hazemeyer Bofors (heavy units with self-contained predictors) or the equivalent, and the maximum number of twin power Oerlikons. Deputy

Controller rejected what he saw as an attempt to turn these very cheap ships into 'full-grown warships of the "sloop" class'. In 1945, ships scheduled to deploy to the Far East were ordered armed with single Bofors in place of the Oerlikons at the break of the forecastle. In October 1945 these guns were listed on board *Awe*, *Inver*, *Nith*, *Neas* and *Tay*. *Barle* had one, and *Usk* had three. *Swale* had two single 2pdrs. The number of single Oerlikons varied, the maximum being ten (in, for example, *Bann* and *Dart*).

The after 4in magazine was designed to be oil-tight, so that it could be converted into an additional oil tank for increased endurance. The ship had to be able to fly a barrage balloon (twenty-two were so fitted). Two radars, one for short-range surface/air warning and one for surface warning, were required (later only one, Type 271, was fitted). In mid-1942 it was confirmed that the destroyer air-warning radar set, Type 286, was not needed. Ships were later fitted with Type 277 on a lattice mast.

These ships were initially called Fast Corvettes, then Twin Screw Corvettes. In February 1943 they were redesignated again, as Frigates, and this name finally stuck. During the Second World War the frigate was a sort of second-rate sloop. After the war, however, the name was attached to all long-range ocean escorts; ultimately it was not at all clear how frigates could be distinguished from destroyers. Frigates clearly required more resources than corvettes, but they were much closer to what was needed. Moreover, one frigate escorting a convoy all the way across the Atlantic might equate to two

corvettes on the legs to and from Iceland. Frigates were so vital that by 13 December thirty corvettes of the projected 1941 War Programme (1940–1 Estimates) were cancelled in favour of them (three were later re-ordered as corvettes). Another twenty-nine were included in the 1941/2 Programme, and another 15 in the 1942/3 Programme (forty of which were cancelled). Total British production was fifty-seven.

There was still some interest in higher performance, on the ground that no existing type could cover fast troop convoys (for which endurance should be 6,000nm at 15kts). Even the new US destroyer escort, then under design, was not credited with more than 6,000nm at 12kts (when diesels were substituted for steam turbines, range was extended to 12,000nm, but that was not known at the time). Initially it seemed that the requirement for a continuous seagoing speed of 20kts (which meant 22kts in trials condition at half-oil displacement), would be revived; but DNC argued again that this speed would mean a destroyer-size ship equipped with scarce high-powered turbines. Moreover, the first ship of any new design could not be ready before 1943.[16] Instead, DNC offered a modified version of the new fast corvette. Simply omitting the after 4in gun and using its magazine for tankage (total 500 tons) would increase endurance to 4,750nm at 15kts under

[16] A sketch design showed 350ft (waterline) × 38ft 6in × 10ft, with a standard displacement of 1,800 tons. A total of 715 tons of oil fuel would give an endurance of 6,000nm at 15kts under operational conditions, or 8,500nm at 15kts clean (compared to 4,180nm and 5570nm for the new twin-screw corvette as then designed). Armament would be no more than that of the twin-screw corvette: two 4in dual-purpose, two single 2pdr, two Oerlikons.

The Canadian 'River' class frigate *Antigonish*, July 1950, with a twin 4in gun forward. She has US electronic equipment: an SU surface-search radar in the masthead radome, and a DAU HF/DF. Another 'River' and a Canadian 'Cr' class destroyer are alongside.

operational conditions and 6,330nm under trial conditions. Making certain store-rooms oil-tight and omitting minesweeping gear would increase tankage to 640 tons (6,080nm at 15kts under operational conditions, 8,100nm under trials conditions). Some estimates placed seagoing speed as high as 20kts.

The first twenty-four ships were the only units of the class fitted to operate as Fleet Minesweepers. It was argued for a time that their existence made it unnecessary to retain TSDS in fleet destroyers. Only once were the ships used for offensive sweeping, during the invasion of North Africa (November 1942), when five of them formed the 10th Minesweeping Squadron, a shadow (temporary) unit. By February 1944, those fitted for sweeping were so scattered that it would take a month to assemble eight of them, and another month to work them up. It was therefore decided to land the sweep gear, including the winches and the motor-generator for the magnetic sweep. One implication was that TSDS was still needed in destroyers. All later units were to pure ASW configuration with increased operational endurance (given as 5,400nm rather than 3,500nm at 15kts). The first of the class, HMS *Rother*, had an endurance of 4,608nm at 15kts, 5,904nm at 12kts, and 6,528 at 10kts.

As with the corvettes, the Canadians built 'River' class frigates, becoming aware of the frigate project in December 1940, and asking for its specifications in March 1941; by May their Naval Staff had decided that in future it wanted only frigates, not corvettes. In October 1941 the Canadians planned thirty frigates, of which they immediately ordered twenty-three. They ordered another three in April 1942. In June they expanded the programme by ten ships (they ordered fourteen frigates that month). All of this was in addition to ten ships ordered for the Royal Navy under Lend-Lease (two of which were retained by the US Navy). Because Canadian shipbuilding capacity was limited, it seemed that only fifteen ships would be delivered in 1943, of which the Royal Navy would receive the first ten. Another nineteen would be delivered in 1944, and another six in 1945.

The Canadians actually did far better. They completed all ten Royal Navy ships in 1942–3 (two in 1942) and sixteen of their own in 1943. In June 1942 the estimate for 1944 was increased to twenty-six and then to thirty-one (the actual figure was forty-four). When the deadline was extended to June 1945, the initial estimate was that forty-two ships could be completed. Another eight could be built using a new central outfitting yard in Quebec to serve two smaller yards, a concept which the British would later adopt for their 'Loch' class. Diverting Davie Shipbuilding from cargo ships to frigates would increase the total to sixty-eight (reduced to sixty-four by the Naval Staff). A new programme submitted in November 1942 therefore called for sixty-four frigates (and twelve *Algerine*s) to be completed by June 1945, including ships already on order. New orders let in January–February 1943 amounted to forty-four named ships, of which twenty-four were cancelled in December 1943 (the Canadian official history refers to sixty-four ships ordered by February, so presumably there were twenty more unnamed ships, all cancelled in December). Another nine unnamed ships were apparently ordered later in 1943 and cancelled that December. Another

The Australian 'River' class frigate *Gascoyne* is shown in wartime, with a mixture of British (Type 271, atop the bridge) and US (SC-1 air-search, at the masthead) radars.

HMAS *Gascoyne*, shown in the 1960s, was refitted heavily, with a deckhouse built forward of the bridge as a Squid magazine. Her single 4in gun relocated to a bandstand, and double Squid (removed by the time of this photograph) placed in B position. (Jim Freeman via John Mortimer)

forty-four may have been projected but not ordered. In addition, in March 1943 the British ordered thirty-six 'Castle' class corvettes for construction in Canada, none of which was built. In addition to ships built in Canada, the British transferred seven ships in 1944 (see above).

The first fifteen Canadian ships followed the British design, except that they had twin power-operated Oerlikons instead of singles. The remaining four had their forward 4in guns replaced by twin mounts and their after guns by 12pdrs. All had four twin Canadian-made power-operated Oerlikons. In February 1942 the Admiralty asked that Canadian 'River' class ships be built to the long-endurance design, without sweep gear. This and the armament of the last of the original batch seems to have defined the modified Canadian version, forty-five of which were built. Some Canadian ships used inferior

grades of steel, due to the tight control of steel exercised by the United States. Ships were refitted for Pacific service beginning in May 1945. The early ships had their forward single 4in replaced by twins (except for *Matane*, refitted in the United Kingdom after battle damage); they retained the single 4in aft. The others were to have had their 12pdrs replaced by US-type twin Bofors (to be delivered at the rate of six per month beginning in April 1945), but few if any received these weapons before the end of the war. The twin power Oerlikons would remain. Refits provided Types 144Q and 147B sonars. These ships also received US radar (SU) and HF/DF (DAU).

In mid-1941 the Australians decided to build six 'River' class frigates, the first pair of which were ordered on 16 August. Another sixteen were added during 1942, but ten were cancelled on 4 April 1944 as the result of an October 1943 re-

The United States also built 'River' class frigates, adapted for mass production at Great Lakes shipyards by the Maritime Administration. Some were transferred to become the British 'Colony' class. Outwardly they differed considerably from their British prototypes, with three single 3in guns instead of 4in guns, but they shared the roomy hulls of the British ships. Thus, unlike 'Captain' class frigates, they were spacious enough for roles such as amphibious flagships, and some were adapted as weather ships. They could also accommodate more topweight. *St. Helena* is shown in September 1944, with two twin Bofors at the break of her forecastle plus nine Oerlikons, three of them in a zareba (gun tub) on her fantail.

view of escort requirements (in their place the Australians planned to build 'Hunts' and a *Dido* class cruiser, but that was abandoned because none would have been completed in time for the war). The Australian version had four more Oerlikons (two in the waist, two on the quarterdeck), and the two single 4in were in high-angle mounts. As refitted between October 1944 and mid-1945 (*Gascoyne* in May 1945), the first five ships had three single Bofors (one forward of the bridge atop a revised 4in gun crew shelter, one on a new deckhouse at the break of the forecastle, and one on the quarterdeck). The four Oerlikons in the waist replaced by power-operated twins and the two on the quarterdeck relocated to abeam the Hedgehog. The last three ships (*Barwon*, *Diamantina* and *Macquarie*) were completed in this form. They were given a funnel cap. This refit in turn was the basis for an early postwar modernisation in which the forward 4in gun was relocated to a bandstand on the forecastle, and double Squid placed in B position (the gun crew shelter was converted into a Squid ammunition space). Other Bofors positions were two alongside the bridge and one on the centreline (on a new deckhouse) superfiring above the after single 4in gun. By April 1950 the standard allowance was a total of seven single Bofors, but it appears that ships typically did not carry all of them in peacetime. Probably the seventh gun position was on the quarterdeck, in place of depth charges landed when Squid was installed. Sonars were Types 144Q and 147B. At least *Barcoo* (1946), *Barwon* (April 1947), *Hawkesbury* (November 1945 through April 1946) and *Lachlan* (Squid refit April 1948) were involved. *Barwon* at least was refitted after decommissioning (31 April 1947), and probably the ships were rearmed as a war reserve measure. The October 1947 issue of the official British list of Commonwealth warships attributes the dual Squid armament to *Barcoo*, *Burdekin*, *Diamantina*, *Gascoyne* and *Hawkesbury*. By April 1950 this armament was attributed to all the RAN 'Rivers', so probably *Barwon* and *Macquarie* were also refitted soon after the war. Four more ships were completed to a radically modified anti-aircraft design (see below).

The US Navy was sufficiently impressed by the design to order 100 from the Maritime Commission, on the theory that, unlike the contemporary destroyer escort, such ships could be built to merchant ship standards (the Maritime Commission designator was S2-S2-AQ1). These ships had US armament (three 3in/50, two twin Bofors, up to eleven Oerlikons, a Hedgehog, eight throwers, and two depth-charge racks). The twenty-one ships transferred to the Royal Navy were given 'Colony' names.

At the end of the war, the British 'Rivers' were quickly laid up or sold, because they were considered obsolescent. Perhaps the first bid for them was a Royal Indian Navy request in June 1945 for eleven (two for training, two for surveying). HMS *Helmsdale* replaced *Kingfisher* as tender to the Asdic development centre at Fairlie. Conversion ordered on 28 March 1945

included replacement of the 4in gun by double Squid (three salvoes) with Type 147F Asdic and installation of a power-stabilised Hedgehog. She was used for trials with the 'Nightshirt' propeller silencer.

A New Weapon and A New Asdic

As noted, Hedgehog had never been entirely satisfactory to its users, so the ahead-throwing depth charge mortar was revived in February 1942 as Squid. This idea seems to have been suggested by a committee formed in September 1941 to explore the advantages of the ahead-throwing weapon then entering production. Initially the favoured Hedgehog successor was a modified Fairlie mortar, Mortar A (Parsnip), firing twenty projectiles to a range of 250 yds; it ran trials on board HMS *Ambuscade* in February 1943. It was dropped because Hedgehog was good enough. Mortar B (Squid) was a parallel project for a non-contact weapon. Squid fired three 400lb projectiles (200lbs of explosive each), sinking at high speed (42ft/sec) to form a triangle 120ft on a side, at a mean range of 275 yds ahead of a ship. The standard pair of mountings fired two layers of projectiles forming a sandwich with a vertical separation of 60ft apart. Like Hedgehog, the mounting was roll-stabilised; tilting the three barrels allowed limited aiming. Squid ran sea trials on board *Ambuscade* in May 1943. They showed that her double Squid was the best ASW weapon to date, far superior to Hedgehog. The U-boat situation was considered so urgent that production had already been ordered. Squid was first installed on board HMS *Hadley Castle* in August 1943. Theoretical kill probability was about 70 per cent for a shallow submarine and 45 per cent for one at 900ft depth. In practice, in 1945 effectiveness was 40.3 per cent, compared to 26.3 per cent for Hedgehog and 7.5 per cent for depth charges.

Due to the effort involved, Squid would be fitted only to ships requiring either large repairs or, in the case of destroyers, beginning conversion to long-range escorts. Installation would be deferred until Squid proved itself in operations, due to the substantial loss of anti-aircraft firepower involved (the *Black Swan*s were dropped from the programme for this reason). In June 1943 Deputy Controller ruled it impractical to install Squid on board a 'Flower'. A 'River' class conversion proposed in July 1943 envisaged moving the 4in gun to a bandstand on the forecastle so that it could still fire down over the bow. Double Squid (150 projectiles, twenty-five salvoes) would occupy B position. Fifteen depth charges, the minimum acceptable, was also the maximum which could be retained. Conversion would require four to five months. By the time the design was ready, yards were fully occupied, so no 'River' class frigates got Squid. A design was drawn for the related 'Colony' class, but by the autumn of 1944 all were earmarked for conversion to fighter directors (which did not happen due to the end of the war). A design for the 'Captain' class had dou-

ble Squid in B position (138 projectiles, twenty-three salvoes). The two remaining 3in guns would be replaced by 4in or 4.7in guns, and the AIO would have been modernised.[17] Because alteration was expected to take 10 months, this project was abandoned. A *Black Swan* could be similarly fitted at the expense of her A mounting (or, alternatively, aft). Again, nothing was done during the war.

Squid required better information as to submarine depth, so that the charges could be set properly. A depth-finding Asdic had already been proposed in November 1941 (an earlier depth-finder installed on board HMS *Kingfisher* in 1939 was removed when she was involved in the Dunkirk evacuation). Interest in depth-finding increased as U-boats dived deeper; because Asdic measured the slant range to the submarine, without depth information it could seriously mis-estimate the horizontal range, which in turn determined the point at which weapons should be released. The successful concept, to use a steerable beam broad in the horizontal but narrow in the vertical, was tested in the spring of 1942. The depth-finding Type 147 was called the 'sword' because it was housed in a separate streamlined dome shaped like a vertical sword. Sea trials were conducted in May 1943. It had a depth recorder analogous to the usual range recorder.

There was also a need to extend Asdic coverage downwards so that U-boats could not escape by diving deeper (the first confirmed report of a U-boat diving below 700ft, in June 1943, led to rapid modification of depth charge and recorder settings). A late 1943 Staff Target called for the ability to counter U-boats diving to 1,200ft (increased to 1,300ft in 1944), but the deepest recorded in wartime was 780ft. The solution was the Q attachment to an Asdic (which was given a Q suffix to its Type number; Q2 indicated a more powerful transmitter). It produced a narrow vertical wedge-shaped beam about 3° wide in the horizontal. Mounted under (and training with) the main transducer, it extended angular coverage from the usual 10° (in the vertical) to 45° and later to 60°. A ship with the Q attachment would not lose contact at close range with a U-boat at a depth of 300–700ft. The Q attachment was developed roughly in parallel with Type 147, but was ready a few months earlier (it was tested in February 1943). Both transducers trained together.

U-boats still had to be dealt with when surfaced, particularly at short range. Thus both ahead-throwing weapons *and* the 4in gun could be considered ASW weapons. It was particularly important that the gun be able to depress for minimum range. That was why, in a 'River' class frigate, it occupied B rather than A position, placing the Hedgehog on the forecastle, the worst possible place for it from a maintenance and manning point of view. A special 4in shell, Shark, was designed not to ricochet on hitting the water, and then to penetrate a

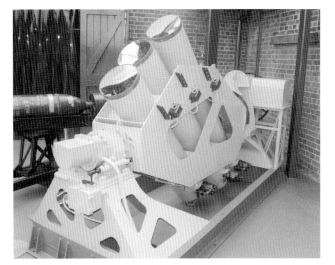

Squid was the most important late-war anti-submarine weapon, and it equipped many ships after the war. This example is at the Explosion! museum at Gosport. The three barrels are splayed out slightly to form a triangular pattern in the water, and the barrel assembly is stabilised on trunnions. Tilting the barrels moves the aim point slightly, from port to starboard, but range is fixed. (Author)

U-boat's pressure hull.[18] Despite design efforts, the 4in gun could not depress beyond a certain point, leaving the field to the ship's light anti-aircraft weapons. By mid-1943 there were complaints that Oerlikons failed to discourage submarines from closing with escorts to ranges (typically within 200 yds) where their heavier guns were ineffective. In July 1943 a range of possible weapons was compared.[19] They included a 6pdr automatic gun, which was ordered installed on board 'River' class frigates and 'Flower' class corvettes as well as on board 'Hunts' and 'A' to 'I' class destroyers assigned to escort duties. However, few were actually installed.

Limbo (Mortar D) was the postwar successor to Squid, conceived as a gun which could be aimed at a moving submarine. Like Squid's, Limbo's barrels were stabilised on trunnions running fore and aft. However, unlike Squid's, the barrels could also be tilted fore and aft, and range could be adjusted by valves through which propelling gas could be vented. Reloading was mechanical, so Limbo could fire rapidly. This example is at the Explosion! museum at Gosport. (Author)

---

[17] This plan was given in a TSD memo dated 13 December 1943 in the 'Captain' Class Cover.

[18] Shark entered service at the beginning of 1944. The standard outfit was ten live rounds per ship (all ready-use) plus five inert for practice. Initially issued to twenty Western Approaches ships armed with 4in Mk XIX guns, it was to be provided to all 4in escorts, with 4.5in and 4.7in versions under consideration.

[19] ADM 1/12530. The first corvette to receive a 6pdr Hotchkiss gun was *Gentian* (July 1943). *Mourne* received an experimental 6pdr Mk II on her bridge. DA/SW listed further possibilities: a short-range (cold-running) torpedo (already in use), a homing torpedo, a small jet-propelled torpedo, a rocket with a stable underwater trajectory, a rocket depth charge, a recoilless rifle, a 3½pdr automatic gun, and a 40lb bomb on a special mounting in the eyes of the ship (Unicorn). October 1943 Unicorn trials on board the frigates *Exe* and *Moyola* and the destroyer *Keppel* were apparently disappointing. Squid and Hedgehog were rejected because, given their fixed range, they would be very difficult to use against a fast-moving target.

Roughly parallel with Squid, a new Asdic, Type 144, appeared. Work had begun in May 1941, and it entered service in the summer of 1942.[20] It introduced a bearing recorder to supplement the earlier range recorder. The Asdic offered a degree of automation (in measuring the bearing of the submarine) which freed the operator to concentrate on listening and watching the range recorder, which in turn made early detection much more likely. Once set by the operator, the transducer, gyro-stabilised as in pre-war sets, stepped automatically in 5° intervals over the usual 80° arc to either side of the ship (in 2½° steps at the ends). The operator started a scan and set it in reverse after it ended.

The width of the bearing recorder paper represented a 150° arc, and it advanced each time the Asdic pinged. The rate at which paper was fed through the bearing recorder and the keying interval were set by the measured range to the submarine. The operator pressed a key whenever he heard an echo, marking the paper of the bearing recorder. With the sonar training in one direction, the mark on the paper indicated one end of the target; the mark made on the return pass indicated, at least in theory, the other end. The marks were where right and left cut-ons (for bearing) would normally be applied. The bearing recorder provided, in effect, a memory of the bearings – in modern terms, a waterfall display – which made it easier to maintain contact. Turning the transducer back and forth to determine where the submarine was, the operator aligned two parallel optical cursors (lines of light) along the right and left cut-ons. The two light cursors ran down the two ends of the targets, and (at least in theory) the

line midway between them indicated the centre of the target. The cursor settings could be read off a curved scale. The slope of the line of bearing marks indicated the rate at which the submarine was moving across the line of sight (actually, of sound); a vertical line indicated that the ship was on the desired collision course with the submarine. The range recorder had its own optical cursor, which was used to measure range rate (the slope of the line of range marks). The improved range recorder improved the accuracy of range and time to fire for both ahead-thrown and depth-charge attacks. In practice it proved difficult to discern the edges of the target, a failure which ultimately led to split-beam sonar, the Type 170 associated with the post-war Limbo ASW mortar.

The bearing recorder showed not only the bearing of the centre of the target, but also the appropriate course to steer for an ahead-thrown attack. Even if contact was lost during an attack, the ship could maintain course by keeping the bearing recorder lined up to the traces already made (it did have to be accepted the U-boat might have manoeuvred away). The course to steer was automatically transmitted to the captain's bearing instrument, which also showed the ship's bearing and that of the transducer, and thence to a 'helmsman's indicator' at the wheel. This degree of automation reduced the CO's workload and made it easier for him to concentrate on fighting the ship. He could, for example, follow the course of an attack on the ARL plot adjacent to the Asdic compartment.

There were normally two operators, only one of which was normally present (the other joined once a submarine was detected, for an attack). Once the attack was being carried out, a senior rating (Higher Submarine Detector, HSD) would join the two operators. The first operator would hold the contact. With the full crew in place, one operated the range recorder,

[20] Hackmann, *Seek and Strike*, pp 271–4 and the December 1942 'Monthly Anti-submarine Report', reprinted in Jak P Mallmann Showell (ed), *The U-Boat Archive Vol. 2: Weapons Used Against U-Boats During World War II* (U-Boot Archiv and the Royal Navy Submarine Museum: 2002).

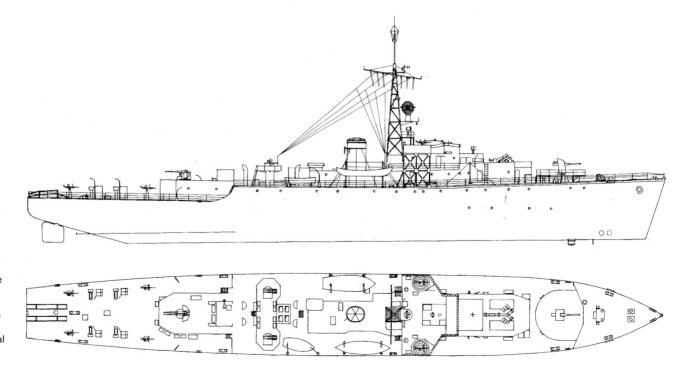

The 'Loch' class was the mass-production successor to the 'River'. This is the design for the class. Note that at this stage the ship would have had both double Squid *and* a substantial depth charge battery (two tracks and four throwers). The radar is Type 277, which in this drawing was labelled Type 273 Mk V, its original designation. (A D Baker III)

The 'Loch' class frigate *Loch Ard* is shown on 18 May 1945 as the South African *Transvaal*, in her original form with a single 4in gun forward.

a second the bearing recorder, and the HSD the 'echo push' recording each echo. Contact could be maintained with one edge of the target by pressing the 'echo push' each time the appropriate echo was heard. The operator could look at the range recorder to help him decide whether what he was hearing was the right echo (as opposed, for example, to reverberation, or to a whale). The training knob was used only to shift from one edge of the target to the other. The bearing recorder made it easy to train the transducer rapidly to the bearing of either cut-on.

Type 145 was a portable-dome version of Type 144 for corvettes and other small ASW units. The post-war Type 164 (prototype Type 160X), derived from Type 144, was the last of the British step-across (to find the bearing of the target) sets. It incorporated radar control of Squid, a means of dealing with a surfaced submarine within Squid range. An updated Type 166 was intended for the later *Daring*s incorporated a secondary set, Type 174, described alternatively as a passive set and as a simple searchlight sonar with a range recorder but no bearing recorder (also used with the post-war Type 170). There were two new range plotting scales, 3,000 yds for search and 1,500 yds for attack.

The last major wartime Asdic development was Cockchafer (Type 162), in effect an imaging set to detect a bottomed U-boat. Conceived in 1945, Type 162 swept a fixed narrow beam across the target as the detecting ship moved ahead, the range recorder trace showing, in effect, a silhouette of the U-boat. It entered service in 1948, using three strip transducers mounted flush with the hull near the bow.

Affecting Asdic performance were the anti-torpedo meas-

ures adopted to deal with the German T-5 homing weapon, which the British called GNAT (German Naval Acoustic Torpedo). One was a towed noise-maker, Foxer, which directly interfered with a ship's Asdic (the post-war Type 182 was tunable to avoid this problem). Publican was a 3in rocket-thrown noisemaker developed by DUW in July 1944; by August 1945 it was on board 'Loch', 'Colony' and 'River' class frigates. There were also tactical countermeasures, such as 'step aside,' some of which exploited the torpedo's inability to home on slow enough (*ie* quiet enough) targets.

The 'Loch' Class

The need for numbers conflicted with the need for increasing capability, which meant greater size: fewer than half as many 'Rivers' as 'Flowers' were built. By October 1942 it seemed that the answer was prefabrication, which would extend the industrial base building the ships. The new Twin Screw Corvette for Rapid Production became the 'Loch' class. In effect it was a 'River' updated and modified for prefabrication. A Staff Requirement (TSD 1657/42) was approved in January 1943. To simplify production, it was ordered sealed (fixed) for two years, a considerable sacrifice at a time of rapidly-changing technology.

Production of 200 ships by the end of 1944 was approved, including both frigates and a new 'Castle' class corvette. The 1942/3 Programme included six ships, one originally ordered as a 'River', but the 1943/4 Programme included 113 (of which eighty-three were in the programme as initially submitted in October 1942). In addition the 1943/4 Programme included eighty-six single-screw corvettes (described below; forty-

F 433

F 429

five in the initial programme), for a total in that programme year of 199 ships. Canadian plans to build 'Loch' class frigates were cancelled in 1943 in favour of continued construction of the 'River' class.

A new longitudinal hull structure was developed by Mr J L Adam, CBE, Chief Surveyor of the British Corporation, in effect the source of standard specifications for British merchant ships. In modern terms, this was a distinctly 'non-MilSpec' project.[21] Messrs Henry Robb & Co studied the necessary simplification. DNC rejected their most radical suggestions, for largely straight lines, but the hull form was considerably re-

designed. The usual slight hollow forward was flattened out, and the tumblehome of the 'River' design eliminated. Perhaps surprisingly, these changes had very little effect on ship performance. Decks were given a flat camber (two sloped sides and a flat top). Compared to the 'River', the boiler room was slightly lengthened (by 2ft 6in). The chairman of the production group, Wilfrid Ayre, was sent to study American prefabrication methods. To suit mass production and assembly at shipyards, units were kept to within 29ft × 8ft 6in × 8ft 6in for rail and road transport, and to weights of no more than 2½ tons to suit cranes. About 80 per cent of the hull structure was prefabricated. Because the ships were not built in warship

[21] Watson, 'Corvettes and Frigates'.

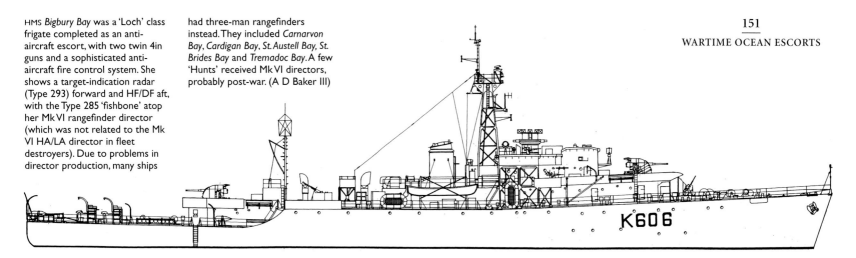

HMS *Bigbury Bay* was a 'Loch' class frigate completed as an anti-aircraft escort, with two twin 4in guns and a sophisticated anti-aircraft fire control system. She shows a target-indication radar (Type 293) forward and HF/DF aft, with the Type 285 'fishbone' atop her Mk VI rangefinder director (which was not related to the Mk VI HA/LA director in fleet destroyers). Due to problems in director production, many ships had three-man rangefinders instead. They included *Carnarvon Bay, Cardigan Bay, St. Austell Bay, St. Brides Bay* and *Tremadoc Bay*. A few 'Hunts' received Mk VI directors, probably post-war. (A D Baker III)

yards, the Admiralty set up two separate outfitting bases.

Armament was largely settled at a Deputy Controller conference at Bath on 4 November 1942. Ships would be used primarily for ASW, so they would have surface-search radar (Type 271) and HF/DF. The main ASW armament would be two Squids in B position, the 4in gun moving to the foredeck. Of the twenty salvoes required by DTM (120 projectiles), one was stowed in the mortars, two were ready-use, and there was space for another eleven in the forward magazine. The other six had to be stowed aft, in space normally used for depth charges. It became available because, given the effectiveness of Squid, the depth-charge battery was cut to two throwers (six charges) and one rail (nine charges), a total of fifteen depth charges. Ships completed before the mortar was in production would have Hedgehogs and a heavier depth-charge battery (two rails and four throwers, and perhaps sixty charges on the upper deck).

To allow the 4in gun to fire over the bow at a range of only 1,000 yds, it was placed on a high bandstand. Rocket flare projectors were fixed to the sides of the gun shield (with forty-eight 'Snowflake' rocket flares), and the ship would also have two rocket projectors (eight parachute and cable [PAC] anti-

aircraft rockets and sixty-four flares). In effect the after 4in gun in the 'River' was replaced by a multiple anti-aircraft gun. Initially the US type twin Bofors was chosen, but it was replaced by a quadruple pompom on the odd ground that the US Mk 51 director was unsuited to smaller warships. Lighter weapons were two single Oerlikons on the bridge and two twin power Oerlikons sided aft. Positions for four more single Oerlikons were reserved in case ships were used for 'a special mission', presumably meaning one in waters more subject to air attack. Most ships received a pair of single Bofors in 1945 in place of the twin Oerlikons.

The powerplant was the same pair of reciprocating engines which powered a 'River'. Speed would be about as in a 'River:' 20.5kts in standard condition, 19.5kts with half oil, 18.5kts deep (17kts when six months out of dock in the tropics). Endurance would be greater: 7,000nm at 15kts (estimated as 5,400nm when six months out of dock in the tropics).

In April 1943 a combined (British/US/Canadian) committee on Standardisation of Design was set up in Washington.[22] The intent seems to have been to standardise warship designs between Canada and the United Kingdom, the committee sit-

[22] ADM 1/12502.

HMS *St Brides Bay*, newly completed, is shown in 1945. The object in A position is her Hedgehog. The object on the small platform projecting forward from her lattice mast is her IFF interrogator, which was vital for air defence. Her long-range air-warning radar (Type 291) is on a topmast; the mainmast carries her HF/DF antenna.

HMS *Morecambe Bay* is shown on 11 March 1949. Her air-warning radar occupies her mainmast.

ting in Washington because the British Admiralty Delegation (BAD) to the United States was also responsible for Canada and because it was concerned with some US production types. The Admiralty view was that enough frigates were now built or building to meet the requirements approved for mid-1945, so that it was time to develop ideal types for continued production. In response to a request on 17 March 1943 from the British Admiralty Delegation to the United States, DASW prepared a list of desired characteristics for escorts to be laid down in 1944.

The ship should be fast enough to overhaul a U-boat on the surface (full speed 24/25kts). In effect the low speed of the 'Loch' class was accepted as part of the price for mass production. Endurance should be 6,000nm at 15kts under operational conditions. Initially the gun was to be effective at 8,000 yds, but this was changed to able to force a U-boat to dive at 8nm range. The gun was also to be effective against a surfaced U-boat at 100 to 2,500 yds, and against dive and torpedo bombers. Such requirements ruled out the inexpensive 4in Mk 19 on new escorts. It was soon pointed out that no existing gun could meet the conflicting long-range and dual-purpose requirements, and the 8,000-yard range was reinstated. As sent in May, the characteristics included two sided high-velocity guns (about 6pdrs) capable of lethally damaging a submarine at close range. The A/S battery was to be double Squid (twenty-two salvoes) plus fifteen depth charges (five-charge pattern).

The first meeting proposed reducing the number of designs for future construction to two, the 'Loch' class and the turbo-geared escort (presumably the *John C. Butler* class, then being built in the United States; the Royal Navy never received such

ships). British comments on the Characteristics (US Staff Requirements) of the new destroyer escort then on offer revealed some of the lessons of the Battle of the Atlantic.[23] It seemed more or less comparable to a 'Loch', but the emphasis, for example on anti-aircraft firepower, was very different (two 5in/38, two twin Bofors, five to six Oerlikons, with more Oerlikons if practicable), plus a triple torpedo tube. The British wanted all ASW command and control facilities adjacent to the open bridge: the Asdic office, an A/S plot (ARL plot), and communications and equipment to control ASW weapons. That was more true of the earlier destroyer escorts than of the new type described by the Characteristics. The British pointed out that recent trials had shown just how noisy the high-revving US-supplied 'Captain' class was, so they wanted a clause inserted to hold RPM as low as possible.[24]

Other Frigate Roles and the 'Bay' Class

At its meeting on 1 March 1943 the Future Building Committee instructed DTSD to develop Staff Requirements for conversion of 'River' and 'Loch' class frigates to anti-aircraft ships for use in the Far East once the war with Germany was over. Far East convoys would need far better anti-aircraft protection, given the scale of Japanese air attacks, but it seemed that there were more than enough ASW escorts to handle Japanese submarines. DTSD issued a Staff Requirement, TSD 2546/43, on 26 April 1943. Requirements became more concrete in 1944; at the Octagon Conference in Quebec that year, the British committed themselves to creating three division-sized amphibious forces for Southeast Asia Command. They were also

[23] ADM 1/13479.
[24] US ships had thirty turns per knot compared to ten for British frigates.

interested in creating an amphibious force for their Pacific Fleet, but that was a more remote matter. As of mid-1944, it was estimated that each assault division required twenty-eight AA escorts. There were enough for one, but not for the projected second and third forces. Two such forces would probably operate simultaneously, so a minimum of fifty-six escorts was required.

DGD having just said that a twin radar-controlled Bofors was better than a 4in gun, DNC offered to replace both 4in guns with twin US-type Bofors with radar directors. The ships would also have the existing Oerlikon battery: two singles on the bridge wings and two twins sided aft. Another four to six single Oerlikons could be added. The new prefabricated 'Lochs' could have two or three twin Bofors: one or possibly two in place of Squid and one aft. If Squid was needed, it could be moved down into the position otherwise occupied by the unneeded 4in gun forward. DASW argued that the Japanese still presented a submarine threat, and that it would be foolish to convert the most capable ASW ships. He therefore preferred 'River' to 'Loch' class conversions.

Not too much later DGD reversed himself: with new fuse-setters the 4in gun was once more to be preferred to the Bofors (and it was certainly preferable for area defence). Now it was a question of how many 4in guns the ship could accommodate. In April 1944 the Canadians proposed modifying ships then under construction. DNC began developing plans for

both British and Canadian conversions, but work on the British version stopped in July in favour of modifying the 'Loch' class (see below). On 8 August 1944 the Canadians decided to complete all 'River' class frigates as ASW ships; any AA ships would be conversions of completed frigates.

DNC pointed out that with 2ft less beam a 'River' could not match a converted 'Loch'. Even so, in September he offered to add a twin 4in gun aft, or alternatively to replace the usual single 4in with a twin mount, adding a twin Bofors (Mk V with austerity director), reducing the Oerlikons to four singles. Even with the original armament, adding a much more sophisticated fire control system would make a considerable difference, albeit at a high cost in topweight. The proposed system incorporated a sloop-type rangefinder director (with Type 285 radar) and a computer (AFCC). Target-indication radar (Type 293) and the destroyer air-warning set (Type 291) would be fitted. To provide the necessary internal space, the deck houses on the forward superstructure and the bridges would have been dismantled and rebuilt. Offices for the Types 291 and 293 radars would be built over the galley. The gun decks would have been stiffened, and permanent ballast was needed. The Canadians were asked to convert ships on this basis.

Compared to a 'River', a 'Loch' was longer and slightly beamier, hence better able to take a heavier gun armament: two twin 4in with RPC and a twin Bofors (Utility mounting, with separate director) on the centreline (originally two sided twins

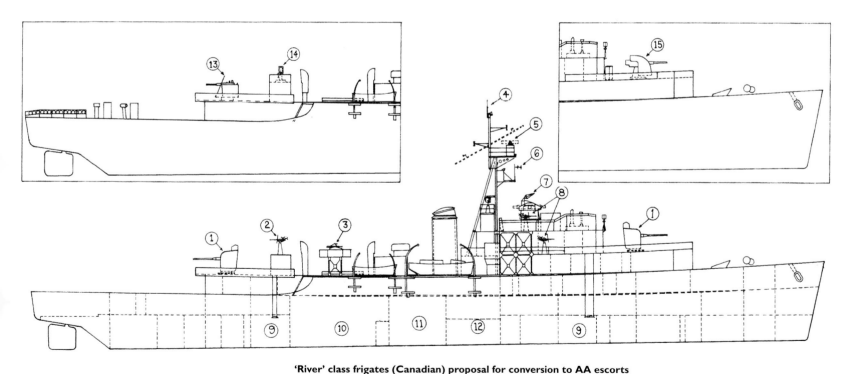

'River' class frigates (Canadian) proposal for conversion to AA escorts

In 1944 DNC developed a proposal for an anti-aircraft version of the 'River' class, to be produced in Canada by converting existing ships. Although the conversion did not entail a much more powerful gun battery, it did provide much better fire control. The project died because Canada produced the system involved, which was also wanted for the more satisfactory 'Bay' class. (A D Baker III)

Admiralty
DNC 30/A/R.C/72
Oct. 1944
Version 1:
1. Single 4in Mk XXIV mounting
2. Single 20mm Oerlikon (C/L)
3. Twin 20mm Mk V ('Boffin') mountings (P&S)

4. Type 291
5. Type 293
6. Type 242
7. AA director with Type 285 radar
8. Single 20mm Oerlikons
9. 4in magazines
10. Engine room
11. Boiler room No 2

12. Boiler room No 1, flanked by oil fuel tanks and by diesel generator compartment to port on upper level
Version 2:
13. Twin 40mm Bofors Mk V (C/L)
14. Simple Tachymetric Director
15. Twin 4in Mk XIX mounting

HMAS *Culgoa* was the Australian equivalent to the British 'Bay' class, a redesigned 'River'. Her masthead radar is an American-supplied SC.

The Australian improved 'River' class as at March 1952.

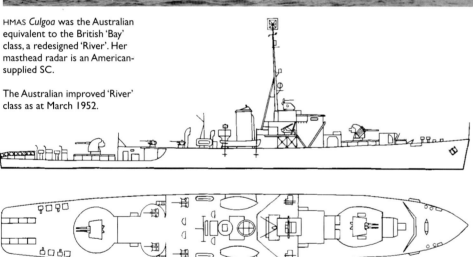

were wanted), plus the maximum possible number of Oerlikons. As in the projected 'River' conversion, the ships were fitted with sloop-type directors and computers, and with Type 293 radar. At least for early ships, the additional generators needed for RPC were not available. As in the 'Loch' class, single Bofors were added in 1945. In March 1946, for example, *Esard Bay* had two twin 4in, two twin Bofors, four single Bofors and two single Oerlikons. Since the ship would not have Squid, she had Hedgehog (ten salvoes) plus fifty depth charges (ten-charge pattern), the latter reduced post-war to allow for more guns.

The Staff Requirement (TSD 3122/44) was approved in June 1944. Conversion was to take into account possible fu-

ture re-conversion to the A/S role. Fighter direction capability, which had been desired, was abandoned, because antenna requirements would have clashed with anti-aircraft requirements, and there was insufficient internal space for an Aircraft Direction Room and a Target Indication Room. Nor was it likely that enough personnel could be accommodated (the anti-aircraft role added forty-five men).

Conversion of up to thirty new 'Loch' class frigates completing in 1944–5 was ordered late in May 1944, reduced to twenty-six in June. The Admiralty wanted the Canadians to convert twenty 'Rivers' to supplement them, and sketch plans were drawn.[25] Unfortunately both any Canadian conversions and the converted 'Lochs' would use the same Canadian-made fire-control systems. Since a converted 'Loch' was superior to a converted 'River', the idea was abandoned.

In January 1945 the British expected to have the following escorts with long-range anti-aircraft guns:

	Suited to Pacific and Indian Ocean	Limited to Indian Ocean
RN AA Sloops	24 (2 due June 1945)	—
RIN AA Sloops	—	6
'Bay' class (converted 'Loch')	12 (1 due May 1945)	—
'Hunt' II	—	25
'Hunt' III and IV	15	4 (Allied)
	51	35

[25] ADM 1/16145. The approach to the Canadians was approved on 12 June 1944. Three alternatives were proposed on 28 October. A had two single Mk XXIV guns and two twin and five single Oerlikons. B had a twin mount and a single mount (in X position), plus the Oerlikons. C had only the twin mount, plus a twin Utility Bofors and four single Oerlikons. The key difference from an existing 'River' was in fire control.

HMS *Portchester Castle* as completed, with Type 272 radar.

HMS *Porchester Castle* was the corvette equivalent to the 'Loch' class, with a single Squid forward. She is shown as built (November 1943), with a minimal depth charge battery aft, and with the unsatisfactory Type 272 surface-search radar (in the 'lantern'). The device on the fore side of the lattice mast under the 'lantern' is the associated IFF interrogator. (A D Baker III)

If only the ships in the left-hand column were counted, without the converted frigates ('Bay' class) and the 'Hunts' the deficit was about thirty escorts, which would be reduced to about eighteen in December 1945. An official paper commented that it could be further reduced if all eight 'O' and 'P' class destroyers were rearmed (as was the case with HMS *Petard*) and declassed to AA escorts. The deficit of ten ships indicated above was not enough to warrant pressuring the Royal Canadian Navy for conversions.

Some of these ships were needed for the new Pacific Fleet. In February 1945 C-in-C Eastern Fleet wanted eighteen 'Hunts' and thirty AA escorts such as sloops as operational escorts. Against that requirement he had twenty Group II 'Hunts', ten sloops (six Royal Indian Navy), ten 'Bay' and ten 'River' class frigates without cutting into Pacific Fleet requirements.

The Australians redesigned their later 'Rivers' as anti-aircraft escorts with two twin 4in guns (the forward gun on the forecastle deck, the after gun on the quarterdeck), plus three single Bofors at the break of the forecastle, and two twin power Oerlikons at 01 level. The bridge was redesigned as a square structure without wings.

When the war ended, several 'Loch'/'Bay' class ships were incomplete. Two were completed as despatch vessels (for the Mediterranean and Pacific Fleets) and four as survey ships. *Luce Bay* and *Mounts Bay* were initially ordered disposed of unless acquired by Belgium (which did not happen), but ultimately both were completed (*Luce Bay* as a survey ship).

Like the 'Flowers', the 'Rivers' were considered, but not chosen, for conversion to small monitors. The Royal Navy was aware of US projects to rearm destroyer escorts ('Captain' class frigates). It considered the US programme to rearm them with

two 5in/38 the best-balanced use of their hull, and in June 1944 it asked the US Navy to rearm twenty of them. The work would be done after the end of the war in Europe. The US Navy had barely enough 5in guns for its own destroyer escorts, but that bottleneck would ease in 1945. As of July 1943 there was also interest in modifying 'Rivers' to carry critical cargo and a few passengers, similar to the warships which had carried critical cargo to Malta. Capacity would have been about 200 tons and fifty-two passengers (four officers, eight senior ratings). Only four Oerlikons would have been retained, for self-defence. This was not pursued.[26]

Another role was that of assault group HQ, to provide communications for a brigade until its headquarters could be established ashore. Two of these LSH(S) were required per assault division. The concept was first discussed at a Controller's meeting on 20 September 1943. Staff Requirements (TSD

---

[26] According to a paper in the 'River' Class Cover (volume 645D), the idea emerged at the 7 June 1943 meeting of the Inter-Services Committee on Development and Production of Special Equipment For War Against Japan.

3070/44) were first stated on 25 January 1944 for both 'River' and 'Captain' class frigates. They had to provide temporary accommodation for twelve officers and sixty enlisted men, plus communications spaces, all as close as possible to each other and to the compass platform. Also wanted was a visual fighter direction position, separate from, but close to, the compass platform, with a good all-around view. The ship would accommodate one beaching craft. The 'River' would have her 4in removed, her armament being reduced to five twin and six single Oerlikons. Conversions for D-Day were two 'Rivers' (*Nith* and *Waveney*), two 'Captains' (*Dacres* and *Kingsmill*), and two 'Hunts' (*Goathland* and *Albrighton*). Six ships would be needed for the three Southeast Asia Command assault units. The 'River' class hull was suited to modification for the Far East, but the 'Captain' would have insufficient accommodation space. 'Hunts' would have to surrender their main batteries and would need complex internal rework. Combined Operations wanted to retain the four existing 'Captain' and 'Hunt' class flagships (the 'Rivers' could easily be modified) for senior officers of the build-up forces for the amphibious forces, as otherwise they would be tied down in one port or another just when they needed to be able to move from port to port at will (the 'Hunts' were needed even more for anti-aircraft firepower in the Far East). Unfortunately the British had only five 'Rivers' in home waters, and hence available for conversion, but all were Escort Group flagships and could not be spared. Instead, the Canadians were asked to return four of the 'Rivers' they had recently received: *Meon*, *Ettrick*, *Exe* and *Chelmer*.[27] *Exe* and *Chelmer* were assigned at the end of the war to Werf Gusto Firma A.F. Smulders in the Netherlands, and were cancelled on 10 August 1945. Proposed reconversion of *Ettrick* to a frigate was later cancelled. In these ships the forward 4in was replaced by a single hand-worked Bofors gun. The after gun was removed. The former twin Bofors (Mk V) and twin power Oerlikons were replaced by two more single Bofors. Hedgehogs were removed, but the ships retained fifty-four depth charges on the weather deck. The corresponding conversion for a 'Captain' involved removing one 3in/50 gun and retaining thirteen Oerlikons (twin Bofors not being available). The ships involved were *Dacres*, *Kingsmill* and *Lawford*.

Another frigate role, closely connected with the war in the Far East, was Fighter Direction, planned for the US-supplied 'Captain' and 'Colony' classes. In a 'Captain', two of the three 3in guns would have been landed, and the light armament increased to two twin Bofors (ex-'Colony' class, in B and X positions) and six single Bofors; the ships would have retained forty depth charges (four throwers, two rails) and their Hedgehogs. A US SA surface-search radar would have replaced the usual HF/DF, and Type 277 radar would have been fitted. Ships involved were *Bentinck, Bentley, Braithwaite, Cotton, Fitzroy*

and *Rutherford*. Ships undergoing conversion were all reduced to reserve as of 17 September 1945; none ever served in that role. However, diesel-electric 'Captain' class frigates were allocated for conversion to electric generator ships for newly-liberated Hong Kong (*Rowley, Stockham* and *Tyler*) and Singapore (*Hotham* and *Spragge*). Because of this role, *Hotham* remained longer in British hands than other US-supplied escorts, which made her available for assignment to what turned out to be an abortive post-war gas turbine experimental project.

Finally, *Loch Assynt* and *Loch Torridon* were completed as coastal forces depot ships, renamed *Derby Haven* and *Woodbridge Haven*. They had additional superstructure forward of the bridge and abaft the break of the forecastle. Armament was reduced to one twin Bofors and five single Oerlikons.

The 'Castle' Class

Not all slips could take the 'Loch' class frigates, so a scaled-down corvette version (the 'Castle' class) was designed, this time by Reed, who had designed the 'Flower' class. Because the smaller yards building this class were unlikely to be equipped to assemble prefabricated structures, the 'Castles' were built in traditional fashion. The design offered maximum commonality with the frigate, for example using the same prefabricated wireless office. As with the frigate, once the Staff Requirement had been approved, it was sealed for two years. Like the 'Loch', it was armed with a double Squid, so the 4in gun had to be relocated to the forecastle.[28] As in the frigate, the depth charge battery was two throwers (three charges each) and one rail (nine charges). The ship could not accommodate a Bofors gun, but she would have two single Oerlikons on the bridge and two twin power mounts aft; positions for four more would be provided.

The new corvette was larger, hence was expected to have better seagoing performance. Because she was longer, she was faster, even though she was also much heavier. Estimated speed was 16.5kts (14.5kts deep and dirty in the tropics). By this time in the war, the ship could have water tube rather than Scotch boilers. However, the main engine was unchanged. She was expected to offer longer range than a 'Flower', 7,500nm at 12kts compared to 4,596nm (6,725nm with water tube boilers).

Of ninety-six 'Castles' ordered in the United Kingdom and Canada, fifteen British and all thirty-seven Canadian ships were cancelled. Another five British ships were completed in 1944–5 as convoy rescue ships with 'Empire' names, manned by merchant seamen. Given their excellent seakeeping, four 'Castles' became weather ships in 1960, replacing 'Flower' class corvettes.

---

27 ADM 1/17196.

28 The armament envisaged in October 1942 was one 4in, two twin and four single Oerlikons, Hedgehog, and fourteen-pattern depth charges. Displacement was 1,015 tons standard and 1,500 tons deep. The ship was larger than a 'Flower': 225ft × 36ft (soon increased to 36ft 6in) × 17ft 6in. A single corvette engine was expected to drive her at 16kts.

CHAPTER 8
The Post-war Destroyer

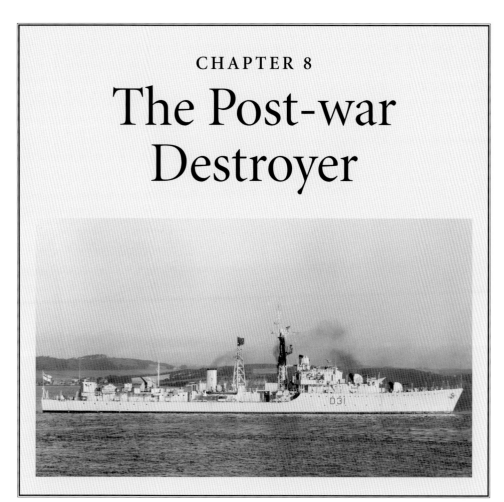

Of the wide variety of destroyer projects developed during the first post-war decade, only the fleet aircraft direction escort (FADE) or radar picket came close to fruition, and even that was in a very limited version. The need to extend the fleet's radar horizon was so urgent that the four 'Weapon' class destroyers were fitted with Type 965 long-range air-search radars, with little other modification (except that configuration was standardised, with all 4in guns forward). This is HMS *Broadsword*, on 6 October 1958. Many other ships, such as *Leander* class frigates, were fitted with similar radars for the same reason.

By the end of the Second World War, destroyer roles had changed and multiplied. A 'lessons learned' paper written by the commander of the British Pacific Fleet showed a need for a large destroyer force. The four-carrier fleet had a twelve-destroyer screen, plus eight destroyers for extraneous duties and four for air-sea rescue. Even more destroyers would be needed if the fleet faced attacks by the new fast submarines, such as the late-war German Type XXI and its projected Type XXVI successor, as it could no longer simply side-step submarines in its path. If the units in the screen could not leave their (anti-aircraft) positions to pounce on a submarine penetrating, then additional destroyers would have to be stationed within the screen as 'pouncers'. US operations in the Pacific demonstrated a need for radar pickets (aircraft-direction ships); the wartime British force had used two cruisers for this purpose. There was clearly a need for a fleet anti-aircraft escort. In 1949, moreover, British naval intelligence reported that the Soviets, the likely future enemy, had begun a large cruiser programme (which produced the *Sverdlov* class and included larger abortive ships).[1] Given British experience dealing with German surface raiders, convoys would need anti-ship escorts, most likely torpedo-armed destroyers.

The Royal Navy ended the war with a large but clearly ob-

[1] As reflected in the entry in the *Tiger* Class (cruiser) Cover explaining the decision (later reversed) to fit torpedo tubes.

solete destroyer force. The war had, moreover, effectively bankrupted the United Kingdom. The depth of the financial problem became clear only slowly, between 1945 and 1949, but it was immediately obvious that most of the new construction planned in 1945 had to be cancelled. The only relief was that the Soviets clearly were not ready for war either. In 1947 the British Joint Intelligence Committee estimated that the Soviet Union would not be ready until 1957, and that date became the target for British naval modernisation. For example, it set the initial timetable for development of the Seaslug anti-aircraft missile. In effect, setting the timetable meant acceptance of a basic limitation: Britain could develop new weapons or she could produce existing ones in quantity, but not both. This forced choice explains why it was so difficult to rearm when the Korean War broke out in 1950, apparently disproving the 1947 assessment.

New Machinery

As in all destroyers, machinery was key for the post-war designs. Machinery design had not figured very heavily in most wartime classes because E-in-C had been extremely conservative, but by 1943 the Naval Staff was demanding something new: British plants were heavier and much less efficient than their US Navy counterparts using high steam conditions. The *Daring* plant was an initial response. In 1945 E-in-C joined with industry to form the Parsons-Admiralty Turbine Research and Development Agency (PAMETRADA), to solve the turbine design problem. It was argued that the Parsons Marine Steam Turbine company, which designed all British warship turbines, had become far too conservative. Some other turbine makers, such as English Electric, offered alternatives. Yarrow, the main boiler developer, received a contract to design a new-generation integrated steam plant, which became Yarrow-English Electric Admiralty Development (YEAD.1). As described in 1949, YEAD.1 would match US technology and correct some faults experience had revealed in US machinery. It was to be available within three years for a destroyer, cruiser or carrier (60,000 SHP on two shafts). YEAD.2, with more advanced steam conditions, could be ready as a prototype for shore tests in five or six years. As a measure of the advance involved, where the *Daring* plant offered an endurance of 2,840nm, YEAD.1 would offer 3,810nm, and YEAD.2 would offer 4,910nm.[2]

To be more efficient, the new plants would be far more integrated than their predecessors. That limited the ship designer's flexibility. For example, although an earlier type of plant might be rated at 40,000 SHP, a slightly more powerful boiler might raise that to 44,000 SHP, and slight changes in turbine design (*eg* adding some stages) could raise that to 50,000 SHP. The boiler and turbine were separate elements which could be combined as needed. However, for efficiency,

[2] T225/1412.

all elements of an integrated plant had to be fixed. This kind of limitation would continue with gas turbines. It probably first became apparent in the cruiser-destroyer design, which used the developmental YEAD.1 plant. Furthermore, E-in-C was reluctant to place this new technology in production ships before a prototype had tested it at sea; the post-war slow-down in warship construction seriously delayed that. The new machinery was developed by Yarrow-Admiralty Research Department (YARD or Y-ARD). It was responsible for steam and gas turbine powerplants, and also for British nuclear powerplants. Plants received Y numbers. beginning with the Y.100 frigate plant (see Chapter 10).

The steam plants were considered interim, while the true post-war plant, a gas turbine, was developed. Gas turbines (jet engines) were the single greatest British wartime propulsion development. As early as 1943 E-in-C proposed an MTB gas turbine plant based on turboprop technology. To make up for the very high fuel consumption of the gas turbine, a low-powered diesel would be used for cruising, in a combination which would now be called CODOG. By 1946 E-in-C saw the gas turbine as a powerplant for ships of all sizes. That May he pressed the Treasury to release development money to avoid falling behind the Americans (who had sets on order for both warships and merchant ships) and the Swiss (Brown-Boveri was working on an engine). To regain the lead, E-in-C proposed an engine in the 4,000–8,000 SHP range, larger than anything built abroad but practicable without any abnormal difficulties in design and manufacture, and also of great potential interest for merchant ships. The huge British merchant fleet would provide a large market whose orders would pay for development.

For a test plant, E-in-C proposed using turbo-electric drive, which would eliminate any need for reversing turbines or gears. He therefore wanted to install a prototype in the US-built 'Captain' class frigate HMS *Hotham*, which had two-screw turbo-electric drive. She was still in British hands because she had been used as a generator ship in Singapore. The US Navy offered informally to extend the loan if they were allowed to send observers and if they received the results of the tests. It seemed that the experiment would last about five years. A contract for a long-life 6,000 SHP plant was let to English Electric (EL 60A) in September 1946. PAMETRADA received a long-term contract for a 15,000 SHP destroyer plant, the prototype being ordered in July 1948. Metropolitan Vickers (Metrovick) and Rolls Royce (RM 60A) received contracts for 6,000 SHP coastal forces engines. By 1948 it was clear that the distinction between a short-life MTB engine and a long-life engine for a frigate or something larger was illusory. The PAMETRADA contract was cancelled when the promise of the RM 60A became obvious.

E-in-C kept DNC's designers informed. In November 1946, for example, a junior designer in the destroyer section recorded that the design of a 'future ship' had been received from

DNC with a specific request to investigate fitting a gas turbine.[3] This project seems to have been intended as part of a larger exploration of future trends. E-in-C was offering a 6,000 HP unit for 55 tons. The designers therefore estimated that a 50,000 SHP destroyer plant would weigh 460 tons, compared to 740 tons for the 54,000 SHP lightweight plant in a *Daring*. In March 1948 E-in-C circulated a description of a futuristic 50,000 SHP four-shaft plant with a spectacularly low dry weight (200 tons, 4lbs/SHP) but very high fuel consumption (14 tons/hr of diesel oil).[4] At half speed, E-in-C estimated that it would consume at 3.3 tons/hour. The 4,500nm at 15kts then being required of new frigates would equate to 300 hours steaming at 3.3 tons/hour, or 990 tons of fuel, which was well above what could be accepted. Harrington, the designer asked to evaluate the plant, proposed a CODAG arrangement, in which all engines would run together at full speed, but only the diesels would be used at low speed. Four Rolls Royce gas turbines (5,000 SHP each) would be geared to the centreline shaft, and four of the new 4,000 BHP lightweight Deltic diesels (0.45lb/SHP/hr fuel rate) geared to each of two outer shafts, for a total of 52,000 SHP. The main design problem would be the very high speed of the turbine, which could not be geared down to an efficient propeller speed. The minimum beam for the plant seemed to be 40ft. A 360ft × 40ft destroyer (2,100 tons) would make about 33kts. A typical frigate (320ft × 40ft, 1,900 tons) would make 33kts on 53,000 SHP. None of this was spectacular, but it was certainly promising.

US shore trials revealed some serious problems, which EL 60A seemed to share. By September 1952 the *Hotham* project had therefore been cancelled. The parallel RM 60A was far more promising. Tested at sea in the spring of 1953 on board the fast gunboat *Grey Goose*, it operated for 1,500 hours without a failure. E-in-C concluded that he could move on to a frigate engine, an upgraded RL 75 (7,500 SHP). He proposed powering a frigate with two of them. She would be the first all-gas turbine ship of her size. He justified the project to the Treasury for its enormous export possibilities as well as for its fighting value (the lighter the machinery, the greater the weight available for weapons). However, it was clear that future gas turbines would be uneconomical, hence would have to be combined with more economical cruise plants.

Adopting gas turbine boost engines seemed to be the way to cut powerplant weight and size. In September 1952 Staff Requirements were issued for a Y.102 combined steam-gas turbine plant, producing the same 30,000 SHP per shaft as YEAD.1. At this time estimated weight of the YEAD.1 plant was 26lbs/SHP. The Y.101 developed for the Type 14 frigate, in effect a slightly heavier version of Y.100, weighed 30lbs/SHP.

---

[3] Notebook 609/7.
[4] Notebook 442/6 (J W Harrington), referring to an E-in-C letter to DNC dated 12 March 1948, forwarded to H G Holt, the preliminary design chief, with a DNC memo of 9 April 1948. E-in-C described the new machinery as at the earliest stage of development, years from even experimental installation.

RM 60 weighed 5.5lbs/SHP and a projected 15,000 SHP version of Metrovick's G5 might weigh only 1.86lbs/SHP. The Y.102 gas turbine was initially to have been Metrovick's G4 (5,000 SHP), but later the 7,500 SHP G6 was selected instead. These engines were considered conservative, as crosses between steam and aero engine practice. Two alternative steam plants were considered, one based on YEAD.1 and one on Y.100 (30,000 or 15,000 SHP per shaft). Despite its complexity, Y.102 was expected to weigh only 20lbs/SHP.[5] As will become clear, as the engine was developed it grew both larger and heavier, to the point where its superiority was no longer nearly so clear. Probably it survived because most of those involved realised that some sort of gas turbine would ultimately prove far superior to steam. The first two shore-test plants were completed in 1958. Y.102 powered the 'Tribal' class frigates and the 'County' class destroyers.

The Future Fleet Destroyer

Many in the fleet, already unhappy with the size of the 'Battle' class, rejected the much larger *Daring*. DNC was asked how the trend towards greater size could be reversed. Destroyer officers were willing to move both the wheelhouse and the A/S cabinet (sonar space) below the weather deck, dramatically reducing the size of the bridge structure. However, control space requirements were growing, for example with the addition of the new Gun Direction Systems (GDS). Topside design would be complicated by the need to limit interference between radars; the ultimate hope was to combine different functions, such as air search and target indication, in a single set – as in the US Navy. DNC complained that destroyer officers wanted divided machinery, which cost length, even though often it did not add survivability. Adopting higher RPM, as in US ships, might also cut machinery weight, but at the expensive of greater radiated noise. DNC considered the new twin 4.5in too big and too heavy for a fleet destroyer (destroyer officers seemed willing to accept 4in guns). If the ships had to have 4.5in guns, then their high rate of fire might justify reducing close-range weapons. Officers still wanted more torpedo tubes, and even reloads, but DNC argued that adding reload gear would cost guns. Pacific War experience showed that ships needed more fresh water; DNC pointed out that nothing increased the size of a ship so quickly, yet with so little apparent advantage, as increased liquid capacity.

To show what could be done, DNC developed a sketch design (A1) for a small destroyer.[6] There was apparently a parallel large destroyer design, probably the one described below under Radar Picket. A1 was scaled down from the most recent design, *Gallant*, by reducing armament to two twin 4.5in guns, two self-contained twin Bofors (STAAGs or Busters), one set of torpedo tubes (pentad), and a single Squid (ten

salvoes). It had the same 40,000 SHP powerplant. It appeared that all this could be accommodated on the length of 320ft which DNC considered the minimum for a destroyer intended for world-wide deployment.[7] Deep displacement would be 2,188 tons. This was much the size of the pre-war 'A' and 'B' classes. Because displacement was less than that of *Gallant*, speed (deep) would increase from 29.75kts to a more acceptable 31.25kts. Probably some structural weight could be saved by welding and by accepting higher stresses. Given effective underway replenishment, more weight could be saved by cutting the number of rounds per gun (reducing from 400 to 300 per 4.5in barrel would save about 3 tons in displacement). The same rationale would justify cutting stores.

A1 was too small. Attention therefore turned to the maximum acceptable standard displacement of about 2,500 tons, something like a 'Battle' (and nearly twice the displacement of A1).[8] DGD could offer either a new 5in gun or a lighter new twin 3in/70 (about the size and weight of a twin 4.5in upper deck mounting), which would provide better anti-aircraft performance but was not considered effective against ships. A majority of those present at a 1948 meeting wanted to retain torpedo tubes: the minimum effective anti-ship salvo was eight (DoD suggested two fixed tubes, with one or two reloads each). DTASW wanted both the new ASW mortar, Limbo, and the new ASW homing torpedo (Bidder), but admitted that not all fleet destroyers would need them. DoD wanted a combination of A/A and A/S weapons and increased speed, 35kts at normal load. DNC pointed out that four twin guns, two pentad tubes, single Limbo and *Daring* speed would bring displacement to an unacceptable 4,000–5,000 tons. On 2,500 tons he could provide 300 tons of armament: two twin 4.5in or 3in/70, two quadruple torpedo tubes, two STAAGs, some Oerlikons and some depth charges (single Limbo, at 30 tons, was far too heavy). The meeting formally adopted a design broadly similar to *Gallant*, with two main gun mounts, one pentad torpedo tube, and single Limbo. By this time DNO was promoting the 5in gun as the future destroyer (and cruiser) weapon, so in the end the proposed main armament was two single 5in (DNC wanted to consider an alternative armed with 3in/70s), a small close-range battery, up to eight torpedoes (possibly with fixed tubes), and single Limbo. Unfortunately DNO lacked the resources to develop the single 5in; in 1948 he was concentrating on a twin mount for cruisers, far too massive for the 2,500-tonner. In the end the main significance of the 2,500-ton design was that it was the destroyer used in comparisons with possible future ('1960') cruisers, hence as part of the process leading to the cruiser-destroyer described below.

Destroyer construction was a long-term proposition: given a life of sixteen years, ships to replace those ordered in 1940

---

[5] Notebook 337/15 (W G John).
[6] Submitted 3 May 1946, but clearly consonant with the later paper.

[7] Remarks to Controller in connection with Design A1, 5 June 1946, in General Destroyer Cover.
[8] Meeting on the future destroyer, chaired by DTSD, 18 August 1948.

RIGHT: The mast of a Type 15
frigate shows the two standard
radars of the time: Type 293, at the
masthead, for target designation
(short-range air search) and Type
277, at the foot of the mast, for
surface search. Type 277 could be
tilted upward and thus could also
be used for height-finding. At the
masthead is the standard HF/DF
'birdcage', which the Royal Navy
considered a vital ASW sensor.
The dipoles at the yardarms are
for VHF radio, and the whips
below are for HF. At this time, in
the 1950s, the Royal Navy had not
yet adopted UHF (the shift from
VHF to UHF, particularly for ship-
to-air communication, was quite
expensive; it was undertaken
largely because the US Navy
switched). The array on the stub
mast aft is the ship's IFF
interrogator. The object in the
foreground is part of the shield of
the ship's twin Bofors gun, atop
her bridge. (Alan Raven)

would have to be ordered in 1956. Director of Plans estimated that beginning that year, the Royal Navy would have to
order six destroyers each year. Until then the fruits of the war
programmes would give the Royal Navy more destroyers than
it needed.

The A/S Escort

Destroyers could not be made large enough to be multi-purpose, so specialised types, including a fleet A/S escort, were
needed. In March 1944, in connection with the 'G' class design, DTASW pointed out that that existing and planned ships
could harass but could not kill submarines. Those which survived might penetrate a dispersed screen to attack. If Asdic
could be used successfully at high speeds, some destroyers
might usefully trade torpedoes for ASW weapons. The British
sonar development establishment (A/SEE Airlie) already knew
that smoothing water flow over at least 100ft back from the
bow would help. The British therefore eliminated paravane
fittings and also SA gear for protection against acoustic mines.[9]
Adopting all-welded construction in the 1944 destroyers was
also expected to improve flow. By late 1945 the British had a
100in dome which they hoped would make it possible to use
existing Asdics at up to 30kts.

In December 1945 Mr Baker, the chief preliminary designer, asked for a sketch design (designated N2/1, presumably

ABOVE: HMS *Cavalier*, on display at
Chatham, shows some standard
destroyer electronic systems of
the 1950s. The topmast carries the
UA-3 ESM system, employing
quartets of microwave horns of
different dimensions (stacked
vertically) to cover three bands
(from bottom, S, C, and X). A
single display was switched among
the three bands, and there was an
audio output which made it
possible to measure the pulse rate
and also the sweep rate (the
operator could compare radar
input in one ear with a reference
output in the other). There was no
attempt to measure frequency
directly. This combination was
adequate as long as relatively few
radars were encountered. The
audio element explains some of the
NATO nicknames for Soviet
radars, such as Owl Screech
(which must have been meant
literally). The 'cheese' antenna
serves a Type 293Q target

indication (short-range air search)
radar, which worked with a TIU 2
target indication unit, designating
targets to the Mk 6 director at
bottom right, with the two lenses
of its Type 275 radar. Unlike the
early Mk 6 on late-war destroyers,
this one lacks an optical
rangefinder. It does, however, have
a bubble for an observer who
could slew it to a target he saw,
which the search radar might have
missed. The yardarms carry
'candlesticks' (Outfit AJE) for UHF
radio: transmitters on one side,
receivers on the other, typically
one channel per 'candlestick'. The
yard just under the Type 293
'cheese' carries a 'sword' antenna
used for VHF communications
interception. The smaller radar on
the lower platform is the Type 974
surface-search (and high-definition
surface-warning) set, whose
functions included periscope
detection. (Author)

companion to A1) of a 1,500-ton 'escort destroyer' with moderate endurance and reasonable firepower on a waterline length
of 300ft.[10] A rough arrangement showed a long forecastle, extending abaft X gun, to gain internal volume. Armament would
be four single triaxially-stabilised 4.5in guns (with 200 rounds
each, well below the usual allowance) on the centreline (A, B,
X and Y positions), with Squids (ten salvoes) on either side of

[9] DASW 16 July 1943, *Daring* Class Cover. SA gear was not then being used by fleet
destroyers.

[10] Notebook 554/7 (E A Steane).

the deckhouse below B gun, and four twin Bofors (later amended to four singles). In addition to the Squids, the ship would carry ten depth charges. There was not enough weight for a desired pair of triple torpedo tubes. The ship would have the usual 40,000 SHP plant, but the two boiler rooms would be abaft the engine room, placing the single funnel well aft. In February 1946 Haslar confirmed disappointing powering estimates: the ship was much too heavy for her length. She would likely make 29.75kts on 40,000 SHP at 2,100 tons (deep load). She would gain 1.5kts if she could be lengthened 20ft. Baker added 15ft at each end, but only to the underwater hull, presumably to limit added weight. The bizarre result was a very pronounced ram bow and a stern sharply tapered in profile. Probably the point was that the armament planned for the ASW destroyer added up to 240 tons, not far short of the 258 tons in a 'Weapon' and far beyond the 174 tons in an 'O' class Emergency Destroyer, but the projected deep load displacement was closer to the 2,175 tons of the 'O' than to the 2,702 tons of an 'Weapon'. She was much less feasible than the small anti-aircraft or anti-ship destroyer. Stretching her properly to 330ft would make her too large.

A more viable approach, first proposed in December 1945, was to complete the surviving 'Weapon' class destroyers as prototype Fleet ASW ships, double Squid replacing one twin 4in mount. Later they could have the projected Bidder homing torpedo and high-speed Asdic. This Emergency size destroyer was attractive in this role partly because it was considered more manoeuvrable than a larger destroyer. Given the small number of 'Weapons' left uncancelled, on 8 December Director of Plans suggested converting four 'U' or 'W' class destroyers to make up a full flotilla. ACSN(W) said that was unaffordable; the 'Weapons' would be integrated into the fleet and would not form a separate flotilla. First Sea Lord approved the project on 11 January 1946.

The ships had an enlarged Asdic compartment in the keel suited to the new sets then under development, and an enlarged Asdic control room on the bridge. The new 100-inch dome was installed. By March 1946 the approved battery was two twin 4in (either fore and aft or both forward), two twin STAAG Mk II, two single Bofors, two pentad torpedo tubes (for possible use by Bidders), double Squid (twenty salvoes), and one depth charge rail (fifteen charges). Two ships were completed with their Squids in B position and two with their Squids in Y position; the use of X position was rejected. The fleet ASW escort concept was revived in the 1950s, as an early application of the gas turbine (see below).

The Fleet Aircraft Direction Escort

The Fleet Aircraft Direction Escort (FADE) was another specialised type. ACSN(W) suggested converting *Daring* or 'Battle' class destroyers, but Deputy Controller wanted a fresh design, and in January 1946 Deputy Sea Lord agreed. To hold down

size, guns would be sacrificed for radar, although Squid was wanted for self-protection. The ship would have new Types 980 and 981 long-range radars and a receiver for the radar image from early-warning aircraft (which were already in US service but not British). With its fan beam narrow in azimuth but broad in elevation, Type 980 might be considered a target indicator for fighter control.[11] Type 981 was the corresponding height-finder. Fighter control against one target required a pair of these radars, because Type 981 (or the successor Type 983) could measure only one height at a time. These radars did not enter service; the Royal Navy used Types 982 and 983, with similar antennas. There was also a new Type 960 long-range wide-beam (air-search or air-warning) radar.

Initial sketch designs of combination Fighter Directors and Anti-Aircraft Escorts using the new radars were based on the *Daring* (FADE I) and 1942 'Battle' (as in HMS *Armada*: FADE II) classes. A *Daring* could have Type 980 at the after end of the compass platform and Type 981 further forward or aft. In the latter case she would sacrifice her after twin 4.5in gun and her torpedo tubes. She would gain a third BUSTER and four single 40mm guns, but would lose all her Oerlikons (not in fact fitted in *Daring*s as completed). A 'Battle' would sacrifice at least her 4in gun and her four after twin Bofors, as well as her torpedo tubes. In two versions of the design she also sacrificed her B 4.5in mount (in one it was replaced by double Squid).

The *Daring* version was preferable, though not quite large enough. By April 1946 DNC offered FADE III, based on a *Daring* hull lengthened 8ft, armed with two twin 4.5in, four twin Bofors (BUSTERs), and two single Bofors. Deep displacement would have been about 3,370 tons. FADE IV was similar, but had two Type 980 forward and a single Type 981 aft. It was 4ft longer than FADE III, and would have displaced about 3,313 tons, with a speed of about 31.5kts in deep condition. FADE V showed that the *Daring* hull was too small.

DNC also considered what sort of fleet destroyer could be produced from FADE III, probably as part of his exploration of future destroyer design. He increased beam to 43ft. The ship would have displaced 3,523 tons fully loaded, compared to 3,450 tons for a *Daring*, with a somewhat heavier battery: three twin 4.5in with a Mk VI director, four STAAG (two aft, two on the bridge wings), two Pentad torpedo tubes and a Limbo. There was apparently enough interest for DNC to order studies of a rearrangement with torpedo tubes on the upper deck (as in a *Daring*) and a midships deckhouse (again, as in a *Daring*) with two STAAGs forward of the after funnel and two single Bofors abaft it instead of two STAAGs.

In June 1946, DNC was authorised to go forward with FADE III, using a modified *Daring* hull form (383ft × 42ft 9in × 22ft 6in, 2,635 tons light and 3,428 tons deep) and a *Daring* pow-

[11] In December 1946 DNC remarked that one Type 980 would be used for gun target indication, since no masthead position was available for Type 293.

Probably the greatest single electronic gap in post-war British destroyers was the absence of an adequate small-ship air-search radar. Marconi's commercial design was accepted in preference to US and Dutch radars to become Type 965, shown here on board a *Leander* class frigate. Initially it was credited with a range of only about 70nm. However, early versions could detect a Canberra bomber at 20,000ft at 120nm. Type 965M, introduced about 1960, had the original antenna but an improved receiver (noise factor 4.5 rather than 8 dB), a longer pulse (10 rather than 3.8 microsec), and an improved feeder (1 dB improvement), which together extended range to 200nm at 45,000ft. This was the version installed on board the first radar pickets (converted 'Weapon' class), the first series of 'County' class missile destroyers, and the *Leanders*. Ultimately the concept was that escorts operating with the fleet would greatly extend its radar horizon, reporting back the aircraft they detected (ultimately, in the missile ships, entering it into the fleet's computer data base carried by ADAWS systems). Type 965P, on board the 'Battle' class pickets, the later 'Counties', and Type 42s, had a 'double bedstead' antenna, in effect two of the original type on atop the other. That added enough antenna gain to extend the tip of the first lobe to 280nm at 100,000ft. This sort of range was needed to provide sufficient warning of fast-moving jets. However, no UHF radar like Type 965 could detect low fliers, and it also lacked any means of detecting moving targets against land masses. That badly limited its value in the Falklands. (Alan Raven)

RIGHT: Given the limitations of Type 965, the Royal Navy sought an alternative. After several unsuccessful attempts, it bought here on board a Type 42 missile destroyer. This radar combined a British antenna with electronics from the Dutch (Signaal) LW-08 radar – a descendant, in effect, of the LW-02 which had been rejected in favour of Type 965. (Alan Raven)

erplant. FADE IIIB incorporated the new Type 960P air-search radar. In September the Board approved development into a sketch design with two pairs of aircraft-control radars (Types 980/981). Each pair would feed one interception position with its own big Skiatron display. There would also be four PPIs and a dead-reckoning table. An additional first-class visual direction position would have its own air plot and a pair of PPIs switchable between radars. Such facilities required a great deal of deck space in a large Aircraft Direction Room, which would be combined with the Operations Room and, preferably, the Target Indication Room, all contiguous with (preferably alongside) the main Wireless Office. Much more space was needed to accommodate all the personnel handling and maintaining the radars. Records of a meeting in July 1947 on the draft Staff Requirements mention that a complement of 400 would make the ship too large and hence too expensive. FADE seems to have been the Royal Navy's introduction to volume-critical ships, which have been the rule ever since.

Fighter direction facilities were entirely apart from the usual destroyer radars, Type 293 (target indication), Type 275 (medium-calibre fire control), and Type 262 (Bofors control).[12] Armament would be two twin 4.5in, four STAAGs, two single Bofors (Mk VII) and Limbo. Limiting the ship's weapons to self-defence (February 1947) saved little. DGD insisted that the two 4.5in mounts be fore and aft, leaving no blind spot. Successive versions of the Staff Requirement reduced the close-range battery to three STAAGs, then to at least two power Bofors, and it was then crossed out altogether: DGD considered that within a decade these weapons would become useless. Limbo was dropped, but an anti-torpedo weapon was added. Even the requirement that the ship be of destroyer rather than cruiser size was abandoned. At this point Types 982/983 superseded Types 980/981, and Type 960 was added. The ship would have an aircraft homing beacon, the US-supplied YE. Only the *Daring* powerplant was suitable. The original requirement for 31.5kts in clean trials condition in temperate waters was changed to 29kts full loaded in the tropics, three months out of dock. DNC pointed out that propeller silencing would cost at least a quarter-knot. Endurance was set at 3,500nm at 20kts deep and dirty (4,000nm in earlier draft crossed out). Presumably the lessons of the 1946 Bikini atomic test were reflected in a requirement that the primary conn be enclosed, with an open navigating bridge. In a departure from earlier practice, the wheel did not have to be in the fore end of the bridge, but might be anywhere convenient

The corresponding FADE IIIF sketch design would have displaced 2,660 tons light (3,462 tons fully loaded); a destroyer version would have displaced 3,495 tons fully loaded. It seems to have been close enough to what was wanted to justify detailed stability calculations. Its forecastle was extended all the way aft to provide sufficient volume accommodation. Using a flush upper deck had the side benefit of greatly reducing stresses in the hull, since it added hull depth. This version had a single Squid aft (twenty salvoes), as in a *Daring*. As FADE IIIF was nearing the detailed design stage, British finances crumbled. At a meeting on 22 July 1947 Controller said that no FADE could possibly be laid down for a long time, so work on the Staff Requirement could be deferred to July 1948

---

[12] The armament planned initially was three Mk VI twin 4.5in and two STAAG, with a Mk III director and CRBF I; radars were two Type 982/983 pairs and a Type 960 long-range air-search set. Notebook 648/6.

(Director of Plans still hoped that a FADE would be laid down during the next three years).

The Fleet badly needed some sort of FADE, if only to develop tactics. In March 1947 DNC offered FADE VI: conversion of the fast minelayer *Abdiel*. She was of roughly destroyer performance and large enough to accommodate radars and a big operations room. She would not match a ship built for the purpose, but she would come close enough for tactical trials. Her forward boiler and No. 1 funnel would be removed, the latter to allow for a larger bridge. The boiler would be replaced by a 350 kW turbo-generator and one 180 kW diesel generator, with a second 180 kW diesel generator in an oil tank forward. Another 180 kW generator would be installed aft. DNC hoped for 54,000 SHP (30.35kts), but with only two boilers efficiency would be reduced. Actual output would be 48,000 SHP (29.75kts clean in trial condition at 4,000 tons, 28.5kts six months out of dock in the tropics). Armament would be two twin 4in and possibly also two hand-worked Bofors, probably with one long-range and one short-range director. The modern director was important because gun direction was integral to the FADE organisation envisaged. The ship would have Type 960 and two Type 983 height-finders, but possibly no Type 982s to cue them. As of April 1948 the conversion design was proceeding at high priority.

In August 1948 the Ship Design Policy Committee decided that because no new FADE could be built in time, an existing warship should be converted, as a combatant rather than a test ship. The light cruiser *Scylla* was chosen, presumably because her non-standard 4.5in main battery made her much less valuable than other light cruisers. She could accommodate all necessary facilities and weapons because she was considerably larger than *Abdiel*. In December DNC was told to arm the ship with two gun mounts (ultimately 3in/70, 4.5in as interim) controlled by the new GDS 3 system with the Type 992 radar. It proved impossible to incorporate the massive Type 984 radar then under development (as a replacement for the Type 982/983 pair). As money became tighter, in April 1949 the Board promulgated a new 'Revised Restricted Fleet' plan – which did not include any FADE. Design work on both the *Abdiel* and the *Scylla* conversions was abandoned.

In the aftermath, DND pressed for a Fleet Aircraft Direction Frigate armed with a pair of twin 3in/70s. To DNC, it was an illusion. It could not be smaller than a fleet destroyer if it had the requisite speed and self-protection. A rough design for conversion of a fleet destroyer to an A/D frigate had already been drawn up as a guide to writing Staff Requirements, but it was no more than a convoy escort (it was the basis for the later abortive Type 62 design, described in Chapter 10). The FADE saga showed that no satisfactory FADE could be derived from a fleet destroyer. There may have been some feeling that carriers and cruisers could provide the fleet with aircraft direction on an interim basis. Convoys would lack such resources, so they needed the A/D Frigates described in Chapter 10.

The Cruiser-Destroyer

The 1945–9 studies showed that little could be done on an acceptable displacement. ACNS Rear Admiral Edwards proposed a solution in a 1949 paper, 'Ships of the Future Navy', written for the Ship Design Policy Committee: amalgamate the cruiser and destroyer categories to produce something affordable yet effective, accepting drastically reduced cruiser and destroyer numbers. In peacetime the ship would carry out the cruiser policing mission and would show the flag; Edwards saw it as 'small enough to go to most ports and large enough to command respect', like the pre-war 'C' class light cruisers 'that did so much foreign service in the past'. She would handle whatever surface threat the Soviets managed to mount, without making the far more urgent and numerous ASW force unaffordable. 'The Russian cruisers are not expected to be of high quality and are known to have poor endurance.'

Crucial to this 'cruiser-destroyer' was a new 5in/62 gun, with a projected unit weight of 90 tons. It had begun in DGD's 1947 studies of replacements for both the existing (and projected) 6in cruiser gun and for the destroyer gun. Already under development was a faster-firing replacement for the twin 5.25in battleship secondary weapon (and primary armament of the *Dido* class). Although the 5.25in calibre was abandoned, the new mount was considered worth developing (it could be scaled to whatever calibre was chosen). By 1947, DNO wanted to standardise calibres with the US Navy, which used 5in guns. In wartime only the United States could provide enough of the expendable elements of the gun system: certainly the ammunition and possibly also the barrel. The US Navy was working on a twin 3in/70, and the British expected the corresponding medium-calibre gun to be a 5in/70, which would replace the existing 5in/54. At the Fourth US/UK Gun Standardisation Conference (February 1949) both sides agreed to settle on 5in calibre, and the British were interested in the US 5in/54. DNO was interested in a single destroyer mount suited to the 2,500-ton ship then being considered, but there was also interest in a twin mount.

The US 5in/54 was expected to go on trials by August 1950. In November 1951, with four cruisers expected in the near-term programme, plans were to test the prototype on board HMS *Cumberland* by 1955. However, DNO decided not to pursue the 5in/54 due to its low muzzle velocity and rate of fire (hence poor anti-aircraft performance), and instead selected a 5in/62 in November 1951. Unfortunately, so much was being spent on production due to the Korean War emergency that little was left for the new gun mounting. The Ministry of Supply formally closed the order for the 5in mount in September 1952, and terminated the contract in May 1953. The project was cancelled altogether in September 1953 'consequent on decisions recently taken on future new construc-

tion', presumably the abandonment of the cruiser-destroyer. However, Controller was still interested in a 5in cruiser, and he ordered development of a larger cruiser design based on the *Dido* class. Some studies conducted as late as 1954–5 still embodied 5in guns, presumably because nothing else was in prospect. When the projected guided missile cruiser was re-designed in 1956, one of the selling points was that it was now armed with the existing twin 6in gun, so there would be no delay (and expense) associated with developing the 5in which had figured in the earlier version. Roughly in parallel to the 5in, DNO decided to adopt the new L70 Bofors (70 calibres long) to replace the wartime L60. The same gun was adopt-ed by the British army. Although L70s appeared in numerous designs, by the time the gun was available in the late 1950s it had been superseded by the Seacat short-range defensive missile (see Chapter 9).

All of this was still in the future in the spring of 1949. Edwards argued that, based on DGD data, a ship armed with the 5in rapid-fire gun would have enormous hitting power, at least as good as a *Tiger* class cruiser (then being redesigned with two twin automatic 6in guns), sufficient for two such ships to overwhelm the existing Soviet *Kirov* class cruiser.[13] Edwards envisaged a ship armed with two twin or four single 5in guns, displacing about 5,000 tons. Although the ship would normally pass submarine targets to specialised units, he also pointed out that, with the advent of trainable ASW weapons (Limbo) and long-range homing torpedoes (the promised Bidder), a larger and less manoeuvrable ship might still be an effective submarine-killer. She might not need escorts. In Edwards' view the closest existing ship to the cruiser-destroyer was the *Dido* class cruiser. He proposed modernising her gun fire control and adding some ASW capability, while stopping modernisation of all larger cruisers (it would still be worth-while to modernise the later 'Battle' class destroyers).

Edwards proposed fifty cruiser-destroyers at half the unit cost of the projected 12,000-ton cruiser (the '1960 Cruiser' re-cently sketched as a guide to future characteristics) and less than twice the unit cost of a destroyer. Impressed, the Admiralty Board ordered further investigation of Edwards' ideas, look-ing towards construction in 1955 (*ie* under the 1953–4 Programme). Work on destroyers and the FADE was stopped.

Given Edwards' ideas, on 30 June 1949 DTSD asked DNC to sketch a ship with three single 5in guns (the twin 5in was too heavy), each with its own director (with four-channel GDS), and with two close-range mountings (comparable to STAAGs), each with its own director.[14] The ship would also have single Limbo, essentially for self-defence, and anti-ship torpedo tubes (DNC planned eight fixed tubes). Radars were the long-range air-search set (Type 960), the new target indi-cation set (Type 992), and the surface search and height-find-

ing set (Type 277Q). DTASW wanted new sonars (Type 170 and Type 172 or the new long-range set [which became Type 177]). He also wanted silencing and the new anti-torpedo weapon then in prospect (Ruler). Other requirements were a speed of 30.5kts (deep and dirty) and an endurance of 4,500nm at 20kts. Overall length was set by armament arrange-ment. DNC proposed placing all the guns on deck, with ma-chinery units (each with its own funnel) between them. He adopted a flush deck to gain internal space while reducing su-perstructure which would interfere with gun arcs. It would make for a drier ship. Fuel would be stowed in a cruiser-type inner bottom, which would further stiffen the ship. The ship was entirely unprotected. The projected powerplant was two sets of E-in-C's new 30,000 SHP YE.47A steam plants (pred-ecessors of YEAD.1), substantially more compact and eco-nomical than the *Daring* plant. On this basis in August 1949 DNC reported a 4,600 ton (deep) flush-decked design, 465ft × 48ft × 34ft (hull depth). DNC estimated cost as £2.5 million, compared to £5.5 million for the '1960 Cruiser' and £1.75 million for a repeat *Daring*. These figures were very ap-proximate because they involved ordnance, machinery and other equipment that did not yet exist.[15]

DNC's study showed that Edwards' idea was feasible, so a formal draft Staff Requirement (TSD 147/49) was issued on 18 January 1950.[16] The ship was to be kept as free of obstruc-tions as possible, to present an impressive appearance, as the ship would be used to show the flag in peacetime. It was con-sidered desirable to combine the bridge plot, operations room, and aircraft direction room (DGD wanted the gun direction room included in the operations room or opening off it). At least the bridge and operations room would be protected. All three single 5in guns had to be able to train through 360° at all angles of elevation. One 5in control system would have full AA and surface (SU) capability; two would have full AA and limited SU. Each of three close-range mounts (designers de-cided these would by US-type 3in/50s rather than the much heavier 3in/70) would have its own control system. The guns would be supported by a six-channel version of GDS 3 (Type 992 radar). Other radars would include the Type 982/983 fight-er-direction sets, as well as the long-range Type 960. Instead of a starshell gun, the ship would have two Rocket Flare Launchers. There would be eight 21in torpedo tubes on the broadside and a single Limbo, supported by Asdics Types 170 (for Limbo) and 172 or other long-range sets. There would also be an anti-torpedo weapon, later specified as Double Ruler (a rocket launcher). The ship would have ESM equipment and two radar jammers.

This cruiser-destroyer was barely feasible; DNC saw prob-lems in her great length and in the great endurance required. When fleet endurance speed was raised to 22.5kts, it seemed

---

[13] DNC's notes in DNC papers Vol 78, National Maritime Museum (Brass Foundry).
[14] DNC papers, Vol 78.

[15] In September 1950 E-in-C said that a *Daring* plant redesigned to what he called YEAD II standards would save 270 tons on machinery plus fuel and 18ft on length.
[16] Notebook 767/2 (J C Cooper).

The Cruiser-Destroyer, as presented to the Admiralty in February 1951. Ruler, in X position, was an anti-torpedo weapon firing rockets. Such weapons were included in many British designs of this period, as antidotes to the coming generation of guided anti-ship torpedoes. These projects were ultimately dropped because contemporary sonars produced too many false alarms. The breaking-point probably came in 1954, when a Royal Navy study showed that a frigate crossing the Atlantic would need more anti-torpedo weapons than anti-submarine weapons. As anti-submarine ranges increased, the homing torpedo threat seemed to recede, and reliance was placed on decoys. Five decades later it is still extremely difficult to fix and kill an incoming torpedo.
(A D Baker III)

Cruiser-destroyer Design 1
February 1951

1. 5in MC/DF Mk 1
2. 'Ruler' anti-torpedo launcher
3. Rocket flare launcher
4. MRS 3 gun director
5. Type 960 radar
6. 3in/50 single (P&S)
7. Type 992 radar
8. Type 277Q radar
9. Type 932 radar
10. Limbo ASW mortar
11. 5in gun magazine
12. Fresh water tanks
13. Oil fuel
14. B engine room
15. B boiler room
16. Diesel generator room
17. A engine room
18. A boiler room
19. Stabiliser compartment
20. Limbo magazine
21. Diesel fuel
22. Sonar transducer compartment
O.F. Oil fuel
F.W. Fresh water

that she could no longer be built within the desired 4,600 tons.[17] It seems odd in retrospect that the 4,600- or 4,750-ton limit (deep load) was so important to the Royal Navy. Many tables describing the new cruiser-destroyer compared it to the considerably larger (476ft, 4,770 tons) US *Mitscher* (DL 2) class then under construction, full details of which had been given to the British.

Late in March 1950 DTSD held a meeting to prune the Staff Requirements to get down to the desired tonnage. He was willing to accept an endurance of 3,000nm at 22.5kts (deep and dirty), leaving the ship slightly longer legged than a *Daring* but considerably better than a modernised *Dido*. Director of Plans hoped that with emergency tanks she could achieve 3,500nm. DGD rejected D of P's suggestion that the gun battery be cut to two 5in: the ship would lose half her main battery if one mount failed. DGD was willing to give up one close-range mounting. DTSD defended Limbo as second in importance only to the 5in guns and the A/S torpedoes. DNC observed that the ship was too wide for revolving torpedo tubes. He could not provide the desired eight tubes on each broadside. DTASW then described four anti-ship torpedoes on each broadside as an irreducible minimum. On the other hand, because the ship would fire only one ASW torpedo at a time, one tube on each side plus reloads would be satisfactory. DTASW wanted one anti-torpedo Ruler, firing over all arcs around the stern up to 45° either side of the bow. For DND the minimum radar requirement was Types 960, 277Q and the new high-definition surface-search set (which became Type 974). However, he wanted a fighter-direction radar, the massive proposed new three-dimensional Type 984, which could replace both Types 982 and 983 and, to a considerable extent, even Type 960. This set had been far beyond the capacity of the destroyer-size FADEs.

By October 1950 three preliminary designs had been done, all armed with three single 5in guns controlled by MRS 3 systems, with two US type 3in/50, with two quadruple torpedo tubes, single Limbo (twenty salvoes), and Ruler (twenty four-shot salvoes). Radars would be Type 960, Type 992 (for GDS 3), Type 932 (for precision splash-spotting, a new radar), and Type 974. Sonars would be Types 162, 170 (for Limbo), 175 (for Ruler), 176 and 177. All of this would take considerable electrical power: a 350 kW turbo-generator in each boiler room and a 150 kW diesel generator in each engine room, plus a 150 kW diesel outside the machinery spaces.[18]

The baseline design (4,709 tons deep load) had the guns on the weather deck (A, Q and Y positions). A second design (4,764 tons), for FADE, had two massive Type 984 radars, fore and aft (19 tons each, at this stage). Because length was limited, No. 2 gun was made superfiring and the torpedo tubes were fixed (four sets of twins forward and aft, to maintain an eight-torpedo broadside). Design 3 (4,768 tons) was also a FADE, but with the more modest Type 982/983 combinations replacing Type 984. In addition to the 3in/50 mount on either side, this one had one on the centreline. Length seems to have been an even more serious problem, since the gun positions were indicated as A, B and C (*ie* C superfiring over A and B). A final three-mount version (July 1952) brought displacement to 4,800 tons.[19] DNC decided to limit the ship to 4,750 tons on completion, so that she would not exceed 5,000 tons throughout her lifetime. To that end, on 30 July he ordered the designers to adopt destroyer design practices.[20]

A new Legend dated 5 August 1952 was associated with a new Staff Requirement (TSD 2230/52) dated 8 August 1952. Changing to two twin 5in mounts reduced length and saved

[17] Notebook 767/2 shows alternative approaches taken in March 1950, all leading to depressing conclusions.

[18] Notebook 1030/2.
[19] Notebook 673/2. Other armament was two twin L70 Bofors, a single 4.5in gun for starshell, Limbo, two sextuple torpedo tubes, and the Camrose anti-torpedo weapon.
[20] Notebook 337/15 (W G John).

One version of the cruiser-destroyer design (Study II) was equipped as a FADE, with two of the new three-dimensional Type 984 radars. These very heavy units were ultimately mounted only on board carriers, but in 1951 it seemed that they might be much more widely distributed. The bar shown atop the main radar nacelle is an IFF interrogator. The radar atop the mast is Type 992, successor to the wartime Type 293 as a long-range target acquisition set for the new gun control system. The dishes are Type 903s for gun fire-control. Note the short-range gun in the waist, and Limbo aft. The ship in the background is a *Sverdlov*, the type of cruiser the cruiser-destroyer might face in wartime convoy defence. The cruiser-destroyer was expected to be viable in the face of such ships because the Royal Navy expected its gunnery to be far better than theirs; in June 1958, for example, the new edition of the tactical section of *The Fighting Instructions* reported that 'in the majority of firings that have been reported on, rates of fire have been slow … If those firings are typical of the Soviet Navy as a whole … Soviet ships are unlikely to develop an early and high rate of hitting'. (Courtesy of D K Brown)

internal space, which was at a premium. As in the past, the guns were controlled by a GDS 3 (six-channel) system. The Staff Requirement did not define the ship's close-range armament; the best the designers could do within the available weight was two L70 twins with simple (SGS 1) directors. Other weapons were a single 4.5in starshell gun, six fixed torpedo tubes on each beam (as revised again in September, the Staff Requirement showed two quadruple revolving tubes), single Limbo, and four triple Camrose anti-torpedo weapons (replacing the now-abandoned Ruler). Radars included the long-range Type 960 and the Type 982/983 aircraft-direction combination. This ship was 435ft × 50ft × 34ft; the 60,000 SHP plant (probably 56,000 SHP in the tropics) would have driven her at 30.75kts deep and dirty in the tropics (33.75kts on trial). Endurance was cut to 3,050nm at 22.5kts. The only weight which could readily be cut (to meet DNC's requirement) was ammunition. There was some hope of adopting E-in-C's new lightweight Y.102 steam/gas turbine powerplant, but this was soon abandoned.

A typical late effort, Design Study 25 (24 April 1953), was designated 5in light cruiser, with cruiser-destroyer crossed out. Deep load displacement was 4,750 tons (draft 13.5ft). The hull form was based on that of a *Daring*, but it was flush-decked. There was no protection of any kind. Providing an inner bottom of reasonable depth (3ft 6in) would have required a deeper hull weighing 77 tons more. Estimated speed was 30kts deep and dirty in temperate waters (29.5kts in the tropics). Gun armament matched that of the August design, the 4.5in starshell gun being in B position; there were two quadruple torpedo tubes and Limbo, but no anti-torpedo

weapon. Radars included those listed for 1952, plus Type 277Q and GDS 3/Type 992 for target indication, with MRS 3 for each twin 5in mount. Sonars were the Type 174 search set and Type 170 to control the Limbo. The electronics required considerable power: two 1,000 kW turbo-generators and three 200 kW diesel generators to carry the harbour load. With 900 tons of fuel, the ship would barely make 3,000nm at 22.5kts deep and dirty. The designers considered a variety of weight-savers, such as replacing the starshell gun with 5in rocket flare launchers, using fixed torpedo tubes, and omitting the Type 983 radar. The ship was too large, with too little capability, and not quite fast enough. Adding protection would push the displacement up through 5,000 tons: typically that meant adopting heavier scantlings and 20lb (half-inch) plating over operational spaces. The ship might be given 2ft more beam and a double bottom. To maintain speed the ship would need 62,000 SHP, but that would be difficult to provide.

As a last gasp, a fresh cruiser-destroyer design, to destroyer standards, was ordered on 23 April 1953, for submission to Controller on about 13 May. It would take into account the increased estimated all-up weight of the twin 5in mount, 270 tons. The design was so tight that to save 10 tons the 4.5in starshell gun was replaced by a single 5in rocket flare launcher.

In the wake of the failure of the cruiser-destroyer, the Naval Staff asked DNC to define the spectrum of feasible destroyers because the 1956 deadline for restarting destroyer construction was approaching. DNC offered three basic alternatives: a smaller general-purpose destroyer and fleet A/S and A/D escorts (in effect the general-purpose ship was the fleet A/A escort). To define the general-purpose ship, W G John,

in charge of preliminary destroyer design, asked what could be done on 4,000 tons.[21] As a first step, he asked for a *Daring* brought up to date. The ship was considered obsolete in gun direction; in secondary gun armament (wartime-type L60 rather than the new L70 Bofors); in radar, including air warning radar; in grouping of AIO offices; in maintenance and ship facilities; and in not providing for resulting increases in complement and in electrical power. She would be updated with cruiser-destroyer fire control, direction, and radar. Experience designing the flush-decked cruiser-destroyer had convinced the destroyer designers to give up the usual forecastle break near amidships. Its structural discontinuity was dangerous (the British had been experimenting with under-the-keel explosions which often snapped a ship in half at just that point). Furthermore, modern electronics would be demand more enclosed space, both for the equipment and for additional personnel to use and maintain it. John decided to extend the forecastle back to the after gun mount. A year later this concept helped lead to the 'Super-*Daring*' described below.

To match the cruiser-destroyer the ship needed two separate but equivalent channels of main battery fire: two MRS 3 directors, each with its own transmitting station (computer compartment) below decks, two separate close-range control systems, and a four-channel version of GDS 3, with Type 992 radar. By this time it had been accepted that such ships also needed a long-range air-search set (Type 960), as well as the usual low-altitude/surface-search set (Type 277Q) and the high-definition surface-search set (Type 974). Of the cruiser-destroyer radars, only the Type 982/983 combination was missing. Cruiser practice, with its eight fixed torpedo tubes (four each broadside) would be accepted (owing to beam the ship could not have revolving tubes). Unlike the cruiser, this design showed the Squid carried by *Daring*s. These improvements would add 50 tons to armament weight (from 435 to 485 tons).

A first estimate (20 May 1953) showed a 4,300-ton ship (405ft × 48ft × 13.4ft) with an endurance of about 3,000nm at 22.5kts. A 60,000 SHP cruiser-destroyer plant would drive her at 30.5kts deep and dirty; the 54,000 SHP *Daring* plant would drive her at 29.5kts. This design was reported to DNC in June 1953. The July 1953 report of possible future cruisers and destroyers to the Naval Staff included it as an updated 400ft (4,250-ton) *Daring* armed with three twin 4.5in guns (two MRS 3), two twin L70 Bofors (each with its own MRS 3), with a four-channel GDS 3, with four fixed torpedo tubes on each side, and with a Squid (twenty salvoes). With a 60,000 SHP YEAD.1 steam plant, the ship could make 30kts deep and dirty, with an endurance of 4,400nm at 20kts on the same basis as that used for the *Daring*.

The next step was to see what armament a *Daring*-size hull powered by YEAD.1 could accommodate, allowing for slight

enlargement to accommodate more generating capacity and more fresh water. Endurance would be 3,000nm at 22.5kts, as in the cruiser-destroyer. Displacement would be little different from *Daring*: 3,550 tons rather than 3,567 tons deep load. There was enough weight for one twin or two single 5in (155 tons vs 180 tons for the 4.5in) with one or two main-battery control systems, three or two Bofors L70s (96 tons vs 64 tons), a four-channel version of GDS 3, Squid and *Daring*-type Asdic (with Limbo as alternative), and two pentad torpedo tubes, with 5in rocket flare launchers rather than a starshell gun. Total armament weight would be 364 tons for the twin 5in (382 tons with Limbo) or 388 tons for the two single 5in. Radars would be Type 960 for long-range air search, Type 277Q for low-level search, Type 974 for high-definition surface search, and Type 992 for target indication. The two-gun version (3,560 tons, 400ft long) was included in the July 1953 report for the Naval Staff. YEAD.1 would have driven it at 30.5kts. Armament weight was given as 390 tons, compared to 435 tons in a *Daring* as built and 485 tons in the redesigned *Daring* described below (and 530 tons for the cruiser-destroyer with twin 5in guns).

With the 5in gun dead, by October 1953 the Naval Staff was planning a 3,600-ton escort destroyer, which would be laid down in 1957–8. In the autumn of 1953 DTSD and the Ship Design Policy Committee discussed a possible multi-role destroyer, probably on the basis of the study described above of the modernised *Daring*.[22] John estimated in mid-October that the ship would be about 4,400 tons. DTSD concluded that no such ship was practicable: 4,400 tons was too large for a screening ship. Future fleet escorts would have to be specialised. However, work continued for a time. The larger tonnage allowed for the Swedish twin 4.7in, already in use with the Dutch navy, which DNO favoured as a replacement for the defunct 5in. A British version would be heavier because it would incorporate features such as shock-hardening, flash zones, atomic/chemical protection, improved habitability, spraying arrangements and mechanical hopper loading in the magazine.[23] On 22 July 1954 John ordered a quick study of a ship with three such mounts, capable of 30.5kts deep and dirty, with *Daring*-class endurance. In effect this was the modernised *Daring* with the new gun. Secondary armament was two twin L70; the fire control system employed four MRS 3 directors, four-channel GDS 3, and a separate simplified director, the Tachymetric One-Man Director (TOM). The ship would also have the twelve fixed torpedo tubes and eight reloads and the single Limbo of the contemporary A/S Fast Escort (see below). Total estimated armament weight was 660 tons. John proposed using the new Y.102 steam/gas turbine powerplant. Minimum length would be 415ft to achieve 30.5kts deep and

---

[21] Studies requested by John 18 May 1953. A F Honnor notebook.

[22] Notebook 372/9 refers to a DTSD discussion dated 30 November 1953, but the comment 'earlier' is pencilled in. The relevant SDPC paper was numbered 53004.
[23] Including ammunition, the twin 4.5in in a *Daring* weighed 81.75 tons. The twin 4.7in in a Dutch destroyer weighed 97.45 tons. The twin 3in/70 weighed 99.95 tons. The estimated weight of an Anglicised 4.7in mount, with ammunition, was 108.3 tons.

dirty. Estimated deep load was 4,250 tons. That was a great deal, so John also tried two 12cm mounts on 4,000 tons, and then a ship with a single mount and one L70 twin on 3,500 tons (roughly comparable to the Fleet A/S Escort described below). The designers concluded that the 3,500-ton (375ft) and 4,000-ton (400ft) ships would be quite practicable, with speeds of 31kts and 30.5kts and endurances as *Daring* and 4,400nm at 20kts, respectively (the three-mount ship would probably grow beyond 4,250 tons). The two-mount design seemed to be the best all-round proposition.[24]

Another response to the failure of the cruiser-destroyer was to scale her up into a true cruiser. The first stage was to add 850 tons of protection, two more L70 Bofors, and another

Type 668 jammers at the foot of the mast of a *Leander* in 1988. This jammer was intended to screen high-value units from approaching Soviet anti-ship missiles; it was not a means of ship self-defence. As built, *Leanders* had two jammers, to cover S and X bands, but ships with UA-13s had one of the jammers removed to make space for the UA-13 search position. Note the empty platform under the Type 668 box. The two-band jammer, Type 667, was code-named Cooky. Visible under the platform is an optical target designation sight. On the fore side of the mast can be seen a 'sword' antenna, for communications interception (VHF). (Alan Raven)

500nm of endurance (total 3,500nm). These relatively minor changes (armament weight increased from 530 tons to 790 tons) required a 490ft (7,900-ton) ship. Since power could not be increased, speed would fall to 28kts. Estimated cost was £6.5 million, compared to £5.5 million for the last unarmoured design. These data were included in the July 1953 surface combatant report. This cannot have been an attractive result, but the idea of a 5in light cruiser survived for another year, a version being prepared specifically for the autumn 1954 Sea Lords' book of design alternatives.[25]

---

[24] The single-mount Ship A (DNC 7/759) followed the layout of the A/S Fast Escort. Ship B (DNC 7/760) had two guns, Ship C (DNC 7/761) had three. Ship B was offered in two versions: one with 4.7in guns in A and Y positions and twin Bofors in B and X, and one with 4.7in guns in A and B positions, twin Bofors in X and Y, and two additional single Bofors abreast the bridge. No copies of these studies were circulated. In these design designations, 7 indicated DNC Section 7 (destroyers).
[25] According to a note in a list of sketch designs (probably prepared mid-1955), 'the 5in twin was a DNO design study of a mounting, details of which have since changed'. Armament was three twin 5in with two MRS 3 Mod 1 fire control systems, one six-barrel L70 Bofors (MRS 3 Mod 2), two twin L70 Bofors (TOM), GDS 3 (Type 992 radar), and four triple torpedo tubes (UCSF 2 fire control and Type 177 Asdic). Other radars would have been the long-range Type 960, Type 277Q and Type 974. Displacement was 8,000 tons (550ft × 57ft 6in × 34ft 6in × 16ft), using a Y.102 powerplant to make 29.5kts deep and dirty (30.5kts deep and clean), with an endurance of 3,600nm at 20kts. Accommodation would have been 675.

The Fast A/S Escort Revived

The July 1953 design spectrum ranged from a 15,000-ton missile ship down to fleet A/S and A/A escorts. The A/S escort was 375ft long (2,910 tons), with a maximum speed of 30kts deep and dirty (endurance 2,000nm, presumably at the new fleet speed of 22.5kts), armed with one twin 3in/70, one twin L70 Bofors, six fixed torpedo tubes and double Limbo, with a complement of 200. Sonars would have been Type 170 for Limbo and the long-range Type 177. Radars would have been Types 976Q and 992 (for GDS 3). The corresponding A/D escort was 390ft long (3,600 tons), with a speed of 30.5kts (endurance 2,000nm). Armament was two twin 3in/70 (no close-range weapons), six fixed torpedo tubes and Squid, with a complement of 250. Radars would have been the long-range Type 960, the Type 982/983 fighter-control combination, Type 992 for target indication, and Type 974 for short-range surface search. Sonars would have been Types 166 and 147F for Squid. Each ship would have had two MRS 3 directors (in the A/D ship a second 3in/70 in effect replaced the L70 of the A/S ship). Armament weights were given as 300 tons for the A/S ship and 420 for the A/D ship. The latter design seems to have been worked out in some detail, since the sheet showed a probable cost of £4.5 million (no figure was shown for the A/D escort).[26]

Although a new FADE would have to be built, interest initially concentrated on the fleet A/S escort. E-in-C was strongly promoting the new Y.102 steam/gas turbine powerplant. At a meeting of the Ship Design Policy Committee on 21 October 1953 DTSD was asked for characteristics for a fleet A/S escort using the new Y.102 powerplant. E-in-C discussed the new engine with DNC representatives, headed by Mr. John, at a meeting on 27 October.[27] Past studies had shown that the projected fast A/S escort would require about 50,000 SHP, and the projected fleet A/D escort would need 60,000 SHP. E-in-C saw little difference in space and weight between the two, so he fixed power at the higher figure. Normally ships would use steam power, relying on their gas turbines for boost. Steam turbines could be throttled back as gas turbines cut in, to provide intermediate power levels with reasonable efficiency. E-in-C was, however, anxious to avoid constant cutting in and out, and hence wanted steam turbine power well above that required for cruising speed. He expected that the plant would be far more economical than, say, YEAD.1, since it would normally run at optimum power. As an indication of what the new plant could offer, E-in-C estimated that Y.102 would weigh 665 tons (Part IV weight, not including some machinery items) compared to 750 tons for YEAD.1 and 816 tons for the somewhat less powerful *Daring* plant. For 2,000nm at 22.5kts, the new fleet cruising speed (35 per cent power), Y.102 would require 560 tons of oil fuel, compared to 630 tons for YEAD.1 or the *Daring* plant. Total length, as then imagined, was 92ft

---

[26] None of the notebooks preserved in the Brass Foundry seems to show any trace of either of these designs, which presumably used steam powerplants.
[27] Notebook 372/9 (C H Penwill).

for Y.102, compared to 126ft for YEAD.1 and 124ft for the *Daring* plant. E-in-C offered the plant within 43ft beam, but the constructors asked him to rearrange it within 40ft beam.[28] So modified, the plant's length grew to 105ft, and Part IV weight to 700 tons.[29]

The new ship was designed around the Bidder homing A/S torpedo, under development since the war. It was the only weapon which it seemed could exploit the Type 177 sonar, then nearing maturity.[30] Ultimately Bidder proved disappointing, but that was not obvious in 1953–4, when it was only a projected weapon. The A/S escort Staff Requirement thus called for A/S torpedo tubes, long enough to provide space for future wire dispensers (20ft for 16–17ft weapons). The first proposed torpedo-tube arrangement was four fixed tubes in the quarterdeck facing aft, with four more below them, the remaining tubes firing on either bow, in superimposed pairs, as in a submarine. DUW much preferred enclosed torpedo tubes, which would be protected against nuclear and chemical attack, would be easier to service, would be easier to protect against cold weather, and could be reloaded. DUW wanted the tubes arranged so that the ship could fire torpedoes at maximum speed (clean and light, 35kts). At some point the idea of placing the tubes underwater was raised. One question was the least height from which guided torpedoes could be launched to ensure that their tails would clear the tubes before their heads entered the water, and also that the torpedo would not 'belly flop' to be damaged on hitting the water. It was generally agreed that torpedoes could not be fired from No. 2 deck above the transom due to the stern wave. Firing

from the weather deck was more promising.

Free-running ASW torpedoes would typically be fired in salvoes of four, wire-guided ones singly. Ships would carry one type or the other, not a mix of the two. Superintendent of Underwater Launching Equipment (SULE) observed that wire guidance might require that torpedoes be fired aft. All should be fired at the same angle, to minimise tension in the wire. By early 1954 DTASW wanted a 22ft tube, to cater for both types. The 24ft anti-ship Fancy was also under development. It could give a Fast Escort significant long-range anti-ship capability, but to accommodate it the deckhouse carrying torpedo tubes would have to provide 20 per cent more tube and loading space.

Ultimately the preferred arrangement was tubes angled aft in the after deckhouse. The next best was on the quarterdeck, either fixed or in two triple tubes training outboard at a fixed angle. A third, for salvoes of two free-running torpedoes and one wire-guided, was on No. 2 deck forward (if impractical, on the weather deck amidships, oriented forward). By early 1954 the planned battery was twenty torpedo tubes at weather deck level, either all in a deck house aft, firing on both quarters, or sixteen in the deckhouse and four in swivelling mounts on either bow. A few months later the battery was cut to twelve tubes, all in a deckhouse aft, with reloads.

DTSD issued outline Staff Requirements on 6 November 1953 (TSD 4270/53). They included 20ft fixed A/S torpedo tubes and the variable-depth sonar (VDS) then envisaged.[31] Five alternative armaments, P through T, all included single Limbo, TCSF 2, and the same sonars (Asdics Types 162, 170, 176 [passive, for torpedo protection], and 177, with provision for VDS). Speed was 30kts deep and dirty and endurance was 4,000nm at the new standard fleet speed of 22.5kts (until recently the standard had been 2,000nm at 22.5kts). Other armament was:

	P	Q	R	S	T
Fixed TT	12	20	12	20	20
Twin 3in/70	1	1	—	—	—
Six-barrel L70	—	—	1	1	—
Twin L70	1	1	1	1	2
Gun Direction	976	976	GDS 2*	GDS 2*	GDS 2*

Q had the heaviest armament, at 345 tons (P was 335 tons, R was 287.5 tons, S was 297.5 tons, and T was 260 tons). Adopting the lightweight armaments (R, S and T) would unbalance the design. Since the number of torpedoes would depend on arrangement, on 10 November 1953 John asked for two designs with the maximum possible number, giving salvoes of three. One version had the gun armament in P, which roughly corresponded to that of the Stage II A/S frigate (described in Chapter 10). It followed that the 360ft length of that ship would accommodate all of the weapons involved. The alter-

---

[28] The two units of this plant (56ft and 36ft long) could be as much as 36ft apart. The forward unit comprised a 16ft long boiler room and a 40ft long steam turbine room with two 350 kW generators abeam the turbines. The after unit contained gas turbines and two 500 kW diesel generators. With 14ft propellers (the worst case) the plant could be accommodated within the same height as in a *Daring* with about a foot to spare.

[29] In this case there was a separate gearing room (17ft) between the forward engine room (two 400 kW turbo-generators) and the after engine room (reduced to 32ft in length, with two 200 kW diesel generators). DEE wanted four 350 kW turbo-generators and three 200 kW diesel generators in a fleet A/S escort and four 500 kW turbo-generators and three 200 kW diesel generators in a fleet A/D escort.

[30] The Staff Requirement was TSD 4257/53 of 29 October 1953. British work on anti-ship acoustic torpedoes began in 1940 but had low priority. In 1943 two passive ASW torpedoes were under development, the air-launched Dealer and the ship-launched Bidder. A 1946 Staff Target required Bidder to deal with submarines running at speeds up to 25kts, and at depths to 1,500ft. Launch range would be 8,000 yds, far beyond lock-on range for any passive system which could fit into a torpedo nose. Bidder would therefore run out (at maximum speed) to a preset point before beginning to home. To reduce self-noise while searching, it would then slow to listening, but once a target had been detected it would accelerate back up to maximum speed to limit the target's ability to escape. This seems to have been the first use of a currently common technique which makes it possible for torpedoes with limited search speeds to deal with very fast targets (the US Mk 48 is a case in point). The developers imagined firing Bidder either at a target detected by sonar, hence at a more or less precisely known position, or as a search weapon at a less definite target position, such as one indicated by HF/DF or passively. By 1951 Bidder was running initial trials. As of August 1950 expected dimensions were 21in × 114in (1,120lbs), with speeds of 24kts and 15kts, but ultimately the surface-ship version (Mk 20E) was 162in long and weighed 1,800lbs, with a 196lb charge. Performance: 20,000 yds at 16kts or 6,000 yds at 23kts; the torpedo ran out at 23kts and slowed to 16kts to listen. Bidder was finally ready for service in 1958. Performance was disappointing, even within the limits which had been accepted. It was effective only against a noisy submarine, which meant one cavitating near the surface or snorkelling. The Mk 20S submarine version survived longer (single-speed: 12,000 yds at 20kts). Details from Advance Information on Mk 20E (ADM 239/552) and from the 1959 edition of Particulars of British and Commonwealth War Vessels, CB 01815. Range could be extended by providing mid-course guidance using a trailing wire; a 1953 Staff Requirement called for guidance out to 15,000 yds at 30kts (it led to development of Mk 24 Ongar/Tigerfish, which initially but not ultimately had a surface-ship version). An alternative Super-Bidder under consideration in 1953 used HTP propulsion for a very fast run-out. There was also an abortive proposal to reduce run-out time by flying the torpedo to its initial search position (the contemporary US Navy had much the same idea). British missile development resources were far too limited for such a project. The later Ikara reflected much the same idea.

[31] The first VDS used over-the-side installations, but the British were interested in a futuristic installation then being promoted by the US Underwater Sound Laboratory at New London, using a fish housed in a recess under the hull, streamed from a 35–40ft hinged tail. Estimated weight was 16,000lbs. This form of VDS also figured in the slightly later missile destroyer design.

native had a second L70 Bofors instead of the twin 3in/70 (this armament was soon dropped). Since neither version had a gun capable of firing starshell, the ships would also need rocket flare launchers. With a Y.102 plant, a 360ft ship would make 29.75kts deep and dirty; 750 tons of oil would give an endurance of 3,130nm at 22.5kts dirty (3,600nm clean). To get 30kts with the fixed output of the Y.102 plant, the ship had to be lengthened 15ft (370ft and 380ft versions were also evaluated). That in turn would provide more fuel volume, so that endurance would grow to 3,800nm clean at 22.5kts or 4,050nm clean at 20kts. A sketch shows a flush deck and a deckhouse aft (in most versions, containing the fixed torpedo tubes). There were two funnels.

The armament of the A/S Fleet Escort amounted to an unusually small fraction of displacement. DTSD suggested water displacement of fuel to increase the ship's allowable military load (the ship would not need any margin of stability to compensate for reduced stability as fuel was burned). That was feasible only for diesel oil tanks feeding the gas turbines, because light oil would float on water admitted below it. The designer complained that the staff did not understand that the limit was not stability but strength: water displacement would not help at all.

A table of Fast Escort designs shows initial Studies 1 through 4 (DNC 7/533, 536, 537, and 540) completed in November and December (Study 4) 1953. All had one twin 3in/70 and one twin L70 Bofors, both with MRS 3 fire-control systems, plus single Limbo and twelve A/S torpedoes (in six tubes in Studies 1 through 3, in twelve tubes in Study 4). The only radar was Type 976. Study 1 (360ft × 42ft × 30ft 6in × 12ft 6in) was a first estimate to develop a sheer line. Its Limbo was forward, and the torpedo tubes were in a deckhouse firing forward. Machinery in Study 1 was 105ft long. Study 2 was an incomplete attempt to reduce hull depth to 27ft 9in. Study 3 had enlarged machinery (115ft long) with a hull depth of 28ft. Study 4 corresponded to Armament P. Limbo was moved aft and enclosed in the deckhouse with the A/S torpedoes (which now fired aft). Work on this series stopped after John visited DNC on 3 March 1954.

A further preliminary sketch (DNC 7/620, numbered out of sequence some time after being completed) done in March 1954 had 105ft machinery and torpedo tubes firing through the transom. Length increased to 375ft and beam to 43ft. As this sketch developed, John chose to place twelve torpedo tubes and eight reloads in an after deckhouse; the single Limbo would be in the open.[32] Not long afterwards the Ship Design Policy Committee decided to add SPS-6C air search radar and

space and weight for a VDS, at that time envisaged as mounted in the keel. Powered by a Y.102 plant, such a ship would make 30.5kts in temperate waters or 29.75kts in the tropics (54,000 SHP), deep and dirty. With steam turbines alone she would make 26kts. A fuel load of 700 tons, including 250 tons of diesel oil, would provide an endurance of 3,600nm at 20kts operating with auxiliaries connected, six months out of dock in temperate waters or 4,720nm (reduced to 4,500nm) at 20kts clean under temperate conditions with auxiliaries connected, or 5,550nm (5,300nm as reduced) at 20kts under trials conditions in temperate waters with auxiliaries not connected. On this basis a draft Legend was provided for the Sea Lords.[33]

The Y.102 plant kept growing. In December 1953 E-in-C wanted 116ft rather than the 105ft offered some months earlier.[34] Increased length bought a reduction in height which made it possible for the deck above the machinery to be made flush, rather than having a projection over the boilers. Even so, at this point Y.102 offered a 22.5 per cent space saving compared to a *Daring*. However, further substantial increases would be announced in February 1955. An estimate of June 1954 showed that the ship could be expanded slightly (to 4,000 tons, about 400ft length) while retaining her speed (30.5kts deep and dirty), to provide a more powerful armament (445 tons, enough for a second twin 3in/70, perhaps also a second twin L70 Bofors). Thus on 4,000 tons it might be possible to combine the three fleet escort roles (A/A, A/S and A/D) and still maintain fleet escort speed. This was a very rough estimate, and it would still have to be confirmed that the ship was large enough. However, the concept was worth discussing with a DTSD officer, Commander Weston (24 June). He thought the Staff would be quite interested, and the idea worth discussing with his director. This estimate helped lead to the design of the 'Super-*Daring*' described below.[35] By this time there was some question as to whether the Fast Escort would be built as planned. Without it, there might be no initial application for Y.102. On 7 September 1954 E-in-C proposed refitting the ex-US frigate *Hotham* with the gas turbines of the Y.102 plant

Probably the last version was a 405-footer (3,800 tons) developed on DNC's instructions (12 May 1955) and shown to the Controller on 16 May. It was credited with a speed of 31.5kts

[32] The first such design, to TSD 4270/53 of 6 November 1953, was DNC 7/630: 3,555 tons (370ft × 42ft 6in × 27ft 9in × 13ft), capable of 30.5kts deep and dirty, with endurance given as 3,300nm at 22.5kts dirty (under new rules, with auxiliaries running). This version had 116ft machinery spaces. Accommodation to *Daring* standards would have been 300. Copies of this drawing were sent to Departments and to SDPC, and DNC sent one to Controller on 24 March 1954. Another 370ft design, DNC 7/741, was completed in July (3,585 tons, 370ft × 43ft × 28ft × 13ft 3in) to meet the Staff Requirements agreed at the first 1954 SDPC meeting (TSD 2254/53 of 11 August 1954). This design was dropped on 13 October 1954 when John decided to work to 375ft length.

[33] This was the first of the series to have accommodation (in its case, for 325) to approved rather than *Daring* (ie cramped) standards. It was sent to Controller on 5 November 1954. It was also the first version credited with twenty torpedoes (twelve tubes). Designers' notebooks include the SPS-6C air-search radar, but a data table shows only short-range sets (Types 974 and 976 or 293).
[34] Notebook 372/9. Both Y.102 and YEAD.1 were still being developed, so all figures were preliminary. For Y.102, the added length was due to the 20ft gearing room and 40ft after engine room (YEAD.1 used two units, each a 16ft boiler section and a 36ft turbine section). Beam would be 40ft vs 50ft for YEAD.1. Pt IV weight plus reserve feed water (20 tons for Y.102) was now 675 tons, compared to 705 tons for YEAD.1; but the gas turbine plant would need 750 tons rather than the 975 tons of oil fuel.
[35] The preliminary design organisation designated this Ship Z (DNC 7/729), and it was not officially circulated. It seems to have been an internal initiative to develop a combination A/S, A/A, and A/D Fast Escort. The ship would have displaced 4,000 tons deep (400ft × 45ft × 27ft 6in × 13ft), with a Y.102 plant for 30.5kts deep and dirty. Armament was two twin 3in/70 (two MRS 3 Mod 1 fire control systems, which implies that these guns were in A and Y positions) and two twin L70 Bofors (two MRS Mod 2 fire control systems), single Limbo, and twelve fixed torpedo tubes. Asdics included Type 170 (for Limbo) and Type 177. Radars would have been SPS-6C, Type 293 and Type 974.

deep and clean (30.5kts deep and dirty) and an endurance of 3,000nm at 20kts. Accommodation was for 350 personnel, suggesting that earlier versions were considered somewhat crowded. This version seems not to have been taken very seriously, since a DNC design list describes it as a preliminary investigation, only a profile being drawn. By this time interest had shifted to the multi-function 'Super-*Daring*', at least partly because of the results of studies of enlarged A/S escorts.

The 'Super-*Daring*' or Fast Escort

In 1954 it was assumed that the future anti-aircraft weapon would be the big Seaslug missile, far too large to fit anything short of a substantial cruiser. So in that case the best ship to build in the near term might be the specialised anti-submarine escort. In September 1954 Director of Plans drew a very different inference. For the moment, gun ships were still needed. The ageing cruisers would provide Cold War shore-bombardment firepower, but unless they were modernised, at considerable expense, they could hardly deal with modern air threats. Yet the fleet needed something effective against a *Sverdlov*, with seakeeping and endurance to match existing large 6in cruisers, and with weapons effective against 1960s aircraft. Two *Daring*s could probably deal with one *Sverdlov*. They would be far less expensive than a large cruiser, probably with a smaller total complement. This was much the same argument which had been made five years earlier in favour of the cruiser-destroyer. In effect the *Daring* was the smallest 'general purpose' ship which could operate with a strike fleet. The fleet had only eight. It might make sense to build more, to a modernised design.

In October, DTSD asked DNC for alternative destroyers armed with the only existing gun, the twin 4.5in Mk VI, which could be had in the near term:[36]

> 1: A repeat *Daring* with modified Staff Requirements because margins had been exhausted.
> 2: A redesigned *Daring* as offered in July 1953, with a YEAD.1 plant.[37]
> 3: A redesigned *Daring* using the Y.102 powerplant.

The designers asked Commander Weston of DSTD what armament he wanted in an updated *Daring*. They ended up with much the same battery as in May 1953: two MRS 3 to control

the three twin 4.5in (a full Mod 1 forward, a reduced Mod 2 aft), with separate directors (the simple CRBF instead of MRS 3) to control each of two L70s. On the other hand, Weston would settle for a relatively simple target-indication system like that of the *Daring* (GDS 2* with Type 293Q radar) rather than the more elaborate GDS 3 (Type 992 radar) of earlier designs. He also wanted single Squid (ten salvoes), Asdics as in a *Daring*, and winterisation. Armament weight would be 490.5 tons, compared to 435 tons in a *Daring*, approaching that of the Y.102 Fast Escort already worked up. Moreover, *Daring* lacked generating capacity: the projected ship needed four rather than two 350 kW turbo-generators and two 200 kW diesel generators rather than the three 150 kW units of a *Daring*. The Fast Escort already had sufficient generating capacity (four 500 kW turbo-generators, one 200 kW diesel generator). To hold displacement down to that of a *Daring* would require considerable pruning: one less 4.5in mount, less effective 40mm directors (TOM), one rather than two pentad torpedo tubes, and single rather than double Squid. Even then the ship would displace 3,644 tons, which was still

The Royal Navy ended the Second World War with the 4.5in twin Mk 6 gun in advanced development. One great question was whether it would be replaced by a new 5in dual-purpose weapon or, for anti-aircraft purposes, by a British equivalent to the US twin 3in/70. Mk 6 survived both challenges. This twin 4.5in mount is at the Explosion! museum at Gosport. (Author)

too much, and would probably lack sufficient space for modern AIO facilities. Mr John now asked whether the characteristics of the modernised *Daring* could be provided on 4,000 tons rather than 4,250 tons by substituting the Y.102 plant (760 tons, including reserve feed water) for the steam plant (860 tons). A quick estimate gave 4,080 tons (John decided not to promise less than 4,100 tons). The ship would gain a quarter-knot deep and dirty.[38]

Thus began the 'Super-*Daring*' or 'Improved *Daring*' which ultimately became the 'County' class missile destroyer. The design had a variety of designations, such as the All-Purpose Destroyer, the Replacement *Daring*, the Improved *Daring*, and the Fast Escort (as opposed to the A/S Fast Escort).

Given encouraging first estimates, Director of Plans pro-

[36] TSD 4277/54 of 19 October 1954.
[37] This sheet listed seventeen designs under the headings of 'GW Ship,' 'Heavy Cruisers' (columns 2 through 5), 'Medium Cruisers' (including *Tigers*, columns 6 through 8), and 'Light Cruisers, Destroyers, Fleet Escorts' (columns 9 through 17). Column 11 was the redesigned *Daring*, 4,250 tons (400ft), capable of 30kts deep and dirty, with three 4.5in twins, two twin L70 Bofors, eight torpedo tubes (presumably fixed), and Squid. Estimated cost was £5 million, compared to £4.25 million for a repeat *Daring*. The late version of the cruiser-destroyer, with two twin 5in, at a cost of £5.5 million, was column 8 (*Daring* was column 9). The largest of the heavy cruisers was an 18,200-tonner (675ft) with four twin 6in mounts, probably the basis of the missile cruiser ultimately selected and then cancelled. Estimated cost was £13 million (equal to 2.6 redesigned *Daring*s). A slightly smaller (660ft, 16,850 tons) cruiser, with three twin 6in, would cost about £12 million. The sheet also included cruisers armed with four twin 5in (650ft and 620ft long) and with the two twin 6in of the modernised *Tiger*. In September 1954 one of the 5in ships was the preferred basis for a gun/missile cruiser.

[38] Sketch DNC 7/803, completed in October 1954, was described as a preliminary study of a re-designed *Daring* using a Y.102 plant. The ship would have displaced 4,100 tons (400ft × 45ft 6in × 28ft × 13ft 3in) and would have made 30kts deep and dirty (endurance 4,400nm at 20kts in clean trials condition). Armament was three twin 4.5in (two MRS 3 Mod 1), two twin L70 Bofors (MRS 3 Mod 2), eight fixed torpedo tubes (not enclosed), and Squid. Radars were Types 960, 277Q and 974. This sketch was not circulated.

posed requirements for a new destroyer.[39] Functions, in order of importance, would be

> 1: Surface attack (hence 4.5in guns); a pentad torpedo tube for anti-ship torpedoes (with twenty reloads) might be desirable.
> 2: Long-range A/S detection and attack (hence Type 177 and torpedo tubes, plus single Limbo [twenty salvoes] for short-range attack); the proposed battery was six fixed torpedo tubes and six reloads. By this time the anti-torpedo weapon had been abandoned.
> 3: A/A and A/D: for self-defence, she would need a twin 3in/70 and twin L70 Bofors, plus US-supplied SPS-6C and Type 277Q radars, with two intercept positions in the Operations Room

At least since the Second World War, manning has been the main problem in maintaining the Royal Navy. A major goal of the 'Way Ahead' internal review of 1955–6 was to reduce manning; First Sea Lord Admiral Lord Mountbatten emphasised that the Royal Navy seemed to be less efficient than the US Navy in this respect. The fleet plans produced in 1957 were designated not by the number of ships or the cost per year but by the number of men required: the '80 Plan', for example, was for a fleet with 80,000 personnel. Not surprisingly, there has been enormous emphasis on automation. In the 1960s a new automated gun mount, the 4.5in Mk 8, was introduced, its weapon based on a contemporary army howitzer. Growth designed into the mount may allow it to be upgunned with only limited modification to 155mm calibre for land attack. This Mk 8 is shown at Portsmouth, 1988, with the 'County' class destroyer *Kent*, reduced to harbour training duties, in the background. (Alan Raven)

Speed should be 30.5kts deep and dirty, with the endurance of the Fast A/S Escort, 3,600nm at 20kts. Accommodation would be 450.

Immediately, Mr John said that this would add up to 5,000 tons, in effect an unarmoured cruiser. It would be rejected as too large to be unprotected, or if protection were added it would grow much larger, hence more unsatisfactory. He offered two 4,250-ton alternatives, each with two twin L70 Bofors, GDS 3 (three- or four-channel with Type 992 radar), SPS-6C and Type 974 radars, single Limbo, torpedo tubes, and the appropriate Asdics. Alternative A would have two twin 4.5in guns, B would have two twin 3in/70 plus Type 277Q radar and two intercept positions in AIO. The most obvious difference between the alternatives and Director of Plans' 'all-in' ship was the third gun mount (twin 3in/70) in the latter, weighing about as much as a twin 4.5in. Mr. John estimated that the 'all-in' ship would displace at least 4,500 tons, quite aside from any growth required by her topside arrangement. To estimate size, he proposed starting with 4,750 tons and a length of 450ft (to get 30.5kts deep and dirty using Y.102 machinery). This was very close to the US *Mitscher*, which was used as a check on weights.

[39] Notebook 372/9, describing a meeting on 9 November 1954 at which he (Penwill), John, Pound (another DNC designer), and Commander Weston of DSTD were present.

John was not far off; an initial estimate was 4,710 tons.

The Staff rejected John's ideas. A draft Staff Requirement dated 8 November 1954 described an 'all-purpose destroyer' with two twin 4.5in Mk VI forward controlled by MRS 3 Mod 1, one twin 3in/70 aft, and two twin L70 Bofors, all controlled by a four-channel GDS 3 (Type 992 radar), plus six fixed torpedo tubes (twelve torpedoes) and single Limbo (twenty salvoes). Radars would include SPS-6C, to support limited fighter control. Armament weight, 620 tons, approximated that of the cruiser-destroyer. E-in-C's new Y.102 was expected to drive the ship at 30.5kts deep and dirty; endurance (dirty operational – *ie* with auxiliaries running) would be 3,600nm at 20kts. The ship would be about 460ft long. Designers were asked to consider cutting endurance to 3,000nm to reduce overall size.

In November 1954 a book of design studies, including the 8,000-ton cruiser and the 5in destroyer, had been assembled for the planned Sea Lords' meeting. The designers suggested adding the super-destroyer, and Mr John ordered it developed as a 460ft 5,000-ton ship with a double bottom under her machinery (by no means usual in destroyers), capable of 30kts (later 30.5kts) deep and dirty. A tentative requirement for 3,600nm at 20kts could be relaxed to 3,000nm if necessary. An initial sketch showed a 460ft × 48ft × 31ft ship (5,000 tons) large enough for a crew of 490. Armament was that of the draft Staff Requirement, except for twelve fixed torpedo tubes (no reloads). The twin L70s were on each side forward of her bridge. DUSW was willing to accept a cut to six, if necessary, as it was not a requirement to have salvoes of anti-submarine or anti-ship torpedoes ready on each beam. A drawing for the Sea Lords book was given to DNC on 27 November 1954, then to Controller on the 30th, and then to the Sea Lords for their meeting on 17 December 1954. DNC considered this ship too large for destroyer standards of maintenance, stores and amenities – and too large to be completely unprotected. She should not have to depend on frequent access to a base or to a depot ship. She also lacked typical cruiser amenities. That the ship would be seen as a cruiser but would lack cruiser qualities was DNC's almost constant theme throughout the evolution of the 'Super-*Daring*' design into the 'County' class missile ship.

A quick look to see what could be obtained on 6,500 tons with cruiser standards of stores and victuals showed a length of 525ft using a Y.102 plant. There was enough weight for limited protection: 60lb (1½in) sides, 40lbs (1in) over magazine sides and crowns, and 25lb over the operations room, chart house, and bridges. John called this ship an Improved *Daring* cruiser.

DNC now proposed cuts to the 'Super-*Daring*'. The projected SPS-6C radar was eliminated (the ship could not serve as a fighter director). GDS could be cut from four to two channels. Complement could be cut to 475, and endurance to

3,000nm. In studies begun on 10 December the preliminary designers found that the planned armament could be accommodated on a length of 435ft, the minimum for 30.5kts deep and dirty with a quarter-knot margin. A quick weight analysis showed that 4,500 tons (435ft × 48ft × 30ft × 14ft) would suffice. This ship could have six torpedo tubes.[40] Based on her length, she could accommodate 450–475 men.

John discussed the new design with DNC on 14 December 1954. An initial Staff Requirement (TSD 4331/54) issued 20 December 1954 reflected the 4,500-ton study, deleting SPS-6C and one intercept position in the AIO. The Board approved deleting fighter-control capability because it decided to convert existing destroyers into radar pickets. The L70 Bofors mounts were cut to one, forward of the bridge (soon it, too, was eliminated). The ship would have six fixed torpedo tubes. She did retain Type 170 Asdic for her Limbo plus the passive Type 176; she would also have either the long-range Type 177 or the new VDS. Endurance was cut to 3,000nm. Tonnage could be held to 4,500 tons if the ship had no stabilisers, no air-conditioning except in the operations spaces, and Board Margin held to 45 tons (1 per cent). If the ship were allowed to grow to 4,600 tons, she could have a full 2 per cent Board Margin (75 tons), and the 15 tons disposable margin would suffice for a second Bofors (with simple directors rather than the MRS 3 planned for the single mount). On 4,750 tons she could have either stabilisers or full air-conditioning. To get both it would be necessary to raid the Board Margin. Length would grow to 445ft to provide sufficient fuel. Formal Sketch Staff Requirements were finally issued on 30 December 1954 (TSD 2292/54). The resulting design was given to DNC on 24 January 1955, and forwarded to Controller the next day. It was presented to the Sea Lords on 28 January 1955.

The growth of E-in-C's new Y.102 continued. By January 1955 it was 125ft 6in long, and its depth had increased 1ft 6in. Within a few months it was even longer, as much as 133ft 6in in the final version of the A/S Fast Escort. The ship would probably grow to the point where the Board no longer considered it worthwhile. In March 1955 John's successor, Purvis, pointed out that the compactness of the original Y.102 had made the cruiser/destroyer/Fast Escort a viable proposition. For Controller, the failure of the cruiser-destroyer had shown that such ships could not be steam-powered. The estimated weight of YEAD.1 had just grown by 200 tons (machinery plus fuel). As bad as Y.102 might be, it was the only possible option.[41]

The figures in the following table were assembled in a memorandum dated 22 January 1955 giving the state of the design.

Photographed about 1988, a *Leander* displays the standard British naval ESM arrays of the 1970s and 1980s. The flanges on the topmast separate the four sets of directional ports feeding UA-8/9/10. The cross-trees below carry the short cylinders of the associated omni-directional antennas for frequency measurement. UA-8 covered S-band, UA-9 X-band and UA-10 C-band. The combination was called Porker, presumably an ironic reference to the ambiguities of ESM information (as in 'porkies,' slang for lies). Up to five signals could be tracked simultaneously. Analysis (by looking at and adjusting the displays) took about a minute, compared to about a second in later automated systems. The four canted Yagis and the cone at the top of the mast serve UA-13, a separate set which extended UA-8/9/10 coverage to lower frequencies (25 to 1,400 MHz). At least five British *Leanders* (*Apollo, Ariadne, Cleopatra, Minerva* and *Phoebe*) and three Dutch *Leanders* (with UA-13 designated SPR-02) were fitted. UA-13 required a separate operator position, which squeezed out one of two jammer control positions. The big radar is the Type 993 'quarter cheese', a replacement for Type 293. The smaller radar is the surface-search set, Type 1006. In addition to the 'candlesticks' (UHF radio) is a rectangular plate covering a wired array for VHF. At left is a similar rectangular array, in this case not covered. The object at the foot of the mast is a Type 668 jammer. At bottom right is the ship's MRS 3 gun director. (Alan Raven)

[40] A table of design data shows twelve fixed tubes and SPS-6C for this ship, but the designers' notebooks indicate the shift to six tubes and the suppression of SPS-6C (made formal in January 1955).

[41] Steam was worse. An undated comparison sheet showed the latest US Navy steam plant (70,000 SHP in the *Forrest Sherman* class) required 140.5ft. and 143 per cent of the volume of the 54,000 SHP *Daring* plant (124ft long). E-in-C's latest Y.102, 125.5ft long, was 106 per cent of the volume of the *Daring* plant; the earlier 116ft version used 90 per cent of *Daring* plant volume.

This crude profile of the Fast ASW Escort was taken from a Constructor's notebook. This drawing was scaled for calculation of side areas, but otherwise not at all detailed; no other drawings of this project seem to have survived. Gun armament was one twin 3in/70 forward and one twin L70 Bofors aft, with Limbo and homing torpedoes (in the big deckhouse aft).

	4,500 ton	5,000 ton	5in Cruiser-Destroyer (Study 25)	*Mitscher* (US)
	— Improved *Daring* —			
LWL	435ft	460ft	435ft	476 ft
BWL	48ft	48ft	50ft	48ft
Mean Deep Draft	14ft	14ft 6in	13ft 6in	14ft 6in
Hull Depth	31ft	31ft	34ft 6in	30ft
Deep	4,500 tons	5,000 tons	4,750 tons	4,770 tons
SHP	60,000	60,000	60,000	80,000
	Y.102**	Y.102	YEAD.1	
Dirty Oper.	3,000nm @ 20kts	3,600nm @ 20kts		
Clean Trials			3,250nm @ 22.5kts*	4,500nm @ 20kts*
Complement	475	490	475	403
Equipment	385 tons	400 tons	380 tons	294 tons
Machinery	815 tons	825 tons	850 tons w/RFW	986 tons
RFW	20 tons	20 tons	—	71 tons
Armament***	575 tons	630 tons	502 tons	524 tons
Hull++	2,025 tons (45%)	2,265 tons	2,068 tons	1,957 tons
FO	635 tons	775 tons	900 tons	816 tons
B Margin	45 tons +	85 tons	50 tons	122 tons
	4,500 tons	5,000 tons	4,750 tons	4,770 tons

+ Full BM is 75 tons for this ship.

++ Hull weights were based on detailed calculations, and had protection over a larger area than in *Daring*.

* Figures roughly equivalent to 3,000nm @ 20kts dirty operational.

** With 2 × 500 kW turbo-generators and 2 × 500 kW gas turbine generators, as agreed for the A/S Fast Escort, which DEE thought might suffice for the Improved *Daring*, but two rather than one 200 kW diesel generators outside the machinery spaces. Machinery weight is 760 tons for the A/S Fast Escort.

*** Note armament is 12.8 per cent compared to 12.1 per cent in *Daring* as completed.

ABOVE: The balance between escorts and high-value units changed drastically for the post-carrier Royal Navy. At the same time anti-ship missiles proliferated. Thus it became much more important to provide individual destroyers and frigates with self-defence jammers. The radome below the SCOT satellite radome on this Type 21 frigate (probably HMS *Avenger*), at Portsmouth in 1994, is a Type 670 self-defence jammer. (Author)

RIGHT: In the 1970s a new kind of high-precision communications intercept and direction-finding system offered a way of locating Soviet naval units beyond the horizon. The Royal Navy adopted the US Navy's Classic Outboard system, with the twist that the frigates in a formation forwarded their data to the accompanying light carrier for analysis, thus limiting the burden each carried. Classic Outboard VHF and UHF arrays occupy the masthead of this Batch II Type 22 frigate in 1988. Below these arrays is the standard pair of multichannel UHF antennas (Outfit AJK), one for reception and one for transmission, separated by a flange to protect the receiver from transmissions. The yard below carries standard single-channel UHF antennas ('candlesticks' or 'Christmas trees'). The latter eventually could carry multiple channels, but with wider separations in frequency. The rectangular object on the yard below is a VHF antenna. Visible on the yard below are the insulators of classic wire antennas for HF. (Alan Raven)

ABOVE: The standard systems of the 1970s, on board *Bristol* and Type 42s: a Type 992 target-indication radar is shown above a UAA-1 ESM array, in 1988. Note that Type 992 had sufficient range to designate targets to Sea Dart. Ships were equipped with longer-range radars, such as Type 965, to provide the fleet with early warning of aircraft, and thus to support interceptions. The small cylinders at the top yardarm are for omnis for the four bands of the UAA-1, to measure the frequency of a received signal. UAA-1 was the first British ESM system to incorporate this feature, and it was computer-driven. Ships with the upgraded UAT systems lack the omnis because each directional channel has its own frequency-measurement element. The yardarm below carries UHF 'candlesticks' and a VHF dipole (Outfit APH).

Even the 4,500-ton ship seemed large. To cut displacement to about 4,000 tons (400ft × 45ft), the Sea Lords were willing to eliminate a twin 4.5in mount and the L70 Bofors, leaving one twin 4.5in and one twin 3in/70, six torpedo tubes and Limbo. This armament was included in a draft Staff Requirement of 10 February 1955, TSD 2294/55. DTSD estimated that the ship would need a complement of 441. However, estimated capacity on a length of 400ft was only 425 men (probably 375 to 400 when details were worked out). The 4,000-ton ship could have neither stabilisers nor air-conditioning, nor the double bottom of the earlier studies.

At about the same time (28 January 1955), the Sea Lords asked for longer endurance (3,600nm). DNC tried to hold them off, arguing that 3,000nm dirty, with auxiliaries running, equated to 4,550nm clean without auxiliaries, which was comparable to the 4,400nm design figure for a *Daring* (4,100nm in fact as completed). DTSD was unhappy with DNC's 'barracking'. Work on this version was suspended on 6 February in favour of larger ships. A 415ft version would have an inner bottom. On 435ft the ship could gain the desired 3,600nm endurance.

The four-gun design was developed in considerable detail and presented to the Ship Design Policy Committee on 30 February 1955. Variants were a 4,250-ton (415ft) ship without double bottoms and a 4,350-ton (425ft × 47ft 6in × 31ft 9in hull depth) ship with double bottoms. The latter had the longer (by 3ft 6in) and deeper machinery spaces E-in-C now required, and its machinery block, bridge and twin 4.5in gun were pushed 4ft 9in further forward. By April 1955 the 415ft version had grown to 418ft 6in (with a 1ft 6in deeper hull) to accommodate the longer machinery, and then another 5ft (to 423ft 6in) to accommodate 3 per cent more personnel (beyond the original 375). Both versions had endurances of 3,000nm at 20kts; estimated speeds were 30.6kts and 30.65kts deep and dirty.

Just as the Fast Escort with two 4.5in mounts and a twin 3in/70 was most clearly comparable to the earlier cruiser-destroyer, the new more austere design might be compared to the Fast Escort. Each had two gun mounts (4.5in and 3in in the new ship, 3in and L70 in the A/S escort); each had two MRS 3 (Mods 1 and 2 for gun control) and GDS 2* (with radar Type 293Q) for target indication; each had torpedo tubes (twelve in the A/S ship, six in the destroyer, with twenty and six torpedoes, respectively); each had single Limbo with twenty salvoes; each had the new UCSF 2 underwater fire-control system. Each had the same sonars (Types 162, 170 for Limbo, 176, and the long-range 177). The destroyer had long-range radar (SPS-6C) and Type 277Q, plus possibly Type 992 in place of the surface-search set (Type 976) of the A/S escort.

A typical comparison, made late in January 1955, was:

	A/S FE Legend	New Design
LWL	375ft	400ft
Beam	43ft	45ft
Draft	13ft 6in	13ft 6in
Standard Dispt	3,600 tons	4,000 tons
Complement	325	425
Endurance	3,600nm	3,000nm
Armament	350 tons	430 tons
Equipment	250 tons	345 tons
Machinery	760 tons	795 tons
RFW	20 tons	20 tons
FO	700 (675) tons *	610 tons
Hull	1,470 tons	1,710 tons
Margin	50 tons	90 tons
Standard Dispt	3,600 tons	4,000 tons

* To maintain same endurance

For a time, three designs (four- and six-gun Fast Escorts and the A/S Fast Escort) were pursued in parallel. A new Staff Requirement for the six-gun ship (TSD 2292/54 of 4 February 1955) reinstated the air search radar and used an improved gun (Mk 6* Mod 1 rather than Mk 6*). A design to meet the requirement was shown to Controller on 22 April (450ft × 49ft/50ft [at weather deck] × 32ft [hull depth] × 14ft). It was expected to achieve 30.5kts deep and dirty, and endurance was 3,000nm at 20kts. Accommodation might be as great as 497. A 1:96 scale model was built specially for the First Sea Lord's visit to Bath on 17 May 1955, and a print was sent to DNC for the Sea Lords meeting of 26 May 1955. Thus the larger of the two versions of the Fast Escort seems clearly to have been favoured. A further Staff Requirement (TSD 4158/55) instructed John to produce a 4,800-ton version of the 4,500-ton ship. This was the version which evolved into the 'County' class missile destroyer described in Chapter 9.

The parallel four-gun version used a 4,350-ton hull (430ft × 47ft 6 × 32 × 14ft) capable of 30.5kts deep and dirty (31.5kts deep and clean), with an endurance of 3,000nm at 20kts. This ship could accommodate 395, compared to 475 in the larger ship. It too was shown to DNC (on 12 May) and to Controller. It was not, however, shown to First Sea Lord. On this basis DNC decided in May to get back the second 4.5in gun by giving up all the ASW weapons (retaining long-range sonar for evasion), to produce a 'gun Fast Escort'. Compared to the six-gun ship, length was the 435ft of the earlier studies (435ft × 48ft × 31ft × 14ft); performance would have matched that of the four-gun ship. The drawing was intended for the First Sea Lord's visit, but only a profile was completed.

The A/S Fast Escort was also still alive; it was needed if the larger Fast Escort lost its torpedo tubes. On his visit to the preliminary designers on 12 May 1955, DNC asked for a new version with twelve fixed torpedo tubes (no reloads) and with the air-search radar then planned for the larger Fast Escort. Desired performance was 30.5kts deep and dirty and of 3,000nm at 20kts – but under operational conditions. The question was whether such a ship could be designed within the 3,600 tons of earlier Fast Escort studies. There was also a

quick study of a 3,750-ton ship (405ft × 45ft). Once gun escort had been rejected, the separate A/S ship lost its rationale.

DNO still had hopes for a simplified twin version of the 5in gun, so there were also studies in which the 4.5in and 3in/70 guns were replaced by two 5in (all-up weight 90–95 tons, compared to 80 tons for the 4.5in). Three might be accommodated in the 4,500-ton ship, the issue being space rather than weight. Because this gun did not exist, such studies had no impact on a programme intended to lay down destroyers about 1957–8.

FADE Revived: The Radar Pickets

When the aircraft direction role was deleted from the fast escort, the requirement for something like a FADE remained. Again and again exercises showed that the fleet was vulnerable to low-flying attackers. The Type 62 conversion (see Chapter 10), which had already been abandoned, had offered far less capability than the abortive FADE. The next best thing, it turned out, was a radar picket.[42] The picket could provide low-altitude cover beyond the horizons of the major units in the force, for which purpose the existing Type 277Q radar, which many frigates had, would suffice. It could also extend high-altitude cover. In theory airborne early warning (AEW) aircraft could do both, but they had real limitations, and British carriers could not easily accommodate many of them. To some extent the picket role was tied to adoption of a longer-range air-search radar for British destroyers and even for some frigates. As of 1954 the minimum force requirement was four pickets (plus AEW aircraft), for which a total of six ships were required. This figure was based in part on a decade of US experience with radar picket destroyers (DDR).

In 1954–5 both major fleet commanders urgently requested pickets in their reports of almost every fleet exercise. Without some such ships in service it was impossible even to be certain of what characteristics were needed. As short-term makeshifts, DND offered a cruiser (used in Exercise PHOENIX) or a Type 15 frigate, which had a Type 277Q (in Exercise CROSSBOW), or conversion of early non-Limbo Type 15s. He considered the latter the best interim option, requiring only an AEW terminal, SPS-6C (in lieu of Type 293Q), Type 974 (already fitted), and two JW displays in the Operations Room. Such ships admittedly would not be survivable in war. Moreover, it was planned to pay off Type 15 ships to man the new Type 12 frigates. DTSD doubted that it was worth converting ships which would then have to go into reserve. The Type 61 Aircraft Direction frigates were coming, but given their very low speed they could not provide a fleet with any serious cover.

For DND the ideal picket would be a cruiser, but he could not get the only modern ships, the *Tigers*. Next best would be a *Daring* class, which could retain a useful close-range anti-

aircraft battery as converted. Next after them were the 1943 'Battle' class (better than the 1942 version for close-range anti-aircraft fire), with the 'Weapon' class least attractive. DTASW objected that the *Daring*s and the 1943 'Battles' were the best British surface-strike units. The British 1955–65 plan called for full modernisation of the eight 1943 'Battle' class destroyers, extending their effective lives to 1970. The 'Weapon' class, scheduled for modernisation with Limbo, would be the only fully modern A/S destroyers until the advent of the new fast escorts. If pickets really were vital, then DTASW reluctantly agreed to convert the *Daring* and 'Battle' classes – but not the 'Weapons'. The two fleet commanders were desperate enough to press for Type 15s, but DND made it clear that no such conversion could suffice.

The key to picket conversion was a suitable radar. DND proposed a Staff Requirement for a small-ship multi-function (including air defence) radar as early as May 1950.[43] In February 1952 attention turned to air search alone. By March 1953 the US SPS-6C had been selected as the only available set approaching the desired range of 90nm to an altitude of 60,000ft. By 1955 the assistance programme under which it would be supplied was already running down, and the US Navy considered SPS-6 obsolescent; so spares would likely become a problem. Other possibilities had to be investigated, including increasing Type 992's range by slowing its scanning rate (which might also simplify maintenance). The two other alternatives were the Dutch LW-02 and a Marconi UHF (metric-wave) set with a fairly narrow beam (broader, however, than SPS-6C or LW-02). The Marconi set was credited with a range of about 70nm, compared to 75nm at 35,000ft for LW-02 and only 50nm at 15,000ft for SPS-6C. Acceptable minimum range was set by techniques of fighter interception as then understood. Once it had detected an inbound bomber, the system would need two minutes of 'appreciation,' meaning initial target tracking and analysis, then two minutes for a fighter to fly an average of 20nm from the carrier, then a minute for the fighter to turn and a minute to intercept the target. During those six minutes the enemy aircraft inbound at 500kts would fly 50nm. To destroy it at least 20nm from the carrier, radar range should be at least the 70nm of the Marconi set. LW-02 was rejected as potentially unsuitable, so the Royal Navy chose the Marconi radar. It was designated Type 965, the familiar 'bedstead' of the 1960s and 1970s. Unfortunately its beam was fairly broad, and it lacked any provision for moving target indication. It could not therefore distinguish aircraft flying over land, as when they approached fleet units during the Falklands War. Type 965 was ultimately abandoned not because of its limitations but because its emissions interfered with those of television stations (and vice versa): it could no longer be used near European coasts.

The 1955–65 plan called for modernising the four 'Weapons'

---

[42] ADM 1/26007 describes the picket programme.

[43] ADM 1/23426, a 1952 file.

1943 'Battle' class destroyers conversions to fleet pickets

Schematic profile as of Sept. 1958

1. Squid triple ASW mortar
2. Seacat GWS 20 quadruple launcher
3. Seacat missile ready service magazine
4. Guided Weapons Director Mk 21
5. Type 277Q height-finding radar
6. Pole mast supporting UA 8/9/10 intercept arrays and UHF D/F antenna
7. Type 667 jammer arrays (P&S)
8. Communications offices
9. Type 965P early-warning radar (with IFF antenna above)
10. Type 293Q search radar
11. Type 978 navigational radar
12. Mk 37 gun fire-control director with Type 275 radar
13. Operations room (charthouse to starboard; electrical annexe to port)
14. Sonar (ASDIC) control room
15. Wardroom
16. 4.5in gun bays
17. Twin 4.5in Mk 4 dual purpose gun mounts
18. Seacat missile magazine
19. Gearing room
20. Steam turbine engine room
21. No 2 boiler room
22. No 1 boiler room
23. Sonar (ASDIC) hoist compartment

and then the first four 1943 'Battles', the latter beginning about 1958. By March 1955 'Weapon' class modernisation was less attractive than had been hoped. They would need considerable work, and they could not be taken in hand any sooner than planned, and probably not so soon. If they were not modernised, they would have to begin extended refits about September 1956. Given the urgent need for pickets, DND urged abandoning 'Weapon' modernisation in favour of converting the 1943 'Battles' into pickets. The first could be taken in hand in September 1957, with three more in April 1958 and the other four in April 1960, providing eight pickets which could serve through 1969–72. DTSD agreed, and the project was included in the 1957 fleet plan (the '80 Plan'). Estimated unit was £2.55 million. This was not an easy decision, as the 1943 'Battles' were also the only earlier destroyers which could easily be fitted with Limbo, the only available weapon suitable for urgent attack which did not endanger the firing ship (at the cost of a twin L70). There was some interest in modernising the 1942 'Battles', but there was insufficient design capacity to do that very quickly.[44]

The 'Weapons' were refitted instead of being modernised, but there was a twist. Given the strong appeals of the two fleet commanders, the refit added Type 965 radar, though not any special interception facilities. Thus modified, the ships were described as 'third-rate', lacking full radar range and any means of height-finding or fighter direction. Compared to ships with the earlier Type 960 radar, their main advantages were better high cover (to 60,000ft) and improved discrimination (narrower beam). The ships were standardised with both 4in mounts forward. Planned installation of Limbo proved impossible (but *Scorpion* retained her prototype Limbo). The

idea that distributing high-capability radars around a fleet added considerable picket capability led to the provision of Type 965 in the *Leander*s a few years later.

The 'Battle' conversion turned out to be difficult. As understood in June 1954, at a minimum the single 4.5in gun, the pentad torpedo tubes, and the Type 293 radar would be landed. The forecastle would be extended aft, as in a Type 15 frigate. Long-range air-search radar (SPS-6C at this time) and Type 277Q would be installed; desirable additions would include an AEW terminal and V-UHF/DF. Full conversion would add a high-definition surface radar (Type 974), a modernised AIO with two rather than one intercept positions, new sonar (Asdic Types 164 and 174 or 176), and new close-range armament (three twin Bofors L70 with simple directors). There would be five rather than three ship-to-air circuits.

Soon after the new fleet plan had been promulgated, it became clear that, given their short remaining lifetimes, all eight were not worth converting. The choice was to take four ships in hand simultaneously under the 1959/60 Estimates, extending their lives to 1965–6, after which surface pickets would probably become too vulnerable for fleet operations (they would still be useful in limited-war amphibious operations). It was hoped that they would be replaced by a new AEW system. Ships standing off 120nm from a carrier could detect targets 200nm from the carrier, providing valuable early warning and doubling interception time against low fliers. They would be useful against both the pre-1963 Mach 0.9 threat and the successor Mach 2.0 threat expected to be valid through 1970.

Estimated unit cost was now £1.75 million. The crucial item was the new 200 kW diesel generator (two installed in place of 100 kW), with a two-year lead time. As in previous plans the single starshell gun, the light anti-aircraft guns and the

[44] ADM 1/26417.

The only true fleet pickets were the four converted 1943 'Battle' class destroyers. This is HMS *Agincourt*, newly completed in July 1962. She has both the long-range version of Type 965 forward and a Type 278 height-finder on her stub mainmast, facing aft. Below the big double bedstead is a Type 293 gun target indication radar, with Type 978 below it. The object on what looks like a small helicopter deck aft is a Seacat launcher, with its visual control position on the roof of the adjacent deckhouse.

torpedo tubes would be removed. One twin 4.5in mount would also be removed, as the ships would have insufficient electric margin under current policy (this was reversed). Two L70 STAAGs would be added (by 1958 they had been replaced by one Seacat). A Type 965P radar, with a larger antenna than in a 'Weapon', was installed on a new lattice foremast. Other radars were Type 293Q and Type 277Q for height-finding, and Type 978 instead of Type 974. There was provision for an AEW terminal. ABCD (atomic, biological, chemical defence, now called NBC defence) measures were air filtration to the citadel and limited external control of machinery (control from the gearing room) plus limited external boiler control. There was limited pre-wetting. The ships received the latest type of noise-reduction propellers.

The four ships were *Agincourt*, *Aisne*, *Barossa* and *Corunna*.[45] Clearly they were not enough to protect a fleet. By this time plans also called for installing Type 965 on the only frigates with fleet speed, the remaining Type 12s. That did not happen, but when Type 12 was redesigned as the *Leander*, it gained a Type 965 search radar. It had no special picket capability other than the radar – in effect it replaced the 'Weapon' class pickets – but placing such radars far from the centre of the battle group provided useful early warning. That was also why Type 42 and Type 82 missile destroyers had Type 965. Air control, the other element of FADE, was provided by the missile destroyers.

[45] T225/982 and ADM 167/150, Memorandum B.1169 of 26 September 1957, enclosing sketch DNC 11/584.

CHAPTER 9
The Missile Destroyer

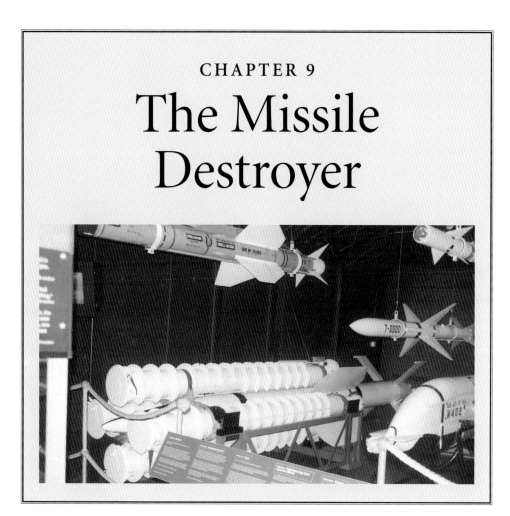

Seaslug as displayed at the Explosion! museum at Gosport, with its four boosters clustered around its nose, and its wings barely visible. One of the boosters has a section cut away. To the right of Seaslug is an Ikara ASW missile. (Author)

The Missile

Like the US Navy, the Royal Navy became vitally interested in guided missiles during the Second World War. In its case the motivating factor was the German use of glider missiles and stand-off bombs, beginning in 1943, which were released outside anti-aircraft gun range. That year work began on LOP/GAP (Liquid-Oxygen Petrol/Guided Anti-air Projectile), later GAP and then, by 1947, Seaslug. The Admiralty Signals Establishment (ASE), responsible for radar development, was already working on gun fire control sets capable of locking onto a moving target. ASE suggested that a missile could ride the radar's beam to the target. The US Navy used a similar beam-riding technique in its roughly contemporary Talos and Terrier missiles. As in every other country which developed such weapons, the timescale and cost of development were grossly underestimated. In March 1945 DNO expected to be running trials using a modified 3.7in anti-aircraft gun mounting within about two months, and that the operational two-rail GAP mounting would be somewhat bulkier than a twin 5.25in gun. GAP plus its tandem solid booster would be about 19ft long (DNO likened it to a torpedo), making stowage awkward. The desired rate of fire was six per minute. Given an estimated time of flight of 30 seconds, three missiles might fly simultaneously towards the same target (estimated lethality was about a third). As of April 1945 the Staff Target called for

engaging aircraft at up to 500mph and at altitudes up to 40,000ft, at a maximum missile weight of 500lbs.[1]

The Staff Requirement of 29 July 1949, to which the missile was designed, called for maximum and minimum ranges of 30,000 yds and 5,000 yds, respectively; desired maximum altitude was 55,000ft, with 45,000ft acceptable. Later the desired range was 30,000–60,000 yds, with a 40 per cent kill probability at maximum range against large 600-knot (ultimately 650-knot) bombers and smaller, faster fighter-bombers. They were expected to weave (at 1G) as they approached, so the missile would manoeuvre at 4G at sea level, and at 2.5G at 40,000ft. Inked into the 1949 document is a requirement to discriminate between multiple targets. An interval of 6 seconds was allowed between taking control off one target and steadying on the next. The missile would self-destruct as it coasted after burn-out, when it decelerated to Mach 1.5 or when it left the guidance beam. The designers settled on a range of 30,000 yds, including 6,000 yds of coasting after the motor burned out, the missile retaining a useful speed, about 50 per cent beyond that of the roughly contemporary US Terrier. To exploit its range, Seaslug needed a radar that could detect a target at 50,000–55,000 yds, beyond the capability of Type 992. Initially it seemed that three missiles would be fired at each target, hence that a triple launcher would be used. Later a twin-rail launcher was chosen, apparently because access to the middle rail would have been difficult.

Priority was placed on the densest possible missile stowage, the explicit choice being to trade length for diameter. Thus wrap-around boosters were chosen over the original tandem booster (for simplest launching). As fielded with four wrap-around boosters, Seaslug was 20ft long (16.1in diameter) and it weighed 1,980lbs (4,400lbs including boosters); fin span was 56.6in. The boosters were inside the envelope defined by the wings and fins. The missile had six feet on which it could be moved on rails within a magazine system. British experts considered it about the largest missile which could easily be handled at sea, although the US Talos was somewhat longer. The US Terrier was 13.5ft long and had a diameter of 13.5in, but it had a 25.8ft booster.

Given the 1957 horizon for fleet modernisation, an oper-

[1] ADM 1/22320 is a DGD paper dated 6 April 1945 on the development of guided weapons for the Royal Navy. AVIA 54/2074 summarises Seaslug Staff Requirements and general policy. Apparently GAP was soon named Seaslug; Seaslug I originally referred to a test vehicle for the guidance system, to be launched along the line of sight, the understanding being that the operational missile would be vertically launched. In March 1947 the overriding requirement was to have a prototype missile by 1949, so that the system could be ready for service by 1957 (in December 1947 DNO pressed for immediate decisions as to configuration). The March 1947 provisional specification required the system to engage five targets in sequence (40 seconds per target). A 21 January 1948 meeting decided that the missile would be a boosted beam-rider using line-of-sight launching, with a 150–200lb warhead. This was initially called Seaslug II and then simply Seaslug (the much later Seaslug Mk II was a very different missile). The 1948 version of the Staff Requirement assumed that three missiles fired together would have a joint kill probability of 80 per cent before the inbound target reached a range of 10,000 yds at 40° sight angle. Size was to be a minimum; it was desirable to reduce length at the expense of diameter for stowage. The 1949 version suggested stowing booster wings separate from the missile proper. The Staff Requirement of 29 July 1949 made the 1956 date for a production model an overriding consideration. Seaslug was given priority over the army's Heathen (later Red Heathen, developed into the operational Bloodhound I) on the theory that in addition to the missile proper the navy needed another five to seven years to develop the necessary ship. If both systems were to enter production roughly simultaneously (about 1956), it made sense to begin Seaslug development first. 1961 data are from DEFE 69/112.

ational system was wanted by 1956 (which could not, ultimately, be achieved). To get the missile into service quickly enough, liquid fuel was initially accepted despite the hazards involved. Fortunately by 1956 solid fuel had replaced it. Development was slow and expensive, and the Royal Navy was tempted to accept US offers to provide the more mature Terrier. For example, the US Bureau of Ordnance offered Terrier to a very impressed Commander P J Hill-Norton (DNO department) when he visited in March 1950. It was about to go into production, to enter service in 1954–5, and it used the much more desirable solid fuel. This offer was repeated on several other occasions, the first of a new missile system to an allied navy.[2] However, the Royal Navy rejected it at least partly for fear of damaging the vital British missile industry, and

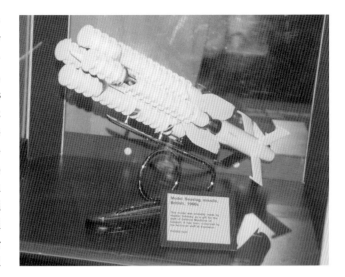

A model of Seaslug at the Explosion! museum of Gosport. One of the boosters has a small section cut away. (Author)

Seaslugs in their twin launcher on board HMS *London* at the 1976 Bicentennial Naval Review in New York. (Author)

partly for fear that future changes in the political climate might affect missile availability.

Seaslug was directed and tactically controlled from the Operations Room, by a Missile Direction Officer and a Missile Controller Officer at adjacent consoles. The Direction Officer selected targets, using selection aids (but not any kind of automated target evaluation). This was comparable to contemporary US systems, such as the one in *Adams* class guided missile destroyers. In the automated GWS 2 system associated with a digital computer combat system (see below), the system automatically evaluated threats and selected weapons to engage them. The command approved each selection and passed target data automatically to the Seaslug system. The only truly manual step was to press the firing button. Seaslug

first demonstrated beam-riding in October 1956. Sea trials culminated in acceptance firings in 1961, including sixteen consecutive successes. The system was GWS 1. In connection with attempts to sell missiles to Germany in the same year, it was claimed that the system had been designed for a single shot kill probability of 0.55, and that the test ship *Girdle Ness* was making 80 per cent hits in realistic tests.

Missile Ships

Seaslug reached maturity as British national – and naval – strategy changed. For about a decade after 1945 the assumption was that a future war, if it came, would broadly resemble the Second World War. That made convoy defence the naval priority, and it explains why the first post-war surface ships were the frigates described in the next chapter. When it first considered the design of a Seaslug ship in December 1950, the Ship Design Policy Committee assigned highest priority to a coastal escort. *Girdleness*, the Seaslug test ship, was initially conceived as the prototype of such a ship. As in the last war, it was expected that it would be coastal convoys that would face the highest threat of air attack. A ship for a task force was a lower priority, at least partly because carrier-based fighters would provide a task force with a measure of air defence.

In 1954 the Royal Navy found itself reviewing its strategy, turning towards an emphasis on limited war in the Third World ('warm war') rather than World War III ('hot war'), and hence from a new Battle of the Atlantic towards concentration on carrier task forces. The new strategy made a task-force missile ship far more important than a convoy ship. Studies of 25-knot missile convoy escorts conducted in 1953–4 must have seemed largely irrelevant by the autumn of 1954.[3] That year Plans Division recommended cancelling six projected Type 15 conversions of destroyers to frigates (to fight World War III). No more ships should be built whose weapons would be outmoded before the end of their lives: a project-

[2] ADM 167/135, memo B.672, 30 October 1950. The memo advocating rejection is B.715 of 22 June 1951, in ADM 167/137.

[3] ADM 1/25609, 'Introduction of Shipboard Guided Missiles into the Royal Navy', 14 April 1954.

ed new class of all-gun cruisers should be abandoned. In June 1955 the new First Sea Lord, Admiral Lord Louis Mountbatten, ordered a further internal Way Ahead study. It seems to have been conceived to pre-empt what he saw as an inevitable ministerial review. The study concentrated on the continuing Royal Navy personnel crisis, exacerbated by the fact that in every category of ship it needed more personnel per ship than the US Navy. Manpower shortages had cost the active fleet forty-eight ships in 1953–4; it would lose nineteen in 1956 and seventeen more in 1957–60.[4] If future war would be neither global nor protracted, the shore establishment could be drastically pruned. The large number of ships required for sea control and to make up for losses could be traded for fewer, much more capable ones requiring far less personnel. In August, Mountbatten told the Board that in connection with the 1956/7 Estimates and beyond, he had just suggested to the Minister of Defence that the service take the calculated risk of reducing the forces and services built for global war.[5]

A decision to cut the carrier force to four ships made a new carrier unnecessary and released money for missile ships. Seaslug was mature enough that an operational prototype could be included in the imminent 1955–6 Programme. Given the new strategy, the provisional building programme shifted from four convoy missile ships to four fleet missile ships, after which convoy ships might be built. In October 1954 a Shipboard Guided Weapon Working Party recommended that the first missile ship have fleet speed, be limited to guns for self-defence, and have a single missile launcher for minimum size. A capacity to control aircraft was desirable but not essential. First Sea Lord considered it most desirable psychologically to include a missile ship in the next year's programme, if only to begin to match US efforts.

Because Seaslug was such a large missile, it was generally assumed that it would require something of cruiser size, which might carry between sixty and ninety missiles. An early design, described in a sheet dated July 1953 listing cruiser and destroyer alternatives, would have displaced 15,000 tons (570ft long), with a speed of 30kts (120,000 SHP). The ship had one twin missile launcher (ninety missiles) and two twin 3in/70 (plus six twin L70 Bofors) but no ASW battery beyond a Camrose for anti-torpedo fire. She required a complement of 900, and would have cost about £10 million.

Admiral Edwards, who had launched the cruiser-destroyer a few years earlier, argued in September 1954 that it would be far better to build multiple small missile ships: four of about *Daring* size, say, with ten missiles each rather than one with sixty to ninety missiles on board. Director of Plans agreed that the missile ship should be the smallest and least expensive possible. A minimum fleet missile ship (GW 24, in a series begun in March 1953) had a single launcher and a minimum missile load of ten or twelve weapons. Gun armament was to be two twin L70 Bofors or a twin 3in/70 or a combination, as in the Fast ASW Escort (eventually it amounted to three L70 and two fixed torpedo tubes; single Limbo could replace one L70). Desired endurance was set at 4,500nm, the typical fleet or frigate figure. An attempt to realise these characteristics on *Daring* dimensions with Y.102A machinery failed. On a deep displacement of 3,550 tons (compared to 3,350 tons for *Daring*), endurance was only 3,200nm at 20kts. Speed would have been 31kts. This design was impracticable, however, because its small hull could accommodate only twenty officers and 260 ratings, but the systems on board required a total of 450. A larger missile cruiser, GW 27, using Y.102 machinery could carry thirty-six missiles on 7,200 tons (450ft×60ft), with a gun armament of two twin 3in/70 or 4.5in and two twin Bofors L70s. A further variation added six fixed torpedo tubes (with six reloads) and single Limbo.

The Sea Lords were shown a range of five missile-ship sketch designs in November 1954, including GW 24, an 18,300-ton cruiser, an 11,000-ton fleet escort (with two twin 3in/70), a 10,000-ton convoy escort, and a converted *Fiji* class cruiser. None of these provoked much enthusiasm, and early in December DNC had to produce another, smaller, cruiser armed with two twin 5in guns (as in the contemporary light cruiser). A crude estimate, using YEAD. 1 machinery, gave a displacement of 8,200 tons (480ft×65ft×17ft 3in). The most interesting feature of the design was a new kind of missile stowage, three rounds high, two wide, and four long, with two blank spaces in each feeding line, allowing any missile to be removed for checking. In earlier designs missiles had been stowed end-to-end in 'tubes' which could accommodate between twelve and forty-eight rounds depending on length. Cruiser designs continued through 1956, the series ending with GW 97.

The Missile Destroyer

As soon as the first sketches of a 'Super-*Daring*' were ready, there seems to have been some interest in a missile version of the ship. The chief of the destroyer section, H W Penwill, recorded Seaslug data obtained from the DNC missile group (Section 5) on 7 December 1954.[6] He was unenthusiastic. Missiles demanded disproportionate space. Small ships would need large protected 'hangars' topside, making for uneconomical dimensions and excessive hull depth to length ratio. Writing to Mr John on 22 December 1954, Penwill advocated a carrier conversion for the missile ship.

However, it was probably inevitable that the missile idea would go ahead. The First Sea Lord, Lord Mountbatten, had been a destroyer officer, and was very interested in destroyers (and modernisation) and he kept himself very much aware of developments in the US Navy. An early Way Ahead report in-

[4] ADM 1/26068.
[5] ADM 167/141.
[6] Notebook 1122/3.

cluded a comparison between three contemporary US warship designs (including the US 'frigate' [large destroyer] project, SCB 129, roughly equivalent to the 'Improved *Daring*') and three British designs: the 'Improved *Daring*,' the new General Purpose frigate (sloop) described in a later chapter, and a missile cruiser armed with two twin 5in guns. Mountbatten was well aware of SCB 142, a missile version of SCB 129, the *Dewey* class, and he apparently asked why the Royal Navy could not do much the same thing.[7]

Probably in response, in May 1955 the missile ship designers (DNC Section 5, the cruiser section) sketched missile versions of the new Fast Escort.[8] They replaced the after guns (two twin L70 Bofors or a twin 3in/70) and the ASW weapons (torpedoes and Limbo) with twelve missiles, a launcher, and a Type 901 guidance radar. Endurance was set at 3,000nm at 20kts; speed was 30.5kts deep and dirty. Accommodation was, respectively, 395 and 475. Overall displacement did not change. The new designs, dated 13 May 1955 (hence predating the Way Ahead papers) were designated GW 54 and 55. A next step, GW 56, added six A/S torpedo tubes without reloads to GW 54. The corresponding upgrade of GW 55 was GW 57. The table below contrasts these designs with GW 53, which was not based on a fast escort, and which was therefore far larger.

Missile destroyer designs, May 1955

	GW53	GW54	GW55	GW56	GW57
Date	5 May 1955	16 May 1955	16 May 1955	16 May 1955	16 May 1955
LWL	500ft	430ft	450ft	450ft	470ft
Beam	71ft	47ft 6in	49ft	49ft	50ft 6in
Draft	17ft 9in	14ft 6in	15ft	15ft	15ft
GM deep	6.9ft	4ft	4ft	4ft	4ft
	9,850 tons	4,550 tons	5,000 tons	4,900 tons	5,400 tons
Launcher		————————1————————			
Missiles	36	————————12————————			
Type 901/2		————————1————————			
4.5in twin	2	1	2	1	2
Bofors L70	4	—	1	—	1
A/S TT	0	0	0	6	6
Radars	Types 982/3, 960	Type 960	Types 960, 277Q	Type 960	Type 960, 277Q
Machinery	Steam	————————Y 102————————			
SHP/shafts	70,000/2	————————60,000/2————————			
	29.25/ 28.25kts	————————c.31/30kts————————			
Hull	4,620 tons	2,170 tons	2,340 tons	2,405 tons	2,575 tons
Equipment	860 tons	340 tons	395 tons	360 tons	430 tons
Armament	730 tons	315 tons	475 tons	365 tons	530 tons
Protection	600 tons	—	—	—	—
Machinery	1,300 tons	850 tons	865 tons	850 tons	865 tons
OF	1,570 tons	780 tons	825 tons	820 tons	890 tons
RFW	40 tons	20 tons	20 tons	20 tons	20 tons
BM	130 tons	75 tons	80 tons	80 tons	90 tons
Deep	9,850 tons	4,550 tons	5,000 tons	4,900 tons	5,400 tons
Accommodation (Officers/Ratings)	65/735	395	475	405	485
Required	65/833				

Seaslug required more than just the massive Type 901 guidance radar. Because it could not scan rapidly in elevation, the fire-control system needed three-dimensional target data. Moreover, the target had to be found and tracked at very considerable range. Thus GWS 53 had the standard pair of fighter-control radars, Types 982 and 983, but the ideal solution was the much larger Type 984. Having figured in early studies of the cruiser-destroyer, in 1955 it was the only prospective British three-dimensional radar. It was by no means clear that it could be installed on board a missile destroyer (the projected, but ultimately abortive, missile cruiser did have it). On the other hand, the missile destroyer was intended to screen a carrier, and in 1955 the Royal Navy planned to put Type 984 on those ships. The projected analogue CDS tactical data system employed a digital data link, DPT. Missile destroyers could receive three-dimensional target data via DPT, in what amounted to an early form of what is now called network-enabled or network-centric operation.[9]

Visiting the designers in Bath on 12 May 1955, DNC reassigned the modified Fast Escorts to the destroyer section. Only the larger of the two alternatives (GW 57) was pursued, becoming the basis of the 'County' class. This design was shown to Mountbatten when he visited Bath on 17 May, and prints were sent to DNC for the Sea Lords' meeting on 26 May. This version showed stowage for twenty missiles. Two days later DNC asked whether Limbo could replace the Bofors gun and the torpedo tubes. Missile stowage was rearranged. On 17 July Mountbatten visited Bath specifically to see this design. Somewhat later it was again modified: adding two twin Bofors (and MRS 3s) would cost 10ft of length and 100 tons. At this point the ship could accommodate no more than 485 men, but DTSD already wanted thirty more. Adding the Bofors guns would require even more personnel. There was some feeling that ultimately missiles would displace all guns, so in June a fully 'missiled' ship, with launchers fore and aft, was sketched. Only a topside layout was developed, and prints of the resulting sketch were sent to DNC. The Staff Requirement included a 'long range short time of flight' anti-ship weapon, but as long as it was not available, First Sea Lord wanted tubes for homing torpedoes. Thus the design was further modified after a Sea Lords' meeting in July 1955, with four fixed torpedo tubes and Limbo (forward), but without any Bofors guns. The ship would have the long-range Type 177 sonar; First Sea Lord really wanted the under-bottom VDS then being discussed. A waterline model (to 1:32 scale) was made.

In July 1955 a formal sketch design was ordered. Draft Staff Requirement TSD 2304/55 (29 June 1955) called for Y.102 machinery with a sustained speed of not less than 30.5kts and

[7] David Andrews RCNC, formerly of the DGS design organisation, attributed the missile destroyer concept to Mountbatten. The 'County' class cover has not been released, and the available designers' notebooks do not make it clear how the idea originated.
[8] Details largely in the Notebooks of R J Daniel (631 series), in charge of the missile ship section.
[9] ADM 1/26038, a DGD paper dated 2 August 1955 on data link requirements of the new missile destroyers. Development of 16- and 24-track CDS/DPT for cruisers, missile ships, and A/D frigates, using the Types 960, 982, 983 and 277 radars, was approved in 1953 (RE 390/53). The system had one analog memory per track, hence greater track capacity required a physically much larger system. Because the memories were separate, the system could not compare tracks, *eg* to decide which was most threatening.

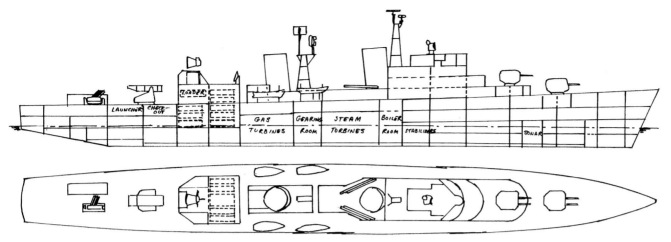

endurance of 3,500nm at 20kts deep and dirty under temperate conditions. The ship would have stabilisers. She was required to have good Asdic performance at speed and in bad weather, as well as the best possible manoeuvrability, for A/S. That is, she had to be the smallest possible ship capable of carrying the missiles at the appropriate speed (which determined minimum length). The designers chose 5,400 tons (470ft × 50ft 6in × 14ft 6in). When the Board approved the design it showed Limbo forward and the Seaslug launcher aft. There was some fear that vibration might reduce missile accuracy, so the Board suggested moving Seaslug forward and placing Limbo aft, but that could not be done. At this point accommodation was probably the major problem, so Mr John proposed lengthening the ship 20ft (to 490ft). The ship would now displace 5,600 tons and accommodate about 475; eliminating the proposed bottom VDS would add another twenty-five men. The new sketch included the four fixed anti-ship torpedo tubes (with UCSF 2 fire control) and missile telemetry

Some new items were added when the Draft Staff Requirement was revised in August 1955:

- Provision for the future Blue Slug anti-ship missile: a larger transmitting station (computer room) and added test equipment (probably about a third larger than that needed for Seaslug).
- GDS 5 (Type 992 radar) instead of GDS 3 (Type 992).
- The new short-range Type 978 surface search radar (instead of Type 974).
- An after capstan.
- A radar recorder outfit (REJ).
- DPT (data link reception) was now 'under consideration'.
- Television (recreational).
- Automatic telephone exchange.
- Telemetry.

Further items to be discussed were:

- Eight fixed torpedo tubes for the 'Fancy' anti-ship torpedo.
- Full picket (FADE) equipment (adding an intercept position in the Operations Room and also more communications).
- A twin L70 Bofors gun each side.
- Under-bottom VDS.
- Enlarged Limbo arcs (135° rather than 115°).

Other items of interest were air-conditioning of all living spaces, a wooden deck, full course-corrected degaussing, and a prefitted missile system transmitting station and Type 992 office.

Because the ship looked like a cruiser, the designers had to provide cruiser-like flag facilities, in the form of an Admiral's suite with dining for twelve, an Admiral's sea cabin (not on the Admiral's bridge), a wooden deck for official receptions, space for five staff officers, a staff office, and even a band. It appeared that on the new length of 490ft, everything could be accommodated. except the under-bottom VDS, DPT, the wooden deck, and the prefitted offices. The projected displacement of 5,600 tons, however, was too low (weights added up to 5,750 tons, including a 100-ton Board Margin). Thus a ship a thousand tons beyond what had seemed tolerable in the cruiser-destroyer, was accepted. This was exactly what several designers had tried to avoid, a cruiser-size ship with all the limitations of a destroyer, such as dependence on a base or a tender.

To cut back this rather large ship, DCNS proposed eliminating stabilisers (45 tons) and the AEW terminal. That such small cuts were being entertained suggests how overweight the ship seemed to be. The chief designer, Penwill, said that the design was now well balanced. Surely DTSD would understand that any major change in requirements would entail a new design – with further delays. Accommodation was the sore point, because it was connected with the ship's length.

DTSD did allow some reductions (such as four staff officers instead of five), but added twelve staff ratings and two additional boats. Eliminating Limbo would save ninety ratings, but DTSD still wanted space for 542 personnel as a private ship, and accommodation for another thirty as a flagship, a total of 572. Clearly 490ft would not do, so Penwill added 15ft and tried a displacement of 6,000 tons. After a meeting between Mr John, DNC, DCNS and Controller, it was decided to retain Limbo but to hold accommodation to 535 and to cut the Admiral's facilities. For example his day and dining cabin would be combined, and there would be no separate Admiral's plot (only a sea cabin). Staff officers were cut to three. To help accommodate the desired features, beam was increased to 51ft. A 500ft × 51ft (6,000-ton) design was reported in November 1955. Length seemed to be the minimum for the desired topside layout, albeit with inadequate accommodation. The

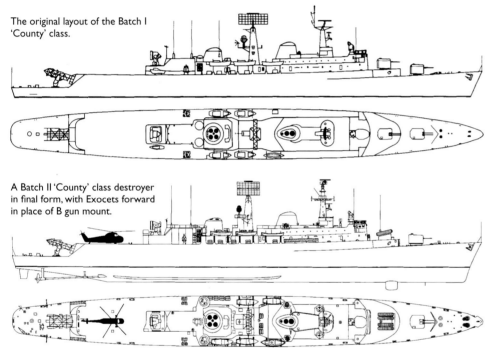

The original layout of the Batch I 'County' class.

A Batch II 'County' class destroyer in final form, with Exocets forward in place of B gun mount.

chosen draft, 16ft, was the maximum which could be accepted given the height of the machinery spaces (the deck above which had to be well above the waterline, for safety). That height in turn helped keep the feet of the outboard gas turbines within the turn of the bilge. Greater draft would require deeper machinery spaces, hence a deeper hull girder. Alternatively, the gas turbines could be staggered lengthways, but that would require a longer ship.

This design was submitted to the Board in November 1955, armed with two twin 4.5in guns, two twin L70 Bofors, eight fixed torpedo tubes, and single Limbo, plus Seaslug. She was expected to displace 6,000 tons deep (500ft × 51ft [waterline]/52ft [weather deck] × 32ft × 16ft). Expected speed was 30.5kts deep and dirty (30kts with noise-reducing propellers), and endurance was 3,500nm at 20kts deep and dirty under

operational conditions in temperate water. This last figure was equivalent to 5,000nm clean under trials conditions. It could be extended to 6,500nm by running 20kts half way on steam, then 15kts the rest of the way. Accommodation was 550 without air-conditioning (535 with it). Space problems due to personnel persisted throughout the design. The designers commented that the only way to cut personnel was to change British operating practices, making the same ratings maintain and use their equipment (presumably this issue was related to the persistent manning problem).

The design was further improved by moving the Admiral's quarters to the bridge structure from the amidships deckhouse; the forecastle deck could be used for large parties, B gun deck for small ones. This would save space, since the Admiral's sea cabin could be eliminated. DTSD liked the idea, which placed the Admiral close to the Operations Room, and his cabin could be used by the ship's CO if the Admiral were not on board. The earlier position conflicted with the use of No. 1 deck aft for crew recreation. The forward superstructure was lengthened 8ft by moving the machinery aft, the corresponding reduction in distance between the after funnel and the after end of the deckhouse being accepted. This change was accepted by First Sea Lord late in November, subject to holding displacement below 6,000 tons.

On 22 March 1956 DNC met with his two chief designers, John and Purvis. He approved the latest version of the design as the basis for a formal sketch design, ordering that the displacement be given as 5,950 tons. The sonar would be the long-range Type 177. About the same time it became evident that the big VDS was far too immature to be included. However, provision for it was retained, at the cost of raising displacement to 6,000 tons and increasing length to 505ft.

At this point DNC ended a long debate about missile stowage by approving tube stowage, very different from what had been contemplated earlier. Tube stowage covered much of the ship's length, but initially the designers tried to keep the stowage area could be kept short, limiting the portion of the Fast Escort to be redesigned. For GWS 57 three alternatives were proposed. The one shown to Mountbatten, and initially adopted, stowed twenty missiles in a space one missile long, with five levels, each 32ft wide, providing space for two missiles on either side of the lift well. Another twenty-missile scheme used a hangar below the weather deck, two missiles long and six wide (with a centre space occupied by a lift). An earlier twelve-missile hangar scheme used a space one missile long, two high, and six wide, for a total of twelve in a 24ft × 35ft × 12ft space. Missiles would feed into a traverse/lift which brought them up to the loader. The twenty-missile scheme was much better than the designers had imagined the previous December. At that time the missile cruiser used continuous tubes in which missiles would be stowed nose to tail along the upper decks. The destroyer designers rejected such

stowage on the ground that it would require a considerably larger ship (not to mention redesigning much more of the Fast Escort). Yet Vickers-Armstrong, which was developing missile stowage systems, reported in November 1955 that it had insufficient designers to develop separate systems for the cruiser and the destroyer. Although he wanted to develop a single scheme for both cruisers and destroyers, DNO accepted that the destroyer could not accommodate tube stowage.

Even so, at Controller's meeting on 15 February 1956, DNO expressed dissatisfaction at deep hold stowage. Controller asked DNC how many missiles could be carried in DNO's tubes, with and without Limbo. Work done since the last design study made comparison possible. Probably to general surprise, it seemed that there was no great difference. The Staff Requirement was for twenty missiles. Tube stowage could accommodate eighteen with Limbo, or twenty without (because its absence added tube length). Eliminating Limbo added no missiles to deep stowage but did buy accommodation, which was in short supply.[10] Generally deep stowage was associated with a flush-deck ship, the tube with a long forecastle (the launcher being abaft the break of the forecastle). Given a 500ft × 52ft × 32ft hull, with Limbo fitted either form of stowage required a displacement of 6,000 tons. Eliminating Limbo in a tube scheme cut displacement to 5,960 tons.

By this time deep stowage was no longer so attractive. It en-

tailed large open spaces deep in the ship, compromising her watertight integrity. The magazine space would so fill the hull that the usual bilges might be difficult to provide. Even if the missiles were stowed deep in the ship, the system would still require a large topside volume (loader and probably inspection spaces). Deep stowage also required a complex mechanism. A topside magazine was simpler, and saved 12 tons of lifts and six men. Much of the enclosing structure would contribute to hull strength. Shock hardening would be relatively simple: the tubes could be connected to the hull structure at only a few points, where shock hardening could be interposed. The tube was also much safer. The structure in which the tubes lay could be subdivided by flash doors, and sprays and blow-off plates could minimise magazine dangers. Propellant fires would be easy to vent.[11] DNO much preferred tube stowage, and it was adopted.

The tube covered much of the ship's length, including the machinery spaces. E-in-C approved splitting the boiler and gas turbine uptakes around the tubes. Hull depth increased slightly. Maintaining sufficient freeboard aft made it possible to work in an additional deck level abaft the machinery spaces. Further features added in April 1956 were warm-up and missile loading and discard spaces. Each tube (built up from openwork girders) accommodated one of two side by side 'chains' of missiles stowed complete, nose to tail.[12] The missile space was divided by bulkheads into four spaces, fore to aft (lengths and capacities on each side in parentheses): check room (40ft), magazine (154ft: seven missiles), ready-use and traversing

[10] Notebook 372/10 (Penwill): 'it had been expected that the higher position of the stowage in the ship, and the greater space required, would make the new scheme unprofitable, but means have been found to overcome expected difficulties to a large extent'. Vickers had developed several deep and horizontal stowage schemes. Scheme A, using chain lifts, seems to have been the first deep-hold type (twenty missiles, 153.5 tons). Scheme E was the most mature deep-hold type, with eighteen missiles (148.5 tons). Schemes B and C were horizontal stowage, presumably hangar schemes, for eighteen and sixteen missiles respectively (148.5 tons and 143.5 tons). Scheme D (twenty missiles) weighed 153.55 tons. There were also schemes with two twin magazines (twenty-two missiles, 158.5 tons) and with tube stowage (eighteen missiles, 148.6 tons).

[11] Arguments taken partly from DEFE 69/112, containing papers written about 1961 for the Germans, who were nominally interested in buying the missile.
[12] Based mainly on manual, BR 954(4)(A), for GWS 1 Handling Machinery Mk 1-0, December 1962, ADM 234/851.

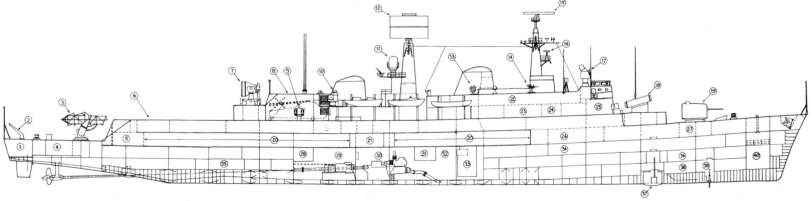

Internal profile of a Batch II 'County' class missile destroyer as modernised with Exocets, shown in May 1976. Note the great proportion of her length occupied by the Seaslug magazine. Not shown are the ship's ESM system (typically UA-8/9 on a fore topmast or under the Type 992Q radar) and her Type 667 jammers (at the base of the mainmast). Ships ultimately had a pair of SCOT antennas at the base of the mainmast.
(A D Baker III)

1. Steering machinery room
2. Crane for Type 182 torpedo decoys
3. Twin launcher for Seaslug Mk II missiles
4. Laundry
5. Seaslug missile loading space
6. Helicopter flight deck
7. Type 901 radar missile director (for Seaslug)
8. Helicopter hangar (opens to port)
9. Quadruple launchers for Seacat surface-to-air missiles (P&S)
10. GWS 22 radar directors (Type 904 radar) for Seacat (P&S)
11. Type 278M height-finding radar
12. Type 965M early-warning radar
13. 3in Mk 4 Knebworth-Corvus rocket launchers (P&S)
14. 20mm Oerlikon AA (P&S)
15. Type 992Q search radar
16. Type 978 navigational radar
17. MRS 3 radar director, for 4.5in guns (P&S)
18. Four MM 38 Exocet anti-ship missile launch containers
19. Twin 4.5in dual purpose gun mount Mk 6
20. Seaslug Mk II missile magazines
21. Seaslug missile checkout
22. Officers' cabins
23. Wardroom
24. Captain's suite
25. Admiral's suite
26. Operations room (CIC)
27. 4.5in gun bay
28. Gas turbine control room
29. Gas turbine room (two G6 gas turbines)
30. Gearing room
31. Main engineering control
32. Steam turbine room (two sets 15,000 SHP steam turbines)
33. Boiler room (two Babcock & Wilcox boilers)
34. Operations room annexe
35. Seacat missile magazine
36. 4.5in shell room
37. Hull outfit 18 (Type 184M sonar, shown retracted)
38. 4.5in powder magazine
39. Hull outfit 21 (Type 162M sonar)
40. Cable locker

space (66ft 6in: two missiles), and loading space (25ft). There were two side lanes outboard of the ready use space, and two smaller discard spaces outboard of the loading space. When the system was required to accommodate nuclear rounds, two were stowed in each side lane so that they would not disrupt the firing cycle of conventional missiles. They were moved onto the main lanes by a traverser which could accommodate two more missiles, for a total capacity of twenty-four. Missiles were rammed by hydraulic pole rammers until they reached the loader, then by chain rammers in the loader, which elevated to line up with the twin launcher. The inspection room had a bogie trolley for one missile taken from the reserve magazine (the three forward missiles in the magazine), running on athwartship rails which could align with either tube, or between them. No spare missiles were stowed in the discard space outboard of the loading space, because there were no flashtight doors between it and the loader. The 30-second loading cycle applied to the first four two-missile salvoes, from the ready-use space.

The radical shift from deep stowage to tube stowage caused DNC to order an entirely new hull form. In each case the problem was to find a good compromise between efficiency at high speed and efficiency at cruising speed (22.5kts): the best for one was bad for the other. The choice was difficult because power output was fixed. Efficiency depended heavily on prismatic coefficient, a measure of the fullness of the hull. A very full form (0.68) gave a maximum speed of 30.65kts, but required 19,000 SHP at cruising speed. A much slacker form (0.55) gave a maximum of only 29.5kts, but required only 14,000 SHP at cruising speed. A lower prismatic coefficient offered better seakeeping – but that would reduce stability (metacentric height) unless the waterline was filled out. The deep stowage initially chosen required fullness near the missile magazine. Because machinery was all below No. 2 deck, the ship needed a generous bilge. A full section was also needed in way of the Asdics forward (to accommodate inboard electronics). On the other hand, all versions of the missile system entailed considerable topweight. The first form selected (December 1955) had a prismatic coefficient of 0.61, described as the minimum acceptable for good sea-keeping, and the maximum providing a sufficient turn of the bilge. This coefficient also made for better sections at the ends of the ship. However, a month later DNC opted for a lower coefficient (0.58) with the fullest possible midships section (draft increased from 15ft 6in to 16ft). This was the lowest figure consistent with deep-hold missile stowage and was more efficient at cruising speed. Once topside tube stowage had been adopted, the cross-section aft could be reduced, and prismatic cut back to an optimum (for cruising speed) figure of 0.56.[13] The new hull form (April 1956) was drawn partly because a new estimate of required power showed that the existing one was

unacceptable.

In March 1956 it was decided that the ship would not need provision for 'special' (nuclear) Seaslug warheads, at least initially (provision would be handled as a post-completion alteration). It turned out that DPT could easily be accommodated, as it did not require much space. Overall, space was so short that a new method of stowing the anchors had to be adopted, right forward at the deck edge. That in turn made it possible to move A and B mountings forward 10ft. Their magazines and shell rooms were placed one over the other, a change DNO accepted. Multi-fin stabilisers were adopted, weighing more than had been expected (to overcome the ship's considerable metacentric height), but saving space. Air-conditioning was now included in the Staff Requirements. There were some detail improvements. A more accurate estimate of hull weight made it possible to allow for the use of aluminium where possible. Departmental spaces were enlarged.

Rewritten Staff Requirements (TSD 32/56) called for eighteen missiles and Limbo, and included DPT. Complement was set at thirty-six officers and 454 ratings. DNC decided that the sketch or preliminary design should be completed by December. Reviewing the design in June, DNC decided that there would be three funnels, one forward and two (side by side, to clear the missile hangar) aft. He wanted missile capacity raised to twenty if possible (he had guaranteed eighteen). When the Board reviewed the design in September 1956, it demanded that displacement be held at or below 6,000 tons. At this point the ship had eighteen missiles plus Limbo (twenty salvoes) and eight torpedo tubes.

In October First Sea Lord suggested that a helicopter be substituted for Limbo. Rather than the Fairey Ultra-Light then being considered for frigates, Controller proposed the much more massive Sikorsky S-58 (later adopted as the Wessex). DAW considered this large helicopter too valuable for the limited role of carrying a few lightweight torpedoes. Almost certainly the key advantage of the larger helicopter was that it could carry a dipping sonar, providing the ship, in effect, with a VDS. The British had been experimenting with helicopter dipping sonars since 1952, and were about to deploy them on board carriers.[14] The constructors offered a hangar large enough for the current S-55, at the expense of one Bofors (the remaining one would be relocated to the centreline). For the moment, the Staff preferred DAW's Fairey Ultra-Light (soon to be replaced by the Westland Wasp).

First Sea Lord was also interested in the US ASROC stand-off ASW weapon. A preliminary estimate (September 1957) showed that it could be fitted at the expense of Limbo, the

---

13 Notebook 372/10 (Penwill) contains, in effect, a 'County' class design history.

14 ADM 1/23064 describes initial trials by the Mediterranean Fleet in January 1952 using a Sikorsky S-51 and a US sonar. The dipper might reach below the shallow summer layer and perhaps also overcome bad winter weather. The 'County' class designer's notebook includes a 1 February 1957 report of tests of the large S-55 on board the Canadian frigate HMCS *Buckingham* by the US Operational Development Force. The S-55 was unsuitable, but the report concluded that day operations by the right helicopter would compare with those from a carrier. The new Wessex (S-58, the US Navy's HSS-1) seemed suitable.

Bofors guns and the helicopter landing space, the Type 901 guidance radar being moved aft. A new smaller anti-aircraft missile, Green Light (later Seacat), was a possible alternative to the Bofors L70.[15] Derived from an anti-tank missile, Seacat was proposed in 1955. It was developed so quickly that the Royal Navy never bought the L70. The 'County' class designers received the relevant data sheet on 7 December 1956, suggesting that substitution for the L70 was proposed at about that time. Although it was subsonic, Seacat gained a large lethal radius from its continuous-rod warhead. It was expected to be able to shoot down the first-generation Soviet air-launched anti-ship missile, Komet (NATO AS-1), which by 1957 figured prominently in threat assessments. Because it was command-guided and had a short range, Seacat also offered anti-ship capability, which turned out to be equivalent, on a round-for-round basis, to a 4.5in gun. Seacat was widely used in the Royal Navy from the 1960s on.

The problem of insufficient radar remained, so late in November the Ship Design Policy Committee asked whether the ship could be fitted with a Type 984 three-dimensional radar. DNC doubted that a ship to destroyer standards was really appropriate for so valuable (and massive) a device, so as a first shot he asked for the characteristics of the smallest cruiser which could accommodate Seaslug, 4.5in guns and Type 984. He thought that it would have to displace 11,000 tons deep. Work on a missile destroyer with Type 984 radar continued up to March 1957, based on the current missile destroyer design. Initial estimates showed that on the missile destroyer hull it was possible to have Type 984 and 4.5in guns, but no Seaslug, or Seaslug and Type 984 without 4.5in guns. It might be possible to carry one twin 3in/70.[16] A somewhat later proposal offered two Type 901s aft, giving two channels of fire. None of these proposals was very acceptable, because the ship had both cold and hot war duties. Guns were essential for the cold or 'warm' war. They could not lightly be sacrificed. As for the cruiser, on 11,000 tons it would probably be limited to 29kts. In order to make the desired 30kts deep and dirty it would have to grow to 13,000–14,000 tons.

By January 1957 the nuclear warheads had been re-introduced, the requirement being to carry four of them as well as eighteen Seaslugs. A helicopter (for the moment, the Fairey Ultra-Light) had, at least in theory, replaced Limbo. The torpedo battery had been cut to four in twin swivelling mounts. First Sea Lord confirmed these changes and asked for some more: provision for Green Light in place of the Bofors guns (which would be retained pending its availability), retaining

Seacat was the other missile system introduced at the end of the 1950s. This standard quadruple launcher, with two missiles on it, is in the Explosion! museum at Gosport. The radome in the centre of the launcher is the command guidance antenna. The launcher was normally stowed this way, and trained and elevated to fire. (Author)

two rather than four torpedo tubes, and compensating for lost accommodation by making the ship a deck higher amidships. That is, missile stowage was moved up from the hull into the superstructure, other superstructure elements, such as the Type 901 radar, being moved a deck higher. The twin launcher had to be moved up a deck to continue to line up with the loader, so the hull was made flush-decked. The necessary weight would come out of the Board Margin.[17] The first sketch in January 1957 showed eighteen missiles and incorporated the 100-ton Board Margin. It still showed the big British VDS then under test (Type 192), Limbo, and eight torpedo tubes; displacement was 6,160 tons. Another version traded off 40 tons of that margin to buy space and weight for four nuclear warheads. The Limbo mortar was eliminated and torpedo tubes cut to four. A further modification (February 1957) cut the margin to 50 tons (displacement 6,095 tons). The torpedo tubes were eliminated, but the ship could land the large Wessex helicopter.

The Sketch Design was formally approved by the Board on 11 April 1957 (Minute 5110) after a meeting on 14 March 1957 (Minute 5103). Controller thought the technical advantages of having two funnels aft more than compensated for a slightly blocked view from the bridge, which could be overcome by adding a small flying bridge. DNC told the Board that Type 984 could be installed at the cost of the 4.5in guns, and the Board asked for a study. There was some question as to whether Green Light was worth fitting in view of its limited maximum range (7,000 yds as then estimated). At this rather late date,

---

[15] The original weapon emerged from 1951 discussions at RAE Farnborough on a visually-controlled (command to line of sight) missile to attack targets with low crossing rates, which included aircraft heading directly for a ship as well as tanks. Seacat was first test-fired in 1958. Maximum range was 5,000 yds (minimum 1,500 yds), and maximum altitude was 3,300ft. The simplest version (GWS 20 system) was controlled by a standard set of target designation binoculars. Blind-fire versions were GWS 21, GWS 22 and GWS 24, of which GWS 22 was based on the standard MRS 3 gun control system. In the anti-ship role, Seacat was tested against the *Algerine* class minesweeper HMS *Acute*. Seacat was exported to sixteen navies. It was credited with destroying eight Argentine aircraft during the Falklands War.
[16] Notebook 1039/9. The reference to the cruiser concept is in Notebook 372/10.

[17] Meeting with First Sea Lord, 15 January 1957. The earlier changes were recorded on 11 January.

HMS *Devonshire* fires a Seaslug. Note the side, rather than aft-facing, door in her helicopter hangar, which made helicopter handling delicate.

there was also a question as to whether Seaslug should be abandoned altogether in favour of the army's Green Flax (Thunderbird Mk 2). Considerable energy went into showing that this would be unwise.[18]

The missile destroyer had been developed alongside a much larger missile cruiser. By March 1957, however, the cruiser was being abandoned as unaffordable. It was therefore proposed that the missile destroyer be redesignated the Guided Weapon Ship. As he had often argued in the past, DNC pointed out that the missile destroyer was an extremely large ship to hold to destroyer standards, and that she would probably be used as a cruiser. However, to build and equip such a ship to cruiser standards would increase her displacement to about 8,000 tons. Given fixed power output, she would lose speed.[19]

There was continuing effort to provide more missile stowage. Late in October Controller asked whether forty missiles could be carried, probably because comparable US missile 'frigates' (large destroyers) carried that many Terriers. Given tube stowage, the ship had to be lengthened; he was told that she would displace 6,650 tons. On the other hand, extending the superstructure out to the ship's side at No. 1 deck did provide increased hangar space, sufficient for twenty-four missiles, at very little cost in displacement. DNC thought the ship's appearance would suffer, but he admitted that this version offered advantages in the face of nuclear attack, with better

shielding of internal spaces and smoother topsides which would make it easier to flush away fallout (pre-wetting). A secondary advantage was that No. 1 deck became the strength deck, making the ship girder deeper, hence stronger for a given weight of steel. Given a model showing how missile capacity could be increased from eighteen to twenty-four by widening the superstructure, the Board approved the idea on 13 November. It also formally abandoned any hopes of armouring the ship. Even at this late date DNC was proposing eliminating the 4.5in guns altogether, on the ground that the ship was intended only to protect the carrier against air attack.

Vickers found a solution to increased missile stowage in December 1957 after considering variations on the existing tube concept (*eg* with four tubes side by side, and a larger traverser). Beginning with the third ship, only the after two sections of the magazine held fully-assembled (ready-use) rounds. Each of two tubes carried two ready-use rounds and three main magazine rounds; two missiles were carried in each of two side lanes, and two missiles were carried on the traverser. Forward of the tubes was a space for missiles without wings or fins, in latticework crates, stacked two high, four across, and three deep, with one space left open for access, for a total of twenty-three more missiles. Capacity was thus thirty-nine missiles in a space originally considered sufficient for only twenty-four, albeit with fewer ready-use rounds.

On 31 October 1957 DUSW wanted the Staff Requirement for underwater warfare changed. The ship's ASW armament would be Bidder homing torpedoes (three or possibly two on a side in fixed tubes) and a big S-58 (Wessex) helicopter carrying US-supplied Mk 43 homing torpedoes. To DNC's protest that he could provide a helicopter pad but not a hangar, DUSW replied that the carrier the destroyer was screening would maintain the helicopters. The big helicopter should also go

[18] ADM 167/152, memo B.1215 of 30 May 1958; also ADM 167/149 and ADM 167/150. In late 1956, when Green Flax was being proposed as a naval missile, Seaslug had a range of 15nm (30nm for Seaslug II). Guidance range was no problem because Seaslug was a beam-rider. The semi-actively guided Green Flax was the follow-on to the army's Bloodhound. There was some question whether it could reach its projected range of 30–35nm against a Mach 1 target because no sufficiently powerful illuminator existed, even in the United States (where semi-active guidance was furthest developed). Furthermore, adapting Green Flax to naval use might cost more in money and manpower than completing Seaslug development. For the long-range requirement (the 100nm range offered by Blue Envoy), Controller agreed to consider the US Talos.

[19] Bringing the ship to cruiser standards would raise her deep displacement to 6,660 tons. Adding 60lb (1½in) protection to magazines and over machinery would add another 650 tons. Heavier machinery would weigh 1100 rather than 895 tons. Other changes would be doubled workshop area, 50 tons more in maintenance, and Grade II flag facilities, including communications.

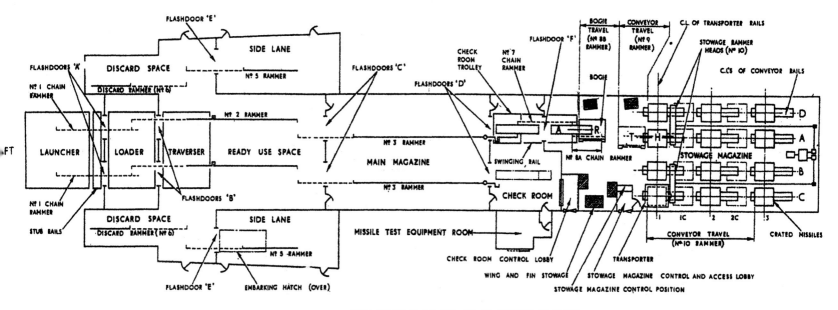

aboard frigates (that proved impossible). VDS was clearly not yet mature enough, so it was eliminated. Without Limbo, the ship would not need Type 170. The projected Type 184 would provide both long-range detection and torpedo warning, so the passive Type 176 could be eliminated. However, it might not be available until 1963, so at least the initial ships would need Types 176 and 177, hence two sonar domes.

First Sea Lord saw the Wessex as no more than an interim alternative to his preferred long-range ASW weapon, the US ASROC. At a meeting on 9 December 1957 he confirmed DUSW's elimination of the under-bottom VDS and Limbo. A big helicopter deck was created in place of Limbo, which had been located atop the missile magazine; the Type 901 director was moved closer to the after uptakes. The designers objected that the Wessex would seriously block the depression arcs of the Type 901 radar and also the missile firing arcs. The ship would have three Bidder tubes on each side, and ultimately the Green Light (Seacat) short-range missile would replace her 40mm guns.

Notes of these decisions (dated 2 January 1958) included some new requirements. First Sea Lord suggested that one ship in a group of four carry the Type 984 radar. There was interest in a Canadian lightweight over-the-stern VDS, CAST (ultimately adopted, though not in this class, as Type 199). The ship was to be arranged so that the very large Type 2001 sonar, then being developed for British nuclear submarines (but ultimately not installed on board any British surface warship), could be installed. As of January 1958 there was also a possibility of restoring Limbo.[20]

As approved by the Board in May 1958, the design showed a new 'turret' type bridge and a new type of multi-fin stabiliser. It incorporated the Wessex helicopter but no hangar. The

Wessex would be used for search and strike, so it needed more fuel for longer and more frequent flights (6,048 gallons rather than 500 gallons). Lightweight torpedoes were cut from forty to twenty-four. The Wessex would use arresting gear like that the Canadians were then developing for their frigates. DNC's initial solution to the helicopter hangar problem was a telescoping structure abaft the Type 901 director. This hangar was incorporated in building drawings approved by the Board on 5 June 1958 (Minute 5237). However, it was later rejected, probably because it would have blocked Type 901 at low angles of elevation. Instead, a helicopter hangar was worked in *forward* of the Type 901 deckhouse, the helicopter being moved out sideways. This was clearly an unhappy solution: positive control was required as the helicopter moved along the narrow gangway alongside the hangar. That may have been acceptable in view of the intention to replace the helicopter with ASROC. The 4.5in guns had two-thirds of the usual ammunition outfit (225 rounds per gun). Armament included two Seacat mountings (sixty missiles).

The AIO and other vital command spaces were moved below the 01 deck level, connected by elevator to the bridge. With the AIO deeper in the ship, it was no longer so important for much of the superstructure to resist splinter damage: it could be built of aluminium, reducing topweight. In approving the building drawings, the Board asked whether a television link between the bridges and AIO might be provided as an alternative to, or a supplement to, the elevator.[21] Functional streamlining, a predecessor to the later work study concept, was applied to these ships to improve their internal layout. A lift from the underway replenishment area ran directly to the provision room and cold and cool rooms, which in turn were directly below the preparing space and galley, to which

Missile handling and stowage spaces in a later 'County' class missile destroyer, as shown in a Seaslug Mk II manual, with fore-and-aft lengths drastically reduced to make the picture more compact. The key to increased stowage was to crate some missiles so that they could be stacked one atop another, three high. One space had to be left free so that missiles could be moved around inside the storage area, but that left space for twenty-three, plus the ready-use weapons in the main magazine and the ready-use spaces to the left. (A D Baker III)

20 Notebook 1122/2 (Sharpe).

21 ADM 167/152, memo B.1215 of 30 May 1958.

the dining halls were adjacent. Officers' quarters, wardroom, offices, and galley were all grouped together in the forward superstructure.

These ships required much more electric power than their predecessors. It was supplied by two 1,000 kW turbo-generators, two 1,000 kW gas turbine generators, and one 750 kW gas turbine generator, the latter on an upper deck with its own switchboard. Although this third gas turbine unit was classed as a salvage generator, it fed into the ship's main electrical supply system. Performance of the gas turbine generators proved disappointing in the tropics, and in all but HMS *Hampshire* the two 1,000 kW units were replaced by 1,000 kW Paxman diesel generators.

The design was still in flux. By July 1958 there was interest in adding a second Type 901, either in place of A gun mount or alongside the existing director. A proposal to add a second helicopter died because it would have required a complete revision of superstructure arrangements in the building drawings.[22] As the design stood in the autumn of 1959, the ship would have twenty-four Seaslugs and sixty Seacats (with visual directors: GWS 21 system), and two twin swivelling tubes for Bidder torpedoes.[23] The torpedo tubes were soon abandoned as weight compensation for the four nuclear missiles.

There was considerable interest in modifying missile stowage. The tube magazine arrangement, called Phase I, used 290ft of the ship, from the centreline of the missile launcher to the fore end of the magazine at the foremast. Phase II envisaged a forward launcher and a total capacity of sixty-two missiles, including fourteen on an endless-chain loader. Phase III, as envisaged in 1959, would use a US-style twin revolver loader (as in the Mk 10 system on the *Leahy* and *Belknap* classes) carrying twelve missiles on each revolver. Presumably they were a projected further development of Seaslug with an integral booster, the NIGS or SIGS mentioned below. Forward of the revolvers would have been further stowage for another thirty-six missiles, for a total of sixty in a space only 129ft long. There were several other proposed arrangements.[24]

For the next series of missile destroyers, the Board initially asked for a steam-powered ship to cruiser standards, with protected missile and other vital spaces (60lbs vertically, 40lbs horizontally, worked structurally).[25] Endurance was to increase to 4,500nm at 20kts. The new powerplant, designated Y.121, would have weighed about 1,000 tons, compared to 895 tons for gas turbines. As in previous attempts to modify the missile destroyer to cruiser standards, this one would have displaced over 8,000 tons (8,621 tons in this case, beam increased to about 58ft). Speed would have been 28kts deep and dirty (30kts clean). Instead a modified version of the original ship was chosen, the main changes being the new digital data system and Seaslug Mk II. Improved missile stowage would have accommodated thirty-nine Seaslugs; the ship also would have had thirty Seacats.

22 ADM 167/151.
23 Dimensions were 520ft 6in OA /505ft LWL × 53ft 6in × 16ft (6,100 tons deep). Speed under trials conditions was 31.5kts. On 718 tons of bunker and diesel oil, endurance was 3,450nm at 20kts under operational conditions (5,000nm under trials conditions). Stores endurance was forty-five days. Complement was thirty-six officers and 459 ratings. The ship had full ABC defence including pre-wetting (washdown), and all living spaces were air-conditioned. She had stabilisers. Data from Notebook 1071/8, from a comparison with the US *Dewey* and *Leahy* classes requested by Purvis, 19 October 1959.

24 This was Scheme 1. Scheme 2 had a ten-missile indexing (vertical) loader, with a total length of 101ft. Scheme 2A had a thirteen-missile indexing loader, for a total of fifty-two missiles (108ft). Scheme 3 used twin ten-missile indexing vertical loaders, carrying fifty missiles in 54ft. Scheme 3A used sixteen-missile vertical indexing loaders (56ft, thirty-six missiles). Scheme 4 carried fifty-six missiles, using twin eight-missile revolving loaders (101ft total).
25 The study is undated, but it was numbered 22A, in a series in which studies of missile ships for Australia, conducted in 1960, were numbered 19 and above.

The Digital Combat System and Batch II

By 1960 a fully-digital combat direction system, Action Data Automation Weapon System (ADAWS [DAB]) was being developed to replace the analogue CDS. It was derived from the digital Action Data Automation (ADA, coded DAA) system under development for the modernised carrier *Eagle*. Like CDS, ADA kept track of the targets detected by the carrier's air-search radar, and it could accept radar plots and tracks from other units. Unlike CDS, it could easily compare data on different targets, to decide which were most threatening and also which the carrier's fighters could engage. The project was apparently inspired by plans for the electronically-scanned Type 985 radar, whose outputs could not have been handled manually. Work on both shipboard computers and on frequency and phase scanning radars began in 1957. The radar was cancelled, but the computer system survived. In the destroyer the system was extended to control missiles and ASW weapons, hence was designated ADAWS. It included a threat evaluation/weapons assignment function, the CATE (Computer-Assisted Target Evaluation). It was considered necessary for Seaslug because, with only a single guidance channel, the ship would be tied up by one target. After completion of ADA, ADAWS development for the destroyers took 4½ years. ADAWS typically used two computers, one for track-keeping and the other for weapon control, and it was developed slightly later than the simpler US Naval Tactical Data System (NTDS), which did not include integrated weapon

control or automatic plot extraction. British ADAWS ships had the TIDE (Link 11) data link required for interoperability with US NTDS ships. That in turn required the Ships Inertial Navigation System (SINS) for precise positioning so that they could report radar and sonar targets accurately over their data links. ADAWS was extremely ambitious. Trials aboard HMS *Fife* (1967) were marked by computer crashes and failures of the auto-detection software, which proved unable to reject the clutter in which real targets were embedded. HMS *Glamorgan* also went to sea with the original system. ADAWS 1 Mk 2 was much more manually-based. Instead of depending on the automatic system, operators were provided with buttons allowing them to inject targets manually, and they could set the level of clutter the system would automatically reject. Special displays monitored the compilation of the tactical picture. A second surface picture table (a JYC), standard in other ships, was added, the implication being that ADAWS could not handle ASW operations entirely automatically. Software was heavily rewritten. This version was successfully tested on board HMS *Norfolk* in October 1970.[26] The Royal Navy considered ADA/ADAWS so valuable that it was initially to have been extended to all British surface combatants, including the contemporary *Leander* class frigates. That proved too expensive, and initially ADAWS was limited to missile ships (ADAWS Mk 2 for the Type 82 missile destroyer HMS

---

[26] DEFE 67/59, an account of the operational evaluation of the HMS *Norfolk* combat system in Exercise Lime Jug.

HMS *Norfolk*, a Batch II 'County' class missile destroyer, as modified with Exocets, 1979. This series could be easily distinguished externally by its double-bedstead Type 965P radar antenna. Alongside the mainmast are the twin radomes of the ship's SCOT satellite communications system. The Royal Navy was a leader in using such systems. Visible abaft the after funnel are a Seacat director and launcher.

Bristol, Mk 3 for the abortive carrier CVA 01).

The last four 'Counties' (Batch II) had a new Seaslug II controlled by ADAWS. It had more powerful boosters and sustainer, and was credited with greater range (49,000 yds rather than 30,000 yds) and altitude. The Type 901M guidance radar generated a third beam to guide the missile independently of the target-tracking beam, as well as a television to observe very low-altitude targets. The missile itself had three fuses: proximity (IR), impact, and command-detonation using coded pulses, and it had a continuous-rod rather than conventional HE warhead. The missile could be commanded to dive or glide to engage a low-altitude or surface target.[27] Unlike Mk I, it could engage supersonic aircraft and the Soviet stand-off anti-ship missile, 'Kennel' (AS-1). There is, however, some question as to whether Seaslug II was ever fully certified for service.[28]

A projected Blue Slug anti-ship missile, which would have been fired from the Seaslug launcher, using the same shipboard guidance equipment, had been cancelled in 1956 after a major Defence Review. VCNS claimed that it and other naval projects had been killed to make the much larger list of RAF cancellations acceptable to that service. Seaslug II could be fitted with a nuclear warhead largely for the surface and anti-ship attack roles; it was credited with a range of 36,000 yds against ships. Contemporary US anti-aircraft missiles also required nuclear warheads to attack ships.

The sonar associated with ADAWS was Type 184. It offered Type 177 performance but used a cylindrical transducer for an all-around view. It was considered much more likely than the planar Type 177 to be able to track a fast submarine flashing past. There were two displays, sector (PPI) and Doppler, the latter indicating target motion (opening or closing

Doppler). Type 184 used long pulses for maximum range, and a string of shorter pulses which, it was hoped, would indicate target aspect. The combination of aspect (in effect, course) and Doppler (speed) would indicate the submarine's track. An operator could place two electronic markers on detected targets on the PPI for direct transmission into ADAWS (one target could be transmitted from the Doppler display). Initially Type 184 was criticised for reverberation problems in shallow water, for poor performance against slow targets (little Doppler), and for a limited ability to gain contact. In tests in 1963, Type 177 outperformed it substantially, and the earlier sonar featured in many 1964 designs. At that time Type 184 was expected to go on board only eleven ships: three carriers, the last four missile destroyers (because they had ADAWS), and four frigates (late *Leanders* which were expected to have some form of ADAWS). By the late 1960s the problems had been cured, and Type 184 replaced Type 177 altogether in British service. Other improvements in Batch II were the Integrated Communication System (ICS) and an improved version of Seacat. These ships, but not the initial units, later had B gun mount replaced by four Exocets.

Programmes

The first four ships (*Hampshire* or 'County' class) were built to the original design under the 1955–6 and 1956–7 Estimates. In the new numbering scheme, they became DLG 01 through DLG 04, in analogy to contemporary large US missile destroyers. Ten were originally projected. By 1958 there was interest in a new small aircraft carrier, the Escort Cruiser, which would accommodate the carrier's ASW helicopters and the destroyer's Seaslugs. In November 1960 the Defence Board formally cut the last four projected missile destroyers on the theory that Seaslug Escort Cruisers would be built instead in 1965/6 through 1969/70, approving the construction of two more (DLG 05 and 06) in the 1961/62 Programme (with some long-lead money in the 1960/61 Estimates).[29] The new ships would have Seaslug II, which was so much better than Seaslug I that six ships so armed would be more effective than nine armed with Mk I. They would be the minimum air defence required for a single-carrier task force by mid-decade.

By 1962 it was no longer so apparent that the Escort Cruiser would be built at all. Even though the much better Sea Dart was coming, two more ships, DLG 07 and 08, were built as stop-gaps until it entered service. Unfortunately for the Royal Navy, Sea Dart had begun as an entirely separate programme. Unlike the US Navy, it could not modernise its first-generation ships to fire a second-generation version of their original missile (as Standard was a second-generation successor to Terrier/Tartar). Replacing Seaslug with Sea Dart meant prematurely scrapping the first-generation 'Counties'.

Plans initially called for modernising the first four ships to

---

[27] Performance claims varied. About 1972 Seaslug Mk II was credited with an effective range of 40,000 yds (compared to 34,000 yds for Mk I) and a maximum altitude of 50,000ft (however, the report of Woomera trials mentions a maximum of 65,000ft). Minimum range was 10,000 yds. Minimum altitude was 100ft at 15,000 yds (200ft for Mk I). Maximum speed was the same 2,000ft/sec as in Seaslug I. Mk 1 had a blast-fragmentation warhead (230lbs) lethal to 120ft; Mk II had a continuous-rod warhead. Neither missile is still in service. For 1960 claims, see DEFE 2/30. As described in ADM 239/711, the GWS 2 handbook, the missile used a new constant angle of sight mode when engaging targets too low to be suitable for the usual line-of-sight guidance. The system tracked the target in bearing, its line of sight fixed just clear of the sea-reflection zone. The missile was commanded to dive near the interception point, the instant of dive being determined by a separate dive computer fed with the range difference (between missile and target) and the depression angle as measured on a television monitor in the Transmitting Station (missile control space). For surface fire, ADAWS had to be 'informed' by manual injection. Other modes were midcourse guidance for targets at altitudes of 500–800ft, which would be above the reflection zone at normal range but not when the missile was fired. In this case the missile would be fired in constant angle mode, then switched to full beam-riding when the target rose above the reflection zone. This mode was called MICAWBER (Midcourse Constant Angle of Sight with Beam Riding). The missile could also be commanded to follow an up-and-over trajectory against a long-range surface target, the guidance radar being made to follow a programme depending on range difference. It could not follow the target directly, and was kept aligned with the Type 903 gun fire control radar. At the end of its path the missile would glide (*ie* would not be controlled by the shipboard guidance system).

[28] Note that, although it was present on board HMS *Glamorgan*, Seaslug was apparently not used as an anti-aircraft missile in the Falklands War. Seaslug trials are described in P Morton, *Fire Across the Desert: Woomera and the Anglo-Australian Joint Project 1946-1980* (Australian Government Publishing Service, Canberra: 1989), pp 342–5. In initial trials many missiles broke up when their boosters separated or lost wings in flight, but that problem was solved by reducing the missile's violent roll and by reinforcing key parts of its structure. Acceptance trials in 1965 both at Aberporth and at Woomera were successful. However, a new series of trials began in September 1971 to cure a new problem of missiles breaking up when their boosters separated (they also tested a new capacitive proximity fuse). It appeared that the problem was that boosters did not separate at the same time (they used aerodynamic forces generated when their motors burned out), but attempts to duplicate the problem failed. This series ended in November 1972, and there were no further Seaslug trials.

[29] DEFE 2/30.

Seaslug II status, with digital combat systems, at their first long refits. These improvements would keep them operational into the 1980s. Arguing against them in 1966, VCNS feared that they would spend a quarter of their first decade in refits. Chief Scientist said that, the carriers having been cancelled, missile ships were even more important. The Board approved the refits.[30] However, they would be very expensive, so on 31 March 1967 the Board limited them to the second pair of ships.[31] It accepted that the first two would end their lives in the late 1970s; they would never get digital combat systems. The two remaining refits were reviewed in January 1968.[32] This time it was argued that missile ships were too important to immobilise for fifteen-month refits. Projections showed heavy pressure on the Royal Navy budget in the early 1970s, particularly 1972/73. None of the four Seaslug I ships was ever modernised.

The Next-Generation Missile

Sea Dart was not directly related to Seaslug because the originally planned second-generation missile was a separate project. In the mid-1950s it had been a navalised version of the land-based Blue Envoy, the 'Stage 1 3/4' missile. Blue Envoy was cancelled in the 1957 defence review, on the ground that by the time it was ready the main threat against the United Kingdom would be ballistic missiles, not bombers. It was understood that this argument did not apply to the fleet: the new follow-on to Seaslug was the New Guided Missile System (NIGS). By 1955 there was a proposal for a higher-capacity fire control system analogous to the US Typhon, which ulti-

mately evolved into the current Aegis. This idea probably helped inspire proposals for an electronically-scanned radar, the abortive Type 985.[33]

By September 1959 NIGS was envisaged as a semi-active homer using a 0.64-ton dart with a 0.83-ton booster, fired from a twin launcher, presumably comparable in size to the projected long-range version of the US Typhon, as then understood. By early 1960 it was credited with a range of 150nm. The missile was so much smaller than Seaslug that it seemed a much smaller ship could carry it. No such missile ever entered development, but as of 1959 it seemed to be a very significant future possibility. Typhon may have been a NIGS alternative; a British constructor's notebook shows calculations for a Typhon installation in a 'County' class hull, with sixty-four or eighty missiles.[34]

In June 1959 DNC ordered a sketch design of a NIGS frigate to see how big the ship would be. There was no tentative Staff Requirement. Although the designers began with a Type 12 hull, the end result was about the size of a 'County'. It would have been underpowered (for the usual 28kts deep and dirty) with a Type 12 powerplant. The missile system would have used four surveillance radars, four guidance radars, and four illuminators, serving a twin launcher with forty-four NIGS missiles. In addition there would have been a 4.5in gun aft (ultimately omitted) and two quadruple Seacats (GWS 21). The ASW battery would have been a lightweight helicopter (twelve torpedoes) directed on the basis of a Type 184 sonar. An early estimate was 4,750 tons deep (424ft × 54ft × 15ft). A July 1959 attempt to boost speed to 28kts would have used a

The Batch II 'County' class missile destroyer HMS *Glamorgan*, in 1981. Note that her Exocets have been unshipped and that she lacks SCOT radomes. When these ships were offered for sale, the British government initially was unwilling to export their Seaslugs. It offered a boxed version of the much more capable Sea Dart instead. Ultimately ships were sold to Chile with their Seaslug missiles.

[30] ADM 167/166.
[31] ADM 167/167.
[32] ADM 167/168.
[33] ADM 220/2179.
[34] Notebook 1073/3 includes calculations involving the characteristic Typhon tower with its SPG-59 radar.

missile destroyer powerplant (60,000 SHP) in a 6,160-ton hull (440ft × 54ft × 41ft 6in depth).

An alternative Study 1B used typical Seaslug missile stowage: twin magazine conveyors (fourteen missiles each) and twin loaders (eight missiles each) for 2-ton missiles. Other armament would be a single Mk 5 gun (4.5in) and two Seacats, plus Limbo and twelve fixed torpedo tubes for Bidders. Study 1C omitted the gun. Study 1D added a missile battery aft, so the ship would have forty missiles at each end. This ship would have displaced about 7,400 tons (470ft × 59ft), which was roughly comparable to (but shorter than) contemporary US double-ended missile ships (*Leahy* class). There were also ships with sixty-four missiles.[35] There were several alternative launcher schemes: a Seaslug-type thirteen-missile horizontal loader or twin ten-missile horizontal loaders or a sixteen-missile vertical loader (as in Sea Dart) or twin twelve-missile loaders or a ten-missile vertical drum loader; or magazines for forty-seven or twenty-four missiles or twin eighteen-missile conveyor stowage. The system might provide nuclear warhead stowage for up to 25 per cent of the total. Nothing came of these studies because as early as November 1958 the Fleet Requirements Committee decided that the frigate-sized missile, SIGS (which became Sea Dart) was more urgent, as the future surface fleet would consist mainly of frigates, many of which would have to operate on detached service.

In addition to new missiles, First Sea Lord was interested in nuclear powerplants, presumably inspired by the US nuclear 'frigate' (DLGN, *Bainbridge*) project. The US D1G nuclear powerplant was tried both in the 'County' hull and in a fresh double-ended design. A preliminary drawing (about 1961) showed a 530ft long ship (48ft hull depth including a double bottom) displacing 8,250 tons, and probably capable of 28.5kts deep and dirty. There was also a CONAD (nuclear-steam) study for the Director General of Engineering (successor to E-in-C) using a 20,000 SHP reactor plus a 20,000 SHP pressure-fired boiler; another study considered 30,000 SHP nuclear and 30,000 SHP pressure-fired plants. It is not clear how serious these studies were, but the nuclear theme returned several times later.

For NIGS, nuclear power was important as a way of providing the enormous electrical power that a very large radar system might require. This idea had originated in the United States in the context of the Typhon system, and references

to it occur in the design notebook of W J Holt, a senior British constructor.

Other Missiles

The British were well aware of US progress in adapting missiles to destroyers, and by 1956 the US Navy was anxious to spread the relevant technology to allied navies.[36] When the conversion of the *Gearing*-class destroyer *Gyatt* (using the Terrier missile) was announced in 1956, a DNC constructor was assigned to estimate whether a similar conversion of a 'Battle' class destroyer was possible. A quick estimate showed no problem: the weight of the missile installation was considerably less than that of the guns and mountings it would replace (in the missile age ships were volume- rather than weight-critical). There was also considerable interest in Tartar, conceived as a direct replacement for the twin 5in gun (hence, by extension, for the standard twin 4.5in of similar size and weight). The British had in effect conceived it (see Chapter 12). In October 1956 an analysis was conducted in which Tartar would replace X gun mount in a *Daring* class destroyer. Two Mk 74 directors would replace the after torpedo tubes, and a new lattice mast about 35ft high would be built around the after funnel. At the same time there was interest in installing Tartar on board the new Type 81 frigate, and two years later Tartar was the projected main armament of a new-generation frigate (see Chapter 12).

The Royal Australian Navy

In 1960 the Royal Australian Navy was interested in buying missile destroyers. Nearly all of its ships had been designed by the Royal Corps of Naval Constructors, so when he visited the UK in January 1960, the Australian Chief of Naval Staff asked that two or three ships be built in the United Kingdom, the first two delivered in 1966 and in 1967. The Australians had four recently-completed *Daring*s and they hoped to buy a missile system suitable both for them and for new ships. DNC suggested Tartar rather than Seaslug. The new ships were described as 'Counties' displacing 3,500–4,000 tons. Other requirements were two Wessex (S-58) helicopters, modern ASW weaponry, conventional guns, and a steam plant giving 40,000 SHP and 30kts (no gas turbines). The Australian admiral was warned that this might be asking too much; it might be impossible to combine A/S and missile functions in a single hull of the size he wanted.

Design studies by DGS showed that no worthwhile missile battery could be installed in a *Daring* (at least 4,000 tons would be needed) and that a 'County' modified as asked would displace more than 5,500 tons with Seaslug or more than 5,200

---

[35] Constructors' notebooks mentioned: Scheme 2, 'County' class conversion with sixty-four missiles; Scheme 3, eighty missiles; Scheme 5, two twin launchers, two twin 4.5in guns, twenty-missile horizontal loader and sixteen-missile vertical loader plus twenty-four rounds stowage; Scheme 6, twin launchers with no guns; Scheme 7, variant of Scheme 6; Scheme 8, variant of Scheme 5; Scheme 10, two twin launchers with twin six-missile loaders and fourteen-missile conveyers aft, twin six-missile loaders forward, and no guns (also given as a ten-missile vertical drum forward and twin ten-missile loaders aft); Scheme 11, two twin launchers, twin eighteen-missile loaders, twin eighteen-missile conveyers, and two twin 4.5in guns; Scheme 12, one twin launcher aft (forty-eight missiles) and two twin 4.5in guns forward. Scheme 13 was nuclear powered, with two twin launchers (twenty-four missiles each) displacing 7,700 tons (535ft × 60ft × 17.4ft, 29.5kts deep and dirty), roughly equivalent to the contemporary USS *Bainbridge*, but with fewer missiles. Scheme 14 used conventional steam (7,386 tons, 535ft × 60ft × 17ft, 3,500nm at 20kts). Scheme 15 used a CONAS (nuclear/steam) plant (7,950 tons, 550ft × 60ft × 17.4ft). Scheme 16 was all-nuclear (8,500 tons, 560ft × 60ft × 18.1ft). Scheme 17 had a steam/ gas turbine plant as in a 'County'.

[36] Contemporary French naval documents describe a US offer to provide Terrier on very favourable terms. The French rejected it partly for fear of destroying the nascent French missile industry and partly because it did not cover expensive support. No parallel British discussions have been found, but similar considerations would have applied. Nor have the relevant US documents been found. By 1957 the Italians had bought Terrier and Tartar; the Dutch later followed suit.

tons with Tartar. A sketch dated 1 March 1960 showed a single 4.5in gun (with Mk 6 or MRS 3 fire control), Seaslug (twenty-four missiles, GMS 1 Mod 1 fire control), two quadruple Seacat launchers (GWS 21 fire control), and two Wessex helicopters. There would be torpedo tubes as in the 'County' as then conceived. Length was reduced (to 450ft) by using an all-steam plant (two 20,000 SHP shafts). Many of the missiles would have been stowed deep in the ship. The arrangement would have followed that of the Escort Cruiser then under design, with its missile launcher aft. Estimated displacement was 5,554 tons (450ft × 54ft × 16.8ft). Estimated speed was 26.75kts deep and dirty (27.75kts clean). The Australians then decided that they preferred the US Tartar missile.

On 4 July 1960 the Australians asked for a ship armed with Tartar (two channels of fire), with three Wessex helicopters, two 4.5in mountings (one of which might be replaced by Ikara), twin Seacat, Type 184 and Type 199 (VDS) sonars, digital computer data handling (ADAWS and the TIDE data link [Link 11]), stabilisers, and with steam machinery ('for simplicity of operation') sufficient for 28kts under tropical conditions and giving an endurance of 4,200nm (5,000nm if practicable) at 18kts. But DGS said he could not provide the necessary design effort. The Australians then retreated to ask for something closer to a 'County', but still with Tartar, the sonars, space for ADA and TIDE, and Wessex helicopters (preferably three but two might be accepted). Gas turbines still were not wanted, the alternatives being the steam portion of the 'County' powerplant, a new design for 30,000 to 40,000 SHP and a *Daring* powerplant. DGS estimated that the ship would displace about 5,800 tons. The 'County' class steam plant would give about 27kts clean, and its gearbox would have to be redesigned. The steam turbines would be fundamentally unsuitable because they were designed for integration with gas turbines. The *Daring* plant was rejected as crude and a source of trouble in its current state. The new plant was a type recently approved for the projected escort cruiser. The existing 'County' plant, including gas turbines, was the best alternative.

Some sketch designs were developed. In a *Daring* hull, the existing powerplant would have been replaced by the British twin-screw frigate plant (Y.100). Projected armament was one or two twin 4.5in guns, Tartar (forty-two missiles), two quadruple Seacats and the Australian Ikara ASW missile then early in development.[37] The ship had to be able to land a Wessex. Tartar could make do with slightly less electrical power than Seaslug (350 kW rather than 370 kW), so generator capacity could be cut (to two 1,000 kW steam sets and two 500 kW diesel sets). Accommodation would be 24 officers and 300 ratings. Speed would be 26.5kts to 26.75kts clean, which was probably unsatisfactory. The ship would have displaced about

3,900 tons. An alternative arrangement (19B) had Tartar and Ikara forward, and one twin 4.5in mount aft. The next step (Study 20) was a much larger ship (5,300 tons) armed with Tartar, Ikara (fourteen missiles), and carrying two or three Wessex helicopters. Because the ship could not land her Wessex over the Tartar launchers, she needed a separate 80ft helicopter deck. In this form the ship grew rapidly, to about 6,300 tons on a second estimate. Yet another possibility (Study 26A, 11 July 1960) was simply to substitute Tartar for Seaslug in a 'County' class hull, but DNC suggested that it might not be acceptable to place Tartar right aft. The final DNC effort, Study 28A, would have displaced 5,783 tons (460ft × 53.5ft × 16.8ft at 5,800 tons) using a 40,000 SHP powerplant to achieve 28kts in clean condition (45,000 SHP would have been needed to make the same speed dirty). A 'County' with *Daring* machinery (54,000 SHP) would displace 6,431 tons.

In August 1960 DGS was developing several new designs, such as a carrier and a nuclear submarine. The Australian missile destroyer would be far more than a simple adaptation of the 'County' design. He therefore begged off. He thought that adapting the 'County' without adding considerable staff would stop all work on RN missile ships for two to three years. The Australians were offered three alternatives:

1: Defer the guided missile ship and build *Leander*s instead.
2: Order slightly modified 'Counties' and drop the idea of installing Tartar in a *Daring* hull.
3: Adopt the new escort cruiser instead of the 'County'.

In the end, the Australians decided to buy not only the American missile, but also an American destroyer, the *Charles F. Adams* class. That was despite the fact that the *Adams* lacked some features they badly wanted, such as helicopter capacity. It did however offer a viable Tartar capacity on far less than the 4,000 tons DGS had proposed. The Australians' happy experience with that class led them to buy a later American design, the *Perry* class, as successor to their version of the British Type 12. In effect the British lost an important export market at just about the time their home market was shrinking to the point that exports were becoming vital rather than useful.

As for the Australian *Daring*s, the idea of fitting Tartar was revived during proposals for the 1965–8 Programme, which also included a fourth *Adams*. The Chiefs of Staff decided to replace Tartar with Ikara, the Chief of Naval Staff agreeing only on condition that the fourth *Adams* would be bought.[38] The fourth ship was not bought.

---

[37] This was Design Study 19A, in a series which had reached No. 53 by 1962. The undated study was probably completed during the first half of 1960.

[38] Royal Australian Navy, Project Paper 101/66 (November 1966), Fourth Comprehensive Escort, RAN Naval Historical Branch. Comprehensive meant General Purpose. A separate non-missile escort briefly became the RN–RAN frigate, leading to the Type 21.

CHAPTER 10

The 1945 Frigate and Her Successors

The Type 12 and the *Leander* class frigates, probably the most successful post-war British warships, derived from the 1945 Sloop (later the 1945 Frigate). It in turn can be traced back to requirements set in mid-1943 for the frigates which might be laid down the following year. Two key requirements were enough speed (about 25kts) to run down a surfaced U-boat, and a gun with sufficient effective range to deal with a surfaced U-boat outside of torpedo range (about 8,000 yds). Speed was the difficult requirement to satisfy. The *Black Swans* could make 19.5kts, the 'Rivers' being little faster.

By 1945 the surfaced submarine was no longer a major issue, but the new U-boats were much faster submerged; escorts certainly needed higher speed to deal with them. The new Type XXI could make 15–18kts submerged, while the projected Walter submarine (Type XXVI) would make as much as 26kts. British naval intelligence first detected the new submarines in 1943, and soon rebuilt a few submarines to achieve high underwater speed as targets, to develop tactics against Type XXI. With little real speed advantage over a Type XXI, all existing escorts, other converted destroyers, the 'Hunts' and some of the US-supplied 'Captains' became obsolete. Surely the new enemy, the Soviet Union, which had always been an enthusiastic exponent of submarine warfare, would soon produce large numbers of Type XXI equivalents. This possibility, foreseen in 1945, materialised in the 1950s in the form of the mass-

production 'Whiskey' (Project 613) and 'Zulu' (Project 611) classes. Future escorts would need at least the 25kts wanted in 1943.

In 1947 Director of Plans estimated that 180 modern escorts would be needed in a future emergency: any new frigate would have to be suited to mass production. Production facilities in the United Kingdom might well be bombed, as in the Second World War. Prefabrication could drastically reduce the time during which a ship lay on the slip, vulnerable to bombing. Apparently the wartime prefabrication scheme (for the 'Loch' and 'Bay' classes) had not gone far enough for the concept to be fully evaluated. Given wartime experience and the threat of bombing, Australia and Canada became important potential builders. Both had naval ambitions. At least in the case of Australia, DNC proposed creating new mass production yards on the lines of those built in the United States during the war to produce merchant ships, escort carriers, frigates (destroyer escorts) and landing ships and craft. In 1947 the Australians asked for details of the new A/S frigates (no designs yet existed).[1]

Canada ultimately received the services of a British naval constructor, Sir Roland Baker, who designed a local equivalent of the post-war British ASW frigate, the *St Laurent* class.[2] The Canadian project affected the timetable for the Y.100 steam plant of the British ASW frigate. In 1949 the Canadians were choosing between it and a US plant, and E-in-C pointed out that a Canadian purchase would depend on completion of a British prototype. That was done, and the Canadians chose the British plant.

First Designs

In December 1944, as part of the run-up to the 1945 Programme, Sir Stanley Goodall, formerly DNC and now Assistant Controller for War Production, asked whether new sloops would be needed.[3] Given their many peacetime roles, sloops were worth producing after the war: Director of Plans wanted two per year, beginning with the 1945 Programme. In

[1] A note dated 31 May 1948 in the A/D Frigate Cover admits that as yet there were no A/S structural drawings to offer the Australians. The British were surprised that the RAN had opted for complex steam A/S frigates instead of simpler diesel-engined alternatives. DNC suggested that it might be best for them to begin with a ship using existing plans, such as a 'Battle' class destroyer (he was apparently unaware that they were already doing so). The Canadians also wanted details of the new A/S frigate. DNC ordered the Canadians given copies of Staff Requirements and also sketches of the A/A and A/D frigates (whose designs would probably be ready about September 1948).
[2] According to Brown, *A Century of Naval Construction*, pp 352–3, Baker put much the same components as a Type 12 into a radically different hull with a far more conservative form, beamier with greater displacement. Because he did not follow Holt in using a fine entrance and low prismatic, it had marginally inferior resistance. A flush upper deck and overall smooth surfaces were intended to make de-icing easier. Rounded deck-edges and a turtle forecastle would clear water which got aboard. The midships form was much finer than in a Type 12, with much more V-section in the area subject to slamming. Brown remarks that, with opposite hull forms, the Canadian and British ships were generally considered the best sea-keepers of all NATO frigates. The Canadians planned but did not build an equivalent to the British Type 14 second-rate frigate, which they called the *Vancouver* class. As described at the British 1954 TAS meeting (ADM 189/237), it would have a single-shaft engine equivalent to that in a Type 14, for comparable performance (24kts, 4,500nm at 12kts), and a length of 320ft. ASW armament would match that of a Type 14, except for four US Mk 32 torpedoes instead of British Bidders, and there would be a US SQS-10 scanning sonar in addition to British Types 162 and 170B, with space for a long-range set. However, gun armament would be closer to a *St. Laurent*: one twin 3in/50 and four single power-operated Bofors. Complement would be twelve officers and 194 ratings. However, the RCN built only *St Laurents*.
[3] Cover 830, Destroyers and Frigates. Goodall's query was dated 18 December 1944. He referred to an earlier Controller's Minute, D.016547/44.

war they were the high end of the escort mix, often used as flagships of ASW Support Groups. For DASW, the high performance of the new submarines would make lower-end ships useless. On 21 April 1945 DTSD ruled that the ships would be called frigates rather than escorts or sloops. The only distinction, if any, within the escort category would be between fleet and trade-protection roles. Perhaps the future sloop would also be the future fleet submarine-killer. DASW wanted a speed of 25kts in deep condition. Endurance should be the 4,000–5,000nm of an unrefuelled escort run across the Atlantic. Neither high speed nor long endurance in itself was a major problem. The 'Hunts' were already considerably faster than 25kts. Wartime frigates and sloops already exceeded the 4,500nm endurance eventually adopted. However, the combination of high maximum speed and long range at considerable speed (18kts, later 15kts) proved quite difficult. To see what it would mean, DNC estimated what it would take to propel a *Black Swan* at 25kts: 15,000 SHP, rather than the 4,300 SHP of the existing ship, in a 325ft 6in (waterline) rather than 283ft hull, with slightly more beam (40ft 6in rather than 39ft). Given typical wartime practice, a larger hull would attract more light anti-aircraft weapons, so DNC's weight estimates showed 20 per cent more close-range guns. Estimated standard displacement was about 1,650 tons, compared to 1,429 tons for a *Black Swan*.

On 15 January 1945 DASW proposed providing alternative ASW and AAW armaments, as in the 'Loch' and 'Bay' classes. The AAW version would provide AA cover for convoys and also for minor offensive operations for which fleet destroyers were unsuited, and would assist in ASW operations. Both versions would direct Coastal Forces craft, as had often happened in the Channel. The only new ASW weapon then in prospect was the Bidder torpedo, and the Shark shell designed to attack a surfaced submarine still seemed worthwhile (it would be abandoned within a few months). The only suitable new anti-aircraft weapon was BEN, a short-range missile which in the event proved abortive (see Chapter 13).

For mass production, initially it was hoped that the new sloop could be limited to 1,400 tons standard, despite DNC's initial estimate. The ship's length would decide how many yards could build her. Of twenty-nine potential frigate yards, only nine could handle ships 350ft long; eight more could handle ships up to 325ft, and twelve more could handle 300ft ships. Of nineteen corvette slips, six were nominally limited to 200ft, and nine to 250ft. A typical modern merchant ship was 450ft long. The United States had avoided this sort of limit during the war by creating new prefabricated-ship yards, but Britain probably would not enjoy that option. To mass-produce the necessary high-powered machinery in wartime it would probably be necessary to create a shadow production organisation in peacetime.

The best existing ASW weapons were double Squid (with

Hedgehog next best) and Bidder; depth charges still seemed useful. For the ASW frigate, DASW wanted double Squid (twenty-five salvoes, in B position), six Bidders, a gun battery capable of firing Shark, preferably on ahead bearings, and a depth charge battery (five-charge pattern, but only half the usual outfit, twenty-five rather than fifty charges). Two of the very heavy Mk X charges were desirable but not essential. Surface-search radar took priority over air-search, because it offered ASW capability in the form of snorkel detection. For the AAW frigate, DASW was willing to accept split Hedgehog instead of double Squid, but wanted more depth charges (ten-charge pattern, fifty charges).

DGD wanted the AAW ship to have provision for the BEN missile. The 4.5in gun having been adopted as the future standard, he wanted two twin radar-controlled (RPC) mounts, backed by two twin Bofors and as many hand-controlled twin

HMS *Lynx* was a Type 41 anti-aircraft frigate. The side view (opposite) was taken in April 1957, the overhead in July 1961. Earlier ships of the class could be distinguished by their shallower (in plan view) bridges.

20mm as possible. As in some destroyer designs, there was some interest in a single 4.5in dual-purpose mount, but there was no realistic hope of developing one. The minimum would be three twin 4in, as in a 'Hunt', but these guns were already at the limit of their development and they could not take full advantage of proximity (VT) fuses. For the ASW role, the order of preference for guns reversed (two twin 4in or one twin 4.5in), with one twin Bofors and the maximum number of hand-worked 20mm, and BEN.

Draft Staff Requirements issued at the end of January 1945 required 25kts (deep, six months out of dock: 'deep and dirty') and an endurance was 4,500nm at 18kts (six months out of dock in the tropics). Endurance speed was later cut to 15kts. Demanding high performance under badly fouled (tropical) conditions would be quite expensive: DNC now wanted 25,000–30,000 SHP, half a *Daring* class plant. The ship would have to be unusually long, hence heavy. It was soon clear that an AAW ship could be somewhat slower. The ASW version would need a full AIO. A new proposed feature was pro-

vision for temporary replacement of one gun mounting (in the AAW version) by triple torpedo tubes, for use in inshore operations (as with the wartime 'Hunt' class). This change was to take no more than 48 hours. DNC pointed out that the torpedo tubes could not simply replace depth charges; they would have to be an alternative to Hedgehog.

To hold down size, DASW and DGD had to offer up cuts, which gave an idea of their priorities. DASW considered Squid most vital, followed by depth charges and the heavy Mk X (1-ton) charges. Space and weight should be provided against future development of Bidder. To reduce topweight, Squid could go in A position, the forward gun in B. For the ASW ship, DGD wanted a single 4.5in gun and a single Bofors or one twin 4.5in plus 20mm guns. For the AAW version, he wanted two twin 4.5in or three 4.5in barrels, preferably a twin forward in A position and a single aft, plus BEN, one single Bofors gun, and the maximum number of hand-worked twin Oerlikons. Instead of replacing a gun mounting, a triple torpedo tube on the quarterdeck could replace the depth charges there. DASW offered Hedgehog as an alternative to BEN if the latter were not available.

A third mission was raised: fighter direction. Convoys in coastal or enclosed waters (such as the Mediterranean) unaccompanied by a carrier and outside the range of land radar would have to direct shore-based fighters. In an amphibious assault, land echoes would often blank the fighter-direction radars on board flagships, so pickets would be needed to provide early warning of low-fliers. Important convoys would need pickets for early warning and interceptor control. DND argued that satisfactory Aircraft Direction (A/D) could not be conducted by the AAW frigate.

Purvis, the preliminary designer, tried two approaches: an AAW frigate (with an ASW version) and the opposite. The AAW ship had the heavier armament. To accommodate two twin 4.5in, one twin STAAG Bofors, four twin hand-worked 20mm, a long-range rocket illuminator, BEN, and depth charges (four throwers and rails for ten-charge patterns, fifty charges) took 1,660 tons (standard; 2,335 tons deeply loaded) in a 335ft hull. The ship needed 23,000 SHP to make 25kts deep and dirty (26.5kts deep and clean, 28.5kts clean at standard displacement). As an ASW frigate (1,605/2,225 tons), with slightly more oil capacity (endurance 4,650nm), the ship could accommodate Bidder, but not BEN. Cutting cruising speed to 15kts would reduce displacement of the ASW version to 1,610/2,155 tons. That the ASW version was slightly faster suggested that a ship derived from the ASW requirements would be slightly smaller. Armed with three twin 4in, a STAAG and four hand-worked twin 20mm, plus BEN and four depth charge throwers (fifty charges), it came to 1,535 tons (2,065 tons fully loaded). The corresponding AAW version was not developed. A ship limited to 1,400 tons could not reach the desired 25kts at all; on the 19,000 SHP which could

be provided, she would make 24kts. Nor could she accommodate 4.5in guns. She would have one or two twin 4in (one in the ASW version); the only other guns would be hand-worked twin 20mm (two in the AAW version, one in the ASW version). The ASW version would have the full ASW battery except for the Mk X charges.

In February 1945 ACNS(W) ordered a study of the reduced AAW battery in the ASW hull. As before, the AAW version offered only the twin 4in gun. Slightly less power (21,000 or 22,000 SHP) would be needed. These designs met the endurance requirement, 4,500nm at 15kts. ACNS(W) considered the ASW ship too big. All he could do to hold down size was to secure agreement that the ship would have no fleet role, to hold down unit size and complexity.

Approval was obtained to include four ships in the 1945 Programme. Staff Requirements would also be drawn for a new corvette, the mass production low end of the usual high-low mix as in 'Loch' and 'Castle' classes (these Staff Requirements have not been found, if indeed they were ever written). The later (and unrelated) Type 14 was the low-end ship corresponding to the 1945 frigates. By this time a fourth frigate function was being proposed: the SNO ship, for the Senior Naval Officer of a convoy. She would need improved accommodations, facilities to control an A/S screen, accommodation for staff, communications ratings and aircraft direction personnel. They could not be accommodated in the AAW ship or, it seemed, combined with the A/D role.

By June 1945 the 4in gun had been rejected. That month Staff Requirements were set out for a common (1,600-ton) hull armed with twin 4.5in guns controlled by the latest destroyer fire control system (Mk VI/Flyplane as interim for the MRS series then under development) with GDS 2 and Type 293 target indication radar. The A/A ship would have two twin 4.5in, the others one. For the A/D ship, the twin 4.5in was interim for the planned new Medium Range mounting (which later materialised as the twin 3in/70). All versions would have a twin blind-fire Bofors and the maximum possible number of single Bofors. By January 1946 the BEN missile had been resurrected as Longshot. The A/S frigate would have double Squid (twenty-five salvoes) and six (later ten) Bidders plus a five-charge pattern (later cut to three-charge) with twenty-five charges (cut to fifteen). Initially it was assumed that Bidder would be in single upper-deck tubes, but early in 1946 DASW asked for pentad tubes (a single pentad with reloads rather than two pentads). The SNO ship would be armed like the A/S ship, but without 20mm guns, with six Bidders and twenty-five depth charges plus two Mk X depth charges. Her main special feature was added accommodation for officers, communications ratings and aircraft-direction personnel. The A/A frigate would have Hedgehog (three torpedo tubes as alternative), and a five-charge pattern (fifteen depth charges).

The A/D ship was conceived as a redesigned version of the A/A ship. First plans showed provision for two day and one night interceptions, but a revision of Staff Requirements in August 1945 made her Aircraft Direction Room comparable to that of a small cruiser. The radars and other equipment involved did not yet exist, but they would be massive. As of November 1945, DNC offered one twin 4.5in and one twin blind-fire Bofors on 1,600 tons. By that time the ASW battery was single Squid (ten salvoes). Design was somewhat simplified in that it was acceptable for speed to be only 23kts with propeller silencing fitted but not working.

Initially it seemed that four frigates would be included in the 1945 Programme. Their construction would reveal likely problems in wartime production. The SNO ship (convoy flagship) was ruled out as little more than an A/S frigate with more accommodation and better communications (at the expense of armament). Director of Plans wanted two A/S (to form a tactical unit) and two A/A ships (DTSD wanted one A/A, and one A/D). Then the programme was cut to two frigates, the right being reserved to insert two more in a future programme. DTSD asked for one A/S and one A/D. The A/S ship was needed to help develop new ASW weapons. Even without new equipment, the A/D ship would be useful for tactical trials. Without new equipment, however, nothing would be learned by operating an A/A ship. Foregoing her would not save design effort, because designing the A/A frigate was a prerequisite for designing the A/D ship derived from her. Given limited resources, on 19 January 1946 the decision was to build both ships to the A/S design. Given the country's severe financial problems, the second ship would not be ordered until it became desirable to place the order so that the builder would be able to preserve the general balance of its work.

New ASW Weapons and Sensors

In October 1945 DASW stated that nothing short of Squid could deal with future fast submarines; he believed most fleet destroyers should replace their depth charges with it. Furthermore, double Squid (ten salvoes) should replace the Hedgehogs and depth charges previously specified for the A/A and A/D ships. But Squid was now a minimum rather than a maximum weapon, because even it could not effectively engage a fast submarine. The ship firing had to be aimed within 20° of the target. DASW pointed out that this would become nearly impossible if the target could cross the escort's path at better than 15kts. Squid had to be turned into a gun: trainable, with variable range, firing multiple shots in quick succession.[4] Repeated shots would be needed: the Squid suc-

cessor had to be capable of fairly rapid fire. The initial requirement was for range variable between 250 and 2,000 yds; the weapon actually fielded, Limbo (initially Mortar D and later Mortar Mk 10), was conceived as an interim solution effective between 380 and 1,000 yds. It became standard in British ASW ships. Limbo was conceived as a single-barrel rapid-fire gun, but as deployed, it had three barrels per mounting like Squid. A valve on the combustion chamber, which could vent some of the gas used for propulsion, set range. The weapon was trained by tilting the barrels from side to side. The standard double Limbo, like Squid, produced a pair of triangular patterns which sandwiched a submarine (and, incidental-

HMS *Salisbury* was the prototype Type 61 aircraft-direction frigate. These two views make it clear just how cramped the ship was. The foremast carried a Type 277Q height-finder. The mainmast carries the new Type 960 long-range air search set, with the short-range Type 293Q below it. Abaft this mast is the Type 982 ('hayrake'), in effect a target-indication set for fighter control. Note that the ship could not accommodate the Type 983 height-finder intended to complement Type 982. This ship has the earlier type of frigate bridge; note the difference from HMS *Lynx*.

[4] Malcolm Llewellyn Jones, 'The Royal Navy and the Challenge of the Fast Submarine 1946-1954' in R Harding (ed), *The Royal Navy 1930-2000: Innovation and Defence* (Frank Cass, London: 2004), pp 140–2, credits Captain N A Prichard RN, of DASW, with the idea of redesigning Squid. Only a depth charge could drive off or deter a submarine (the submarine would not be aware of a passive homing torpedo fired at it). The depth charge had to be fired from a trainable gun. Against a fast submarine there would be no time for cut-on/cut-off direction-finding. Thus even without Limbo, split-beam (effectively instant) direction-finding was essential.

ly, made up for depth inaccuracies in the fire control sonar).

Limbo control required a new kind of sonar: Type 170 ('four square'), the first of a new generation of sonars development of which began in 1945, for completion within five years (which proved rather optimistic), to deal with Type XXI and similar submarines (15kts submerged, diving depth 1,000ft).[5] The British assumed that within a few years much faster submarines powered by closed-cycle engines would be in service. In 1950 a new Staff Target was set: 25kts submerged, 1,500ft diving depth. Type 170 locked onto and tracked a target by comparing adjacent horizontal and vertical beams.[6] Compared to predecessors like Type 147, it required much more internal space. A prototype four-square sonar successfully tracked an 11-knot submarine in 1946, and the Type 170 prototype was tested in 1950. Others in the new family were the interim search/attack sonar, Type 174 (an improved Type 164, a direct descendant of the wartime Type 144) and the dual-frequency (12 to 15 and 39 kHz) passive Type 176 intended mainly as a torpedo warner.[7] By September 1946 Limbo was being required for the 1945 ASW frigate (the A/A and A/D versions would have to make do with the second-best Squid). The prototype was tested on board HMS *Scorpion*. It was very successfully demonstrated by HMS *Rocket* at Key West in August–November 1952.[8]

Although it was not ready until the late 1950s, the projected new long-range search sonar, Type 177, much affected the new frigate designs. Earlier Asdics had been searchlights: they sent out a ping in one direction and waited for an echo before training in another direction. That would not do against a fast submarine. In 1943 the British began work on a scanning sonar which could look in many directions more or less simultaneously (the US Navy began a parallel effort at the same time). Given an array of transducers, a beam in any one direction was created by adding up the outputs of many of them with the appropriate phases. In the US sonars, beginning with the late-war QHB, the beam was created by a rotating commutator which applied the phases to a few of the staves at any one time to create a single listening beam. The Royal Navy developed, but did not adopt, a Type 172 sonar of this type, and it tested the US QHB (which became standard in early post-war US ASW ships). The drawback to such operation was that the sonar would hear only a fraction of the echo from any one target, as for most of its scanning cycle it was not listening in that direction. The British opted instead for what would now be called an array of preformed beams. Transducers were wired together to produce a set of beams staring in multiple directions simultaneously. This approach limited the number of beams which could be created by hardwiring, but it was well-adapted to complex waveforms the beam would be looking in the same direction throughout transmission and reception) and also to listening.

Type 177, design of which was completed in 1949, used a trainable planar array 4ft wide and 3.5ft deep, covering a 40° sector, which was divided into 10° beams. This group could be trained to cover 160° in 40° steps. Type 177 extended effective Asdic range from the 2,500 yds of the Second World War to 8,000 to 16,000 yds (maximum range was 20,000 yds) by operating at much lower frequency than earlier sets (6, 7.5, or 9 kHz rather than 14 to 26 kHz). Type 177 seemed adequate against the sort of fast submarines the Germans had introduced in 1945, but not the much faster craft which seemed likely to appear in the post-war years, which might well spend too little time in even a 40° sector to be tracked and attacked. The much greater range of Type 177 in turn made it worthwhile to devise long-range ASW weapons like Bidder and helicopter-delivered torpedoes (MATCH).

Command Arrangements

The new frigates were the first British warships to have AIO facilities designed into them. The plot in the Operations Room showed the wide-area tactical situation, based largely on plots relayed from the Radar Display Room. The plot in the Asdic Control Room showed the underwater situation. To many COs neither plot could show the close-in situation and hence could be used when ships were manoeuvring rapidly at close quarters. Without any means of instantly reproducing either the Operations Room plot or the Asdic plot on the open bridge, it seemed that the CO had to choose between access to the close-in situation and the long-range or underwater situation. COs generally rejected the idea, based on Pacific War experience, that the command should move from the open bridge to the Operations Room. The first step was to require that all the main internal command spaces (Operations Room, Radar Display Room, Asdic Control Room [analogous to Radar Display Room], Target Indication Room [target assignment to guns], and Aircraft Direction Room) be adjacent, either horizontally or vertically. By February 1946 the A/D frigate (and probably the others) were to have their Operations Room and Aircraft Direction Room (ADR) immediately below the compass platform, with the main radio room adjacent to the Operations Room.

5 Hackmann, *Seek and Strike*, p 339.
6 Four-square was proposed by two British sonar development teams in May 1943 to replace both search sonar and the depth-finding 'sword' (147F). The concept was tested on board the trawler *Icewhale* in July 1944 and then on board the corvette *Kingfisher* in December 1944 through April 1945 (ADM 259/429). Type 170 was generally installed alongside a search sonar such as Type 177 or Type 184.
7 Type 175 was intended to support the Camrose anti-torpedo weapon, which fired a salvo of fast straight-running mini-torpedoes in the direction it indicated. The previous anti-torpedo weapon, Ruler, had fired rockets at the projected torpedo position, based on Type 175 bearing and on a range given by an abortive Type 175 pinger. Type 175 could give an approximate range based on the ratio of received signals at its two frequencies (sound would attenuate differently at the two frequencies). It scanned its 40° beam (at 12.5 kHz) at 7 RPM. The beam could also sweep back and forth in a 90° sector. ADM 189/235, materials from the 11th TAS Conference (1952). Type 176 survived the demise of Ruler because it was valued as a passive detector.
8 ADM 167/143. This was also a test of Type 170. On the last day the target submarine *Odax* had complete freedom of depth (150–300ft), course, and speed, but was held without a break for 1½ hours, until her battery overheated so badly that she had to surface. American visitors to the Admiralty said that they preferred Limbo to their own Weapon Alfa (DNC papers, Brass Foundry, Box 46, Vol 73, April–September 1947). Alfa's problems were tolerated partly due to (misplaced) confidence in the US equivalent to Bidder, the developmental Mk 35 homing torpedo. Nor was the US Navy as impressed with the fast submarine, given its extensive experience both with ex-German Type XXI U-boats and with its own Guppies. It emphasised the limited high speed endurance of a fast battery submarine and the severe problems of a peroxide submarine (the Royal Navy had no Type XXIs to test).

The 1946 Bikini nuclear tests, which the British observed, seemed to show that the open compass platform was no longer acceptable. The Operations Room had to be protected from blast, perhaps even relocated below the forecastle deck. DGD argued in November 1947 for a single enclosed command post with Operations Room adjacent, plus an open bridge if necessary. If, as expected, future ASW tactics would an attack plotter, a case could be made for merging the Asdic Room with the Operations Room. DTASW pointed out in February 1948 that the future threat, the fast submarine, could not be tracked visually. He proposed eliminating the orthodox bridge altogether, minimising any above-decks structure liable to sea damage at the necessary high speeds. A single command station, streamlined to limit resistance to head seas, should be placed on the forecastle, running the full width of the ship. It could accommodate a command position, an action information centre, Asdic, radio, and other offices. This reasoning explains the squashed-down appearance so characteristic of the post-war British frigates.

The first post-nuclear frigates, the converted destroyers *Rocket* and *Relentless* designed in 1947, had DTASW's command position, located in the centre of the Operations Room, raised sufficiently to give a view through a bubble and through a row of bridge windows. Pushing the bridge structure down into the ship required that the helmsman be buried in the hull. The idea of eliminating the helmsman's view altogether, rejected in connection with the *Daring* class, was revived. The new 1945 frigates had their Operations Rooms below their enclosed compass platforms (bridges), with the Asdic Control Room, Bridge Wireless Room, 3rd Wireless Room (radio countermeasures) – and steering position – adjacent to it.

By early 1950, opinion had veered back to emphasise an unimpeded ahead view and seaworthiness, so the Staff wanted a separate closed bridge above the Operations Room. Its height would be limited to avoid interference with the 4.5in director and also to provide acceptable ahead views for the lookout sights and for the 20in searchlight/projectors. DND proposed a policy of minimising the bridge but retaining easy access to the Operations Room, Aircraft Direction Room and compass platform. Despite nuclear threats, DND wanted to retain an open platform for ship handling.

Associated with the new sonars and with the threat of fast submarines was a new automated ASW tactical command system, Cambria (also called the Automatic Surface Plot, or ASP), in effect an ASW version of the CDS system later installed on board missile destroyers.[9] Automation became more and more

essential as the tempo of operations (and, for that matter, the number of ships and aircraft) increased. Cambria offered a geographically-stabilised display of own-ship movements and the raw surface radar picture on a flat plotting surface, with selected enemy range and bearing data superimposed. Information generated in the plot could be passed automatically to the ship's weapon control systems. The plot would also indicate whether own forces were endangered by the weapons, which was likely to become a major issue because the ship was to be armed with homing torpedoes. Because the system had, in effect, a memory, it could rapidly re-centre its display and change its range scale. Although all the system computers were analogue devices, Cambria (like CDS) initially included the new DPT digital link, which would enable ships in a group to share information. In July 1950, with the new technology approaching maturity, DND proposed it for the new frigates. The A/S frigate would have the full ASP, with associated inter-ship and air-to-ship plotting facilities. In April 1952 a simplified ASP without DPT was chosen for the new Second Rate A/S frigate.

The A/D Frigate was initially to have received the air picture and to have transmitted air warning via DPT. The A/A frigate would automatically receive the air picture (in effect the external air picture would act as her air warning system). As the ships' design developed, they lacked the necessary space for the associated CDS. The requirement to receive the digital data link (DPT) was abandoned. CDS and DPT were limited to the carriers HMS *Victorious* and HMS *Hermes* and to the first four 'County' class missile destroyers, and a decision to fit most British frigates with DPT was reversed.

Design Development

During the autumn of 1945 the ship grew. E-in-C wanted greater hull depth (4ft) over the full machinery space, not just in the way of uptakes as initially. DNC admitted that he was holding displacement down to 1,600 tons by expedients such as specifying speed in cold water rather than in the tropics, and by omitting generators (55 tons) from the original weights. It could be argued that the ship was so large because a single hull and its machinery had to meet several incompatible requirements. The A/S version clearly needed the 25-knot speed, but did she really need the 4.5in dual-purpose gun? Did the A/A version really have to maintain 25kts deep and dirty? Did the A/D version really need the specified speed or armament? In January 1946 DNC estimated that the displacement of the A/A version (with two twin mounts) would be 1,750 tons. Displacement could be cut by reducing speed (to 23kts deep and dirty) or armament (by replacing one of the twin mounts with a proposed single biaxially-stabilised 4.5in gun, and by replacing single Bofors). DNC suggested splitting the project into a 20-knot frigate (A/A and A/D) and a 25-knot frigate (A/S and SNO). To the surprise of DNC representatives, a

[9] Development of the Automatic Surface Plot was approved in March 1951. As of 1952, the frigate version used an electronic plotting table (replacing a standard ARL table) with six markers. The system projected ahead the motion of targets indicated by the markers, and could change scales as required. By this time the ship to ship data exchange feature had been abandoned. In service the plot was designated JYA. JYA(1) and (4) used a single table and marking facilities. JYA(2) and (5) had two tables. JYA(3) and (6) used a single table and no marking facility. JYA(7) used two tables with individual marking facilities. JYA was associated with MATCH. JYB was a simpler alternative, an ARL table (Mk 18) on which a raw radar image could be projected. The list of JYA variants is from ADM239/833, the summary of British and Commonwealth ship characteristics dated 1973.

meeting preferred the 1,750-ton ship. The common hull seemed too attractive to abandon. It made possible shifts in the distribution among functions to meet changing wartime needs, as the 'Lochs' had given way to the 'Bays' in 1944–5.

As of February 1946 the common hull was 330ft LWL/335ft OA × 40ft 6in × 27ft 6in to the forecastle deck and 20ft to the upper deck). Four versions were developed: A/A, A/S, and two different A/D (one twin or two single 4.5in). Eliminating one gun mount in the A/D ship saved 12 tons directly, but the single-mount version would displace 32 tons less (1,597 tons vs 1,629 tons standard). All versions had one STAAG, four single Bofors, Long Range Rocket Flares, and the Longshot defensive missile. The A/S version showed double Squid (twenty-five salvoes), one pentad torpedo tube (ten Bidder), and fifteen depth charges. By July 1946 double Squid had been replaced by the much heavier double Limbo, with the same twenty-five salvoes (the ship retained pentad tubes for Bidder). The depth charges were gone. The A/A version had single Squid (ten salvoes). The A/D version initially had only depth charges (ten of them), but later both A/A and A/D showed single Squid, and no depth charges at all.

Radars in the A/A and A/S versions would be the wartime Type 291 air-search set and Type 293Q for target indication. The long-range Type 291 was later eliminated from the A/S frigate. The A/D ship began with the better Type 960 air search set and Type 277Q as well as Type 293Q. By July 1946 a second new set, Type 981 (for long-range target indication), had been added, and Type 960 had been replaced by the longer-range and antijam Type 960P. The A/D ship had radar DF (RU4), an aircraft a homing beacon (Type 251P/X), and VHF/DF (for fighter control).

Compared to earlier versions, this one offered larger machinery spaces and increased beam (to give good stability despite increased armament weight and decreased machinery weight), and a smaller deep draft to give a good range of stability. When critics asked why the new frigates were so much larger than the 'Hunts', which produced much the same horsepower, their designer, Purvis, pointed out that a 'Hunt' carried

substantially less armament, and that its machinery was much less economical (its 277 tons of oil fuel gave an endurance of only 1,500nm at 15kts deep and dirty in the tropics).

The A/A version would displace 1,632 tons (2,078 tons fully loaded), the A/S version 1,595 tons (2,033 tons fully loaded). On 18,000 (temperate)/19,200 (tropics) SHP, the A/S version would make 25.25kts deep and dirty, and 27.75kts clean at standard displacement. A fuel load of 305 tons would suffice for the required 4,500nm at 15kts. Later it was decided that ships should make full speed with propeller silencing (Nightshirt) operating. That required more power, both to overcome more drag and to generate the air used to screen off propeller noise.

By mid-1946 it seemed that a keel might be laid early in the next financial year (1947/8), which would have meant mid-1947 (this was not done). There were still no final Staff Requirements, and in August 1946 DCNS admitted that it would probably be fifteen months from the start of sketch design to keel-laying. The Staff would have to stop dithering. At a meeting on 23 August DNC showed drawings of the three versions. DCNS now favoured the A/D ship over the A/S ship: some key ASW weapons, such as Bidder and Limbo, were nowhere near ready. DGD pointed out that the ship would have to have the existing Mk VI director instead of the planned MRS; she would land the single Bofors as weight compensation. Later it might be possible to add a second director (MRS 2) to provide a second (independent) 4.5in fire control channel. It too would be installed at the expense of single Bofors guns. For the moment, DGD agreed to delete the short-range Longshot missile, which would be restored (in place of the STAAG) if it proved successful, but work on this weapon was soon abandoned.

The deciding factor was the powerplant. The only existing plants offering sufficient efficiency were diesels. In 1946 the Admiralty was developing its Admiralty Standard Range of such engines, the highest-powered of which was based on a 1937 design for a 1,300 BHP high-speed submarine engine produced by the Admiralty Experimental Laboratory

Type 41 as designed June 1950. The *Leopard* class were completed in very nearly this form, but the bridge was enlarged and the projected rocket flare launcher forward eliminated. Note that this design has only the short-range Type 293Q target-indication radar, not the Type 960 long-range air-search radar later placed on the mainmast. All ships had fin stabilisers, not shown here. (A D Baker III)

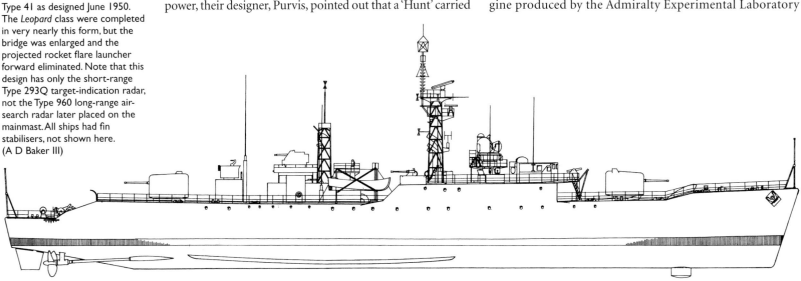

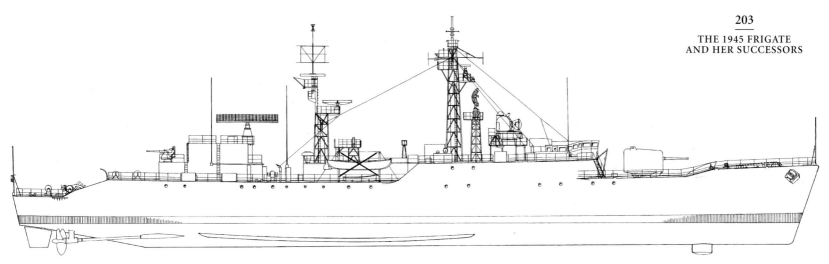

in West Drayton; Chatham Dockyard produced a sixteen-cylinder prototype. The war stopped development, but the design was revived for the new requirement. A turbocharged version offered 2,000 BHP. Alternative versions had eight and six cylinders, in each case offering 125 BHP/cylinder. Detailed design began in 1947, and a prototype was completed in 1949. The first ship using the engine was the frigate-sized survey ship HMS *Vidal*, which had a twelve-cylinder version.

In February 1947 DNC asked E-in-C to lay out alternative diesel plants, using eight 2,000 BHP units (which might produce 2,250 BHP for about two hours at a time). In the tropics, output would be reduced to 14,000 SHP. This plant would drive a 2,075-ton ship using the hull already developed at the 23kts deep and dirty speed which had already been accepted for the A/A and A/D frigates. At the two-hour rate the ship would make 24.5kts deep and dirty (the Staff would probably reject the two-hour performance as irrelevant). At the very least, it would take 18,000 BHP to drive a common-hull frigate at the required 25kts. Existing diesels could not provide that power within the sort of weight assumed for the steam plant in the sketch designs. DNC concluded that while the A/A and A/D ships could be diesel-powered, the A/S ship would need a steam plant – which did not yet exist. E-in-C could not vouch for any of his developmental compact efficient steam plants until the prototype, in the *Daring* class, had been tested at sea – in a few more years. DNC's solution was adopted at DCNS' technical staff meeting on 7 March 1947. A/A and A/D speed was cut to 23kts. It was formally accepted that no long-range frigate would be able to make 25kts deep and dirty within the next five years.

The common hull was dead; the two A/S frigates on order could not be built. A meeting in First Sea Lord's War Room on 19 July 1947 proposed switching both to A/D frigates, as that function was the least understood of the projected ones. He asked DNC to produce new sketch designs for the A/D Frigate without reference to the Staff Requirements, as those would have to be amended anyway. Priorities were A/D (including a high-performance height-finder), Squid, and then

The Type 61 frigate HMS *Lincoln* is shown as completed, with her long-range target-indication radar (Type 982M). There was insufficient space or weight margin to accommodate the Type 983 long-range height-finder forward, so she had Type 277Q, normally a surface-search set (due to its beam, narrow in the vertical) but tiltable for height-finding. The air-search set at the maintop is Type 960. What looks like a search radar just below Type 960 is the associated Mk 10 IFF interrogator. Below that is the Type 293Q target-indication radar. The 'cheese' on the foremast is for the Type 268 surface-search set. There is no ESM system. *Lincoln* was unique in having a large deckhouse aft, intended for Seacat (which was not fitted), with a single Bofors

gun; the others in the class all had twin STAAG mountings in the same position, on the weather deck. *Lincoln* was also unique in this class in lacking fin stabilisers. In the ships' first major refit (beginning with HMS *Salisbury*, 1961–2, followed by *Chichester* in 1963–4, *Llandaff* 1964–6, and *Lincoln* 1966–8) Type 960 was replaced by the Type 965P 'double bedstead' on a plated-in mainmast. At the same time Type 293Q was moved to the top of the foremast, and Type 982M was raised on a higher pole mast (as in *Lincoln*). In *Salisbury* the STAAG was replaced by the lighter twin Mk V Bofors mounts. The UA-8/9 ESM system was fitted on the fore topmast. In a second series of refits the foremast was plated-in, Type 667 ECM being fitted (in *Chichester*

and *Llandaff*), and Type 293Q replaced by Type 993, with its distinctive 'quarter-cheese' antenna. *Lincoln* and *Salisbury* (which had a similar raised deckhouse) received Seacat (GWS 20) in place of their Bofors. In *Lincoln* Squid was landed, presumably as weight compensation. These two ships were fitted with two single Oerlikons. Their final refits were completed in, respectively, 1968 and 1970. The other two received Mk V Bofors instead of their STAAGs. All four received Corvus chaff launchers at the base of the foremast. *Chichester* was converted in 1973 as Hong Kong guardship, her air-search radar removed from her mainmast. (A D Baker III)

guns (and target indication for them). No design would be ready in time for the 1948 Estimates. Given the inevitable delays, and the well-understood relationship between the designs, it was no great stretch for the decision to shift again, this time to one A/A and one A/D ship (22 September 1947).

Diesel Frigates

The new frigates were among the first warships that, like current ones, were volume- rather than weight-critical. That was partly because they had much greater electronic content than their predecessors, and partly because the Royal Navy's response to the atomic bomb was to move as much as possible into the hull. To provide as much hull volume as possible, the ships had a very long forecastle, leaving only a short quarterdeck for Squid and other fittings. The long forecastle bought stability (extending the range of inclinations before the deck edge went into the water), buoyancy and better seakeeping. According to the description provided to the Board, the ships had been given about a foot too much beam to gain volume. They would be unusually stiff (metacentric height 5.2ft in compensated light condition for A/A, 5.5ft for A/D), hence would be fast rollers. Greater initial stability did provide an

ample growth margin, and fin stabilisers would handle the quick roll. Had beam been reduced, internal volume could have been clawed back only by lengthening the ships – which would be undesirable from a production point of view. The hull form was based on the bow of the pre-war destroyer *Amazon* and the stern of the pre-war cruiser *York*. The stern had a novel underwater form to accommodate large-diameter slow-turning propellers.

The ships' appearance reflected the need to simplify construction. The usual sheer line running continuously from the bow aft was replaced by two steps connected by a short ramped straight section. The height of the forecastle was chosen for seakeeping, but there was also a requirement (to deal with nuclear blast) to keep down the height of the superstructure. The view from the bridge still had to extend over No. 1 gun mounting. Instead of raising the bridge, the deck was cut down forward of it to lower the gun mount. All of the 1945 frigates used this arrangement. To deal with nuclear fallout, the ships had rounded weather deck edges for easier washdown after an attack and had provisions to decontaminate both structure and personnel. This was the first British class to exploit the results of the early post-war ship target trials. All-welded longitudinally-framed German destroyers had performed better than transversely-framed British ships. The new frigates had lighter hulls using widely-spaced transverse frames and closely-spaced longitudinals.

Construction of the A/A and A/D frigates was expected to provide experience in mass-production techniques. In the A/A Frigate, the fire control, radar and radio compartments normally adjacent were deliberately separated so that each could be completely fitted-out before installation. That was expected to minimise the need for scarce electrical labour by concentrating it in the factories rather than at the shipyards.[10] The ship would be somewhat larger (much as in current MEKO frigates), but DNC argued that she would thereby gain larger reserves of stability and buoyancy. Ultimately it proved impractical to prefit electronic spaces.

To a far greater extent than a steam plant, a diesel powerplant could be subdivided against underwater damage. It was not clear how worthwhile that would be, because some weapons, such as torpedoes, would probably destroy the entire powerplant if they hit amidships. On the other hand, some weapons, such as inert underwater-penetrating rockets, had very localised effects. In choosing a machinery arrangement, DNC analysts worked in terms of two kinds of damage, with effective lengths of 70ft and 40ft. The latter was typical of small mines (60–100lb charges). All proposed arrangements had the eight diesels grouped in pairs, two pairs (one before, one abaft) driving each shaft through a common gearbox. The choice initially fell on a single machinery space with auxiliary

spaces fore and aft, so that diesels did not have to be coupled through bulkheads. DNC objected that even a single rocket hit could immobilise the ship; ocean escorts should be able to reach harbour on one shaft. He won: the diesels were placed in overlapping spaces, each of the two L-shaped. The diesels themselves were on resilient mountings, driving the gearshafts through flexible hydraulic couplings. Some of the measures to limit noise and vibration had been developed for the new frigate-like survey ship *Vidal*.

The L-shaped bulkhead involved did allow asymmetric flooding which could have made a ship list badly, particularly since she had very little stability when tanks were empty. This arrangement recalled the use of centreline bulkheads, which had led to the loss of several British cruisers during the war. To maintain stability, tanks were intended always to be 100 per cent full, whether of fuel, water, or a combination (fuel floating on the water, which was acceptable for diesels). An unusual feature of the design was the use of water compensation (as in a submarine) to maintain stability if all main machinery spaces were flooded. Estimated endurance at 15kts was 5,000nm for the A/A version and 4,500nm for the A/D version.

Sketch designs were sufficiently mature to be submitted to the Board in December 1947. On 13/14 January 1948 Controller decided that one would be built at Portsmouth and one at Devonport. Using Royal Dockyards would limit the cost of post-contract changes. The design was approved by the Ship Design Policy Committee on 9 February 1948, and the two Frigate sketch designs were approved by the Board on 27 May 1948.

By this time estimated standard displacement of the A/A version, the heavier of the two, had grown from 1,650 tons (May 1946) to 1,773 tons. Some of the gain could be traced to normal design development, which made for more accurate calculations. The main growth was in machinery, up from 295 tons to 418 tons. Armament (including radar) grew far less, from 227 tons to 252 tons. The hull lost weight thanks to extensive use of aluminium (922 tons vs 956 tons), and equipment gained only slightly (146 tons rather than 140 tons). Complement had increased from 240 to 255. The lighter A/D version also grew; by mid-1948 its estimated standard displacement was 1,655 tons, slightly over the 1,600-ton limit set earlier. Compared to the A/A version from which it was derived, it had a slightly lighter hull (917 tons) and much less armament (148 tons vs 260 tons) as well as much less radar (5 tons vs 12 tons). Both versions required considerable water to compensate for fuel usage: 250 tons in the A/A version, 270 tons in the A/D.

Both the A/D and the A/A frigate continued to grow during detailed design. By the time the Board had approved the final designs in August 1950, the projected standard displacement of the A/A frigate was 1,835 tons (about 60 tons' growth) and

[10] Unit dimensions (29ft × 8ft × 6ft, 5 tons) were set by road and rail limits. Large firms could have accommodated heavier units, but the lower limit made it easier to distribute work in an emergency.

that of the A/D frigate was 1,704 tons (about 50 tons' growth). Contributory factors included some further increase in machinery weight (to 443 tons) and considerable growth in armament and radar (300 tons vs 257 tons in the A/A version).

Plans initially called for fin stabilisers like those of the 'Hunt' class, albeit on a larger scale. Stabilisation was then dropped because the new fire-control system (MRS series) would itself have been stabilised. However, it would take much more power than might be available for such a set to track a fast target from a rapidly rolling and pitching ship. It was far easier to split the problem into limiting ship motion (the fin stabiliser) and separately tracking a fast target from a nearly-stable platform (MRS). The new stabilisers were tested on board the trials cruiser HMS *Cumberland*.[11] All of the anti-aircraft frigates had retractable fin stabilisers. Those on board the aircraft direction frigates were not, apparently, retractable (an unofficial source claims that only *Lincoln* lacked them).

After the basic design was completed, it was proposed in August 1948 to use larger slower-turning propellers, which would be inherently quieter (quiet speed was roughly doubled from the previous 6–8kts). They were also considerably more efficient. The ships were now expected to make 24.5kts rather than 23kts deep and dirty, which approached the originally required A/S Frigate speed.[12] By this time the decision had been made to use a steam plant in the A/S frigate, and the required speed had risen. Designs for both diesel frigates were submitted to the Board in August 1950.[13]

As the A/D frigate was being designed, new systems were being developed. Instead of waiting for technology to stabilise, the Royal Navy planned to build and equip its standard frigates in Stages. Stage I, using existing (interim) equipment, would apply to ships ordered in 1948 (for delivery in 1952–3). Stage II would use equipment under active development, listed under 'Later Ships' in the official 'Goal for the Armament of the Fleet'. It would appear on ships delivered in 1954–5. Stage III ('ultimate' 1957 phase) used equipment for which requirements were firm, but which were not yet fully under development. Stages would be introduced during the ship production stream, rather than being retrofitted to individual ships.

The most important Stage II weapon was the new Medium Calibre Close Range gun, the twin 3in/70, which would replace the twin 4.5in. Stage I ships were not designed to accommodate it, but considerable effort was devoted to proving that it could be fitted without requiring a larger (hence unacceptable) hull. Other equipment was the new L70 Bofors gun; the MRS 3 director replacing the wartime Mk VI; and GDS 3 with

TIU III (Type 992 radar) replacing GDS 2* (Type 293Q). Stage II for frigates was delayed because the *Tiger* class cruisers, under reconstruction, had a much higher priority for new equipment. That was fortunate: the 3in/70 gun was not particularly successful, whereas the twin 4.5in proved quite reliable – and much more useful for the roles the ships actually played, in which shore bombardment was vital. The most significant Stage III equipment was the analogue Comprehensive Display System (CDS), with its Digital Plot Transmitter (DPT). The A/D Frigate would probably need something like CDS to handle the massed jet raiders of the future. Other examples were anti-torpedo weapons and Asdic Type 177. Some improvements outside the Stage system were widely retrofitted. Thus in 1954 the standard sonars were 170B (for Limbo) and 174, but the passive Type 176 and the long-range Type 177 were expected by mid-1955.

Communications requirements exploded. By January 1953 the A/D frigate needed seven (rather than the original two) ship-to-air UHF channels (VHF having been superseded) and seven ship to ship channels (three VHF, four UHF). The other two types needed six two-way ship-to-ship V/UHF channels (plus one receive-only), doubling the most recent requirement. Projected installation of the US Tacan (URN-3), for a time a very high-priority item, was ultimately abandoned.

Generator capacity had to be increased. The initial four 360 kW diesel generators gave the A/A frigate no electric power margin for growth; its action load (830 kW) exceeded the capacity of two of its generators (DNC rejected the idea of a 100 per cent power reserve in a mass-production ship). Only the first four ships (A/A and A/D: *Lynx*, *Panther*, *Puma* and *Salisbury*) had the original units. The next four (*Leopard*, *Jaguar*, *Chichester* and *Lincoln*) had the 500 kW units associated with Stage II (earlier A/A ships had two 360 kW units replaced by 500 kW units). By this time E-in-C was developing gas turbines for propulsion, and a gas turbine generator was a good way of gaining design and operating experience. Thus in January 1952 it was decided that later ships would have one 600 kW (later 500 kW) gas turbine unit in place of one of the diesel generators. That applied to HMS *Llandaff*. Performance in the tropics was apparently disappointing, both in this ship and in the 'Tribal' and 'County' classes.

The first ship, *Salisbury*, had the original small bridge. *Lynx* and later ships had an improved design with much better visibility. In the A/A frigate, the most visible change during construction was installation of a long-range Type 960 radar at the cost of two single Mk 9 Bofors (about February 1954). As might have been expected of ships with considerable new equipment on board, these frigates turned out quite heavy. At deep load *Lynx* displaced 2,515 tons, compared to the projected 2,185 tons; *Salisbury* displaced 2,330 tons rather than 2,110 tons. When production of these classes was cut short, DNO decided in 1955 that instead of the projected Stage II L70s, the

---

[11] Existing stabilisers used DC power; the new frigates used AC. To operate at convoy speeds (12–15kts) the stabilisers needed either longer fins than earlier ones or else multiple ones (which would replace most of their bilge keels).
[12] The 12ft (rather than 9ft) propellers turned at 160 rather than 290 RPM; estimated efficiency increased from 67 to 72 per cent. On trial in bad weather, *Lynx* made 23.8kts on 12,165 SHP at 199 RPM at 2,217 tons. *Salisbury* made 23.9kts on 12,380 SHP at 199 RPM at 2,240 tons. Due to diesel and gear characteristics, ships could not operate below 7kts.
[13] ADM 167/135, Memo B.658 (A/A Frigate) of 16 August 1950 and B.659 of 17 August 1950 for the A/D frigate.

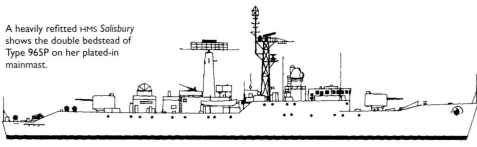

A heavily refitted HMS *Salisbury* shows the double bedstead of Type 965P on her plated-in mainmast.

Lynx and *Puma* were modernised in 1962–3 and May 1963–June 1964 respectively, emerging with plated-in mainmasts, Type 965 (single bedstead) in place of Type 960, and Type 993 in place of Type 293Q. UA-8/9 ESM was fitted to a fore topmast. *Leopard* was refitted between October 1964 and February 1966, and *Jaguar* in 1966–7. The big STAAG twin Bofors shown abaft the lattice mainmast was replaced by a single Bofors in HMS *Jaguar*, and the others were similarly rearmed. Seacat was never installed, although it was apparently planned for these ships.

The A/S Frigate

Once the common hull was abandoned, and a steam plant accepted, it was clear that the ideal speed for an A/S frigate was considerably higher than 25kts. One of the first SDPC projects (October 1948) was to estimate required speed and endurance as a guide to E-in-C for machinery development.[14] The coming threat was a 17–18kt diesel-electric submarine, which might ultimately be superseded by a 25-knot submarine with a closed-cycle powerplant. An Escort Group should include ships 10 knots faster than the submarine: 27-knot escorts (35kts in the more distant future). Although power for 27kts would be difficult to provide in a compact yet efficient plant, it was considered an 'irreducibly firm' figure. This speed had to be maintained in tropical, rather than temperate, conditions, further raising the required power. The Committee wanted the 4,500nm endurance of the 1945 frigates, but was aware that a steam plant could not be as economical as a diesel. It therefore accepted a lower endurance speed, 12kts, as a minimum for a 10-knot transatlantic convoy. Long endurance was justified on the grounds that replenishment would probably be impractical in wartime owing to the shortage of tankers. If the endurance figure could not be met, it would be better to sacrifice it than speed.

No immediate construction was contemplated, but the SDPC did not want to wait indefinitely (past, say, 1955) for a prototype. Because the new high-powered steam machinery might not be suited to mass production, the SDPC asked E-in-C to develop an insurance design which could be in production within six years, *ie* by 1954. It became the 30,000 SHP Y.100 plant.[15] The Board approved this project in November 1948. By that time the A/S frigate was far more than a distant possibility. The Soviets had blockaded Berlin, which seemed to be a step towards a new war, in which ASW would certainly be a very high priority. The British-led Western Union, the forerunner of NATO, had been formed.

The A/S frigate could be designed very quickly because it was effectively a modified diesel frigate with the new steam powerplant. Features such as the low superstructure and the odd stepped sheer duplicated those of the A/A and A/D frigates. As in the A/A and A/D frigates, the gun was controlled by the best available director, Mk 6, which was located atop the low superstructure forward of the mast and the funnel. Double Limbo was placed on the quarterdeck, not an ideal location, but one sheltered by deckhouses port and starboard which continued the forecastle aft. There was provision for four fixed torpedo tubes and twelve torpedoes (later changed to twelve

final ships in both classes would be armed with the same STAAGs as earlier units. In the aircraft direction ships (Type 61), the one STAAG was later replaced by a single Mk 9 Bofors, which in turn was replaced by Seacat. Their mainmasts were plated up to accommodate double-bedstead Type 965 radars (anti-aircraft ships, and *Salisbury* as first refitted, had the single-bedstead version).

There were some minor problems. Ships had difficulty going astern (*Lynx* was unable to, at least on trials) due to loss of circulating seawater in main and generator engine cooling systems due to entrained air in pumps, causing a loss of suction. The problem was solved by fitting additional inlets and air separators. Given problems with the diesel powerplant, there was a proposal to abandon it in favour of the steam plant of the A/S (Type 12) frigate. The Type 12 hull could easily accommodate the A/A and A/D payloads, but its powerplant needed just too much deck height to fit into a Type 41 or 61 hull. By the time the issue was raised, the Royal Navy no longer wanted A/A and A/D frigates very badly, so nothing was done. The last ships in each class, *Lincoln* and *Jaguar*, were unique in having controllable-pitch propellers.

[14] ADM 167/129, memo B.569, 1 October 1948. Board approval was Minute 4255, 5 November 1948.
[15] In May 1948, 20,000 and 30,000 SHP alternative powerplants were being considered, consuming (at 3,000 SHP, presumably for cruising speed) 0.92 and 0.95lb/SHP/hr. The Staff Requirement was still 25kts deep and dirty and 4,500nm at 15kts six months out of dock in the tropics, as in the A/A and A/D frigates. However, the relevant entry in Notebook 442/6 gives power for the later requirement of 27kts: 28,000 SHP for a 330ft standard frigate, which needed 14,400 BHP to make 23.25kts at 2,090 tons. Carrying 220 tons of weapons, such a ship was expected to displace 2,025 tons deep. The 330ft ship would need 19,700 SHP to make 25kts. That would have required at least eleven diesels.

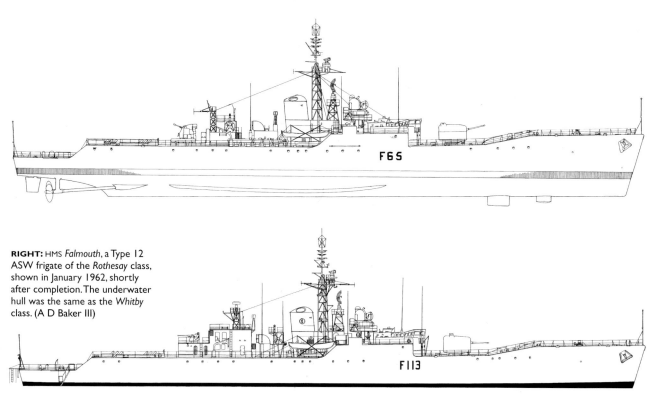

RIGHT: HMS *Falmouth*, a Type 12 ASW frigate of the *Rothesay* class, shown in January 1962, shortly after completion. The underwater hull was the same as the *Whitby* class. (A D Baker III)

tubes, eight of them fixed, plus two trainable twins).[16] The Staff Requirement was completed in 1949, and the design was presented to the Board in April 1950.[17]

To drive easily, the ship was given a long narrow forebody with fine lines above water, with weight and buoyancy concentrated as far aft as possible. This was almost as though the diesel common hull had been compressed (the steam plant was more compact), but given an extension forward (in D K Brown's phrase, a hydrodynamic aid, much as some ballistic missiles have aerospikes which increase their effective length). For high speed in bad weather, the A/S frigate had reduced prismatic coefficient (0.59), great length (high length-displacement ratio), and a long fine entry. Flare was minimised to reduce pitching in waves (hence the rounded superstructure). Given the narrow hull form forward, the massive twin

[16] Two tubes were made rotatable because there was not enough space both for fixed tubes and for reloading. The history of the torpedo requirement was convoluted. When Staff Requirements were reviewed in June 1952 the requirement changed to salvo-firing (three per salvo). Type 12 was satisfactory, but Types 14 and 15 were not. Type 14 was changed from two swivel tubes on each side to three lightweight tubes on each side, and Type 15 from four fixed tubes on each side to six lightweight tubes on each side (which entailed weight problems). ADM 1/24114. The fire control system, UCSF 1, was a surface equivalent to a submarine fire control system, with a target position-keeping element and ballistic computer. It was wanted because the torpedo tubes might fire several different weapons, such as the fast anti-ship torpedo, and it also controlled Limbo. This type of system was first proposed by DUW in a 1948 paper, and a Staff Requirement was approved in principle in June 1949; UCSF 1 was an interim (less ambitious) system. The design was largely complete by 1953, and trials were scheduled on board HMS *Undaunted*. Unfortunately torpedoes were not ready by mid-1954, when she was needed for Type 177 trials, so UCSF 1 was first tested on board HMS *Blackpool* in 1958. By that time many were on order for Type 12 and Type 14 frigates. Because she lacked a Type 177 sonar, *Blackpool* could not fully test the system. UCSF 1 had been approved for Type 14 frigates in 1953 because they and Type 12s were expected to fire more advanced torpedoes, such as Ferry and Pentane, in addition to Bidder. They were later cancelled. Type 15s lacked space for UCSF 1, so a much simpler TCS Mk 11 was ordered in 1955 for them. There had always been sceptics doubting the value of the full torpedo calculator, and in 1955 HMS *Vernon* (the torpedo development establishment) proposed simplifying it by eliminating one of its two calculators. By 1959 *Vernon* wanted to scrap UCSF 1, and many COs in the fleet had no use for Bidder. Its projected (abortive) successor, the surface version of Ongar (Mk 23 Tigerfish), would not be available, as then expected, until the mid-1960s. ADM 1/27489.

[17] ADM 167/135, 13 April 1950, designed to TSD 2078/49. The Board approved the Legend and sketch design on 20 April 1950. As an indication of the urgency of the project, building drawings were submitted on 8 December 1950 (memo B.682).

The twin Bofors aft was replaced by a single mount: HMS *Whitby*, with enlarged funnel casing.

4.5in gun had to be placed well aft. That pushed the bridge to about amidships, where a ship has the least motion in a seaway, hence is the most comfortable. Pushed so far aft in a compressed part of the ship, the superstructure had to be short. Thus, as in the diesel frigates, the Operations Room had to be placed below the bridge (hence did not meet the Staff Requirement that it be adjacent). Also as in those ships, the wheel was buried in the hull, just forward of the Operations Room. Carrying the freeboard well abaft the bow helped account for the ships' outstanding seakeeping, since waves tend to come aboard abaft the bow. The high freeboard section forward made a convenient location for the diesel generators, and placed them as far as possible from the steam machinery spaces, for survivability.

The hull was made deep for seakeeping and to accommodate large slow-turning propellers. This hull form was quite different from that chosen pre-war for destroyers.[18] The pre-war ships had high prismatic coefficients (typically 0.63) and the maximum section was carried well forward of amidships. The ship had maximum freeboard forward subject to a requirement that the water one cable (600 yds) ahead be visible from the bridge. The forward end of the superstructure was rounded for easy driving through head seas, with two breakwaters to protect it. A large slow-turning propeller (12ft diameter, 220 RPM) was selected for silencing. DNC promised good acceleration and maximum fuel economy at convoy speed.

A deep hull with low prismatic coefficient made for high rise of floor (the angle at which the sides of the ship begin to rise from the keel). That concentrated weights relatively high in the hull. When the ship was fully loaded, the weight of her fuel would maintain her stability. To avoid contaminating tanks, E-in-C banned flooding them with water as fuel was burned (this practice was permissible with diesel oil, which would float atop the water). The ship therefore had water ballast tanks under her oil fuel tanks. They were filled at light load to keep the ship stable. Without them, the ship could not have accommodated as much topweight. There were soon complaints that the 53 tons devoted to water ballast could better have been devoted to fuel oil.[19] The *Leander* class relied on filters and tank-stripping technology to permit tank flooding, but that was apparently unsatisfactory. Tanks were left empty in *Leander*s converted to configurations with much-reduced topweight. Because the design was completed very quickly, it had some odd flaws. An error in calculation would have given a 6ft trim by the stern. Detected very late in the design, it had to be corrected by adding tankage forward.[20]

The ship was armed with a twin 4.5in gun forward (with Mk 6M director) and a STAAG aft (later replaced by a single Mk 9). Stage I ASW armament was Double Squid (controlled by the early post-war Type 166 sonar). However, the ships were all completed with Limbo and its Type 170 sonar (plus Type 164 in *Whitby* and Type 174 in the others). Bulkheads in the hold were arranged so that a large (150in) second sonar dome could easily be added for the projected Type 177 long-range sonar. The Asdic Instrument Room on the lower deck forward was made large enough for both sets (some storeroom space would have to be surrendered when Type 177 was installed). Space for a proposed third dome, for an anti-torpedo sonar, was not provided.

Stage II would include the 3in/70 gun with its MRS 3 fire control system, GDS 3 with Type 992 radar, the new Type 976 radar, Double Limbo, new sonars to match (Types 170 and 174 [176 when 177 was fitted], plus 162), ASW torpedoes (six torpedo tubes on each side) with their fire control system, the Nightshirt propeller silencer, and the Unifoxer torpedo decoy plus thrown decoys. For Stage III the ship would get further-improved longer-range sonars (Types 172 and 177) and the Ruler anti-torpedo system (with Type 176 passive torpedo-detecting sonar). Stage II was formally abandoned about February 1955 as part of the attempt to cut the cost of the massive Korean War rearmament programme. However, considerable new equipment, such as Stage III sonars, could be fitted without major redesign. Of the six Type 12s, all but

---

18 M K Purvis, 'Post War RN Frigate and Guided Missile Destroyer Design 1944-1969' in *Transactions of the Royal Institution of Naval Architects* (1974) and D K Brown and George Moore, *Rebuilding the Royal Navy* (Chatham Publishing, London: 2003), pp 75–6. The hydrodynamic aid phrase is from D K Brown, *A Century of Naval Construction*.

19 Notebook 767/4 (J C Cooper) analysed possibilities for gaining endurance by eliminating the ballast. Unfortunately some ballast was needed in deep condition simply to keep the ship upright.

20 ADM 167/143: Controller memo B.866 of 2 December 1953: a calculator 'missed out a nought'. The same problem made Type 14 overweight, probably costing between half a knot and a knot at deep load. Due to pressure early in the rearmament programme to 'get on at all costs' Controller (Rear Admiral R A B Edwards) and DNC (V G Shepheard) agreed to suspend the usual practice of doing all calculations in duplicate. That was partly because, against an authorised strength of 250, the RCNC had only 187 constructors. DNC could not contract the work out, because the yards had too few sufficiently skilled naval architects. DNC no longer had the capacity to offer the Board design alternatives. Controller estimated that ending the accelerated practice had slowed work by about 25 per cent.

HMS *Eastbourne* shows the full torpedo battery planned for the Type 12s: four fixed (forward-firing) and two revolving tubes on each beam. Note the foremast ESM array. This photograph was taken on 23 September 1959.

Whitby and *Torquay* received the torpedo tubes (*Scarborough* was the first, the others being retrofitted). With the failure of the Bidder torpedo, the tubes were all removed by 1963. Ruler proved so disappointing that it was abandoned in the mid-1950s.[21]

The seventh and later ships constituted the *Rothesay* class, a modified Type 12 recognisable by the raked funnel introduced in HMS *Torquay* and by a larger superstructure block aft. The redesign was paid for by cancellation of Stage II. Electrical power was increased, with two 400 kW rather than 350 kW turbo-generators and two 300 kW rather than 200 kW diesels. Crew accommodation was improved (partial bunk sleeping) and some parts of the ships air-conditioned. In November 1955 DNO ordered follow-on Type 12s (from the seventh ship on, *ie* the *Rothesay*s) armed with the twin L70, controlled by the new MRS 8 director. Since L70s were not

immediately available, *Rothesay* received a Mk 5 utility twin on an interim basis (the others had single Mk 7s instead). In fact the L70 never appeared, because the Royal Navy bought Seacat missiles instead. In December 1957 the Board ordered Seacat installed on board the Type 12 (*Rothesay* class) frigate bought instead of the last A/D frigate, HMS *Coventry*. As completed ships had a large after superstructure intended for Seacat, but they had Bofors guns. Like the earlier Type 12s, these ships had twelve torpedo tubes (with the twins forward of rather than abaft the fixed singles). As in the earlier ships, they did not last for long. After the first nine, later *Rothesay*s in turn were reordered to become the early *Leander*s.

Beginning with *Rothesay* in 1966, the ships were modernised with a flight deck and hangar for a Wasp helicopter (the forward Limbo well was decked over and the after superstructure replaced by a hangar). The lattice foremast was replaced by a taller plated mast and the funnel was raised. MRS 3 replaced the Mk VI director, and the Type 277 radar removed (Type 293Q was replaced by the improved Type 993). As mod-

---

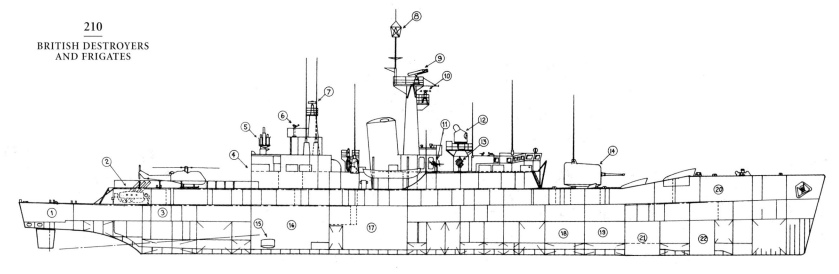

HMS *Brighton*, a modernised *Rothesay* class frigate, is shown in 1972. Major changes were the helicopter, Seacat, the plated-in foremast, and an MRS 3 director in place of the earlier Mk 6M. The Type 978 surface-search radar replaced the earlier Type 277Q, and Type 993 replaced Type 293Q. Not shown is the UA-3 (not UA-8/9) ESM array which many ships of this class carried on the fore topmast under the HF/DF array. Ships did not receive jammers, but they did receive Corvus for self-defence. *Brighton* was rebuilt beginning in August 1968. Modernisation completion dates for the class were: *Rothesay* 5 July 1968, *Yarmouth* 30 September 1968, *Plymouth* 28 February 1969, *Londonderry* 19 December 1969, *Lowestoft* 29 May 1970, *Falmouth* 18 December 1970, *Berwick* 13 March 1971, *Brighton* 18 February

1972, and *Rhyl* 16 June 1972. *Falmouth* tested a prototype DA-5 towed array in 1978, and *Lowestoft* tested a prototype Type 2031 in 1981–2. *Londonderry* was converted into the Admiralty Surface Weapons Establishment trials ship in November 1975–October 1979, emerging with three plated-in masts (the after one being portable), her gun being removed. She was given pump-jet propulsion. (A D Baker III)

1. Steering machinery room (twin rudders)
2. Triple Limbo Mk 10 ASW mortar
3. Limbo projectile magazine (to port)
4. Helicopter hangar
5. Quadruple Seacat GWS 20 surface-to-air missiles launcher

6. GWS 20 optical director
7. IFF interrogation antenna
8. Mk 5 HF D/F array
9. Type 993 search radar
10. Type 978 navigational radar
11. 20mm Oerlikon AA (P&S)
12. MRS 3 radar gun director (Type 903 radar)
13. 3in Mk 4 Knebworth-Corvus rocket launchers (P&S)
14. Twin 4.5in dual purpose gun mount Mk 6
15. Fin stabilisers
16. Engine room (two sets geared steam turbines)
17. Boiler room (two Babcock & Wilcox boilers
18. 4.5in gun powder magazine
19. 4.5in projectile magazine
20. Diesel generator room (two 500 kW sets)
21. Hull outfit 20 (Type 174 sonar)
22. Hull outfit 15 (Type 170B sonar)

ernised, these were among the first British ships to carry the Knebworth Corvus chaff rocket launcher.

Type Numbers

As had been expected, the steam A/S frigate was expensive, but there was no reason to imagine that fewer such ships would be needed. In August 1949 the ACNS, Rear Admiral Edwards, suggested that it might be possible to build a substantially less expensive ship by eliminating everything but the primary ASW weapons. This second-rate A/S ship is described in Chapter 11. It was cumbersome to describe ships as first- or second- (or, later, third-) rate, particularly when some of them, like A/A and A/D frigates, might not be quite comparable to the A/S ships being built in large numbers. Edwards proposed the alternative designation system which the Royal Navy has used ever since for its frigates.[22]

ASW ships were numbered in a 10 series, beginning with 12 for the first-rate A/S frigate (Type 11 presumably could have been confused with the 'Hunt' Type II). Nor was unlucky Type 13 used. Thus the second-rate frigate became Type 14.

The converted destroyer conceived as an interim first-rate frigate (see below) became Type 15. A second-rate version became Type 16. A somewhat more elaborate conversion, still short of Type 15 standards, became the abortive Type 18. However, destroyer modernisation, which provided something not too different from Type 16, received no Type number. Perhaps to show that they were not comparable to the ASW ships, the A/A frigates were designated Type 41. The A/D ship became Type 61. A war-built destroyer converted into an A/D ship (conceived but not executed) became Type 62.

The Royal Navy also began to number ships under construction with US-style hull numbers (which were not the pennant numbers painted on ships' hulls). Type 12 and her successors were numbered in an FSA series, policy documents referring to FSA 15 or 25, for example.

Programmes

Until June 1950 the Royal Navy planned for reconstruction by 1957, the 'year of maximum danger' (of war). An early plan, prepared in March 1948 (when the idea of the 1957 target year seems to have originated), showed a total of fifty-three destroyers and 217 frigates (including fifty-nine converted destroyers). In addition to the two frigates (one A/A and one A/D) approved under extensions of the 1945 Programme, two more A/A frigates, three A/D frigates and four A/S frigates would be built, for totals of four Type 12, three Type 41 and four Type 61.[23] By January 1949 the planned figure for A/S frigates had grown to eleven, the prototype being built under the 1949/50 Programme. Most construction under the plan would begin in 1954. This 'Revised Restricted Fleet' plan was in force when the North Koreans invaded South Korea in June 1950.

Suddenly it seemed that World War III might be at hand –

22 ADM 167/135, memo B.653, 25 July 1950. When the Board approved the sketch design of the second rate Frigate, 11 May 1950, it asked for alternatives to the first and second rate titles. Edwards suggested using a Type number until the first of the class had been completed. His idea was approved after discussion on 27 July and 1 August 1950. Probably the Type number was first applied when the Board approved the Type 12 drawings, Minute 4473 of 14 December 1950.
23 ADM 167/129. The 1948 plan called for the first A/S frigate in the 1949/50 programme and for six frigates in 1951/2 (three A/S, two A/A and three A/D).

almost seven years too early. It was shocking that Stalin had been willing to start even a regional war in the face of US nuclear deterrence (his spies may have told him that the United States had relatively few bombs). In October 1950 the Admiralty telescoped re-equipment to 1951–4, in effect bringing the planned build-up forward by two years.[24] The US government had recently brought forward its version of the 'year of maximum danger' to 1954. The NATO Medium Term Defence Plan of November 1950 embodied the British October plan.

In December 1950 the British government decided to accelerate rearmament with a £4,700 million three-year plan (£1,610 million for the Royal Navy) covering the 1951–2 to 1953–4 Programmes Acceleration proved difficult, so late in 1951 the plan was stretched to include the 1954–5 Programme. Because of bottlenecks and the competition of a recovering civilian economy, defence prices rose; the total increased to £6,652 million. Some items were cut or postponed during the winter of 1951–2. It had to admitted that British forces could not be completely re-equipped until April 1958.

The first Type 12, HMS *Whitby*, was ordered under the last pre-Korea programme (1949–50). No frigate was included in the 1950/51 Programme, presumably to allow for tests of the prototype. Once war broke out, a Supplemental 1950/51 Programme added a second Type 12. Four more in the 1951/2 Programme brought the total to six. The Supplemental also provided four Type 41 frigates (two in 1951/2, two in 1952/3), for a total of five, including the 1945 prototype; and three Type 61 (one in 1951/52 and two in 1952/3), for a total of four. Plans also called for the first two Type 14 (second-rate A/S) in the 1951/2 Programme, with another ten (reflecting estimated shipyard capacity) in the 1952/3 Programme.

Because the Korean attack was widely considered the beginning of a larger war, the British concentrated on the force they would have to contribute to NATO in that event. In 1951 that included thirty-eight escorts. To meet commitments under the NATO Medium Term Plan the British would have to build thirty-two destroyers or Type 12 equivalents and 144 ocean escorts (Types 14, 41, 61 and lesser ships). These figures took no account of Middle Eastern or Home waters. The Admiralty decided to accelerate and expand frigate production with thirty-six more ships: six Type 12 (two each in 1953/4, 1954/5 and 1955/6) and thirty other ocean escorts: four Type 41 A/A (two in 1955/6 and two in 1956/7), three Type 61 A/D (one in 1954/5 and two in 1955/6), twenty Type 14 (in two series of ten), two Type 17 (prototype plus the first production ship, the former moved from 1953/4 to 1954/5), and one Type 42 (prototype in 1954/5).[25] The frigate and destroyer force would be modernised. These were very ambitious for a country still recovering from the Second World War, with food rationing still in place. As noted in Chapter 9, by 1954 British strategists had

decided that global war really was not too likely, so the budget could be cut. The Board decided to delete the World War III ships, *ie* the follow-on Type 14s and a prototype ocean minesweeper in the 1953/4 Programme.

To avoid turbulence in the shipyards, the pace of first-rate frigate construction would be maintained. In fact construction was proving slow, so as late as 1956 many of the ships in the 1952/3 Programme had not yet been laid down. It was therefore relatively painless to keep rearranging the frigate programme. Plans calling for four frigates in 1953/4 and five in 1954/5 were cut to meet a financial limit imposed in 1953. Five frigates (plus one of the 1951/2 Programme) were allocated to the Indian Navy. Although not included in the building programme, in effect they competed for British shipyard capacity.[26] The two Type 12s of 1953/4 were moved forward to 1954/5. One of the Type 41s, HMS *Panther*, was sold to India before completion as the first of three such ships. Then two of the four ships of that year's programme were re-ordered as Type 41s, so that the totals of A/S and A/A frigates would have been ten each. Then the balance between the two

swung back. First one of the 1955/6 Type 41s was replaced by a Type 12, then the two 1954/5 ships reverted to Type 12, and then a second Type 12 was added in 1955/6 (total four), for a total of fourteen Type 12s. The remaining 1955/6 Type 41 replaced HMS *Panther*. Two more Type 41s remained in the programme, scheduled for 1956/7. Plans called for three Type 61 (two in 1954/5 and one in 1955/6).

Plans Division argued that gun air defence would soon be obsolete, so that Type 41 would become pointless; nor was a slow Type 61 worthwhile. All of these ships should be replaced by Type 12s, bringing the class total to twenty (presumably the last ship would have replaced World War III frigates, Types 14 and 42. Reviewing the programme again in July 1955, the

HMS *Rothesay* was a modified Type 12. One major change was to place the fixed tubes abaft the revolving ones, firing aft. Note that the twin Bofors is a Mk V rather than the considerably heavier STAAG. The tubes did not last long.

---

24 ADM 167/137: this Fraser Plan was approved 12 October 1950 (Minute 4407).
25 DEFE 7/753, an August 1951 discussion of the 1952–3 programme, and ADM 167/137, referring to COS(51)24.

26 ADM 167/142. Minute 4838 of 6 January 1955 and Memo B.953 on the 1955/6 New Construction programme and previous programmes.

Board decided to concentrate on Type 12.[27] Because of continuing delays, as of March 1956 the second pair of 1954/5 ships was moved to 1955/6 and three of four 1955/6 ships to 1956/7. Type 12 now replaced one of two 1956/7 Type 41s; another ship added to the 1956/7 Programme probably replaced the planned Type 42 and one Type 17. Thus the planned total

Two views of HMS *Yarmouth* as modernised, with hangar, Seacat, MRS 3 director and plated-in foremast.

of Type 12s had grown to sixteen.[28] Many of these ships had not yet been laid down. Of the other classes, four Type 41 were building, plus one in the 1955/6 Programme and one planned for 1956/7. Four Type 61 A/D frigates were building, with another (not yet laid down) contracted for under the 1953/4 Programme, and a sixth planned for 1956/7. The Staff argued against building the 1956/7 Type 41 because guns would be inadequate against the post-1962 threat as it was then understood. Naval members of the Board agreed that the last two Type 41s might well not be worth building.[29] These ships survived in the programme mainly because industry could not

build another missile destroyer instead. It also seemed that guns would probably remain worthwhile, though of declining value after 1962. The Staff wanted the Type 61s cancelled because their low speed made it impossible for them to operate effectively with a battle group.

Of the ships still to be built, as of December 1956 Type 41 and 61 frigates had already been ordered from Portsmouth and Devonport Royal Dockyards. An A/D frigate had recently been ordered from Fairfield, and an A/A frigate from Vickers Newcastle (February 1956). No work had been done on either ship, apart from ordering material. Quite apart from other arguments, by this time the early diesel frigates had encountered considerable problems, whereas the Type 12 steam plant was very satisfactory, and the ship was considered much more useful because she was so much faster. On the other hand, the Staff badly wanted pickets, even slow Type 61s. At some point the Royal Dockyard Type 41 was switched for the Fairfield Type 61. Thus the two Royal Dockyard ships were to have been Type 61s named *Exeter* and *Gloucester*. Given the ease with which a Royal Dockyard ship could be reordered, in January 1957 they became the Type 12s *Rhyl* and *Plymouth*, making a total of eighteen such ships. To replace one of the A/D frigates lost at a Royal Dockyard, the Staff proposed reordering the Type 41 at Vickers as a Type 61. Soon, however, the attractions of the slow picket faded. Cancelling HMS *Coventry* at Vickers would cause less disruption than cancelling the one at Fairfield. That was done in October 1957.[30] Ultimately the ship was ordered in 1961 as HMS *Leander*. The Fairfield ship, apparently to have replaced the HMS *Panther* sold to India, was cancelled. Thus in the end the Royal Navy received only four each of Types 41 and 61.

In approving these changes, the Board asked DNC to investigate placing the only available frigate-sized anti-aircraft missile, the US Tartar, on board future frigates.[31] This question ultimately led to the *Leander* design (see Chapter 12). About 1956 there were no plans for frigate production beyond the last Type 12s, which would provide a total of about twenty ships. It was clear that the desired number of frigates could not be maintained without a rolling programme of new construction, probably three ships per year. Given an expected sixteen-year lifetime, that would eventually support a total of forty-eight frigates. From time to time there were attempts to boost the annual rate to four ships. These figures were far below what was wanted at the time.[32] There would be little point in a high-low mix. Instead all frigates would be of a single standard type evolving over time, much like the pre-war destroyers of the A through I cycle. The first ships involved in the new programme concept were the 'Tribal' (Type 81) frigates

[27] ADM 167/141, meeting of 14 July 1955.
[28] ADM 167/146, Memo B.1056 of 6 March 1956.
[29] ADM 167/146.

[30] ADM 167/150.
[31] ADM 167/146, Minute 5080. The Staff Memo was Bl1121 of 18 December 1956.
[32] ADM 167/143 includes the desired size of the fleet, including sixty destroyers/fast escorts, sixty first-rate frigates, and 120 ocean escorts (presumably Type 14 equivalents), all credited with a sixteen-year life. To maintain this fleet the average annual programme would have been 3.75 destroyers, 3.75 first-rate frigates, and 7.5 ocean escorts. The best the Royal Navy did in later years was three to five escorts per year.

BELOW: Late in 1975 the Indian Type 12 frigate *Talwar* had her 4.5in gun mount replaced by Styx missiles from an Osa-class missile boat; her sister *Trishul* was similarly fitted in a 1977–8 refit. Later both ships were further modified, Limbo being removed and a helicopter deck and hangar added.

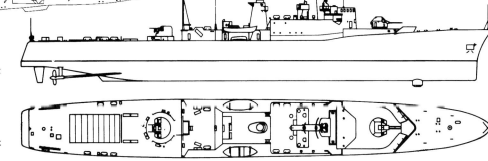

RIGHT: The first post-war Canadian frigates were equivalent to the British Type 12, with the same powerplant. The Canadian ships had almost turtle-back forecastles to clear freezing spray. Anchors were recessed, with covers, so that they could not ice up. The hull form was as opposite as possible to that of a Type 12, and the Canadians clearly rejected the British view that the bridge should be squeezed down into the hull to avoid nuclear threats. Reportedly they told their RCNC constructor to make the ships distinctively Canadian. Dimensions were not far from those of a Type 12: 366ft x 42ft (2,000 tons

standard, 2,600 tons full load). The *Restigouche* shown here was an improved version of the original *St Laurent*, with a 3in/70 rather than the forward 3in/50 twin mount, and thus might be seen as equivalent to the original version of the British *Rothesay*. The Canadians regarded her armament as equivalent to that of a Type 12: a twin 3in/70 forward (which the British had considered the ultimate replacement for the 4.5in gun, for better anti-aircraft performance) and a twin 3in/50 aft (which the Canadians preferred to the British twin Bofors). The folding door on deck aft protected two Limbos from

spray. The tower foremast carried a US SPS-12 air-search radar, a US SPS-10, and the Canadian Sperry Mk 2 navigational set. In November 1956 the US Navy considered HMCS *St. Laurent* 'potentially as effective as any ASW ship in existence' but

criticised poor visibility for the commanding officer. She was considered noisy up to 21kts due mainly to her machinery, but quiet at high speed (21–29kts) despite noisy propellers. The ship had two twin 3in/50, two 40mm Boffins, two Limbos, and two lightweight

torpedo launchers for US Mk 43 torpedoes. Sonars were the British Type 162 (bottom search) and 170 (Limbo fire control) and a US SQS-11 scanning sonar, the 100in dome shown accommodating both 170 and SQS-11.

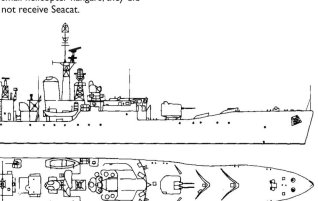

BELOW: This US Navy drawing represents the *Rothesay* class as planned, with the original small superstructure aft for Seacat. Only the two Royal New Zealand Navy ships of this type, *Otago* and *Taranaki*, were refitted in this configuration, and only they had the two single Bofors L60s. These ships were delivered with 21in torpedo tubes and a single Bofors, but later were fitted with the planned Seacats but not with the helicopter hangars of the modernised British ships. Note the unusual deck shape forward,

typical of Type 12 and its derivatives. The three South African ships of this type, *President Kruger*, *President Pretorius* and *President Steyn*, were all heavily rebuilt with plated-in foremasts, massive plated-in mainmasts carrying French Jupiter long-range air-search radars, new Italian main battery fire controls (NA 9C), and small helicopter hangars; they did not receive Seacat.

ABOVE: The 1961–6 reconstructions of the Canadian *St. Laurents* may be likened to the *Rothesay* modernisations. A hangar and helicopter pad replaced one of the two Limbos, and variable-depth sonar (the same type adopted by the Royal Navy). In this case, however, gun armament was drastically reduced. The *St. Laurents* had two twin 3in/50s, and one was removed. Instead of the small Wasp, they were fitted to operate the very large Sea King, which had a dipping sonar and thus could search independently for submarines. In British practice a Sea King was operated only by a

carrier or a helicopter cruiser. The hatched area on the flight deck is a grid into which the helicopter could insert a probe, to allow it to land on a pitching deck. The Royal Canadian Navy regarded its ability to operate such large helicopters from relatively small ships as a major triumph. Visible under the flight deck is a triple tube for lightweight Mk 44 torpedoes. Conversion added about 200 tons to deep load displacement, and the old US SQS-11 sonar was replaced by a more modern Canadian SQS-503A. Canadian and US ESM sets (UPD-501 and WLR-1) were added.

HMCS *St. Laurent*, the Canadian equivalent to a Type 12, using the same machinery and much the same armament (note the double Limbo aft) – but a very different hull form.

described in Chapter 12. How many ships of a given class would be built would depend on how long it would be before a new class was wanted.

Exports

India and New Zealand each received two British-built units. One of the two for New Zealand had been ordered for the Royal Navy as HMS *Hastings* (both New Zealand ships were actually built to the modified *Rothesay* design). South Africa received three *Rothesay*s.

The Royal Australian Navy ultimately built six Type 12s as part of its shift towards an ASW orientation. Its initial (1947–52) post-war Five Year Plan had envisaged a force in commission comprising two carriers, two cruisers, six destroyers and three frigates, *ie* essentially a pair of carrier task forces. This force justified the construction of the two 'Battle' and four *Daring* class destroyers. However, by 1949, with the Cold War being waged intensely, interested shifted to shipping protection. That year a navy analysis suggested an urgent need

for eighteen fast modern escorts. On hand were eight modern destroyers which could be modernised for a primarily ASW role: three 'Tribals' and five ex-RN 'Q' class (which the Royal Navy gave to the Australians when the latter announced they would pay for Type 15 modernisation). As in Britain, the matter became urgent when the North Koreans invaded South Korea in June 1950. In August the Australians announced a three-year programme (for a 1953 global war) including six Type 12s (the 1949 plan required at least ten), which were named the 'River' class. A contemporary ASW plan included local forces (each one 'Q' class destroyer and two 'River' class frigates) to protect four focal areas (the approaches to Sydney, Moreton Bay, Fremantle and Port Phillip).

The Type 12s were to be built in batches, the first four being ordered in 1950. As DNC had warned, the Australian shipbuilding industry had limited capacity; the first ship could not be laid down until 1953. The Australians therefore considered an alternative, the Canadian *St Laurent*, roughly equivalent to a Type 12. Four could be built in Canada, and the

remaining pair (plus two more envisaged) built in Australia. This idea was formally proposed to the Cabinet Defence Preparations Committee in March 1952, but it was abandoned because the estimated price for the Australian-built ships was two and a quarter times that estimated for the Type 12s in 1950. Falling Australian foreign-currency reserves made it impractical to order the ships in Canada.

As in the UK, the Australians found themselves unable to complete their planned programme. In 1952 it was stretched out and expenditure capped. Further cuts were made in 1953: one of the planned 'Tribal' modernisations, the fourth *Daring*, and the fifth 'Q' class. The Type 12 programme was cut to four hulls, although the last two ships were not formally cancelled until 1956 (construction was reconsidered in 1958). Cuts were partly to maintain carriers and to buy new ASW aircraft (Gannets) for them. Long delays in construction made it possible for the Australians to adopt different equipment. As completed the first four ships incorporated the improvements in the *Rothesay* class, and had MRS 3 gun fire controls and Dutch Signaal LW02 air-search radars (atop a high foremast). The second pair had the forecastle extended aft to the stern, adding accommodation. *Stuart* was the first to receive Ikara (in place of one Limbo), and *Derwent* was the first RAN ship with Seacat. All four ultimately received these weapons. *Yarra* had her Type 177 sonar replaced by the prototype Australian Mulloka. In 1968 plans were made to modernise *Parramatta*, *Stuart* and *Derwent*, and to give *Yarra* a half-life refit. In each case the goal was to extend operating life by a decade. The Dutch M22 'egg' (rigged to control Seacat as well as the gun) replaced MRS 3 except in *Yarra*. Limbo was removed, and in all but *Yarra* it was replaced by a pair of lightweight torpedo tubes, the torpedo aim point calculated by the Ikara computer. The Australian Mulloka sonar replaced British types (Type 170 was retained, but not manned, as a reserve system).

Reordered in June 1964, *Swan* and *Torrens* were initially to have been repeat *Derwent*s, the object reportedly being to replace HMAS *Voyager*, which had been sunk in a collision with the aircraft carrier HMAS *Melbourne* on 10 February 1964, as quickly as possible. Within six months it had been decided to redesign them completely, the result corresponding roughly to the British *Leander*, with that ship's Y.136 powerplant. They had substantially enlarged superstructures and forecastle decks extending all the way aft. Both had Ikara as completed. Construction of another pair was considered but rejected in 1969, as necessary components were no longer in production.

In October 1973, when the Australians were considering buying the US *Perry* class frigate, they considered building or modifying 'Rivers' with US weapons. A January 1974 design study showed that it would be feasible to replace the 4.5in gun with a lightweight US 5in/54 Mk 45. The plated-in foremast could accommodate a US Mk 92 'egg', equivalent to the Signaal 'egg'. Alongside the superstructure aft would be a pair of

quadruple Harpoon launchers. Roughly abeam them would be a Signaal LW02 long-range air-search radar. Abaft it would be two CIWS, port and starboard (sketches showed a twin mount like an Emerlec-35, Phalanx not yet having been fully defined). The ship would have two triple lightweight torpedo tubes. Freeboard was carried right aft, and the hangar would accommodate a pair of Lynx helicopters. The sonar would have been the recently-developed Australian Mulloka. Deep

TOP: HMAS *Paramatta*, the Australian version of a Type 12, as modernised with Ikara (the Ikara data link is in the radome immediately above the bridge).

ABOVE: HMAS *Yarra* in October 1984, showing her Ikara launcher. (RAN photo by LSPH W McBride)

HMAS *Swan*, representing the ultimate version of the Australian Type 12.

displacement would have been slightly less than that of a modified Type 12, 2,735 tons rather than 2,756 tons. An alternative version would had a Tartar launcher (Mk 22; the larger Mk 13 could not be accommodated) forward and the single 5in/54 right aft. The long-range air search radar would have been the US SPS-49, and the Mk 92 'egg' would have been supplemented by an SPG-60 dish for missile control. Given the gun aft, the hangar would have been shorter. This version was not too far from the US frigate, and it had more firepower.

More British colonies became independent, beginning with Ghana in 1957. On 27 May 1960 C-in-C South Atlantic and West Indies reported that the Ghanaians wanted a frigate/despatch vessel (and presidential yacht), and he laid out basic characteristics. They included a twin 4in gun and Squid, with a searchlight sonar (Type 164/174). The ship would not operate a helicopter, but she needed a landing platform, since VIPs would generally come aboard that way. A successful design might well appeal to the other newly-independent African country, Nigeria, and might have further export potential (the Nigerians bought a Dutch frigate instead). Controller asked DGS to develop a design suited to New Commonwealth countries, which at least initially would have little naval infrastructure. A Staff Requirement (TWP 4124/61) was written, and variants displacing 1,570–2,055 tons devel-

oped.[33] DGS chose a hull based on that of the Type 41 frigate, powered by eight ASR I diesels. The basic design was completed in 1962 and the ship ordered in 1965. Reportedly to have been named *Black Star*, she was cancelled in 1966 when President Kwame Nkrumah, who had ordered her, was deposed in a coup. She was launched without being named and then completed and laid up. A vigorous sales campaign found no buyers. In May 1970 the Royal Navy considered converting her to an MCMV Support Ship, as an alternative to HMS *Abdiel*, but the project was not pursued. By 1972 it was accepted that she would never be sold; she would either be scrapped or taken up by the Royal Navy. The navy acquired her to replace HMS *Puma*, due for a refit which would have been more expensive than acquiring the frigate. Later she was sold to Malaysia.

Vosper apparently saw an opportunity for commercial sales to the emerging countries at about the same time, conceiving a modular series of corvettes and frigates. They may have been follow-ons to the company's earlier large patrol craft. In August 1960 the company approached the British government in hopes of securing sales support, citing long-standing inquiries from some Commonwealth and NATO countries for a small

---

[33] Weights of the variants are listed in Notebook 337/16 (W G John). Other details are from the Cover for HMS *Mermaid*.

general-purpose ship.[34] The company envisaged a small ship which could be completed with various armaments: (i) GP (4in single submarine-type or 3.3in Coastal Forces gun, Seacat or Bofors twin L70 or two single L70); (ii) torpedo boat (single 4in gun, four or six torpedo tubes, Seacat or L70); (iii) GP Training Ship; (iv) patrol and VIP. At this stage it was a 175ft, 430-ton ship driven by two-shaft diesels, with a complement of fifty. Two Mk 1 corvettes were built for Ghana (4in gun, Squid, Bofors), and a gun version (four Bofors, no Squid) for Libya. Mk 2 was a more sophisticated version of the same ship. It may have been the very fast gas turbine corvette offered to Canada in 1962 (see Chapter 12). Mk 3 was a 202ft corvette with a twin 4in gun and two Bofors; two were built for Nigeria.

Vosper then merged with Thornycroft, which was more interested in fast frigates. The series then split into fast light frigates and derivatives of the earlier designs. Thus Mk 5 and the slightly larger Mk 7 were small frigates powered by gas turbines and diesels; four Mk 5 were built for Iran, and one Mk 7 for Libya. Mk 9, however, was a corvette not much larger than Mk 3, also for Nigeria. Mk 10 was a much larger frigate for Brazil. Mks 5 and 7 made a considerable impression, and helped inspire the choice of a Vosper Thornycroft design for the Royal Navy's Type 21. Vosper Thornycroft's second-gen-

eration design, 'Vigilance', was sold to Oman as the *Quahir al Amwaj* class. From the late 1970s on, Vosper also built a corvette-sized *Vita* class fast attack boat (for Egypt, Kenya and Oman; it was the basis for the US *Cyclone*), but it was not related to the standard corvettes and frigates. A corvette version (*Khamronsin* class) was built for Thailand.

The Vosper and Vosper Thornycroft designs were developed in partnership with Vickers, but in the early 1970s Vickers promoted a somewhat similar class as the 'Vickers Vedette.' It was offered unsuccessfully to Indonesia, and a version was developed in Australia using US systems.

Yarrow, another important destroyer builder, seems to have drawn a parallel conclusion. Its Yarrow Frigate was slightly larger than Mk 5 or Mk 7, with half the power (one gas turbine and one diesel rather than two of each). One was sold to Malaysia, and a slightly larger and more heavily armed version to Thailand. Yarrow's YARD design arm developed several major foreign frigate designs.[35] A 'Yarrow corvette' developed in the late 1980s (and marketed beginning about 1990) was bought by Brunei and Malaysia.

The new standard frigates were far too expensive for export. In 1959 Vosper began to develop a much less expensive corvette specifically for emerging navies. The Nigerian *Enyimiri* is shown at Portsmouth on 14 November 1979. She was a late version of the Vosper Thornycroft series (Mk 9). Visible right aft is her lightweight Seacat launcher. Forward are a 76mm gun and a Bofors ASW launcher, and aft is a 40mm gun. Such corvettes enjoyed far more export success than the 'Commonwealth frigate' based on Type 41, which was sold only to Ghana (and then cancelled as soon as the regime which had bought her was deposed). Even so, in the early 1960s it seemed that the New Commonwealth navies offered considerable sales opportunities for such ships. (James Goss via John Mortimer)

---

[34] DEFE 7/1097, a file on warship sales.

[35] Known examples are the Dutch *Tromp*, the Danish *Niels Juels* (KV72), and the Osprey 55 patrol craft (for Denmark, Greece, Morocco and Senegal). See, *eg* the in-house Yarrow history. The Dutch warship design history suggests that in the case of *Tromp* YARD was responsible for machinery design. According to the Yarrow history, export warship sales were killed mainly by very high inflation between the late 1970s and the mid-1980s. That was roughly the period of government ownership of the yard (1977–85).

CHAPTER 11

The Search for Numbers

One solution to the lack of fast escorts was to rebuild existing destroyers. HMS *Virago* is shown on 15 October 1952.

The British 1949 fleet plan called for a total of 182 frigates, including ships for trials and training: 107 A/S, fifty-nine A/A and sixteen A/D. This was a drastic reduction from the 1947 estimate that forty-six twelve-ship Escort Groups (552 ships) would be needed in war, thanks to assumed US assistance, but it was still a huge force. By early 1948 the envisaged wartime escort force was fifteen groups, each reduced to eight ships (120 operational frigates). On hand in 1949 were sixty-eight A/S and ninety-five A/A frigates, their proportion the opposite of what was needed. The A/S ships were two *Rocket* class (destroyer conversions), nineteen 'Loch' class, twenty-five 'Castle' class, and twenty-two 'River' class (with nine others already on the disposal list) which were clearly obsolete; almost none had been refitted since the war. The A/A ships were twenty 'Bay' class (including the despatch ships), HMS *Pelican*, twenty-four *Black Swan* class, and forty-nine 'Hunt' class. By October 1946 plans called for retaining 'Hunts' Types II, III, and IV; Type I 'Hunts' would be retained pending replacement by modern ships.[1] All the anti-aircraft ships had obsolete fire-control systems, and hence required modernisation. Given the high cost of maintaining ships in reserve, in May 1950 the Admiralty Board approved disposal of early 'Hunts' and the worst 'Rivers'. However, as soon as war broke out in Korea, disposals were stopped on the theory that the Soviets

would begin World War III with submarines comparable to those the Germans had used during the Second World War. Older ships were no longer so expendable – for the moment.

Under destroyer policy set in the spring of 1947, the surviving 'O' and 'P' class and the 'Tribal' to 'N' class destroyers which could economically be repaired were derated to escorts, subject to conversion.[2] The pre-war ships were soon disposed of and the War Emergency classes brought into the conversion programme. Controller asked for Staff Requirements for conversions to escorts. Against the calculated shortfall of thirty-nine A/S and sixteen A/D frigates, plans in 1950 called for building twelve new A/S and four new A/D frigates, leaving twenty-seven A/S and twelve A/D destroyer conversions. After transfers to friendly navies, a total of five 'M', five 'N', six Intermediate ('O' and 'P'), and forty-one 'Q' to 'Z' class War Emergency destroyers were available.

'Hunt' Class Modernisation – 1946

Apparently the 'Hunts' were the first ships considered for modernisation. On 15 August 1946 Director of Plans asked DNC and DUW to work out details of conversions of older destroyers and Type III 'Hunts' to A/S escorts. Approval would be sought for two conversions of each type in 1947 as prototypes.[3] The ships had grown appreciably in service, and an important issue was whether the required extra generating capacity (typically two 80 kW sets to replace the existing 60 kW, or a third 60 kW set) could be accommodated. The tentative Staff Requirement was under consideration by the end of 1946.[4] On 19 December 1946 DGD asked DNC to evaluate three alternative 'Hunt' class modernisations, the highest priority

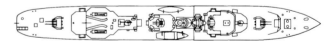

A drawing of a 'Hunt' class destroyer modified for the Royal Norwegian Navy gives some idea of abortive plans for upgrading Royal Navy ships of this type. The two Type II ships were taken over on a four-year loan basis in 1952 (it was made permanent in July 1956). They were refitted in 1954, X gun mount being replaced by double Squid. The light anti-aircraft battery was one twin Mk V and two single Mk 3 hand-worked Bofors. They retained two depth charge rails, six throwers, and fifty-seven depth charges. Similar ships transferred to the Royal Danish Navy were not fitted with Squids.

[1] 'Hunt' Class Cover, citing PO/OL 0157/45 of 21 October 1946.

[2] Note from Controller (Rear Admiral R McGrigor) to Dof D, DOD and DTSD, 3 April 1947, in answer to a query of 18 March.
[3] PD 023/46 of 15 August 1946, cited in 'Hunt' Class Cover. Notebook 528/8 (A W Wetherall) describes a proposed 'Hunt' III class A/S escort. X gun (twin 4in) would be replaced by a STAAG and the pompom by a Mk V twin Bofors. The single Bofors on the quarterdeck would be replaced by Double Squid, and ten Bidders would be carried; Type 144 sonar would be installed. The torpedo tubes, thirty depth charges (and four throwers and two rails) and the stabiliser would all be landed. Foxer and HF/DF would be installed. The modified ship would displace 1,240 tons, including 40 tons of ballast. A proposal dated 30 August 1946 was to replace Squid with Limbo (twenty salvoes) on the after deckhouse (in place of the STAAG), the Bidders being cut to six.
[4] DNC papers in the Brass Foundry, Vol. 78: DCNS turn-over notes, 21 January 1947.

going to a combination AA/AS ship. Version (i) had a twin 4in mount forward, controlled by an MRS (or a US Mk 61, an abortive director), a single Squid aft, and as many single Bofors as possible, with a Type 293 radar/TIU combination and a Type 277. Alternative (ii) had both one after twin 4in and the single Squid. Alternative (iii) had the two twin 4in, one twin Bofors capable of firing aft, and as many single Bofors as possible, but no Squid and no Type 277 radar. Sketches showed the forecastle extended well aft, with the Squid or the 4in gun mount (in option (iii)) on the quarterdeck. The forward 4in was raised to B position. In version (ii) a STAAG was in X position aft. Conversion would entail installation of a new bridge structure, and much of the new structure would have to be aluminium, to save weight. Displacement would have risen considerably, to 1,345 tons (light) and 2,125 tons (deep) in version (i) or 1,362 tons and 2,141 tons in (ii); no detailed calculations were done for (iii), which DNC considered the best of the lot.

'Hunt' class modernisation was still being investigated, albeit with low priority, in 1949. In September 1950, after rearmament had begun, an analysis of possible ASW upgrades showed single Squid on the after deckhouse in the A/A version and single Limbo in the same place in an ASW version. Neither figured in the frigate modernisation programme then being planned.

Destroyer Modernisation: Type 15

There was also interest in converting 'T' and later classes of destroyers to ASW ships. As understood early in 1947, the main features would be Limbo or Double Squid, six Bidder torpedoes, the latest Asdic, the latest anti-homing torpedo decoy (Foxer), modern communications, radar, AIO facilities, and a single twin 4in dual-purpose gun with blind-fire control.

A full Staff Requirement was developed in 1947 (TSD 2012/47) for conversion of HMS *Rocket* and *Relentless* to prototype A/S convoy escorts. Initially they were an interim alternative to the new-construction 1945 A/S Frigate, which had been abandoned due to lack of a suitable powerplant (see Chapter 10). Another forty-five ships would receive much

more modest conversion. In 1949, however, in connection with cuts accepted in the overall naval reconstruction plan (for achievement by 1957), the decision was taken to rebuild all fifty-seven available hulls to full standard.

The *Rocket* design (marked 'pre-T conversion') was presented to the Board in March 1949.[5] DNC observed that even though this was much like a new ship, no sketch design had been presented. The influence of the recent Bikini nuclear test showed: as much as possible was sheltered below decks, and the bridge extended only one level above. As required, the Operations Room was directly abaft the bridge, slightly lower in the ship. Lowering it provided a view aft through the bridge windows. There was no separate Gun Direction Room or chart house. The Bridge Wireless Office had to be placed below the Operations Room, because there was not enough space for it at forecastle-deck level. The ship's wheel was buried in the hull, on the upper deck immediately below the bridge.

The ship could be fought entirely closed-up, the CO using a periscope and the lookouts working from inside plastic bubbles. The revolutionary step was that they were designed to be fought from the fully-enclosed Operations Room rather than the bridge. That made good sense, particularly if the ship was co-operating with aircraft or with other ships. In practice, however, if nearby ships were manoeuvring fairly radically at high speed, the plot in the Operations Room gave insufficient information to avoid collisions. Naval officers on an open bridge judged the courses of nearby ships by their inclination, *ie* by their apparent courses. Typically an experienced officer always had to be kept on the bridge to ensure safety.[6]

To provide sufficient internal volume, the forecastle was extended aft. The forward superstructure went all the way across the ship. Its fore end was strengthened and curved to drive through waves breaking across the deck. To protect it, another breakwater was built across the forecastle. The fore end of the ship was strengthened against pounding, so that the ship could maintain 25kts in rough weather (she could meet the

[5] ADM 167/133, memo B.582 of 14 March 1949.
[6] Llewellyn Jones, 'The Royal Navy and the Challenge of the Fast Submarine 1946-1954' in R Harding (ed), *The Royal Navy 1930-2000: Innovation and Defence* (Frank Cass, London: 2004).

HMS *Rapid* was a standard Type 15 conversion. She is shown in 1953. The most striking feature was the very low superstructure, adopted to limit the effect of nuclear blast. She was fitted with Squid because Limbo was not yet available in quantity. The foretopmast carries UA-3 ESM under the HF/DF; both passive systems were considered useful submarine detectors (ESM could pick up a submarine's radar). (A D Baker III)

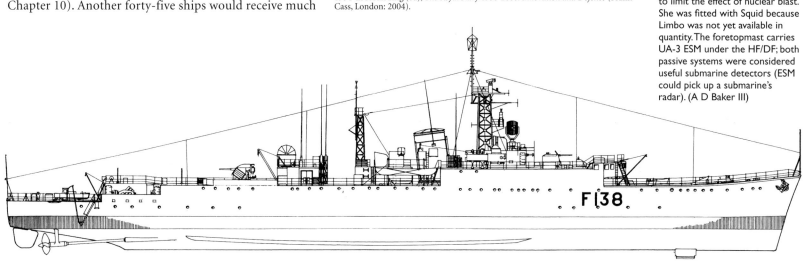

The planned main armament was double Limbo (aft) and ASW homing torpedoes. Limbo was placed on the upper deck, the two mountings being staggered, between high bulkheads with freeing ports to avoid creating a wave trap. Adjacent stowage held enough projectiles for twenty-two salvoes. The Staff Requirement called for three fixed torpedo tubes on each side (twelve torpedoes), but that was written when weapons were expected to be quite small; by 1949 they were expected to be more like 21in torpedoes. The 1949 requirement was two tubes and eight reloads. They could not fit on the upper deck, so instead eight single tubes (without reloads) were placed on the extended forecastle deck. This arrangement was shown in the building drawings, with the notation that any increase in weight (for more tubes) would require compensation. This armament was cancelled in 1953. Only HMS *Ulster* received the tubes, for tests of the system, which was planned for Type 12 frigates. Sonars were Types 170 and 172. Limbo required a stabiliser and plane-converter compartment and also an Asdic Instrument Room. Like the Stage I frigates, these ships initially had Squid rather than Limbo. The design included an allowance for a future anti-torpedo weapon.

Given their heavy steam plants, the Emergency Destroyers could not accommodate the big twin 4.5in gun, so the gun ar-

ABOVE: HMS *Relentless* was one of two Type 15 prototypes. This view emphasises her low bridge, adopted to minimise nuclear effects and curved so that seas could easily pass over her forecastle. She is shown on 23 July 1951.

The original low bridge was disliked for ship-handling, so the last few Type 15s had higher bridges similar to those of the new frigates. HMS *Ulster* is shown on 11 March 1957. The objects below her HF/DF array are her ESM antennas (UA-3/4 series).

The two prototype Type 15 conversions, HMS *Rocket* and *Relentless*, were intended to carry long ASW torpedoes. This is the arrangement envisaged. In fact the torpedoes were not available in time, and ultimately they were deleted from Type 15 (one ship, *Ulster*, tested them). (A D Baker III)

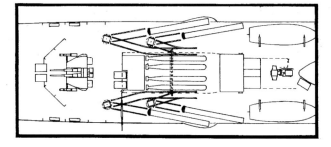

Staff Requirement, 28kts deep and dirty in the tropics). Internally, although the main transverse bulkheads were unchanged, practically all minor ones were new, and aluminium alloy was used extensively.

mament was cut to a twin 4in and a twin Bofors. Both had austere fire control systems: a blind-fire director for the 4in (CRBF) and the very simple STD for the twin Bofors. The twin 4in gun was placed aft to keep it dry and to avoid obstructing the view from the bridge. For gun direction, the ship had a Type 293Q target-indication radar feeding a TIU 2 in the Operations Room. The twin Bofors was placed atop the bridge. To limit superstructure forward, and to gain space and weight for the required Type 277Q surface-search radar, the visual and radar directors for the Bofors gun were amalgamated.

The two 155 kW turbo-generators were kept unchanged, but considerable additional diesel generating capacity was added: two 150 kW instead of one 50 kW in No. 1 Boiler Room,

HMS *Ulster* shows her original ASW armament, two Limbos and eight fixed tubes to fire Bidder homing torpedoes. The Bidder project predated Limbo, and through the 1950s it was the great hope for a weapon compatible with the coming generation of long-range sonars.

one 150 kW in No. 2; the 50 kW diesel in the Gearing Room was retained (it was impossible to provide a diesel generator outside the machinery spaces, for survivability). All of this needed fuel, but the new 4in magazine aft displaced some of the original fuel tankage. Given minor improvements expected to increase efficiency by 10 per cent, estimated endurance was 3,350nm at 15kts, six months out of dock in the tropics, which more than met the Staff Requirement of 3,000nm at 15kts. Nightshirt propeller silencing would be fitted. The result was considered quite successful, adding as much as twenty-five years to the ships' lives.

The draft version of the 1949–50 fleet plan showed twenty-seven Type 15 conversions: the two prototypes under the 1949/50 Programme, then six in 1950/1, three in 1951/2, four in 1952/3, four in 1953/4, four in 1955/6, and four in 1956/7. The programme accelerated after war broke out in Korea. Eleven ships were included in the 1950/1 supplemental programme, to be followed by another thirteen: one in 1951/2, six in 1952/3, and another six in 1953/4. By mid-1951 twenty conversions were planned, in addition to the two prototypes. Then there was interest in shifting to a simplified Type 18 (see below). As noted below, that was given up. Two ships initially earmarked for austere Type 16 conversions were replanned as Type 15s (only one was completed as such). For a time the programme totalled twenty-five ships. Like other parts of the rearmament programme, it encountered bottlenecks, the last of twenty-three ships not being completed until 1956.

The two Commonwealth countries which received

Emergency destroyers ordered analogous conversions. The wartime transfer of five 'Q' class destroyers to Australia was made permanent in June 1950 when the Australian government offered to pay for their Type 15 conversions. *Quadrant*, the first, had Squid; three others had Limbo. They differed slightly in appearance from the British ships, with round-fronted bridges and the twin Bofors forward of the bridge. *Quality* was not converted. The Canadian *Algonquin* and *Crescent* were converted on the lines of the new *St Laurent* class, *ie* analogously to Type 15 but with a very different appearance, and with a mix of British and US equipment, *eg* a US twin 3in/50 instead of a twin Bofors, and the forward mount on the forecastle. As in a Type 15, the helm and engine room telegraph were buried in the hull, in this case two decks below the bridge.[7] The ship was completed with Squid but was scheduled to receive Limbo (with Type 170 Asdic), and she was also scheduled to receive US-type fixed tubes for homing torpedoes (four tubes for twelve Mk 35s). The third ship, *Vancouver*, was completed with two separate Limbo wells aft, and with four single Mk 32 torpedo launchers for the US Mk 43 lightweight torpedo. In addition to her 3in guns, she had four single Bofors aft. South Africa bought *Wrangler* after she had been converted; the purchase of two other Type 15s (one would have been *Roebuck*) was cancelled.

---

[7] Evaluating HMCS *Algonquin* as an ASW ship in January 1954, US officers noted that placing these items deep in the ship eliminated the distractions of irrelevant noise and communications, but also eliminated the US Navy's preferred direct visual contact by the Officer of the Deck. Voice tubes imposed delays. This account makes no mention of the British practice, in Type 15s, of driving the ship from the Operations Room (CIC).

The Limited Conversion: Type 16

In January 1949 Director of Dockyards suggested that it might be faster to do the ten destroyer conversions following the first two to a more limited standard.[8] Conversion would begin in 1950/1, although much of the preparatory work would be included in the 1949/50 Estimates (some of it in the 1948/9 Programme). A sketch design was presented to the Board in March 1949.[9] Instead of extending the forecastle aft and cutting down all superstructure, only the bridge above the superstructure deck (formerly the signal deck) would be removed, replaced by a new structure topped by an enclosed bridge. The Operations Room would be immediately below the bridge. As in Type 15, there would be no separate Gun Direction Room or Weapons Control Room, these functions being performed from the Operations Room. containing the AIO and radar offices. The existing after deckhouse would be extended forward to add space, for example for a Bofors magazine. One twin 4in gun would be mounted in A position, and a twin Bofors in Y, with double Squid atop the after deckhouse. The forward quadruple torpedo tube would be retained to fire homing weapons. New sonar domes and sonars (Types 144Q2 and 147F to suit Squid) would be fitted. As in Type 15, the ships would have Type 277Q surface-search radar and Type 293Q target-indication radar (for TIU 2). The fore end would be stiffened against pounding in a head sea, and Nightshirt fitted.

However, cuts in the 1949/50 Estimates made this project impossible. Although it was soon concluded that three could be done to a lower standard within about a year beginning in 1949 (without modern radars, which would not be ready), the Staff decided that the limited conversion was not worthwhile; on 30 May 1949 the Board decided that it would be better to wait for full conversions. But that did not quite kill the idea of the austere conversion. A discussion in June 1949 revealed that it would take eighteen months to get a full conversion prototype, and sixteen months or more for follow-ons.[10] Compared to the new construction first-rate frigate which was about to be built, the full conversion offered similar Asdic and radar, but a less powerful gun and torpedo armament, at a somewhat lower price (£550,000–£600,000 compared to £1.33 million), more quickly (new construction would take 2½ years).

Controller argued that the Royal Navy would never get enough money for sufficient fast ASW frigates. On his own initiative he had Staff Requirements drawn up for the simplest and cheapest possible destroyer conversion, at an estimated cost less than half as much as a full conversion. Funds could be added to the 1950/1 Programme to convert HMS *Tenacious* on this basis. Controller saw her as the prototype of a vastly-expanded programme, to be undertaken 'whenev-

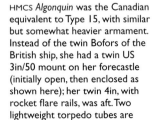

ABOVE: HMCS *Crescent*, shown early in 1962, was the Canadian equivalent to Type 15. Both she and her near-sister *Algonquin* had their main guns on the forecastle rather than aft (4in in her case, 3in/50 in *Algonquin*'s). The gallows aft is associated with a VDS, probably the SQS-504 adopted by the Royal Navy as Type 199 or CAST (Canadian Sonar, Towed). Radars are the US-supplied SPS-10 and -12 (air search).

BELOW: HMAS *Quickmatch* was the Royal Australian Navy version of the Type 15 frigate conversion. Note the raised wheelhouse, which was not as large as that in the last few Royal Navy Type 15s (*Troubridge*, *Ulster* and *Zest*).

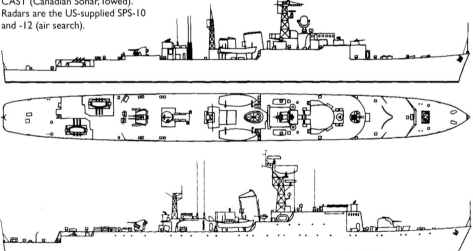

HMCS *Algonquin* was the Canadian equivalent to Type 15, with similar but somewhat heavier armament. Instead of the twin Bofors of the British ship, she had a twin US 3in/50 mount on her forecastle (initially open, then enclosed as shown here); her twin 4in, with rocket flare rails, was aft. Two lightweight torpedo tubes are shown in her waist, and she has a pair of Limbos aft. The two Bofors guns abeam the funnel were in Boffin mounts (adapted twin power Oerlikon mounts). The other Canadian ship, HMCS *Crescent*, had her main armament in opposite positions, the 4in guns being forward. Like the new Canadian frigates, these ships had prominent superstructures rather than British-style structures nearly buried in their hulls. The big air-search radar was a US SPS-12. The ship is shown as refitted with a prominent funnel cap, whose absence initially distinguished her from her half-sister.

[8] ADM 167/133, memo B.592 of 10 June 1949.
[9] ADM 167/133, memo B.583 of 14 March 1949, based on Staff Requirement TSD 2052/49 of 6 January 1949, and sketch DNC 38/270.
[10] ADM 167/135, memo B.623 of 4 Februxary 1950.

er the financial situation allows or the political situation requires'. He asked for Board approval. First Sea Lord supported him: even the full conversion had real limits, and it would have a short life when completed.

DNC presented the conversion design in July 1950, just after the outbreak of war in Korea apparently presented exactly the political situation Controller had had in mind. It was designed to minimise dockyard work. Existing gun foundations would be used. Because the bridge would not be rebuilt (but the director would be removed), potential AIO size was limited. The AIO and the former Asdic Office were combined to form a new Operations Room, a new Asdic Control Room being built in the old signal office and part of the cross passage (a new signal office replaced the earlier Type 291 radar office). The view trunk from the bridge down to the plot was moved to suit the position of the new ARL table (dead-reckoning

table) in the Operations Room below. The ASW battery would be the same as that proposed a few months earlier, double Squid and, potentially, four homing torpedoes from the remaining quadruple tubes. The wartime Asdics would be upgraded, Type 144Q2 being replaced by Type 166Z and Type 147B to Type 147F; Type 162 would be fitted. The fore end would be stiffened and the machinery improved, as in Type 15. The only additional generating power was a 50 kW diesel generator in No. 2 boiler room (a 150 kW unit was being considered). DNC thought that single Limbo could later replace double Squid, but that was ruled out on weight grounds. Later it was pointed out that Limbo required much more internal space – which was not available – for an Asdic Control Room for its Type 170. The twin 4in mount was placed in B position. Single Bofors would replace the Oerlikons on the bridge wings and on the searchlight platform; a twin Bofors with

HMS *Orwell* was a minelaying destroyer converted into a Type 16 frigate. She is shown as completed. By 1954 the three single Bofors and the Squids had all been removed. She had retained her minelaying capability. A near-sister, *Petard*, was converted into a minelayer after having undergone Type 16 conversion (completed September 1957 as a minelayer). (A D Baker III)

Type 16 was the low-end equivalent to Type 15. HMS *Tenacious* is shown in December 1952.

The smaller 'O' and 'P' class destroyers could not accommodate as many Bofors guns. HMS *Paladin* is shown on 3 March 1954.

STD director was on the Bofors platform in lieu of the previous pair of single Mk III guns. Another single Bofors was in Y position on the quarterdeck. This heavy anti-aircraft battery was the sole advantage the limited conversion enjoyed compared to a Type 15. HMS *Tenacious* (1950/1 Programme) was designated Type 16, the limited or partial conversion.

Nine more ships were included in the Korean War supplemental programme, plus another seven projected as of August 1951, for a total of seventeen. Once *Tenacious* had been completed in 1952, she was criticised for her very cramped bridge and Operations Room. In July 1953 a meeting chaired by First Sea Lord agreed that the rest of the Type 16 programme should be cancelled as too expensive and not worthwhile. The class was to have included all of the Intermediate destroyers, too small to be Type 15s or 18s. Cancellation left three in the programme (*Orwell*, *Paladin* and *Petard*); in September the Board decided to retain the other three (*Opportune*, *Obedient* and *Obdurate*) as fast minelaying destroyers. *Paladin* (in 1957) and *Orwell* were fitted as minelayers, with a capacity of thirty mines. Three more Emergency Destroyers (*Termagant*, *Tuscan* and *Tyrian*) had already been completed. Type 16 conversion could not easily be halted in three ships (*Teazer*, *Terpsichore* and *Tumult*) in hand at private yards. They were, however, improved with a redesigned (frigate-style) bridge an enlarged operations room. In September 1953 two War Emergency destroyers (*Troubridge* and *Savage*) scheduled for conversion were shifted, for the moment, to Type 18s. *Troubridge* would be taken in hand at Portsmouth in September 1953, and progressed as economically as possible. *Savage* would not be taken in hand until September 1955. *Troubridge* ended up as a Type 15 (see below), but conversion of *Savage* was can-

celled when priorities shifted in 1955.

Pakistan received three 'O' class destroyers, of which *Onslow* and *Onslaught* were converted to Type 16s using US MDAP funds under an agreement dated 29 April 1957. Australian and Canadian ASW conversions of surviving 'Tribal' class destroyers might be considered a step down from Type 16. The Australian conversion entailed installation of single Squid on the quarterdeck in place of Y 4.7in gun mount; the anti-aircraft battery was one twin Mk 5 and four single Mk 7 Bofors.[11] Ships received modern fire-control systems (Mk VI directors with Flyplane) and modern sonars (Types 170 and 174). Search radars were Type 293Q and Type 974. The torpedo tubes were retained. *Arunta* and *Warramunga* were converted, but conversion of *Bataan* was cancelled due to the high cost of the first two.

Canada retained seven 'Tribals', all of which were modernised immediately after the Second World War. They had originally differed from the British version in that the pompom was mounted on the after superstructure. Of the four built in Canada, the first pair essentially duplicated the British version, with six 4.7in and two 4in anti-aircraft guns and the Mk III(W) director. The last two Canadian-built ships, *Cayuga* and *Athabaskan*, were completed with four twin 4in

[11] The Australian modernisation project began in 1949 (Admiralty comments are dated January 1950). Sacrificing one gun mount for Squid accorded with Admiralty preference for double rather than single Squid. The RAN proposed to keep the existing fire control system in the expectation that it would be replaced in three or four years, to retain the existing pompom (to be replaced by two Bofors when available), to fit six power-worked single Bofors (Mk VII), to retain torpedo tubes if possible, and to replace the existing Type 144 Asdic with Type 164. Given the potential for a modern dual-purpose fire control system, the Admiralty proposed replacing the 4.7in guns with 4in, as in the Canadian ships. Substituting a Mk V twin 40mm gun for the pompom would simplify the ships' close-range batteries. The ships would get with new Type 293Q radars. The Australians wanted an air-search radar to replace their old Type 286, but the Admiralty advised them to forego such a set altogether (the Australians wanted their fleet destroyers to carry out the 'Tomcat' and 'Watchdog' picket functions). Completed later than her two sisters, *Bataan* had a US SC-2 air-search radar and six single Bofors in addition to her pompom.

The last few Type 16s had new frigate-type bridges. HMS *Teazer* is shown on 16 May 1955.

and Mk VI directors, the pompom being replaced by a Mk V twin Bofors, with four single Bofors replacing the wartime 20mm guns. The first ship to receive ASW modernisation was HMCS *Micmac*, severely damaged in a collision on 16 July 1947. She received double Squid in A position and a US-type quadruple Bofors in B. When ships were rebuilt, their Y mountings were replaced by a double Squid (possible due partly to the ships' greater beam). In the early 1950s the earlier ships had their 4.7in guns forward replaced by twin 4in, so the class had a uniform armament (although the earlier ships never got Mk VI directors). An additional modernisation (1951–5) left these ships with two twin 4in forward and a US-type twin 3in/50 aft, plus four single Bofors, the quadruple torpedo tubes, and Squid. The 4in guns were controlled by a US Mk 63 system, which included an on-mount radar dish for B mount. It replaced the old DCT, the raised director (Mk III or Mk VI) remaining. Ships were fitted with US SPS-6C air-search radars and with Canadian Sperry surface-search sets. In addition the

last pair of Canadian-built ships retained their British Type 293 radars. Canada applied a kind of sub-Type 16 conversion to one Emergency destroyer, HMCS *Sioux* (ex-*Vixen*). She retained her forward 4.5in guns and her forward superstructure, but her after superstructure was replaced by a large deckhouse carrying double Squid.

Type 18

Because funds were being freed for rearmament, it is no surprise that attempts were made to develop something more satisfactory than a Type 15, but not as expensive. This became Type 18. The key issue was whether Limbo could be installed in a fleet destroyer at a cost less than that of Type 15. At the end of June 1950, before Type 15 was presented to the Board, DTSD asked whether that could be done in a Type 16. That turned out to be possible; Limbo could replace the torpedo tubes, or it could be placed atop the after deckhouse. The issue became critical when DTASW reported that recent trials had

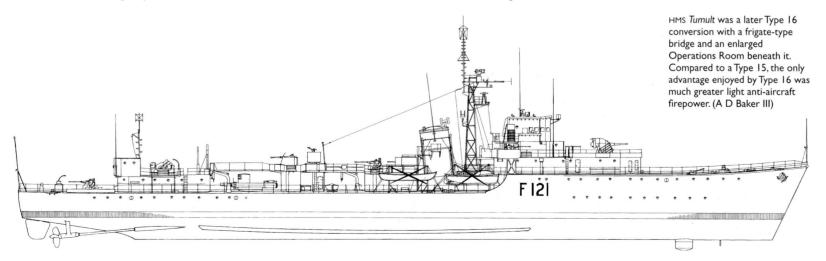

HMS *Tumult* was a later Type 16 conversion with a frigate-type bridge and an enlarged Operations Room beneath it. Compared to a Type 15, the only advantage enjoyed by Type 16 was much greater light anti-aircraft firepower. (A D Baker III)

shown that against a fast submarine double Squid was not an acceptable austere alternative to double Limbo. DNC argued against wasting valuable destroyer hulls with second-rate conversions, while Director of Plans feared the effect on the overall programme of a third conversion design. However, if Type 18 were good enough, it could replace both Type 15 *and* Type 16 at a considerable saving. A Staff Requirement (TSD 4376/50) was issued on 25 August 1950, and Controller approved a

HMCS *Sioux* was a Canadian equivalent to a Type 16. She is shown on 21 January 1954. The two shrouded objects aft are her two Squids.

sketch of this 'fused' conversion on 29 August. DTSD asked that design work begin in November. Instead of the planned twelve Type 15s and fourteen Type 16s, DNC proposed stopping Type 16 at six ships (after *Tenacious*) and doing all twenty others as Type 18s. That was approved, and in April 1951 DNC expected that the design would be ready in 1952.

The sketch design was presented to the Board in July 1951 as a replacement for Types 15 and 16, with much the capability of Type 15 (except for the fixed torpedo tubes and Type 277Q radar) but with reduced habitability (albeit somewhat better than Type 16).[12] Reducing habitability eliminated the need for the expensive aft extension of the forecastle of the Type 15. The Type 15 bridge having been criticised as too low, the bridge (with adjacent Operations Room) was raised one deck above the forecastle. Bridge arrangements were similar to those in Type 15 but with open wings. It was 100ft from the stem, rather than 80ft back as in Type 15. The Operations Room was only slightly smaller than in a Type 15 (550 sq ft vs 580 sq ft). As in Type 15, it provided weapons direction.

Gun mounts used existing gun supports wherever possible: the Bofors was on a bandstand in A position (with a simple STD director atop the bridge) and the 4in in Y position.

As in a Type 15, the ship had GDS 2* (lacking in Type 16), the existing Type 293M radar being modernised to Type 293Q. As in a Type 16, a set of quadruple torpedo tubes was retained for homing weapons, but Type 18 had the desired Double Limbo (in the position of the previous torpedo tubes), with Asdics to match (Types 170, 172 and 162, as in Type 15). Because the new long-range Type 177 sonar was nearing reality, Type 18 offered what neither Type 15 nor Type 16 did, provision for a large (150in) second dome, and a large enough Asdic Control Room. Diesel generator capacity was slightly less than in Type 15, 400 kW rather than 500 kW, but far more than in Type 16 (250 kW). Estimated speed was 29kts deep and dirty in the tropics, with endurance of 3,620nm at 15kts. Type 18 was expected to cost two-thirds as much as Type 15 and to save three months. The £200,000 saving was about half the cost of a Type 16 conversion.

At a meeting on 31 May 1951 in advance of Board consideration of the new design, the SDPC suggested that it be substituted at once for Type 16, but perhaps not for Type 15. Plans called for twenty-seven Type 15 (including the two prototypes) and eighteen Type 16. The SDPC proposed substituting Type 18 for eight Type 16. Nothing was done for the moment, because even Type 16 conversions were being slowed by the sheer size of the rearmament programme. In December Controller delivered an unpleasant shock. Perhaps unsurprisingly, the rather capable Type 18 would not be too much less expensive than a Type 15 (at this point, £800,000 vs £950,000). Worse, Type 18 would consume the one resource in really short supply, design effort. Controller suggested abandoning Type 18 altogether, using the money on as many Type 15s as possible. He hoped to lose only two or three ships in the process. For the available £8.8 million he could have eleven Type 18s or nine Type 15s or six Type 15s and five Type 16s (with the improved bridge).

The ships scheduled for Type 18 conversion were the five surviving 'N' class (*Noble*, *Napier*, *Nizam*, *Norman* and *Nepal*) and six Emergency Destroyers (*Zest*, *Zealous*, *Zephyr*, *Zambesi*, *Troubridge* and *Savage*). *Troubridge* was already in hand at Portsmouth, and *Zest* was soon to be taken in hand. Controller ordered both completed as Type 15s, and proposed doing the next four ships (presumably the Emergency class). The rest of the programme could be decided in a year's time.[13] The Board agreed; Type 18 was dead. The only surviving trace of Type 18 thinking was redesign of the last three Type 15s (*Troubridge*, *Ulster* and *Zest*) with a new enclosed frigate-style bridge raised to the top of the superstructure deck (as in Type 18) and the twin Bofors relocated to the forward end of that deck.

Type 62

As not enough new A/D frigates could be built, a destroyer

12 ADM 167/137 (1951), Memo B.712 of 2 July 1951, in accordance with Controller's approval on 29 August 1950 of the proposal in DTSD 4376/50 of 25 August 1950.

13 The 'N' class were similar to, but hardly identical to, the Emergency destroyers, hence would have required new drawings.

conversion (Type 62) was planned. The initial choice fell on the 'M' class. They differed enough from the other surviving wartime destroyers that new plans would have had to be drawn for any type of conversion, hence they could not simply duplicate the other A/S conversions. In their case the necessary space would be provided by extending the forward deckhouse forward and aft to a total length of 80ft.[14] A twin 4in gun would have been mounted on the forward extension of the super-structure deck. Another level would be built atop it, and a new enclosed bridge (with wings) atop that, with a CRBF director on top. On the level below the bridge were the Operations Room, Bridge Wireless Office, and the chart house. The after deckhouse was also considerably enlarged. A twin Bofors would have been mounted on the quarterdeck (with STD director on the deckhouse), and two single Bofors on either side of the deckhouse. Squid would have been placed in a recess on the side of the after deckhouse. The forward lattice mast would have been raised and strengthened to take a Type 293Q radar and the new Type 974. A new pole forward of the mainmast would have carried a YE aircraft homing beacon. Other radars would have been Type 960 and the Type 982/983 picket radar combination. To provide sufficient power, three 150 kW units would have replaced the 60 kW diesel generators. The other ships proposed were the 'Z' class, including the leader *Myngs*, but excluding *Zest*, which received the ASW conversion. These ships were considerably smaller than the 'Ms'. A sketch design showed a twin 4in in B position, as in the 'M' class conversion, but only a twin Bofors aft, and single Squid. The lighter Type 277Q radar would have replaced Type 983.

By July 1952, three of the Emergency destroyers had been dropped from the programme. DTSD wanted the remaining Emergency hulls for A/S frigates; because they were smaller than the 'Ms' they would make unsatisfactory A/D ships.

[14] Notebook 848/3 (T E Darby).

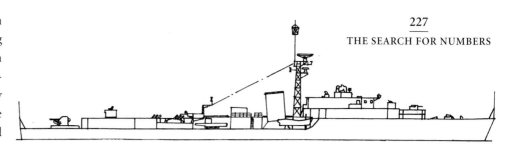

By mid-1953 only the five 'M' class conversions remained. The project was killed during the 1955 review; the destroyers were sold to Turkey. It may have been argued that the new Type 81, with its limited picket capability, could effectively replace Type 62.[15]

Anti-Aircraft Frigate Modernisation

Existing anti-aircraft frigates were fast enough for convoy operations, but they needed new fire control systems. In July 1949 Controller noted that the Western Union (predecessor of NATO) gave priority in anti-aircraft modernisation to frigates (DNO preferred destroyers). Plans for the two most valuable classes, the *Black Swans* and the 'Bays', showed the new MRS 3 fire control system, with CRBFD as an alternative. However, MRS 3 would not be available until 1954, and maximum CRBFD production for the next two years had

[15] The initial version of the 1955 Radical Review cut four A/D frigate conversions, presumably leaving only one, which would not have been worthwhile.

BELOW: Australian 'Tribal' class as rebuilt post-war, with Squid aft.

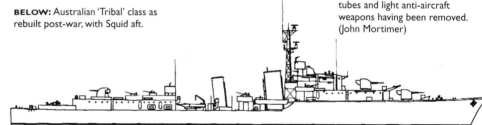

Type 18 was a compromise between the sophisticated Type 15 and the more affordable Type 16; note the torpedo tubes of the latter, and the Limbo, low bridge, and limited gun armament of the former. This sketch is based on a profile in the National Maritime Museum. (Author)

BOTTOM: The Royal Australian Navy modernised two of its three 'Tribal' class destroyers for ASW capability, replacing the after twin 4.7in mount with double Squid. HMAS *Arunta* is shown on January 1969, in reserve; her torpedo tubes and light anti-aircraft weapons having been removed. (John Mortimer)

That was extended in 1951 to the entire 'Bay' and *Black Swan* (and very similar HMS *Pelican*) classes. Director of Plans wanted to rearm the best of the ships the 'Bay' class, with US-supplied 3in/50 guns and, presumably, with MRS 3 fire controls. The earlier ships would have retained their 4in guns (one being surrendered as weight compensation) and would have had the Mk 6M/Flyplane combination. All structure above the signal deck would have been rebuilt. A new enclosed bridge (with open wings) would be similar to that in a Type 41 frigate. The deckhouse on the quarterdeck would be rebuilt to provide a new sickbay, moved up from the mess decks to relieve overcrowding. The funnel would be moved 12ft aft to reduce the director's blind arc aft, as one of the two 4in mounts would be in Y position (the other would be in B position). Single Squid would be installed. As in other contemporary conversions, increased generator power would be needed, in the form of 160 kW turbo-generators to replace the earlier 70 or 80 or 100 kW units, and a 150 kW diesel generator instead of the 70 kW unit abreast the engine room. The relevant Staff Requirement was approved on 27 August 1951 and a sketch design presented to the Board in July 1953.[16]

Bottlenecks in the rearmament programme drastically slowed this project; in January 1953 it had been reduced to two *Black Swans*. Detailed study showed that they would be quite expensive (about £500,000); in December 1953 the Board was not sure it was affordable. A draft of cuts to be made due to the 1955 Radical Review included substitution of eleven partial *Black Swan* modernisations for the original full ones. Little could be done, but the *Black Swans* survived into the 1960s because they were valued for the policing role which survived the abandonment of preparations for World War III (*ie* for convoy ASW). The 'Bays' were not modernised.

Full modernisation of the 'Hunts' was not planned, but in December 1952 DGD pointed out that they were hardly capable of self-defence. US Mk 63 systems might be sought under the MDAP programme.[17] Director of Plans agreed that their high speed made them potentially useful. It might be worth seeking 3in/50s for them. Again, nothing could be done.

ASW Frigate Modernisation

Initial Korean War mobilisation plans (September 1950) included modernisation of the 'Loch' class, with a better sonar (Type 144Q2 or Type 164) and a better radar (Type 277Q in place of Type 277). A twin 4in would have replaced the single mount forward, a twin Bofors Mk 5 would have replaced the pompom, and four single Bofors would have replaced the Oerlikons. The radar office would have been enlarged, and the wheelhouse converted to an Operations Room. The Korean War supplemental programme envisaged thirteen modernisations (the prototype to be taken in hand in 1951). In 1951

ABOVE: HMCS *Micmac* was trials ship for Squid in the Royal Canadian Navy. When repaired after collision damage, she was fitted with a single Squid in A position and a US quadruple Bofors in B. *Micmac* is shown in February 1950. Note the US-type HF/DF at her masthead. As modernised, Canadian 'Tribals' retained their twin 4.7in guns forward and had their Squids aft. (RCN)

RIGHT: The Royal Canadian Navy modernised 'Tribal' class destroyer *Cayuga* (218), which retained the British Mk VI director, and was fitted with a US SPS-6 air-search radar (unlike others of the class which had the US Mk 63 anti-aircraft fire control system, with a radar dish on B gunshield). All modernised ships had US twin 3in/50s aft. *Haida* of this class survives as a museum ship in Toronto.

already been allocated. The alternative, which was also being adopted for the new construction frigates, was the much bulkier combination of a Mk 6 director and Flyplane (FPS 5), equivalent to most of a destroyer fire-control system. It required nearly doubling the space in the below-decks computer room (Transmitting Station). The director would weigh 10.5 tons rather than 3.5 tons, and weight compensation would have to be found, *eg* by removing the STAAG planned for the *Black Swans*. DNO wanted to defer modernisation until at least a majority could get MRS 3. Destroyers could accept the new fire control system at a more limited price in other armament.

The Korean War swept such arguments aside, not least because it was assumed that new fire-control systems could be made much more quickly. Under the Korean War supplemental programme, nine frigates were to receive A/A modernisation (work on the prototype to begin in October 1952).

[16] ADM 167/143, Memo B.853 of 24 July 1953.
[17] ADM 1/23485.

Although the Royal Navy did not modernise its 'River' class frigates, the Royal Canadian Navy did; many of its ships were younger, and in effect were equivalent to the British 'Loch' class. This is HMCS *Jonquiere*. Her two Squids are under the hatches on deck aft, her forecastle having been extended alongside them.

that expanded to full modernisation of all nineteen 'Loch' and twenty-four 'Castle' class.

A 'Loch' class modernisation programme begun in 1953 was limited to seven ships (*Loch Alvie*, *Loch Fada*, *Loch Fyne*, *Loch Insh*, *Loch Killisport*, *Loch Lomond* and *Loch Ruthven*). Their single 4in gun was replaced by a twin mount with a director at the after end of the bridge, and the close-range battery replaced by one twin (Mk V) and four single Bofors. Type 277 radar was retained but communications equipment was modernised. The 'Castle' class was not modernised. Under the abortive plan, the single 4in gun would have been replaced and Type 293Q radar (*ie* GDS 2) installed. At least as initially proposed, homing torpedoes would have been provided. Ships remaining in service after the war did get improved radar and single 40mm guns in place of their 20mm. In the 1950s ships received Type 974 high-definition surface-search radar (as a snorkel detector).

As an indication of what might be envisaged in a wider mobilisation, a list dated March 1951 of ASW equipment for ships unable to carry Limbo and the associated Type 170 sonar included installation of Squid (with fifteen rounds) in place of the 4in guns of existing *Algerine* class ocean minesweepers. These ships already had the wartime destroyer sonars (Types 144Q and 147B) needed to control Squid. At least four ships were so fitted: *Espiegle*, *Mutine*, *Orestes* and *Pluto*. Their gun armament was reduced to four Bofors; in effect they were corvette replacements. Other ships had their 4in guns landed but did not have Squids fitted: these were *Hound*, *Lennox*, *Plucky*, *Recruit*, *Rifleman* and *Wave*. *Chameleon* and *Waterwitch* may have had Squids. Note that the abortive 1954 Ocean Minesweeper would have had one Squid with thirty-four rounds, including those in the barrels. Consideration was also given to fitting trawlers with Squids; that would have involved considerable difficulty.

Although the Royal Navy seems not to have considered modernising the well-worn 'Rivers', the Canadians rebuilt

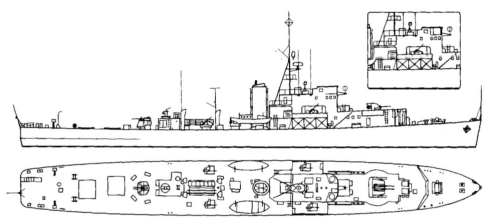

many of theirs. When war planning became urgent after 1948, ships which had been placed on the sale list, and transferred for sale, were frozen by government order and designated a strategic reserve. Modernisation began during the Korean War. HMCS *Prestonian* was the prototype (rebuilt 1951–3). Her forecastle was extended right aft to enclose a pit containing double Squid, and her bridge considerably enlarged, the funnel being raised to keep it clear of smoke. The twin 4in was kept in B position, other anti-aircraft weapons being one twin (Mk V) and four single (Mk 9) Bofors. Twenty more were converted during 1958, the only exceptions among surviving Canadian 'Rivers' being the weather ships *St. Catherines* and *Stonetown*. The Australian 'River' class frigates were fitted with Squids under an earlier programme (see Chapter 7).

The Royal Canadian Navy rebuilt 'River' class frigates in the early 1950s to this *Prestonian* class design. British 'River' class frigates were considered too tired to be worth modernising.

Destroyer Modernisation

The 1949 fleet plan called for thirty destroyers (twenty-six 'C' class and four 'Weapon' class) to be modernised to the point where in wartime they could lead A/S Support Groups. Command and AIO facilities would be improved as much as possible. By May 1950 the Admiralty Board had approved fitting a second automatic plot to maintain a wide-area ASW picture. Habitability would also be improved. Although not counted as frigates, ships so modernised would be somewhat

superior to the austere Type 16s (albeit with surface rather than anti-aircraft firepower).

Initial attention focussed on the 'Ca' class, the least capable of the 'Cs'. For AAW, ships would receive the Mk VI director (which DGD considered essential), even though they lacked space for the full Flyplane system (180 sq ft in their transmitting stations, compared to the 400 sq ft required). Ultimately a new compact version of Flyplane was installed. The 4.5in guns were fitted with the associated RPC. As in the 1942 Emergency Destroyers, weight compensation for the new director would be one set of torpedo tubes. That was controversial, because as these plans were being drawn British naval intelligence was reporting that the Soviets had begun a large cruiser programme. War experience showed that destroyer torpedoes were often the only defence a convoy could have

against such ships, and it would take a salvo of at least eight of them to be sure of hitting a single freely-manoeuvring high-speed target. However, the ASW torpedo salvo would be only one or two (with reloads). In May 1949 a staff meeting on Staff Requirements accepted that the cost of effective AAW and ASW modernisation (the Mk VI director and Squid) would be one set of tubes. DGD hoped that given a future lighter version of Mk VI (for which no development capacity was available), the second set of tubes could be restored. The four Oerlikons could be replaced by single Bofors, but STAAG could not replace the existing twin Bofors. Weight compensation, the two single Bofors around the bridge, would have left the ship with a large blind arc forward. DNC had favoured eliminating just these guns to expand the bridge structure to accommodate Asdic, AIO and radio spaces. Ultimately space

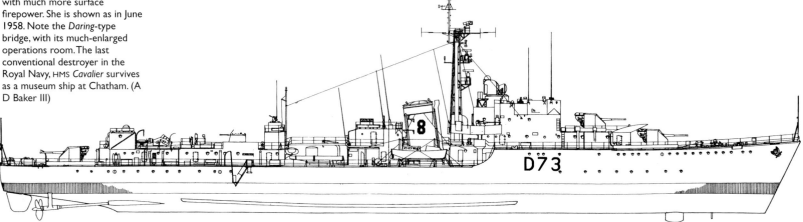

HMS *Cavalier* was extensively modernised to something approaching Type 16 standard, but with much more surface firepower. She is shown as in June 1958. Note the *Daring*-type bridge, with its much-enlarged operations room. The last conventional destroyer in the Royal Navy, HMS *Cavalier* survives as a museum ship at Chatham. (A D Baker III)

As modernised, 'Ca' class destroyers might be considered one step down from Type 16, or one step up to fleet capability. HMS *Cavendish* is shown on 4 March 1957, double Squid having replaced her X 4.5in gun. The *Daring* type bridge provided much more operations room space.

The second group of four 'Ca' class ships modernised (*Caesar*, *Cambrian*, *Caprice* and *Cassandra*) had enclosed frigate-type bridges and only a single Bofors (if any) aft. It was to have been replaced by Seacat, but that was done in only two ships. HMS *Cambrian* is shown in the Straits of Johore in April 1964 during the Indonesian Confrontation.

would be provided by installing a new bridge structure similar to that in the *Daring* class. It would provide an enlarged Operations Room, A/S Room, and 3rd Wireless Office. The only available near-term ASW weapon was Squid. Double Squid could replace No. 3 gun or single Squid No. 4. In either case the ship could not retain all four 4.5in guns. The much superior double Squid was chosen although the remaining gun had worse arcs than No. 3. Ammunition supply was ten salvoes (sixty rounds) in a new structure atop an extended after deckhouse which replaced the after set of torpedo tubes. Asdics were Types 147F, 166 and 172, and Type 162 to detect bottomed submarines.

The ship would be fitted for both TSDS and the Unifoxer torpedo decoy. Provision was also made for later installation of the Nightshirt propeller silencer. The two 155 kW turbo-generators were retained, but the 50 kW diesel generators in the boiler rooms were replaced by 150 kW units (the 50 kW diesel in the gearing room remained). Provision for additional diesel fuel somewhat reduced oil fuel capacity. As of August 1950 recent inclining experiments showed that the 'Ca' class had grown 115 tons, so some weights had to be cut. The close-range anti-aircraft battery had to be cut (to two) by two single Bofors guns and allowance for reload anti-submarine torpedoes eliminated. Approved Staff Requirements were issued in January 1951 and building drawings submitted to the Board in January 1952.[18]

Meanwhile DTSD decided, as noted above, that nothing short of Limbo could deal with a fast submarine, and DUW agreed. DNC estimated that a 'C' class destroyer could take one Limbo mounting in place of each of her two after gun mounts. Both sets of torpedo tubes and all depth charges would

be surrendered. Alternatively, one Limbo mounting could replace No. 3 gun (in place of double Squid), but in that case the twin Bofors would have to be surrendered, leaving the ship no close-range anti-aircraft weapon firing aft. In fact Limbo was reserved for new ships and for some destroyers converted for ASW.

Plans initially called for taking the prototype, HMS *Carron*, in hand in March 1952, and the next four in January 1953. However, the initial programme was cut short at four ships. Modernisation of the other four affected overall destroyer planning later in the 1950s.[19] The last pair, *Caesar* and *Cassandra*, were not completed until 1959. Five ships were fitted for rearmament with Seacat instead of the 40mm gun (*Cavendish*, *Cavalier*, *Carysfort*, *Cambrian* and *Caprice*), but only *Cavalier* and *Caprice* were actually so armed.

Of the later 'C' class, in 1950 plans called for partially modernising seven 'Ch' and six 'Co' class: one in 1952–3, four in 1953–4, and eight in 1954–5, leaving one 'Ch', two 'Co' and two 'Cr' class for full modernisation. The other 'Cr' class ships had all been transferred abroad, and the two survivors assigned to the 3rd Training Squadron at Londonderry. In 1948 B gun was replaced by a deckhouse. Both had been laid up by 1954; they were sold to Pakistan in 1958. The projected full modernisations were never carried out. All of these ships already had Mk VI directors, which were to be replaced by the new MRS 7 (combining Mk VI with a new computer). The existing close-range anti-aircraft armament would be replaced by one twin Bofors and four single mounts (two forward, two amidships). Double Squid would replace No. 3 gun mount, the forty-two projectiles (not the sixty of the full conversion)

---

[18] ADM 167/138, memo B. 752, 21 January 1952, to TSD 4038/51.

[19] The initial version of the 1955 Radical Review would have eliminated five of the eight 'Ca' class modernisations, but that was cut back to four.

being accommodated in the former depth-charge store. Refits would be carried out at Singapore and Malta in 1952–3.[20] Most of the 'Ch' class were modernised in 1954. Unlike the 'Ca' class, they retained their wartime bridges. Not modernised, *Chivalrous* was transferred to Pakistan. Of this class, *Chaplet* and *Chieftain* were equipped to lay mines, surrendering their torpedo tubes and Y gun when carrying mines. Of the eight 'Co' class, *Constance* and *Comus* were listed for disposal in 1955 and thus were not modernised. Four ships (*Cockade*, *Cossack*, *Consort* and *Concord*) remained in the Far East, unmodernised, returning home only for disposal. *Comet* and *Contest* were modernised and fitted for minelaying.

In 1950, before the Korea War, plans also called for interim modernisation of twelve of the 1942 'Battle' class. For these and the 'C' class, Controller approved on the understanding that equipment was available, that there was sufficient dockyard and design capacity, and that time in hand would not exceed twelve weeks. The Korean War programme envisaged full modernisation of eight of the twelve, but that seems not to have been done.[21] Instead, all were scheduled for interim modernisation. Two STAAGs replaced the Hazemeyers and a single Squid replaced the quarterdeck Bofors. Ships retained four single Bofors (in some cases modernisation included replacement of existing 2pdrs by Bofors guns). The first modernised ship was HMS *Barfleur*.[22] Before transfer to Pakistan in 1956, *Cadiz* and *Gabbard* had their STAAGs replaced by Mk V mounts with separate directors (STDs), a change extended to most of the ships in British service.

As of August 1951 plans called for full modernisation of four 1943 'Battles' plus partial modernisation of the other four. These ships had all been completed with two STAAGs, a Mk V 'utility' Bofors, and Squid on the quarterdeck. Ultimately four ships were converted to radar pickets instead, the other four not being modernised at all. There was some interest in fitting Limbo instead of Squid. In a 1942 'Battle', depending on where Limbo was placed, the alternatives were to land (a) depth charges, two STAAGs and their ammunition or one STAAG and one set of torpedo tubes and one single Bofors; or (b) the depth charges, one set of tubes, and a single Bofors; or (c) the depth charges. In a 1943 'Battle' the price was the single Squid and the single 4.5in gun and, in one case, the after

[20] ADM 167/137, memo by DNC dated 31 May 1951. The Staff Requirement was TSD 2115/49 of 22 December 1949.
[21] Full modernisation would have entailed installation of GDS 3 (or 2 or 2*), Types 166 (or 164 and a US QHB), 147F and 162 sonar, Types 974 and 293Q radar, pentad torpedo tubes, double Squid (ten salvoes), and the Unifoxer torpedo decoy, as well as more modern radios. Additional generators might have been added. The ships would have been converted to General Messing. Interim modernisation programme dates: 1955, *Matapan*; 1956, *Alamein*; 1957, *Dunkirk*; 1958, *Jutland*.

[22] The 1959 official handbook of British and Commonwealth ships (CB.01815) listed *Saintes* as being modernised, the others only interim modernised, but she was listed with the same weapons and sensors as the others. Programme years for modernisation were: 1952, *Cadiz*,* *Gabbard*,* *St. James*,* *St. Kitts*;* 1953: *Barlfleur*; 1954: *Gravelines*, *Sluys*, *Vigo*, ; 1955, *Solebay*; 1956, *Armada*, *Lagos*, *Saintes*;* 1957, *Camperdown*, *Hogue*; 1958, *Finisterre*, *Trafalgar*. Starred ships had completed interim modernisation by 1954. Presumably *Saintes* had been brought up to interim standard under an earlier programme. *St. James* and *Gravelines* were scrapped before ongoing modernisation could be completed.

Later 'C' class destroyers were subject to interim modernisation, in which the bridge structure was unaltered, but X gun was sacrificed for double Squid. HMS *Contest* is shown in 1957. She had been converted into a minelayer, surrendering her remaining torpedo tubes and Y gun. The 'C' class minelaying conversions can be traced to a 1948 request by C-in-C Mediterranean that two of his destroyers, *Chaplet* and *Comet*, be converted so that they could block the Dardanelles in the event of war. Later *Contest* and *Chieftain* were also ordered converted. *Comet* and *Chaplet* were converted at Chatham in 1953 and 1954, and *Contest* at Portsmouth in 1954–5. It is not certain when *Chieftain* was converted.

set of torpedo tubes. In that case a deckhouse containing Limbo ammunition, with single Limbo alongside, replaced the tubes.[23]

Later the Australians became interested in modernising their 'Battle' class destroyers. Their plans suggest just how much potential the design had. There were two options, installation of the Tartar missile system and a limited ASW modernisation. The Tartar project began in 1960. A US Navy study of July 1960 suggested placing the launcher at the after end of X deck, eliminating Squid and two twin and one single Bofors. The alternative of replacing B 4.5in mount was considered undesirable and would not be pursued. Later it envisaged installation of Tartar (Mk 11 twin launcher, forty-two missiles), Seacat (GWS 20: two launchers, fifty missiles), GDS 5 for gun control, the British Cooky/Porker ECM system, the US SLR-2, Type 184 sonar, the JYA ASW plotting system, Ikara, and the Ongar long-range homing torpedo (eight fixed tubes). A long-range Signaal LW-02 air-search radar would be installed, and provision would be made for a helicopter. The forecastle would have been extended. Possible additions included the Type 199 VDS. B turret, the Bofors guns, Squid, and the existing torpedo tubes would all be landed. Initial estimates showed that deep displacement, already over the stress limit at 3,454 tons, would increase to 3,471 tons. The idea was dropped.

The ASW modernisation arose at a meeting at Navy Office on 26 April 1961. The two 'Q' class (Type 15) frigates were reaching the ends of their lives. The proposed replacement was a 'Battle' class with one turret removed and Type 177 sonar installed, using some equipment from the two 'Qs'. A draft Staff Requirement was issued in May, and a final one in September 1961. The Chief of Naval Staff objected to eliminating half the ship's surface firepower, but all the plans called for eliminating B turret. Work was to begin in 1963. By that time plans installation of double Limbo (with twenty salvoes; Types 170, 176 and 177 sonars would replace the existing Types 144Q and 147B), two automatic surface plots (JYB) and two visually-controlled (GWS 20) Seacats (total forty missiles), the latter replacing the after deckhouse and the torpedo tubes. No. 2 (B) 4.5in gun, all Bofors (three STAAG, six single Mk VII), and the single Squid would be removed. Radar would be Type 293Q, Type 978, and the surviving Type 275P on the 4.5in director. To handle the much-increased electrical load, existing generators would have been replaced by two 400 kW turbo-generators and three 200 kW diesel generators. An alternative Scheme II had provision for Wessex helicopter trials, the ship being fitted for but not with the forward Limbo so that it could be installed should the trials prove unsuccessful. The forward Limbo handling room would be converted to stow eighteen Mk 44 torpedoes for the helicopter. One version had only one Seacat mounting. Because single Limbo could not make up for the depth inaccuracy inherent in the Type 170 sonar, there was a suggestion that it be replaced by

[23] Notebook 767/2.

a pair of lightweight triple tubes for US Mk 44 homing torpedoes. Deleting Limbo would eliminate the requirement for Type 170. If VDS (Type 199) were fitted, there might be no need for Type 176, either, and one sonar dome could be eliminated altogether.

Tobruk would have been the first ship. She was reduced to reserve instead of being modernised. Her sister *Anzac* became fleet training ship, with STAAGs and torpedo tubes removed; in 1966 she was fitted with classrooms in place of B mount and another classroom deckhouse aft.

BELOW: HMS *Consort*, shown on 12 March 1956, retained her tubes and Y gun.

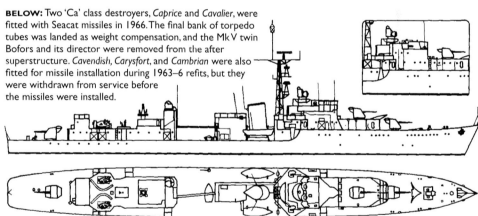

BELOW: Two 'Ca' class destroyers, *Caprice* and *Cavalier*, were fitted with Seacat missiles in 1966. The final bank of torpedo tubes was landed as weight compensation, and the Mk V twin Bofors and its director were removed from the after superstructure. *Cavendish*, *Carysfort*, and *Cambrian* were also fitted for missile installation during 1963–6 refits, but they were withdrawn from service before the missiles were installed.

An Emergency Design

As insurance in the event that an emergency arose before the new Y.100 steam machinery was mature enough to produce, in 1948 an intermediate A/S escort was ordered designed using a hull similar to that of the wartime Emergency Destroyer. In effect this was a new-build equivalent to the Type 15 full-conversion destroyer. It seems to have been assumed that it would be built at once, to test its workability. As in the 1945 frigate programme, the ship would make 25kts deep

and dirty, but endurance at 15kts was cut from 4,500nm to 3,000nm (in effect leaving more weight for machinery at deep load). Gun armament was cut to what was needed for self-defence: either two STAAG or one STAAG and a twin 4in. ASW armament was dsouble Limbo and three fixed torpedo tubes each side for Bidder (six reloads, total twelve torpedoes). Nightshirt was specified, the loss of speed above 23kts not to exceed 0.25kt. The emergency frigate was broadly based on existing destroyers; these sketch Staff Requirements were largely those of the Type 15 destroyer conversion.

There was some question of whether the 'Hunt' class could serve as a basis for the emergency frigate. On 16 May 1948 DNC asked for a rough estimate using 'Hunt' class machinery. The projected battery (two STAAG, double Limbo, but four tubes and four reloads) would have weighed more than 'Hunt' armament (145 tons vs 117 tons), and the ship would need more equipment (150 tons vs 115 tons). Bringing the 'Hunt' powerplant up to modern standards would add weight (370 tons rather than 295 tons). Keeping within 'Hunt' class displacement, to maintain reasonable speed (24.5kts deep and dirty, well below what was wanted) required a dramatic cut in fuel load, to 75 tons (rather than 295 tons). Moreover, a hull designed to reach the required speed would be long and shallow, its own weight too great. 'Hunt' machinery could not solve the problem.

Type 14: The Second-Rate Frigate

Rear Admiral Edwards' other way to get enough frigates, laid out in his paper of April 1949, was supplement the first-rate frigates (Type 12s) with second-rate frigates, ultimately designated Type 14s (*Blackwood* class). Interest in a minimum ASW frigate predated Edwards' paper, and may have inspired some of his remarks. At an SDPC meeting on 31 May 1949 DTSD was asked to investigate the minimum requirements for an A/S frigate, to see whether it was worthwhile pursuing Edwards' idea. This ship was sometimes called a 'World War III corvette', *ie* as the low end of a high-low mix of ship designs. DTASW wanted a light dual-purpose gun armament, primarily for anti-aircraft self-defence, but also capable of en-gaging a surfaced submarine. DNC pointed out that the 4in gun was practically obsolete, the Bofors hardly effective against a submarine. The ASW weapons were those of the interim frigate: double Limbo (ten salvoes) and six fixed torpedo tubes. DNC estimated that the ship would cost £875,000 compared to £1.1 million for the new First-Rate A/S frigate.

At a meeting on 12 July 1949 First Sea Lord rejected this ship as too expensive: the second-rate frigate should cost no more than half as much as the first-rate. To do that the ship would be given half the powerplant of a first-rate, and size and speed would be cut. If that was not enough, DNC would be asked to propose further cuts. Armament was set at double Limbo (ten rather than twenty salvoes), four fixed torpedo tubes without reloads (at one stage, one tube each side, with a total of six torpedoes), one twin Bofors (self-defence only) with an STD director, and a 2in rocket flare launcher (since there was no gun to fire starshell). Asdics would be Types 162, 170 and 172. Endurance would be the normal frigate figure, 4,500nm, but at 12kts rather than 15kts. It was hoped that on a deep displacement of 1,400–1,500 tons the ship would make at least 24kts deep and dirty. A design was presented to the Board in April 1950.[24]

The hull form had to offer good seakeeping without being too large. It was long and lean to maintain speed into a head sea, with sufficient draft for seaworthiness and to accommodate a large-diameter (12ft) propeller turning slowly (as in the first-rate, for silencing). Length helped the ship make 25kts deep and dirty, a knot over the Staff Requirement. It was greater than needed to meet internal space requirements, so spaces forward were deliberately left empty to keep the fore end light for good performance in a seaway. The unusually long hull had a low block coefficient and a 'peg top' midships section (*ie* with high rise of floor). To avoid overcrowding the ship, space for stores was limited to that needed for forty-five days. DNC proposed 300ft (310ft overall) × 33ft × 18ft 6in, displacing about 1,200 tons. Estimated cost was £652,000, compared to £1.315 million for the first-rate frigate.

[24] ADM 167/135, memo B.634 of 27 April 1950.

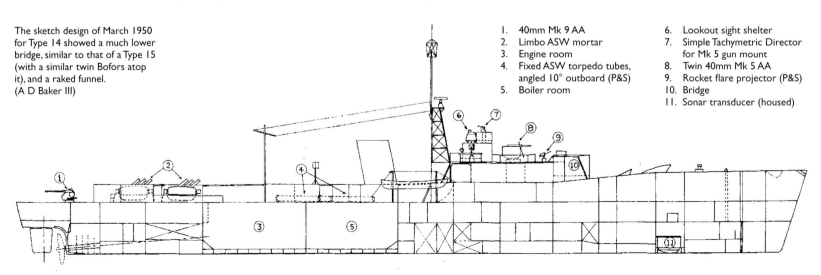

The sketch design of March 1950 for Type 14 showed a much lower bridge, similar to that of a Type 15 (with a similar twin Bofors atop it), and a raked funnel.
(A D Baker III)

1. 40mm Mk 9 AA
2. Limbo ASW mortar
3. Engine room
4. Fixed ASW torpedo tubes, angled 10° outboard (P&S)
5. Boiler room
6. Lookout sight shelter
7. Simple Tachymetric Director for Mk 5 gun mount
8. Twin 40mm Mk 5 AA
9. Rocket flare projector (P&S)
10. Bridge
11. Sonar transducer (housed)

The design showed a low bridge like that chosen for HMS *Rocket*. The SDPC was sceptical, albeit unwilling to demand a change. Could a ship with so low a bridge manoeuvre safely in harbour or in confined waters – or near other ships? There was so much space that accommodation could be to peacetime rather than austere wartime standards, an illustration of the adage that hull steel is the cheapest part of a ship.

The single Y.100 plant would have had only one boiler, but E-in-C insisted on two so that the ship could not be immobilised by a minor accident. This departure from E-in-C's strict standardisation policy added 10 tons to machinery weight. DNC estimated that without Nightshirt operating, the ship would make 25kts deep and dirty under tropical conditions, and 26kts clean on trials. She would not meet the required endurance: DNC estimated 3,900nm at 12kts six months out of dock in the tropics. With emergency oil stowage (32 tons in double bottom tanks) she would make 4,500nm. The extra stowage could be used only under emergency conditions, because to maintain stability the tanks would have to be flooded after it was used (DNC thought this problem could be eliminated during detail design).

Approving the sketch design on 26 October 1949 the SDPC asked for modifications. It disliked the emergency fuel tank, and wanted full endurance without it. Officers would sleep in the wardroom, so noisy machinery should be as far away as possible. Since seas might well sweep over the open weather deck, a destroyer-type catwalk should connect the after superstructure and the forecastle. Finally, DNC should try a design with two sets of Deltic diesels.

Building drawings were submitted to the Board in May 1951. Models run in wave-making tanks showed that the original plan to place the bridge on the forecastle deck level was unsatisfactory. It was raised a deck. The Operations Room (incorporating weapons control) was immediately below the enclosed bridge. A bulwark was added forward to help keep the deck dry. The ship was given a fine forebody to maintain speed in waves. Preferably the deck edge would have been rounded for washdown, but that was impossible because the full width of the weather deck had to be used. At this detailed design stage, two single Bofors had to be substituted for the earlier twin. Placed on each side, they had limited forward arcs at low angles of elevation. DGD reluctantly accepted this limitation because the gun armament was secondary in any case. A third single Bofors was mounted right aft. The ASW torpedo battery was set at two twin trainable mounts. They were fitted only to *Blackwood, Duncan, Exmouth, Malcolm* and *Palliser*. As in other British frigate classes, they were removed in the early 1960s with the failure of the Bidder programme.

Type 14 was put into production as part of the Korean War mobilisation. As in 1938, a less expensive escort was urgently needed because a major war seemed imminent. The first two were included in the 1951/2 Programme, with ten more in the 1952/3 Programme. As of August 1951 plans called for another ten in each of 1954/5 and 1955/6. In this case, the big war did not come. These very austere ships, moreover, did not meet agreed NATO requirements. By December 1953 the programme was being cut. The 1954/5 and 1955/6 series were cut to two ships each before the Staff proposed in 1956 that they be dropped altogether. Foreign sales were limited to three ships ordered by India in 1954.

Type 14 figured in an early NATO frigate design competition. In 1952 the United States planned to supply frigates to Portugal under the Mutual Defence Assistance Program (MDAP). The ships already financed for France (E50/52 classes) and Italy (*Canopo* class) were too expensive. In the US view, the minimum characteristics for an A/S frigate were a maximum speed of 27kts, an endurance of 4,500nm at 12kts, and fifteen A/S salvoes. A discussion of the characteristics for a

HMS *Palliser* shows the full ASW armament planned for Type 14: double Limbo aft and two twin revolving ASW torpedo tubes just abaft the funnel. Note the small bridge raised above the deckhouse which probably originally would have housed a Type 15-like bridge. This photograph was taken on 15 May 1958.

NATO frigate brought out differences of opinion between the major ASW navies. The Royal Navy emphasised the value of low silhouette to confuse enemy attackers. It considered the escort's contribution to convoy AA protection (offered by the 4.5in gun in a first-rate frigate) secondary. The British and the French considered one medium-calibre twin dual-purpose gun with blind-fire capacity sufficient for a first-rate A/S frigate. The Canadians, Italians, Dutch, Portuguese and Americans all wanted two such mounts, fore and aft, plus four single close-range guns. The AIO had to include two automatic surface plotting tables, to show the tactical situation at large and small scale (for co-operation with other ships and with aircraft). Particular emphasis was placed on fast turning, with a tactical diameter of about 437 yds. For a second-rate frigate, a maximum speed of 25kts might be acceptable, with the same endurance as the first-rate, and the same fifteen A/S salvoes.

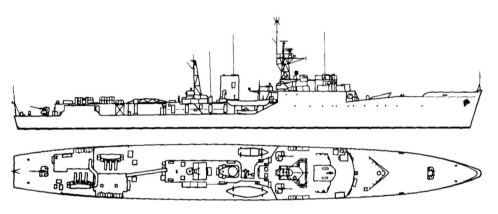

Type 14 as built.

The Europeans considered two twin close-range (blind fire) guns sufficient, but the United States, Canada and Portugal all called for the same two medium dual-purpose mounts as in the first-rate.

The US Navy in effect rejected the British second-rate idea altogether. However, when the US Navy became aware of an actual second-rate frigate, Type 14, in the spring of 1953, the Bureau of Ships liked it for its low cost. *Whitby* was considered too capable (and too expensive) for the projected MDAP programme. One problem in using a British design was that the Royal Navy was unwilling to release key technology to NATO: the silenced (AGOUTI) propeller, Asdic Type 176, ECM equipment or ASW homing torpedoes (these were also an issue for Commonwealth countries). The alternatives to Type 14 were the French E54 (which was never built) and the Italian corvette (light destroyer) then being built by Ansaldo for Venezuela. The Office of the Chief of Naval Operations rejected the British and French designs because they sacrificed anti-aircraft protection almost completely. The Ansaldo design was described as remarkable for its size, but with an unacceptably light hull (which is how it achieved its remarkable load). For the time being, the programme died (later Portugal got three modified *Dealey*s). About 1959 the US official assessment of Type 14 was that they carried too little armament

on a hull about the size (and speed) of a *Dealey*. Crews' berths were 'too far' aft, hence too subject to propeller vibration. Crewmen had to use the open deck to come forward, and food from the galley had to come over the open deck to reach messes aft. The US Navy tended to use the midships area for replenishment at sea, but in the Type 14 the only open space was forward, where it was likely to be wet.

For the Royal Navy, the misfortune of Type 14 was that World War III was never fought; it did not fit the new strategy of the late 1950s and beyond. Ironically, Type 14s figured heavily in a major peacetime British naval operation, the 'Cod War' against Iceland in the 1970s.

Third-Rate Frigates

An even smaller and less expensive third-rate frigate (Type 17) was proposed, roughly in parallel with a proposal for a gunboat frigate (Type 42) to protect convoys in British coastal waters against air and surface attack. The latter was motivated by experience: during the war the Germans had operated motor torpedo boats quite effectively in the Channel and in the North Sea. Type 42 seemed to require a hull about the same size as that of the Type 17, so there was hope that a small common hull might be designed. In fact the two projects were pursued separately, but later an attempt was made to develop a single common hull for both roles. Because neither Type 17 nor Type 42 was built, the Type 42 number was re-used in the 1960s.

Controller asked DNC to design an A/S frigate with about a third the cost of a Type 12.[25] In June 1950 the DNC London section produced a pair of sketch designs, N2/184 and N2/185. N2/184 was a step down from a Type 14, powered by a pair of ASR I diesels (total 4,000 BHP) and armed with a single Limbo (twenty salvoes), four fixed torpedo tubes, and one twin and one single Bofors. N2/185 was a further step down, with a single Squid (twenty salvoes), two fixed torpedo tubes, and the same Bofors armament. The Naval Staff proposed adapting the N2/184 hull as the Type 42 gunboat. Both would make 22kts deep and dirty, using two-shaft diesels (E-in-C preferred a steam plant).[26] Type 17 would have an endurance of 4,000nm at 12kts, Type 22 half that. DNC pointed out that any reduction below 22kts would offer considerable savings, so Type 17 was cut back to DTASW's minimum acceptable speed, 19kts. Its endurance was pushed up to that of a Type 14, 4,500nm at 12kts. Note that Type 17 speed was keyed to tropical conditions, whereas Type 42 speed was keyed to temperate ones (presumably because she was most likely to operate in British coastal waters).

25 Con 474/50. TSD 2153/51 of 9 February 1951 was the Staff Requirement for both types.
26 Alternatives were geared lightweight diesels (Deltics), geared ASR I heavy diesels (as in the diesel frigates), a free piston gas generator feeding a gas turbine, and a geared gas turbine. The Deltic was too expensive and ASR I too large for Type 42 (Type 17 could use two ASR 1 geared to one shaft). The gas turbines were too undeveloped. According to E-in-C, ASR I production probably could not be expanded quickly enough for this mass production ship. It seemed that Type 42 would have to be powered by a geared utility steam turbine.

Even more than Type 14, Type 17 was conceived for rapid production. Thus length was not to exceed 275ft (considered the maximum for quick production); if possible it was to be limited to 250ft. Tonnage was not to exceed 1,050 tons. Armament was that given for N2/184 (with the twin Bofors forward). Like Type 17, Type 42 was not to exceed 275ft or 1,050 tons. Given the anti-MTB role, 22kts was considered a bare minimum. Armament would be two or three MDAP-supplied twin 3in/50s, each with enough ammunition for ten minutes of fire, controlled by US directors (Mk 63) and GDS 2 (Type 293Q radar); plus as many power-worked Bofors as possible. The ASW battery would be a single Squid, although single Limbo might be fitted later. For this ship, but not for Type 17, the bridge would be enclosed with open wings.

Preliminary designs to support preparation of Staff Requirements were prepared in the DNC London section. At this time the London section was largely occupied with preparations to ships for King George VI's tour of Australia (ultimately aborted due to the King's final illness). The Type 42 project was therefore transferred to the Bath DNC organisation in September 1951. Because work on Type 17 continued in London, the two designs soon diverged. A Legend given to Prime Minister Winston Churchill, probably in October 1951, showed the design just before that happened: they had a common 275ft × 31ft 6in hull (deep displacements 950 tons for Type 17, 1,050 tons for Type 42), with a 7,200 SHP twin-screw plant for 22kts and an endurance of 2,000nm at 12kts.[27] At this stage Type 42 had two twin 3in/50, single Squid (ten

salvoes), and two single Bofors.

As in Type 14, the choice of machinery would largely decide the cost of the ship.[28] A quick estimate suggested 4,700 SHP (single shaft) or 4,500 SHP (twin shaft) for 19kts and 8,200/7,800 SHP for 22kts. In 1951–3 E-in-C had three alternatives. One was the 15,000 SHP Y101 of the Type 14 frigate, with two 7,500 SHP boilers. That would over-power Type 42 and require a larger hull (about 5ft longer and 40–50 tons heavier). Cost would be about that of a Type 14. A second possibility was a 2,500 SHP (per shaft) plant being developed for an abortive ocean minesweeper. A third was a 'utility' plant based on commercial rather than advanced naval practice, to develop about 4,500 or 5,000 SHP per shaft. The boilers would be simplified reduced-output versions of those in the Type 14 powerplant (Y101s). It would be impossible to develop both this plant and the ocean minesweeper plant. The 'utility' plant would over-power the minesweeper.[29] E-in-C suggested that one 'utility' shaft could power a Type 17, and two a Type 42. If the usual 30 per cent of deep displacement were devoted to fuel, Type 17 endurance would be 3,000nm (3,400nm if the ship used diesel rather than turbo generators), and Type 42 endurance to 1,300nm (1,400nm with diesel generators).

27 PREM 11/83, undated, but attached to a DRC report (12th) on Developments in Naval Construction (October 1951).
28 Analysis dated 13 November 1951, in Type 42 Cover.
29 A table of machinery sizes and weights prepared in 1953 showed 170 tons for a 7,500 SHP plant, 190 for a 10,000 SHP plant (Y.25) – and 215 tons for 15,000 SHP. A notional 5,000 SHP single-shaft minesweeper plant (Y.20) weighed 190 tons, but was shorter (54ft vs 62ft) than Y.25. Y101 Mk II would weigh 10 per cent less, and a boxed-boiler version (Mk IIA, at least 66ft) was under development. Boxed boilers would protect against fallout and gas; conventional cased boilers could leak intake air, and so contaminate a boiler room.

A stern view of HMS *Duncan*, on 28 July 1960, clearly shows her third single Bofors gun aft. The shrouded object on deck may be a twin torpedo tube.

Thornycroft tried hard to develop designs for the Royal Navy; DNC's records show frequent explanations of why they were not acceptable. Conversely, officers aware of such designs, which often promised far more than DNC's, seem often to have suspected that private builders could do better than the Royal Navy's own designers. This situation was not limited to destroyers. Generally the argument was that private designers had gained their high performance or accommodated unusually heavy weapon loads by limiting less visible factors such as endurance or stores or ammunition. In effect the much later Type 21 represented an official attempt to see whether the builders might actually have it right. In September 1949, for example, DNC C S Lillicrap wrote to Controller than the 40-knot frigate the company had proposed that January reflected unrealistic (tacit) Staff Requirements, and that their machinery and fuel weights were grossly optimistic; there was no weight available for armament.

Lillicrap pointed out that the Thornycroft proposal showed no space for the favoured future weapon, the guided ASW torpedo (or for the necessary workshops); that although it had Limbo, it lacked space for the necessary stabiliser, metadyne, and Plane Conversion (for fire control); that it had no Asdic Instrument Room (and that the Asdic Directing Gear space was too small); that there was no Asdic or Weapons Control Room; that the Radar Office was too small for the desired surface-search set (Type 277); that the ship had far too little electric power (150 kW, less than a fifth that in Type 15 and a seventh that in the new frigates); that there was far too little oil fuel; and that the bridge was not covered (eg against nuclear blast). The ship had too little stores space. All of this probably referred to Thornycroft's design T1526, an 850-tonner with 36,000 SHP machinery (271ft × 27¼ft × 16¾ft). Armament would have been limited to two Limbo

on the forecastle and two single Bofors abaft the funnel (alternatively the Limbos could have been moved aft and a single gun, probably 4in, placed on the forecastle). A somewhat later version, T1617, had two 18in torpedo dischargers (not tubes) and was rated at 39kts. T1687, shown here, was a later, larger, and considerably slower development. It was offered as an alternative to Type 14, shows clear evidence of its Type IV 'Hunt' ancestry. The ship would have used modified *Brecon* machinery to make 26.5kts. Thornycroft argued that it was superior to Type 14 in several key ways. Like the Type IV 'Hunt', it offered covered access to all parts of the ship. The 4in gun forward would be essential in dealing with a surfaced submarine, a common problem at the end of submarine hunts in the Second World War. This design also offered better

protection for the two Limbos aft, and protective plating over the machinery – and unlike a Type 14, it did not require any special alloy steel. Also unlike a Type 14, it had twin screws and twin rudders for manoeuvrability. Thornycroft offered this twin-screw Third Rate frigate as an alternative to the evolving Type 17, Staff Requirements for which were circulated in March 1952. As a result of the Thornycroft proposal, DNC developed a new Legend and Sketch Design in October 1952, and Staff Requirements were revised up to December 1953, leading to the idea of a common hull frigate.
(A D Baker III)

Thornycroft Design proposed frigate

April 1952
Length: 300ft 0in waterline
Breadth: 33ft 0in moulded

Depth: 17ft 6in main deck; 25ft 0in shelter deck
Displacement: 1,250 tons Standard
Speed six months out of dock, foul, at half oil condition: 26.5kts
Endurance: 4,500nm at 12kts
1. 40mm L/70 Bofors (C/L)
2. Port Limbo Mk 10 ASW mortar
3. Starboard Limbo Mk 10 ASW mortar
4. Two fixed ASW torpedo tubes (P&S)
5. 27ft whaler P&S
6. 40mm L/70 Bofors (P&S)
7. Open bridge
8. 4in single gun
9. Weapon control room
10. Operations room
11. ASW control room (to port)
12. Limbo projectile stowage
13. 40mm magazine
14. Engine room
15. Boiler room
16. 4in magazine
17. Sonar hull outfit compartment
O.F. Oil fuel
W. Water

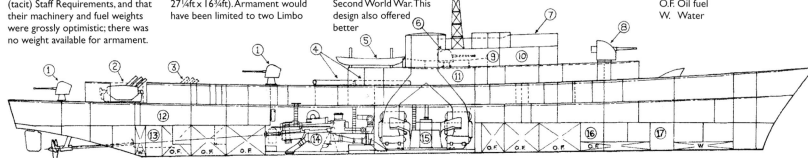

To set appropriate endurance DTSD called a meeting on 8 September 1951. The endurance of the third-rate A/S frigate could not be reduced: all A/S frigates had to be able to cross the Atlantic with convoys. Second- and third-rate frigates offered similar armament, and the second-rate seemed so much better that the meeting recommended abandoning the third-rate altogether. On the other hand there was a firm requirement for the gunboat, which would become even more important when, as expected, the Western Powers adopted a 'forward strategy.' The Type 14 hull and engines should be adapted to the gunboat role under the designation Coastal Frigate.

Type 17

Type 17 was not allowed to die. Controller justified it on the grounds that Type 14 was not really adapted to mass production, and that much of British shipbuilding capacity would be needed in wartime to build merchant ships. Neither argument was valid. In January 1952 N G Holt, in charge of preliminary design, observed that Type 14 was the bare minimum for efficient ASW. A smaller hull would be too slow and too cramped. Its operations room, which would determine how well it could fight, would be crowded, hence inefficient. Its short hull could not take the second dome required for sufficient different Asdics. It would be too slow to deal with a modern submarine. If the machinery were the bottleneck, it

would be better to install a 10,000 SHP plant in a Type 14 hull built of mild rather than high-tensile steel. Since British strategy explicitly assumed that the United States would be a wartime ally, surely the Americans would mass-produce merchant ships as in the Second World War.

An October 1952 study of a faster Type 17 showed a 12,600 SHP plant (250 × 31ft 6in × 9ft 3in, 1,087 tons) offering 23.4kts deep and dirty.[30] A developed version showed endurance limited to 2,000nm at 12kts, six months out of dock – an ASW version of Type 42 limited to European waters. Estimated unit cost was £915,000, compared to £1.1 million for Type 14 (1,381 tons). A 'Joint Naval Staff/Production Paper' issued the following month called for a speed of about 20kts. A quick design study showed a 280ft ship (1,300 tons) requiring 7,500 SHP.[31] It would be about 80 tons lighter than a Type 14, but it would be 5kts slower, with 500nm less endurance, single rather than double Limbo, with 'utility' machinery (7,500 SHP) rather than the 15,000 SHP Y.101 of a Type 14. Accommodation standards would be slightly worse. Built without using special steels or aluminium, the ship would cost about a fifth less than a

[30] Notebook 956 (A S Hetterly).
[31] A typed table in the Holt notebook, presumably intended for DNC, showed five alternatives, I.A through I.F, of which I.A and I.C were 280ft long (10,000 and 7,500 SHP powerplants, respectively, for 22kts and 20.5kts) and I.D through I.F were 300ft long with 12,500, 10,000, and 7,500 SHP powerplants, for 23kts, 22kts and 21kts. All offered endurance of 4,000nm at 12kts, and all had the same ASW armament. Estimated costs were £925,000 for I.A, £885,000 for I.C (the cheapest), £975,000 for I.D, £940,000 for I.E, and £900,000 for I.F.

Thornycroft proposed this third-rate frigate, T1711 in 1955. It would have displaced 966 tons standard and 1,106 tons deep. This design was 50ft shorter than a Type 14, and drew 2Ωft less water. Unlike Type 14, it offered twin screws (the company also offered a single-screw version, T 1712, displacing 954 tons standard). Power was 13,500 SHP (12,500 SHP in the single-screw version); speed was not given. Endurance was 2,000nm at 12kts. (A D Baker III)

Proposed twin screw A/S frigate (third-rate)
Length: 250ft 0in waterline
Breadth: 31ft 6in moulded
Depth: 16ft 3in to main deck; 25ft 6in to upper deck
Standard displacement: 966 tons
Armament:
Single A/S mortar Mk 10
Three single 40mm power-operated single Bofors guns
Tw 2in rocket flare projectors
Four target-seeking A/S weapons (ie torpedoes)

1. Limbo Mk 10 ASW mortar (to starboard)
2. Single 40mm Bofors (C/L)
3. Two fixed ASW torpedo tubes (P&S)
4. 20in searchlight
5. Wheelhouse, forward of signal office

6. Bridge
7. Single 40mm Bofors (P&S)
8. Limbo projectile stowage
9. Engine room
10. Boiler room
11. Sonar Hull Outfit 7A

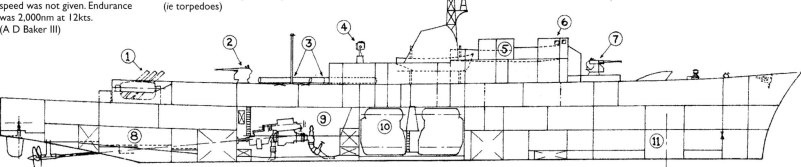

T 1729 (May 1953) was Thornycroft's proposal for an absolutely minimum frigate, below even the level of their proposed Third-Rate. Yet it offered a dual-purpose armament on about the same size as Type 17, which had the same four homing torpedoes but two rather than one Limbo (and no 3in/70). Type 17 did offer L70 rather than wartime-type L60 Bofors. Thornycroft offered 7,500 SHP for 21kts, compared to 10,000 SHP for 21.5kts in Type 17, but endurance was only 2,000nm at 12kts, rather than the 4,000nm

of Type 17. In effect Thornycroft was trading off endurance fuel (100 tons vs 280 tons) for armament (140 tons vs 70 tons). The firm also saved 25 tons on machinery. (A D Baker III)

Proposed single screw A/S frigate (fourth-rate)
Length: 260ft 0in waterline
Breadth: 33ft 0in moulded
Depth: 23ft 6in
Standard displacement: 1,024 tons

Armament:
One single 3in/70 mount
Three single 40mm power-operated single Bofors guns
One ASW mortar Mk 10
Four target-seeking A/S weapons (ie torpedoes)
Two 2in rocket flare projectors
1. Limbo Mk 10 ASW mortar (to port of C/L)
2. Limbo projectile room (to port of berthing space)

3. Single 40mm Bofors (C/L)
4. 30in searchligt
5. Two fixed ASW torpedo tubes (P&S)
6. 3in gun director location
7. Single 40mm Bofors (P&S)
8. Bridge
9. ASW control room (to port)
10. Operations room
11. 3in/70 gun
12. Engines and reduction gearing
13. Boiler room
14. 40mm magazine (to port aft)
15. 3in magazine
16. Sonar Hull Outfit 7A

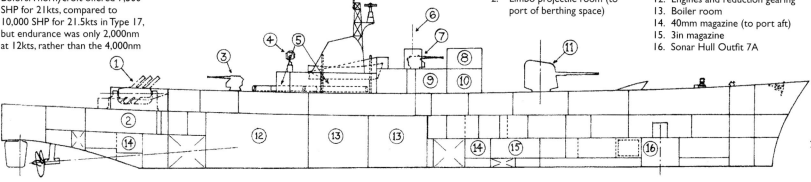

Type 14, perhaps 40 per cent as much as a Type 12. This 'alternative Third Rate' frigate would cost about £40,000 less than a Type 17 because of its much lower SHP.

At a Sea Lords' meeting in November 1952 Controller killed the alternative ship: A/S ships should be as fast as possible; the difference between 19kts and 24kts was enormous. However, it might be worthwhile to distinguish coastal from Atlantic A/S frigates, as the former would not need as much equipment, fuel or personnel. Controller was willing to forego area air-defence weapons in such ships. Soon afterwards (on 3 December 1952) DCNS suggested clear production advantages if Type 17 could have the 10,000 SHP engine being considered for Type 42. Adopting utility machinery would probably claw back the £40,000 difference between the two designs, and more power would add speed. For DCNS the result would be considerably cheaper than a Type 14, and easier to pro-

duce.[32] To reduce Type 17 size, it was decided in June 1953 to eliminate the torpedo tubes, saving six ratings. A month later the decision had to be reversed, as torpedoes were the only available long-range ASW weapons: now two or four twin torpedo tubes replaced Limbo. This version would probably have been 275ft long. An estimate for a dual-purpose version of Type 17 was inspired by a Thornycroft proposal for a 'Fourth-Rate A/S Frigate'. A study dated 4 July 1953 showed a single 3in/70, three single Bofors, four torpedo tubes and a Limbo on a 1,412-ton hull (1,095 tons standard).[33]

---

[32] DCS/578/52, carbon copy in Holt notebook.
[33] Notebook 648/9. The dual-purpose armament was what Thornycroft was proposing for a 'fourth rate A/S frigate:' one 3in/70, three Mk 7 Bofors, four Bidders in fixed tubes, and a single Limbo with twenty salvoes, all in a 260ft×33ft ½in hull at 1,172 tons deep. That compared with 260ft×32ft 6in (1,280 tons) for Type 17, which would have two Mk 10 Bofors (L70 vice L60) and the same torpedoes and Limbo. Thornycroft offered 7,500 SHP for 21kts, compared to 10,000 SHP for 21.5kts in Type 17, but endurance was only 2,000nm at 12kts, rather than the 4,000nm of Type 17. In effect Thornycroft traded off endurance fuel (100 tons vs 280 tons) for armament (140 tons vs 70 tons). The firm also saved 25 tons on machinery. These data were dated 2 May 1953.

Type 42

At the outset (November 1950), DGD wanted at least two and preferably three main battery mounts, each with ten minutes of fire. That the chosen mounting had to be available in large numbers by January 1953 ruled out the 3in/70. That left either the war-built Mk 19 twin 4in (from existing ships) or the US twin 3in/50, which DGD preferred. By January 1952 it seemed that under MDAP the US Navy would not supply more than the eight mounts already on hand (earmarked for the carrier *Victorious*). Buying these weapons would consume scarce dollars better spent on other projects.

There was soon a third alternative, the Vickers single 4in Mk 25.[34] It offered better anti-aircraft performance than the Mk 19, and it would not consume dollars. A prototype was expected late in 1954, with production versions in the latter part of 1955. By January 1952 DGD's minimum armament was two Mk 25, each with its own SGS Mk 1 director, plus two single Bofors L70 (Mk 10); later the secondary battery was two twin and two single Bofors plus a Squid. Vickers persisted with the Mk 25 design after Type 42 lapsed, installing it (as Mk N) on board two Chilean *Almirante Williams* class destroyers. A late proposal (September 1953) to replace Mk 25 with a single 3in/70 was rejected because the latter, which had not yet been built, was expected to be far too heavy. Two single 3in/70 would drive displacement up from 1,350 tons to 1,400 tons; with three such guns the ship would displace 1,500 tons.

Holt seems to have doubted that the armament could be accommodated in a short hull. As a first cut (November 1951) he tried the Type 14 hull with beam increased to 35ft make up for a much heavier armament.[35] The displacement of about 1,300 tons deep load was far beyond what had been hoped for in 1950. A 10,000 SHP single-shaft steam turbine would drive the ship at about 22.5kts, roughly what was required. No such powerplant could be developed in time. The ship would have either the 5,000 SHP (per shaft) utility plant or the 15,000 SHP Type 14 plant. As of October 1952 E-in-C preferred 5,500 SHP for Type 17 and 15,000 SHP for Type 42.

Staff Requirements for armament were still fluid, so on 21 January DNC sent a preliminary design study, with three alternative armaments (each about 168 tons) to DTSD and Controller. He offered both large (300ft) and small (260ft) alternatives. Staff Requirements finally issued on 7 August 1952 (TSD 6026/52) reined back the length for quick production. Armament was now given as three Mk 25 guns, each with its own fire control system, two single L70 Bofors (Mk 10),

and a single Squid. Acceptable speed was reduced to 21kts deep and dirty (temperate). The ship would be built in numbers only in an emergency, hence the design was to emphasise rapid cheap construction.

A preliminary general arrangement showed a 260ft × 35ft × 26ft (to forecastle) ship (1,320 tons deep) carrying 155 tons of armament, slightly below previous figures, but allowing for a 33 per cent increase over the estimated weight of the new Mk 25 mounting. A 12,500 SHP powerplant (occupying a somewhat greater length than had previously been assumed, 72ft) would have driven the ship at 22.75–23kts. Lengthening the hull to 280ft would have given 24kts. Cutting power to 10,000 SHP (62ft long) would make it possible to shorten the ship to 250ft (1,350 tons deep). Hull weight could be reduced (at the cost of survivability) by accepting a lower deck at waterline level.

Plans initially called for including the first ship in the 1952/3 Programme, to be ordered in September 1952 for completion in March 1955. By March 1952 Type 42 had been pushed ahead to the 1953/4 Programme. Then the project died.

The Common Hull Frigate

By December 1953 it seemed that the Royal Navy could not afford the variety of frigates it was building: three kinds of first-rate frigate (Types 12, 41 and 61), a second-rate (Type 14), and projected third-rates (Types 17 and 42).[36] The first-rates were highly effective but too expensive, the second-rate was too expensive and not simple enough, while the third-rate had grown too large. Nor was there any cheap simple engine. It might therefore be best to standardise on the Y100 steam plant used in the Type 12s.

The SDPC therefore recommended using a limited number of first-rate A/S ships as Group Leaders, supplemented by moderate numbers of A/A and A/D frigates. In future a single hull with alternative armaments should be built (it probably could not be used for the A/D function). The benefit of standardisation would outweigh the fact that the ship would be too large for some roles and might seem over-powered and underarmed. The SDPC thus proposed cancelling further Type 14s and endorsed the stop-work order already issued for Type 42 (12 November 1953). The late approaches to the Type 17 and Type 42 design, using the Type 14 hull and engine, would be the basis for the new ship.

New preliminary (sketch) Staff Requirements (TSD 2261/53) were issued on 4 January 1954. The anti-aircraft version would have two 4in twins (Mk 19) with CRBF and TOM (250 rounds per gun) controlled by GDS 2* (Radar 976), two twin L70 Bofors and a single Squid. The A/S version would have twin L70 Bofors fore and aft (TOM fire control), single Limbo (twenty salvoes), four triple torpedo tubes (as then planned

---

[34] The gun is described in ADM 1/25127. DNO initially rejected it because he expected it to have poor remote-control performance, and also because it could not fire on a sustained basis because it was not water-cooled. Vickers was offering it to re-arm the Argentine cruiser *La Argentina* and also for Peru and Chile; it was incorporated in a Italian proposal in June 1954 for a destroyer for Israel. Vickers had recently developed a series of export designs, all tailored to its new weapons: a 1,200-ton sub-hunter, a 2,000-ton fast escort, and a 2,600-ton destroyer.

[35] Notebook 442/6: in November 1951 Holt proposed using the same displacement as Type 14, but increasing beam for stability, since armament weight would be about 160 tons compared to 95 tons for the A/S frigate. E-in-C envisaged using a steam plant something like that in an Emergency Destroyer, but with lower performance 210 tons for a single-shaft 10,000 SHP plant).

[36] SDPC(53) 4th meeting, 16 December 1953, based on the Chairman's paper, SDPC 53007, in Type 42 (gun frigate, not DDG) Cover.

for Type 12 frigates, but never installed), TCSF 2 and the automatic A/S action plot. Asdics would have been Types 162, 170 (for Limbo), 174 and the new long-range Type 177. The powerplant would be that of Type 14.[37] Desired endurance was 4,000nm at 12kts, as in Type 17.

As in the third-rate frigate designs, it was difficult to rein in size. Ships had to be large enough to accommodate not only the weapons but also the personnel. A first cut (290ft × 40ft × 18ft, 1,700 tons) proved too short to accommodate gunboat personnel, so a new version (February 1954) was lengthened to 300ft. The next step used a modified Type 14 hull (300ft × 40ft × 25ft 6in) and powerplant (Y.111, a modified version of the initial Y.101 plant). Even this turned out to be too short to accommodate the expected complement (twelve officers and 230 ratings), so it was stretched to 310ft (1,839 tons fully loaded). Estimated speed was 23kts. The ASW version now had eight large and four lightweight homing torpedoes. A smaller complement (eleven officers, 203 ratings) could have been accommodated within the 300ft hull. A further version had better gun fire control (GDS 2* and CRBFD for Bofors control) at the cost of the four lightweight homing torpedoes.

Controller considered an 1,800-ton ship too large; he asked DNC to make a 1,500-ton ASW ship the basis for both versions, accepting whatever cuts in armament had to be made. On 1,500 tons, the ship could be armed with a single Limbo (twenty salvoes), with four homing torpedoes (controlled by UCSF 2), and with two single L70 Bofors. She would have only a high-definition surface-search radar (974). The machinery plant would be Y.101 without the modifications entailed in Y.111, as E-in-C could not produce Y.111 or any other modified version without a twelve-month design effort (production would require another 2½ years).

Another attempt to cut back was to scale up the last Type 17 design, lengthening it from 260ft to 275ft to accommodate the Y.101 plant (76ft long rather than the 62ft as in Type 17). Deep displacement would be 1,555 tons. This version could accommodate gunboat armament but not even ASW personnel (ten officers and 150 ratings). DNC told the SDPC on 20 April 1954 that accommodation would require at least 1,600 tons. Once Controller allowed 1,600 tons, a new 285ft (1,640-ton) design was prepared based on the *Black Swan* hull. It grew to 305ft to accommodate Y.101 machinery, lengthened from 72ft to 76ft. The ASW version would have displaced 1,819 tons. A 290ft (1,585-ton) June 1954 gunboat version, also based on the *Black Swan*, would have had two twin 4in (CRBFD, GDS 2*) and a single Squid. Endurance would have been cut to 2,000nm at 12kts six months out of dock in temperate waters.

By this time E-in-C had sold the Y.102 plant to the Naval Staff for Fleet Escorts. A constructor's notebook shows a study of a third-rate A/S frigate with gas turbine boost machinery dated about June 1954.[38] It would have had a 17,000 SHP steam/gas turbine powerplant in a 290ft × 38ft 6in hull. Deep displacement would have been 1,625 tons (1,379 tons standard).

Some versions of the Type 42 gunboat were armed with a new Vickers 4in gun, which was ultimately installed, as shown, on board Chilean *Almirante Williams* class destroyers. This gun also figured in several abortive British export designs.

[37] Notebook 648/8 (E F Wood). K J Rawson was then in charge of the design section.

[38] Notebook 999/2 (D K Brown). No power output is specified, but machinery weight was 233 tons (deep displacement was 1,389 tons). A typical machinery weight for such a ship with a somewhat less powerful all-steam plant (Type 14) was 242 tons.

CHAPTER 12

The General Purpose Frigate

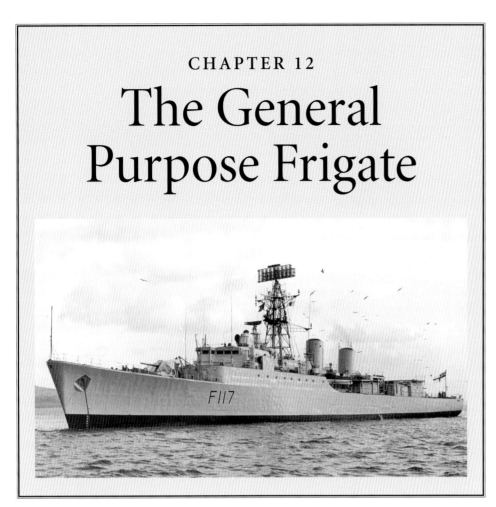

The 'Tribal' (Type 81) class frigates were briefly conceived as replacements for both Type 12 and Type 14, adding a useful long-range radar and limited picket capability. HMS *Ashanti* is shown, newly completed, in November 1961. (RN)

The 'Tribal' Class

Frigate requirements were reviewed again in mid-1954.[1] Given the ongoing shift in British strategy, away from preparing for World War III, the need for large numbers of second-rate ships seemed to be disappearing. The Common Hull frigate was therefore dropped in favour of a larger ship with good second-rate characteristics in both ASW and AAW, which might also be used for Cold War policing.[2] Unlike the Type 14, she needed more AAW firepower to deal with a more powerful Soviet naval air arm. In effect she would be an enlarged Common Hull with both good gunboat and reasonable ASW firepower. The idea was approved by the SDPC at its meeting on 28 October 1954. The design was developed by the DNC London Section rather than at Bath.[3] It was called a Common Purpose Frigate or a sloop (General Purpose Escort) or a General Purpose frigate. The sloop designation, which recalled the earlier ship used in peacetime for policing duties, was being formally applied by mid-December 1954. To emphasise the difference from earlier types of frigates, this one was designated Type 81 in a new General Purpose series. The ships were

given 'Tribal' names, hence the class name.

Work apparently began in July 1954, based on the final steam/gas turbine version of the Common Hull Frigate.[4] E-in-C promoted the gas turbine on the ground that a ship so equipped could get underway instantly in the event of an attack warning, a significant point when the Royal Navy was much concerned with the nuclear threat to its bases (time to get underway could be as short as thirty seconds). Other advantages, not cited at the time, were reduced maintenance and inherent silence (because the plant had neither pumps nor piping through which liquids could gurgle). In August 1954 E-in-C proposed a mixed powerplant with 10,000 SHP provided by a steam turbine and 7,500 SHP by a gas turbine. At this time the Y.102 plant being developed for the fast fleet escorts used 15,000 SHP steam turbines and four 7,500 SHP gas turbines. Ultimately the ships had a 12,500 SHP steam element based on the Y.111 of the Type 14. Requirements imposed before the powerplant was selected included a speed of 24kts (deep and dirty) and an endurance of 5,000nm at 12kts, *ie* some improvement in endurance, but not in speed, over a Type 14. Designers considered alternative single- and twin-screw configurations, the former offering a weight advantage. In December 1954 the Sea Lords approved a single-screw powerplant for the first four ships.[5] The mixed powerplant became the prototype for that in the missile destroyers. An early casualty (a disc failure) in *Ashanti* was particularly helpful in making teething troubles apparent before the destroyers entered service. It became clear that in future repair should be done by replacement, a policy that was later adopted.

As of October 1954 armament was two twin 4in Mk 19 (fore and aft) controlled by GDS 2*, two L70 Bofors, single Limbo (twenty salvoes), eight torpedo tubes (with UCSF 2), and two 2in rocket flare launchers. To meet its limited A/D requirement, the ship would have the US SPS-6C radar. Sonars would be Types 162, 170 for Limbo, 176 for self-protection, and the long-range 177, in two sonar domes, with the automatic A/S Plot. Propellers would be silenced. The initial sketch showed a 330ft × 42ft 6in × 28ft flush-decked hull.[6]

Changes ordered in November 1954 were better 4in fire control (MRS 3 instead of CRBF); a British radar in place of the US SPS-6, supply of which was increasingly problematic; a fin stabiliser; a second twin Bofors; and a wooden deck

---

[1] According to a brief history of 'investigations leading to the GP frigate' in ADM 205/183, a series of 1957 newsletters to flag officers produced by Mountbatten.
[2] The General Purpose Staff Requirement was TSD 2290/54, dated by one official source on 16 February 1954 (probably a misprint for 1955), describing a ship 'capable of reasonable, but not first class, performance in all functions of A/S protection, A/A protection, and fighter direction'.
[3] D K Brown, the historian of the Royal Corps of Naval Constructors and of British warship design, was preliminary designer. The relevant notebooks begin with 999/2.

[4] The initial orders for the design seem to have been dated 27 June 1954 (Notebook 993/2, K J Rawson). The notebooks do not make a clear distinction between the Common Hull frigate and the new design.
[5] However, a constructor's notebook shows a study dated 13 November 1956 of a twin-screw version using Y.100 machinery, as in a Type 12 frigate. That would have required more depth in the machinery spaces and therefore increased beam to maintain stability. The Y.100 plant would have been redesigned to meet ABCD requirements, which would lengthen it to 80ft. Armament would have been reduced to one twin 4in and one twin Bofors, the latter aft. There was also a brief study of a sloop with an alternative 40,000 SHP plant offered as an alternative to the 20,000 SHP plant actually chosen. Alternatives were 350ft and 375ft long (2,600 tons or 3,000 tons).
[6] The initial requirement was apparently for a 1,600-ton A/S frigate using the 10,000/7,500 SHP COSAG powerplant. Armament was two twin 4in, one twin Bofors with TOM, eight A/S torpedoes, and Limbo; radars were SPS-6C, Type 974 and Type 262, and Asdics were Types 170 (for Limbo), 162, 176 (torpedo warner), and 177 (long-range search). Given the desired small tonnage, the first estimate was 270ft × 38ft 6in. That was insufficient, so the design grew: to 285ft × 38ft 6in, then 290ft × 37ft (and 37ft 6in), then the 330ft × 42ft 6in of the initial Common Purpose Frigate.

HMS *Gurkha* is shown with the lightweight Wasp helicopter (stowed in a very small hangar below the flight deck) and the Canadian Type 199 VDS aft. Note the two Oerlikons forward of the bridge.

(deemed important for the ceremonial side of a sloop's role). The resulting 2,600-ton ship was about the same size as a Type 12, with a more general-purpose armament, but substantially slower (24kts rather than 27kts deep and dirty). Dimensions at this stage (January 1955) were 340ft × 42ft × 27ft 6in (hull depth). The ship kept growing longer, so late in March it was 350ft × 42ft 6in × 26ft 6in × 11ft 3in (2,417 tons). This was slightly shorter and lighter than Type 12.

The 4in gun, which was becoming obsolete in 1954, seems to have been chosen because it figured in the Type 42 designs; the only other gun in production, the twin 4.5in, was far too massive. In August 1954 DGD and DNO proposed an alternative solution.[7] Single 55° 4.5in mounts were becoming available as older destroyers were discarded. Unless this weapon were adopted, by the 1960s the new frigates would be the only ships in the fleet retaining 4in guns. It would be far better to standardise on the 4.5in gun. By that time guns would no longer be effective for anti-aircraft in any case, so the 55° elevation limit would not be very important. Moreover, the 4.5in would be more effective in shore bombardment, an important policing role, because it was more accurate and fired a heavier shell. The proposal was accepted.

When the sloop was presented to the Sea Lords in May 1955, they asked whether 24kts deep and dirty would be enough.[8] In 1948 Type 12 design had been required to make 27kts,

the caveat being that higher, not lower, speed might well be needed in the future. Approval of the new design was held up. A 27–28kt version would displace about 3,300 tons. DTSD remarked that modernising Type 12 and giving it a General Purpose capability would require about as much tonnage.[9] Type 81 was much smaller, hence much less expensive. There could never be enough frigates, but adopting a less expensive one would help. DTSD left the caveat that the balance between it and a true first-rate frigate might have to change as the Soviets deployed their expected nuclear submarines.

Type 81 might be acceptable because it was no longer so obvious that higher frigate speed would be worthwhile. Maximum Asdic speed was 25kts.[10] Silencing was unlikely to gain much. Future submarines might well be capable of 30kts, but at such speeds they would be deaf. They might find 15kts an effective limit while attacking, both to be able to listen and also to run at shallow enough depths to be able to fire torpedoes. Once detected, however, a submarine would use her full speed to evade. Doing so might break up a screen, leaving ships vulnerable to other submarines. With no realistic hope of achieving a sufficient speed advantage over a 30-knot nuclear submarine, the only defence would be a stand-off weapon or a helicopter – both then under active consideration. The sole remaining ASW argument for high frigate speed might be the ability to evade torpedoes (and homing torpe-

[7] ADM 1/26040. The October 1955 docket date is probably an error. The design shown to the Board in June showed 4in guns, but the notebooks suggest that the decision to substitute the 4.5in gun was made the previous February (certainly by July 1955). The Way Ahead policy review had just killed the ships armed with 4.7in gun mounts, which could be converted into 4.5in mounts. In August 1955 DTSD could not say why the Staff had originally favoured the obsolescent 4in gun. DGD's discussion of the armament alternatives (ADM 1/24610) was started in October 1953, but the detailed discussion is dated July 1954.
[8] ADM 167/141. The version offered was Design Study S.7, DNC 1/329, the 1 indicating the London Section.

[9] ADM1/26419, a paper by DTSD dated 22 June 1955, assisted by DUSW, Director of Plans, and Director of Naval Intelligence.
[10] Even under good conditions, the new Type 177 long-range sonar and the Type 176 passive torpedo warner were ineffective above 24kts (at 28kts Type 177 range fell from 8,000–10,000 yds to 3,000 yds). The projected Type 192 VDS, not yet nearly ready (it never entered service), would buy another 1–2kts. According to a 1956 paper, the maximum speed for attack sonars (Type 170) was about 27kts. A fast ship might be able to close with a submarine but she could not hold contact. It seems not to have been envisaged that a very fast ASW ship could employ 'sprint and drift' tactics (detection at maximum range, then run-in).

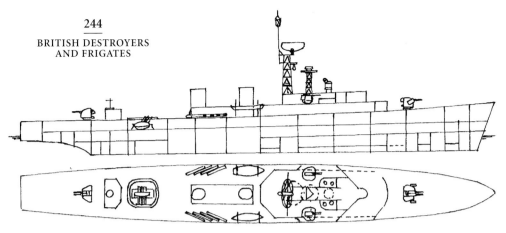

DNC 1/329, the drawing of Type 81 presented to the Board of Admiralty in mid-1955. This drawing was dated May. Note the two twin 4in guns, the forward of which has rocket flare launchers on its sides, the two twin L70 Bofors, the fixed torpedo tubes, and Limbo. Although this design called for combined steam and gas turbine propulsion, it showed only a single engine room (the other machinery space was marked 'gearing room'). The big search radar is recognisably the US SPS-6C, at the time the favoured small-ship air-warning and interception set. Ships got Type 965 instead. The drawing's designation, with its DNC 1 prefix, indicates that the design was carried out by Section 1, DNC's own London office. At this time Section 5 was responsible for cruisers (the missile cruiser sketch circulated at this time was DNC 5/6158), and Section 7 was responsible for destroyers. The frigate section was separate from the destroyer section, as these two types still seemed quite distinct. (Author)

does could not as yet be very fast). The new Type 182 decoy was expected to reduce torpedo effectiveness.

On this basis, in July 1955 the Admiralty Board agreed that the project should proceed. In April 1956 First Sea Lord, Lord Mountbatten, by then an enthusiastic supporter of the project, was told that the ship would probably make 25kts deep and dirty (28kts on trials).[11] A new paper on frigate speed

[11] ADM 205/109.

argued that 24kts was not only the maximum for efficient Asdic use, but also the maximum safe speed in the face of acoustic homing torpedoes. At a meeting called by First Sea Lord on 29 May the Board agreed that a clear case had been made out for the 24-knot speed.[12]

The Legend and sketch design were presented to the Board in December 1956.[13] The design had been made possible by adopting seawater ballasting of fuel tanks when they were emptied. Superstructure, masts, funnels and some internal structure was of aluminium. Against that, the hull was somewhat heavier because only mild steel was used, to avoid delays due to the use of special steels. As in previous escorts, the hull was stiffened forward to cut through head seas. The ship was stabilised. The enclosed bridge had a new Delta form. The Operations Room was immediately below it, with ladder access. Aircraft and Gun Direction facilities were inside the Operations Room, with the Asdic Control Room adjacent, as in other frigates. Cambria would not be available for the first ship, so the standard plotting table would be substituted on a temporary basis. In a departure from previous practice, the wheel was placed, not adjacent to the Operations Room, but rather on No. 2 deck immediately abaft the Machinery Control Room. When his ship visited the United States, the CO of Ashanti was asked why the helmsman had not been moved all the way back to the steering-engine room (as some US Work

[12] ADM 167/146, memo B.1119A of 19 December 1956 by VCNS and Controller.
[13] ADM 167/146, memo B.1119 of 17 December. The Board approved the drawings and Legend on 20 December (Minute 5076). It agreed to sacrifice a new broadband HF radio system (common aerial working, using the ship's funnels and masts as antennas) to get the small-ship air-search radar.

Off Hampton Roads on 26 March 1964, HMS Tartar displays her unusual Limbo arrangement, the flight deck aft being folded back to provide the opening through which the mortar fired. Note also the single 40mm gun alongside the base of the lattice mast. (USN)

Study engineers had proposed). He replied that the steering-engine room was extremely uncomfortable in rough weather and at high speeds. Given his comfortable location, it was unnecessary to provide a second (lee) helmsman for such conditions. The others on watch in the machinery-control room could see whether the helmsman was ever incapacitated. The US Navy was also impressed by the ship's ABCD citadel, which was far in advance of US practice. Habitability was considerably improved, all living and most working spaces being air-conditioned. All ratings would sleep in bunks rather than hammocks, and all would mess cafeteria-style.

DNC emphasised the need to get the gas turbine to sea. To speed construction he would provide advance information to the builders so that they could mock-up the machinery spaces. Against a required speed of 22kts deep and dirty in temperate waters (with 24–25kts desirable), Type 81 was expected to make 24kts (22kts on steam turbine alone, 19.5kts on gas turbine alone). She would have a 500 kW turbo-generator in her boiler room, a 500 kW gas turbine generator in her gearing room, and a 250 kW diesel generator in the hold forward, to meet the requirement for electrical power from outside the machinery spaces. Ultimately ships had two 750 kW diesel generators plus the steam and gas turbine units.

There were also some other issues. Could the new Green Light (Seacat) missile replace the twin 40mm guns? Could the new lightweight variable-depth sonar (CAST, later Type 199) be installed? Could the US Tartar anti-aircraft missile, advertised as equivalent to a 5in mount, replace the after 4.5in gun? DNC could offer everything except Tartar (the British single 4.5in was far smaller and lighter than the US 5in/54 Tartar was designed to replace). The ships were ordered armed with Seacat, but two single 40mm were mounted as interim until it was available. Only *Zulu* was completed with the missile. *Ashanti* and *Gurkha* had Type 199 VDS (CAST), installed in 1968 and 1969 respectively.

As of 1956 four ships were planned for 1955/6 and three more for the 1956/7 Programme; it seemed that the next twenty-eight frigates would be built to the sloop design. Given nervousness about the ship, VCNS and Controller suggested stopping construction for evaluation. They argued that 1956/7 was the right break point because it was important to order seven sets of machinery together: the gas turbine 'is best with intricate licensing arrangements'. It would be uneconomical to stop at the first four ships and then start a new two-shaft design.

The speed issue having been revived, First Sea Lord argued that the new long-range sonars, beginning with Type 177, made it possible to engage submarines using stand-off weapons. The ship no longer had to be fast enough to close with the submarine (although Mountbatten did not say so, there was little prospect of building a frigate fast enough to get within Limbo range). The required frigate speed should depend on the speed of whatever was being escorted, not on the speed of the target submarines. With Type 177 close to fruition, Mountbatten ordered a Working Group to devise a commensurate weapon. The only existing stand-off missile was the US RAT, carrying a Mk 43 torpedo to a range of 5,000 yds, beyond which its error margin exceeded torpedo homing range. The US Navy was considering a longer-range missile to deliver a nuclear depth bomb (ultimately developed as ASROC), but in 1956 the British considered such weapons of limited value given the threat of damage to the ship firing them. Mountbatten's strongly-favoured alternative was a lightweight helicopter carrying homing torpedoes. The ship would vector the helicopter into attack position based on sonar and radar data co-ordinated in her Action Information Centre.[14] The helicopter was an imaginative and very flexible addition to the frigate. The Royal Navy bought a small helicopter-launched anti-ship missile, the French SS-12 (later replaced by Sea Skua in the larger Lynx). That the helicopter could not fly in bad weather was considered acceptable.

DUSW agreed. In November 1955 he proposed using the Fairey Ultra-Light (Director of Naval Air Warfare [DNAW] considered it too small for the North Atlantic). The great advantage of the Ultra-Light was that a frigate needed only limited modification to accommodate it, such as a 20ft × 20ft pad aft. It was successfully operated from HMS *Grenville* after the ship completed her refit at Chatham in December 1956. Three Ultra-Lights were to have been ordered, but then the larger Saunders-Roe P.531 (later redesignated Wasp) was substituted. It could carry two torpedoes rather than one, and its radius of action was 80nm rather than 30nm. Meanwhile the Canadians showed that a much larger helicopter, a US Sikorsky S-55, could operate from their frigate *Prestonian*, a modified 'River'.

Initial trials having succeeded, on 30 September 1958 the Fleet Requirements Committee recommended as its highest priority that Type 12 and also the new Type 81 with the Type 177 sonar be fitted to carry the new helicopter. The helicopter system was called MATCH (Medium Range Torpedo Carrying Helicopter). Note that helicopter direction based on sonar data was not demonstrated until September–December 1959, on board HMS *Undaunted*. DNC found that in a Type 12 the main penalties were the loss of one Limbo, increased congestion of fittings on the quarterdeck, and replacement of about 10 tons of ship fuel with helicopter fuel. The helicopter upgrade was combined with the project to replace Bofors guns with the Seacat short-range missile. As the first Type 177 ship, HMS *Falmouth* became the first Type 12 (actually a *Rothesay*) with a helicopter hangar.

To accommodate the helicopter in Type 81, Limbo was raised from the well originally planned to No. 1 deck. That improved the layout on No. 2 deck and provided space for

---

14 Details of the operational need and the experiments are in ADM 1/26968.

F133

more accommodations. The helicopter deck was arranged atop the after deckhouse, inside which sat the Limbo mortar. It folded back to allow Limbo to fire. About 1960 the planned fixed ASW torpedo tubes were eliminated. No record of that decision has been found. Most likely, as in *Leander*, they were traded for the new Integrated Communication System (ICS).

MATCH was bought in preference to the US ASROC missile (successor to RAT). Director of Underwater Weapons Materiel (DUWM) objected that it could not grow beyond 10,000 yds range, hence could not fully exploit the Type 177 sonar. Furthermore, it would be expensive because it was understood to require the associated US SQS-23 sonar. The US alternative to ASROC was the ill-fated DASH helicopter drone. In effect MATCH was a manned DASH, the pilot making the system vastly more flexible and reliable. Type 81 was retired due to the 1979 Royal Navy manpower crisis, although some were brought back into service following the Falklands War.

A New Generation of Escorts

Decisions on the future frigate programme coincided with the 1957 defence review, which included naval policy. The fleet that emerged was characterised not in terms of how much it might cost but in terms of the number of personnel involved. The initial 90 Plan (90,000 adult personnel) accepted deep cuts in the NATO commitment, in view of the shift towards 'warm war' thinking. The resulting fleet would be built around four Task Groups (Home, Mediterranean, East of Suez [actually Indian Ocean], with one more refitting), each comprising a carrier and a cruiser screened by four destroyers and four frigates. Thus the frigates were now fleet units rather than trade protection ships. Only Type 12s and converted destroyers were really suited to this role. The Eastern force would be supported by an escort maintenance ship and a 'Commando Carrier' based either at Malta or at Singapore. Additional Far Eastern surface forces (presumably for Cold War) were a cruiser, four more destroyers, and four more frigates, in effect a Task Group without a carrier. Another six frigates were needed for the Gulf (two permanently on station, one within seven days), with more for the two Western Hemisphere

stations (four for the South Atlantic, two for the West Indies). Trials and training would require another destroyer and fifteen frigates. In an attempt to save money (the 75 Plan, promulgated in what Mountbatten called the 'Ides of March') the spare task forces was eliminated.[15]

Finally a compromise 88 Plan was accepted. Destroyers amounted to thirteen for the Home and Mediterranean Fleets (nine *Daring* and 'Battle' and four radar pickets), five for the Far East (modernised 'Ca' class), one for trials and training (modernised 'Ca' class), three in operational reserve, and four in extended refits and modernisation. Of these, the 'Ca' class would reach the end of their lives in 1968. The later *Darings* would be replaced by missile destroyers. The new radar pickets would not have to be replaced until 1972, perhaps by aircraft. Each of the two main fleets would have a total of twelve frigates in three squadrons, each comprising three Type 12s plus a Type 61 A/D frigate. Other frigate requirements were five in the Far East, six for the Gulf cycle, four for the America/West Indies cycle, and four for the South Atlantic and South America cycle. Additional ships were needed for trials and training (fifteen), fishery protection (four), as spares in operational reserve (five), and as cover for refits and modernisation (nine).[16] To maintain these levels the Royal Navy needed twenty-six destroyers and sixty-four frigates, a total of 90 escorts (a 68-frigate figure was also used). Note that this force was well short of what NATO wanted as a commitment of resources two months into a war. These figures justified an annual programme of three frigates, representing an extension of the nominal sixteen-year destroyer or frigate lifetime. A ten-year extension by modernisation was being proposed at this time, in which case something under 2.5 frigates per year would have sufficed.

At this time, against the 64-frigate requirement, the Royal Navy had fifty new ships built, building or on order: nineteen Type 12, twelve Type 14, four each of Types 41 and 61, and the twelve Type 81 (soon to be seven plus five of a new design). A

---

key new assumption was that frigates with fleet speed should both fill this gap *and* replace the ageing 'Ca' class destroyers. 'Tribals' were clearly too slow. Reordered as a Type 12, the A/D frigate *Coventry* (1955/6 Estimates) became temporarily the twentieth and last Type 12 as HMS *Weymouth*. Then the Type 81 programme was capped at seven ships, leaving five planned units available for a new class. The former *Coventry* could now become the lead ship of that series. A rolling programme was envisaged: two per year in the 1962/3 to 1964/5 Programmes, then three per year in 1965/6 to 1968/9, then a final two in 1969/70. This new study took into account the most recent approved fleet plan (the 88 Plan). British planning was based on the prospect of limited war, which the Royal Navy might have to fight independently against recent Soviet weapons in Third World hands (or even in the hands of Soviet 'volunteers'). Such wars might be characterised by a substantial air threat. In 1956, in approving replacement of the A/A and A/D frigates by Type 12s, the Board had asked whether the ships could be equipped with the only existing frigate-sized anti-aircraft missile, the US Tartar.

The Fleet Requirements Committee began to discuss a new frigate in the autumn of 1958.[17] DNC pointed out that any entirely new design would take two to three years to prepare. Much of DNC's manpower was about to concentrate on detailed design of the new missile destroyer. However, there was an opportunity to redesign Type 12 during the year-long gap before that work began. Such a design would have to impose minimum changes on Type 12, and it would use only current equipment. It would have little or no margin for additional equipment, hence would offer little potential for growth.

[17] ADM 1/27384 contains the Fleet Requirements Committee papers for 1958–9. The paper was FRC(58)12, circulated to the members of the Board by order of First Sea Lord as Memo B.1253, and discussed by the Board on 21 January 1959 (ADM 167/153).

DUSW rejected the idea. Money should be used to develop next-generation weapons. The numbers gap should be filled by the simplest possible ships. For DUSW this would be a sloop with somewhat longer endurance (6,000nm at 12kts) and with sonar limited to the new lightweight variable-depth type.[18] Speed would be 24kts. Armament would be one 4.5in gun, Seacat, and a new heavy torpedo (Ongar, later Tigerfish or Mk 24, which ultimately was produced only in a submarine version). The ship would have the latest habitability features, including air-conditioning, and the latest ABCD protection. She would be about the size of a Type 14: initial sketches were based on that hull, armament being much lighter than in a Type 14, 136.4 tons rather than 290 tons. In October 1958 DTSD listed the sloop requirement alongside that of a new General Purpose frigate, but the idea was rejected. The Royal Navy could not afford to build frigates which could not be deployed as needed.

The October 1958 General Purpose frigate was still described primarily as an escort. To the new limited war role of ASW/Aircraft Direction/Anti-Aircraft were added a new Cold War mission of limited army support in minor operations. The last might justify the twin 4.5in gun even after it became obsolete for anti-aircraft use (as DGD soon said would occur in the 1970s). The combined roles justified the new frigate helicopter, because it could deliver small air-to-surface missiles as well as lightweight anti-submarine torpedoes. It was thought that, adapted to frigates, the new ADAWS digital combat direction system would provide the flexibility to handle the new fast submarines. It was associated with Type 184 sonar and with the Canadian CAST variable-depth sonar

[18] Details from Notebook 1073/3, date implied by Purvis Notebook entry of November 1958 referring to characteristics of a new sloop on R/S TSD 4333/58 of 22 October 1958.

HMS *Gurkha* shows the cut in her transom and the handling equipment for her Type 199 VDS, installed in 1968, and the Wasp helicopter on her small flight deck. Also visible is the Corvus chaff launcher just abaft her bridge. The prominent hooded objects abeam her after funnel are Seacat missile directors (all ships of the class had been fitted with this weapon by 1977). The missile launcher is barely visible at the after end of the superstructure deck, in this photograph just below the lattice mast.

(Type 199 in British service, SQS-504 in Canadian). The next-generation torpedo associated with Type 184 was the wire-guided Ongar, which ultimately entered service only as the submarine-launched Tigerfish.

DTSD offered two alternative surface armaments: Tartar with one Seacat aft or one twin 4.5in and two Seacats. Underwater weapons would be Limbo and A/S torpedoes, supported by new long-range sonar (Type 184 and CAST) and by the Limbo attack sonar (Type 170). For the limited aircraft direction role (as in the 'Tribal') she would have a Type 965M radar (HF/DF was an alternative). She would also have a target-indication radar (Type 293Q or Type 992), a surface-search set, and EW capability. All would be co-ordinated by a digital

HMS *Dido* shows some major *Leander* features: the plated-in mast (carrying diesel generator exhaust), the topmast carrying ESM antennas (in this case, UA-3) and HF/DF, and the Type 965 long-range air-search radar aft, to extend the fleet's radar horizon. The quarter-cheese radar is Type 993, replacing Type 293, and below it is the Type 978 surface-search set, with a strip of radar-absorbing material to reduce interference from its backlobe and sidelobes.

combat direction system. The ship would be air-conditioned, with full ABCD protection. To operate the helicopter, she would be stabilised. DTSD wanted a speed of 27kts deep and dirty and a range of 5,000nm at 12kts (when six months out of dock).[19] Something much larger than a 'Tribal' was needed.

The Fleet Requirements Committee adopted DTSD's specification in November, and DNC was asked to develop a sketch design. In December, the committee asked to what extent its requirements could be met simply by modifying the existing Type 12 frigate. DNC (A J Sims) thought that there was a good chance of doing so, based on an ongoing study of how to incorporate improvements in the Type 81 frigate into the larger Type 12. If the number of heavy torpedo tubes were cut from twelve to four, weight would be freed allowing No. 1 deck

to be extended right aft to form a flush deck, adding space. The existing water ballast tanks would be used for fuel. In all about 3,000 sq ft would be gained, of which about 2,000 sq ft would be needed for air-conditioning and improved armament. Other space would provide the desired cafeteria messing and bunk sleeping.

DME and DEE had not yet stated their revised requirements, but it was clear that the machinery space would have to be lengthened. ABCD protection required boxed and remote-controlled boilers, air to which would be trunked in so that the ship could otherwise be closed up completely. DEE wanted to consolidate electrical and machinery controls in one space, but DME preferred to place the switchboard outside and above the machinery control space (where it would interfere with the large open space needed for cafeteria messing). DGS's solution was to place the switchboard either forward or inside the machinery space (in a separate new Machinery Control Room). DEE expected to need larger turbogenerators. Overall, extra space would make it possible to move heavy equipment lower in the ship, improving stability and offering a greater margin for added topweight.

Compared to a follow-on Type 12 (the *Rothesay* class), a modernised version would displace slightly more (2,660 tons rather than 2,595 tons) but would have similar performance (28kts+, 4,500nm at 12kts). She would have more modern main-battery fire control (MRS 3 with GDS 5 rather than Mk 6M with GDS 2*) and would lack the fixed torpedo tubes of a Type 12 (she would retain the two twin swivel tubes). Both ships would have the same UCSF 2 underwater fire control system, but only the modernised ship would have Type 184 and CAST. She would have single rather than double Limbo (twenty salvoes), but she would also have the light ASW helicopter, with twenty-four Mk 43 torpedoes. Furthermore, only the modernised ship would have a long-range air-search radar (Type 965M) in addition to the short-range Types 978 and 293Q for target indication. Only the modernised ship would be able to carry troops on a short passage.[20] This redesign was encouraged by the experience of redesigning the Type 12 for the Royal New Zealand Navy. It added air-conditioning at a slight expense in standard of accommodation. None of this addressed the question of installing the Tartar missile, however.

The Committee dithered. Initially it decided that the modernised design was not worthwhile. Work therefore went ahead on a fresh design. Further estimates, completed by February 1959, suggested that a length of 370ft overall (as in Type 12) would be adequate. Type 12 also offered the desired endurance of 4,500nm at 12kts. DME wanted another foot of beam (to 43ft) to allow for full ABCD protection of the boilers. Type 12

[19] DTSD 4333/58 of 22 October 1958. Requirements were stated for both a frigate and for a follow-on sloop.

[20] Some of the armament changes were ordered only on 27 November, probably in response to the Fleet Requirements Committee specification: removal of the forward Limbo, of the Bofors guns and their directors, of all the torpedo tubes and torpedoes. In their place were added a permanent hangar and the lightweight helicopter, lightweight torpedoes (twenty-four Mk 43 or eighteen Mk 44), four torpedo tubes (and, if possible, eight Bidders), two Green Lights (sixty rounds total) with directors, and the CAST VDS.

HMS *Jupiter*, a broad-beam *Leander*, shows her single Limbo recessed into her helicopter deck aft, and her Seacat launcher. The objects on the lower sides of her plated-in foremast are Type 667 jammers. Her topmast carries the cylindrical arrays of the UA-8/9 ESM system associated with the jammers. Less visible is a Corvus decoy launcher on a platform abeam the mainmast.

machinery would certainly meet the 27kts requirement. By this time DTSD was calling the ship a General Purpose frigate. DGS that the ship bore absolutely no relation to the previous 'general purpose' frigate, the Type 81 'Tribal'.

Requirements began to grow. On 1 April DTSD presented a new set of Staff Requirements to the Fleet Requirements Committee. It wanted the much larger (15,000lb) Wessex helicopter then being projected for the missile destroyer, the only British helicopter capable of both search (using a dipping sonar) and attack. It required an 80ft × 40ft landing area and a 43ft × 19ft × 17ft hangar. The ship might be armed with the US ASROC stand-off missile then being considered as the ultimate replacement for the Wessex helicopter in the missile destroyer. The projected torpedo was the big Ongar. The ship would also have the usual Limbo. She would make 28kts deep and dirty, with an endurance of 5,000nm at 12kts.[21] DTSD hoped that the ship could be built on 2,500–3,000 tons; the Staff was apparently reluctant to go over 3,000 tons, considering that a Type 12 displaced about 2,600 tons. However, an initial estimate suggested 3,050 tons (375ft). On that length it would take 32,000 SHP to achieve the desired 28kts. With the existing Y.100 plant (30,000 SHP) the ship would make only 27.5kts.[22] The extra half-knot would require entirely new

machinery, at considerable expense in money and time. Conversely, a 395ft ship (probably 3,200 tons) would make the extra half-knot on 30,000 SHP.

In May 1959 one of DNC's naval architects pointed out that apart from higher speed (presumably to work with the fleet), the gun armament (a twin 4.5in), and the sonar, the desired frigate was not too different from a 'Tribal'. Knowing that a Type 81 could accommodate most of what was wanted except for the twin 4.5in gun, he took the 'Tribal' length (350ft), deducted the machinery length, added back the machinery length of a Type 12 (the only available powerplant), and also added 12ft for the twin 4.5in gun.

The machinery would have to be changed to some extent. Boilers would be boxed to protect the boiler rooms from radioactive or poisonous air, and remote controls would be added. Gearing would be reinforced (presumably there had been problems with Type 12s in service). Cruising turbines could be eliminated. That would add about 10 per cent to machinery length, and weight would increase from 437 to about 467 tons. Length would have to increase to at least 372ft.

Alternatives were presented at a meeting DNC called on 13 May 1959 to discuss future frigates:

---

[21] Figures for February 1959 in notebook by R E Pitt.

[22] Notebook 337/16 (W G John). He was then in charge of preliminary design. That the new powerplants were in effect modular, hence that power could not easily be slightly increased, was not yet automatically taken into account.

1959 FRIGATE ALTERNATIVES

	A	B	C	D	E	Type 12
LWL	400ft	375ft	400ft	390ft	360ft	360ft
Beam	45ft	44ft	45ft	44ft	44ft	41ft
SHP	30,000/34,000	30,000/34,000	30,000/34,000	30,000/32,000	30,000/31,500	30,000
Speed	27.25/28kts D&D	27.25/28kts	27.25/28kts	27.25/28kts	27.25/28kts	28kts
Endurance	5,000@12kts					4,500@12kts
Fuel Oil	560 tons	540 tons	560 tons	510 tons	510 tons	400 tons
Sonar	184				177	177
VDS	CAST (Type 199)				None	None
Torpedo	ONGAR			—	—	12 Mk 20
Helicopter	WESSEX with Mk 43 or 44			Wasp	—	
A/S Missile	ASROC	—	—	Limbo	Limbo	2 Limbo
SSGW	Yes		No	No	No	No
Air/Surface GW	Yes			No	No	No
Gun	—	—	Single 4.5in		4.5in twin	4.5in twin
Air Radar	965M				277Q	277Q
TI	293Q or 992			992	992	293Q
Surface	978		—	974	—	—
Dispt	3,600 deep	3,300	3,600	3,100	3,000	2,600
Armt (%)	12.3	11.8	12.3	12.2	11.0	11.1
Hull (%)	50	49	50	46	44	44
Accom	—	300	—	—	—	281

In this table, powers above 30,000 SHP were the ones required to make the desired 28kts deep and dirty. D was a conventional frigate along the lines already being proposed for the later Type 12s, with the variable depth sonar, Seacat and a Wessex helicopter. E was an even more conventional ship, with a lightweight ASW helicopter (Wasp) instead of the big Wessex. SSGW was an undefined Small Ship (AAW) Guided Weapon, presumably represented by Tartar. In these studies Seacat was eliminated wherever SSGW was mounted, since SSGW would cover Seacat range (because DTSD did not take this view, Seacat was carried on board the missile destroyers). Seacat was so light that adding it would make very little difference. ASGW was the helicopter-launched air-to-surface missile, twenty-four of which were to be carried; at this time it was associated only with the big Wessex. Later it was carried on board the much smaller Wasp.

Replacing the 4.5in gun with a twin 3in/70 would have increased armament weight from 306 tons to 337.5 tons, increasing displacement to 3,250 tons, and forcing length up to 400ft. Replacing the 4.5in with Tartar would require additional radars: SPG-51 for guidance and a three-dimensional set (the US SPS-26 or its successor, SPS-39). They could be accommodated on a 370ft hull (about 3,060 tons), which would make 27.25kts. A quarter-knot could be gained by reducing displacement to 3,000 tons by reducing oil so that range would fall to 4,200nm.

At the meeting, Purvis, who was in charge of frigate design, pointed out that Tartar was the only available SSGW. Given the radiation hazard created by its radars, any nearby gun would have to be enclosed. In the absence of a simple fire con-

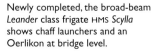

Newly completed, the broad-beam *Leander* class frigate HMS *Scylla* shows chaff launchers and an Oerlikon at bridge level.

F 58

trol system, the only suitable gun would be the twin 4.5in with MRS 3, as in Type 12. Tartar was expensive, and the only possible simplifications were to use one director instead of the usual two or to cut the number of missiles.

Purvis argued that DTSD's requirements were impractical: his ship would need a new powerplant and would displace 4,000 tons. A 3,000-ton ship with the standard 30,000 SHP plant could make 28kts if lengthened to 380ft, but she could carry only 167 tons of armament on that tonnage. She would therefore have to be either an A/S, an anti-aircraft, or a limited general purpose type.[23] Nor could she carry enough oil to reach the desired 5,000nm at 12kts (that had to be cut to 4,200nm). The main items forcing up the size of the ship were the longer and heavier machinery required to reach 28kts; increased fuel oil for the longer steaming range; and new weapons (the Wessex with its large pad and hangar, Tartar and ASROC). Whatever the horsepower, DME still wanted ABCD protection; in June he asked for two more frame spaces in both engine and boiler rooms, adding 18ft to the original machinery length of 72ft.

The Redesigned Type 12: *Leander*

The calculations showed that Sims had been right six months earlier: it would be relatively easy to redesign the Type 12, but very difficult to do as much as was wanted. Moreover, the Royal Navy was very reluctant to buy Tartar, officially because it was too complex and too expensive. It seems likelier that available dollars, never in great supply, could better be spent on more urgent items, such as the new nuclear powerplant for the sub-

marine HMS *Dreadnought*. Although work continued on a new frigate design, it must have been clear that a further evolution of Type 12 made far more sense.[24] The alternatives were full or partial modernisation and retrofitting (on paper) with newer weapons. The design had already been modified to take a lightweight helicopter (at the cost of one Limbo) and one Seacat (GWS 21). The ship still had twelve torpedo tubes for the Bidder homing torpedo, substantially lighter than Ongar. Deep displacement was 2,634 tons.

Full modernisation would provide full air-conditioning (rather than none), full (rather than partial) bunk sleeping, full cafeteria messing (rather than such messing only for senior rates), a revised fuel system with fuel tank ballast instead of separate ballast tanks, a separate machinery control room, a raised quarterdeck, and full ABCD except for boilers. This version would have MRS 3 instead of the earlier Mk 6M main battery director, two Seacat launchers, single Limbo, four torpedo tubes, a lightweight helicopter (with push-hangar and twenty-four US-type Mk 43 torpedoes), and stabilisers. Type 184 sonar would replace the earlier Type 177, and the ship would accommodate the CAST VDS. The ship would have a Type 965M radar, not because each ship needed long-range air-search or air-direction capability, but because in 1959 the Naval Staff wanted one frigate in four to have it. The easiest way to accomplish that was to install the radar in the next four frigates. Once that had been done, the rest of the class was so fitted. Deep displacement would rise to about 2,700 tons. Compared to Type 12, metacentric height would increase somewhat (2.7ft rather than 2.3ft).

The partial version had the raised quarterdeck, but kept the separate ballast system, the partial bunks, and the partial cafeteria mess. It had no ABCD features. A retrofit would remove one Limbo and the eight fixed torpedo tubes, adding two Seacat launchers and a lightweight helicopter. Sonars would

HMS *Hermione*, a Batch III *Leander*, is shown as of July 1968. The objects on the side of her tower foremast are Type 667 jammers to screen major fleet units. Below the HF/DF array at her foretop is a UA-8/9 ESM array associated with the jammers. The tower mainmast carries a Type 965 radar, for task force early air warning, and the 'sword' antenna used for communications interception. Aside from the twin 4.5in forward, her only gun armament is a pair of Oerlikons, one of which is visible just abaft the MRS 3 gun director. A second MRS 3 aft controls her Seacat. Just visible on the flight deck are the protruding barrels of her Limbo, and equipment aft is for her Type 182 torpedo decoy (part of her Type 199 VDS sonar is visible through her transom). Note her large fin stabiliser and the pair of sonar domes, one for her Limbo fire-control sonar (Type 170) and one for her long-range search sonar (Type 184). (A D Baker III)

---

[23] Purvis pointed out that any SSGW would consume about 140 tons, leaving only 27 tons. If the DNC margin were cut to an impossible 13 or 14 tons, the ship could also have either ASROC, or a lightweight helicopter and Seacat (GWS 21), or a Wessex with torpedoes and fuel. Substituting a twin 4.5in gun (104 tons) for the SSGW would leave 43 tons, since in that case the ship would need a Type 992 radar (about 20 tons). That would buy two Seacats (GWS 21) or CAST (VDS) and a light A/S situation was, if anything, grimmer, since even two Seacats (for self-defence) would consume 38 tons. Within 177 tons, more than was allowed, the ship could then have CAST (25 tons), a Wessex (20 tons plus 50 tons of fuel), and ASROC (41 tons), plus a Type 293Q radar for target indication. For AAW, there were two alternatives: SSGW plus one Seacat or the twin 4.5in gun plus two Seacat and a lightweight helicopter. If the ship was not required to operate a big Wessex, her length might be cut to the 360ft of a Type 12.

[24] One constructor's notebook carries a note dated 29 September 1959 that he had decided to investigate a 390ft × 43ft × 28ft 6in ship, but there was no follow-up.

be unaltered. Deep displacement would be 2,620 tons, and metacentric height would be somewhat less (2.2ft at deep load).

The full modernisation was chosen. In a memo in July 1959 DG Ships argued that this would be a better choice than building more 'Tribals'. Type 81 offered better habitability and had some valuable Cold War qualities, but it was slower and had untried machinery. A description of the redesigned ship was given to the Treasury on 7 September 1959, when formal agreement was sought to include three ships (FSA 21–23) in the 1959/60 Long Term Costings. A Legend dated 22 December 1959 was circulated for Board approval on 11 February 1960, to apply to future frigates (FSA 21 onwards). The Board approved the sketch design in March 1960.[25] It specifically commended DGS on the ingenuity of the design. No Type number was chosen because the class name, *Leander*, had already been assigned.

Deep displacement was given as 2,700 tons. Dimensions and hull form matched those of a Type 12, but internally the ship was totally redesigned. Greater stability made it possible to improve arrangements, particularly in the CO's and officers' accommodation. The bridge was modelled on that of the Type 81 frigate, for a better view aft. The Operations Room was moved a deck down and given unimpeded access to the bridge via a ladder. Armament was the usual twin 4.5in gun plus two Seacat launchers (GWS 21 with twenty-five missiles per launcher), four fixed torpedo tubes (with Mk 20 Bidder

torpedoes), a lightweight helicopter (sixteen Mk 43 torpedoes), and single Limbo (twenty salvoes). Cruise turbines were eliminated, and the 400 kW turbo-generators were replaced by 500 kW units. The two 300 kW diesel generators were moved from the eyes of the ship to the hold, exhausting through the new plated-in mast. Later units such as HMS *Phoebe* had 450 kW diesels, and the later broad-beam units had 750 kW turbo-generators. Endurance was 4,500nm at 12kts in temperate waters, oil fuel having been increased to 450 tons. The old water ballast tanks were eliminated in favour of ballasting with seawater as fuel was expended. That made it easier to provide for future growth.

In the course of design the superstructure was integrated to make better use of space, also improving appearance and eliminating traps for pre-wetting water. A new turret-type bridge, based on that of the 'County' class missile destroyer, replaced the frigate-type bridge. A revised Legend showed a displacement of 2,720 tons (2,240 tons standard). Expected cost rose slightly due to increased labour costs (a 42-hour week was instituted in March 1960), the increased cost of the Seacat missile (GWS 21), and the inclusion of electronic warfare systems (UA-8/9 ESM and Type 667 ECM, from FSA 21 onwards).[26] Rather surprisingly, given all the agony over speed, the ship was credited with 28kts deep and dirty six months out of dock. The difference was that this was under temperate, not tropical, conditions.

In July 1960, in connection with the decision to build four *Leanders* instead of modernising four *Daring* class destroyers (see below) it was stated that the *Leanders* would be fitted with

Although not conceived for export, *Leanders* enjoyed considerable export success. This is the Indian *Taragiri*, with an enlarged helicopter hangar and Dutch rather than British radars, yet clearly still a *Leander*. She is shown in February 2001. (John Mortimer)

[25] ADM 1/27563. The memo for the Board is B.1318 of 11 February 1960 in ADM 167/156. Minute 5393 of 3 March 1960 (ADM 167/156) explicitly mentions the decision not to build any more Type 81s. The building drawings were approved on 30 June 1960 (Minute 5424).

[26] ADM 167/156, Memo B.1343 of 21 June 1960.

The Indian Navy went furthest in developing the *Leander* theme. *Godavari*, shown in October 1988, combined a recognisable *Leander* hull with a mixture of Russian and Western systems. The main search radar is Dutch, the radar forward is Russian (to control a SAM system forward of the bridge, retracted into the deck), and the main battery is four Russian-type Styx missiles. The helicopter hangar aft has been enlarged to support British Sea King helicopters. This version of the *Leander* was further developed as the current *Bramaputra* class. (John Mortimer)

the new Integrated Communication System (ICS) at the expense of the planned torpedo tubes. That was justified on the ground that Mk 20E torpedo performance had been very disappointing.

All of this mattered because on 28 May 1959 the Admiralty Board had accepted Fourth Sea Lord's recommendation, based on the costing of the new overall fleet plan (88 Plan), that work should resume in October on the twentieth and last Type 12 frigate then on order, HMS *Weymouth* (which had replaced the aircraft direction frigate *Coventry*, ordered under the 1955/6 Programme). She became HMS *Leander*. Three earlier ships (FSA 14, 16 and 19) were reordered as well: *Fowey* and *Hastings* became *Ajax* and *Dido*; the third ship had not yet been named. These were the only ships which could be altered while under construction, although *Weymouth* could not have the new turbo-generators without accepting a six-month delay. Machinery for three more frigates (FSA 21–23) would be ordered in October so that the ships could be laid down in October 1961.[27] The frigates would be ordered in tandem with two more missile destroyers , as the next slice of the new construction programme. New frigates, rather than modernised *Daring*s (see below) would replace the postponed DLG 7 through 10. A substantial frigate-building programme was coming. It would consist entirely of the new type.[28]

Another three ships were ordered under each of the 1961/2 and 1962/3 Programmes (FSA 24–29). The 1962/3 ships had machinery redesigned for better access, as experience had shown that the operational availability of Type 12 frigates was limited by access to their machinery. They were to have introduced a small-ship version of the ADA combat data system (plus SINS to work with it), but these features were omitted as too expensive. However, Type 184 sonar, designed to work with ADA, was substituted for Type 177.

In May 1962 the Cabinet Defence Committee agreed to continue at this rate of three frigates each year over the next three years, 1963/4, 1964/5 and 1965/6. The point at which the series ended depended on progress with the Sea Dart missile, which was supposed to arm follow-on frigates (which ended up as the massive destroyer *Bristol*; see the next chapter). The programme was extended to two ships in 1966/7, the third frigate that year being the first Type 82, HMS *Bristol*. With the cancellation of further Type 82s three more *Leander*s were ordered (1967/68 Programme) to keep shipyards alive: two last units for the Royal Navy, *Ariadne* and *Apollo*, and a third for the Royal New Zealand Navy (HMNZS *Canterbury*). Plans for another three were abandoned in favour of building the new Type 21. The ten 1964/5 to 1967/8 ships were built to a modified 'broad beam' design. DG Ships wanted added stability (from 2ft more beam) to allow for future modernisation. That added 25 tons of deep load and cost less than a quarter-knot at deep displacement. The existing layout was kept, but the added beam relieved some congestion, *eg* in the wardroom. The change was proposed on 10 January 1964 and approved in August.[29]

[27] ADM 1/27498 summarises the situation late in 1959, after the *Leander* design had been chosen.
[28] ADM 167/156, Memo B.1339 of 13 June 1960 on the Long Term Costing through the mid-1960s. Tartar was specifically rejected at this time. The rolling programme was not initially envisaged. Initial costings of the 88 Plan (1958) showed only four frigates in the 1960/1 through 1965/6 programmes; by 1963 the Royal Navy hoped for eighteen. The increase of fourteen was attributable to deferments (one from 1958/9, one from 1959/60), adjustments (four ships) to even the flow of construction, and progressive replacement of earlier ships (eight ships) which had not been included in the original 80 Plan. The rolling plan ensured production of large numbers of more or less identical ships.

[29] ADM 1/31008.

The *Leander* class was extremely successful. In addition to the twenty-six built for the Royal Navy, six each were built for the Royal Netherlands Navy and the Indian Navy, and two each for Chile and New Zealand. India built a further three, armed with Soviet systems, as the *Godavari* class, and three

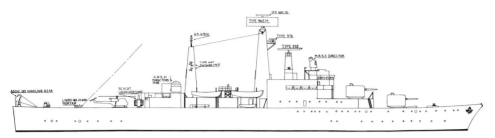

more with further modifications as the *Brahmaputra* class. As late as the 1980s, Yarrow offered a redesigned *Leander* to the Royal Australian Navy for what became the ANZAC class. Of all post-war British frigate classes, the *Leanders* were the only ones never assigned a Type number.

DGD, however, was also right. The result of all this effort was still a gun-armed frigate, albeit with a long-range sonar and a stand-off delivery system in the form of a helicopter. By the 1970s it would be obsolescent at best. Future British frigates would need a small-ship missile system. Tartar was definitely rejected in 1960, and the Royal Navy began to develop its own Sea Dart, the question being whether it should arm frigates or something larger.

Destroyers vs Frigates

Probably the clearest indication of the new status of the big frigates was the demise of a proposal to modernise the first

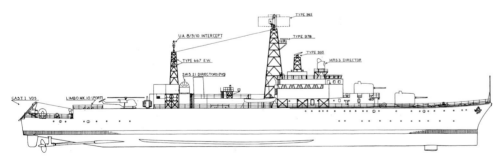

four (DC electrical system) *Daring* class destroyers. A draft Staff Requirement was issued in March 1956. The ship would get long-range sonar (Type 177 or VDS plus Type 170 for Limbo and Type 176 for self-protection). Her one remaining set of torpedo tubes would be modified to fire long-range anti-ship homing torpedoes (Fancy); alternatively she might have four fixed tubes on each side. Limbo (with at least twenty salvoes) would replace Squid. The existing 4.5in fire-control system would be replaced by MRS 3 with GDS 5 (using Type 293Q radar). The unreliable Flyplane computer, with its many vacuum tubes, would be eliminated. The ship would be fitted with the new small-ship air-warning radar (ultimately designated Type 965). DNC observed that the Australian *Darings*

had both No. 3 gun mount and Limbo, whereas it appeared that in the British ships No. 3 mount would have to be landed when Limbo was installed. By October 1957 plans called for replacing both sets of torpedo tubes with a deckhouse containing eight fixed tubes. Apart from the gun armament (two twin 4.5in and two twin Bofors) this was not too different from the slightly earlier Fast A/S Escort.

Under the '88 Plan' approved in 1957, the *Daring*s were to be replaced on a one-for-one basis by 'County' class missile destroyers, the first four of which would be ready by 1966.[30] In 1959 there was a new factor: construction of the later missile destroyers (DLG 7–10) was being deferred. Since DGW and the Ministry of Supply were considering a more advanced missile system, NIGS, for the late 1960s, they might be further deferred to be armed with it. That left a hole which four *Daring*s could fill; they would be needed for the whole of 1962–70 and in operational reserve for some time afterwards. The Staff now saw the eight *Daring*s, suitably modernised in 1960–4, as the core fleet ASW force. The four later (AC) *Daring*s, forming the 5th Destroyer Squadron (DS 5), were undergoing an extended refit. They would receive updated fire-control systems and minor improvements, but were hardly being modernised. They would therefore be quite inadequate for the extended service now contemplated. The other four *Daring*s (DS 2) would be taken in hand in 1961. They would have to be modernised or partly modernised or new ships built. Anything but considerable modernisation would leave them seriously deficient against the threats of the 1960s. Even without a full refit, the elderly and now unreliable FPS 3 computer would have to be replaced simply to keep the ships effective. The ships could be modernised at Royal Dockyards in 1961–4 (these yards were more flexible than private ones).

Installation of Type 965 radar was particularly desirable, as it would add considerably to task group or convoy air defence. At this point full modernisation also entailed provision of long-range sonar (Type 177 or Type 184), the light helicopter to deliver a torpedo using that sonar, six fixed A/S torpedo tubes and Limbo. One twin 4.5in mount would be landed. Seacat (GWS 21) would be fitted.

With no new destroyer design ready (and nothing short of a missile destroyer in sight), any replacement ship would be a frigate. Both existing types, Types 12 and 81, lacked firepower. However, a combination design might provide good ASW capability and long-range air-warning with fleet speed. It would also offer some anti-aircraft support to the fleet, though that might be marginal by the late 1960s. Thus what amounted to a *Leander* became, remarkably, the explicit alternative to an expensive destroyer modernisation. This equivalence was raised implicitly in an April 1959 paper for the Board which described the modernised destroyers as combining in one hull the best qualities of Type 12 and Type 81: fleet speed,

[30] ADM 167/153, B.1270 of 5 June 1959.

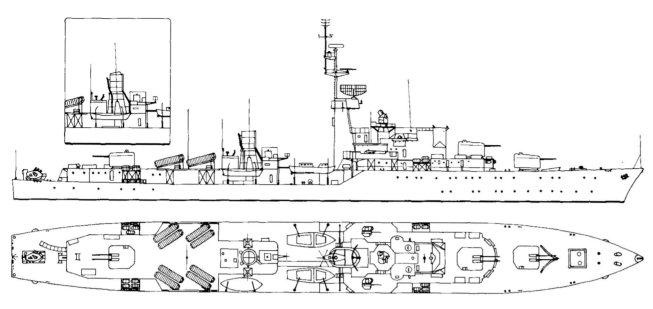

good A/S capability, and a long-range air-search radar. For the moment, the Fleet Requirements Committee recommended modernisation of DS 2. The Board approved modernisation that June.[31]

Modernising the four ships would cost £12 million, or £14 million with ABCD improvements required by the Board A more limited modernisation would omit both the long-range sonar and the helicopter, and the ships would have only four fixed torpedo tubes and Limbo. Sonars would be limited to 170 for Limbo and 174. This version still had the two twin 4.5in, Type 965M radar, and Seacat (GWS 21). The price for all four would fall to £6 million. A simple refit (£4 million) would leave the ships with much their original armament (except for two visual-only Seacats, GWS 20) and a self-defence sonar (Type 176 in addition to the original Type 164). The ships would retain one pentad torpedo tube and Squid. They would need another refit in 1968.

At this time a Type 12 cost about £3.5 million: full modernisation of a *Daring* would cost about as much as a new frigate, and the ship would be much more expensive to man. She would be somewhat faster, but would not last nearly as long. In July 1960, therefore, the Board decided to abandon the project, explicitly comparing it to the new *Leander* (which had the same sonar and the same helicopter), four of which would cost only £5 million more.[32] Ideally the four DC ships would simply be discarded when the AC *Darings* rejoined the fleet after their refits.

In fact the four DC ships were refitted beginning in 1958, their after torpedo tubes being replaced by a deckhouse offering additional accommodation. Partial modernisation (1962–4) replaced the other set of tubes with another deckhouse. The STAAGs were replaced by lighter Utility Mk V Bofors, and the Mk VI directors by the lighter MRS 3. In this configuration the ships deployed for the first time East of Suez, presumably

because they now required far less maintenance. They remained in service until 1967–9. The four AC ships were refitted in 1959–60, their STAAGs replaced by single Bofors and their Mk VI directors by MRS 3s. *Decoy* had a prototype Seacat missile launcher installed in place of her Mk V twin Bofors, her CRBF director modified to control the missile. The refit prepared the other three for a similar missile installation, but that never happened, and the *Decoy* missile was removed in 1962 after the trials. *Duchess* was transferred to the RAN to replace HMAS *Vampire*, lost in 1964. Of the other three, *Diamond* survived as Portsmouth harbour training ship until 1981. The other two were rebuilt for Peru in 1973, their foremasts plated in and new AWS-1 air search radar installed.

RAN plans to modernise the four Australian *Darings* can be compared with the British project.[33] After the Australian Chiefs of Staff rejected a proposal to install Tartar missiles, they approved installation of Ikara. A March 1966 project directive for half-life modernisation of HMAS *Vendetta* and *Vampire* called for removal of X gun mount, both twin Bofors, and the torpedo tubes. Ikara (twenty-five missiles) and the US SQS-23 (Type 177 was an alternative) sonar would be installed, plus two Seacats. Existing British radars would be replaced by Dutch Signaal sets: the M22/6 'egg' for gun fire-control, M44 for Seacat control, and LW02 for air search. The ship would have one JYA and one JYB plotting table, with radar inputs switchable between LW02, the 'egg', and the navigational radar. Although neither was part of a digital system, the Staff Requirement included provision of (or space for) a digital data link. The existing bridge would be replaced by one similar to that in a Type 12 frigate. As in the British project, the long-range air-search radar would give the ship a limited radar-picket capability. Both ships were modernised in 1970–3, but apparently without Ikara or the long-range sonar.

---

[31] ADM 167/155, Minute 5325 of 11 June 1959.
[32] Board Minute 5434, 28 July 1960. The decision was due in part to the steep rise in the expected cost of modernisation.

[33] Naval Board Project Directive 5/66: Half Life Modernisation of *Daring* Class Destroyers, March 1966, RAN Naval Historical Branch.

CHAPTER 13

The Second Post-war Generation

Sea Darts on board HMS *Bristol* on 25 August 1986. All RN Sea Dart ships used the same launcher, as hopes of developing a special lightweight type for Type 42s were abandoned. The only difference between systems on board different classes was that Type 42s had many fewer missiles on board, twenty-two rather than thirty-eight. Missiles were stowed vertically below the launcher and rammed hydraulically up through blast doors, the launcher arms being vertical, as in the US Mk 26 system. (Maritime Photographic)

The Small-Ship Guided Weapon

From about the end of the Second World War, the Royal Navy sought a missile suited for a frigate, on the theory that nothing else could defend against the rising threat of anti-ship missiles. The earliest was the short-range 100–150lb BEN (named after its inventor, Benson), an adapted air-to-air missile. Described as a 5in rocket with an IR seeker, it had some impact on early US studies leading to the Sidewinder air-to-air weapon. In 1946 it seemed that Longshot (ex-BEN) might be available in 1948/9, so a Staff Requirement for a missile to arm frigates and destroyers was issued, but it failed to make the shortlist of projects worthy of scarce development resources, assembled by the Defence Research Policy Committee. By May 1947 the short-range missile Staff Requirement was apparently associated with the name Popsy. Since nothing was known of Soviet efforts, the proposed weapon was designed to deal with either wartime German weapons (which were presumably the basis for Soviet developments) or with projected British and US weapons, ship- and air-launched, which might parallel Soviet efforts. We now know that the Soviets ordered work on an air-launched anti-ship missile in September 1947. It emerged in 1954 as KS (NATO AS-1 'Kennel').

Popsy was seen as the step beyond Seaslug, an anti-missile weapon with secondary anti-aircraft capability, offering the low-altitude firepower Seaslug lacked. Unfortunately the Ministry of Supply, responsible for British missile development, was already overloaded with its four projects: Seaslug, the army's Red Heathen, Blue Boar, and the air-to-air Red Hawk (Blue Sky). None of the four could easily be cancelled. Some features of Red Hawk, particularly its homing system, might benefit the Popsy project, but the missile itself could not be adapted to the Popsy role. Since resources were not available in the short term, in September 1948 the Royal Navy withdrew the 1946 Staff Requirement and replaced it with a Staff Target.

The alternative to Popsy was a conventional anti-aircraft gun, DACR (direct action close range), a joint Anglo-American programme. However, a study in September 1948 showed that guns could not deal with incoming missiles. The prospective 3in/70 could kill a non-manoeuvring target, but a manoeuvring missile would defeat it: even a 1G Blue Boar would reduce its net kill probability between 3,000 and 2,000 yds to about 20 per cent. The rapid-fire DACR (a notional 34mm gun, 4,000 rounds/min), whose shells could not accommodate a proximity fuse, was much worse: it had to fire 1,500 rounds at over 10,000 rnd/min to have a 94 per cent chance of hitting a Blue Boar flying a straight course between 2,000 and 200 yds. To so as well against a missile manoeuvring at 1.5G, it would have to fire 3,000 rounds at 20,000 rounds/min. These were impossible figures.

A small British working group was therefore formed to consider a missile solution. It reported on 1 April 1949.[1] Popsy was envisaged as an unpowered dart accelerated to speed by its booster. A subsonic version would be 5ft 8in long (weighing about 300lbs). With detachable control surfaces and wraparound boosters, 110 of them could fit in the forward 4.5in magazine of an anti-aircraft frigate. The supersonic version would be 7ft long with wrap-around boosters (400lbs); sixty-six could be accommodated in a 4.5in magazine. The missile would be semi-actively guided, using very short wavelength (Q-band, 8.6mm) to overcome reflections off the sea surface. A target would be acquired at 12,000–14,000 yds, the CW guidance system locking on at 10,000–12,000 yds. The launcher, locked to the illuminator, would begin to track the target at 8,000 yds. The subsonic version would engage a typical target at 3,000–4,000 yds (supersonic at 5,000 yds). At such ranges Type 992 (modified for higher elevation) would suffice for surveillance and target indication. Against the big Mach 0.85 Blue Boar stand-off bomb then being developed, a single Popsy with a miss distance of 25ft would offer a kill probability of 75 per cent (two would raise that to 94 per cent). Later estimates envisaged a 60ft miss distance (65 per cent single-shot kill probability).

Popsy was thus vital but the British were unlikely to develop it. DNO's solution was to approach the US Navy. Beginning in July 1950 a British team visited the US Navy's

[1] ADM 1/27591 is a 1949 account of Popsy.

Bureau of Ordnance to sell Popsy. Having examined several US projects, such as a guided shell, they pronounced Popsy significantly better. The British contribution to a US programme would be the superior Q-band radar technology essential to engage low-fliers. However, the US Navy was more interested in an escort function than in Popsy's self-defence role. The British team discovered a US Navy programme to develop the large air-to-air Meteor, which seemed quite suitable for the Popsy role. Making the dart powered would roughly double its range, making it a serious rival to all anti-aircraft guns. The British team persuaded MIT, which was developing Meteor, to change its CW guidance radar from wide- to narrow-beam, the remaining difference from Popsy being that it was X- rather than Q-band.[2] The British designated the joint project Mopsy. The US Navy rejected it, but the British would later say that this was the origin of the US Tartar – which the Royal Navy considered in the mid-1950s for the Popsy role. It homed semi-actively like Popsy but used lower-frequency radar. In 1950 the threat was scaled down from a fast missile like Blue Boar to the slower and larger Loon (a US V-1 copy), and guns became more attractive. The Bofors L70 thus seems to have filled the planned Popsy role, at least temporarily.[3]

The Popsy idea survived, to be revived about 1954 as Orange Nell, when it seemed that resources would soon become available because Seaslug development was almost complete.[4] A formal Staff Requirement (GD 45) was issued in 1956, but little was done. However, in 1958 the Fleet Requirements Committee pointed out that within a decade any frigate not armed with a missile would be obsolete. Tartar, the only available weapon, was soon rejected. That may well have been due to lack of dollars (as opposed to Sterling, which would pay for development of a British missile). Tartar was described as too

expensive and as lacking development potential. The latter would have been a distinct surprise to navies who now operate the Standard Missiles directly descended from Tartar. NATO had just issued a requirement, NMBR 11, for a frigate missile. Within the Royal Navy it was argued that a less elaborate, hence less expensive, missile could be developed. Development funding was justified at least partly by the hope that an austere British solution would be attractive to other navies. The Staff claimed a market for as many as 150 missile-armed frigates, saying their hopes had been raised by several recent proposals by British firms. It wanted the Staff Requirement rewritten (simplified) and the overriding Royal Navy requirements restated to the Ministry of Aviation, which would contract for development.

A staff paper describing this SIGS (Small Ship Guided Weapon) was circulated in October 1960.[5] The missile system would fit a 3,000-ton frigate and cost less than £1 million excluding search radar. It would arm frigates joining the fleet from 1968–9 on. Potential targets were low-altitude aircraft, air-launched stand-off missiles (like the Soviet AS-1), medium- and high-altitude bombers, frigate-sized surface targets, and ship-launched anti-ship missiles. Minimum altitude would be as low as 50ft. The First Sea Lord approved the programme on 5 December 1960.

The main candidates were Bristol's new CF 299 ramjet and an enhanced version of the army's Rapier (PT 428).[6] Bristol's tandem-boosted semi-actively guided ramjet was chosen, and christened Sea Dart. It was expected to engage Mach 3 targets at a range of 20,000 yds (low altitude) to over 30,000 yds (high altitude). Actual maximum altitude was 65,000ft. Mach 1.1 targets could be engaged down to 50ft. Minimum range was 10,000ft, rather than the 10,000 yds of Seaslug. Speed was 2,900ft/sec at high altitude and 2,500ft/sec at low altitude, compared to 2,000ft/sec for Seaslug. Absolute maximum range, set by aerodynamics, was 39nm. Sea Dart was credited with twice the kill probability of Seaslug. It had twice the target-handling capacity (destroyers had two illuminators), and had limited but real anti-ship capability. In 1966, estimated salvo (two-shot) kill probability against the Soviet AS-2 'Kipper' anti-ship missile was 0.8 to 0.9, compared to 0.35 to 0.55 for Seaslug II; figures for a 'Blinder' bomber were 0.5 to 0.8 compared to 0.3 to 0.5.[7] Partly because it was much faster, Sea Dart could engage more targets in a stream attack: typically seven rather than three supersonic aircraft or missiles. It could handle far greater crossing rates due to its collision-course guidance. Studies (1968) suggested that a two-channel Sea Dart

[2] The British conceived the idea of making Meteor the basis of Popsy in May 1950. According to the British report, Meteor weighed 360lbs. and was 109in long. In air-to-air form it used a 165lb booster; the surface-to-air version would use a 340lb booster; total lengths were, respectively, 161in and 181in (span 34in in either case). Against a Mach 1 sea level non-manoeuvring target the air-to-air version had a range of 3nm in a tail chase and 8.4nm head-on (figures for a manoeuvring target were 2nm and 5.9nm).
[3] According to AVIA 54/2103, the BuOrd/DNO conference in the UK agreed that the British would develop a fast-firing anti-missile DA gun for both navies. At the eighteenth meeting of the DACR Weapon Analysis Panel (August 1949) it was agreed that it would be impossible to meet the requirement for a 40,000 rnd/min 34mm gun firing for 5 seconds. In 1950 the joint view was that the supersonic target (like the British Blue Boar) was unrealistic, so attention shifted to subsonic missiles like the US Loon (V-1 copy), which were far easier to hit. About this time details emerged of the US T131 gun-assisted rocket, the same weight of ammunition of which offered the kill probability of a British 42mm gun (Red Queen) then being developed, but with a much lighter mounting. Other possibilities at this time were discarding-sabot shells, gun-assisted rockets, rocket darts (like the US Loki), and unguided rockets. The Royal Navy ruled out several possibilities because it did not want to risk damage by the sabots which shells or rockets might discard near a gun muzzle. At this time a quadruple Bofors L70 seemed to have a 22 per cent chance of sufficiently damaging a Loon, compared to 33 per cent for the slightly heavier Red Queen. A contemporary British army study gave the twin L70 a Figure of Merit of 42, compared to 54 for Red Queen and only 37 for a 3in/70.
[4] AVIA 54/2103 includes a September 1954 paper describing Orange Nell as a derivative of Mopsy/Popsy, for 1,500–2,500-ton frigates and as a secondary battery for Seaslug ships. Targets were subsonic and supersonic missiles and piloted aircraft penetrating the Seaslug screen at altitudes between 50–15,000ft. Single-shot kill probability against aircraft was to be better than 30 per cent at ranges beyond 12,000 yds, with a cumulative kill probability of 80 per cent before the target reached minimum range (about 2,000 yds). As of 1952 estimated missile characteristics were a maximum body diameter of 10in, length 10ft (6ft missile, 4ft booster, both solid-fuel), and a total weight of 500lbs (270lb missile). The missile would be wingless, with 25.5in tail span for tail control. Maximum lateral acceleration would be 25G, and the warhead would weigh 40lbs. Slant range would be 9,700 yds. On 18 November 1955 DNO asked for an assessment of Orange Nell as a high priority. The Staff Target for Popsy had been the supposed 1960 threat: a supersonic missile, to be engaged outside 2,000 yds, and a subsonic missile outside 4,000 yds (piloted aircraft would be engaged at the maximum possible range).

[5] ADM 1/27647.
[6] As of January 1961, PT 428 (Rapier) used a quadruple launcher with a total of fifty-six or fifty-eight missiles, each 242lb, typically with two directors forward. At this time CF 299 (768lb missile) also used a quadruple launcher. Vickers-Armstrong was promoting a version of Tartar (1,172lb) using a twin launcher. Each system was associated with its own search radar. Ultimately Sea Dart weighed 1,200lb.
[7] DEFE 48/7, a 1966 analysis of fleet air defence, completed before Sea Dart entered service. These figures were probably over-optimistic for both Seaslug II and Sea Dart. The 1968 study was described to the Operational Requirements Committee, DEFE 10/942.

system was equivalent to eight Phantoms on combat air patrol. An upgrade to handle sea-skimmers was ordered in 1971. Initially it appeared that a 3,000-ton frigate could accommodate thirty to forty missiles. During the Falklands War, Sea Dart was credited with destroying seven Argentine aircraft. During the 1991 Gulf War, HMS *Gloucester*'s Sea Dart destroyed two Silkworm cruise missiles fired at the US battleship *Missouri*.

Seaslug had proven surprisingly expensive to develop. When the proposal for the new missile came before the Operational Requirements Committee, the first question was whether it was a Seaslug replacement. The Royal Navy knew that the new weapon was far superior, but it was reluctant to kill the Seaslug programme before ships armed with the weapon could come into service. The answer was that the new missile was not in the same category (it was far superior). The DRPC endorsed

An Ikara missile, as shown at the Explosion! museum at Gosport. The missile in left background is Seawolf; to right, partly visible, is an Exocet. (Author)

full development in 1962; work began in the spring of 1963. The missile was re-endorsed by the Operational Requirements Committee on 15 December 1966. This GWS 30 system armed the new Type 82 frigate/destroyer, HMS *Bristol*, as well as the Type 42 destroyers and the *Invincible* class carriers.

The Sea Dart ship would have a new three-dimensional surveillance radar, Broomstick (British Type 988) being developed by the Dutch.[8] It was considered essential to battle-group air defence, but unnecessary for Sea Dart itself. For the Dutch, Broomstick was to be a key element of a new missile ship. Both navies were already collaborating on a new small-ship combat direction system. It is not clear how far the latter project

went; the British and the Dutch did jointly propose a new data link (ultimately Link X or Link 10), cheaper than the Link 11 developed by the US Navy, and the character of the link seems to have been connected with the choice of 24-bit computers (albeit different ones) by both navies. Given this collaboration, and their purchase of Broomstick, the British hoped the Dutch would adopt Sea Dart, extending its production run and reducing unit cost. At this time it was estimated that the radar would cost about as much as the combat direction system and half as much as a two-director Sea Dart system. The British were shocked that the Dutch rejected Sea Dart in favour of the US Tartar system (Standard Missile), reportedly largely because unit price had risen to £30,000 in 1967/8 from the 1962 estimate of £25,000.[9]

Attempts to sell Sea Dart to several other countries, including Germany, South Africa, Spain, and Turkey, all failed. China came close to buying a boxed version about 1982 to refit existing destroyers, apparently mainly for the anti-ship role, but lost interest after supposed missile failures during the Falklands War (it has also been suggested that the Chinese decided to develop their own equivalent; this project apparently failed). The only customer was Argentina, for two Type 42 destroyers. Argentine knowledge of the system probably caused their pilots to adopt very low-level attack tactics against the British task force in the South Atlantic. These tactics saved many aircraft, but they probably also helped the Royal Navy. Bomb fuses had to be delayed to protect aircraft against their own bomb explosions, so bombs from very low-flying Argentine aircraft often hit before they could arm.

Ikara

In the late 1950s the Royal Navy was also interested in a stand-off ASW weapon. Initially the only alternative, which was rejected in favour of helicopter delivery, was the US ASROC. In 1959, without any input from the Royal Navy, the Australians began developing Ikara, a rocket-powered missile carrying a

8 The Type 988 project was endorsed by the Defence Research Policy Committee in 1962, and a Letter of Understanding exchanged with the Dutch in March 1964. Each navy would pay for its own prototype, and the British would finance half of the design effort. Between 1964 and 1967 the project suffered heavily from inflation, the unit price rising from £1.475 million to £2.75 million, in each case including spares. DEFE 10/532.

9 DEFE 69/482 describes an Anglo-Dutch meeting at The Hague on 26 May 1966. The Royal Navy claimed that Sea Dart offered faster reaction, better range and better ECCM (J-band radar rather than G-band in the US Standard Missile, the Tartar successor). The British also claimed that their unique combination of an interferometer and a dish in the missile was equivalent to a 14in dish, far larger than the 11in of the US missile. To provide gain equivalent to that of Sea Dart in J-band Standard would need a 20in dish. Thus Sea Dart could enjoy much better accuracy. Furthermore, Standard intercepted after its fuel burned out, flying Mach 1.3 at low altitude, compared to the Mach 2.3–2.7 of Sea Dart. At this time the US system was not backed by any automated command system, so it reacted much more slowly (30 seconds vs 12 seconds for Sea Dart). The Dutch expected to back either missile with an automated command system, in which case they expected the solid-fuelled Standard to react faster. Dutch satisfaction with the US Terrier system was apparently a major factor in the Dutch decision against Sea Dart. In November 1965 British manufacturer Hawker Siddely Dynamics submitted a budget at Dutch request. On 25 April 1966 the Dutch asked for a firm fixed price; they wanted to know the costs to the Royal Navy of the first two frigate systems, including forty missiles each, twelve for practice, and three for blast trials. Other papers in DEFE 69 include the claim that upon seeing the British unit cost for Sea Dart the US Navy had under-priced Tartar (Standard) in order to undercut the British. See also DEFE 13/558. The Dutch ship is described in S G Nooteboom, *Deugdelijke Scheppen: Marinescheepsbouw 1945-1995* (Europese Bibliotek, Zaltbommel: 2001), a semi-official history of post-war Dutch naval development (p 113). She would have had a single-director system and a French 100mm gun rather than the British 4.5in; the sonar would have been a modified version of the EDO 610 on board the Dutch *Leander* class frigates. The search radar was Broomstick. Eventually the Dutch planned to adopt the same Ikara ASW system as the British, albeit without the nuclear depth bombs planned for (but never adopted for) the British ships. Complement was 345 rather than the 390 of the British ship. The evidence for the approach to Spain is a 1963–4 file listed by The National Archives but not opened, ADM 1/28558. The unsuccessful approach to the Germans is in DEFE 69/112.

lightweight homing torpedo. It offered a range of 20,000 yards, which was about the maximum achievable by sonars like Type 177. A ship could launch Ikara on the basis of another ship's sonar data, so that the missile's maximum range could be exploited. Unlike ASROC, Ikara was controlled throughout its flight, and thus could deal more effectively with a rapidly-manoeuvring submarine. Typical reaction time against a target at a range of 10,000 yds was two minutes. Like other missiles, Ikara had a minimum range, generally estimated as 3,000 yds, so to deal with a submarine slipping within this range or on the bottom (hence immune to lightweight torpedo seekers) British Ikara ships also had single Limbo.

In 1962 the Royal Navy decided to adopt Ikara under the codename Blue Duck.[10] The project study was formally approved in 1963, the missile being scheduled to enter service about 1970 and to last about twenty years. The NSR 7668 Operational Requirement was formally approved in May 1963. The British version differed from the Australian in that it used a digital fire-control system embodied in the ADAWS combat direction system, which in turn embodied a ship-to-ship digital link. Ikara was to equip not only the new Type 82 destroyer (six ships, at that time), but also the new carrier and eight escorts (Ikara destroyers). The system designation, GWS 40, indicated that it was developed immediately after Sea Dart (GWS 30) but before Exocet (GWS 50) was bought. In 1962 an Ikara system was expected to cost about half as much as a two-director Sea Dart system.

A major issue was whether Ikara would also be armed with the nuclear depth bomb being developed for frigate helicopters. This option was abandoned in 1966, having figured heavily in frigate designs. Ikara was eventually retired to avoid paying for redesign to carry the British Stingray lightweight torpedo; it was much simpler to modify helicopters.

The Missile Frigate: *Bristol*

The expectation in 1960, when SIGS/Sea Dart was conceived, was that when the system matured frigate production would shift from *Leander*s to missile ships, without changing the rate of production. After all, the missile would simply replace the ship's gun. The missile ship would be somewhat more expensive than a *Leander*, but not cripplingly so.

The new ship project began in April 1961 as the 'CF 299 Frigate' or 'New Frigate,' becoming the Post *Leander* Frigate when a Draft Staff Requirement was issued on 8 March 1963. As an example of what was initially planned, a SIGS frigate sketched in May 1961 had the *Leander* powerplant.[11] Desired deep displacement was 3,500 tons, desired speed was 28kts deep and dirty, and desired endurance was the 5,000nm at 12kts of the 1959 studies. Armament was one SIGS system with forty missiles, perhaps supplemented by Seacat, plus Limbo or two lightweight helicopters. The ship would have a data handling system. She would have a new smaller radar

HMS *Bristol* was the sole survivor of an ambitious programme to produce missile destroyers. She is shown in May 1982. The big radome forward covers a Type 909 missile-control (illuminator) radar; another is visible abaft her after funnel. The small radome alongside the bridge controls the Ikara anti-submarine missile, whose launcher is hidden in the structure abaft her 4.5in gun. The big radar atop the bridge, Type 965P, replaced the abortive Anglo-Dutch Broomstick (Type 988), a version of which equipped the Dutch *Tromp* class. The radar atop the mainmast is Type 992, for missile and gun target indication. There was no separate gun fire-control system.

[10] ADM 302/483. Versions of Ikara had M designations, M3 carrying Mk 44 only and M3+ adding the British Mk 31. British plans had initially envisaged using the US Mk 46 lightweight, but Mk 31 was preferred. These versions could not lift heavier torpedoes such as the new British NAST 7511 (which became Stingray). According to DEFE 24/239, on 20 October 1966 the Admiralty Board Ship Committee chose 'M-4 Minus,' which deleted provision for the nuclear depth bomb but could later deliver NAST 7511. The latter, which could deal with a 35-knot submarine at depths to 2,000ft, was considered essential if the system were to remain viable. M5 was a follow-on Australian version to carry the US Mk 46 torpedo, which was considerably heavier than Mk 44. When Mk 31 was cancelled, the British Mk 46 option had to be revived. The British version had different electronics than the Australian M5 and thus involved some new design effort. The Australians developed a surface-to-surface version under Project Womba (their Naval Staff Target 11/70, to enter service in the late 1970s), but it never figured in British plans for post-carrier anti-ship missiles. It would have become operational in the late 1970s. The Australians were also interested in the anti-ship potential of the Mk 46 torpedo Ikara carried.

[11] Notebook 337/16 (W G John), dated 24 May 1961, titled '1980's Ship'.

(2.5–3.5 tons, presumably a replacement for Type 965 and Type 992) and the usual sonars (Types 184 and 170). Initially it seemed that a version of Sea Dart which could replace a twin 4.5in on a one-for-one basis would simply have its missile capacity reduced from thirty-eight to twenty-six weapons. When the Indian Navy asked for exactly that version, DGS suddenly discovered that Sea Dart had grown beyond what a *Leander* could accommodate: the Sea Dart ship would have to be a fresh design.

There was apparently some interest in fitting Sea Dart to even smaller ships; at least one design study (51A) placed it on board a modified Type 14 frigate. The resulting ship would have displaced 2,050 tons (325ft × 37ft × 11ft 9in), and the 15,000 SHP Type 14 powerplant would have propelled her at 24.5kts deep and dirty. She would have had a single fire-control radar and thirty-two missiles; the ASW weapon would have been a Bofors rocket launcher (eighty rounds). The sonars would have been Type 170 (for the Bofors launcher) and Type 177. This ship would have cost slightly more than a *Leander*, £5.8 million in 1962 terms. In effect Study 51A demonstrated just how much Sea Dart itself cost.

Initially plans called for building separate Sea Dart and Ikara ships. Then it seems to have been decided that, whatever Ikara ships were built, the Sea Dart destroyer would have it. That enormously increased unit size and cost. The Royal Navy persevered with the project because it was deemed the most economical, and the quickest, way of getting both weapons into service.[12] To estimate the need for the new ship, in 1962–3 the Fleet Requirements Committee conducted a study of task-force defence in the early 1970s East of Suez, which was con-

sidered the main theatre for likely wars, which would be fought against Soviet proxies (such as Indonesia).[13] The British force comprised two carrier battle groups operating within 50nm of each other for mutual support, one underway replenishment group, and an amphibious group up to 200nm away (hence requiring its own missile escorts). Since the primary role of the carrier would be strike, she probably would not maintain a combat air patrol; her fighters would be launched on warning provided by three pickets, each 100nm away. Each would need her own Sea Dart missiles for self-defence. One Sea Dart ship could handle the assumed threat, an attack by five closely-spaced aircraft. A single ship at the centre of the task force could cover all sectors, but range against low-fliers was only about 20,000 yds. Even though the nuclear threat might be limited, ships would be dispersed at kiloton range (*ie* at sufficient distances so that a nuclear hit on one would not destroy the others). That made it impossible to rely on a single ship at the centre of a task force. The ideal would be at least three ships, each 5nm (10,000 yds) from the centre of the group. To allow for refuelling, submarine hunts, etc, it would be best for each force to have four missile escorts. Fitting Sea Dart to the new carrier, as was then planned, would somewhat alleviate the situation, since it would place a Sea Dart system at the centre of the battle group. Plans also called for each carrier to be accompanied by an escort cruiser armed with Sea Dart. The cruiser would carry the group's ASW helicopters.

On this basis, each carrier would have three Sea Dart-armed escorts. The amphibious force would need four missile escorts of its own, one of which could be armed with Seaslug. The carriers might make do with five pickets in all, if they operated close enough together. All of this suggested a need for four-

---

[12] Although the two-hull solution was referred to in justifying the Type 82 design, no trace of an early Ikara frigate was found in the constructors' notebooks, which seem to show all other contemporary designstudies. The separate Ikara ship was revived later.

[13] DEFE 8/24, FRC/M(62)-4 of 22 April 1963.

Type 82 as designed, with the massive Type 988 'Broomstick' radar forward, and with early 1960s EW systems on her mainmast: the Porker ESM system and the Cooky jammer. None of these systems was fitted. Note also the 'bird cage' HF/DF antenna on the maintop. VDA indicates the Type 199 towed sonar, also not fitted; Type 182 was the standard torpedo decoy. In an earlier version of the design, the mainmast was a pole carrying only the HF/DF array, and the ship carried no EW systems at all. (PRO: drawing from DEFE 24/38)

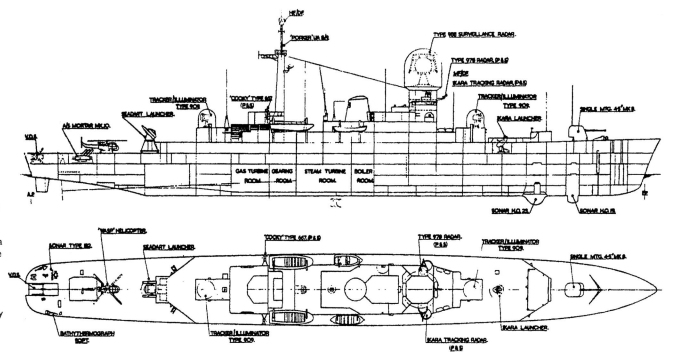

	53A	53B	53C	53D	53E	53F	53G	53H
Powerplant	S	S	S	S	G	G	C	S, Increased Complement
Deep Load	4,100 tons	3,600 tons	3,920 tons	3,440 tons	4,200 tons	3,600 tons	4,310 tons	4,300 tons
Length	400ft	375ft	395ft	370ft	400ft	375ft	410ft	440ft
Beam/GM deep	45ft/3.7	45.7ft/3.6	45ft/3.6	45.7ft/3.6	45ft/3.5	45.7ft/-	45ft	45ft
Draft	14.6ft	13.2ft	14.2ft	12.9ft	14.8ft	—	—	—
Speed (D&D)	c.28kts	c.28kts	26.4kts	26.7kts	c.28	—	—	—
Endurance/18kts	5,000nm	3,000nm	5,000nm	3,000nm	5,000nm	3,000nm	5,000nm	5,000nm
SHP. thousand	40	40	30	30	40	40	*	40
Accom				20/255				25/325
Hull	1,733 tons	1,667 tons	1,712 tons	1,641 tons	1,752 tons	1,689 tons	1,827 tons	1,866 tons
Equipment	245	243	245	243	245	243	245	290
Armament				275				
Machinery	635	635	530	530	462	462	710	635
Fuel	927	530	892	512	1,200	705	967	940
RFW	40	40	30	30	5	5	30	40
Margin	245	210	236	209	261	221	256	254
Cost, £ million	8.5	8.4	8.2	8.1	—	—	—	8.75

* two 12,500 SHP steam turbines and one 7,500 SHP gas turbine.

teen Sea Dart ships, all operating together East of Suez. British deployment patterns required at least two ships in service for every one deployed in the East, with an additional allowance for long refits. That suggested a need for about thirty Sea Dart frigates. At this time plans called for placing the first three Sea Dart ships in service in 1967, with another four in 1968, ten in 1969, and six in 1970. These figures presumably included the carrier and the escort cruiser, leaving thirteen Sea Dart frigates. Clearly in 1962 it was still expected that Sea Dart would impose a relatively minor cost on the projected *Leander* follow-on frigate.

The British considered it likely that the Soviets would either provide their proxies with nuclear submarines or even introduce 'volunteer' submarines into a local conflict, as Chinese 'volunteers' had entered the Korean War little more than a decade earlier. ASW protection of a carrier group would require a nuclear submarine in direct support, at least two helicopters airborne and one ready (on board the escort cruiser), three frigates armed with Ikara and Limbo (with long-range sonar like Type 184), and another Type 184 ship (which might be a 'County' or a *Leander*). The slower underway-replenishment group, much easier to attack, would need six escorts, at least two with Ikara, two with MATCH, and at least four with Limbos. The situation for an amphibious force would be similar. That added up to at least eight Ikara ships. The navy later claimed that design studies of separate Sea Dart and Ikara ships, included among forty conducted between April 1961 and mid-1963, showed that the most economical solution was to combine both systems in one hull.

Sketch Staff Requirements, the first ship requirements to be considered by the Operational Requirements Committee, were written early in 1962. Like earlier missile destroyers, the new ship would both directly defend a surface force and function as a radar picket supporting carrier-based fighters. The initial Staff Requirement also included such general purpose frigate roles as ASW and policing. At this stage project-

ed armament was Sea Dart (thirty-eight missiles) with two tracker-illuminators, Ikara (twenty missiles), Limbo (sixty projectiles), and the French short-range SS-11 wire-guided surface-to-surface missile (seventy-six missiles), the latter to deal with small craft but useless against anything larger. The sonars were Type 170 for Limbo, Type 184 for Ikara, and the US SQA-10 variable-depth sonar, plus the usual Type 162 to detect bottomed submarines. The big Anglo-Dutch radar was the only air-search set.

The Fleet Requirements Committee was offered versions of the current Design 53 (in the series of all contemporary preliminary design studies, including those for carriers and cruisers) with alternative two-shaft powerplants.[14] In the table above, S is steam, G is gas turbine, and C is COSAG. Speeds are for the deep and dirty (tropical) condition.

Cost was just short of twice that of a *Leander*. The staff requirements for 28kts and an endurance of 5,000nm at 18kts effectively ruled out all but 53A and 53E; 53F was intended for comparison with 53A. The all-steam 53A was chosen. In April 1963 YARD received a contract to design a 40,000 SHP steam plant (91ft × 45ft). The design was designated Type 82 at this time, the number indicating the general purpose character of the ship as a follow-on to Type 81 and to the *Leander*. Later the designation changed from Type 82 Escort (July 1964) to General Purpose Escort to Destroyer (March 1965).

This was hardly the inexpensive mass-production missile-armed *Leander* successor originally envisaged; it was close to cruiser size and cost. Much the same thing had recently happened to the 'County' class. DGW pointed out that from the weapons point of view the ship was more cruiser than frigate. DGS cautioned that it was an overgrown frigate or destroyer, not a true cruiser: Frigate standards meant limited protection: machinery was not unitised (to survive an underwater hit) and there was no splinter protection. In effect the ship had to be considered expendable. She lacked the

14 ADM 1/28960.

HMS *Bristol* fires an Ikara ASW missile. The ship's great (ultimately excessive) size was due to the decision to combine two missile systems, for ASW and AAW, in one hull. Although that was less expensive than building separate Sea Dart and Ikara ships, the size and cost of the resulting single unit proved unacceptable. In post-carrier planning *Bristol* was, in effect, scaled down to a single-missile destroyer (which emerged as Type 42 and as Ikara *Leander*) and scaled up to a command cruiser (the *Invincible* class, with helicopters rather than Ikara, but incorporating the key group command facilities on board *Bristol*). Note the SCOT satellite communications radome visible alongside the ship's foremast. (RN)

cruiser's stores endurance and ability for self-sustainment. She also lacked amenities.

The ship would be much slower than the 'County' class destroyers she was clearly intended to replace. In January 1963 the Fleet Requirements Committee asked what it would take to increase speed to 32kts. DGS offered three higher-powered steam plants. DS 300 used a cruiser-style (unitised) 90,000 SHP plant for 33kts.[15] The ship would displace almost 2,000 tons more (5,900 tons) and would cost £12.75 million. That seemed excessive, so DGS tried a 60,000 SHP plant. In non-unitised form (DS 302) it would add only 500 tons, and the ship would make 31kts (£11.5 million). In unitised form (DS 303) it would add 700 tons (to 4,800 tons), the ship would make 30.5kts (roughly like a 'County'), and would cost £11.75 million. None of these alternatives was pursued, but speed was clearly an issue.

The missile battery was one twin Sea Dart launcher (thirty-eight missiles with ten additional – presumably nuclear – warheads) and Ikara (at least twenty-four missiles, four of them carrying nuclear depth bombs [this requirement was eliminated by 1965]). Sea Dart was supported by two Type 909 illuminators, so it could handle two targets simultaneously. The search radars were the Anglo-Dutch 'Broomstick' (Type 988) and the Type 992 target designator, plus the Type 978 high-definition surface-search set. Supporting the missiles would be a new version of the ADAWS combat direction system. The ship would have austere tactical data links (Links 12 and 13, which were Anglo-Dutch alternatives to the US-supported Link 11; both later evolved into Link X/Link 10). ADAWS with data links in turn required a ships inertial nav-

[15] The Design Studies series began in 1963, DS 301 being a 'SIGS frigate'. The previous cycle of design studies had two-digit numbers, a series of Type 82 studies being Study 53, with various suffixes.

igation system (SINS), because ships had to know their positions more precisely if they were to exchange tactical data effectively. In addition to Ikara, the ship would have single Limbo (double Limbo was ruled out as an 'overindulgence'). Sonars specified initially were Types 162, 170B (for Limbo), 176 (torpedo warning) and 177, a variable-depth sonar to be specified (but probably the US EDO 610), and the Type 196 sonar-intercept set. The final choice was Types 162M, 170B and 184M in two sonar domes; the ship got neither an intercept set nor VDS. EW systems were the UA-8/9 and Type 667 combination standard in Leanders. As a cost-saver, the ship would not have any satellite communication system. Nor would it have MATCH, although it did have facilities to land and fuel a Wasp helicopter. The major saving, compared to a 'County', was in complement: twenty-three officers and eighty-two senior and 220 junior ratings.

By May 1963 the Staff Requirement also included a 4.5in Mk 5 gun (150 rounds), as in a 'Tribal', with its own MRS 3 Mod 3 fire control system, alongside the missiles. The required Gun Direction System used a Type 993 (updated 293Q) radar. Length grew to 430ft and displacement to 4,975 tons (this version was coded DS 321). Given the cruiser weaponry, a quick calculation was done to see what unitising the steam plant would entail. It would employ 33ft engine rooms alternating with 28ft boiler rooms, for a total machinery length of 122ft if no space were left between the two units. Displacement would rise from 4,975 tons to about 5,175 tons and length from 430ft to 450ft.

As of May 1963 expected cost was £12 million for the first ship (at 1963 prices), nearly three times as much as a Leander. The ship was justified as the smallest hull which could combine the three crucial new systems: Sea Dart, Ikara and Type

HMS Bristol on 7 April 1986, with her two Type 909 missile directors uncovered. The platform on her mainmast carries a pair of Type 670 defensive jammers. She has platforms for the SCOT satellite system, but it is not installed; SCOT was cross-decked as needed. Visible forward are two broadband HF antennas, which look like shallow cones atop their supporting single struts. The adoption of such antennas made it possible to eliminate the numerous HF whips characteristic of earlier ships. (Maritime Photographic)

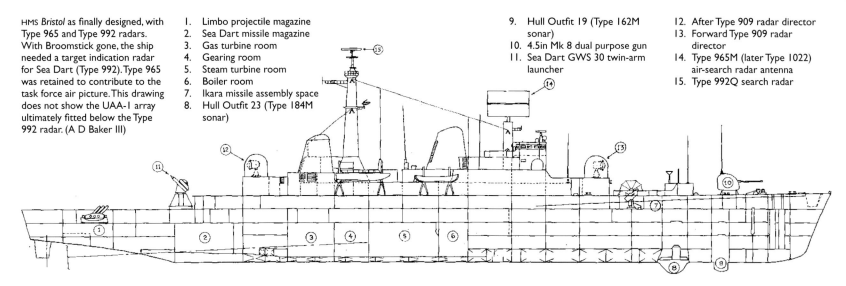

HMS *Bristol* as finally designed, with Type 965 and Type 992 radars. With Broomstick gone, the ship needed a target indication radar for Sea Dart (Type 992). Type 965 was retained to contribute to the task force air picture. This drawing does not show the UAA-1 array ultimately fitted below the Type 992 radar. (A D Baker III)

1. Limbo projectile magazine
2. Sea Dart missile magazine
3. Gas turbine room
4. Gearing room
5. Steam turbine room
6. Boiler room
7. Ikara missile assembly space
8. Hull Outfit 23 (Type 184M sonar)
9. Hull Outfit 19 (Type 162M sonar)
10. 4.5in Mk 8 dual purpose gun
11. Sea Dart GWS 30 twin-arm launcher
12. After Type 909 radar director
13. Forward Type 909 radar director
14. Type 965M (later Type 1022) air-search radar antenna
15. Type 992Q search radar

988, and thus the quickest way to get all three to sea. This argument was raised in the face of objections that she was too large to pass financial muster. This was not too different from the argument used at the same time to justify the large new carrier, CVA 01, which would have been Type 82's stablemate. When the Admiralty Secretary suggested that something smaller might be much easier to sell to the government, the Board response was that smaller was not really at all efficient; to get the same military effect, more ships, at a much higher total cost (and with many more personnel) would be needed. That was true in both cases, but the Secretary better understood the political reality that unit costs, not overall fleet costs, could doom large ships.

By October 1963 beam had increased from the 45ft of early 1963 to 50ft. Clearly more power was needed. DME went 'back to the drawing board' to provide a new COSAG powerplant, which Controller accepted. The new machinery design was based on the 'County' class layout and length (114ft), with two main boilers in one space. It combined a 30,000 SHP two-shaft steam plant and a pair of Olympus gas turbines, a new-generation type offering more power within limited dimensions. Because the ship could run on either powerplant, it enjoyed improved survivability against underwater hits, roughly matching that of a 'County'. Controller considered but rejected as premature an all-gas turbine powerplant. Beam increased to 52ft (which meant greater displacement and a need for even more power) and a double bottom was adopted (which reduced the width of the machinery space, since it was wrapped around the hull). Beam increased to 54ft by August 1964 (the final figure was 55ft). As built, the ship displaced 7,700 tons fully loaded and was 490ft long. Speed was about 30kts.

An agreed Staff Requirement emerged in October 1963.[16] Controller submitted the sketch design in January 1964.[17] The Board approved the Type 82 building drawings and final Legend on 15 July 1965.[18] When submitting the design,

Controller argued that it was needed to meet the much tougher environment to be expected in the 1970s; nothing less would survive, even in the Third World, against modern Soviet equipment supplied to proxy states like Indonesia and Egypt. Type 82 incorporated some features of the new carrier, and early completion would help that project. Approval seemed particularly urgent because the Dutch were demanding firm news by the first week of November 1964 if they were to continue collaboration on the Type 988 radar. In fact it proved necessary to defer an approach to the Cabinet Defence Committee due to the ongoing Defence Review.

About August 1964 a new Appendix on availability was added to the Staff Requirement; this may have been the first such specification. The interval between long refits was to be eight to nine years. The interval between short refits (from completing one to beginning the next) would be thirty months, each refit lasting twenty-four weeks including tests, tuning and trials. The maximum continuous time at sea or at short notice would be forty-five days, the maximum continuous availability would be 105 days, and the duration of maintenance between continuous availabilities would be fifteen days. These figures presumably reflected standard current practice; they help explain why so many frigates were needed to maintain a limited number always at sea.

During this period the planned Mk 5 gun was replaced by a new Mk 8 unmanned weapon.[19] The Staff Requirement involved was reviewed in November 1964, so the gun had probably first been proposed a few months earlier. The Royal Navy argued that a gun was necessary for tasks such as gun fire support, surface action, illumination, ECM fire (using chaff-carrying shells) and for general Cold War policing. Mk 8 was attractive because it could use existing naval ammunition, 4.5in being the largest calibre which could use fixed ammunition. Vickers proposed a simple solution based on its army 105mm gun. The 105mm itself was rejected, as were the army 155mm (too large and not available in time) and the US

[16] DEFE 5/229.
[17] ADM 167/163, Memorandum B.1478 of 29 January 1964.
[18] ADM 167/165.
[19] DEFE 10/457, minutes of the Operational Requirements Committee.

5in/54 (twice as expensive). An important selling point in 1964 was a pledge that Type 82 would have either no fire control at all or else a very rudimentary system; but it proved possible to integrate the gun into ADAWS and thus to use the ship's surface-search and missile-control radars. Mk 8 became the standard British destroyer and frigate weapon.

By the autumn of 1964 the ship was expected to cost more than a 'County'. Programme cost could be cut by reducing the number of Type 82s to those required for aircraft control. The surface picket mission was already being questioned. In the standard scenario, DOR suggested collective air defence of both carriers by three or four Type 82s. Each of the other two groups would have a single Type 82 for air control. A less expensive Sea Dart ship, using a simpler radar (Type 992P) could supplement it. Given normal refit and rotation policies, a total of thirteen would be needed to provide five for the two carrier groups. If only one of the ships in each carrier group were a Type 82 (the others could be lower-grade Sea Dart ships), the total would fall to three, and six or eight Type 82s might suffice. The programme was accordingly cut to that level.

In 1964 it was assumed that the first of the class would be ordered in 1965, to be followed by five more ships. One would be deployed with each carrier group and one with each amphibious group East of Suez. A typical carrier battle group would be screened by one 'County', one Type 82 (carrying the escort commander), three Leanders and two Type 12s, supported by a nuclear attack submarine. The Type 82 would steam about 5,000 yds ahead of the main body. This force offered far too little missile firepower; presumably it was expected that simpler and more affordable Sea Dart ship would later be built. Later the projected force rose to eight ships.

In 1966 the next-generation British carrier was cancelled. The eight-ship programme survived for a time, but ultimately only one Type 82, HMS Bristol, was built. The Royal Navy withdrew from the Broomstick radar programme on grounds of cost, complexity and uncertain reliability. The Type 82 design was modified to provide a two-dimensional target-designation radar (Type 992P) and the long-range Type 965P, the latter to offer some radar picket capability (Type 992P sufficed for Sea Dart target designation and for 4.5in control). Given her very capable ADAWS system, Bristol served as a 'gateway' between the network of Royal Navy ships with the Anglo-Dutch Link 10 and NATO, mainly US, ships using the more capable Link 11. Although conceived for the frigate-type combination of UA-8/9 and the Type 667 jammer, Bristol was completed with the much more advanced Abbey Hill (UAA) ESM system (but without a new jammer).

For the future, the Royal Navy was interested in nuclear power. The issue had come up several times and had been deferred. This time a design study of a nuclear frigate with Type 82 characteristics, which would cost about £250 million, was approved as a basis for further analysis.

The Helicopter Ship

Beginning in the late 1950s there was interest in both the Royal Navy and the US Navy in multiplying the effect of a frigate or missile ship by using large helicopters, such as Wessex, with dipping sonars. The British had two different approaches. One to enlarge a frigate to carry several large helicopters, something approached with the Type 23 in the 1980s. For example, in response to the Fleet Requirements Committee, in June 1959 a Type 12 frigate was redesigned with a five-helicopter hangar and a lift to the flight deck. The result was a Type 12 back to the bridge and also below the hangar deck. It had Type 12 armament (except for MATCH and Limbo), and it retained its Seacats and might even have lightweight triple torpedo tubes. A quick estimate showed that displacement would rise about a thousand tons, to 3,800 tons. A revised version would have displaced about 3,600 tons. The frigate option was dropped in favour of a large cruiser-carrier (armed with Seaslug as well as helicopters).

Another approach was to build helicopter carriers (cruisers) combining long-range anti-aircraft weapons with air capability. This class became the Escort Cruiser (which could accommodate helicopters otherwise based on board a carrier) and then the Invincible class. In January and April 1959 helicopter carriers or cruisers were sketched, supporting fifteen or eighteen helicopters. In 1962, as money was clearly becoming tight, the question was raised of whether it might not be better to build such cruisers than Type 82.[20]

A June 1962 comparison between a version of Type 82 then being considered and an escort cruiser showed:

TYPE 82 AND THE ESCORT CRUISER COMPARED

	Type 82	Escort Cruiser
Displacement	6,000 tons	10,000 tons
Chinooks	4	4
Sea Dart systems	1	2
SS 11/12	Yes	Yes
Dutch radar	Yes	Yes
ADA/TIDE	Yes	Plus Ikara
Sonars	Types 182, 184, 185	Same
SHP/Config	36,000 /two non-unitised	45,000/two unitised
Speed	26.5kts	27kts
Endurance	3,500nm @ 20kts	4,500nm @ 20kts
Built to	Destroyer standards	Cruiser standards
Accommodation	50/500	85/800
C2 facilities	Full	Full
Stable helo platform	Marginal	Satisfactory
Emergency troops	c.500	c.1,000
Cost	£10 million	£15.6 million

The maximum for destroyer design practice, as reflected in Type 82, was 6,000–6,500 tons. Above that the steam plant had to be unitised to avoid extreme vulnerability. The harbour load (taking into account salvage load) would be such that it would no longer be economical to use multiple diesel generators. Steam would have to be kept up constantly in har-

[20] ADM 167/154, from VCNS's memorandum on how to handle the 1962 Long Term Costing.

HMS *Bristol* is shown in September 1990, with a US type OE-82 satellite dish (the 'wash basin') visible between her two after uptakes. A second OE-82 was mounted forward of the ship's bridge, for full coverage. Unlike SCOT, it was typically not cross-decked. *Bristol* acted as a gateway ship between British warships carrying only national communication systems (such as SCOT and Link 10) and NATO allies using other systems, such as Link 11 and the US naval satellites. Also visible here are two types of decoy launchers, the British Corvus (on the 02 level, against the forward Sea Dart radome) and the fixed US type, just below Corvus on the 01 level. (Maritime Photographic)

bour, and that added boilers and men. The difference between the two possibilities, £5.6 million, was two-thirds the cost of a Sea Dart frigate. That would buy the equivalent of a second such frigate in terms of Sea Dart and Ikara. The cruiser would be steadier, would have much longer range, would be markedly less dependent on base, and would have a useful design margin. VCNS recommended it, but Type 82 survived.

The Escort Mix

In 1964 the Royal Navy envisaged a fleet of eighty-nine escorts, but all could not possibly be expensive Type 82s. In 1963 the Fleet Requirements Committee was told that given available funds the escort fleet would ultimately collapse to only forty, far too few to cover British global commitments. The only solution was the one Admiral Edwards had proposed in 1949, a high-low mix. Given the nominal hull life of twenty-one years, it would take an annual programme of nearly 4.5 ships to maintain a ninety-escort fleet.[21] In 1975 there would be eighty modern escorts, a shortfall of nine: thirteen missile destroyers (eight 'Counties' and five *Bristol*s), forty first-rate frigates (twenty-five *Leander*s and fifteen Type 12, nine of them with MATCH), seven General Purpose frigates ('Tribals'), eight slow frigates (A/A and A/D), and twelve Type 14s. To make up the shortfall, the navy projected another nine frigates of undetermined type,

to be built alongside the Type 82 programme.

In January 1963 Plans Division produced a quick paper proposing the low end of a high-low solution, a Second Rate Escort, which it suggested should be called a corvette.[22] The estimated cost of a Type 82 was £10.5 million, twice the cost of a *Leander* and about three times the cost of a *Rothesay* in current terms. On the basis of a DGS estimate (done in 24 hours), Plans Division proposed an 1,800-ton 27-knot ship with limited endurance (3,000nm at 18kts) whose cost would be cut by limiting her to the A/S role. She would be armed with Ikara and with Seacat (GWS 22). There would be no anti-ship weapon as such, but it appeared that Seacat could be modified to provide some capability out to 3,000 yds. Limbo (which was a kind of gun) could fire sub-calibre rounds. Their accuracy would be limited because they would fall steeply, but they could be proximity-fused. The homing torpedo delivered by Ikara should offer some capability against a surfaced submarine. Sonars would be the high-capability Type 184 and VDS combination, but radars would be limited to Type 993 (for Seacat direction) and to Type 978 for periscope/snorkel detection. Hull life would be sixteen years, *ie* the ship would not be worth a long refit. Estimated cost, £4 million, would make a large escort force affordable. In support of this admittedly very rough estimate, Director of Plans noted that DOR had recently estimated that a somewhat comparable 1,500-ton ship would cost £3.3 million.

The idea was deemed worth pursuing. The future first-rate

[21] Nominal hull life, including one long refit, was sixteen years. Extension to twenty-one years assumed two long refits, which in turn cost operating time. The Committee asked whether a third long refit could extend life to twenty-six or even twenty-eight years. The consensus was apparently that ships that old would no longer be useful. The alternative later proposed was to eliminate the long refit so as to increase the fraction of time a ship was available, reducing lifetime to 13½ years. Much of the work in a long refit, rehabilitating the steam plant, was eliminated when gas turbines replaced steam. The last Type 42s will have served about thirty years before they are discarded.

[22] This paper dated 17 January 1963 and the table of the escort spectrum are in ADM 1/28609, the Fleet Requirements Committee papers for 1963.

frigate would be a specialist ship with one major weapon system. At this time the two major weapon systems were Sea Dart and Ikara. The future second-rate ship would have limited escort capability but good Cold War peace-keeping capacity, at a limited cost. Early in 1963 DTWP (successor to DTSD) remarked that the choice would be between first and second rate ships deficient in one or more areas or a mix of specialised first-rate ships. The first-rate A/S ship would have a single screw (for minimum cost), the latest sonars (including VDS), the best A/S weapons (Ikara and Limbo), a gun and/or missile for self-defence, and essential communications and data handling systems. DTWP envisaged an annual programme of 2.5 first-rate and two second-rate ships. That would halve the rate of Sea Dart introduction into the fleet, and even so it would be necessary to build mainly Sea Dart ships without Ikara. Time and money could be saved if the existing *Leander* hull could be adapted to the new weapons.

For the Fleet Requirements Committee, DGS produced a series of alternative sketch designs ranging from a very simple corvette up to Type 82 (see table overleaf). The existing *Leander* was included as a reference point. DS 352 was what could be obtained within the £4 million proposed by the Plans Division. It was rather less capable than had been imagined. The powerplant was the cheapest available, a pair of 10,000 BHP Rushton AO16 diesels (which figured in many of the design studies). It barely matched the standard NATO requirement for a short-range ASW escort, NBMR 25: 24kts, 3,000nm at 18kts). DGS considered its 20,000 BHP the upper limit for a single-screw ship (which was the cheapest possible). A heavily-loaded single screw would cavitate at lower speeds (DTWP noted, however, that the US Navy was building single-screw destroyer escorts with 35,000 SHP powerplants).

The ship was armed only with double Limbo and a single Bofors gun, and had no VDS. However, she had a computer tactical data system (B2, the NATO committee then considering a version of the US NTDS) and a data link (TIDE), by means of which she could pass her sonar data to ships armed with Ikara. This simple form of what would now be called network-centric warfare would make her useful in a screen. DOR argued that omitting a VDS was a false economy. Providing it (and the data link) would roughly double the overall probability of detecting a submarine trying to penetrate a screen. Providing the ship with a bare minimum of A/A firepower, a single 4.5in gun with MRS 3 control, would add £500,000. A VDS would add another £250,000.

The US Navy was considering buying its first point-defence missile, a navalised version of the US Army's Mauler. Sea Mauler would thus become available to the Royal Navy. Unlike Tartar, it would make few demands on a ship. Given very limited information, it was assumed that Sea Mauler would cost about £1 million per ship. In fact in 1964 the entire Mauler

project was cancelled as excessively expensive. The US follow-on, Sea Sparrow, was not considered for British use; the British developed their own high-performance point defence weapon as Seawolf. It made considerable demands on a ship.

DOR suggested that the Royal Navy was over-insuring against the air threat but under-insuring against submarines, so the next step up was DS 338, the minimum Ikara corvette. It also had the minimum surface armament, the single 4.5in gun of a 'Tribal'. Its minimum Ikara system stowed all weapons on the upper deck, hence had no capacity for nuclear depth-bombs (which required deep stowage). Manning was minimised by accepting that all weapons could not be manned simultaneously (otherwise the ship would have been larger, with space for thirteen officers and 259 ratings). DS 340 added VDS and/or deep stowage for nuclear depth bombs. Given a fixed powerplant, growth reduced speed to 25kts.

That raised the further question of just how fast the escort should be. Fleet speed was 28kts. However, some of the formations requiring escort, such as amphibious groups, underway replenishment groups, and convoys, might well operate at 18–20kts. A separate analysis undertaken for the Fleet Requirements Committee suggested that for such groups an escort speed of 24kts might suffice. However, would it really be wise to build escorts which could not be used both with the fleet and with those special formations?

The next step up (DS 342) increased manning to provide full capability. That pushed up size, so to avoid further loss of speed it adopted the *Leander* twin-screw steam plant. That increased speed to the 27kts of a *Leander*. Otherwise DS 342 matched the ASW battery in DS 340. This study showed that true capability depended as much on manning (which meant hull volume for accommodation) as on the weapons and systems placed aboard the ship. DS 342 did not meet the NATO requirement for an Ocean ASW Ship (NBMR 20, 4,000nm at 18–20kts). To gain back endurance the ship had to grow further (DS 343), but with her fixed powerplant she lost speed. To obtain both endurance and speed the ship had to grow further and to adopt a new powerplant (DS 344). In effect DS 344 was the ultimate first-rate A/S frigate.

DS 347 and DS 336 added limited missile batteries: point defence Sea Mauler in DS 347, a reduced version of Sea Dart (twenty missiles, one tracker-illuminator rather than two) in DS 336. DS 336 had a short-range air-search radar (Type 992P) sufficient to support her Sea Dart missile system, but lacked any longer-range radar for picket purposes. In effect she represented an expansion back to a limited general-purpose capability. DOR considered the limited missile load-out in DS 336 insufficient for fleet air defence.

The full anti-aircraft equivalent was DS 345, which had a full Sea Dart system (thirty-eight missiles, two tracker-illuminators), but only the short-range two-dimensional radar. It was not really wanted, but it was included for completeness.

The Escort Spectrum, 1963–4

DS	352	338	340	342	Leander
Deep	1,960 tons	2,520 tons	2,700 tons	3,080 tons	2,880 tons
Standard	1,760 tons	2,298 tons	2,360 tons	2,670 tons	2,384 tons
Length	322ft	385ft	383ft	355ft	360ft
Beam	37ft	37ft	39ft	42ft	41ft
Hull Depth	29ft	29ft	29ft	32ft	28.25ft
SHP (thousands)	20/1	20/1	20/1	30/2	30/2
Machinery	D	D	D	S	S
Speed	26.5kts	25.5kts	25kts	27kts	27kts
Endurance	3,500nm @ 15kts	3,500nm @ 15kts	3,500nm @ 15kts	3,500nm @ 15kts	3,800nm @ 15kts
Limbo	x	x	x	x	x
Ikara	—	x	*	*	MATCH
AA	—	—	—	—	GWS 22
SU	1×40mm	1×4.5in	1×4.5in	1×4.5in	Twin 4.5in
Sonar (Type)	170, 184	170, 184	170, 184	170, 184	170, 184
VDS	—	SQA-10	SQA-10	SQA-10	199
Radar (Type)	993, 978	993, 978	993, 978	993, 978	965M, 993, 978
Data Handling	B2, SINS	B2, SINS	B2, SINS	B2, SINS	—
Comms	ICS, TIDE	ICS, TIDE	ICS, TIDE	ICS, TIDE	ICS
EW	Limited	Limited	Limited	Limited	UA-8/9, 667
Accommodation (Officers/Ratings)	12/197	12/225	12/225	13/259	17/244
Cost (£ million)	4	5.5/5.75	6	6.5	5.25 ex Wasp

DS	343	344	347	336	345
Deep	3,580 tons	3,850 tons	4,050 tons	4,500 tons	4,400 tons
Standard	2,720 tons	2,940 tons	3,020 tons	3,510 tons	3,420 tons
Length	360ft	365ft	385ft	420ft	395ft
Beam	42ft	42ft	44ft	46ft	47ft
Hull Depth	32ft	32ft	32ft	32ft	32ft
SHP (thousands)	30/2	40/2	40/2	40/2	40/2
Machinery	S	S	S	S	S
Speed	26.5kts	28.5kts	28.5kts	28kts	28kts
Endurance	5,000 @ 18kts	5,000 @ 18kts	5,000 @ 18kts	5,000 @ 18kts	5,000 @ 18kts
Limbo	x	x	x	x	x
Ikara	*	*	*	*	—
AA	—	—	Sea Mauler	Sea Dart(20)	Sea Dart(38)
SU	1×4.5in	1×4.5in	1×4.5in	1×4.5in	1×4.5in
Sonar (Type)	170, 184	170, 184	170, 184	170, 184	170, 184
VDS	SQA-10	SQA-10	SQA-10	SQA-10	SQA-10
Radar (Type)	992P, 978	992P, 978	992P, 978	992P, 2×978	992P, 2×978
Data Handling	B2, SINS	B2, SINS	B2, SINS	B2, SINS	B2, SINS
Comms	ICS, TIDE	ICS, TIDE	ICS, TIDE	ICS,TIDE	ICS, TIDE
EW	UA-8/9, 667	UA-8/9, 667	UA-8/9, 667	UA-8/9, 667	UA8/9, 667
Accommodation (Officers/Ratings)	13/259	13/259	14/266	21/269	20/280
Cost (£ million)	6.75/7	7.5	8.5	9	8.25

DS	321 (Type 82)
Deep	4,975 tons
Standard	3,910 tons
Length	430ft
Beam	48ft
Hull Depth	32ft
SHP (thousands)	40/2
Machinery	S
Speed	28kts
Endurance	5,000nm @ 18kts
Limbo	x
Ikara	*
AA	Sea Dart (38)
SU	1×4.5in
Sonar (Type)	170, 184
VDS	SQA-10
Radar (type)	998, 993, 2×978
Data Handling	ADA
Comms	ICS, TIDE
EW	UA-8/9, 667
Accommodation (Officers/Ratings)	23/302
Cost (£ million)	11.25

In the table, the asterisk for Ikara indicates the version providing upper deck stowage for the twenty-four missiles and torpedoes and deep stowage for four nuclear depth-bombs. B2 was a NATO combat direction project, in effect a small-ship version of the US NTDS. It maintained a track file and could feed an automatic data link (TIDE), but it did not control weapons. Thus it was comparable in concept to the British CAAIS. TIDE was the NATO data link, Link 11. SINS was the inertial navigation system associated with a co-operative data system, necessary because ships had to give their own positions when sending data. ADA in Type 82 referred to a version of ADAWS, in which weapon control was integrated with data handling. ICS was the Integrated Communications System, which incorporated radio teletype and other high data rate (for the time) features. SQA-10 was a US variable depth sonar body. Presumably it was intended for integration with

Type 184 (in US service it was integrated with the roughly comparable SQS-4 series). Unlike the Canadian Type 199, which was based on the Type 170 transducer, it offered all-round scanning capability. Some related studies did not make it into the table.[23]

———— • ————

At a Fleet Requirements Committee meeting in July 1963 ACNS asked whether Sea Dart could be installed on board a *Leander*. That would be difficult at best: the *Leander*s had already used up their growth margins. Asked about installing Ikara, DGS produced a study, DS 356, with Ikara forward and a single 4.5in gun aft in place of the helicopter hangar (the ship retained her Seacat missile system). The VDS and Limbo were retained. The ship would need 50–60 tons of ballast to retain her stability, and for DGS this proved that such an installation was not practicable.

There was, however, an important caveat. The existing ships had used up their reserves of stability, to the point where they needed considerable water ballast. They had no space in which to add electric generating capacity. Their machinery lacked ABCD protection in the form of remote control and isolation of boilers from the interior of the ship. However, stability could be recovered by adding 2ft to the ship's beam. That would make it possible to rearrange the machinery to provide a reasonable degree of ABCD defence, and also to add electric generating capacity. This point, made almost casually to explain why the *Leander* should not be the basis for the next-generation frigate, seems to have led directly to the 'broad-beam' *Leander*. These ships were never armed with Ikara, but the extra space and weight did make it possible to fit them out with next-generation sonar and with Seawolf.

Design development continued through late 1963. About November single- and twin-screw corvette designs, both using paired 10,000 BHP Rushton AO 16 diesels, were developed. The single-screw version (DS 358: 350ft × 40ft × 11ft 6in, 2,300 tons) was expected to make 26.5kts deep and clean. The twin-screw alternative (DS 359: 365ft × 40ft × 11.95ft, 2,400 tons) would make 27.25kts. DS 362 (December 1963) was another corvette, with a 4.5in gun (MRS 3 fire control) and a Bofors ASW mortar instead of Limbo. The ultimate development in this series was DS 363 of December 1963 (320ft × 37ft × 19ft hull depth). She had the same paired Rushton diesels, the de-

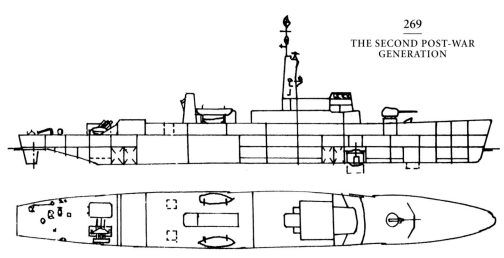

Design Study 363, the 'corvette' of the 1963–4 series of frigate concepts. This drawing was dated January 1964. The ship would have been 320ft (wl) x 37ft, displacing 2,075 tons, with 20,000 SHP engines. The gun is the Bofors 75mm; as at that time British industry had produced no lightweight automatic frigate gun. Work on the 4.5in Mk 8 began only the following year, in connection with the Type 82 destroyer. Not shown are four decoy launchers spaced around the bridge structure. The two big spaces in the hull are the engine room, forward of the auxiliary room. The plated-in mast carries, at its head, the usual HF/DF, with a UHF/DF array below it, and Porker (UA-8/9) below that. The top of the tower carries the ship's only radar, a Type 978 for surface search. The platform well down the face of the mast carries an MF D/F array. Although not indicated as such in the official drawing, the object on the side of the mast is presumably the Cooky fleet protection jammer. The sonars indicated are Types 170 (forward, to support Limbo) and 177 (the array shown retracted). The object on the stern is the Type 182 torpedo decoy, with its rather substantial handling gear. This design was significant as the forebear of the Type 19 low-end frigate, which ultimately led to Type 21 and to a further low-end ship, the Future Light Frigate. (Author)

signers having considered and rejected a Proteus-Olympus gas turbine plant because it would not be ready in time. The ship was too large to meet the 28kts demanded in the Staff Requirement (she would make 26kts deep and dirty in the tropics). She would meet the required endurance, 4,000nm at 18kts. Endurance was forty-five days (stores) or 4,000nm at 18kts (260 tons of fuel). Armament would have been a single Bofors 75mm L56 gun (300 rounds) using a remote visual sight and one Limbo (ninety rounds). The sonars were Type 170B for Limbo and Type 177 for long-range search. Complement would have been ten officers and thirty senior and 120 junior ratings, which was more than the Board considered affordable. It seemed odd that a ship whose Staff Requirements were little better than those of a Type 14 was so much larger. the main reasons were that she had three times the communications spaces, four times the space devoted to her electrical system (including generators), and 12 per cent more machinery space. Unlike a Type 14, she was fully air-conditioned, in accordance with current requirements (and as was necessary in the sort of Third World operations the Royal Navy contemplated). Communications and operations spaces were adapted to computer data handling (B2 system, sixteen-track capacity), which made the corvette a potential fleet sensor platform. DUSW wanted a VDS as well, which would give the ship MATCH capability.

The corvette figured in the long-term costing produced in 1964, a projection of what ships the Royal Navy planned to build. The armament of the second-rate A/S corvette was mod-

[23] DS 301 was a small Sea Dart escort based on a Type 14 hull, to meet a requirement dated 25 October 1962; dimensions were 285ft × 38ft × 10ft 1in (1,460 tons, speed about 18kts on 4,000 SHP). Work on an Ikara frigate began at least as early as February 1963; very brief notes on a DS 309 survive. It would have been armed with Ikara and with Seacat. Other frigate studies were DS 310 and 311, of which DS 310 was a large ship (420ft × 46ft 3in × 15ft 11in, 4,850 tons) with two-shaft COSAG propulsion (40,000 SHP). These figures suggest that she was a COSAG variant of Type 82. Apparently DS 325 and DS 326 were similar to DS 309. These studies may have supported the conclusion that the Type 82 destroyer was far more economical than a two-hull solution, or they may have been the beginning of an attempt to provide sufficient Ikara if Type 82 was limited to a few ships. Known corvette studies were a 'baby corvette' (DS 328, undated, 340ft × 37ft × 29ft, with a complement of fifteen officers and 150 ratings) and DS 346 of June 1963. Like the earlier austere Sea Dart ship, DS 346 was based on a Type 14 hull. Armament was a single 4.5in gun with MRS 3 director and Type 992P radar and Limbo; the only sonar was the Type 199 lightweight towed set (in effect a towed Type 170, hence compatible with Limbo). Improved habitability standards reduced the numbers that this small hull could accommodate, possibly to the point where the design was no longer feasible.

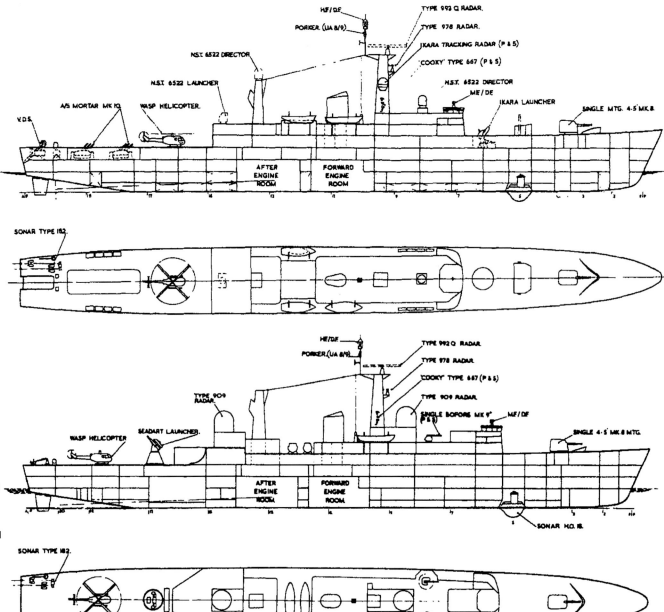

The 1964 escort spectrum study projected a single hull which could be completed as either an Ikara missile ship (381) or a Sea Dart ship (382). Systems were located as in HMS *Bristol*: Ikara was forward and Sea Dart was carried aft. These designs used diesel power; the decision to adopt all gas turbine plants was not made until 1967. These ships would have been designated Types 17 and 42.

ified to meet the requirements of the 1970s (*ie* Seacat was replaced by the projected Seawolf).

At an annual level of £28 million the alternatives were:

28A: One Type 82, one GP frigate (DS 336), two second-rate A/S frigates (DS 352).
28B: One Type 82, one A/S frigate (DS 340), two second-rate A/S frigates (DS 352 modified with Seawolf).
28C: Two GP frigates, one A/S corvette (DS 352), one second-rate A/A corvette.
28D: One GP frigate, one A/A corvette (DS 343 modified with reduced Sea Dart), two A/S corvettes.
28E: Two A/S and two A/A, both modified forms of DS 343.

Given the decision that Type 82 would be built in any case, the choice fell between A and B. Programme A would give Sea Dart ships most quickly, but not sufficient pickets soon enough. This programme included the maximum allowable range of designs (three): destroyer (Type 82), frigate, and corvette.

The choices for the next lower level of funding, £24 million per year, were starker:

24A: One Type 82, three second-rate A/S (DS 352 with VDS).
24B: One GP frigate, one A/S frigate, two second-rate (modified DS 352).
24C: Two A/S and two second-rate (DS 343 and DS 352).
24D: Two A/A frigates and two A/S frigates (alternative

forms of DS 343 and 352, entailing an overspend of £250,000).

24E: Two second-rate A/S and two second-rate A/A (modified DS 340 with Sea Mauler).

Alternatives from 24C down did not include any 28kt ships, hence could not contribute to fleet defence.

These ranges figured in Board discussions throughout 1964. In January 1964 DCNS called for a mix of six Type 82, thirty A/S frigates (DS 344), and forty-five corvettes (DS 363), a balance between first- and second-rate frigates similar to that of the existing fleet. It would provide substantial capability even if Type 82 and the three-dimensional radar were abandoned. It gave DCNS's minimum force of thirty Ikara ships, but not his desired thirteen Sea Dart installations. In effect DCNS had chosen 28B.

The A/S frigate was tentatively designated Type 17 and the corvette Type 18. In March and April 1964 DGS produced two Type 17 designs: DS 365 and a diesel version, DS 369, plus a modified broad-beam *Leander*, DS 368. All had grown as space requirements were worked out in detail Thus one version of DS 365 was 400ft × 44ft (4,125 tons on trials). DS 365 was compared to a new design being developed for a Dutch frigate armed with a gun, Sea Dart and Ikara, based on a Type 41 hull. DS 368 was lengthened to accommodate an increased complement of fourteen officers and sixty-three senior and 207 junior ratings. Considerable attention went into alternative corvette designs. DS 377 (May 1964) had a 4.5in gun and the projected Seawolf point-defence missile. One price of greater capability was an unacceptably larger crew; the ship could accommodate sixteen officers and 210 ratings.

The phasing of the programme would depend on the balance between air and submarine threats. Given the emphasis on operations East of Suez, the air threat was considered dominant, hence Type 82 construction was particularly urgent. In defence of Type 82, the Board was told that the US, Italians and French were all facing similar problems and were all building very large destroyers in the same 7,000-ton class. The new corvette was criticised for its large hull accommodating weaponry which had been limited to hold down its cost. The large hull had been needed to carry out the worldwide function, and the vital training function – and to be declarable to NATO as a frigate to meet British commitments.

Board deliberations began with a study which VCNS reported on 20 February 1964. The goal of eighty-nine escorts within a likely manpower limit of 103,000 ruled out a force consisting mainly of Type 82s (twenty-seven officers and 386 ratings). If the new carriers were to be built, most or all escorts would have to be limited to an average of about ten officers and 186 ratings. Discussion was deferred in May but resumed in June 1964.[24] For the moment, the Board decided to approve

[24] ADM 167/164.

Type 82 as the best way to get Sea Dart and Ikara to sea, and because there was an unquestioned need for a 'County' class successor.

The overall concept of the first-rate Ikara frigate (Type 17) seems to have been considered satisfactory. A design (DS 381) completed in September 1964 gives some idea of what was wanted. She would have displaced 4,400 tons (440ft × 46ft × 38.5ft [hull depth]), with the hull form of a 'Battle' class destroyer. Four Rushton AO16 diesels on two shafts would have driven her at 28.5kts deep and dirty. Endurance was 3,500nm at 18kts. There were two 250 kW diesel generators. Armament was a 4.5in gun, a Seawolf point defence missile with two directors, Ikara (twenty-four missiles plus four nuclear depth-bombs, at that time the standard load-out) and double Limbo, supported by Types 170, 176, 162 and 177 sonars plus VDS, and by Type 992Q and Type 978 radars. The gun was forward, the Ikara launcher aft around the break of the forecastle. The same director would control both gun and missile. The ship would support a Wasp helicopter (MATCH). Armament would have been supported by a fully-automated combat direction system with automatic data links (ADA and TIDE). All of this was far too expensive in manpower terms: estimated complement was eighteen officers and 307 ratings (also estimated as nineteen officers and eighty-four senior and 235 junior ratings). Estimated unit cost was £9.75 million.

The designers were then asked to place Sea Dart in the same hull. That was not entirely possible, but they came close with DS 382 (completed 12 October 1964), offering Sea Dart (aft), a 4.5in gun, two single Bofors (Mk 9), and MATCH on 4,500 tons. The big Dutch radar had to be abandoned, leaving the short-range target-indication set (Type 992Q) and two fire-control radars (Type 909, as in the big destroyer). Complement was twenty officers and eighty-six senior and 216 junior ratings, not too far from that in the big Type 82.

Although Type 17 certainly figured in discussions of the future escort mix, the corresponding Sea Dart destroyer apparently did not, perhaps because raising that possibility would insure abandonment of Type 82. However, the existence of this design study almost certainly affected Royal Navy thinking two years later, when the carrier was cancelled and the fleet had to be redesigned. In effect it presaged Type 42, although there is no direct evidence of a connection between the two designs. The corvette seems to have been far less satisfactory; the Board was left searching for something better but not significantly more expensive.

The Escort Mix Working Party reported late in November 1964. The requirement for fourteen Sea Dart, fourteen Ikara, and eight Type 988 systems led to a proposal to build eight Type 82s for completion between 1970/1 and 1975/6. They would be followed by a new high-quality escort with a complement of about 285. In parallel with the Type 82s and the

new quality escort, large numbers of a new Small Escort would be built. Available money and manpower would limit it to a unit cost of £5 million and about 110 personnel. It would reinforce the high-value units, but at minimum cost. This ship became Type 19.

Although in theory the new-construction carrier programme had been accepted, clearly there were fears that it would be cancelled. Studies made since July 1964 were cited in November as proof that Type 82 was needed even without a carrier. The Navy Minister (equivalent to the old First Lord) warned against calling ships escorts, for fear that they would be linked too closely with larger ships (which, by implication, might disappear). Ships up to 4,000 tons would be classed as frigates; those over 4,000 tons would be called destroyers. The arbitrariness of this distinction made it obvious that the old difference between the two categories was gone.

Type 19 was oriented towards Third World policing and presence operations. It could not carry much in the way of sophisticated armament, but it could carry a useful sonar. Because sonar ranges were relatively short, a Royal Navy study of ASW showed a need for at least fifty medium-range sonars, many more than it needed ships with major ASW weapons. To make a contribution to an escort screen, the ship needed some form of semi-automatic data exchange (ultimately a two/three-man version of ADA). Given the ability to pass sonar data, another ship with Ikara or with MATCH could usefully prosecute Type 19's contact, passed over a data link. Later it would be argued that the ship should have at least MATCH capability. The escort role also required a defensive missile (Seacat, to be replaced by Seawolf when the latter was available); and EW equipment (when suitable automatic equipment became available, given the requirement to hold down manpower). Endurance should be about 2,000nm at 18–20kts. Fleet speed was 28kts; a ship operating only with slower amphibious and underway replenishment groups might make do with 24kts. However, much higher speed might be valuable. In the 1970s Soviet nuclear attack submarines might appear even in limited wars, so that every available escort might be needed to screen fleet units. High burst speed might make up for the ship's lack of Ikara. A fast enough escort could quickly redeploy, could quickly reach a distant datum, and could quickly return to station. Too, frigates were losing their speed advantage over merchant ships, whose typical speed had increased by about a fifth over the last five years. Higher burst speed might be required to escort such ships.

These points were part of a larger argument advanced by the Staff for high burst speed, which was made possible by the compact but powerful new Olympus gas turbine. They may have been inspired by Vosper's claims for a 177ft 50-knot corvette, described in November 1963 as the antidote to the nuclear submarine. It was powered by two 22,000 SHP Marine Olympus engines, the type which had just been adopted for

the Type 82 frigate (there were also two Deltic diesels for cruise).[25] In 1964 the Royal Navy was involved in just the sort of 'Warm War' it had been predicting for years, the undeclared confrontation with Indonesia over the fate of Malaysia. Like other Third World countries, Indonesia had been armed with small combatants, in this case fast missile boats. It was also important to be able to intercept fast gun-runners supporting enemy guerrillas and insurgents. The Naval Staff became interested in a very fast frigate capable of running such craft down. A recent (March 1964) staff paper had highlighted the Royal Navy's lack of small fast combatants. The navy could afford neither sufficient numbers of such craft nor their tenders and bases. The Staff considered fast destroyers or frigates a viable counter, particularly since even craft rated at 40kts could not achieve such speeds in the open sea. Also, high speed would make it possible for the ship to reach the scene of action quickly enough. By November 1964 the Staff envisaged a small frigate capable of 40kts in burst mode. DCNS considered that speed quite valuable. Nor was the Staff alone. The Royal Australian Navy, also involved in the Confrontation, was formulating a very similar requirement for its General Purpose Escort.[26] The two navies later briefly collaborated on such a ship, the RN/RAN Frigate (see Chapter 14).

A feasibility study showed two Olympus gas turbines and two Paxman-Ventura diesels per shaft (driving controllable pitch propellers) in a 1,900-ton ship (340ft × 35ft), much smaller than a *Leander*. Maximum speed would be 39kts (endurance 700nm, all gas turbines on line). The ship would make fleet speed with one gas turbine on line (endurance 1,100nm). Alternatively, the gas turbine could be run at lower power for a speed of 20kts (1,700nm). Two diesels on each shaft (without gas turbines) would drive the ship at 18.5kts (4,700nm), and endurance at 15kts would be far beyond the requirement, 7,500nm. By way of comparison a *Leander* had an endurance of 1,200nm at 28kts and 3,530nm at 18kts.

Armament would be the new unmanned 4.5in gun (with at least 400 rounds) then planned for Type 82, Seacat, and a single hand-worked Bofors. There would be no Limbo, but the ship would have MATCH capability. Triple lightweight torpedo tubes might later be added as a sort of Limbo alternative. Unlike earlier escorts, this one would have only a single sonar, the ageing Type 177 instead of the new Type 184. Radars would be the missile fire-control radar plus the high-definition sur-

25 The Vosper corvette did not figure in contemporary Board minutes or in the papers of the Fleet Requirements Committee. It seems to have been offered to (and rejected by) the Royal Canadian Navy as early as July 1962, as a logical follow-on to that navy's hydrofoil projects, and it was publicised a year later in the magazine *Engineering*.
26 Antony Preston, in R Gardiner (ed), *Conway's All The World's Fighting Ships 1947-1995* (Conway Maritime Press, London: 1995), p 16, describes the Australian General Purpose Escort (GPE): 1,800 tons deep, 330ft × 34ft × 11ft, 37kts on a two-shaft CODOG plant, 5,200nm at 12kts. Armament was one 5in/54, one Seacat, two single 20mm, and two triple lightweight torpedo tubes (one version had a 40mm gun instead of Seacat). Radars would have been the Dutch LW02 and M22 then being planned for *Daring* refits and installed on board Type 12 frigates, and the sonar would have been Type 177 or the new Australian Mulloka. Design work continued at least through October 1966, which suggests a direct connection with the RN/RAN frigate of 1967–8. A drawing of a DDL (presumably the GPE) in the *RAN Centenary History*, p 200, is the sketch Vosper used to illustrate the standard version of its Mk 5 frigate. The contract for preliminary design of the RAN's follow-on DDL was awarded in July 1970.

Although initially *Bristol* was conceived as a follow-on standard frigate, it was soon clear that she was too expensive to build in numbers. At about the same time Vosper Thornycroft produced a series of export frigates which seemed to be exactly the low-end ship needed to complement the high-end *Bristol*. The Iranian *Saam*, shown at Portsmouth on 15 May 1977, displays an eclectic collection of weapons and sensors. The export ships were the first to mount the Mk 8 single 4.5in gun, but its development had initially been ordered for HMS *Bristol*. The twin mount aft is a 35mm Oerlikon. The missiles in the box launcher aft are Italian-made Sea Killers, for which Iran was the sole customer. The fire controls atop the bridge are a Swiss Contraves system, but the big radar is a British commercial AWS-1. A British Limbo is barely visible between the missile launcher and the gun aft. Not visible forward of the bridge is a Seacat launcher. This was a very impressive armament on 1,250 tons. Contemporary observers were also impressed by the high rated speed, 40kts, claimed for this type, using the new Olympus gas turbine as powerplant. Unit cost was cut to about two-thirds of that of a comparable Western warship by eliminating what would later be called Mil-Spec requirements. (John C Callis via John Mortimer)

face radar, Type 978. To cut manning, both sonar and radar would automatically detect their targets as soon as that capability became available, feeding their data into the ship's automated combat direction system. To hold down complement (to six officers and thirty senior and seventy-four junior ratings), there would be sufficient personnel to man only the gun, but not Seacat, at action stations. There would be a two-man version of the standard automated combat data system, ADA, without any weapons control. It would have a semi-automatic rather than an automatic data link. There would be only single lookout, with all-round view. The ship would accommodate thirty troops (a platoon). As presented to the Operational Requirements Committee in February 1965, Type 19 (NSR 7025) would supplement Type 82 (no mention was made of the Ikara frigate).[27] For the primary peace-keeping role, the ship would need a medium gun, a light helicopter (for reconnaissance and communications), a stabiliser, spare accommodation (for an army platoon or for refugees), and a work boat with good beaching capability. She would need the sort of long endurance (over 5,000nm) associated with Type 82, and the ability to get underway quickly associated with a gas turbine or a diesel. To operate in small harbours, she would need to be very manoeuvrable and robust (so that she could not easily be damaged when going alongside). The global role clearly entailed good sea-keeping. An added requirement associated with the global mission was impressive appearance. Plans called for approving the Staff Requirement in mid-1965, completing the sketch design in 1966, and ordering the ship at the end of 1967 for completion at the end of 1970. The first would be completed in 1970/1 (with the last two *Leander*s), then two in 1972/3, two in 1973/4, two in 1974/5, and three in 1975/6, a total of ten in a rolling programme.

27 DEFE 10/461.

Early estimates proved grossly over-optimistic. Preliminary Design revealed that a more realistic displacement was the 2,600 tons of a *Leander*, with an unacceptable complement of 154 and a price of £6.3 million. Given lengthy explanations of why the earlier estimates were hopelessly wrong, in July 1965 DGS convinced a reluctant Admiralty Board to reconsider. The ship now offered was somewhat shorter (336ft overall) and beamier (38ft maximum). Four Olympus (19,000 SHP each) could indeed drive it at 40kts for 16–17 hours (temperate conditions, clean) or 35kts under tropical conditions (dirty). This machinery (including the Paxman diesels) would cost more than twice as much as that of a *Leander*. Calculated endurance was much as before: 10,000nm at 28kts, 2,000nm at 20kts, 8,000nm at 15kts. A late version of the design was DS 387, presented to the 1966 Future Fleet Working Party. It would have displaced 2,600 tons (360ft × 39ft); in 1966 its unit cost was given as £6.5 million, compared to £9.75 million for the simplest Ikara frigate, DS 390. The Type 19 heritage showed in the powerplant, an Olympus (and two Paxman Ventura diesels) on each shaft, for a maximum speed of 30kts. Like Type 19, she had a very limited armament, one 4.5in gun forward, Seacat and a MATCH helicopter, plus lightweight torpedo tubes in effect replacing Limbo. An unusual feature, at least of the 1966 version, was the use of a Dutch 'egg' search/fire control radar (M29) in place of British equipment (she would have had Type 993 aft, however).

The next step was to retreat to a 28-knot ship, which might be powered by diesels, or by two lower-powered Proteus or Tyne gas turbines (prices, respectively, would have been £5.75 million and £5.8 million). Alternatively the ship could use a *Leander* class steam plant, the only existing one on offer. But all such plans were thrown into turmoil when, in 1966, the carrier, the centrepiece of the fleet, was cancelled.

CHAPTER 14

The Post-Carrier Generation

As the Royal Navy retrenched, the Soviet Navy was growing dramatically. Here HMS *Glasgow* shadows a huge Soviet *Kirov* class nuclear-powered cruiser. The advent of such ships recalled the fears of Soviet commerce-raiding cruisers of the early 1950s. *Glasgow*'s Sea Darts did offer some anti-ship capability, but a proposal to increase it was rejected on the ground that the resulting weapon would lose anti-aircraft capability, which was also badly needed.

In 1966 the Labour Government cancelled the new aircraft carrier, CVA 01, as unaffordable. First Sea Lord Sir Varyan Begg formed a Future Fleet Working Party under ACNS to re-design the fleet. It assumed that everything but the fleet's non-nuclear strike roles would remain. The United Kingdom still had to exercise a world naval presence. To provide ships in enough places at the same time the Royal Navy would have to build low-end frigates like the Type 19 proposed a few years earlier. In the face of serious opposition they would fall back on more powerful forces: cruisers working with area air defence destroyers. Initially the Working Group wanted Type 82s as the area air defence ships, but they were rejected as unaffordable. The group therefore offered a destroyer which could be armed with either of the two Type 82 weapons, Sea Dart or Ikara (the other Type 82 system, the Broomstick radar, was abandoned). Production could shift from Sea Dart-armed destroyers to Ikara-armed ones once enough Sea Dart ships had been completed.

The cruisers would provide local command and control, and they would also support the big Sea King helicopters which the Royal Navy was developing specifically to prosecute submarines – which could not operate from the new small destroyers and frigates. The Working Party suggested that they were also natural platforms for the new P.1127 VTOL jet, then being tested, which could carry anti-ship weapons. It went so

far as to sound out the RAF staff to make sure the RAF would not attack the cruisers the way it had killed the large-deck carrier. The then Defence Minister, who had considered elimination of the carriers a major cost-saving accomplishment, was less than pleased, and so the First Sea Lord felt compelled to disown the Working Party study and to fire ACNS.[1] It then became possible quietly to implement the Working Party programme, a fleet consisting of three warship classes: a large cruiser, a destroyer and a low-end frigate oriented towards presence.

The design alternatives embodied in the Working Party study pointed the way ahead. Inflation had increased the cost of Type 17 (DS 381) of 1964/5 from £9.75 million to an unacceptable £12 million. The corresponding Sea Dart frigate had risen to £12.5 million. Revised versions ships inverted the previous weapon arrangements, with Ikara aft in the ASW ship and Sea Dart forward in the AAW ship. Both had Type 177 rather than Type 184 sonar, presumably because it was considered superior within its narrow sector. To cut cost to £10.5 million, Type 17 was pared to 3,500 tons (390ft × 45ft × 30.5ft). Endurance would be about 4,000nm at 20kts, and speed about 28kts deep and dirty. The price was helicopter capability. The gun would be controlled by the Seawolf search radar (presumably Type 967) on a track-while-scan basis suited to surface but not air targets. Complement was reduced to about 210, which must have been closer to what was acceptable. The corresponding Sea Dart ship, DS 391, would have MATCH but would give up Limbo and the variable depth sonar. Her Sea Dart system would be cut to twenty-six missiles and one rather than two directors. Unit cost would be about £10.25 million.

The next level down was to eliminate the 4.5in gun, in the 2,500-ton (360ft × 40ft × 29ft [hull depth]) DS 389 and DS 390. These ships could be squeezed to such small dimensions only by adopting gas turbine (Olympus-Tyne) powerplants. They would have made the same 28kts deep and dirty (tropical) as the others. DS 389 carried her Sea Dart aft on her forecastle deck, in the same 26-missile version as in DS 391. DS 390 had her Ikara aft, in a well, with Seawolf for self-defence. Both would have had single Bofors on the forward superstructure. The main radar was the projected Type 965 replacement, which did not materialise. Prices would have been £9.5 million (DS 389) or £9.75 million (DS 390).

The Working Party also considered two versions of a 1,200-ton patrol vessel costing less than half as much as a frigate: DS 919 and DS 920, each 1,200 tons (260ft and 270ft × 33ft). The basic DS 919 (£4 million) had a 4.5in gun, Seawolf and a helicopter pad, but no sonar. Trading a Type 184 sonar for the gun (a single 40mm was substituted) would have saved £500,000. The powerplant was one Olympus and two Tyne

[1] For the Working Party studies, including lists of ship characteristics, see DEFE 24/149, DEFE 24/194, and DEFE 24/235. For the firing of ACNS, see E J Grove, *Vanguard to Trident* (Naval Institute Press, Annapolis, Md.: 1987).

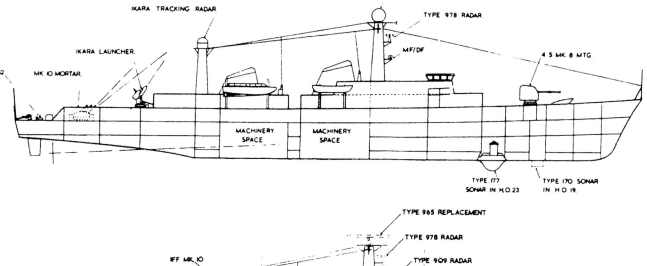

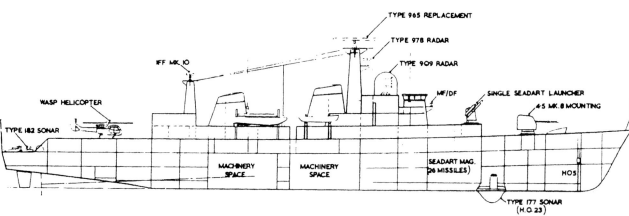

Design Studies 391 and 392 were attempts to reduce the costs of the initial Ikara and Sea Dart studies by eliminating the variable-depth sonar in Type 17 and one of the two Type 909 radars in the Sea Dart ship. The Sea Dart launcher is marked 'single Seadart launcher' and was probably to have been a redesigned unit proposed at the time by Vickers (Type 42 ended up with a standard twin-rail launcher). In effect Type 42 began as a gas turbine equivalent to Design Study 391. The absolute minimum was represented by another pair of designs, Studies 389 and 390, in which the 4.5in gun was eliminated. (PRO DEFE 24/238)

gas turbines; speed would have been 28kts. Endurance would have been half that of the frigates, 2,000nm at 20kts. Such short-legged ships would be unaffordable in a world in which the Royal Navy had fewer and fewer overseas bases. Because ships would operate alone, all of them had to be armed with at least a 4.5in gun (nothing was being done to develop a promised anti-ship missile).

A new factor in any frigate spectrum was the advent of the Vosper Thornycroft commercial designs. To many in the service, these frigates were an attractive alternative to DGS's designs. The Vosper Mk 5 was included in the Working Party's list of alternatives. The emergence of its Mk 7 stablemate was probably an important factor in the decision to build the Type 21 frigate to a commercial design.

At about the same time British machinery policy was re-evaluated. It was assumed that ultimately nuclear power would be adopted for surface ships, but until that became practical the choices were steam, mixed, diesel and gas turbine plants. Steam was increasingly unattractive, not least because it required long periodic refits which drastically reduced the number of available ships. Big diesels, such as the Rushtons of the 1964/5 studies, offered better fuel economy, but they were also far bulkier (and noisier, unless specially silenced). The only real drawback of the gas turbine was inefficiency at partial power. That was cured by adding a low-powered cruise engine. Given its experience with first-generation plants, the Royal Navy adopted a policy of gas turbine repair by replacement. To make that economical, gas turbines had to be standardised across the fleet, in a SYMES (Systematic Machinery

Programme) adopted in 1966. The boost engine was the Olympus, adopted in HMS *Bristol* after tests on board the Type 14 frigate *Exmouth*. The cruise engine was the Tyne, derived from the turboprop in the Vickers Vanguard airliner.[2] A third engine with intermediate power was considered but rejected as not worthwhile. SYMES is why Types 21, 22 and 42 all had the same powerplants.

Carrier aircraft had delivered the Royal Navy's anti-ship weapons. The 1966 White Paper announcing the end of the carrier mentioned acquisition of a frigate anti-ship missile, but for the moment it seemed that frigates would make do with whatever missile their helicopters could carry.[3] By 1969, however, there was considerable interest in a missile primarily to be fired by submarines.[4] It was accepted that surface ships also needed such a weapon, which would be a version of the submarine missile. A formal Operational Requirement, NST 6533, endorsed by the Operational Requirements Committee

[2] The cruise turbine had to produce about 5,000 BHP to power a small destroyer or a frigate at about 20kts; at that output it had to have a specific fuel consumption of 0.5 or better. In 1967 the only available engine with such characteristics was the new free power turbine version of the Tyne, offering 4,350 HP and 0.49lb/SHP/hr. Existing engines, such as Proteus and the US Pratt & Whitney FT 12A, fell somewhat short of the desired output and had 25 and 45 per cent, respectively, too much fuel consumption. Tests of a marinized Tyne began in 1966. For gas turbines as interim before nuclear power, see T225/3473.
[3] According to DEFE 24/528, note dated 14 March 1967, the 'small SSGW' of the White Paper was a long term project. The Future Fleet Working Party (DEFE 24/238) listed four missiles: the Norwegian Penguin, the Israeli Gabriel and the notional Fleetfoot Feasibility Study and a longer-range weapon. Fleetfoot was a 1,700lb missile with a range of 20–25nm and a 250–350lb warhead, using command-to-line-of-sight midcourse guidance and active terminal homing. It could enter service in 1976. Exocet (1,650lbs, 364lb warhead) roughly met this requirement. The other missile, with a data link for mid-course guidance, had a range of 100nm (weight 2,500lbs with a 500lb warhead), for ships or aircraft. Expected unit price was £125,000 (Penguin was £8,000). Otomat, which roughly filled this requirement, was about the size of Exocet, but gained considerable range thanks to its turbojet engine. The missiles contemplated in the January 1969 Staff Target for Type 21 (in DEFE 10/943) were quite small: the Norwegian Penguin, the French SS 12 and the Italian Seakiller.
[4] DEFE10/947.

in September 1969 set required range at the horizon (20–23nm for a surface ship). To meet the desired in-service date of June 1970, the missile had to come off the shelf.[5] The Royal Navy was already interested in Exocet, to which the French were committed; the first meeting with the French to consider acquisition was probably held on 6 August 1969. The alternative was a submarine-launched (waterproofed) version of the Martel anti-radar missile. The Royal Navy Tactical School favoured Exocet because it was considered technically mature. Sub-Martel stayed alive in view of serious technical problems in adapting Exocet for submarine launch, but probably it would not be available until 1978. Given its lack of submarine capability, Exocet (GWS 50) was chosen as an interim weapon to cover the period 1973–8. Its submarine/surface ship successor was the US Harpoon (GWS 60).

Soon the surface-ship missile seemed more urgent, given what seemed to be a huge number of Soviet ship-launched anti-ship missiles.[6] NATO strategy was to deter by showing that the Alliance could counter the Soviets at every level, including limited conventional war at sea. Ships operating alone at the outbreak of war had to be able to deal with nearby enemy surface ships. A Naval Staff study begun in December 1969 standardised missile arrangements, with four per ship.[7] Despite some discussion, there was never any serious possibility that ships would be provided with reloads. Because the successor

Harpoon was more compact than Exocet, a ship could carry eight. It first appeared on board Type 22 Batch II frigates.

These missiles would be targeted by ESM systems, which were also recognised, by the mid-1960s, as a vital fleet AAW sensor. They often detected signals refracted from well beyond the horizon. By the late 1960s the standard system was Porker (UA-8/9). In Exercise Phoenix (1964), average range against aircraft was 225nm, compared to 140nm for radars; they detected 75 per cent of possible contacts. They were also a vital means of resolving air situations badly confused by fast high-flying civilian aircraft (as in Kuwait in 1961 and in Malaysia during the 1963–5 Confrontation). In Exercise Calpurnia (November 1965) UA-9 detected five of six low-level Buccaneer attacks, in one case at a range of 230nm, even though the aircraft were flying at 200ft. The exercise report cited UA-9 as the only fleet sensor offering adequate early warning. In the same exercise these sensors detected thirteen of eighteen possible submarine contacts (exploiting emissions from the submarines' radars). On the other hand, lacking automated signal processing, they could be confused when many similar radars were present (they got only 25 per cent of contacts in Exercise

---

[5] In view of arguments made a few years earlier in favour of Abbey Hill, it seems surprising that longer ranges using ESM were not taken into account.
[6] Most of the Soviet blue-water surface combatants were armed with a missile NATO called SS-N-10, which was assumed to be an anti-ship weapon. Never having been seen outside its tubes, it turned out to be an ASW weapon (NATO SS-N-14) – which later turned out to have, in at least one version, a limited anti-ship capability. As it turned out, this was a low point in Soviet surface anti-ship capability: soon the very capable SS-N-22 (Moskit) would appear on board *Sovremennyy* class destroyers.

[7] The Operational Requirement was for a ship to have better than a 50 per cent chance of inflicting Category B damage on a 3,000-ton target, and better than 40 per cent for a 4,000–5,000-ton target (Soviet destroyer and cruiser, respectively). Such figures were difficult to verify, particularly as there was no way to estimate the effect of Soviet ECM on missiles. Initial plans for 680 to 800 missiles on board sixty-one ships were abandoned as unaffordable; 300 would equip thirty-seven ships. Projected installations (with number of missiles per ship in parentheses): HMS *Tiger* (four), five 'Counties' (DLG 04–08, four each), HMS *Bristol* (four), up to eight Type 42 Batch I (four), eight *Leander* Batch II (six), up to eight Type 22 Batch I (six), and six Type 21 (two). The total missile buy could not be changed once the contract had been signed, but plans changed considerably. *Tiger*, *Bristol*, the earliest of the 'Counties' and the Type 42s were all dropped. One Batch II *Leander* was sold to New Zealand without having been rearmed. *Leanders*, Type 21s and Type 22s had four missiles each. Surplus missiles armed five Batch III *Leanders*, four more Type 22 (Batch II), two more missiles more Type 21s. Type 42 was probably dropped in view of the anti-ship capability of Sea Dart (which was not enhanced for fear of reducing anti-aircraft capability).

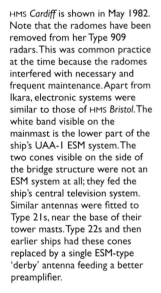

HMS *Cardiff* is shown in May 1982. Note that the radomes have been removed from her Type 909 radars. This was common practice at the time because the radomes interfered with necessary and frequent maintenance. Apart from Ikara, electronic systems were similar to those of HMS *Bristol*. The white band visible on the mainmast is the lower part of the ship's UAA-1 ESM system. The two cones visible on the side of the bridge structure were not an ESM system at all; they fed the ship's central television system. Similar antennas were fitted to Type 21s, near the base of their tower masts. Type 22s and then earlier ships had these cones replaced by a single ESM-type 'derby' antenna feeding a better preamplifier.

Aigrette). When Exocet was introduced, the Royal Navy also introduced a new low-band UA-13, whose very prominent antennas appeared on board four *Leander*s (*Apollo*, *Ariadne*, *Cleopatra* and *Phoebe*), and on three Dutch *Leander* class frigates.

The next step was the more automated Abbey Hill (UAA-1), which incorporated instantaneous frequency measurement (IFM) so that it could distinguish more easily between radars. Manual operation was too laborious, too slow and too limited, and it became less and less acceptable as more and more signals were detected. Automation made it possible for one man (rather than two as in the UA series) to operate the system, and he had a 200-emitter library against which to compare the signals detected. The system could warn automatically if it detected up to six designated signals, and it could steer the associated Type 668 jammer. Compared to Porker, Abbey Hill was a third the size and a quarter the weight. Its data were injected into a ship's computer combat system (ADAWS or the new CAAIS described below). Unlike the earlier systems, it could handle the new frequency-agile and pulse Doppler signals. It was modular, hence could be extended to new frequency bands without the dockyard work required by Porker. Finally, Abbey Hill offered sufficient precision and signal-handling capacity to be used for electronic intelligence gathering, which was not possible with Porker. The Phase I feasibility study began in October 1965.[8]

The associated jammer was the spot-noise Cooky (Types 667 and 668) intended to produce false targets. It could prevent a standard S-band air to surface radar, APS-20, from detecting a carrier beyond 25–35nm, and it could screen an aircraft carrier against X-band radar to 10nm. It could screen a destroyer to 5nm in S-band, and completely in X-band. Screening (counter-targeting) was intended to force a Soviet bomber to close to within anti-aircraft range before it could identify its target to launch missiles. Later a more powerful Type 675 produced false targets to deceive Soviet targeting radars, including, apparently, those on radar satellites.

When the Soviets introduced anti-ship missiles, the Royal Navy equipped some ships with a masthead repeater, Type 669 (Bexley), whose antenna resembled a searchlight at the top of the ship's mast. It bounced its signal off the sea near the ship. The missile was expected to home on the centroid of the total signal it received, including the repeater signal, which would lie somewhere between the ship and the bounced reflection. Only four Type 669s were bought. The next step was a programmable jammer, Millpost, which would presumably fill both the self-defence and screening roles, complementing Abbey Hill. Modern anti-ship missiles set a range gate around the target and ignore signals from outside. In the self-defence mode a jammer like Millpost would send spurious signals to 'walk' the gate away from the target and into a chaff cloud.

As Millpost was not expected to appear before the late 1980s, an interim commercial self-defence jammer, which became Type 670 (Heather), was bought. Millpost itself was dropped, probably about 1980, as too expensive.

Many of the frigates of the 1964 study had digital combat direction systems. Because ADAWS was too expensive for them, they had the notional B4 version of the US NTDS then being offered to NATO, with sixteen-track capacity. The projected *Leander* ADA system would have cost about £300,000. In 1966 the Royal Navy issued a Staff Requirement for a simplified CAAIS (Computer Assisted Action Information System) for future frigates.[9] The existing *Leander* manual/analog system cost £160,000, so the CAAIS cost target was £100,000 (plus £20,000 for a data link). Apparently CAAIS was conceived as a parallel to the central tactical system in the new Nimrod maritime patrol aircraft, both using an Elliott 920C computer. By about 1968 the Royal Navy had shifted to a Ferranti computer like that in ADAWS.

The acronym indicated that CAAIS was only a way of improving the existing system (it replaced the JYA(7) plotting table and most of the TIU 5/GDS 5 gun target indication system). In fact what had been too expensive a few years ago (ADA in a *Leander*) was now quite affordable, mainly due to the falling cost of computer power.[10] Unlike ADAWS, CAAIS did not control weapons and it lacked fully automatic radar target extraction (the system could extract tracks on a limited-area basis). Operators generally entered targets manually from their PPIs, as in the US NTDS system. As in ADAWS, targets, including those received via data link, were tracked on a rate-aided basis. Sonar data were injected semi-automatically when an operator placed one of two trackers on a target (trackers gave range, bearing, Doppler speed and range and bearing rates). The system displayed the surface and underwater pictures corresponding to the tracks it carried, providing back-tracks, rippled markers and lines of bearing. It could solve relative velocity problems (triangles). The ASW plotting function included target indication for MATCH and Limbo and the selection of tracks for transmission via data link. CAAIS also displayed EW targets, hence could automatically triangulate Exocet targets at maximum range. CAAIS thus corresponded to the contemporary US Navy NTDS, but on a smaller scale (48nm rather than 512nm range). Capacity

---

[8] DEFE 10/533.

[9] DEFE 10/533, discussion of NSR 7934 for CAAIS, 1967. CAAIS was offered as a much less expensive alternative to NTDS and to the Dutch DAISY (SEWACO), both of which cost about £300,000. It was presented to the NATO countries at Brussels in November 1967, and a prototype demonstrated off Zeebrugge on board HMS *Wakeful*. The ship demonstrated the system for the Belgian, Danish, French, Norwegian and Swedish navies, in a cruise completed 27 November 1967. As of October 1968 other navies which had either requested or received demonstrations were the RAN (twice, in connection with the RN/RAN frigate), Germans, Italians, Argentines, Indians, Portuguese, Turkish, South African, Pakistani, New Zealand, Canadian and US. A paper dated 25 October 1968 for the Operational Requirements Committee (DEFE 10//942) describes the completed study authorised by the Weapons Development Committee on 13 September 1967.

[10] In much the same way, when the US Navy provided an automated tactical data system to the *Perry* class frigates and to some modernised *Adams* class destroyers it wanted to avoid comparison with the expensive NTDS. The new system was called Junior Tactical Data System (JTDS) or, with a data link, Junior Participating Data System (JPTDS). In fact JPTDS was not too different from NTDS, but with a much more compact and much less expensive new-generation computer.

The short hull of the original Type 42 made for wetness forward. This is HMS *Glasgow*, in a photo released in May 1982.

was also smaller, at sixty tracks, including twenty auto-tracks (compared to 128 or 256). CAAIS was associated with a simplified Link 10 (Link X) digital data link, which was also used in the new Type 42 destroyers (neither had the more complex Link 11). Given CAAIS, a *Leander* could link data from the new digital sonar (Type 184) to an Ikara ship.

The basic system (£110,000 as envisaged in 1967) had six consoles and accepted inputs from up to two radars. A Weapons Direction Console showed all EW bearings plus the air picture out to 48nm. Its operator would assess the tactical situation, select targets, and indicate them to the gun or the Seacat; he also controlled the ship's jammer. In Seawolf ships this console was replaced by a Seawolf (GWS 25) console, which carried out some air-tracking tasks. Connected to its own computer, it was fed directly by the Type 967 radar and could pass up to forty tracks to the ship's CAAIS.

Roughly in parallel with CAAIS, Ferranti, Elliott and Decca began work on a private-venture system for the new Vosper Thornycroft export frigates. It used much the same hardware as the Royal Navy's CAAIS (once the Royal Navy had decided to adopt the Ferranti computer), but apparently at least some of the software was proprietary. Production of the private-venture version began in 1969. The first unit went to sea on board the Argentine carrier *25 de Mayo*, now discarded

(the Argentines wanted compatibility with the ADAWS/Link Y on board their Type 42s). The Royal Navy version, DBA 1, entered service on board Batch II *Leander*s in 1974.

The Destroyer-Frigate Force

In 1970, in the wake of the 1966 Defence Review, the authorised destroyer-frigate level was sixty-eight ships, above the fifty-nine envisaged two years earlier. Given a lifetime of twenty-one years, to maintain it would require three ships per year. The 68-ship force level sufficed to maintain twenty-four fully-efficient ships for the Western Fleet and overseas. Typical overseas commitments included six frigates East of the Cape, including one on the Beira Patrol to blockade Rhodesia (with a seventh ship planned), two in the West Indies, six in the Mediterranean, and one in the new NATO Standing Naval Force Atlantic.[11] There was interest in increasing presence East of Suez (East of the Cape after the Canal was closed following the 1967 Middle East War) to balance the new Soviet presence in the Indian Ocean. Passage time overseas cut into availability: four months to keep a frigate East of the Cape, six months for the Gulf. Twelve frigates were in long refits or at extended notice at any one time, and the equivalent of another thirteen in normal short refits (every 2½ years for a frigate,

[11] T225/3604 includes details of the operating cycle given in August 1972.

every 3½ years for a missile destroyer). A three-ship Standby Squadron was maintained to provide for emergencies and for premature retirements as ships wore out due to hard usage. Another five were used for peacetime sea training (three for Dartmouth cadets), and three more for trials (one for radar/communications, one for propulsion including silencing, *eg* pumpjet trials, and one for sonar development). Thus thirty-six of the sixty-eight ships were not available at all. Another eight were working up or on passage.

The 36-ship overhead was insurance against emergencies and losses. Without the overheads, for example, the Royal Navy could not have fought even the 'Cod War' against Iceland. Overheads made up for heavy losses in the Falklands. However, since 1970 analyses have focussed on the need to maintain a set operating force. The main new factor was that gas turbine ships did not need the short machinery refits, typically eighteen to twenty weeks for a *Leander* but up to thirty-six weeks for a diesel frigate. There was hope at the outset that gas turbine ships could make do with a four-year cycle.

At the end of 1971 new rules cut maximum time away from the base port from twelve to nine months, further exacerbating the situation. Total time overseas in any thirty-month period was not to exceed fifteen months, down from eighteen. In 1971 the Royal Navy was short 3½ ship-years, and could meet only half of the British commitment to NATO. The Royal Navy needed more hulls: eighty-one rather than the existing seventy. The NATO force goal itself would rise to eighty-one by 1975, driven by the rising Soviet naval threat. One solution then being considered was forward basing, to reduce the usual 3:1 ratio of ships to deployed ships to 1:1 except for refits.

The October 1973 Middle East War led to a dramatic rise in the price of oil (the 'oil shock') which threw Western economies into recession. The Defence Review conducted by the new Labour Government which entered office in 1974 deleted nine of the frigates and destroyers planned for 1975–84; the first being two Type 42s of the 1975/6 programme. The 1974 review set the destroyer/frigate force level at sixty-five, all formally declared to NATO (fifty-two for SACLANT, thirteen for CINCCHAN). SACLANT considered this force level inadequate. To further complicate matters, five ships had recently been added for shipping defence in the South Atlantic.

Most importantly, the Defence Review rejected the separate out-of-area role: henceforth British forces would be shaped entirely by the country's NATO commitment. An internal study of the long-term size and shape of the Royal Navy by the Fleet Requirements Committee, suspended pending the outcome of the Review, was resumed in October 1974, producing a report in May 1975.[12] The report acknowledged the out-of-area role, but pointed out that no separate out-of-area force could be afforded; the Navy would have to use NATO forces for any such mission. In 1969 the British Chiefs of Staff had approved a planning concept in which a NATO war would

be the most violent phase of escalation, beginning with a three-month period of tension, followed by a one-month period of much greater tension and perhaps limited engagement. War itself would last only a week, which really meant until one side or the other credibly threatened to go nuclear.

The wartime fleet would be concentrated in two carrier task forces built around two of the three small carriers (only two would ever be available simultaneously). They would cover vital convoys and they would also support the NATO Strike

[12] DEFE 24/687, the Long Term Structure of the Fleet (LTSF), produced by a sub-committee of the Fleet Requirements Committee chaired by Rear Admiral P E C Berger. Work had begun on 22 February 1974. The report breaks down naval tasks and then lists alternative ways to carry them out, showing relative costs. The study looked toward the period 1985–99. Estimates were based on DOAE studies; clearly there was no independent Royal Navy analytical organisation. It was assumed that the Soviets would have over 1,000 naval aircraft (280 with missiles), over 100 surface combatants (ninety with anti-ship missiles), over 100 fast patrol boats, and a massive submarine force (over 250 in 1985, over 180 of these with anti-ship missiles). This force would be spread over all the Soviet fleets, so the Royal Navy would face only part of it. The air threat was up to two regimental (twenty-missile) attacks per day, plus occasional attacks by surface ships or submarines. Up to four air-to-surface missiles might be fired at one area air defence ship in each of six groups. A detailed table showed three kinds of air threat: steep-diving supersonic missiles (AS-4 and AS-6, four appearing in 15 seconds), medium diving trans- and subsonic missiles (AS-5 and SS-N-3, 4 missiles in 15 seconds), and low-flying trans- and subsonic missiles (SS-N-7, -10, -11, and -12, four missiles in 15 seconds, without ECM support). Of these, SS-N-7 was a submarine-launched pop-up missile. SS-N-10 was later called SS-N-2C; it was fired by 'tattletales'. SS-N-12 was a better version of SS-N-3. SS-N-11 was an ASW missile (SS-N-14) misidentified as an anti-ship missile. It was significant because it armed a large new class of surface combatants ('Krivaks'), and the numbers involved greatly inflated the perceived surface anti-ship threat. It was assumed that one to two escorts would attract four missiles, that one to two high value targets or RFAs would attract eight, that a carrier would attract twelve, and that ten merchant ships would attract eight, twenty would attract twelve, and thirty would attract twenty missiles. In addition to the tasks mentioned in the text, the report spent considerable time on the requirement to protect the British strategic deterrent by controlling access to its bases, which included possible measures such as fixed shallow-water acoustic arrays. This task explains the renewed interest in defensive mining. It later emerged that the estimates of anti-ship missiles in surface ships and submarines were excessive, but the Soviet naval air arm was certainly well-equipped with such weapons. The study estimated that the United Kingdom could build about 2.5 surface ships per year, and that a surface ship could be expected to last twenty-eight years with two modernisations, so the surface fleet (destroyers and frigates) could be no larger than seventy ships (this did not take cost into consideration). A new surface ship design could be produced every three years, a new submarine design every seven, and six seemed to be the optimum batch or class size. Surface ship numbers for various tasks were based on an assumption that 60 per cent of surface ships (and submarines) would be available at 15 days' notice. Thus seventeen towed array escorts would equate to ten operational ones. Fewer than 2 per group were acceptable because of the long expected range of the array.

Type 42 was designed to be completed fitted 'for but not with' some important subsystems. Shown in 1980, HMS *Birmingham* lacks the UAA-1 ESM system later installed on the mainmast below the Type 992 target-indication radar. Type 992 fed targets to the ship's Sea Dart system. The longer-ranged Type 965P forward was installed to support the fleet's air picture via the ship's data link. Given the link, Type 42s could use their radars while higher-value units remained silent. HMS *Sheffield* was acting as radar picket for HMS *Hermes* when she was hit by an Argentine Exocet missile in the Falklands. The ship's foremast carries her two stacked UHF antennas (Outfit AJK), one for transmission and one for reception. Present but not visible above them is the HF/DF 'birdcage'. The mainmast carries the previously standard 'candlestick' (Outfit AJE) UHF antennas. Note the triple lightweight ASW torpedo tubes abeam the mainmast, which were not envisaged in the ship as originally conceived.(RN)

Force Atlantic, consisting of US carriers assigned to attack Soviet naval targets. Each task force might have to split into two or three separate elements for convoy protection, so enough ships would be needed for six surface formations, which might be far enough apart to need separate area air defence.

However, during the periods of tension the fleet would be far more dispersed. Moreover, operations at this time might be crucial, as they might convince the Russians that further escalation, at least at sea, was pointless. The 1975 study argued that the United States was withdrawing forces from the Eastern Atlantic, and that no other NATO country could contribute much to NATO naval strength in the north-eastern maritime flank of the alliance. It followed that, at least at the outset, the main naval burden would fall on the United Kingdom. The study also argued that, from a deterrent point of view, the northern (mainly maritime) flank of the Alliance was as important as the Central Front in Germany.

A new factor in this study was the towed array, recent tests of which suggested that it could detect submarines at distances as great as 100nm. The great question was whether towed arrays should be operated primarily by submarines or by surface ships. If they were operated by surface ships, then aircraft of some sort would be needed to prosecute such distant contacts: should they be helicopters flying from ships or long-range maritime patrol aircraft? Another question raised by the study were how the fleet was to meet the threat of Soviet long-range missile bombers flying into its operational area. The combination of Soviet missile bombers, surface missile shooters, and missile-armed submarines seemed to demand much more powerful missile defences within the British fleet.

During the periods of tension, the Royal Navy would conduct surveillance in the Greenland-Iceland-UK (GIUK) Gap and it would trail ('mark') Soviet surface combatants, which were assessed as a major anti-ship threat. The Chief of the Soviet Fleet, Admiral Gorshkov, had written about the importance of the initial attack in a missile war at sea, and his 'battle of the first salvo' concept suggested that it would be vital to keep Soviet ships ('tattletales') from marking major British units. It followed that the Royal Navy should include ships fast enough to keep station with the fastest Soviet surface warships, and the 1975 study called for building eleven 36-knot missile-armed marker/counter-marker ships. As for surveillance, the study concluded that to cover the GIUK Gap the fleet should include five nuclear submarines north of the Gap and twelve surface ships south of it, where they could more easily be protected against hostile air attack. Each of the two carrier groups would have its own towed-array ships, a total of seventeen being required. In theory, a towed-array ship operating with a carrier would not need much in the way of short-range weapons or sensors (torpedoes and a duct sonar), because the other ships would provide for it. However, if the pre-war period of tension – which might be at least as vital as

the war itself – was taken into account, ships would have to be able to operate independently.

The scale of air defence needed was daunting. A total of thirty-seven area air defence systems (Sea Darts) was needed to cover the four task groups which might be formed to cover vital convoys, but only twenty-nine were planned (including the three on the carriers and one on HMS *Bristol*). It might well pay to place two systems in a future destroyer (hence Type 43, described below). The best existing combination of systems for ship self-defence was a double-headed Seawolf (with projected ECCM improvements and an electro-optical director), as in a Type 22 frigate, plus a jammer and radar/IR decoys. Unfortunately that combination made for a very expensive ship, so the report suggested that something simpler was needed, in the form of a close-in weapon system (CIWS). That would soon be available in the form of the US Phalanx and the Dutch Goalkeeper.

The 1975 study concluded that there was no point in low-end frigates; it explicitly killed the 'future light frigate'. It showed just how important organic aircraft could be, and it emphasised the potential role of a follow-on Sea Harrier in fleet air defence. This aircraft could be so important that it would be worthwhile to move the big ASW helicopters from the small carriers to accompanying underway replenishment ships. This idea led to the construction of the *Fort Victoria* class. Another new idea was that large-scale ASW mining was the only economical way to deal with the Soviet submarine force beyond the GIUK Gap. Accordingly the Royal Navy negotiated with the US Navy to obtain Captor mines for wartime use, and it planned to convert cross-Channel ferries into wartime minelayers. For the future, perhaps the most important conclusion was that nuclear attack submarines were so important that the future fleet should include twenty of them. Given their cost, they would inevitably squeeze down the scale of surface combatant construction.

The existing fleet plan would provide twenty-six missile destroyers (including fifteen basic Type 42s and ten modified ones) and thirty-nine frigates (eight Type 21, seven Type 22, and twenty-four *Leanders*) in 1990. It also envisaged nineteen 'Bird' class patrol vessels (which might be thought of as low-end frigates or corvettes) and five 'Island' class OPVs; in fact five 'Bird' class and seven 'Island' class were built.

The 1975 report developed an alternative Baseline force, admittedly not affordable but useful as a yardstick. Through 1977 the Fleet Requirements Committee produced two attempts at a more affordable fleet plan, Fleet 3 and Fleet 4. Throughout, the emphasis remained on high-end ships. This view was not universal. Many senior officers doubted that the high-end ships could be built in sufficient numbers. DG Ships' Forward Design Group was increasingly interested in minimum-cost warships. Another new factor was the need to replace the four Polaris submarines. Studies were conducted so

Photographed on 23 January 1989, HMS *Cardiff* shows Type 1022 radar instead of her original Type 965P forward and Type 996 instead of the earlier Type 992 on her mainmast. The radomes at the foot of the mainmast are Type 670 self-defence jammers. The triple lightweight torpedo tubes have been eliminated as weight compensation. (Maritime Photographic)

secretly that they were not reflected in the long-term building plans. When Trident emerged, no special provision had been made for its costs, so they had to be borne by the rest of the fleet.[13]

By late 1978 a new long-range destroyer/frigate plan had been developed.[14] The pre-war marking and counter-marking roles were abandoned, as was wartime surveillance of the GIUK Gap. It was assumed that the Soviets would have moved most of their submarines south of the Gap well before war began: pre-war but not wartime surveillance was worthwhile. Thus frigates on surveillance duty could move to the carrier task forces once hostilities escalated. The need to stretch frigate endurance to embrace both roles during a period of rising tension and then war justified the armed *Fort Victoria* class replenishment ships, which could keep frigates 'up threat' in the Gap. These changes cut up to twenty-three frigates from the ultimate force: eleven for marking and counter-marking, and twelve for wartime Gap surveillance alongside the seventeen reserved for carrier force operations. Basing frigate numbers and characteristics entirely on the hot-war role entailed a considerable saving. As noted in 1975, ships intended always to operate with the carriers would be little more than tugs for towed arrays, not needing additions such as short-range (duct) sonars, guns and anti-ship missiles. Ships operating in the pre-war Gap surveillance role could similarly be simplified. Aside from their arrays, ships in both roles needed effective anti-missile defence in the form of Seawolf. This

change was reflected in the shift from designs for general-purpose towed-array frigates like Types 24 and 25 (see below) to the very austere towed array 'tug', the original Type 23 (which actually succeeded Types 24 and 25).

The Maritime Tactical School and DOAE now agreed that there should be five Type 42 and five towed-array Type 22 for each light carrier, which meant seventeen ships of each type. Under current plans, there would be enough missile destroyers to meet the Task Group requirement by 1983–4, the total then rising to twenty-two, which would provide air cover for other formations. Plans called for updating Sea Dart in stages, initially with a new long-range radar, STIR (NSR 7946), and then with a successor system (NST 6505). Sea Dart Mk II (GWS 31) and STIR would be installed in as many of the first ten Type 42 destroyers as possible during three-year refits. The successor Type 43 would have STIR, GWS 31 and the new SM1A gas turbine; it would later be fitted with the Future Command System (NST 7868). The Millpost jammer would be installed as widely as possible from 1986 on. As an interim fit, a commercial jammer would be installed in up to seventeen ships under NSR 7373 (see above). A new NATO Seagnat decoy would be installed from 1982 on, offering infra-red as well as radar protection. A future offboard jammer might be built with NATO assistance. There was a new requirement for ships to carry the Classic Outboard HF intercept and D/F system (two per carrier). This was a battle-group system: the carrier the ships accompanied would process its data to greatly extend the group horizon.

To put the new Type 2031 towed array to sea as soon as possible, it would be installed on an interim basis on board four *Rothesay* class frigates during major refits in 1981–2. The mass production programme would consist of as many Type 22s as

[13] Dorman, *Defence Under Thatcher*, pp 21–2. Dorman (p 86) notes that the US decision to phase out Trident C-4 in favour of the larger D-5 forced the British to redesign and to push their own Trident programme out to the 1990s, leaving more money in the long-term costings of the late 1980s for conventional naval forces.
[14] DEFE 24/1114, dated 5 December 1978, a paper intended to justify increased production of Type 22 frigates before the Operational Requirements Committee the following year. It was described as consistent with a current DOAE Force Mix Study, DOAE Report 253.

HMS *Glasgow* is shown in June 1996, with Type 670 on the side of the forward tower supporting her Type 1022 radar, with SCOT, and with a Phalanx CIWS abeam her funnel. The wrap around her foremast is radar-absorbent material to reduce reflections into her Type 1022 radar. (Maritime Photographic)

possible (on construction) and also five Batch III *Leanders*. To gain sufficient towed array Type 22s, eleven Type 42 hulls in the 1978 long-term costing would be shifted to Type 22s. That would have little effect, because the two types cost about the same. Apparently Batch I Type 22s were not suited to towed arrays. Because Type 21s lacked sufficient margin for towed array installation, they would be retired early (at thirteen years, between 1987 and 1991), without major refits. They survived slightly longer, probably because the Nott cuts had eliminated new frigates which would have replaced them.

The 1980–90 plan proposed at this time showed a final total of nineteen Type 42s, with the first three Type 43s entering service in 1989, and five in service in 1990. Type 22 numbers would rise to fourteen by 1989 and to sixteen in 1990. Twelve Batch II (and later) Type 22s and five converted Batch II *Leanders* would provide the desired seventeen towed arrays using the production system, Type 2031Z. Presumably further Type 22s or a successor would replace the Batch III *Leanders* as they retired, as the revised Long-Term Costing envisaged at least fourteen such ships. Clearly the marking and counter-marking roles were still interesting, because an accompanying commentary noted that although all future frigates should be capable of at least 30kts, a recent study had showed the value, in some, of speeds of at least about 35kts.

The Conservatives came into office in May 1979 planning to rebuild the fleet. There were not enough escorts, and Soviet anti-ship capability, particularly in bomber-launched missiles, was growing. Supreme Allied Commander Atlantic (SACLANT) Admiral Harry Train USN suggested routeing

shipping as far south as possible. They might thus operate beyond the range of Soviet bombers. Any Soviet submarines forced to operate far to the south would have to spend most of their time in transit from their bases, hence would have little time left to patrol against shipping. For their part, convoys would spend four more days in transit. There were not enough NATO escorts to stay with them across the Atlantic; instead escorts would concentrate on the leg from Madeira to European ports. To many in the Royal Navy this was suicidal: historical experience showed that convoys had to be escorted all the way across the Atlantic. C-in-C Fleet, Controller and Navy Minister Keith Speed all wanted more numerous escorts.[15] They therefore proposed a high-low mix of Type 44 and Type 42 destroyers and Type 22 and new Type 23 frigates. The Board, remembering Type 14, was apparently divided.

The British economy fell into recession in the winter of 1979–80; high inflation cut into export orders. One paradoxical effect was that firms which might otherwise have balanced defence orders against others were free to complete defence work much more promptly. Forward defence plans had been framed on the assumption of a slower pace of production and about 20 per cent late delivery, hence late payment. MoD found itself short of cash. The navy now emphasised platform numbers over systems, favouring such less expensive ships as Type 23 and a new diesel submarine. Weapon programmes, including the Sea Dart upgrade, Millpost and a Sea Skua upgrade, were cancelled to maintain the numerical strength of the fleet, the theory being that as long as the platforms survived they

[15] Dorman, *Defence Under Thatcher*, p 34.

could be upgraded later.[16] Destroyers and frigates which had been added to the long-term costings as insurance were dropped. However, an attempt to cut £4 billion from overall spending for 1980/1 failed. When the defence team failed to offer sufficient cuts to the Treasury, the matter came before the Cabinet. Prime Minister Thatcher now dropped her previously uncompromising support for defence.[17] For the moment, the navy simply discarded ships already in reserve, but it was clear that a full-scale defence review was coming. In 1981, of the three services, the Royal Navy was the most over-extended in the long-term costings.

John Nott was made Defence Minister in January 1981 specifically to cut defence costs while improving capability. Nott's approach was described as more analytical than those of other defence ministers. Unlike his Prime Minister, he had no interest in out-of-area operations; he wanted to concentrate first on the defence of the United Kingdom itself and second on the NATO commitment. Nott's first reform was to rein in the long-term costings by allowing only the NATO-mandated growth of 3 per cent per year through 1985/86, with no growth thereafter. That made the looming resource problem more obvious. Nott seemed particularly hostile to the navy, and he seemed to have no understanding of the significance or value of surface warships.[18]

On the basis of a DOAE analysis, Nott reversed Admiral Train's logic, arguing for concentration on the GIUK Gap rather than on any escort operation built around the carriers. If the convoys ran well to the south, then Soviet submarines could not disperse there much before hostilities began. Instead, they would have to conserve their available patrol time; blocking the Gap would once more be well worthwhile. DOAE's arguments strongly favoured nuclear submarines and Nimrods,

supported by fixed arrays of increasing effectiveness, for this purpose. New surface construction would be limited to low-end towed-array ships (Type 23s). Nott soon announced that he was cutting the Royal Navy's proportion of the budget from 29 to 25 per cent by the end of the 1980s.[19] That the reduced figure included Trident made the cut much worse. When he protested (not having been consulted by Nott), Navy Minister Keith Speed was forced to resign.

The navy had to cut manpower by a quarter to a third. Without the NATO carrier group mission, Type 44 was abandoned, and at least two projected Type 42s cancelled. Nott was willing to retain two carriers (and thus some escorts), more for out-of-area operations than for strike fleet support, but that did not require expensive high-end anti-aircraft capability. In effect the retained carriers were his sop to the Royal Navy. The Type 22 frigate programme was stopped in favour of the low-end Type 23. All mid-life modernisation was abandoned. That killed the project to place towed arrays on the last five Batch III *Leander*s. The amphibious force would be abandoned (the Norwegian support mission was already being questioned). The Royal Navy lobbied its allies, particularly the US Navy, to protest the surface ship cuts.[20] After considering destroyer/frigate figures as low as thirty, Nott announced a reduction from sixty-five (of which fifty-nine were declared to NATO) to forty-two (plus eight at long notice in Operational Reserve) over a period of three to four years. Nott was forced to retreat somewhat as he lost influence with the Prime Minister, and he felt compelled to order another Type 22 frigate in February 1982.

Nott later wrote that he saw little point in wartime shipping protection designed to guarantee that NATO armies in Europe could be resupplied.[21] All analyses showed that within seven days of the outbreak of war losing NATO armies would be compelled to use nuclear weapons. Why bother with what came after that? Nott had missed the point, which the Admiralty had made as early as 1954 in its strategy paper. The Soviets might build an army capable of mobilising and overrunning Western Europe, but the prospect that it would touch off a nuclear war would probably deter them from deliberately starting a war. If it came at all, war would come by miscalculation, probably out of an unexpected explosion in the Soviet empire in Central Europe. In 1968, for example, as the Soviets sent forces into Czechoslovakia, they feared a NATO response. Both sides would feed forces gradually into such an unexpected war, and it might be precisely NATO's ability to reinforce (using seaborne resupply) which might be decisive.

---

[16] Dorman, *Defence Under Thatcher*, p 50, quoting 1980–1 Parliamentary testimony by Admiral Sir Raymond Lygo.

[17] According to Dorman, *Defence Under Thatcher*, p 54, the Prime Minister was convinced by her bad experience with the Stingray torpedo programme that defence was grossly inefficient. Britain and other NATO members had all pledged in the late 1970s to increase defence spending in real terms by 3 per cent per year, a pledge which would expire in 1985/6. Nott makes it clear that such figures were, at best, confusing, not least because Britain was experiencing rampant inflation. Thus the 1981/82 defence budget of £12.3 billion was equivalent to only £9.7 billion in 1980 terms (*ie* 27 per cent). His account (p 207) is complicated by an apparent confusion between growth in real (constant pound) terms and in inflated terms. Thus about 1982, after the Falklands, the Chiefs of Staff wanted 12 per cent growth, and were disappointed that they were getting only 7 or 8 per cent; but this was in current rather than real terms. It suggests that inflation was expected to run at about 9 per cent.

[18] According to Speed, who was not involved in the review, Defence Minister John Nott was unimpressed by the argument for numbers of surface ships, arguing that unit quality (weapons) was more important than numbers (platforms). Dorman, *Defence Under Thatcher*, p 67, says that he simply did not understand surface ships. According to Dorman, *Defence Under Thatcher*, p 70, DOAE in particular rejected the logic of the navy re-equipment programme on the ground that it failed to deal with the anti-ship missile threat to ASW ships. Dorman argues that DOAE was particularly important in this exercise because none of the services was willing to volunteer cuts or changes. He points out that DOAE's analysis of the GIUK Gap strategy had two defects, one of which the Royal Navy challenged, the other being allowed to pass. The challenged claim was that the Soviet submarines would pass through the gap only *after* war had broken out; otherwise the barrier would be pointless until submarines had to return to rearm. The point not challenged was the assumption that the Soviets would leave the SOSUS system in Iceland, on which the Nimrods depended, intact.

[19] This was presented, among other things, to the Chiefs of Staff on 16 March 1981 in a one-page 'Bermudagram': Dorman, *Defence Under Thatcher*, p 71. In his memoir, *Here Today, Gone Tomorrow* (London: Politico's, 2002), Nott claims (p 205) that excluding Trident the naval share of the British defence budget had grown from 25 per cent in 1950/1 to 27 per cent in 1970/1, to 28 per cent in 1978/9, and to 29 per cent in 1982/3, and that in 1982/3 the naval budget was 60 per cent larger than in 1950/1. He also claims that the torpedo programme cost about £2 billion, in his terms 80 per cent of the entire 1950/1 budget. Comparisons over so long a period are difficult because alternative measures of the British inflation rate are radically different. Furthermore, the 1950/1 budget was unusually small because it was pre-Korea.

[20] Dorman, *Defence Under Thatcher*, pp 77–8.

[21] Nott, *Here Today, Gone Tomorrow*, pp 205–6, citing Soviet exercises which demonstrated plans for an armoured thrust into Western Europe. The great fear at the time was that the Soviets might be able to launch such an attack without giving NATO much warning by mobilising. The deterrent effect of nuclear weapons would have remained, however. Nott says that he and his colleagues considered war unlikely, but he did not draw the conclusion that war would more likely come by miscalculation rather than by intent. At least in the United States, this possibility had been raised some years earlier within official circles. One of the author's then think-tank colleagues, Frank Armbruster, produced a widely-discussed scenario for a war beginning with an East German uprising, both sides very unwillingly being dragged in.

Later in 1982 the Falklands War showed just how valuable naval flexibility could be, and Nott's ideas were reversed: the importance of out-of-area operations was now evident. Nott's decision to stop Type 42 construction stood, largely because the loss of HMS *Sheffield* to a single dud Exocet made further construction of that class politically unacceptable.[22] As of 1985 the Type 42 successor was to have been a Type 23 variant, to be ordered from the mid-1990s on. Given its earlier problems, the Admiralty became interested in a collaborative programme which would be difficult to cancel. That eventually emerged as the NATO Frigate, leading indirectly to the current Type 45. Meanwhile, the ships built after the war to replace lost units, including two lost Type 42s, were Type 22 ASW frigates.[23] Three frigates scheduled for scrapping were retained, and four standby ships retained in commission for service in the South Atlantic. By that time the Royal Navy had additional overseas commitments, such as the Armilla Patrol in the Gulf.

The Falklands War coincided with a radical shift in British naval strategy. It became clear that the Soviets regarded their strategic submarines as a key asset, to be protected against NATO attacks. Instead of spreading their attack submarines into the Atlantic at the outset of a crisis, they would call these ships home.[24] The US Navy espoused an offensive maritime strategy, which the Royal Navy found quite attractive. The NATO Strike Fleet Atlantic, assisted by the British carrier task force, would have a major role in applying pressure, as would British and US nuclear attack submarines. Blocking the GIUK Gap would indeed be extremely important, because only well into a war would the Soviet submarine force come out to fight in the sea lanes (there was also a real hope that naval pressure might make it difficult for the Soviets to overrun NATO land forces nearly as quickly as had previously been imagined).

[22] For Nott (*Here Today, Gone Tomorrow*, p 203), the Falklands War justified his belief that surface ships could not survive against modern missiles, as some DOAE studies already suggested. This was disingenuous. The two Type 42s were lost due to economies taken in their design and construction, and the Type 21s could hardly be considered first-line ships. The Seawolf anti-missile system proved quite effective, albeit not against missiles (which were not fired at Seawolf ships or formations defended by them).
[23] According to Dorman, *Defence Under Thatcher*, p 92, the Royal Navy would have liked two replacement Type 42s and two Type 22s to replace the lost Type 21s. The Treasury argued for four Type 21s or Type 23s. The navy beat back the Treasury by arguing that Type 21 was no longer in production and that Type 23 was not yet ready for production; it chose four upgraded Type 22s.

[24] It is difficult to say exactly when perceptions changed, either in the US Navy or in the Royal Navy. The only quasi-official account is C A Ford and D A Rosenberg, 'The Naval Intelligence Underpinnings of Reagan's Maritime Strategy', in the special Cold War at Sea edition of the *Journal of Strategic Studies*, 28 (April 2005), pp 379–409. At least since 1968, on the basis of Soviet unclassified writings, scholars such as Robert Herrick had argued that Soviet naval strategy was fundamentally defensive, but that did not convince those who saw an expanding Soviet fleet capable of blue-water operation and of contesting control of vital sealanes. Ford and Rosenberg claim that the fruits of unprecedented 'deep penetrations' into Soviet naval communications in the 1970s and early 1980s convinced the US naval leadership of earlier claims that the Soviets valued their strategic nuclear submarines *and* felt compelled to defend them in bastions. That in turn offered valuable naval leverage. The Soviets might well soon realise that they ought to contest the sea lanes, but the bastions made it possible to force them to concentrate their anti-shipping forces at home. The author recalls considerable British scepticism in the mid-1980s, as some saw the Royal Navy being forced to follow its larger ally.

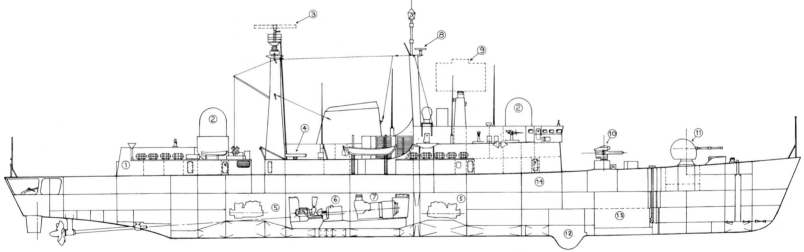

Batch I Type 42 as designed, with both Type 909 tracker/illuminator radars. Note how the ship's Operations Room (CIC) is buried in the hull for protection, rather than being set adjacent to the bridge, as in some US ships. The ship's UAA-I ESM array is below her Type 992Q Sea Dart target indication radar. Note the SCOT antenna at the base of the foremast. Because it operated at radar-like frequencies, it could produce a false alarm in the ship's ESM system. The latter was therefore shut down while HMS *Sheffield* communicated by satellite – as in the Falklands. That left her open to Argentine attack, but even so she received warning from other ships via her data link. The Exocet which hit the ship during

the Falklands War lodged and burned in her machinery spaces (its warhead did not explode). The situation was aggravated by the use of a gravity-feed header tank; when pipes burst due to the missile hit, fuel was sprayed throughout the machinery space. With some of the gas turbine casings broken, an intolerable high-pitched whine filled these spaces. Some post-war analyses suggested that the burning missile fuel, which could not easily be put out (because it was mixed with its own oxidiser) was actually a worse threat that a small explosive warhead. When smoke filled *Sheffield*'s machinery spaces, the ship lost all power, because she had no emergency generator outside her machinery spaces. The

lack of smoke barriers made it impossible for the crew to remain onboard, even though the single Exocet that hit did not sink the ship. Because the engines were not put out of action by the missile hit, the ship ran herself out of the battle area, being found the following day. By that time she was high in the water, having burnt her fuel, hence relatively unstable. A storm poured water through the hole made by the missile, and the ship sank. The lesson was that even a small modern warship is inherently quite tough; had things gone even slightly better (or had there been better smoke barriers), she would have been saved. (A D Baker III)

1. Helicopter hangar, aircraft weapons magazine
2. Type 909 radar weapons directors
3. Type 992Q search radar
4. Single ASW torpedo tube (P&S)
5. Auxiliary machinery rooms (diesel generator sets)
6. After engine room (two Tyne gas turbines)
7. Forward engine room (two Olympus gas turbines)
8. Type 1006(3) navigational radar
9. Type 965R air search radar antenna
10. Sea Dart GWS 30 twin-arm launcher
11. Hull Outfit 23 (Type 184M sonar)
12. Sea Dart missile magazine
13. Operations room

HMS *Liverpool*, a Batch II Type 42, is shown in 1984. She has the new Type 1022 long-range air-search radar but not Type 996 (aft), and as yet she has no defensive jammers. (Maritime Photographic)

Towed array surveillance of the Gap would be well worthwhile. Thus by the time it was being built Type 23 was seen more as a towed-array surveillance ship than as a carrier escort, even though it had been conceived at a time when the carrier support role was far more important.

With the end of the Cold War, there was intense pressure for a 'peace dividend', which meant sharply reduced naval spending. The irony was that the deterrence which had marked the Cold War was no longer effective. Thus the sort of out-of-area problems traditionally addressed by the Royal Navy were likely to become more common, not less, the most immediate case being the continuing need for ships in the Gulf. Even so, by the early 1990s the authorised destroyer/frigate force level was thirty-five, and it was cut to thirty-two when the large new carriers were announced in 1997. In 2005 it was cut to twenty-seven, presumably to pay for the rising price of the new carriers and of the new Type 45 destroyers.[25]

The Sea Dart Destroyer: Type 42

By 1966 it was clear that Seaslug had to be replaced. The Admiralty therefore concentrated on gaining authority to design and produce a Sea Dart destroyer soon designated Type 42 in the A/A *frigate* series. The Board saw it as a derivative of the Sea Dart frigates designed as part of the 1963–4 escort mix

study described in the previous chapter. VCNS promised a rigid unit cost limit of £12 million when he sold the fleet 'package' in July 1967; Type 82 had cost £17 million. Estimated unit cost in the fall of 1967 was £10.5 million, £3.2 million of it for weapons. Another £0.7 million for hull and £0.5 million for weapons was allowed for contingencies. From the beginning it seems to have been assumed that the ships would have an ADAWS based on the *Bristol* version, but without Ikara.

In the post-carrier fleet, Sea Dart destroyers would be spread among groups of surface ships rather than concentrated, like Type 82s, around a capital ship. They might amount to a quarter to a third of the destroyer-frigate force. They therefore needed general-purpose capability, albeit on a scale far less grand than that of a Type 82. Thus they needed a single 4.5in gun; as in *Bristol*, there was no separate gun fire-control system (in effect the Type 909 missile control radar and the high-definition Type 1006 surface set were the gun fire-control radars). For area ASW they had a helicopter (MATCH) and a modern Type 184 sonar. The self-defence weapon was a ship-launched lightweight torpedo, preset so that it could not home on the ship (MATCH had an effective minimum range of 3,000 yds to preclude self-homing, the torpedo having no safety zone). Although Limbo itself was never proposed, the comparable Norwegian Terne was (and was rejected out of hand). The new Lynx helicopter provided considerable general-purpose capability, because it was large enough for reconnaissance and surface strike (using the French wire-guided AS 12 missile) as well as stand-off ASW torpedo delivery (MATCH). As an economy measure, the usual provision for MATCH to deliver nuclear depth bombs was deleted. Ultimately the Sea Dart ship was affordable because her weapon had been de-

[25] Cuts announced in 2005 were three Type 42s (to be withdrawn by the end of 2005) and three Type 23 (two to be withdrawn in 2005, the last by March 2006). Note that the four Type 22 Batch III are being retained (all earlier Type 22s were sold). An explanation quoted by the House of Commons Defence Committee was that the destroyer/frigate force was sized to meet a series of Standing Tasks, each requiring one destroyer or frigate. Before March 2004 there were seven: contributions to Standing NATO forces Atlantic and Mediterranean, escort in home waters, Atlantic patrols North (Caribbean) and South (Falklands, West Africa), and two East of Suez (one in the Gulf, one in the Indian Ocean and further East). The NATO Atlantic commitment was dropped in March 2004, and the Mediterranean would probably devolve into part of a NATO Response Force. The 2005 cuts would reduce the Standing Tasks to four. Presumably the Standing Tasks were in addition to participation in a battle group built around a carrier.

signed for use in a frigate, hence could be installed in a small hull. Initially it seemed that a special small-ship version would be required, but ultimately the Type 82 system was simply scaled down, with twenty-two rather than thirty-eight missiles. This system accounted for nearly £4 million of the increase in cost compared to a *Leander*.

Because the picket role was still vital, Type 42 had the same Type 965 long-range air-search radar as *Bristol* and the *Leanders* (Type 992 sufficed for Sea Dart target indication). So tight was the planned budget that VCNS initially rejected a second missile director (Type 909 radar), which would double firepower, to save £0.75 million. Also to save money, the ships would have provision for the new Abbey Hill ESM system, but they would not be completed with it.

The most important difference between Type 42 and the earlier Sea Dart frigate studies was machinery, the Olympus-Tyne combination instead of bulkier diesels. Compared to a *Leander* steam plant, the new machinery would be more reliable, would require much shorter refits, and would save manpower. Thus Type 42 was designed for a very long four years between refits; greater availability would reduce the total number needed to maintain a given number at sea. The Tyne cruise engine gave much better endurance and a much higher cruising speed, 18kts.

As presented to the Board on 2 October 1967, estimated unit cost was £11 million in 1967 terms. It was well under-

stood that the fate of the programme depended holding down the price. That was done partly by accepting austerity. No lift was provided between Operations Room and bridge. As offered to the Board, the ship had only a single missile director, with no provision for the second missile director, for the Bexley self-defence EW system, for extra torpedoes, or for an observer for the Lynx helicopter. The only close-range weapons were two Oerlikons. There was no provision for satellite communication. Silencing and shock-hardening standards were those of an improved *Leander*. There was no provision for the usual pre-wetting (against nuclear fallout). There was no provision for underway replenishment (including transferring missiles at sea. The ship would have a single integrated galley (for all officers and ratings) and a single anchor.

Probably to make it difficult to add new and expensive features, the ship was limited in length to 392ft (which was still beyond the 385ft of early 3,500-ton sketches). Compared to a conventional design, the hull was cut back forward of the gun and the missile launcher, leaving too short a run-in from the bow. The full part of the hull needed to accommodate the missile magazine was left too near the bow. Thus the ships were very wet forward, which must have affected the maintainability of the forecastle missile launcher and the 4.5in gun (in at least one Type 42 during the Falklands War, sailors reportedly had to jump on the blast doors to close them after missiles were run up on the rails). The short hull limited speed,

too, to an estimated 28kts deep and dirty in the tropics. Displacement was held to 3,575 tons deep, partly by using water-displacement fuel tanks, as in Type 41 and Type 61 frigates. Apparently hull strength was insufficient: Batch I and II ships had visible deck reinforcements, and Batch III ships were given hull girders.

Probably the only margin was in complement (306 planned, with space for 315). Later complement was reduced to 273, and the provision for 306 was considered sufficient margin. Still later the margin was effectively eliminated, the ship accommodating no more than twenty officers and 260 ratings. In peacetime that would include only one Lynx crew (in wartime the required extra crew would have to double-bunk). Accommodation was at the earlier standard of the 'improved *Leanders*'. By the mid-1980s the usual complement was twenty-four officers and 229 ratings, with capacity for a total of 312.

Controller asked for formal approval of the sketch design on 10 April 1968.[26] First Sea Lord wanted a second director.[27]

[26] ADM 167/168. DNC's presentation is ADM 281/291-292.
[27] According to figures given the Operational Requirements Committee, the missile was so fast that it could successively destroy targets in a stream twenty-four seconds apart at Mach 1. The second illuminator reduced minimum spacing to ten seconds, making saturation far more difficult. If aircraft were closely bunched, the second illuminator would double the number of targets the ship could handle. Typical possible targets were Styx and Kipper anti-ship missiles and Fitter fighter-bombers, all of which might be encountered in the Third World. The requirement was to handle two targets simultaneously, and to kill three out of ten Mach 1 aircraft flying at 50ft altitude within a 10° sector, with targets ten seconds apart. The ship's Type 992 target indication radar lacked moving target indication (MTI) capability: it could not detect aircraft flying low overland. Because the Argentines had Type 42 destroyers, they were well aware that the system could be saturated by pop-up targets appearing suddenly at short range. That was how HMS *Coventry* was sunk by a co-ordinated raid.

In a NATO scenario of dense raids it would double the ship's capability at a relatively low cost. Through May 1968 the navy hedged, providing space and weight for two directors but expecting to install only one. Then the second was added. The Board saw the final drawings on 21 November. It now appeared that the ships could be built for less than the £13.5 million cost reported to the Treasury. Controller reminded the Board of some further sacrifices made to control cost: the ship could never be fitted with the projected EW system and she could have only single rather than the desired triple lightweight torpedo tubes (in fact triple tubes were fitted).

Initially twelve Type 42s were planned, but then the programme was extended indefinitely. Thus the November 1972 long-term costings (*ie* through 1983) showed twenty-six Type 42s (unit cost £19.9 million) as well as Type 21 and Type 22 (£20.4 million each, twenty-one planned) frigates and three small carriers.[28] Type 42 Batch II would begin with the fourteenth ship. In fact the first six Type 42s constituted Batch I. Two of them, HMS *Sheffield* (first of class) and HMS *Coventry*, were sunk in the Falklands. The next four were Batch II. Probably largely due to inflation, costs far exceeded expectations: £30.9 million for *Birmingham* (Batch I), and £60.9 million for *Exeter* (Batch II).

[28] DEFE 24/503. Dorman, *Defence Under Thatcher*, p 18, points out that only the first year of the ten-year Long-Term Costing was the agreed budget. The next four were the Government's intentions reflected in the Public Expenditure Survey (PES). The last five were internal MoD estimates, by no means agreed by the Government. As elsewhere, the services tended to over-estimate available resources (by about 10 to 20 per cent) and to load the most expensive programmes into the out-years, at the end of the decade. There was no slack for unexpected large programmes.

HMS *Liverpool*, photographed in March 1995, shows both new main radars. Note the electro-optical director atop the bridge, visible against the forward Type 909 radome. Note, too, the elimination of the old HF/DF antenna atop the foremast. Instead of the cone shown here, by 2001 *Exeter* had a rounded radome. The slightly raised section visible amidships along the weather deck is not a bulwark; it is deck strengthening, presumably to deal with the increased loads the ship was carrying. (Maritime Photographic)

The last two Batch II ships, *Nottingham* and *Liverpool*, had a new search radar (Type 1022 instead of 965), an improved target-indication set (Type 992R vice 992Q), a new underwater data link (Type 2008JA instead of the Type 185 underwater telephone), Link 11 with two channels (previous ships had only the less capable Link 10, limited to the British and Dutch fleets), Parkhill (secure HF speech), Lamberton (secure UHF speech), and improved HF communications.

Studies for a Type 42 redesign began in 1975, a Working Group being assigned to develop both modified versions of the existing design and a potential successor. This was the origin of the Type 43 design described separately below.[29] It was recognised that the ship was shorter than desirable and too densely packed. There was no indication, incidentally, that (as has often been said) Type 42 had been shortened in the design phase from the preferred length of 434ft.

DGS reported in June 1976, proposing a stretched hull (434ft long, 2ft beamier). Although it would have the same 22-missile magazine as earlier ships, space had been allocated to add fifteen missiles if desired. In the longer hull, the sonar dome (HO 23) could be moved forward to within 105ft of the fore perpendicular, alleviating self-noise. The most important advantage of the enlarged hull, and the reason it was accepted, was that it provided sufficient margin for later upgrades; by 1976 it was accepted that Type 42 was no longer at all adequate. See the later discussion of Type 43 for the problems involved.

Given the additional space in Batch III, DGS reported pro-

[29] The report of the Working Group is in DEFE69/551.

jected weapons and sensors:

Batch III:
STWS 2 vice STWS 1 (lightweight torpedo system; Mk 2 could fire the new Stingray torpedo).
Sonar 2028 vice Type 184 in the same HO 23 dome (this sonar did not materialise).
ICS 2A vice ICS 2.
NATO Sea Gnat decoy system vice 3in RLS (Corvus).
Interim ECM (Millpost Phase 1).
Modified Operations Room Arrangement.
Electro-optic tracker*.

Batch IV:
STIR radar vice Type 1022 or 992R.
GWS 30 improvements (NST 6503)*.
UAA-1 improvements*.
Montana* (electro-optical surveillance system).
FH5/UA-13*.

Starred items had not been studied in detail because of insufficient data, which suggests that they were still quite developmental. Some of these items, such as the Millpost jammer, never materialised, but the list gives some idea of what was wanted.

The last four ships had the stretched hull. It turned out to be somewhat weak, and very visible reinforcing strakes had to be added. For the entire class, many of the austerity measures were reversed. Ships were fitted for satellite communica-

HMS *Edinburgh*, shown on 28 October 1988, was a Batch III Type 42, substantially lengthened but without additional armament. Completed in 1985, at this time she still had her lightweight torpedo tubes and had not yet been fitted with Phalanx. A Type 670 radome is visible behind her port side SCOT radome. (RAN)

HMS *Edinburgh* is shown in July 2001, with Type 675 gone. (Maritime Photographic)

tions (SCOT system), they had UAA-1 ESM systems (eventually replaced by UAT(5)) controlling decoy launchers, they received the defensive Type 670, and later they were equipped with the Type 675 ECM system (removed by 2000). Type 1022 eventually replaced the original long-range Type 965. The three-dimensional Type 996 replaced the two-dimensional Type 992Q or 992R on board most ships, probably significantly improving reaction time by reducing the need for the Type 909 missile director to scan in elevation to acquire its target. Batch III added the electro-optical GSA 7 gun fire-control system (Sea Archer 30) as a back-up to the radars. The original Type 184M hull sonar was replaced by the digital Type 2016 and then by Type 2050 in later and refitted ships.

The only foreign customer was Argentina, which in April 1968 considered asking for alternative armament and propulsion (FIAT gas turbines instead of Tynes). The armament alternatives were the US lightweight 5in/54 and two OTO-Melara 3in/62 Compacts, plus either the Norwegian Terne or the Swedish Bofors ASW launcher (instead of lightweight tubes). In the end the Argentines bought standard Type 42s.

Overall, Type 42 was the bare minimum Sea Dart ship. When two Type 42s were lost in the Falklands War, that was taken as proof that even very sophisticated modern warships could not resist modern anti-ship missiles. The reality was that the losses reflected conscious cost-cutting gambles taken over the previous two decades, such as the decision not to deploy moving target indicator radars and the decision to cut the ship's length (with consequences for launcher availability). Minimum size

made it difficult or impossible, for example, to keep SCOT side lobes out of the ship's ESM system, so when HMS *Sheffield* was transmitting on her satellite link she had to turn off her ESM, and thus miss the warning it would have given that an Argentine aircraft was attacking (inattention to Link 10 denied the ship warnings from other ships in the fleet). *Coventry* was lost to a co-ordinated attack which she could not detect in time because of her lack of an MTI radar. In effect the current Type 45 reflects reality: ships can beat back air attack, but only at a high cost in sophistication.

The Falklands War dramatised the ships' lack of any short-range defensive weapons. The immediate reaction was to fit two twin 30mm BMARC guns and two single GAM-B01 20mm guns. Beginning with HMS *Exeter* in 1987, ships were fitted with two Phalanx close-in weapons. Eventually in Batch I and II ships the triple ASW tubes were landed as weight compensation for various improvements. Limited margin made it impossible to fit the desired Seawolf point-defence missile system, a projected lightweight version of which had been cancelled.

The Ikara Frigate

The dead Type 82 was the only near-term Ikara platform. The planned Ikara destroyer would have to wait, probably about seven years, for construction of the final *Leander*s, the Sea Dart destroyer and a new nuclear submarine. Yet Ikara was the only British all-weather naval stand-off weapon which could deal with fast submarines. It was the best means of dealing with

HMS *Gloucester* is shown in February 1997. The most noticeable change is the massive reinforcing strake at weather deck level; the ship's structure clearly had not been strengthened sufficiently for the extra length. Note too the box structure abaft the funnel for Type 675 jammers. This system was eventually eliminated, presumably largely because likely enemies would not have remote targeting systems comparable to those the Soviets had developed during the Cold War (and against which Type 675 was conceived). The Royal Navy now expects to use an offboard active decoy, Siren, which has the advantage that a missile homing on jamming signals will not hit the ship. In addition to the two SCOT satellite antennas visible forward is an INMARSAT antenna. Note that the ship retained her triple torpedo tubes. (Maritime Photographic)

a fast evading submarine, and the only weapon effective against a transient contact. The solution was to convert existing *Leander* class frigates at a substantially lower price than that of an Ikara destroyer.[30] Ikara was pruned (to M4-Minus configuration) to fit a *Leander*. The initial choice was to fit to either the last five ships or the first five subject to long refits (which would be extended from eighteen to twenty-four months). Retroactive installation would be substantially more expensive than installation in a ship under construction, but it was chosen because the design would apply to more than five ships. The need for more than the five hulls was justified on the basis of the shift towards NATO and the growing submarine threat. The loss of the 4.5in gun was reluctantly accepted, but it would have been less painful given the declining importance of shore bombardment.[31] It was assumed that Ikara could not be installed on the new commercial frigate (which became Type 21).

As in Type 82, Ikara was associated with an automated combat direction system (ADAWS 5, based on that designed for Type 82), which assessed a target before passing it to the fire control system. Given this degree of automation, ships in company could use their data links to rapidly pass their own sonar targets to the Ikara ship for engagement. By this time the Royal Navy wanted to use submarines in direct support of surface ships, passing contacts from their very long range Type 2001 sonars to an Ikara ship via a ship/submarine link. It is not clear to what extent that was done. A quick study showed that it would be far better to replace the 4.5in gun than the helicopter (the Ikara destroyer would have had both gun and missile). The gun director was replaced by an Ikara missile

tracker and data link antenna in a small radome. Limbo was retained. To some extent the loss of the gun was compensated for by a second Seacat (the two launchers were on either side of the ship). The long-range Type 965 radar was landed as weight compensation, the internal space going to ADAWS equipment. Ships which did not already have VDS fitted received it.

Had the new-construction broad-beam ships been chosen, it might have been possible, as DGS had pointed out in 1963, to have both Ikara and a single 4.5in gun. Note that the Royal Australian Navy installed Ikara aft on board its Type 12 ('River') class frigates but retained the 4.5in gun and the helicopter.[32] The most obvious sacrifice was apparently in magazine safety margin; in hot weather the Ikara magazine sometimes had to be hosed down to hold its temperature to within appropriate limits. The Australians also lacked the digital combat systems of the British ships, hence could not as easily exploit sonar data from other ships.

Initially it was decided to convert five ships, but later three more were added. Ultimately the *Leander* class was divided into three Batches: I and II were the original narrow-beam design, of which Batch I (eight ships) got Ikara. In Batch II Exocet in effect replaced the twin 4.5in gun. With the gun removed, the ships had considerably less topweight: the self-compensating fuel system, which had proven difficult in service, could be eliminated. The single centreline Seacat launcher aft was replaced by two launchers (on either side), and a third launcher was mounted on the centreline, forward of the Exocet tubes.

[30] DEFE 24/239.
[31] DEFE 10/941.

[32] Mk F1, on board HMAS *Stuart* and *Derwent*, had an analogue computer and stowage for twenty-four missiles and one test missile. Mk F3, for the other frigates (for refit on board *Yarra* and *Paramatta*, for installation during construction of the redesigned *Swan* and *Torrens*), used a digital computer. It was planned for the modernised *Darings*. Mk F2 was the digital version on board the Australian *Adams* class destroyers. RAN, Fitting of Ikara in DDGs and Type 12 DEs, March 1966, RAN Naval Historical Branch.

Initially the Sea Dart missile destroyer was to have been succeeded by a version armed with Ikara. Instead, *Leander* class frigates were rebuilt. This is HMS *Leander* herself. The long-range Type 965 air-search radar was eliminated, but an independent IFF interrogator was retained in its place on the mainmast. The side of the foremast carries the Type 667 jammer standard at this time. It was intended primarily to screen larger units, rather than to defeat attacks on the frigate. For the latter purpose the ship had a pair of Corvus chaff launchers, roughly abeam her mainmast. The object clipped to the fore masthead, which resembles a small searchlight, is the Bexley (Type 669) self-defence jammer, which projected a replica of the signals received from an incoming missile onto the water near the ship. In theory the missile would home on the centroid of the net radar return, and thus would dive into the water. Not very visible in these photographs is the UA-8/9 ESM array at the masthead, below the masthead array. The structure between bridge and Ikara launcher (in the zareba) was the missile magazine and assembly space; in effect Ikara replaced the twin 4.5in gun. The cut in the stern was for the Canadian-designed Type 199 VDS. Alongside and to port is the handling device for the Type 182 torpedo decoy, the towing aperture for which is visible in the stern quarter view. Defensive armament was limited to the two Seacats aft and a pair of single 40mm guns.

The Type 993 radar and MRS 3 director installed for the gun were retained to control Seacat forward (a second MRS 3 controlled the Seacats aft). The hangar was enlarged to handle the new Lynx helicopter and the flight deck extended aft, at the expense of Limbo. Triple lightweight torpedo tubes were therefore added. The VDS well aft was also plated up. Deep load displacement increased from the original 2,860 tons to 3,200 tons.

Batch III was the broad-beam type, the modified version of which is described below. Modified *Leanders* were given CAAIS and thus could pass sonar data to Ikara ships by digital link.

The Standard Frigate Phase One: Type 21

The third element of the approved fleet was a 'standard' frigate directly descended from the Type 19 of the earlier escort study. Its initial designation of Patrol Frigate reflected its global low-end mission. The main change from Type 19 seems to have been abandonment of high dash speed. Given limited de-

The Fleet Working Party, like the Admiralty two years earlier, badly wanted a low-end frigate which could be built in numbers to meet the navy's global obligations. This role was represented in its report by Design Study 387 (modified), described as a Standard Frigate, and effectively a derivative of the earlier Type 19. Armament matched that of the Type 21, which in effect met this requirement. The ship had sufficient space and weight for two Norwegian Penguin anti-ship missiles. Note the use of a Dutch Signaal 'egg' radar for air search and surface fire-control, as at the time there was no British equivalent, and the use of an optical rather than a radar director for Seacat. (PRO DEFE 24/238)

sign manpower, DGS A J Sims said that he could not develop the new *Invincible* class, Type 42 and the new frigate in parallel (the public explanation was an unexpectedly large workload on the new Polaris submarines). He was later bitterly criticised within the Royal Corps of Naval Constructors for opening the door to outside designs. The Naval Staff reportedly suspected that DGS was unable to resist designing expensive ships; surely industry, which was trying hard to gain export orders, could do better. Reportedly nine private yards lobbying for the contract claimed that they could build a frigate for £3.5 million, compared to £5 million for a *Leander*.[33] Sims may well have hoped to head off a larger disaster by allowing the Staff to discover just how wrong it was on this project. The British government badly wanted to support exports; if the Royal Navy bought an affordable commercial frigate design, surely others might follow. The previous year the Board had observed that press publicity for the Vosper Mk 7 frigate would quite possibly provoke questions about the *Leander* replacement; could a smaller commercial design do? That discussion on 6 July 1967 was probably the origin of the Type 21 project. Also, the Admiralty was reluctant to wait to order new frigates: it was vital to gain momentum for post-carrier programs in a very difficult financial environment. The frigate design was put out to tender. Given their experience in designing export frigates, the only likely choices were Vosper and Yarrow. Vosper was developing a range of export frigates.

Core features were CAAIS, a lightweight 4.5in gun, the standard sonar and MATCH, and Seacat (later to be replaced, it

was hoped, with Seawolf). The short-range ASW system was lightweight torpedoes rather than Limbo. The ship was powered by the new standard Olympus-Tyne combination. There was a strong emphasis on minimum manning. There was some hope that the design might appeal to export customers: New Zealand, India, Pakistan, the Netherlands and South American states. Hopefully the prospect of foreign sales would be an incentive for commercial designers and builders to hold costs down. Although no foreign country bought the design, the Mk 10 frigates built for Brazil were related to it.

The Royal Australian Navy's projected General Purpose Escort seemed to have a good deal in common with the British ship. Staff discussions began in 1967, a Royal Navy team visiting Australia that October.[34] Bringing the RAN into the programme would accelerate it; one consequence would be that the ship would probably be ready before Seawolf and the Lynx helicopter, so that initially it would have Seacat and Wasp instead. It would be fitted for but not with the new Abbey Hill ESM system. At this point the RAN wanted to pay £7.5 million without US equipment, and the Royal Navy no more than £7 million (a repeat *Leander* would cost £6.5 million).

The requirements of the two navies did not quite match. The RAN sought a high-end ship capable of dealing with missiles as well as aircraft at medium and low altitudes and of contributing to group defence against surface ships and submarines. Recalling the recent Confrontation against Indonesia, the RAN wanted to counter fast light surface craft and to control patrol craft. Hence it wanted high sprint speed, 36kts, reminiscent of Type 19. The RAN emphasised operations in the island waters north of the country, and it wanted a long 'ferry' range (5,000nm at 14–15kts) to get there. The Royal

[33] Antony Preston in the United Kingdom section of Gardiner (ed), *Conway's All The World's Fighting Ships 1947-1995*, p 522. According to Preston, Controller backed this claim wholeheartedly, to the extent of trying to keep the Ship Department entirely out of the procurement process. Captain John Lippiett, RN, *Type 21* (Ian Allan, London: 1990), pp 10–12 describes the role of Controller ADM Sir Horace Law in selling the ship to the Board and to the Ministry of Defence, to the extent that it was called 'the Controller's frigate'.

[34] DEFE 24/239.

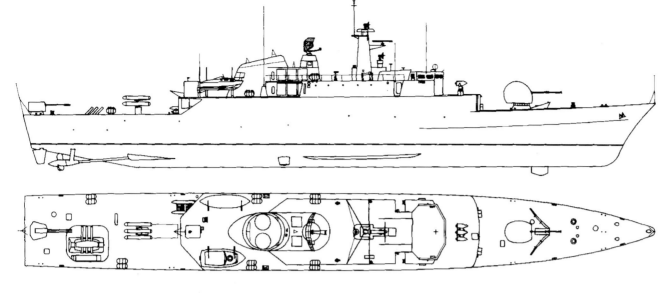

The Iranian *Saam* class seemed to demonstrate how efficient a commercial design could be. It is shown as delivered, with the four-missile Sea Killer launcher aft.

The post-carrier Royal Navy was still designed for world-wide deployment, and most of the force it used would be frigates. Because DGS effort had to be concentrated on Type 42 and *Invincible*, an outside design was bought for an 'interim' austere frigate, Type 21. In effect it was the Type 19 envisaged in 1964, but without the high speed proposed for that ship. Early in her career, this Type 21, HMS *Arrow*, had Exocet missiles, but neither defensive ESM nor lightweight torpedo tubes. She did have Corvus chaff launchers on her 01 level (ships which did not yet have Exocet had them forward of the bridge; when Exocet was added, they were moved to the waist). The only ESM device was the HF/DF array on her tall pole mainmast. The big antenna was for the Type 992 short-range air search (target indication) set. The ship has the two platforms for the SCOT satellite communications system, linked by a gangway, just forward of her uptakes, but the antennas and radomes are not aboard (SCOT was generally fitted only when needed). The Royal Navy pioneered satellite communication for ships below cruiser size.

Navy sought a low-end ship, for which 32kts and 4,000nm at 18kts sufficed.

A design study (Y.217) the RAN commissioned from the British Y-ARD (Yarrow design) company gave a set of possible characteristics. Initially the RAN hoped to hold displacement (with two-thirds fuel) to 2,000 tons, but by October 1967 that had increased to 2,070 tons. The Royal Navy began with a limit of 2,400 tons, but by October it seemed that a compromise could be reached at about 2,200 tons. Although neither navy had made final choices, the RAN preferred US weapons and sensors to match those on board its three US-built missile destroyers: the 5in/54 gun, the Sea Sparrow point defence missile, the Mk 46 torpedo, and an EDO sonar. The

RAN rejected the British Seawolf because it would not be ready in time. Sea Sparrow also greatly outranged Seawolf. The RAN did want a British air-search radar, the commercial AWS-1, but not the Type 992Q preferred by the Royal Navy, on grounds of cost and range. A Signaal surface-search radar was already in RAN service, and could control a helicopter; it was transistorised, and it was smaller than the British Type 978, producing a smaller IR signature (which might be important in night operations inshore). The RAN had no requirement for HF/DF (FH 5). However, it faced Styx missiles in Indonesian hands, and it valued the new Abbey Hill. The RAN considered sonar a very effective means of tracking fast craft with small radar signatures, and it liked the US EDO set which provided a

It was always intended that the Type 21s be upgraded at mid-life, but improvements began earlier than that. HMS *Ardent* shows a subtle but vital improvement, the UAA-1 ESM array surrounding the base of the topmast supporting her two radars (Types 992 and 1016). She has the supports for her Exocet tubes forward of her bridge, but not the tubes themselves, and the triple torpedo tubes at the after end of her forecastle.

Doppler display which might highlight echoes in shallow water. Given shallow waters, the RAN wanted a retractable dome (Type 184 had a fixed dome). The RAN rejected Limbo and other mortars as too heavy and too expensive; it considered lightweight torpedoes an adequate deterrent against submarines. The RAN was interested in CAAIS, but was deterred by its high cost; the British had to convince them that an automated system was worth while. One special RAN requirement was the EXDAK data link to an Ikara ship.

In late 1967 the British naval staff summarised likely requirements:

RN and RAN Frigate Requirements 1967

	RN	RAN
Endurance	4,000nm @ 18kts	5,500nm @ 14kts (one shaft)
Speed	32 +kts	35+kts
Power	(Olympus/Tyne)	
Gun	4.5in Mk 8	US 5in/54
Air Search	992Q	AWS 1
Surface Search	978	Signaal 8GR300 (nav, helo control)
EW	FH5, Abbeyhill	Abbeyhill
Missile	Seacat, then Seawolf (18 rounds)	Sea Sparrow (box plus 24 rounds)
Sonar	184M	EDO 610 (US)
Torpedo Decoy	182	Nixie or Fanfare
ASW	Mk 31 torpedoes or Limbo/Terne	Mk 46
Helicopter	Lynx	Iroquois (Huey)
Combat Data	Elliott 920 CAAIS	JYA, Plessey Displays (might buy CAAIS)
Communications	RN	USN
Complement	162	146
Accommodation	191	169

It seemed that there was enough in common for the two

navies to proceed on an RN/RAN frigate. A design contract was let in March 1968 for a version of the standard Vosper Thornycroft frigate series. The firms would be paid only if a ship were built. The Board feared that the Australians would want too much, and that the ship would be neither the inexpensive ship it wanted nor a good prospect for foreign sales. Conversely, the Board feared that because the RAN timetable had slipped for financial reasons, construction in the UK would no longer be urgent; the RAN might demand that the ships be built in Australia. There was also fear that the ship would not reflect the Royal Navy's real requirements. A joint Staff/designer committee was formed.[35] The firms wanted a finalised Staff Requirement by the end of April 1968. The Staff Requirement was finally submitted to the Operational Requirements Committee in July. By this time considerable design work had been done.[36]

The ship would be completed with Seacat and a Type 992Q radar. With no modern British gun fire-control system in service, she would have a foreign (presumably Dutch) system. The design had to be suitable for modernisation with Seawolf and its more massive Type 967/968 radar. The separate gun director would have to be landed as weight compensation. Ideally the Seawolf director would control the 4.5in gun forward (a mode of operation called GSA 3), but the only acceptable position for the director was abaft the funnel, in the original Seacat director position (the key after arcs from the position forward of the funnel were blocked by the funnel). That left the track-while-scan mode of the Type 968 radar as the only

[35] ADM 167/167.
[36] DEFE 10/942.

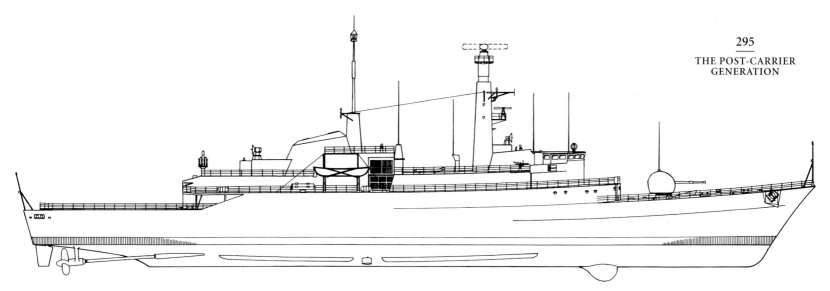

means of gun control in the modernised ship. The gun, the main deterrent against surface attack, would thus become less effective (as yet the Royal Navy had no surface-to-surface missile in prospect). The sonar would be Type 184, in a fixed dome. It would be impossible to install the later Type 2016, with its much larger transducer. The desired thrown ASW weapon (Limbo or the Norwegian Terne) had to be given up due to cost, weight and manpower. Projected complement was eleven officers and 159 ratings, which might be compared to fifteen officers and 234 ratings in a *Leander*. Estimated deep displacement was 2,300 tons.

Given their considerable differences, on 8 November 1968 the RAN withdrew from the project, which was renamed Type 21.[37] In March 1969 Vosper received a 'design and build' contract for the first ship. Not having prepared the design, the Admiralty technical departments were asked to review it. Their criticisms were significant enough for Controller to take the very unusual step of appending the departmental comments to the sketch design when he submitted it to the Board on 24 March 1969.[38] For example, the hull had to be lengthened by 10ft to reach an acceptable standard of stability. The hull depth calculation had not taken into account the fact that the aluminium superstructure could not contribute to hull strength; previous ships were all-steel. Controller had hoped to have the design before the Board at the end of 1968. It turned out that going to an outside commercial source had not cut costs at all. The first ship was expected to cost £7.3 million, a million more than a repeat *Leander*. Although Type 21 was

described as an interim choice before DGS could design a frigate, the Admiralty had seen it as a possible successor to the *Leander* class which might be built in similar numbers. The Board's formal reaction to the criticisms and the price escalation was that the experiment with private design had been less than satisfactory. In that sense Sims' choice had been vindicated. The builder had been left free to choose many subsystems, including the tactical data system. In this class CAAIS fed a separate, specially-developed digital weapons control system (WCS) which controlled the gun and Seacat, using an adapted Italian Orion 10X (Type 912) fire-control radar. Abbey Hill was installed after completion. Endurance was slightly short of the requirement at 3,750nm at 18kts, but that was 350nm better than a *Leander* could do at that speed (there was some hope of making up the difference). Speed was slightly less than required, but it was still 2.25kts greater than that of a *Leander* in temperate waters.

Compared to a *Leander*, Type 21 offered better accommodation (15 per cent more space per man) with a smaller crew (seventy to eighty fewer men, thanks mainly both to adopting gas turbines and a lightly-manned gun and to a policy under which not all weapons and systems had to be manned simultaneously). Controller considered the smaller complement critically important. The margin for accommodation of twenty-two was intended to provide for new systems, particularly Seawolf and Abbey Hill, to be added at half-life. The ship had a somewhat reduced capacity for self-maintenance and would need more shore support. The use of non-standard (commercial) equipment would create logistical problems. However, the Staff Requirement demanded greater availability than in the past. In the follow-on in-house Type 22 the self-maintenance deficiency would be corrected.

Type 21 was very popular in the Royal Navy, perhaps because of the legacy of commercial (export) design practice, such as unusually large wardrooms. On the other hand, they had poor accommodations for ratings, which was also export practice. The ships were driven hard, like sports cars, in service. A reflection of export practice was limited margin for im-

Type 21 was a commercial low-end frigate inspired by the success of the Vosper Thornycroft and Yarrow export frigates. In concept it was a direct descendant of the Type 19 frigate proposed in 1964. This drawing emphasises its very limited capabilities: it was a gunboat with a MATCH helicopter. Only later were anti-ship missiles added, and even then she had only four of them. Initially the ship had no electronic warfare capability beyond the usual HF/DF (on the pole mainmast). Well-liked for its speed and accommodation, the class offered only limited margin for additions, and it was never modernised. The key deficiency was inability to install a towed array. (A D Baker III)

---

[37] The Australian project became the DDL or light destroyer. Its requirements reflected the two most recent Australian naval experiences, the Confrontation against Indonesia and the Vietnam War. By February 1970 the Australians wanted three variants of a common hull: patrol, AAW and ASW. The patrol ship would be used for interdiction and control of patrol boats; to destroy surface targets up to an including missile boats; to control surface strike operations as part of a larger force; and for direct and indirect shore bombardment. It had to be reasonably survivable in the face of air and underwater threats. Primary operating areas would be the Northern approaches to Australia and the waters of the Territory of Papua New Guinea; the ship might also operate in Southeast Asia, the Pacific, and the Indian Ocean. All were temperate or tropical. Although not armed with Ikara, the DDL could pass attack information to Ikara ships. Helicopter capability was vital both for interdiction and for ASW. The Australians planned to adopt the US LAMPS concept, in which the helicopter would use sonobuoys (processed on board the ship) to localise a contact, then drop a homing torpedo on the basis of MAD indication. The British MATCH helicopter carried no ASW sensor, attacking on the basis of the ship's sonar. The DDL preliminary design contract was let in July 1970. A design was ready in 1972, but in 1973 the DDL was dropped in favour of the US *Perry* class, with a redesigned Type 12 as an alternative.
[38] ADM 167/169, which does not list the deficiencies.

provement, despite what was written into the Staff Requirement and the contract. Studies showed that, for example, it was impossible to fit them with Seawolf, at least within Royal Navy standards. However, some constructors' notes suggest a 1977 project to design a modified version with double Seawolf for Iran. What doomed the class, however, was that it lacked sufficient margin to accept a towed array.

Plans initially called for only three ships, to replace the last three projected *Leanders*, FSA 42–45 of the 1968/9 Estimates. At the very least, in 1969–70 it seemed vital to maintain a building rate of better than three frigates and destroyers each year. Type 21 would have to be built until the two companion designs, Types 42 and 22, could be ordered. The lead ship was ordered on 26 March 1969 (nearly at the end of the 1968/9 financial year), and two more were ordered on 11 May 1970. Another five ships were ordered on 11 November 1971. This order seems to have reflected delays in the Type 42 and Type 22 designs.

The loss of two of the eight ships in the Falklands War was widely attributed to their commercial design standards and to the widespread use of aluminium. A bad fire in *Amazon* in 1977 had already drawn attention to the dangers of aluminium construction (it was banned from British warships afterwards). However, aluminium construction does not seem to have contributed to either loss: *Ardent* was torn up over much of her waterline by unguided aircraft rockets, and *Antelope* sank after a large unexploded bomb lodged in her structure went off. Ships of this size probably would not have survived either type of damage. On the other hand, ships did experience hull cracking during the Falklands War.

HMS *Antelope* is shown in the Falklands, shortly after being hit by an Argentine bomb (which made the round hole visible in her side). The bomb did not explode initially, and when this picture was taken the ship was still operational and under way. The 4.5in gun and the Seacat launcher (with its director) are still pointed in the direction from which the attacking aircraft came. Note that the ship has a Corvus chaff launcher instead of Exocets on her 01 level forward of her bridge.

Type 22

By the time DGS began work on the frigate interest had shifted from the global cold or warm-war perspective of 1966–7, when the Working Party did its study, to a more NATO-oriented one closer to that of the 1950s. The ASW escort role was still vital, but the Soviet submarines were far more capable. Frigates would escort and complement the British ASW carrier supporting the NATO Strike Fleet and they would also screen vital convoys. NATO strategy envisaged a series of escalations, the hope being to convince the Soviets not to continue into war or into more intense war. Thus an important naval role was to confront Soviet warships during a period of pre-war tension. To be credible, the ships doing so had to be survivable (*ie* armed with an effective anti-missile weapon) and capable of doing major damage to the Soviet warships. Type 22 was designed with these requirements in mind.

Unfortunately the Royal Navy never made clear within the British government the change in the frigate role. Type 22 was advertised as a *Leander* successor, but it was more expensive than a Type 42. Without a clear rationale for the ship, in 1970–2 the Treasury argued that it should be cancelled outright in favour of more Type 42s (with a smaller total number of destroyers and frigates), and that the Royal Navy should revert to a low-end frigate.

The new point-defence missile was Seawolf, the supersonic successor to Seacat. It was conceived to meet an Anglo-French-Dutch requirement for a short-range self-defence missile to deal with the new anti-ship missiles. The British Staff Target for a Seacat replacement was raised in March 1964 and was approved by the Operational Requirements Committee that year.[39] The British retreated somewhat from

39 T225/2667 includes Treasury scepticism that such a missile would be needed, as at the time (1964) the Royal Navy was still saying that all projected new frigates would be armed with Sea Dart. For the Treasury, the request for the new missile was the first indication that a high-low escort mix including a much cheaper frigate was being considered. T225/3477 includes several versions of the Naval Staff Requirement (NSR 6522). The missile would accelerate to Mach 2.7 by the time it reached 0.8km range, then coast, decelerating to Mach 1.1 at its maximum effective range of 5km (about 2.5nm). Missile length was set at about 2m by the requirement to use existing Seacat magazines. By 1968 hopes of simply adapting the Seacat fire control system and launcher were being abandoned, as modification would have been too expensive.
   The British national feasibility study (Confessor) is dated 15 October 1965 (file ADM 220/2443 in PRO). Discussions began in the summer of 1963, the Staff Target, GD 302(T), being submitted to the Operational Requirements Committee on 9 January 1964. Desired in-service date was 1972. Targets envisaged were typical air-to-surface missiles (ranging from the large Soviet types down to small Western missiles such as Bullpup), fighter-bombers, short-range ballistic missiles (such as the US Subroc, to which it was correctly assumed the Soviets would produce an equivalent), and surface ships (with speeds of less than 100kts, desired range being 10,000m). Desired minimum effective range was 1,000m (2,000m would be acceptable), and altitude limits were 15m and 5,000m. Range against a small missile would be at least 5km (8km against a large one). Four missiles would have to be fired without manual intervention, the launcher being reloaded in two minutes (as built, Seawolf used a six-round launcher; Seacat had four rounds per launcher). Minimum load-out would be eighteen missiles per system. The system had to be able to deal with two small (0.1 square meter) targets spaced no more than six seconds apart. Single-shot kill probability against an aircraft would be at least 0.7, and probability of mission kill against a missile would be at least 0.3. Requirements included the ability to manhandle the missile (limiting it to about 90kg) and that the missile be stowed vertically to limit damage by underwater shock. Since no separate magazines were planned, the missile would have to fit within the normal deck height, which limited its length to about 2m. Overall, the system had to be simple to limit manpower (to about seven for maintenance and watchkeeping). Desired total weight would be no more than 5,000kg above decks and 7,500kg below, at a total cost (including eighteen missiles) of no more than ££600,000.
   A joint Royal Navy/Ministry of Aviation Study Group was formed in April 1964. It looked at alternative point-defence solutions, including guns, jammers and decoys, but soon concluded that only a missile (perhaps supplemented by EW/decoys) would suffice. Guns were ruled out because they would have to deliver about a ton of projectiles in 10 seconds, a conclusion reminiscent of that reached in the much earlier Popsy study. IR guidance (as in Sidewinder and the British air-to-air Red Top) was rejected on the grounds that it was unsuitable against a head-on threat, and also that it would fail in rain or fog. Of existing radar-guided missiles, the US Sparrow III (the basis for the roughly equivalent US point-defence systems) was rejected for its size and weight. That left the French Roland and the US Mauler. It seemed that the French would already have adopted Roland if they thought it could be suitable, and the British correctly guessed that the United States would abandon Mauler. The Rapier (ET 316) missile, already under development (initially as insurance against the failure of Mauler) was rejected on the ground that it was unlikely to hit small fast targets. If it were given a proximity fuse and a larger warhead, it would need a new airframe like that projected for Confessor. Hence the need for a new missile. Given discussions with the French and the Dutch naval staffs, a joint Staff Target replaced the national one in May 1964, the first international meeting being held at The Hague in July. However, the three staffs decided that the British would continue their national effort through October 1965. The British first sketched five possible solutions (December 1964), then rejected three as too large and expensive. However, the third international meeting (Paris, May 1965) agreed to include a third, higher-performance system (System C). System A, the simplest, was intended for very small units such as minecraft, using a combined search/track system also under consideration as a new lightweight gun fire control. It could replace Seacat (GWS 22) directly in larger ships. A used a command to line of sight guided 60kg to 80kg missile. B was a frigate self-defence missile using separate search and track sensors. It could use either the command guidance of System A or semi-active guidance. C would try to intercept by 7km range any target passing within 4km of a ship, ie including crossing targets, using a 140kg semi-active missile or an 80kg command-guided missile. C seems to have been the high-performance solution demanded by the French, which broke up the international project. B was the basis of Seawolf.

the original requirement to make the missile affordable. Shown the feasibility study in April 1964, the French rejected the compromise, and the Dutch later opted for NATO Sea Sparrow (a British file suggests that they would have chosen Seawolf only if it used a Dutch radar). The Germans signed a Memorandum of Understanding after talks in 1966, but withdrew from the programme early in 1967, at least partly because they were unwilling to incur R&D costs. Like the Dutch, they ultimately bought NATO Sea Sparrow. In 1968 the Royal Navy hoped to buy forty to fifty systems, the projected mix (as late as 1971) being twenty-four Type 22 and sixteen retrofits (ten *Leander* Batch III and six Type 21). Retrofits were also considered for the 'County' class and for the two *Fearless* class LPDs.

The British missile was alternatively designated GD 302(T), Confessor, Sinner, PX430 and Seawolf; the system was GWS 25. As conceived, it could be fired from the Seacat launcher, but it needed a much more elaborate fire-control system. As fielded it used a very different sextuple launcher. As a point defence weapon, Seawolf had only very limited capability against crossing targets. Even so, in the Falklands escorts interposed between the threat and carriers effectively defended them. One implication was that such tactics might be extended using a somewhat longer range Local Area Missile System, which might be more practicable against future threats than a long-range area weapon like Sea Dart. Seawolf was credited with destroying five Argentine aircraft. The follow-on vertical-launch GWS 26 arms Type 23 frigates.

In 1968, with the frigate not yet approved officially outside the Royal Navy, the Royal Netherlands Navy offered to share with the Royal Navy the cost of a new 'integrated' frigate that it could not afford to develop independently.[40] This was attractive politically as well as financially. A bi-national pro-

40 T225/3603 and T225/3604.

The simplest type of *Leander* modernisation might be considered comparable to Type 21 in capability, with the twin 4.5in gun replaced by four Exocets. This is HMS *Minerva*. She shows an additional Seacat launcher right forward. The cone and Yagis at her foremast head served UA-13, which extended UA-8/9 ESM coverage to lower frequencies, probably to those used by Soviet radars such as the Top Sail of the carriers and large missile ships. It may have been intended to support Exocet missile targeting.

gramme would demonstrate a British commitment to Europe despite rejection by the French for membership in the then European Common Market (now the European Union). Also, a multi-national programme might be difficult for a British government to cancel. As of early 1969 the projected programme was twenty British and twelve Dutch ships.

A joint design team was set up at Bath (DGS). The two navies agreed to a common hull and common main propulsion (British machinery). Each could choose weapons and equipment, but in some categories both agreed to accept the result of binational competition. The British already suspected Dutch motives, having come out badly in the Broomstick-Sea Dart programme. They suspected that the Dutch had participated mainly to penetrate the British electronics market. In April 1969 the Naval Staff echoed the Treasury: any deal which did not improve British balance of payments should be resisted. Even so, the British were upset in December 1969 when the Dutch decided not to adopt Seawolf. Presumably their decision awakened memories of Dutch rejection of Sea Dart. On the other hand, the abortive Sea Dart frigate deal seems to have led the Dutch to buy Rolls Royce rather than US Pratt & Whitney gas turbines for their *Tromp* class. This time the British hoped to sell the Dutch the Lynx helicopter, its radar, and its new Sea Skua air-to-surface missile. There was mild British interest in Dutch electronics: the L-band long-range radar (later bought as part of Type 1022), IR and optical surveillance systems, and a submarine passive intercept sonar. In one category the Dutch were too interested: they wanted British ECM equipment, but it embodied US secrets which were not releasable.

Once the Dutch decided to buy a different point-defence missile, it became difficult to reconcile such basic parameters as beam, hull depth, location of gas turbine uptakes and downtakes, and displacement. The Dutch cost limit was below what the British expected to spend. Equipment competition was a problem; the Royal Navy argued repeatedly that although some Dutch equipment might be best in the context of the new frigate, buying it would badly upset the logistical base serving the whole fleet. The Dutch particularly insisted on adopting their electrical system, which caused particular problems. It was incompatible with the British system and considerably more expensive. To accommodate it the ship would have to be redesigned, lengthened by 10ft. By April 1970 the agreement was beginning to unravel, the Dutch saying that they were considering an interim class of two to four ships because the British side was so badly delayed, the British that the Dutch could not match their milestones.

By June 1970, the Royal Navy wanted to disengage. It was particularly unhappy about the delays the joint programme was imposing. The Foreign and Commonwealth Office, however, badly wanted to buy Dutch support within NATO and the Common Market. It feared that withdrawal would prove to others that, as the French so often charged, the British just were not interested in Europe. Major industrial prizes such as a share in Airbus were at stake. The Treasury was less enthusiastic. The 1970 Long Term Costings (up to 1981) showed seventeen ships, perhaps with a new design introduced in the mid-1970s.

In November 1970 tank tests showed that the ship had to

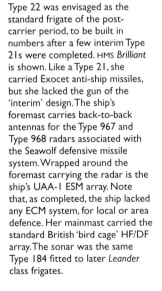

Type 22 was envisaged as the standard frigate of the post-carrier period, to be built in numbers after a few interim Type 21s were completed. HMS *Brilliant* is shown. Like a Type 21, she carried Exocet anti-ship missiles, but she lacked the gun of the 'interim' design. The ship's foremast carries back-to-back antennas for the Type 967 and Type 968 radars associated with the Seawolf defensive missile system. Wrapped around the foremast carrying the radar is the ship's UAA-1 ESM array. Note that, as completed, the ship lacked any ECM system, for local or area defence. Her mainmast carried the standard British 'bird cage' HF/DF array. The sonar was the same Type 184 fitted to later *Leander* class frigates.

HMS *Beaver* was a Batch II Type 22 frigate with a substantially lengthened hull, including the sort of clipper bow (with bow anchor) required to support a sonar dome in her forefoot. Less noticeable is the pair of antennas atop her mainmast, which were part of the Anglo-American Classic Outboard communications intercept and exploitation system. Not visible is another element of the system, a series of small rectangular antennas spaced along the ship's hull. The need for a sufficient baseline for this system may have been the main reason for lengthening the ship. Also not visible is the mechanism for the ship's towed-array sonar, which paid out through a hole in her stern. Compared to the earlier 'birdcage' and its FH 4/5 system, Classic Outboard can handle shorter signals and can also provide much more precise directional measurements. In British practice escorts within a group carried the antennas but not the processors; processing was done on board the command ship, generally the carrier. Notable in this post-completion photograph is the absence of any kind of defensive countermeasure system, other than decoy launchers.

be lengthened (by at least 25ft beyond the 10ft to accommodate the Dutch electrical system) to meet seakeeping requirements. She had already been lengthened (from 112m to 117m) to the point where the Dutch would find her difficult to accommodate in their dry dock at Den Helder. Now the British considered 130m the minimum acceptable to provide some growth margin (waterline length as built was 125.7m). The designers considered an arrangement which could have a short bow for the Dutch or a longer one for the British. The British feared that the very real issue of length would be seen as a pretext for abandoning the bi-national programme. To their surprise and relief, in November 1970 the Dutch announced that they were withdrawing because they could not buy the ships. Their naval architects had already concluded that the ships had to be lengthened.

The Staff Target (NST 7095) had been approved by the Operational Requirements Committee in February 1969, by which time a sketch design had been developed. The Staff Target stressed maintainability, habitability, and growth margin. Type 22 was intended as a high-quality very quiet ASW escort and as a screen flagship, with the large command and operations spaces that required. Her CAAIS tactical data system would allow her to exchange sonar data with other units in the kind of network which had figured prominently in the 1964 escort mix discussions. Because she had been developed up from a low-end ASW frigate rather than down from the Ikara destroyer, her only stand-off weapon was the helicopter.

The main sensor was a new Type 2016 hull sonar, a draft Staff Requirement for which was issued in mid-1968.[41] Work

began in March 1971. Development was urgent because existing sonars using obsolescent technology could not be maintained beyond the end of the 1970s. Like Type 184, Type 2016 used preformed beams, but formed by a computer rather than by wiring. The sonar could thus form many more beams and it could handle many more targets. Digital technology could greatly simplify the operator's task; it was argued that contemporary US sonars such as SQS-26 were so complicated to use that their full capabilities were not exploited. Type 2016 was expected to be effective in 90 per cent of UK coastal waters, compared to 65 per cent for the Type 184M it would replace. In low sea states the sonar would reach out to 20,000 yds. In deep water reliable range would be 8,000 yds in deep water, compared to effective ranges as short as 2,500 yds for Type 177 (for 50 per cent probability of detection). Under some conditions the sonar would reach out to convergence zone. Eliminating existing separate sonars (Types 170, 176 and 177) would in itself cut the number of sonar ratings from seven to three or even to two. The first Type 22s were completed with Type 184 sonar, but all were later given Type 2016. Ultimately Type 2016 was replaced by Type 2050, with the same transducer but with much better signal processing. Analysis showed that a half-diameter transducer, comparable in size to that of Type 184, was not worthwhile: Type 2016 could not be installed on board a Type 21 frigate.

Type 2016 was intended to work with a lower-frequency bottom-bounce/convergence zone sonar using a 150ft × 10ft array on each side of the keel. The medium range sonar offered solid coverage out as far as 10nm. Bottom-bounce seemed to offer solid coverage between 10–15nm and 20–25nm, and the first convergence zone in deep Atlantic water would be at 30–35nm. Such performance was attractive because it might limit the number of escorts needed for a high-value unit.

[41] DEFE 10/953, OR 20/73 of 17 April 1973. The original requirement was endorsed in 1970, but Type 2016 was cut from the programme in July 1971 (reinstated July 1972). It operates at slightly lower frequency than Type 184: 5.5, 6.5 and 7.5 kHz, compared to 6, 7.5 and 9 kHz. Proposed installation of a version of the lower-frequency Type 2001 submarine sonar on board a *Leander* was abandoned: it would have been twice as expensive as Type 2016.

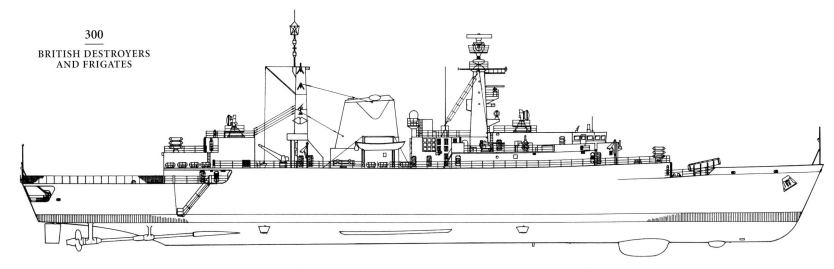

Batch I Type 22, in a late design version as of January 1973. This drawing reflects the decision to double the size of the helicopter hangar, but does not reflect a variety of later changes. (A D Baker III)

However, only a large ship could accommodate the planar arrays. The US Navy was pursuing similar ideas; the two navies conducted a joint project using the specially rebuilt destroyer HMS *Matapan*.

The long-range ASW weapon would be MATCH, using the new Lynx helicopter carrying both torpedoes and nuclear depth bombs (the '600 pound GP bomb'); two depth bombs could be stowed in place of two of the sixteen torpedoes. Type 21 could not accommodate the depth bombs because she lacked the required below-water magazine stowage. Also, Type 22 could fuel an airborne helicopter, whereas Type 21 could not (and she had fewer torpedoes for her helicopter). The short-range ASW weapon was the lightweight torpedo in a triple tube (initial Type 21s were fitted for but not with such tubes, but they were installed during construction in later units).

For self-defence Type 22 had two Seawolf launchers, each with its own director. Although there was no gun, the ship had sufficient reserves of weight to accommodate six Exocets (Type 21 was understood to be limited to two, although in the end both classes got four each). The lack of a gun was considered acceptable because even in 1980 well over half the escort force would have guns. Type 22 but not Type 21 could accommodate a detachment of Royal Marines.

Type 22 would be manned on a sufficient scale to use all weapons simultaneously (Type 21 could not). She would be more reliable and easier to maintain. For example, there was full access to all machinery, with routes arranged for replacement, whereas in a Type 21 access was limited to the main propulsion and main generators. Accommodation would be much better, and the crew considerably larger (215, with accommodation for 250, versus 170 with accommodation for 192). Compared to Type 42, Type 22 would have sufficient margin for a mid-life upgrade. A less obvious feature was hardening against nuclear effects. She was designed to remain operational at a blast overpressure of 3.5 psi (1 psi for Type 21) and to remain mobile at 10 psi (5 psi in Type 21). All generators had ducted (filtered) air, as against half in Type 21. All magazines were deep in the ship (in a Type 21 the only deep

magazine was for the 4.5in gun).

To match *Leander* seakeeping, Type 22 lines were derived from those of the earlier and very successful ship. She was to match Type 42 speed (28kts) and endurance (4,000nm at 19kts) , and to be able to sustain 24kts in Sea State 5. That was also the target for maximum sonar speed (higher than in previous escorts). As designed, Type 22 was considerably larger than Type 21, 410ft × 46ft (3,500 tons) vs 384ft × 42ft (2,600 tons). With the same powerplant, she was therefore a knot slower (30kts vs 31kts). Before any ships were ordered, in 1973 the design was modified to accommodate a second helicopter, at the cost of increased beam (to 48ft 6in). With two helicopters, the ship could cover different roles simultaneously; she could launch a second aircraft within minutes of the first; and she could replace an unserviceable aircraft on deck within about twenty minutes. A fourteen-hour standing patrol could be maintained.

By 1972 the Royal Navy expected to build twenty-two (later twenty-one) ships, beginning with ten in Batch I, the first to be delivered by 1973/4.[42] Numbers seem to have been predicated at least partly on the composition of an ideal task force built around the new *Invincible* class helicopter carrier. In 1966, in the immediate aftermath of the cancellation of the big carrier, the task force would have comprised two cruiser/carriers, a Type 82, two 'County' class destroyers and six standard frigates, plus a nuclear submarine. At this time the Royal Navy hoped to buy six cruiser/carriers, so it needed eighteen standard frigates for three task forces. With the demise of Type 82 and the 'County', the task force would have three Type 42s for air defence and an additional Type 22 as escort flagship, for a total of seven frigates. Three task forces (now with one carrier each) would require twelve Type 42 and twenty-one Type 22, roughly the building plans for these classes.

Because Type 22 was quite expensive, Batch III *Leander*s were rebuilt with much the same weapon systems, but presumably without the flagship capability. They had CAAIS, Type 967/968, a single Seawolf missile system and Type 2016 sonar. Like Batch II, Batch III ships had Exocet in place of their

[42] DEFE 10/955.

4.5in guns. The top of the funnel and some of the superstructure aft were removed, apparently to reduce topweight. The four Exocet launchers were placed directly on deck rather than on raised platforms, and the lightweight torpedo tubes (replacing Limbo) were carried a deck lower than in Batch II. SCOT satellite communication antennas were added. The ships were heavily rearranged internally, presumably to meet the demands of the missile system and of the new sonar. Plans called for rebuilding all ten ships, but the programme was halved in the 1981 Defence Review, only five ships being converted (*Andromeda*, *Hermione*, *Jupiter*, *Scylla* and *Charybdis*). The second group of five (see below) would have had towed arrays.

Only four Type 22 Batch I were built. The fifth and later ships were redesigned under the new destroyer/frigate policy chosen in 1978. These Batch II ships were stretched by 41ft (waterline length) to accommodate two new systems, the US Classic Outboard HF intercept system and the Type 2031Z towed array (not installed initially in all ships). It has been suggested that the additional length was needed to provide a sufficient baseline for Classic Outboard direction-finding, using small antennas spread around the ship's side. The stretch is usually attributed to the need for a larger Operations Room and, presumably, a larger sonar room to accommodate towed-array analysis equipment.

These ships had a new CACS 1 (Computer-Assisted Combat System) tactical data system, proposed by Ferranti as a CAAIS replacement for Type 21s in 1977. It was the first Royal Navy combat system to be developed completely by a contractor. It was also the first British command system intended to handle passive ESM and sonar data. Presumably that meant submarine-style target motion analysis used to create a fully passive tactical picture. There were three computers instead of the two in CAAIS and ADAWS: one for radar/link picture-keeping, one for Seawolf and the gun, and one for the long-range passive sonar/ESM picture. First installed in 1984–6, CACS 1 was not completely operational until 1991. CACS was also in effect an ADAWS successor: CACS 2 (not bought) was planned for upgraded Type 42 destroyers and CACS 3 for the abortive Type 43 destroyer (see below).

The towed array in effect superseded the big planar array envisaged in 1968 for a new-generation ship. The big planar array was an active sonar; the towed array was passive, exploit-

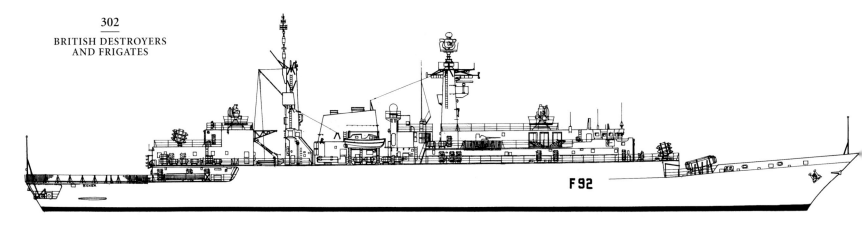

F 92

HMS *Boxer*, a Batch II Type 22 frigate, is shown as in December 1984. Her mainmast carries some of the arrays of the Anglo-American Classic Outboard communications intercept and DF system. Not shown are small elements distributed around her deck edge, making her hull in effect a long-baseline HF/DF array. At the base of the mainmast is a Type 670 self-defence jammer. The ship's foremast carries the back-to-back arrays of the Type 967 and Type 968 radars associated with her Seawolf defensive missile. The sharply-raked bow suggests that she has a sonar dome in her forefoot, rather than further aft, as in earlier British practice. (A D Baker III)

ing technology developed since the 1950s for sonobuoys and for fixed SOSUS bottom arrays. The Royal Navy awarded initial contracts for surface towed array research to GEC Avionics in 1971–2 (a contract for a submarine clip-on array had been let in 1970). As of November 1972 the long-range Royal Navy shipbuilding plan showed three A/S ships, definitely not frigates: A/S 01 to be ordered February 1979 for completion in February 1983, 02 in February 1981 for February 1985, and 03 in February 1983 for February 1987; concept design was to begin in January 1973. They were almost certainly surveillance ships broadly comparable to the contemporary US T-AGOS fleet.[43] They were not built, because it was soon that, far from being a very distant prospect, a tactical towed array was a real possibility.

This was a sudden development, led by the US Navy. A 1974 DOAE proposal for a study of future ASW systems remarked that arrays of various types were important, but it made little distinction between towed and drifting arrays (which would be dropped into the water and then retrieved). The following year the long-range fleet study emphasised towed arrays, pointing out that they might be deployed by either submarines or surface ships. By 1978 the array was the centrepiece of the destroyer/frigate building plan. Prototypes were tested on board the ex-destroyer *Matapan* and the frigate *Lowestoft* in 1978–81. The production Type 2031 was both a tactical and a surveillance set: its array was longer than its US tactical counterpart (shorter than the US surveillance system), and was towed further from the ship (to escape more of the ship's self-noise). Industrial trouble made it impossible to install towed arrays on board the first two (of four) planned *Rothesay* conversions, *Berwick* and *Rhyl*. Scheduling then probably made it easier to install the prototype Type 2031 on board HMS *Cleopatra*, conversion beginning in 1980. Given the necessary design work already done, four *Leanders* (Batch IIB) were con-

verted instead of the *Rothesays*: *Cleopatra*, *Sirius*, *Phoebe* and *Argonaut*. Compensation for the additional 70 tons of top-weight included lowering the Exocet launchers. This interim quartet was to have been followed by five Batch III *Leanders*, but the latter fell afoul of the Nott cancellations. A fifth *Leander*, the Ikara-carrying HMS *Arethusa*, was fitted with a towed array in 1985, the year the towed-array trials ship *Lowestoft* was withdrawn from service.

The main barrier to using the array tactically was the vast amount of computation required to detect each target in each of the array's many beams. The expectation that tactical use would long be impossible was probably actually an estimate of how quickly enough computer power could be made available in a reasonable package. However, a new Curtis system architecture drastically shrank the size of the array's dry end. The system (not just the array) exploiting the new architecture was Type 2031Z, thirteen of which were bought prior to the advent of the Type 23 class (which also received this system). Note that reportedly the four Batch I ships were to have been retrofitted with Type 2031Z, but that their combat direction systems lacked the necessary capacity (the other explanation, that their hulls could not have taken the strain of the array, has been rejected by D K Brown as unlikely; the relevant official papers have not yet been released). In Batch II ships the hull sonar was moved to the forefoot. Later units had an enlarged flight deck capable of taking a Sea King or an EH 101 helicopter.

The 1981 Defence Review capped the Type 22 programme at the seven ships of the pre-1978 plan (three Batch II), partly on the ground that although in theory they were *Leander* replacements they cost about three times as much. The role and future of the class was to be reviewed. In the post-Falklands revival of frigate-building another three Batch IIs were ordered, for the total of six needed for Outboard.

Four Batch III were ordered to replace destroyers and frigates lost in the Falklands. The main improvements were addition of a 4.5in gun, and replacement of Exocet by Harpoon. The combat system was CACS 5. Like Batch IIs, these ships had Type 2031Z towed arrays. They are apparently now considered more valuable than the later Type 23s, and are expected to outlast the Type 42 destroyers.

[43] T225/3604, a general file on destroyers and frigates. DEFE 10/941, ORC 24/68 includes a May 1968 overview of current British sonar research and development for the Operational Requirements Committee which listed the towed array only as a submarine sensor, useful to detect targets in the otherwise blind stern arc. There was no mention that such arrays could achieve very long ranges. The surveillance role is described in connection with plans to install the new Type 2016 duct sonar, DEFE 10/553, paper ORC 20/73. No ORC paper justifying the initial R&D for towed arrays has been found. Dorman, *Defence Under Thatcher*, p 29, suggests that the towed array was the basis for the Merlin (EH-101) Sea King replacement programme begun in 1978, which was about when the array was successfully demonstrated on board a frigate.

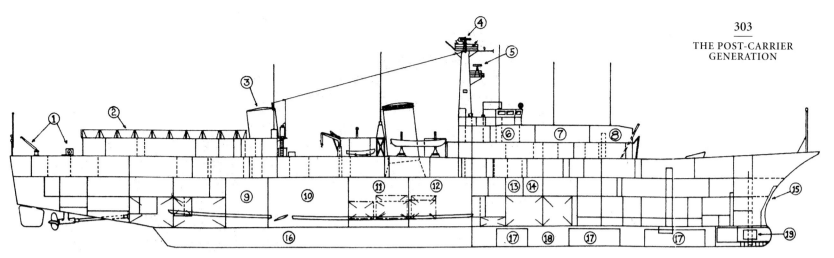

ABOVE: In the early 1970s it seemed that the key to longer sonar range was to adopt lower frequencies, either to bounce signals off the sea bottom or (in deeper water) to allow them to bend around to converge at a great distance, typically 35nm or 70nm in the Atlantic. The Royal Navy believed that such performance required enormous arrays. To develop this concept the 'Battle' class destroyer HMS *Matapan* was rebuilt under an Anglo-American programme. She was in pristine condition, having been laid up (for lack of personnel) after her trials. Arrays were in the massive false keel built under the ship, as shown here. The concept worked, but it turned out that a towed passive array, which could be deployed aboard a relatively small ship (because it was not part of the ship's hull) was even more effective. By 1975 the Royal Navy saw the towed array as the key to future ASW, the only caveat being that the Soviets might ultimately quiet their submarines sufficiently to negate it. (A D Baker III)

1. Davit and winch for Type 182 acoustic torpedo decoy system
2. Helicopter platform
3. Funnel for additional diesel generator sets on main deck to port
4. Type 978 navigational radar
5. Type 944M(2) IFF interrogation antenna
6. Operations room
7. Sonar operations room
8. Scientists' office
9. Propulsion gearing and compressors for Agouti propeller sound-suppression system
10. Engine room with fin stabilisers ports and starboard
11. Boiler room No 2, flanked by water and fuel tanks
12. Boiler room No 1, flanked by water and fuel tanks
13. Passive stabilisation tank No 2
14. Passive stabilisation tank No 1
15. Glass reinforced plastic (GRP) bow fairing
16. Free-flooding portion of GRP underhull fairing
17. Planned location of passive hydrophone arrays, portside only
18. Pressurised portion of underhull fairing
19. Bow Ducting Sonar array

BELOW: Four modernised *Leander*s were fitted with towed-array passive sonars. This is HMS *Cleopatra*, the first ship fitted. Her towing reel is visible right aft. These ships were used both to patrol the GIUK Gap, and as escorts.

HMS *Cumberland*, shown in July 1998, is a Batch III Type 22 frigate. Falklands War lessons are reflected in provision of a close-in defensive weapon, the Dutch Goalkeeper CIWS (abaft her Harpoon launchers), and of a 4.5in gun (left). Instead of the bulky MM 38 Exocets of the two earlier Batches, she has eight small Harpoons abaft her bridge, firing athwartships. (A D Baker III)

F 85

F 86

ABOVE: HMS *Campbeltown* is a Batch III Type 22 frigate reflecting some of the lessons of the Falklands War. Abaft the Seawolf director atop her bridge is a Goalkeeper CIWS, in effect backing up Seawolf. Forward of the Seawolf launcher is a single 4.5in gun, whose value in shore bombardment was proven by the war. Space for the gun was provided by the replacement of the bulky Exocet containers by the much smaller canisters of the successor Harpoon anti-ship missile (not mounted in this photograph). The ship's defensive jammer (Type 670) is barely visible at the base of her mainmast. The platforms for her SCOT satellite antennas are empty.

RIGHT: HMS *Chatham* was the final Batch III Type 22 frigate. Note the two spherical Sea Archer 30 electro-optical gun directors atop her bridge (on either side) and the Harpoon canisters abaft her forward Seawolf director. One of her two SCOT satellite antennas is clearly visible. The bulge protruding from her mainmast, below the exhausts, is the radome of a Type 670 jammer.

F 87

The Cheap Frigate and Type 23

Resources were too limited to build Type 22 on anything like the desired scale. By the early 1970s studies of an inexpensive frigate or sloop, the Future Light Frigate, were being carried out. For example, a 1972 study of a ship for construction after 1978 showed four Exocets, a Lynx helicopter (with a garage hangar, *ie* without maintenance), and two Oerlikons, powered by a single Olympus with two Ventura diesels for cruising. Radar would have been limited to a Type 1006 for surface search, and there would have been no air defence weapon.[44] The 1975 paper on the future fleet effectively killed this project, but the idea of abandoning low-end ships was quite controversial within the Royal Navy. Within a few years there was again intense high-level interest in them. Thus by 1978 DGS was analysing factors leading to high unit costs, in hopes of developing an affordable yet useful ship. This effort is reflected in a paper, 'Cheap Warships are Not Simple' (SNAME Symposium, 1982), by the two men most closely as-

sociated with the project, D K Brown and David Andrews, of whom Brown led the DGS Forward Design team. Brown's key point was that attention to detail was much more useful than simply cutting capability. The DGS programme was paralleled by, and connected with, a US programme, which Dr Reuven Leopold, the civilian head of the then Naval Ship Engineering Center, called the 'headache frigate'.[45]

So as to avoid encroaching on the next frigate, which would be designated Type 23, the designs evolved at this time were unofficially designated Types 24 and 25. Type 24 was inspired by the main British frigate builders, Yarrow, Vosper Thornycroft and Vickers, who were finding it difficult to sell ships of types not bought by the Royal Navy. They wanted something which would repeat the export success of the *Leander* class. A steering committee was chaired by Chief Naval Architect Ken Rawson with the three companies' chief naval architects, to develop a light general-purpose frigate which would be acceptable to the Royal Navy 'if it had the need currently for such a ship'. The initial design by the DGS Forward Design team incorporated the small superstructure they then favoured, as a way of providing space for further development. Yarrow's developed version was presented at the 1979 Royal Naval Equipment Exhibition (RNEE). The company implied that

---

[44] This design study is described in Notebook 1129/1 (R A Snelling) as a follow-on to Design Studies 648 and 649, with a reference (apparently to a sketch Staff Requirement) dated 23 December 1971. Generating capacity would have been three 750 kW, with three 1-million BTU air-conditioning plants. Complement would have been fifteen officers, fifty senior and sixty-five junior ratings, accommodated to nuclear submarine standards, with minimum nuclear and chemical protection beyond a citadel containing the AIO and machinery control room, no special shock protection, and minimal noise reduction. Alternatives to be studied were eight Exocets, 1962 accommodation standards, and two Olympus engines. The basic design, Study 650, would have used a *Leander* hull form (301ft × 36ft 6in × 25ft hull depth). Apparently it offered insufficient space, because some later studies used a hull lengthened to 325ft. At about this time the British adopted metric measurements, so a later ship in the series (June 1973) was 100m (328ft) × 12m × 7.9m. Other variations were to add a single OTO-Melara 76mm/62 gun and to substitute four Pielstick diesels for the mixed powerplant. Displacement was about 2,000 tons. The notebook does not give detailed weights or projected performance.

[45] The author remembers Dr Reuven Leopold, probably in 1975, describing an Anglo-American project, on a small but very high level, to design a really inexpensive frigate. On the American side, it arose from fleet feeling that the *Perry* class, despised as weakly armed, was so large and expensive. See N Friedman, *US Destroyers: An Illustrated Design History* (revised edition: Naval Institute Press, Annapolis: 2004) for details of this 'headache frigate'.

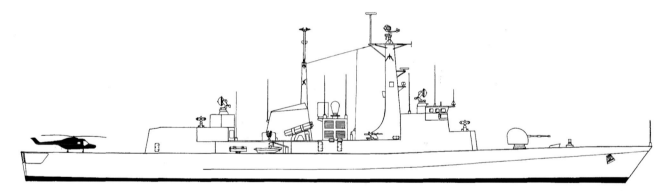

Yarrow's Type 24, as exhibited at RNEE 1979. At the show, Yarrow claimed that the first ship would be completed in 1983, presumably based on a misunderstanding of Royal Navy intentions. The long knuckle running down the ship's hull is reminiscent of recent stealthy designs, and may well have been conceived as an anti-radar measure. The structure forward of the funnel is the downtake for the two Olympus gas turbines, which exhaust through the forward part of the funnel. In the compartment abaft them are the two cruise diesels, with the two diesel generators abaft them. Speed on gas turbines would be 31kts; the ship would cruise at up to 16–17kts on diesels. Range was 7,800nm at 16kts and 9,650nm at 13kts. Yarrow also offered a three- or two-engine COGAG powerplant, eg with Speys. Planned complement was 160 (fourteen officers, forty-seven senior and ninety-nine junior ratings), with space for 190. By the time of the show, the ship was being advertised to China, and there was hope of NATO sales (Canada, Greece and Portugal were specifically mentioned). The RN version would have been a more specialised ASW ship. Yarrow offered the ship for export with four armament and equipment options, which might be described as British, US, French and Italian. The British export option, shown here, had the Mk 8 gun forward, Seawolf (in a new twin launcher automatically reloaded from below), Exocet MM40, and lightweight Mk 44/46 torpedoes. The secondary gun was the Oerlikon twin 30mm which the Royal Navy adopted. At least in the export version, the main air-search radar was Plessey's AWS-5. The fire control sets fore and aft were Signaal's VM40 (STIR), but the sonar was British (Graseby 850, in effect an updated Type 184) and the combat direction system was Ferranti's CAAIS 450, a somewhat less capable version of what a Type 21 had. Also evident here are SCOT satellite radomes and, it would appear, the Type 670 defensive jammer. The hangar could accommodate two Lynx helicopters. The US version offered the standard US NTDS system (with UYK-7 computer, as in a *Perry* class frigate), Harpoon and Sea Sparrow missiles, a 5in gun, the SPS-65 missile detection radar, the Mk 86 fire control system, and the Canadian Westinghouse SQS-505 sonar, which had very nearly been selected for the *Perry*. The secondary gun was Emerlec's twin 30mm. The French version used the French equivalent to NTDS, SENIT; its missiles were Exocet and Crotale Naval, and its guns were the standard French 100mm and the Italian Breda 40mm/70. The main radar was Sea Tiger, the fire control was the French Triton, and the sonar was the French Diodon. The lightweight torpedo would be Mk 44, using Italian Whitehead tubes. Finally, the Italian version would have had Otomat and Aspide missiles plus the OTO-Melara 127/54 gun and Breda 40/70s, controlled by Selenia's IT-10 system; the main sensors would be the RAN-10S radar, SPQ-2D fire-control radar, and Krupp Atlas DSQS-21 sonar. Most of the market Yarrow envisaged was captured by the German MEKO frigate series, which also offered modularity allowing the customer to choose his own weapon and sensor combination. China and Canada rejected foreign designs altogether. (A D Baker III)

the ship would be bought by the Royal Navy, but that had always been a provisional idea. Among other things, Yarrow had eliminated headroom aft under the helicopter deck required for towed array handling. The geared diesel cruise powerplant was not nearly quiet enough.

Yarrow's frigate was conventional-looking, with a large helicopter hangar aft. It had a single 4.5in gun forward and a hangar large enough for two Lynx helicopters aft, with four Exocet launchers on either side of its large funnel. Seawolf would be carried in four new lightweight twin launchers with automatic reloads (this version, which was also projected for upgraded Type 42s, never materialised). There would also have been two sets of lightweight torpedo tubes. The planned powerplant was two Olympus and two Paxman Valenta cruise diesels. Trial displacement would have been 3,100 tons (122m overall, 116m on the waterline × 14.8m × 8.8m hull depth). Maximum speed on both Olympus would have been 31kts (cruise speed would have been 17.5kts). Although Yarrow implied that the Royal Navy was about to buy such ships, that was not the case.

DGS showed its version of Type 24 in model form at the 1979 RNEE. It had a long foredeck (for dryness) carrying a single gun well abaft the bow, with a sextuple Seawolf launcher in B position, its director atop the bridge. Two sets of anti-ship missile launchers were placed alongside it. Abaft the uptakes was a second director, with two more Seawolf launchers abeam the after superstructure. Abaft that were a small hangar and a small landing deck suited to a Lynx. The announced powerplant was two Speys, which, oddly, would form a COGOG plant (one or the other, not both). There was no

mention of a towed array, but the commentator writing in *International Defence Review* correctly observed that the British were surely following the US and Canadian lead in adopting surface ship towed arrays, and that the model showed open space under her helicopter pad suitable for handling them.

Brown's goal in Type 25 was Type 22 capability at two-thirds the cost. He also wanted sufficient margins for long effective lifetime. He wrote that it paralleled the 'Castle' class offshore patrol vessel (OPV) which he had designed.[46] Given its small superstructure and good stability, it could accommodate a wide variety of weapons, up to a modified army 105mm gun, and it could operate a helicopter under most weather conditions. Export customers might first buy an upgraded 'Castle' and then a frigate derivative.

Brown pointed out that using a towed array (decoupled from ship noise and motion) even a small cheap frigate could be an effective submarine detector. The main ship requirement would be silencing, since ship noise would be reflected from the sea bottom into the array.[47] To silence the ship at minimum cost, Type 25 used an inherently quiet diesel-electric cruise powerplant. With no mechanical connection to the propellers, the diesels could be above decks, isolated from the water and thus unable to put noise into it. Thus the ship could be silenced with little special effort. Electric drive also offered extraordinary endurance, which would be very valuable for a towed-array ship conducting surveillance. Type 23 used this electric drive, the same generators being used for propulsion and for the ship's electrical system. For higher speed the ship used conventional gas turbines.

By this time DGS wanted to emphasise two new concepts, reduced radar cross section by reducing the superstructure, and cellularity. The latter was an attempt to reduce the cost and time-lag associated with electronics by designing standard installation cells into a ship. The ship would be somewhat larger than necessary, but it would not have to be redesigned again and again as new electronic equipment was demanded, or as existing equipment changed. Cellularity might be compared with contemporary attempts at greater design flexibility, such as the German MEKO type and the abortive US Seamod programme.

Type 23 was conceived as a minimum towed-array ship supported by the helicopter-carrying armed replenishment ship first proposed in 1975.[48] When attention turned from carrier support to surveillance in the GIUK Gap, the replenishment ship survived, because now it was valued as a way of ex-

This sketch is based on a photograph of the DGS frigate model displayed at RNEE 1979. The objects atop the bridge and the hangar are Seawolf directors; the ship has the standard Royal Navy sextuple launchers, one in B position and two abeam her hangar. The gun forward is unidentified, and is probably intended to be a Mk 8 (which it does not resemble). The usual pair of quadruple surface-to-surface missile launchers are abeam the forward Seawolf. By this time the Royal Navy had selected the US Harpoon to replace its Exocets. Note the big radomes on the tower mast in addition to what

look like SCOT radomes at hangar-top level; they probably represent the Millpost programmable ECM system then under development. The entire superstructure has been pushed well aft to protect it from seas coming aboard. Comparison with a model of a heavily-armed version of the 'Castle' class OPV, also displayed at RNEE, shows a strong family resemblance, although the OPV has a much larger area in B position to accommodate a gun. This design is one in a series of general-purpose towed array ships begun about 1976; by 1977 DGS had at least a sketch of a ship with a gun,

Exocets, double-headed Seawolf, and a towed array. It responded to the 1975 evaluation of British naval requirements, in which towed-array ships had to be capable of pre-hostilities tasks in which they would often operate individually and might well encounter major Soviet surface combatants. That view turned out to be unaffordable, and by 1978 the justification for ship characteristics was explicitly limited to the short envisaged period of intense hostilities, when towed-array ships would be used to escort carriers and high-value convoys. Since other ships would be operating with them, they would not need extras such as guns, Exocets, and short-range (duct) sonars. This cut in requirements made it possible to design a much more austere ship, which became the basis for Type 23. Many officers argued that such specialised ships would be useless most of the time, and that the more general-purpose features should not be dropped. (Author)

[46] This discussion is largely based on D K Brown and George Moore, *Rebuilding the Royal Navy* (Chatham Publishing, London: 2003). In his book, former Navy Minister Keith Speed called the 'Castle' a Third World War corvette, *ie* a low-end frigate. Brown, who was in charge of the 'Castle' design, certainly saw it that way. In 1985 the Government abandoned plans to order six to eight corvettes, presumably based on the 'Castle' class. Dorman, *Defence Under Thatcher*, p 120.
[47] For example, an early US towed-array frigate once tracked a contact for two days up and down the US East Coast, only to discover that it was tracking itself.
[48] Much of this account of the Type 23 design is taken from Admiral Sir Lindsay Bryan, 'The Procurement of a Warship,' *Transactions of the Royal Institution of Naval Architects*, 1984 (paper presented June 1984). Admiral Bryant was then Controller, and he referred explicitly to Type 23 as his example of surface-ship design.

The current standard British frigate is Type 23 ('Duke' class), shown here in preliminary form. Not shown are the fixed lightweight torpedo tubes set into the side of the after superstructure block, where they have access to the same magazine which feeds helicopters in the hangar. Nor does this sketch show the 30mm guns on deck abeam the structure just forward of the funnel. The entire Seawolf battery is concentrated forward, in a 32-round vertical launcher, with eight Harpoons (firing athwartships) abaft it and forward of the bridge. Not apparent in this sketch is the considerable attention paid to minimising radar cross-section, eg by angling the hull sides and superstructure elements. Type 23 began as a simple towed-array 'tug,' with minimal other equipment on board. She was designed in accord with a 1978 destroyer/frigate policy paper which based the size of the frigate force on the requirement to escort the light carriers during a short high-intensity war. Although the previous requirement for surveillance of the GIUK Gap (through which Soviet submarines would have to pass to get to the North Atlantic) was dropped, the choice seems to have been to maintain surveillance during a period of tension, then shift the ships to the escort role once war had broken out. The rationale would have been that whatever submarines were going into the North Atlantic would move there during the period of intense tension, so it was unnecessary to maintain surveillance once war had broken out. Note that the British Type 2031 array, unlike its US cousins, was effective in both the surveillance and the tactical (escort) roles. In both cases, the towed array ship needed some ability to defend herself against air attack: in the Gap each surveillance ship would operate on her own, and when operating with the carrier the array ship would have to be some distance away, so as to avoid interference from the noise of the carrier and her close-in consorts. It was argued that a ship working with a carrier did not need such refinements as a shorter-range (duct) sonar, because other units would have it, nor did it need anti-ship missiles. One factor in the ability of a towed-array force to swing between the two roles was the ship's ability to spend protracted periods in the Gap thanks to support by the new *Fort Victoria* class replenishment ships. General-purpose capability – the duct sonar, the gun, and the anti-ship missiles – was promoted on the grounds that the really important naval contribution to NATO deterrence would come during the transition from tension to war, when ships would operate dispersed, and when they would often be used to trail ('mark') Soviet surface combatants, or to elbow them away from high-value units like the carriers. Attempting to keep the fleet affordable, and probably also to deal with Defence Operations Research conclusions, the Royal Navy felt compelled to withdrew this argument in 1976–8, when Type 23 was initiated. Even so, some early sketch designs showed guns and missiles. (A D Baker III)

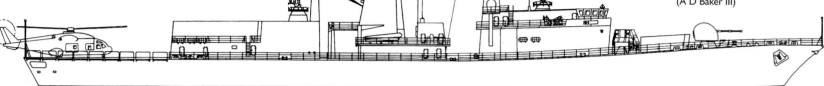

tending surveillance time by limiting the array ship's need to return to port. Initially, then, although the frigate might carry a helicopter, much of the maintenance load would be borne by the replenishment ship. The earliest version of the Type 23 design was 100m long, with SSMs forward and lightweight torpedo tubes amidships. A substantial superstructure included two diesel generator rooms on the main deck.

An outline Staff Target was issued early in 1981. Requirements included reduced radar cross section and a unit cost of £70 million in September 1980 terms. Complement was to be substantially reduced, which in turn significantly reduced mission time. Initially it was arbitrarily set at 150 as a way of capping costs, but that had to be increased to 170, which still left no margins (for training, advancement and board). A major change would be to limit on-board maintenance to rectifying defects. The ship would be maintained mainly by a fly-in team of cleaners who would meet the ship when she came into port, at home or abroad. In the 1980s there were hopes that personnel could be reduced further, perhaps to as few as fifty in a frigate (Type 23 required over 150 personnel, despite her innovative design). The Staff Target emphasised high endurance and silencing for the towed array (which would be streamed at a moderate speed). The ship would have a large enough flight deck for the Sea King successor (the EH-101 Merlin) and the ability to rearm and refuel it. Although the ship was conceived primarily as a towed array platform, she would have to operate at times in water too shallow for an array, hence needed a modern active sonar as well.

Some costs were accepted. Maximum quiet speed was set by the cavitation inception speed, which in turn could be increased by using large slow-turning propellers. Despite the cost, the ship was given two shafts. Propulsor options were fixed pitch or controllable-pitch propellers and a pumpjet. The latter was rejected as too expensive (the British were then using pumpjets on submarines), and the fixed-pitch propeller selected because, for a given diameter, it could be made quieter.

Type 23 coincided with a decision to shift from the Olympus-Tyne combination to the Spey gas turbine, a marinised version of the TF41 used in the US A7 Corsair II attack bomber. It was less powerful than an Olympus but offered greater efficiency and longer life. The rationale was that the Tyne-Olympus combination did not cover the full speed range, whereas a four-engine plant (54,000 to 66,000 BHP, using engines producing 13,500 to 16,500 BHP each) would offer reasonable economy at roughly half power. The first installation was on board the Type 22 frigate *Brave*: Spey replaced her Olympus. Speys (SM1A) were later installed in the Type 22 Batch III frigates. Type 23 uses an uprated SM1C.

Type 23 was announced in the 1981 Defence Review as an inexpensive frigate with export potential. That phrase justified a much more general-purpose ship than the towed-array role would have indicated. It was incorporated in the Naval Staff Target presented to MoD in October 1981. The general-purpose role was used to justify high speed, which would not have been needed for a GIUK Gap surveillance ship (except perhaps for transit to the listening area). However, it certainly was needed for the envisaged escort role, in which the ship would sprint between low-speed (quiet) listening periods, to keep up with her carrier or convoy. At this stage the sketch design showed a 107m ship. Trade-off studies had justified the helicopter hangar and the self-defence weapon (Seawolf). Some reduction in speed was accepted to reduce cost, the ship being powered by one rather than two Speys

HMS *Richmond* is a Type 23 frigate, a very successful attempt to turn a rather specialised ASW ship into a general-purpose combatant. The tubes forward are for vertically-launched Seawolf defensive missiles, with eight Harpoon canisters (athwartships) abaft them. The tower foremast carries her Sea Archer 30 electro-optical gun fire-control system and her Type 996 multi-purpose radar, with the ship's UAF-1 ESM array below the radar. Sponsoned out to one side of the mast is the usual Type 1006 surface-search radar. The two large domes sponsoned out to either side are for SCOT, the satellite antenna. The radome on the fore side of the uptakes is for INMARSAT. Atop the bridge is one of two Seawolf directors. Although Type 23 carries only about half as many Seawolf missiles as Type 22, all are immediately available for launch, and all can tip over to fly in any desired direction, a considerable advance on the two trainable launchers (twelve missiles in all) of a Type 22. Aft, the mainmast carries a UHF/DF array (presumably for aircraft control) above a pair of standard UHF antennas (one to send, one to receive). The 'sword' antenna on the yard to starboard of this mast is for the ship's communications intercept system. The opening in the centre of the sponson is for the ship's towed array sonar. The hull shows considerable flare, which was not a feature of Type 22. Contemporary Soviet surface combatant hulls were flared. When Types 23/24/25 were designed, radar cross-section was becoming an important consideration; flare considerably reduced the ship's radar cross section. The naval architects involved liked flare because it would help maintain the ship's stability as she added topweight during her lifetime. A less obvious naval architectural feature was some turtle back in the forecastle, inspired by the Canadian *St. Laurent* class frigates designed by Sir Roland Baker, which were perceived as better seaboats than *Leanders*.

(with two diesels). Using transverse framing in some areas would cut cost even though it added 40 tons to displacement.

Reviewing the Staff Target, the relevant MoD committees (presumably the Weapons Development Committee and the Operational Requirements Committee) wanted the ship optimised for the Royal Navy ASW mission and given a point defence missile and at least a garage hangar. Studies had shown that such a hangar would triple the number of days a helicopter could be maintained at sea. The simplest version would be a collapsible structure erected only when the helicopter was on deck, but it would fare very poorly in the North Atlantic. Making it a fixed structure would again triple helicopter endurance, making it compatible with ship endurance, but at a considerable price. They accepted an increase in cost.

The design was soon reconfigured with a single-headed Seawolf system and a hangar offering limited second-line maintenance. A close-in weapon, such as Phalanx, became an option. The ship was now 115m (377ft) long. A sketch showed a sextuple Seawolf launcher forward and anti-ship missiles atop the diesel-generator space in the amidships superstructure. At this point the flight deck was sized for the projected Merlin helicopter, but it was too short for the existing Sea

King. Because it was not certain that the Merlin project would proceed, another 3m was added to provide sufficient space to land a Sea King. The extra length (118m total) was used to reduce congestion in the machinery spaces, and also to expand accommodation areas slightly. As submitted to the MoD committees for endorsement early in 1982, the ship had a second Spey (required to provide sufficient speed for the larger ship) and a second Seawolf director. Estimated cost rose to £90 million.[49] Yarrow received a design contract in mid-1982.

The Falklands War demonstrated that much more was needed. A major wartime lesson was the need to contain smoke and fire. Type 23 had been divided into three sections by fire-containment bulkheads. Now the number of such bulkheads was doubled, to divide the ship into five sections. Fortunately ventilators had already been grouped between the main transverse bulkheads, so little had to be done. That is, the zoning idea had already been accepted. The impact of the Falklands experience was to protect it against the usual round of budget cuts. The practice of opening bulkheads below No. 1 deck for cabling was discontinued, to prevent flooding. The ship was lengthened to 123m (403ft LWL, 435ft OA), the maximum which the Devonport Frigate Complex could accommodate.

The war showed that frigates should be general-purpose ships. When the design was submitted to the Board in mid-1983 (approved October 1983), that body approved both a 4.5in gun and a new vertically-launched Seawolf instead of the earlier sextuple launcher. Adopting the new type of Seawolf saved space, which was used to install eight Harpoon anti-ship missiles. That the gun was a late addition is evident from its position so far forward, where it obscures the view of the bow from the bridge and makes the ship wetter than necessary.

Before the design was frozen, YARD was asked to rethink it, to see whether the evolution from towed array ship to general-purpose frigate had resulted in an optimum ship. YARD was to emphasise changes which might reduce unit cost. It suggested that a larger ship might actually be less expensive to build, and would provide more space for personnel. The ship's structure would be heavier but would use cheaper steels. YARD specifically suggested limiting longitudinal framing to the bottom and using transverse framing for the sides. It pointed out that commercial ship structures (transverse) required about a third of the steel man-hours of warship structures (longitudinal). More space would make it easier to install cabling, would simplify fitting-out, and would make command centres less congested. More functions could be buried in a larger hull, thus reducing radar cross-section and offering more siting options for weapons. YARD also proposed substituting a CODOG powerplant for the CODLAG in Type 23. It would have been less expensive, but it would just have met the noise limit, and would not have offered any margin for the future. Some of these ideas were incorporated in the final

Type 23 design.

The major surprise in the programme was the failure of the CACS 4 combat direction system originally planned. The manufacturer, Ferranti, had argued that existing central-computer systems could not continue to grow, and that it was time to adopt a very different distributed architecture. The Royal Navy position was to avoid radical change, probably on the ground that developing very new software would be crushingly expensive and might well take far too long. Before the ships were built, it became clear that Ferranti had been right. Admiral Reffel, the Chief of Navy, took the courageous step of cancelling CACS 4 but proceeding with construction. Thus the first eight ships went to sea without any combat direction system at all, while the Royal Navy chose a successor. This was embarrassing, as these newest British frigates could not be assigned to danger spots such as the Gulf. A new distributed system, SSCS (DNA 1), was developed, and ultimately it was retrofitted to the first eight ships.

Sixteen ships of this 'Duke' class were ordered, the first (HMS *Norfolk*) on 29 October 1984. She was followed by three on 15 July 1986, three on 11 July 1988, three on 19 December 1989, three on 23 January 1992, and three on 28 February 1992. Plans called for maintaining twelve ships in service while four refitted, six with Merlin and six with Lynx helicopters. Ironically, the first ship entered service in 1990, just as the Cold War was ending. With it ended the need for a high-capacity ASW ship, so it was no surprise that plans for twenty-four ships were curtailed. The last six ships were completed without towed arrays. The lesson is the classic one: general-purpose capability is often expensive, but ships finely tuned for one mission often become embarrassingly obsolete as times change.

Types 43 and 44

In March 1976 DNOR ordered initial work on a Type 42 successor. He observed that air defence ships would clearly still be needed, and that Type 42 could not accommodate a Sea Dart successor. The threat had recently been re-assessed.[50] The most dramatic change was that anti-ship missiles, rather than aircraft, were the primary threat. Each attacking aircraft might launch two to four missiles, which it could fire from beyond Sea Dart range. Without fleet fighters to oppose them (the last British carrier, *Ark Royal*, had recently been retired), enemy missile aircraft could survive to attack again and again. Missiles were, moreover, smaller and more difficult targets than aircraft. Saturation air attacks would be supported by massive ECM. Enemy submarines could now launch missiles in surprise attacks *inside* minimum Sea Dart range. The Soviets might well introduce much higher-performance missiles. It is now known that they were working on the Kh-15S semi-ballistic (Mach 5) missile when they collapsed.

---

[49] Dorman, *Defence Under Thatcher*, p 85.

[50] Much of this information is from DEFE69/551, a file completed in 1977. DNOR cited D/DIS 10/3/3 of 3 April 1975 in his March 1976 paper.

Artist's impression of the Type 43. (By courtesy of D K Brown)

These threats were not actually new; the Soviets had been developing air-launched anti-ship missiles for many years. What was new, as DNOR pointed out, was concentration on NATO operations in the Eastern Atlantic and in the Channel. Type 42 could not handle the new threat:

- Sea Dart was very vulnerable to main-beam jamming.
- The ship had no height-finding radar (too much time was lost when the Type 909 illuminator had to search in altitude for a target designated only in range and bearing).
- There were limited facilities for onboard training.
- There were too few channels of fire to handle attacks by supersonic stand-off missiles (AS-4, AS-6).
- The ship had too few defensive missiles; the ship would need replenishment too frequently.
- The missile fuse had not been proven against supersonic missiles.
- Apart from an Oerlikon, the ship had no defence against short-range missiles.

A two-phase Sea Dart upgrade programme had been started, to maintain the missile through the end of the century: modernisation (NST 6503) and a further upgrade (NST 6505), the latter not limited by the Type 42 hull. NST 6503 included a new surveillance and target-indication radar (STIR, the abortive Type 1030) and missile and system improvements. In 1976 NST 6505 (GWS 31) was still embryonic, but possibilities included adding channels of fire, using vertical launchers, adding mid-course guidance to the missile, adding a height-finding radar, developing a new long-range anti-radar version of Sea Dart, and installing a new warhead and fuse.

The mid-course guidance option (making the missile autopilot remotely commandable) would both have increased missile range and provided new channels of fire, as in the US Aegis and New Threat Upgrade systems approaching maturity at this time. Given the commandable autopilot, illumination would be required only when the missile approached its target. The ship could keep several missiles airborne without devoting an illuminator to each on a full-time basis. Many more targets could be engaged in quick succession. As a side benefit, because it would not have to point towards the target throughout flight (to receive reflected illumination), the missile could fly a more energy-efficient path, achieving a greater range. Also, the missile would not have to receive illumination energy until it approached the target: that energy would not have to make a full round-trip between target and ship before being picked up. Illumination could be effective at a much greater range or against a target with smaller radar cross-section.

At least initially attention was concentrated on improvements to the missile proper. Thus a 1978 study of GWS 31 options listed as a maximum a package comprising reliability/serviceability improvements, larger wings and fins, ramjet improvements, titanium components, thrust-vector control (for vertical launching), guidance improvements (acquisition, sensitivity and ECCM), and lethality improvements (fuse and warhead). Lower-cost options included minor changes to the airframe, avoiding the use of titanium; and a package limited to reliability and guidance. System reaction time would be reduced from 23 to 10 seconds. Against a particularly demanding target, interception range could be ex-

tended from 21 to 47km, and overall system effectiveness (reliability x lethality) improved from 0.53 to 0.7. None of the improvements would change minimum interception range, which was 4.1 km, and the improved system still used the same Type 909 or 909M tracker-illuminator.[51]

GWS 31 was killed in the 1981 Defence Review. Although many recommendations of that review were reversed following the Falklands War, Sea Dart was never upgraded as planned. The Royal Navy will receive an anti-saturation weapon only when Type 45 destroyers, armed with the Aster missile, enter service.

The Type 42 combat direction system was fifteen years old. DNOR suggested that a new ship might take advantage of the new micro-processors in a system which could take batter advantage of the expanding tactical horizon (achieved through data linking with other ships and, perhaps, through wide-area information becoming available through some US programmes). He wanted a high-data-rate ECM-proof area surveillance system (which meant electro-optics) and fully-integrated EW, including a stand-off jammer (like the current Siren). The new ship should also have a hard-kill self-defence system. Other desirable features were passive protection (*eg* armour) and facilities to support unmanned air vehicles (called remotely piloted vehicles at that time). Very high speed (35kts) might be attractive for the marking/counter-marking role. As

[51] ADM 219/720, an August 1978 study of GWS 31 interception range and missile options, DNOS Note 4/78. This note does not mention a commandable autopilot.

for some time, it would be vital to reduce manpower. DNOR wanted a preliminary report by October 1976.

The Working Group envisaged introduction of a new design with the nineteenth missile destroyer (DDG-19). DGS incorporated new design concepts such as 'long-low' (meaning minimum superstructure, for minimum radar cross-section, superstructure being restricted to the primary purpose of weapon support) and cellularity (for simpler electronic development). The new ship would be powered by the new standard Spey (SM1A) engine. Other new ideas were:

- Machinery moved aft to integrate up- and downtakes with the after superstructure.
- Due to the above, free space amidships for future weapon additions.
- Concentrate major weapons to reduce vulnerability: Sea Dart forward, Seawolf aft.
- Cellularised weapon zones concentrated in blocks forward and aft.
- Auxiliary machinery spaces well-separated and adjacent to weapon zones.

There was also interest in making the separate weapons blocks more autonomous by including secondary surveillance radar and separate direction systems in the after block.

The helicopter became the major constraint on flexible arrangement. If it were aft, weapons had to be fitted in above

Type 43 was conceived as successor to Type 42, but it was ultimately rejected as too expensive: it would provide numbers of Sea Dart launchers, but not the desired number of hulls allowing that capacity to be spread widely enough. Note the dispersal of armament and sensors fore and aft, for survivability. Of the equipment shown, Abbey Hill was the automated UAA-1 ESM system and Millpost was the abortive companion programmable jammer. STIR was the Surveillance and Target Indication Radar intended to replace both 992 and 965; the prototype Type 1030 had two antennas back-to-back for maximum data rate. Ultimately Type 1022 came closest to meeting the STIR requirement, but ships fitted with it also have Type 996 for target indication. Type 967/968 was the short-range search and target indication combination used for Seawolf, but it could also provide Sea Dart target indication (as is indeed done by the successor Type 996). Seagnat was the standard NATO decoy launcher, for both radar and IR decoys. Note the alternative version in which a centreline Seawolf forward would have replaced the 4.5in gun. SKR was the Sea King Replacement helicopter (which ultimately emerged as the current Merlin). (By courtesy of D K Brown)

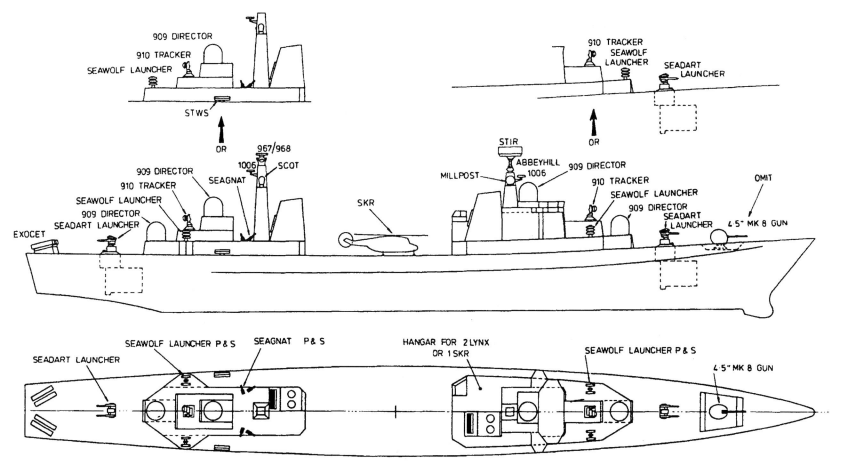

its hangar. The group became interested in placing the helicopter amidships, in the area of the ship least subject to motion. The hangar would be in the forward superstructure. This arrangement was inspired by that of the pre-war 'Town' class cruisers. It was recognised that pilots might be chary of the obstacles presented by the forward and after superstructure blocks, and DNOR asked DNAW and HAD(N) (naval helicopter aviation director) for their advice. Placing generous sitting-out and recreation areas adjacent to the weapon zones would provide a useful working margin for expansion; the Working Group compared this idea with the concept of void 'growth zones' in the US *Spruance* class. There was also interest in developing a 'standard ship' which might be built in either AAW or ASW form, an idea which had arisen several times in the past and which may have been inspired this time by the US *Spruance* programme (the US ships were designed so that they could be completed in either form). DGS cited a parallel study of a ship with a towed array, a Type 2016 sonar, Sea King helicopter, double-headed Seawolf, Exocets and a gun.

The Working Group presented two armament options, Numbers 10 and 22, in its report. Option 10 was a modernised Sea Dart system (NST 6503) with a new surveillance radar (STIR) and a larger magazine obtained at the cost of the gun. Option 22 added Seawolf and retained the gun. Both options could be accommodated only in a stretched hull. The successor could have either Option 10 with the gun, or Option 22. It would have an improved weapon configuration, and would be suitable for the NST 6505 Sea Dart upgrade. The existing Type 42 hull could be refitted with the modernised Sea Dart (NST 6503), or Seawolf could be added at the cost of the 4.5in gun.

A sketch design for the new Type 43 destroyer seems to have been completed about 1978. It provided new missiles by adding a second Sea Dart launcher, and more channels of fire by doubling the number of tracker-illuminators (Type 909s). The short-range problem was solved by providing two or four Seawolf launchers (each launcher or each pair with a Type 910 director). To limit vulnerability, weapons were in duplicate blocks fore and aft. The forward block carried a STIR radar, the after one the Type 967/968 associated with Seawolf (but providing some target indication for Sea Dart). Machinery was split fore and aft, and the helicopter was amidships. Four Exocets were arranged on the extreme stern, for the secondary (marking/counter-marking) anti-ship role. A single 4.5in gun was mounted forward (but not in the version with Seawolf on the centreline).[52] The ship had the new standard Type 2016 bow sonar. Reported dimensions were 172m × 17.8m (6,000 tons). Four Spey SM 1A would have given the ship a maximum speed of 31.5kts (given existing gas turbines, there was no hope of achieving DNOR's 35kts).

Type 43 was also part of an attempt to capitalise on the flex-

ibility of the new Sea Harrier. Given the limited size of the *Invincible* class carriers, the only way to provide enough aircraft to the fleet was to fit ships down to the smallest practicable size to support not only helicopters but also VTOL aircraft. For example, a June 1978 design calculation refers to a design requirement (possibly in a modified version) to support a pair of VTOL aircraft for a 21-day mission, which might include periods of up to seven days between replenishments (requiring 175 tons of jet fuel to support eight sorties per day, 1½ hours per sortie). This was ultimately unrealistic, because a Harrier had very little capability without being able to roll down a deck (or up a ski-jump). It recalls the attempt, in the 1930s, to provide the Royal Navy with enough strike aircraft by placing them aboard battleships and cruisers, launching them from catapults. That attempt, incidentally, is why the Swordfish was required to take off carrying a torpedo at the 60-knot end speed of a standard catapult, and hence why this aircraft had to be a high-lift biplane. The irony then was that the concept was never implemented (floatplane Swordfish were used as battleship spotters and reconnaissance aircraft). The abortive Harrier concept also recalls a contemporary US proposal to place aircraft on board the rather larger Strike Cruiser.

Like Type 82, Type 43 was used as a basis for a possible nuclear surface combatant, as part of a continuing British evaluation of such ships. Both one- and two-reactor plants were evaluated. A typical version was 172m × 17.2m × 14.0m (depth amidships) × 6.6m, displacing about 10,000 tons. These studies seem not to have been very serious.

Type 43 was rejected as not cost-efficient because it could not engage more than four low-altitude high-speed targets before they came within minimum range. However, the future GWS 31 (NST 6505) offered a solution in a smaller ship with a single launcher. The smaller ship could also be built in larger numbers. Type 44 used a Type 22 Batch II hull to carry one Sea Dart launcher with the usual two directors and a single Seawolf launcher aft, plus Exocet (sided alongside and below the forward Sea Dart director). It and GWS 31 were killed in the 1981 Defence Review (see above).

The 'Short Fat Ship'

Beginning about 1979, Peter Thornycroft and David Giles advocated an alternative to the conventional hull form which they called the 'short fat ship' or semi-planing monohull. Initially it was for fast attack craft; later it was advertised as a superior alternative to the usual 'long thin hull'. They claimed that it would be easier and cheaper to build, that it would have better seakeeping and manoeuvrability, and that it offered greater weapon capacity. These claims amounted to a direct attack on DGS. They were supported by an informal committee chaired by Lord Hill-Norton, a former First Sea Lord.

The 'short fat ship' saga reflected the usual service dissatis-

---

[52] This account is based largely on Brown and Moore, *Rebuilding the Royal Navy*, pp 98–100.

faction with its own ships: the operators are inevitably well aware of their limitations. Surely something else would be better. The experience of the Falklands War shocked many British naval officers, who saw their ships as under-armed. The governments of the day had generally ignored the real risks of demanding minimum size and cost. The British government had been more open than most in saying that nuclear deterrence made high-intensity war unlikely and thus justified economies. The Falklands War showed, as the Royal Navy had warned, that locally high-intensity war was still quite possible outside the NATO area.

None of this had much to do with the basic designs of British warships. Understandably, however, some at sea imagined that their problems could be solved by some radical innovation. Technological history seems to be full of brilliant new ideas rejected at first by hidebound officialdom but ultimately accepted. Often a more complete version of history shows officialdom not nearly so hidebound and innovations often promptly adopted, but those entranced by the radical new hull form were largely unaware of that. It is not much of a story if the inventor has no long odds to overcome. Nor was there much awareness of how many of the rejected ideas richly deserved their fates.

DG Ships rejected the short fat concept outright. Well over a century of scientific analysis of hull forms made it easy to assess this one, and to find it badly wanting. There was no question but that a beamier hull would be more stable in a seaway, and that it would offer more deck space. However, it was ludicrous to imagine that a frigate could plane like a small fast combatant; it would need entirely too much power. Remarkably, graphs of resistance published by Giles and Thornycroft showed as much. They seem to have been entirely misinterpreted by those supporting the 'short fat ship'. The graph showed a dramatically upward trend – unfortunately, in resistance per ton versus speed, which was exactly opposite to what a better design would have offered. Apparently it was offered as evidence of merit just because it showed some sort of upward trend. The situation recalled the failed ironclad HMS *Captain* of about a century earlier. In both cases the innovation was backed enthusiastically by those with only limited technical knowledge, as though enthusiasm could trump physical laws.

In the past, as with Type 21, DG Ships' critique would have been accepted at the outset. This time the climate was radically different. The Thatcher Government often proclaimed that government departments at all levels were hidebound, that private industry was more forward-looking and efficient. It was natural to assume that a commercial critique of standard official practice was correct. In effect the Government saw the professionals in DGS as a kind of trade union, jealous of its prerogatives. The possibility that the outsiders were quite unprofessional in their own thinking seems not to have been

imagined. Perhaps it really was unimaginable that anyone would risk making totally unsupportable claims about technology, since such claims could easily be tested and refuted. A cynic might suggest that the real problem was that the decision-makers had little or no exposure to technology or science, hence did not realise just how outrageous the Giles-Thornycroft claims could be. It was certainly surprising at the time that some experienced retired naval officers accepted their statements at face value. They really did not understand some of the more basic aspects of hull performance.

In effect Giles and Thornycroft made DG Ships their rival, rather than the professional advisor to the Admiralty Board. Given the official attitude, it was very nearly up to his organisation to defend itself, not up to the outsider to prove that his idea was worth pursuing. It took an independent inquiry by Lloyd's Register (1988) to establish the reality that the 'short fat ship' was pointless. Cynics at the time suggested that Giles and Thornycroft were actually backed to destroy DG Ships and thus to open the way to commercial designs. The situation was also affected by the change which had created DGS – which was not DNC. Its chief was not necessarily a naval architect, because the different elements of the DGS organisation were, in effect, equal. In this case the chief was a submarine engineer Vice Admiral (*ie* a propelling machinery man) with little feeling for hull design. In theory he relied on his Chief Naval Architect, Ken Rawson, but in this politically-charged case he seems not to have backed him. That made for considerable bitterness. Rawson felt compelled to take early retirement after the controversy ended.

Less than two decades later Type 45 is being designed by BAE, and the new carrier by a consortium of BAE and Thales. However, many of those actually doing the designs are RCNC-

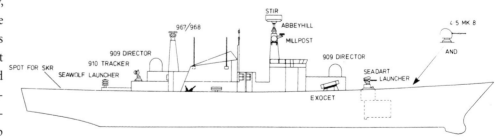

trained, so for a time the DNC legacy survives. There is also increasing recognition that designs should involve MoD leadership and partnership. However, it is by no means clear that the current relatively satisfactory situation can long survive. DGS is no longer a design organisation, and its corporate memory has been wiped out; most of its records are either gone or retired to deep storage. What happens when the last designers who keep some of those records in their heads are gone? At the end of 2005 MoD announced that in future it might be willing to buy its hulls abroad.

Type 44 was the abortive smaller alternative to Type 43. (By courtesy of D K Brown)

CHAPTER 15

The Future

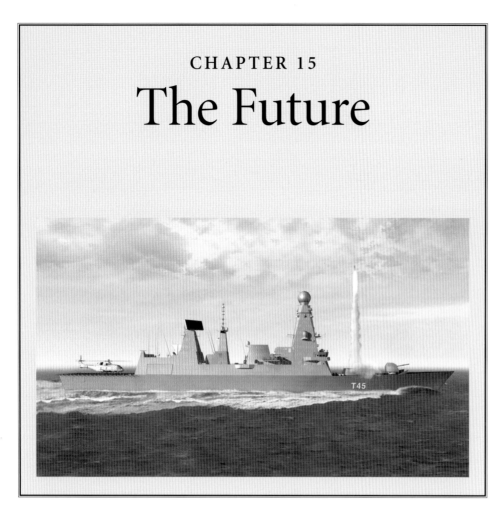

The new *Daring* (Type 45) class will finally provide the Royal Navy with a replacement air defence escort after about a quarter-century of attempts to replace the venerable Type 42. Dimensions, as of early 2005, were 152.4m x 21.2m (18.0m on the waterline), with a full load displacement of 7,350 tons. The 48-cell Sylver A50 vertical missile launcher forward of the bridge is to carry sixteen long range Aster-30 missiles and thirty-two short-range Aster-15s (unlike the US Mk 41 considered as an alternative, this version of Sylver cannot accommodate cruise missiles). Aster-30 was developed specially to meet the Royal Navy's Local Area Missile System (LAMS) requirement, for a system capable of screening other ships (the French and Italian navies use only the shorter-range Aster-15 in their 'Horizon' class frigates). At least in the first ships, the gun is a 4.5in Mk 8 taken from discarded Type 42s. Other armament is two 30mm DS-30B remote-controlled guns (with provision for two Phalanx Block IA) and two fixed tubes for lightweight Stingray torpedoes (which may not initially be installed). The ship is arranged so that two eight-cell Mk 41 vertical

(continued opposite)

The major lesson of the Falklands War, that the Royal Navy still had a global role, and that it needed its own sea-based aircraft for that mission, was certainly taken to heart. Instead of being forced to concentrate on a late Cold War mission, *ie* ASW, the Royal Navy retained its general-purpose character, which has proven increasingly important over the last two decades. The general-purpose orientation is the main reason the navy was not been slashed massively once the end of the Cold War made the large-scale ASW mission obsolescent. However, individual ships cost more and more, and the overall share of the British budget spent on defence is shrinking. The authorised number of escorts has now fallen from Nott's fifty to thirty-five and then to twenty-five or even fewer. Some of this is to free funds for the two new carriers. On the other hand, individual capability is rising, quite dramatically in the case of Type 45. The logic of the high-low mix may well return to create a new class below the destroyer/frigate category, yet filling some of the roles of past destroyers and frigates. However, a fleet limited to one very powerful task force cannot fulfil all national or alliance requirements.

In the 1980s the Royal Navy hoped that its next air-defence ship would emerge from an international programme, NFR 90, to produce a NATO Frigate. The NATO navies had invested heavily in new frigates in the 1960s, so by the late 1980s replacements would be necessary. Like other international pro-

grammes, this one moved very slowly. A project group was formed in December 1979, and a prefeasibility study began in 1981. By that time the US Navy was much interested in convincing other NATO navies to adopt modern anti-aircraft systems somewhat analogous to the US Aegis (SPY-1). The key feature was intermittent command guidance of the anti-aircraft missiles, based on a tactical picture maintained by a Multi-Function Array Radar (MFAR). The system would keep more or less continuous track of multiple targets and of the missiles sent to engage them. Individual missiles could be commanded to approach different targets at much the same time (the radar was, in effect, time-shared). Guidance had to be intermittent to allow time-sharing of a limited number of uplinks. Systems might differ as to how the missiles would be guided into their targets once they got close enough. The US Navy preferred semi-active guidance, an illuminator being switched on only at the last moment (thus the illuminators could be time-shared), while the French-led PAAMS consortium adopted active missile seekers instead (no illuminators to time-share). At least in theory, the NATO programme was driven by the perceived obsolescence of the existing NATO Sea Sparrow missile system in the face of modern Soviet missiles such as the low-flying SS-N-22 (Moskit) and the steeply-diving AS-4 (Kh-22). The eight participants (Canada, the Netherlands, Germany, France, Spain, the United Kingdom, Italy and the United States) formed a joint venture. The target price for the NATO frigate was $500 million in FY89 terms.

The programme envisaged a common hull and combat system architecture within which each participating country could insert its favoured radars, combat-direction system, and missiles. Thus the national elements, which would not be common within the programme, would also be the most expensive ones. Adopting identical or nearly-identical hulls would save very little. The programme therefore collapsed. Britain was the first country to withdraw from the project definition phase, followed by France and Italy at the Baseline Review stage. The remaining five countries terminated the project on 18 January 1990. From the US point of view, the programme had been quite successful, since it started national programmes to produce exactly the sort of systems which NATO navies so badly needed. Thus its products included the Dutch-German APAR, the British Samson, and the Italian EMPAR radars, the French PAAMs and the NATO ESSMS missile systems.

For the Royal Navy, the key national elements of the system were the Samson radar and the distributed command system first developed for the Type 23 frigate. It is not clear to what extent there was interest in developing a British missile to exploit these elements. Britain joined France and Italy in Project Horizon, which used the French-developed PAAMS missile system (the Aster missile). After considerable debate over the character of the ship, the Royal Navy withdrew from the project on 21 April 1999 in favor of building its own

destroyer, Type 45 (*Daring*). This was the first class since Type 21 to be designed outside the Royal Navy. BAE won the design contract on 23 November 1999. Initially twelve ships were to have been ordered in four batches, to replace Type 42s on a one-for-one basis, but in January 2001 MoD announced that the first six would be ordered as a single batch (ordered 18 February 2002). In 2005 it was announced that only eight would be built. The ships will, it is hoped, screen the projected pair of large new aircraft carriers.

The Royal Navy chose to adopt its own version of PAAMS in preference to the US Aegis system. Because the missile is modular (it uses a common upper stage or 'dart', but different-size boosters) the Royal Navy was able to gain the area performance it wanted, where the French and Italian navies have emphasised point performance. The British version of the system uses the Samson radar and a BAE-modified version of the Dutch Smart-L three-dimensional long-range search radar. Later units may have a pair of eight-cell Mk 41 vertical launchers for Tomahawk land-attack missiles.

The next surface ship project is, in effect, to replace the remaining Type 23s as they age. Initially the new ship was simply described as the Future Surface Combatant. Post Cold War reality was reflected in plans to build a large ship capable of firing large numbers of cruise missiles. The other major proposed feature was a new trimaran hull under development by the British Defence Experimental Research Agency (DERA). The main advantage of the trimaran was that it offered great stability (for example, for helicopter operations) even in a relatively small hull; advocates claimed that a 2,000-ton ship could enjoy the stability of a 5,000-tonner. The trimaran was also said to offer higher speed (partly because it made for a slimmer hull and partly because the interference pattern of waves created by the main and side hulls) and a degree of protection against underwater hits. Although said to have been a success, the prototype was sold for commercial use early in 2005.

The Future Surface Combatant has progressed in fits and starts. The planned Initial Gate (project initiation) was deferred in 1999 so that the trimaran concept could be explored. A second attempt (November 2001) using a 9,500-ton ship clearly based on Type 45 also failed. The stated reason was that the ship did not correspond to post-September 11 realities (probably mainly budgetary) of the war against terrorism. The project was re-started in September 2003, the goal being to build eighteen ships, the first to enter service as quickly as possible after 2015. The ship was described as the glue connecting the other major Royal Navy elements: the new carrier, the Type 45 destroyer, the amphibious task group and the submarines. That suggested a multi-role destroyer at a lower unit cost than Type 45. The ship was also described in much the terms used forty years earlier for Type 19: it would support Third World policing and humanitarian functions, pro-

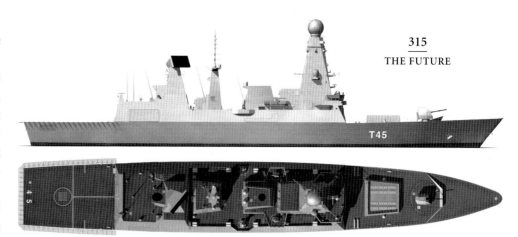

vide limited shore bombardment and small-unit army support (engagement); and it would fill the ASW and ASUW gaps left when Type 23 retired. The ship clearly would need both helicopter and UAV capability. An important new feature might be a more powerful gun.

The two 2001 Baselines which have been published are a 9,500-ton monohull (Baseline 5) and a 9,700-ton trimaran (Baseline 7). The monohull is apparently a stretched Type 45 carrying a heavier gun (155mm) and a larger missile magazine (64-cell vertical launcher) with the same Samson radar, but without the long-range S-1850M radar and with the Rolling Airframe Missile (RAM) for short-range defence. She has the new Type 45 bow sonar (Type 2100) but also the new active towed array (Type 2087), which Type 45 lacks but which is being refitted to Type 23s. The powerplant is the pair of WR-21 regenerative gas turbines planned for Type 45. The trimaran was similarly equipped, but showed podded propellers aft instead of the standard type.

The main problem with these designs was their size and cost, so the developers turned to smaller modular ships which would not carry all desired weapons and systems at all times. A modular monohull, for example, might displace 5,000 tons, a modular trimaran 5,200 tons. These design studies featured waterjet main propulsion. Another possibility considered at this time was a 6,500-ton pentamaran rated at 43kts. There were also initial investigations of future weapons. Examples were a 155mm gun using precision munitions (range 40–80km), the US electromagnetic rail gun (range 200km) and a variety of land-attack missiles.

Any large frigate would likely have been expensive. The situation as of 2004 was not too different from that forty years ago, when the Board had to face the fact that if it wanted numbers of frigates it would have to accept a high-low mix. At that time the result was the Type 19 corvette, which eventually led to the Type 21. This type of solution is probably inescapable. The big Future Surface Combatant was cancelled in 2004, its basic requirements not yet having been settled, in favor of a 'global corvette'. By mid-2005, however, the Future Surface Combatant was back, probably as a two-type programme, the first of which would be modified Type 45s.

launchers can be fitted, to carry Tomahawk cruise missiles. The gun can be replaced by a 155mm weapon (Royal Ordnance has studied modification of the existing Mk 8 mounting to take weapons up to 155mm/52). Alternatively, ships beyond the first three may be armed with the US Mk 45 Mod 4 5in/62 gun. The big radar on the foremast is the Siemens-Plessey Sampson active array; the planar array aft is the BAE-Thales S-1850M. The ship also has a Type 1006 surface-search set, and a Minerva integrated ESM/ECM set. In addition to the radars, the ship has an electro-optical tracker (GSA.8). The sonar is EDO's MFS-7000. There is no towed array or towed body. The ship will have an integrated electric powerplant (primary and auxiliary plants using the same power) driven by two Rolls-Royce/Northrop Grumman WR-21 regenerative gas turbines (33,530 HP each), for a speed of 29kts (two 20 MW motors, equivalent to about 53,650 SHP) and an endurance of over 7,000nm at 18kts. Planned complement is twenty officers and 170 ratings, with a capacity for 235 in all. The plan to order three batches of four ships each was cut in July 2004 to a total of eight, of which six ships had been ordered by the end of 2005. (BAe Systems)

BIBLIOGRAPHY

Published works

Brown, D K, *A Century of Naval Construction* (Conway Maritime Press, London: 1983).

_____ (ed), *The Design and Construction of British Warships 1939-1945* (DNC official history) Vols 1 (*Major Surface Ships*) and 2 (*Submarines, Escorts, and Coastal Forces*) (Conway Maritime Press, London: 1996).

_____, *Nelson to Vanguard: Warship Design and Development 1923-1945* (Chatham, London: 2000).

_____, and Moore, George, *Rebuilding the Royal Navy: Warship Design since 1945* (Chatham, London: 2003).

Canada, Ministry of National Defense, *The Naval Service of Canada: Its Official History* (Ottawa: Ministry of National Defence, 1952; Vol II, *Shore Activities During World War II*, describes the corvette and frigate programmes and the swaps for British ships).

Critchley, Mike, *British Warships Since 1945*, Parts 3 (destroyers) and 4 (frigates) (Maritime Books, Liskeard: n.d. but probably 1984).

Dorman, Andrew M, *Defence Under Thatcher* (Palgrave, London: 2002).

Elliott, Peter, *Allied Escort Ships of World War II: A Complete Survey* (Macdonald and Jane's, London: 1977).

English, John, *The Hunts* (World Ship Society, Kendal: 1987).

_____, *Afridi to Nizam: British Fleet Destroyers 1937-43* (World Ship Society, Kendal: 2001).

Franklin, George, *Britain's Anti-Submarine Capability 1919-1939* (Frank Cass, London: 2003).

Gardiner, Robert (ed), *Conway's All the World's Fighting Ships 1947-1995* (Conway Maritime Press, London: 1995).

Gillett, Ross, *Australian and New Zealand Warships Since 1946* (Child and Associates, Brookvale, Australia: 1988).

Grove, Eric, *Vanguard to Trident* (Naval Institute Press, Annapolis, Md.: 1987).

Hackmann, Willem, *Seek and Strike: Sonar, anti-submarine warfare and the Royal Navy 1914-54* (HMSO, London: 1984).

Hague, Arnold, *Sloops 1926-1946* (World Ship Society, Kendal: 1993).

Hodges, Peter and Friedman, Norman, *Destroyer Weapons of World War II* (Conway Maritime Press, London: 1979).

Jeremy, John, *Cockatoo Island: Sydney's Historic Dockyard* (USNW Press, Sydney: 1998).

Langtree, Christopher, *The Kelly's: British J, K, & N Class Destroyers of World War II* (Chatham Publishing, London: 2002).

Lenton, H T, *British and Empire Warships of the Second World War* (Greenhill, London, and Naval Institute Press, Annapolis: 1998).

Lippiett, John, *Type 21* (Ian Allan, London: 1990).

Macpherson, Ken, *Frigates of the RCN 1943-1974* (Vanwell, St. Catherines, Ontario: 1987).

_____, and Milner, Marc, *Corvettes of the RCN 1939-1945* (Vanwell, St. Catherines, Ontario: 1993).

_____, and Barrie, Ron, *The Ships of Canada's Naval Forces 1910-2002* (3rd Edition: Vanwell, St. Catherines, Ontario: 2002).

Manning, T D, *The British Destroyer* (Putnam, London: 1961).

March, Edgar J, *British Destroyers 1892-1953* (Seeley Service, London: 1966).

Marriott, Leo, *Type 42* (Ian Allan, London: 1985).

_____, *Type 22* (Ian Allan, London: 1986).

_____, *Royal Navy Destroyers Since 1945* (Ian Allan, London: 1989).

_____, *Royal Navy Frigates Since 1945* (Ian Allan, London: 1983 and 1990).

Meyer, C J , *'Leander' Class* (Ian Allan, London: 1984).

Moore, George, *Building for Victory: The Warship Building Programmes of the Royal Navy 1939-1945* (World Ship Society, Kendal: n.d., probably 2003).

Morton, P, *Fire Across the Desert: Woomera and the Anglo-Australian Joint Project 1946-1980* (Australian Government Publishing Service, Canberra: 1989).

Raven, Alan, and Preston, Antony, *Flower Class Corvettes* (Bivouac, London: 1973 [Ensign 3]).

_____, and Roberts, John, *War-Built Destroyers, O to Z Classes* (London: Bivouac, 1976 [Ensign 6]).

Smith, Peter C, *Into the Minefields: British Destroyer Minelaying, 1916-1960* (Pen & Sword Maritime, London: 2005).

Unpublished material consulted at the National Maritime Museum

Designers' notebooks (see footnotes).

David Lyon, *The Thornycroft List*.

Ships' Covers:

(NOTE: most numbers cover multiple volumes)

Destroyers, general cover (376 series).

'Tribal' Class (541).

'J' and 'K' Class (565).

'L' Class (576).

4in 'L' Class (630).

'M' Class (610).

'N' Class (609).

'Hunt' Class (Types I and II: 599; Type III: 633; Type IV: 637).

Intermediates ('O' and 'P' classes) (597).

'Q' and 'R' Classes (625).

'S' through 'U' Classes (642).

'V' through 'Cr' Classes (655).

'Battle' Class (1942 series: 662; 1943 series: 677).

'Battle' Class Radar Picket Conversion (860).

Daring Class (703).

Daring Class Modernisation (890).

'Weapon' Class (697).

Gallant Class (711).

Matapan Conversion (936).

FADE (760).

FADE Conversion (764).

Guided Missile Ships 1945–57 (does not include 'County' Class) (789).

Girdleness, missile test ship (737).

Tiger Class (Cruiser) reconstruction (777).

Frigates, general cover (830, actually 1945 frigate material).

Grimsby Class (501).

Enchantress, Convoy Sloop (516).

Guillemot Class (587).

Black Swan Class (573).

Black Swan Modernisation (796).

'Flower' Class (611).°

'River' Class (645).

Castle Class (686).

Loch Class (687).

Bay Class (714).

Type 14 (827).

Type 15 (808).

Type 16 (809).

Type 18 (810).

Type 42 (gunboat, not missile destroyer) (825).

Type 41/61 (795).

Mermaid (894).

DATA TABLES

Except as noted, these are design data, from Legends. These tables generally do not indicate additional armament and machinery weights for deep load as opposed to standard displacement. Weights in parentheses are as weighed. Data on wartime 'Loch'/'Bay' class frigates are from 1945 tables prepared to assist in the design of the '1945 frigate'. Complement is given, if available, as officers/ratings or officers/senior ratings/junior ratings. It is generally as the ship was designed or completed, not as she was latter operated; numbers could vary considerably. Guns are given as number of mounts (Arabic numeral) × number of barrels (Roman numeral): ammunition figure that follows is rounds per barrel for guns, and total missiles carried for missile systems.

Abbreviations/Contractions Used

ASW	Anti-submarine weapon (excluding depth charges)
DC	Depth charges
DCT	Depth charge throwers
FW	Feed water
LBP	Length between perpendiculars
LOA	Length overall
LWL	Length waterline
MG	Machine guns
RFW	Reserve feed water
Std	Standard
TT	Torpedo tubes
WL	Waterline

I. Destroyers

Class	'Tribal'	'J'/'K'	'L'/'M'	'O'/'P'
LBP (ft-in)	355-6	339-6	345-6	328-9
LWL (ft-in)	364-8	348-0	354-0	350-0
LOA (ft-in)	377-0	356-6	362-6	362-9
Beam (ft-in)	36-6	35-8	36-9	35-0
Depth (ft-in)	28-9/21-6	28-3/20-6	28-3/20-6	28-3/20-6
Draft (ft-in)	11-4	11-9	12-5	11-4½
Standard (tons)	1,882	1,707	1,948	1,570
Deep Load (tons)	2,532	2,326	2,642	2,175
SHP	44,000	40,000	48,000	40,000
Speed Deep Clean (kts)	32.75	31.5	32	32.25
Speed Std Clean (kts)	36.5	36	36	37
Speed Deep Tropics (kts)	—	—	—	30.25
Speed Std Tropics (kts)	—	—	—	35
Oil Fuel (tons)	521	490	568	497
Endurance (nm/kts)	3,950/20	3,700	4,000	3,850
Endurance (CB1815) (nm/kts)	3,700/20	—	—	—
Endurance Tropics (nm/kts)	—	—	—	2,550/15
Endurance (E-in-C) (nm/kts)	—	—	—	—
Complement	190	183	190	176
Weights (tons):				
Hull	910	860	925	839
Machinery	596	525	650	536
Armament	254 (279)	215	260	150
Equipment	94 (174)	90	85	85
Stabilisers etc	—	—	—	—
Ballast	—	—	—	—
Other Loads	—	—	—	—
Generators	—	—	—	—
Protection	—	—	—	—
Margin	—	—	—	—
Std	1,854	1,690 (1,707)	1,920 (1,948)	1,610 (1,570)
Armament	—	—	—	—
Equipment	—	—	—	—
Fuel	524	484	568	500
Diesel Oil	—	6	—	45
Avcat	—	—	—	—

Class	'Tribal'	'J'/'K'	'L'/'M'	'O'/'P'
RFW	—	—	—	—
Deep Load	(2,532)	(2,326)	(2,642)	2,155 (2,175)
Missiles	—	—	—	—
4.7in	4×II (250)	3×II (250)	3×II (250)	4×I (200)
4.5in	—	—	—	—
4in	—	—	—	—
2pdr	1 Mk VIII	1 Mk VIII	1 Mk VIII	1 Mk VIII
40mm	—	—	—	—
20mm	—	—	—	—
MG	2×IV 0.5in	2×IV 0.5in	2×IV 0.5in	2×IV 0.5in
TT	1×IV	2×V	2×IV	2×IV
ASW	—	—	—	—
DCT	—	2	2	4
DC	20	20	42	42

('L' and later class ships with 4.7in were completed with one 4in gun [300 rounds] in place of their after torpedo tubes. In some ships the after tubes were later restored.)

Class	Emergency	'Battle' 1942	'Battle' 1943
LBP (ft-in)	339-6	355-0	355-0
LWL (ft-in)	348-0	364-0	364-0
LOA (ft-in)	356-6	379-0	379-0
Beam (ft-in)	35-8	40-3	40-6
Depth (ft-in)	28-3/20-6	30-3/22-0	30-3/22-0
Draft (ft-in)	12-3	12-11(mean)	15-6 (deep)
Standard (tons)	1,734	2,322	2,380
Deep Load (tons)	2,465	3,153	3,400
SHP	40,000	50,000	50,000
Speed Deep Clean (kts)	31.25	31.25	30.0
Speed Std Clean (kts)	36.5	35.75	—
Speed Deep Tropics (kts)	30.25	29.25	29.0 (temperate, 6 months out of dock)
Speed Std Tropics (kts)	35	34.5	—
Oil Fuel	615	699 (actual: 754)	598 (actual: 743 tons)
Endurance (nm/kts)	4,600	4,400 (actual: 2,600/20, 6 months temperate, 6 months out of dock, post-war)	2,820/20 (temperate, out of dock)
Endurance (CB1815) (nm/kts)	—	—	—

Class	Emergency	'Battle' 1942	'Battle' 1943
Endurance Temperate (nm/kts)	—	—	—
Endurance Tropics (nm/kts)	2,550	2,830	
Endurance (E-in-C) (nm/kts)	—	—	—
Complement	176	17/270	23/290
Weights (tons):			
Hull	890	1,135 (1,157)	1,274
Machinery	530	655 (685)	743
Armament	150	360 (367)	435
Equipment	80	105 (178)	241
Stabilisers etc	—	30	—
Ballast	—	—	—
Other Loads	—	—	—
Generators	—	—	—
Protection	—	30 (21)	—
Margin	—	—	—
Std	1,650 (1,734)	2,315 (2,408)	2,719
Armament	—	—	—
Equipment	—	—	—
Fuel	615	699 (actual, without stabilisers: 37 tons diesel oil; some ships 675 oil, 33 tons diesel oil)	598 (actual: 703 tons oil, 40 tons diesel oil)
Diesel Oil	—	—	—
Avcat	—	—	—
RFW	45	46	43
Deep Load	2,310 (2,465)	(3,153)	3,360 (3,418)
Missiles	—	—	—
4.7in	4 or	—	—
4.5in	4 Mk V	2×II Mk IV	2×II Mk IV, 1 Mk V
4in	—	1	—
2pdr	1 Mk VIII or	—	—
40mm	1 Mk V	4×II	3×II, 2×I
20mm	6×I	2×II, 2×I	—
MG	—	—	—
TT	2×IV	2×IV	2×V
ASW	—	—	1 Squid
DCT	4	4	—
DC	70	60	—

('Battle' 1943 Legend weights are from Lenton, *British and Empire Warships*; no official Legend was found in DNC records examined.)

Class	'Weapon'	*Daring*	'G'
LBP (ft-in)	341-6	366-0	341-6
LWL (ft-in)	350-0	375-0	350-0
LOA (ft-in)	365-0	390-0	365-0
Beam (ft-in)	38-0	43-0	39-6
Depth (ft-in)	28-9/20-9	30-9/22-6	28-9/20-9
Draft (ft-in)	8-2 (fwd)(std) 11-0 (aft)(std) 11-2½ (fwd) (deep) 13-0 (aft)	10-0 (fwd)(std) 11-0 (aft)(std) 12-0 (fwd)(deep) 13-0 (aft)(deep)	12-1¼
Standard (tons)	1,965	2,610	2,000
Deep Load (tons)	2,702	3,352	2,745
SHP	40,000	54,000	40,000
Speed Deep Clean (kts)	30	31.0	29.75
Speed Std Clean (kts)	34	34.75 (design)	33.75
Speed Deep Tropics (kts)	—	29.0 (temperate, 6 months out of dock)	—
Speed Std Tropics (kts)	—	—	—
Oil Fuel (tons)	620	590 (actual: 581)	630
Endurance (nm/kts)	5,000/20	4,400/20	5,000
Endurance (CB1815) (nm/kts)	—	—	—

Class	'Weapon'	*Daring*	'G'
Endurance Temperate (nm/kts)	—	—	—
Endurance Tropics (nm/kts)	—	2,200	—
Endurance (E-in-C)	—	—	—
Complement	—	—	—
Weights (tons):			
Hull	1,038	1,307	1,021
Machinery	540	700	570
Armament	241	408	292
Equipment	103	139	104
Stabilisers etc	—	—	—
Ballast	—	—	—
Other Loads	—	—	—
Generators	30	40	—
Protection	—	30	—
Margin	13	26	—
Std	1,965	2,610	2,000
Armament	17	24	19
Equipment	61	95	57
Fuel	620	590 (actual: 534 oil, 47 diesel oil)	630
Diesel Oil	—	—	—
Avcat	—	—	—
RFW	39	43	39
Deep Load	2,702	3,352	2,745
Missiles	—	—	—
4.7in	—	—	—
4.5in	—	3×II Mk VI (300)	2×II Mk VI
4in	2×II (300)	—	—
2pdr	—	—	—
40mm	2×II, 2×I (1,200)	3×II (1,200)	2×II
20mm	—	—	2×II
MG	—	—	—
TT	2×IV	2×V	2×V
ASW	2 Squid	1 Squid (30)	—
DCT	—	—	4
DC	—	—	50

(Note: 'Weapon' data corrected to 1952, as modified with four 4in forward and Squid aft. *Daring* data also corrected to 1952.)

Class	'Hunt' I	'Hunt' II	'Hunt' III
LBP (ft-in)	264-2½	264-2½	264-2½
LWL (ft-in)	272-0	272-0	272-0
LOA (ft-in)	280-0	280-0	280-0
Beam (ft-in)	29-0	31-6	31-6
Depth (ft-in)	17-2	17-2	17-2
Draft (ft-in)	10-9 deep	—	—
Standard (tons)	1,000	1,050	1,050
Deep Load (tons)	1,314	1,412	1,412
SHP	19,000	19,000	19,000
Speed Deep Clean (kts)	26	25.5	25.5
Speed Std Clean (kts)	27.5	27	27
Speed Deep Tropics (kts)	—	—	—
Speed Std Tropics (kts)	—	—	—
Oil Fuel (tons)	243	277	279
Endurance (nm/kts)	2,300/—	2,560/—	2,560/—
Endurance (CB1815) (nm/kts)	—	—	—
Endurance Temperate (nm/kts)	—	—	—
Endurance Tropics (nm/kts)	—	—	—
Endurance (E-in-C) (nm/kts)	—	1,500/—	1,500/—

Class	'Hunt' I	'Hunt' II	'Hunt' III
Complement	146	164	168
Weights (tons):			
Hull	513 (452)	577 (595)	585
Machinery	290 (285)	295 (295)	295
Armament	90 (87)	112 (136)	100
Equipment	57 (83)	66 (111)	70
Stabilisers	—	—	—
Ballast	50 (52)	30	30
Other Loads	—	—	—
Generators	—	—	—
Protection	—	—	—
Margin	(10)	—	—
Std	1,000 (917)	1,050 (1,137)	1,050
Armament	18	24	17
Equipment	34	45	45
Fuel	243 (248)	277	279
Diesel Oil	—	—	—
Avcat	—	—	—
RFW	19 (16)	16	21
Deep Load	1,314 (1,233)	1,412 (1,430)	1,412
Missiles	—	—	—
4.7in	—	—	—
4.5in	—	—	—
4in	2×II (250)	3×II (250)	2×II (250)
2pdr	1 Mk VIII	1 Mk VIII	1 Mk VII I
	(1,020 design)	(1,800)	(1,800)
40mm	—	—	—
20mm	—	—	—
MG	—	—	—
TT	—	—	1×II
ASW	—	—	—
DCT	2	2	—
DC	40	110	—

(Weights in parentheses in 'Hunts' I and II are from Lenton, *British and Empire Warships*. 'Hunt' I weights are presumably design figures, as they include a Board Margin. The weights given for the 'Hunts' were listed in 1945 to support estimates for the 1945 frigate. Ballast weights given for 'Hunts' II and III are as fitted.)

Class	'Hunt' IV (Thornycroft Design T1306)
LBP (ft-in)	276-0
LWL (ft-in)	283-0
LOA (ft-in)	296-0
Beam (ft-in)	33-4 (at WL; at upper deck 34-0)
Depth (ft-in)	16-3
Draft (ft-in)	10-0 deep
Standard (tons)	1,170
Deep Load (tons)	1,589
SHP	19,000
Speed Deep Clean (kts)	25
Speed Std Clean (kts)	27
Speed Deep Tropics (kts)	—
Speed Std Tropics (kts)	—
Oil Fuel (tons)	286
Endurance (nm/kts)	2,350/20
Endurance (CB1815) (nm/kts)	—
Endurance Temperate (nm/kts)	—
Endurance Tropics (nm/kts)	—
Endurance (E-in-C)	—
Complement	170
Weights (tons):	
Hull	480 (655)
Machinery	260 (305)
Armament	114½ (154)
Equipment	63 (95)
Stabilisers	—
Ballast	—
Other Loads	—
Generators	—
Protection	—
Margin	—
Std	920 (1,209)
Armament	—
Equipment	—
Fuel	278 (286)
Diesel Oil	—
Avcat	—
RFW	23 (20)
Deep Load	1,231 (1,515)
Missiles	—
4.7in	—
4.5in	—
4in	3×II (250)
2pdr	1 Mk VIII
40mm	—
20mm	2×I
MG	—
TT	1×III
ASW	—
DCT	—
DC	50

('Hunt' IV deep load includes 10 tons characterised as 'unforeseen' in the Thornycroft design T1306 weight breakdown as given in David Lyon, 'The Thornycroft List'. No equipment weight is given; 63 tons is the load listed under Standard Displacement. In this category 2½ tons is deducted as 'unforeseen'. Figures in parentheses, from Lenton, *British and Empire Warships*, are presumably actual weights, and suggest considerable changes from the Thornycroft design.)

Class	'County'	Bristol	Type 42 Batch I
	(Estimates for *Kent, London*)		
LBP (ft-in)	—	—	—
LWL (ft-in)	505-0	490-0	392-0
LOA (ft-in)	520-6	507-0	412-0
Beam (ft-in)	54-0	55-0	47-0
Depth (ft-in)	—	—	—
Draft (ft-in)	15.55 (std)	16-7 deep	13-10 (keel)
	16.16 (deep)	23 over sonar dome	19-0 (screws)
Standard (tons)	5,268 (5225)	6,300	3,500
Deep Load (tons)	6,076 (6,210)	7,100	4,100
SHP	60,000	74,000	50,000 (full) 9,700 (cruise)
Speed Deep Clean (kts)	31.5	30	29
Speed Std Clean (kts)	30.5 (deep temperate 6 months out of dock)	—	—
Speed Deep Tropics (kts)	—	—	—
Speed Std Tropics (kts)	—	—	—
Oil Fuel (tons)	780	—	600
Endurance (nm/kts)	4,500/15 (clean temperate)	5,000/18	4,100/18
Endurance (CB1815) (nm/kts)	—	—	—
Endurance Temperate (nm/kts)	3,500/20 (3,450/20 when 6 months out of dock)	—	—
Endurance Tropics (nm/kts)	—	—	—
Endurance (E-in-C)	—	—	—
Complement	37/432	30/367	24/229
Weights (tons):			
Hull	2,700 (2,891) (3,055)	3,630	2,202.2
Machinery	1,065 (1,258) (875)	1,040	631.4
Armament	835 (764) (790)	536	311.4
Equipment	478 (505) (430)	429	392.2
Stabilisers etc	—	—	—
Ballast	—	—	—
Other Loads (Std)	190	—	—
Generators	—	—	—

Class	'County'	Bristol	Type 42 Batch I
Protection	—	—	3.6
Margin	—	—	—
Std	5,268	5,635	3,540.8
Armament	—	—	—
Equipment	—	—	—
Fuel	392	1,071	619.4
Diesel Oil	327	—	—
Avcat	61	—	—
RFW	28	34	—
Deep Load	6,076	6,750	4,160.2
Missiles	Seaslug (39)	Sea Dart (38)	Sea Dart (22)
	Seacat (36)	Ikara	
4.7in	—	—	—
4.5in	2 × II Mk VI	1 Mk 8	1 Mk 8
4in	—	—	—
2pdr	—	—	—
40mm	—	—	—
20mm	—	—	2
MG	—	—	—
TT	—	—	2 × III
ASW	—	—	—
DCT	—	—	—
DC	—	—	—

(Data in first set of parentheses for 'County' class are weighed weights, probably for *Devonshire*, May 1962. The second set of parentheses is the Legend data as presented to the Board in January 1957, for a ship carrying eighteen Seaslugs and two twin L70 Bofors plus a Limbo, but without a large helicopter; her deep displacement was given as 6,000 tons. Her fuel load was 780 tons and RFW was 20 tons; Board Margin was 50 tons. *Bristol* data are from her June 1965 Book of Calculations. The equipment figure includes 28 tons of aircraft equipment. Type 42 data are from the 1978 Book of Calculations for the stretched version. The equipment weight includes 33.4 tons of aircraft equipment.)

Class	Type 42 Batch III	Type 43
LBP (ft-in)	—	—
LWL (ft-in)	—	—
LOA (ft-in)	463-0	573-0
Beam (ft-in)	49-0	59-0
Depth (ft-in)	—	—
Draft (ft-in)	19-0	—
Standard (tons)	—	—
Deep Load (tons)	5,350	approx 6,000
SHP	50,000	68,000
Speed Deep Clean (kts)	31	—
Speed Std Clean (kts)	—	—
Speed Deep Tropics (kts)	—	—
Speed Std Tropics (kts)	—	—
Oil Fuel (tons)	—	—
Endurance (nm/kts)	—	—
Endurance (CB1815) (nm/kts)	—	—
Endurance Temperate (nm/kts)	—	—
Endurance Tropics (nm/kts)	—	—
Endurance (E-in-C)	—	—
Complement	—	—
Weights (tons):		
Hull	2,367	—
Machinery	635	—
Armament	327	—
Equipment	407	—
Stabilisers etc	—	—
Ballast	140	—
Other Loads (Std)	—	—
Generators	—	—
Protection	2	—
Margin	—	—
Std	3,920	—
Armament	—	—
Equipment	—	—
Fuel	620	—
Diesel Oil	—	—
Avcat	—	—

Class	Type 42 Batch III	Type 43
RFW	—	—
Deep Load	4,540	
Missiles	Sea Dart (22)	2 Sea Dart
		4 Sea Wolf
		Exocet (4)
4.7in	—	—
4.5in	1 Mk 8	1 Mk 8
4in	—	—
2pdr	—	—
40mm	—	—
20mm	—	
MG	—	—
TT	—	2 × III
ASW	—	—
DCT	—	—
DC	—	—

(Data for Type 42 Batch III are from the 1978 Book of Calculations. Equipment includes 37 tons of aircraft equipment.)

II. SLOOPS AND FRIGATES

Class	Grimsby	Bittern (1935)	Egret (1936)
LBP (ft-in)	250-0	266-0	276-0
LWL (ft-in)	262-0	276-0	288-6
LOA (ft-in)	266-0	282-0	292-6
Beam (ft-in)	36-0	37-0	37-6
Depth (ft-in)	—	—	—
Draft (ft-in)	6-0 (fwd)(std)	8-7 (fwd)(std)	8-0 (fwd)(std)
	8-2 (aft)	8-5 (aft)	8-10 (aft)
	9-1 (deep)	11-2 (fwd)(deep)	10-8 (fwd)
		10-3½ (aft)	(deep) 10-5 (aft)
Standard (tons)	1,062	1,190	1,242
Deep Load (tons)	1,335	1,605	1,675
SHP	20,000	3,300	3,600
Speed Deep Clean (kts)	16	—	—
Speed Std Clean (kts)	16.5	—	19.5
Speed Deep Tropics (kts)	—	—	—
Speed Std Tropics (kts)	—	—	—
Oil Fuel (tons)	278	386	395
Endurance (nm/kts)	6,000/10	8,450/10	7,500/12
		6,200/15	
Endurance Tropics (nm/kts)	—	—	—
Complement	103	125	188
Weights (tons):			
Hull	685 (633)	680 (711)	737
Machinery	174 (166)	168 (181)	181
Armament	49 (47)	116 (122)	138
Equipment	154 (146)	181 (160)	136
Stabiliser	—	30 (21)	—
Water Ballast	—	—	—
Fresh Water	—	—	—
Margin	—	—	—
Std	1,062 (992)	1,175 (1,195)	1,242
Armament	—	—	—
Equipment	—	—	—
Fuel	278	364	373
Diesel Oil	21	22	22
RFW	—	—	—
Deep Load	1,335	1,605	1,675
Missiles	—	—	—
4.7in	2 (150)	—	—
4.5in	—	—	—
4in	1 × 3in HA	3 × II (250)	4 × II (250)
	Mk III (150)		
2pdr	—	—	—
40mm	—	—	—

Class	Grimsby	Bittern (1935)	Egret (1936)
20mm	—		
MG	8 (2,000)	1×IV 0.5in (2,500)	1×IV 0.5in (2,500), 4 Lewis (2,000)
		4 Lewis (2,500)	
TT	—	—	—
ASW	—	—	—
DCT	—	2	2
DC	4	40	40

Class	Black Swan	Improved Black Swan (1940 Programme)
LBP (ft-in)	283-0	283-0
LWL (ft-in)	295-6	295-6
LOA (ft-in)	299-6	299-6
Beam (ft-in)	37-6	38-6
Depth (ft-in)	—	—
Draft (ft-in)	8-5 fwd (std)	9-1¼ fwd (std)
	8-5 aft	9-5 aft
	10-9 (deep)	11-4 (deep)
Standard (tons)	1,250	1,470
Deep Load (tons)	—	—
SHP	4,300	4,300
Speed Deep Clean (kts)	19	18.75
Speed Std Clean (kts)	19.5	19.5
Speed Deep Tropics (kts)	—	—
Speed Std Tropics (kts)	—	—
Oil Fuel (tons)	415	420
Endurance (nm/kts)	7,500/—	7,000/—
Endurance Tropics (nm/kts)	—	—
Complement	167	210
Weights (tons):		
Hull	715	775
Machinery	190	200
Armament	135	200
Equipment	210	260
Stabiliser	—	35
Water Ballast	—	—
Fresh Water	—	—
Margin	—	—
Std	1,250	1,470
Armament	—	—
Equipment	—	—
Fuel	413	395
Diesel Oil	2	25
RFW	—	—
Deep Load		
Missiles	—	—
4.7in	—	—
4.5in	—	—
4in	3×II (250)	3×II
2pdr	1 Mk VIII (2700)	—
40mm	—	2×II (1,545)
20mm	—	2×II, 2×I (2,700)
MG	4 Lewis (2,000)	—
TT	—	—
ASW	—	—
DCT	2	4
DC	40	110

Class	'River'	'Loch'	'Bay'
LBP (ft-in)	283-0	286-0	286-0
LWL (ft-in)	295-6	297-4	297-4
LOA (ft-in)	301-4	307-4	301-4
Beam (ft-in)	36-6	38-6	36-6
Depth (ft-in)	17-6	—	—
Draft (ft-in)	11-10	12-3½	12-11
Standard (tons)	1,397	1,435	1,592
Deep Load (tons)	1,925	2,260	2,415
SHP	5,500 (IHP)	5,500 (IHP)	5,500 (IHP)
Speed Deep Clean (kts)	17.5	17	17
Speed Std Clean (kts)	20.5	20.25	20.25
Speed Deep Tropics (kts)	—	—	—
Speed Std Tropics (kts)	18.5	19	18.5
Oil Fuel (tons)	441 (647 Long End)	724	724
Endurance (nm/kts)	—	—	—
Endurance Tropics (nm/kts)	3,200/15 (E-in-C)	4,800/15 (E-in-C)	4,800— (E-in-C)
Complement			
Weights (tons):			
Hull	805	811	916
Machinery	385	390	390
Armament	115	134	140
Equipment	92	100	146
Stabiliser	—	—	—
Water Ballast	—	—	—
Fresh Water	—	—	—
Margin	25	36	34
Std	1,397	1,435	1,592
Armament	30	30	30
Equipment	32	35	35
Fuel	441 (647 Long End)	724	724
Diesel Oil	30	29	29
RFW			
Deep Load	1,925	2,260	2,415
Missiles	—	—	—
4.7in	—	—	—
4.5in	—	—	—
4in	2 Mk XXIII (250)	1 Mk III** (280)	2×II (324)
2pdr	—	1 Mk VIII	—
40mm	—	2 Mk V	—
20mm	2 Mk VIIA (positions for 6 more)	2 twin Mk V	6 Mk VIIIA
MG	—	—	—
TT	—	—	—
ASW	1 Hedgehog	2 Squid (25)	Hedgehog
DCT	4	2	4
DC	150	15	60

Class	Type 12	Rothesay	Leander
LBP (ft-in)	—	—	—
LWL (ft-in)	360-0	360-0	360-0
LOA (ft-in)	370-0	370-0	370-0
Beam (ft-in)	41-0	41-0	41-0
Depth (ft-in)	—	—	—
Draft (ft-in)	11-0 (fwd) deep	12-5(fwd) deep	12-1½ (fwd) deep
	13-0 (aft)(13-6)	13-6(aft)	14-6½ (aft)
Standard (tons)	1,814	2,162	(2,305)
Deep Load (tons)	2,425	2,611	2,700 (2,880)
SHP	30,000	30,000	30,000
Speed Deep Clean (kts)	29.0	29.5	
Speed Std Clean (kts)	28.0 (deep temperate, 6 months out of dock)	28.0 (deep temperate, 6 months out of dock)	—
Speed Deep Tropics (kts)	27	—	28
Speed Std Tropics (kts)	—	—	—
Oil Fuel (tons)	394	427	480

Class	Type 12	*Rothesay*	*Leander*
Endurance (nm/kts)	—	—	—
Endurance Tropics (nm/kts)	4,500/12	4,500/12	4,500/12
Complement	20/225 (12/195)	13/199	16/242
Weights (tons):			
Hull	1,088	—	1,240
Machinery	437	—	440
Armament	245	—	285
Equipment	240	—	255
Stabiliser	—	—	—
Water Ballast	187	—	—
Fresh Water	—	—	—
Margin	—	—	—
Std	1,814	—	—
Armament	—	—	—
Equipment	—	—	—
Fuel	394 (314)	350	480 (376)
Diesel Oil	21 (77)	77	(74)
RFW	18	—	20
Deep Load	2,425	—	2,700
Missiles	—	—	2 Seacat (25)
4.7in	—	—	—
4.5in	1×II Mk VI (375)	1×II Mk VI (375)	1×II Mk VI (375)
4in	—	—	—
2pdr	—	—	—
40mm	1 STAAG Mk 3 (1,500)	1×I	—
20mm	—	—	—
MG	—	—	—
TT	12	12	—
ASW	2 Limbo (120)	2 Limbo	1 Limbo (60)
DCT	—	—	—
DC	—	—	—

(Type 12 is from Legend of December 1950. *Leander* data are from Legend dated 22 December 1959. The ship as completed was somewhat different, and did not have the four torpedo tubes of the Legend version. Many *Leander*s had two single 40mm rather than two Seacats as listed.)

Class	Type 41	Type 61	*Mermaid*
LBP (ft-in)	—	—	—
LWL (ft-in)	330-0	330-0	330-0
LOA (ft-in)	339-10½	339-10½	344-11
Beam (ft-in)	40-0	40-0	40-0
Depth (ft-in)	—	—	—
Draft (ft-in)	9-10 (fwd) deep 11-10 (aft)	9-6½ (fwd) deep 11-6½ (aft)	10-11 (fwd) 12-11 (aft)
Standard (tons)	2,223	2,192	2,240
Deep Load (tons)	2,523 (*Leopard*: 2,015/2,284 tons)	2,332 (*Salisbury*: 2,090/2,330 tons)	2,500
SHP	15,200 (temperate) 14,400 (tropics)	15,200 (temperate) 14,400 (tropics)	15,000
Speed Deep Clean (kts)	23.75 23.0 (temperate, 6 months out of dock)	23.75	24
Speed Std Clean (kts)	—	—	24.75
Speed Deep Tropics (kts)	23	23	23.5
Speed Std Tropics (kts)	—	—	—
Oil Fuel (tons)	230 (231)	240 (252)	260
Endurance (nm/kts)	5,700/12 (temperate, 6 months out of dock)	6,150/12 (temperate, 6 months out of dock)	4,000/15
Endurance Tropics (nm/kts)	4,500/15	4,500/15	—
Complement	15/206 (actual: 9/213)	18/199 (actual: 14/224)	—
Weights (tons):			
Hull	1,171 (930)	1,149 (918)	1,280
Machinery	230 (465)	240 (465)	570

Class	Type 41	Type 61	*Mermaid*
Armament	572 (300)	552 (215)	170
Equipment	168 (224)	157 (224)	220
Stabiliser	—	—	—
Water Ballast	—	—	—
Fresh Water	55	65	—
Margin			
Std	2,223 (1,835)	2,192 (1,738)	—
Armament	—	—	—
Equipment	—	—	—
Fuel	—	—	—
Diesel Oil	230	240	260
RFW	—	—	—
Deep Load	2,523 (2,185)	2,332 (2,110)	2,500
Missiles	—	—	—
4.7in	—	—	—
4.5in	2×II (300)	2×I (300)	—
4in	—	—	1×II
2pdr	—	—	—
40mm	2×I (1,200)	—	4×I
20mm	—	—	—
MG	—	—	—
TT	—	—	—
ASW	1 Squid (30)	1 Squid (30)	1 Squid
DCT	—	—	—
DC	—	—	—

(Type 41 data in parentheses are from the Legend approved in June 1950. Drafts are Legend data. Type 61 are weighed weights for *Salisbury*, with August 1950 Legend data in parentheses. Drafts are Legend data. *Mermaid* data are from original Legend, and do not reflect ship as finally built. Type 61 weights are from Book of Calculations.)

Class	Type 14	Type 81	Type 21
LBP (ft-in)	—	—	—
LWL (ft-in)	300-0	350-0	360-0
LOA (ft-in)	314-0	360-0	384-0
Beam (ft-in)	33-0	42-6	41-8
Depth (ft-in)	—	—	—
Draft (ft-in)	8-10½ fwd (deep) 10-11½ aft	10-9¾ fwd (deep) 13-5½ aft	19-6 (screws)
Standard (tons)	1,016	2,300 (as built)	2,750
Deep Load (tons)	1,320	2,700	3,250
SHP	15,000	20,000	50,000 9,700 cruise
Speed Deep Clean (kts)	—	25	30
Speed Std Clean (kts)	—	—	—
Speed Deep Tropics (kts)	—	24	—
Speed Std Tropics (kts)	25	—	—
Oil Fuel (tons)	259	—	—
Endurance (nm/kts)	—	—	—
Endurance Tropics (nm/kts)	4,500/12	5,000/12	4,000/17
Complement	9/156	17/257	13/162
Weights (tons):			
Hull	579	1,295	—
Machinery	236	375	—
Armament	95	270	—
Equipment	120	235	—
Stabiliser	—	—	—
Water Ballast	—	—	—
Fresh Water	—	—	—
Margin	22	54	—
Std	1,016	2,229	2,700
Armament	—	—	—
Equipment	—	—	—
Fuel	259	428	—
Diesel Oil	—	—	—
RFW	9	12	—

Class	Type 14	Type 81	Type 21
Deep Load	1,320	2,700	3,250
Missiles	—	2 Seacat	1 Seacat
			Exocet (4)
4.7in	—	—	—
4.5in	—	2×I (320)	1 Mk 8
4in	—	—	—
2pdr	—	—	—
40mm	3×I	—	—
20mm	—	—	4
MG	—	—	—
TT	4	—	2×III
ASW	2 Limbo (60)	1 Limbo (60)	—
DCT	—	—	—
DC	—	—	—

Class	Type 22	Type 22 Batch II	Type 23
DCT	—	—	—
DC	—	—	—

(Type 22 figures are from the November 1972 Book of Calculations. They are in metric tonnes. The figure for ballast is water in the sonar trunks. Note that Type 23 was designed in metric units, so those are used and translated. Later units have SM-1C Speys with considerably higher output, probably over 25,000 SHP on a continuous basis. Speed is 30kts.)

(Type 14 Legend shows 1,488 rounds for each of two single 40mm guns forward but only 288 rounds for the gun aft. Type 81 weights from Legend in which the ship has eight fixed torpedo tubes but no helicopter and has one twin 40mm gun with 1,500 rpg instead of Seacat.)

Class	Type 22	Type 22 Batch II	Type 23
LBP (ft-in)	—	—	—
LWL (ft-in)	410-0	445-0	—
LOA (ft-in)	430-0	485-7	133m
			(436.2ft)
Beam (ft-in)	48-6	48-4	15m
			(49.2ft)
Depth (ft-in)	—	—	—
Draft (ft-in)	19-11	21-0	5.5m (18ft over screws)
Standard (tons)	4,000	4,200	3,500
Deep Load (tons)	4,500	4,800	3,850
SHP	50,000 (full)	50,000 (full)	34,000 (gas turbines)
	9,700 (cruise)	9,700 (cruise)	7,000 (diesels)
Speed Deep Clean (kts)	30	30	28
Speed Std Clean (kts)	—		
Speed Deep Tropics (kts)	—	—	—
Speed Std Tropics (kts)	—	—	—
Oil Fuel (tons)	—	—	—
Endurance (nm/kts)	4,500/18	4,500/18	7,800/15
Endurance Tropics (nm/kts)	—	—	—
Complement	235	265	—
Weights (tons):			
Hull	2,131	—	—
Machinery	670	—	—
Armament	215	—	—
Equipment	329	—	—
Stabiliser	—	—	—
Water Ballast	33	—	—
Fresh Water	—	—	—
Margin			
Std	3,378	—	—
Armament	—	—	—
Equipment	—	—	—
Fuel	564	900	—
Diesel Oil	—	—	—
RFW	8	—	—
Deep Load	3,950		
Missiles	2 Seawolf (30)	2 Seawolf (30)	Seawolf (32)
	Exocet (4)	Exocet (4)	Harpoon (8)
4.7in	—	—	—
4.5in	—	—	1 Mk 8
4in	—	—	—
2pdr	—	—	—
40mm	2×I	2×I	—
20mm	2×I	2×I	—
MG	—	—	—
TT	2×III	2×III	2×III
ASW	—	—	—

Additional Frigate Weight Breakdowns

	Type 21	Type 22 Batch 3	Type 23
Hull	972.3	1,685.1	972.3
Propulsion	354.9	321.2	354.9
Electrical	215.3	195.1	215.3
Control/Comms	108.0	322.3	108.0
Auxiliary Systems	233.9	410.4	233.9
Outfit/Furnishings	283.5	387.8	283.5
Armament	47.1	50 (Est)	47.1
Variable Load	886.8	1,200 (Est)	886.8
Deep Load	3,101.8	4,571.9	3,101.8

(Note: Weights are all in metric tonnes rather than Imperial (2,204 lbs vs 2,240 lbs each). Note that, in contrast to weights in other tables, all weights are empty weights, eg armament does not include weapons. Variable loads include all consumables, not merely fuel. Type 21 weights are from the CONDES Ship description file dated October 1991. Type 22 weights are from the Type 22 Batch 3 stability assessment dated December 1999. Type 23 weights are from the Book of Calculations dated 7 August 1983. Published (hence unofficial) fuel weights: Type 22 Batch 3: 700 tons plus 80 tons of aviation fuel; Type 23, 800 tons.)

III. Corvettes

Class	Kittiwake	Guillemot	'Flower' (as in 1942)
LBP (ft-in)	234-0	224-0	190-0
LWL (ft-in)	240-0	230-0	196-0
LOA (ft-in)	243-2	233-3	205-0
Beam (ft-in)	26-6	25-6	33-0
Depth (ft-in)	—	—	17-6
Draft (ft-in)	6-3 fwd (std)	7-3½ (fwd) (std)	11-5½ fwd
	6-2 aft (std)	7-7½ (aft)	15-8 aft
	8-5 fwd (deep)	8-8½ (fwd) (deep)	
	7-2 aft	8-6 (aft)	
Standard (tons)	531	585	940
Deep Load (tons)	725	725	1,220
SHP	3,600	3,600	2,750 (IHP)
Speed Deep Clean (kts)	20	20	16
Speed Std Clean (kts)	—	—	—
Speed Deep Tropics (kts)	—	—	—
Speed Std Tropics (kts)	—	—	—
Oil Fuel (tons)	173	131	233
Endurance (nm/kts)	4,000/12	3,000/11	4,596/12
Endurance Tropics (nm/kts)	—	—	—
Complement	60	—	—
Weights (tons):			
Hull	330 (290)	331	491
Machinery	178 (152)	164.5	375
Armament	25 (25)	24.5	17
Equipment	54 (64)	65.1	57
Margin	20	—	—
Std	531	585.1	940
Armament	—	—	—
Equipment	—	—	—
Fuel	173	131	233
Diesel Oil	—	—	—
FW	—	—	40
RFW	—	—	13.5
Deep Load	—	725	—
Missiles	—	—	—

Class	*Kittiwake*	*Guillemot*	'Flower' (as in 1942)
4.7in	—	—	—
4.5in	—		
4in	1 (100)	1 (250)	1
2pdr	—	—	1
40mm	—	—	—
20mm	—	—	—
MG	8 Lewis (2,000)	8 Lewis (2,500)	2 Lewis
TT	—	—	—
ASW	—	—	—
DCT	2	2	4
DC	40	40	60

Class	'Castle'
LBP (ft-in)	225-0
LWL (ft-in)	234-0
LOA (ft-in)	252-0
Beam (ft-in)	36-6
Depth (ft-in)	17-6
Draft (ft-in)	7-3 fwd (std)
	12-7 aft
	13-5 (deep)
	—
Standard (tons)	1,010
Deep Load (tons)	—
SHP	2,750
Speed Deep Clean (kts)	16.5
Speed Std Clean (kts)	17
Speed Deep Tropics (kts)	—
Speed Std Tropics (kts)	—

Class	'Castle'
Oil Fuel (tons)	—
Endurance (nm/kts)	6,200/15
Endurance Tropics (nm/kts)	—
Complement	—
Weights (tons):	
Hull	663
Machinery	230
Armament	56
Equipment	111
Margin	
Std	1,060
Armament	—
Equipment	—
Fuel	480
Diesel Oil	—
FW	—
RFW	40
Deep Load	1,580
Missiles	—
4.7in	—
4.5in	—
4in	1
2pdr	—
40mm	—
20mm	2 × II, 2 × I
MG	—
TT	—
ASW	1 Squid (81)
DCT	2
DC	15

The Type II 'Hunt' class escort destroyer *Tetcott* as completed.

Pre-war and wartime ships are listed in order of ordering date and then alphabetically. Post-war ships are given in hull number order, where available (see below). Commonwealth ships *to British designs* are included for completeness; note that Second World War pennant numbers for all such ships formed a single series.

The first column of dates gives date of laying-down with date of launch below it. The second column of dates gives the date of completion and recommissioning if rebuilt or taken from reserve. The third column is dates of paying-off, which generally means the date of reduction into reserve (it may also be the date the ship arrived in port for reduction to reserve). For ships which spent substantial time in reserve before being reactivated, a second completion date (recommissioning date) and a second (final) date of reduction to reserve are given.

Destroyers marked with double asterisks (**) were leaders, specially equipped as such.

Pennant numbers are given for each ship. The initial letter (flag superior) sometimes changed over time. Pennant numbers were generally painted on ships' sides, but not on leaders. Once Britain joined NATO, destroyers were all given D pennant numbers and frigates all had F numbers. In some cases an initial 1 was added when the new pennants were assigned, *eg* L48 became F148.

Post-war ships were assigned US-style hull numbers, such as DLG 01, but only for record purposes; the numbers painted on ships' sides were always the pennant numbers. The hull numbers are given in the Fates column. Hull number prefixes were: DLG for the 'County' class missile destroyers, DDG for Type 42s, FSA for Type 12 and successors, FSB for Type 14, FA for Type 41, FD for Type 61 (direction) and FGP for Type 81.

Fates

Note: wartime fates of ships under British operational control during the Second World War (FFN, ORP, RAN, RCN, RHN, RIN, RNN, RNLN, RNZN) are given.

break	Expended as breakwater (Canadian frigates)
BU	Broken up (date arrived for scrapping)
C	Collision (peacetime)
Canc	Cancelled
CTL	Constructive Total Loss (write-off, but not sunk); cause in parentheses as in war Losses
disc/reacq	discarded and reacquired (refers to Canadian 'River' class frigates).
FFN	Free French Navy (wartime, under Charles de Gaulle's Free French)
FN	French Navy (post-war)
FRGN	Federal Republic of Germany Navy
HTS	Harbour training ship
IN	Indian Navy
LD	Laid down
Merch	Merchant ship (sold as)
mod	modernised
ORP	Polish Navy Ship
PLAN	People's Liberation Army Navy: Chinese (Communist) Navy
PN	Pakistan Navy (initially Royal Pakistan Navy)
RAN	Royal Australian Navy
RCN	Royal Canadian Navy
RDN	Royal Danish Navy
Reb	Rebuilt/rebuild
Recomm	Recommissioned
Ren	Renamed
Ret	Returned (applies to Lend-Lease ships)
RHN	Royal Hellenic (Greek) Navy
RIN	Royal Indian Navy
RNLN	Royal Netherlands Navy
RNN	Royal Norwegian Navy
RNVN	Royal Navy Volunteer Reserve
RNZN	Royal New Zealand Navy
ROCN	Republic of China (Nationalist) Navy
SAN	South African Navy
STT	Ship Target Trials
S(T)	Sunk as target
Str	Stricken
Susp	Suspended
USN	US Navy
WL	War Loss
WL(B)	War Loss (Bombing)
WL(C)	War Loss (Collision)
WL(G)	War Loss (Gunfire)
WL(M)	War Loss (Mining)
WL(T)	War Loss (Torpedo)

Yards

Ailsa	Ailsa (Troon)
Austin	Austin (Sunderland)
Barclay	Barclay Curle (Whiteinch)
Blyth	Blyth Dry Dock
Brown	G Brown (Greenock)
Burntisland	Burntisland Shipbuilding
Burrard	Burrard Dry Dock (North Vancouver, Canada)
Caledon	Caledon (Dundee)
Cammell	Cammell Laird (Birkenhead)
CanV	Canadian Vickers (Montreal)
Chatham	Chatham Dockyard
Cockatoo	Cockatoo Dockyard (Sydney)
Cook	Cook, Welton & Gemmell (Beverley)
Collingwood	Collingwood Shipyards, Canada
Crown	Crown (Sunderland)
Davie	Davie Shipbuilding (Lauzon, Canada)
Denny	Denny (Dumbarton)
Devonport	Devonport Dockyard
Evans	Evans Deakin (Brisbane, Australia)
Fairfield	Fairfield (Govan)
Ferguson	Ferguson (Port Glasgow)
Fleming	Fleming & Ferguson (Paisley)
Furness	Furness (Haverton)
G Brown	G Brown (Greenock)
Grangemouth	Grangemouth Dockyard
H&W	Harland & Wolff (Belfast)
Halifax	Halifax Shipyards (Canada)
Hall	Hall (Aberdeen)
Hall Russell	Hall Russell (Aberdeen)
Hawthorn	Hawthorn Leslie (Hebburn)
Hill	C Hill (Bristol)
Inglis	Inglis (Pointhouse)
John Brown	John Brown (Clydebank)
Kingston	Kingston Shipbuilding (Canada)
Lewis	Lewis (Aberdeen)
Marine	Marine Industries (Sorel, Canada)
Mazagon	Mazagon Dockyard, Bombay (India)
Melbourne	Melbourne Harbour Trust (Williamstown, Australia)
Midland	Midland Shipbuilding (Canada)
Morton	Morton (Quebec)
Morts	Morts Dock (Sydney, Australia)
NSW	NSW State Dockyard (Newcastle, Australia)
Philip	Philip (Dartmouth)
Pickersgill	W. Pickersgill (Sunderland)
Port Arthur	Port Arthur Shipbuilding (Canada)
Robb	Robb (Leith)
St. John	St John Shipbuilding (Canada)
Scotts	Scotts (Greenock)
Simons	Simons (Renfrew)
Smiths	Smiths Dock (Middlesborough)
Stephen	Stephen (Linthouse)
Swan Hunter	Swan Hunter and Richardson (Wallsend)
Thornycroft	Thornycroft (Woolston)
VA Barrow	Vickers Armstrong (Barrow)
VA Tyne	Vickers Armstrong (Tyne)
VA Walker	Vickers Armstrong (Walker)
VT	Vosper Thornycroft
Victoria	Victoria Machinery Depot (Canada)
Walkers	Walkers Drydock (Maryborough, Australia)
White	White (Cowes)
Williamstown	Williamstown Dockyard (Australia)
Yarrow	Yarrow (Scotstoun)
YarrowC	Yarrow (Esquimault, Canada)

I. DESTROYERS
(List is in order of ordering dates)

'Tribal' Class (no leaders in this class)
Flag superior was variously L, F, and G.
Ordered 10.3.36

No./Builder	Name				Notes
F07	*Afridi*	9.6.36	3.5.38		WL(B) 3.5.40.
VA Walker		8.6.37			
F03	*Cossack*	9.6.36	7.6.38		WL(T) 27.10.41.
VA Walker		8.6.37			
F20	*Gurkha*	6.7.36	21.10.38		WL(B) 9.4.40.
Fairfield		7.7.37			
F24	*Maori*	6.7.36	2.1.39		WL(B) 12.2.42; salved and scuttled 15.7.45.
Fairfield		2.9.37			
F31	*Mohawk*	16.7.36	7.9.38		WL(T) 16.4.41.
Thornycroft		5.10.37			
F36	*Nubian*	10.8.36	6.12.38	12.45	BU 25.6.49. Allocated to STT 21.2.48.
Thornycroft		21.12.37			
F18	*Zulu*	10.8.36	7.9.38		WL(B) 14.9.42.
Stephen		23.9.37			

Ordered 19.6.36

No./Builder	Name				Notes
F51	*Ashanti*	23.11.36	21.12.38	21.8.45	BU 12.4.49. Allocated to STT 21.2.48.
Denny		5.11.37			
F67	*Bedouin*	13.1.37	15.3.39		WL(G, T) 15.6.42.
Denny		21.12.37			
F75	*Eskimo*	5.8.36	30.12.38		BU 27.6.49. Depot ship allocated for 12.45, STT 21.2.48.
VA Walker		3.9.37			
F 59	*Mashona*	5.8.36	28.3.39		WL(B) 28.5.41.
VA Walker		3.9.37			
F26	*Matabele*	1.10.36	25.1.39		WL(T) 17.1.42.
Scotts		6.10.37			
F21	*Punjabi*	1.10.36	29.3.39		WL(C) 1.5.42.
Scotts		18.12.37			
F82	*Sikh*	24.9.36	12.10.38		WL(G) 14.9.42.
Stephen		17.12.37			
F33	*Somali*	26.8.36	12.12.38		WL(T) 24.9.42.
Swan Hunter		24.8.37			
F43	*Tartar*	26.8.36	10.3.39	31.1.46	BU 22.12.48. Accomm. ship Devonport, then reserve, str 2.3.48.
Swan Hunter		21.10.37			

RAN Ships
Ordered 24.1.39

No./Builder	Name				Notes
I.30	*Arunta*	15.11.39	30.4.42	14.6.56	Sold for BU but foundered 13.2.69. Mod 7.50–5.53.
Cockatoo		30.11.40			
I.41	*Warramunga*	10.2.40	23.11.42	7.12.59	BU 63. Mod 11.52–5.10.54.
Cockatoo		7.2.42			

Ordered 5.4.40

No./Builder	Name				Notes
I.91	*Bataan*	30.11.40	25.5.45	18.10.54	Ordered as *Kurnai*, renamed 1944, sold for BU 1958. Mod cancelled 1957.
Cockatoo		15.1.44			

RCN Ships
Ordered 4.41

No./Builder	Name				Notes
G07	*Athabaskan*	31.10.40	15.2.43		WL(T) 29.4.44.
VA Walker		15.11.41			
G24	*Huron*	15.7.41	28.7.43	30.4.63	BU 20.8.65. Refit 1949– 50 (4in guns, Squid) while in reserve then mod 1951–2.
VA Walker		25.6.42			
G63	*Haida*	29.9.41	18.9.43	11.10.63	Museum 1964 (Toronto). Mod 7.50–3.52.
VA Walker		25.8.42			
G89	*Iroquois*	19.9.40	10.12.42	24.10.62	BU 9.66. Refit 1947–9, mod 15.6.50–21.10.51.
VA Walker		23.9.41			

Ordered 4.41

No./Builder	Name				Notes
R10	*Micmac*	20.5.42	14.9.45	24.10.62	BU 6.10.64. First RCN ship with Squid. Mod 30.11.51–14.8.53.
Halifax		18.9.43			
R96	*Nootka*	20.5.42	9.8.46	6.2.64	BU 6.10.64. Refit (4in guns, Squid) 15.8.49–8.50, mod (adds 3in/50) cpl 15.12.54.
Halifax		2.4.44			

Ordered 4.42

No./Builder	Name				Notes
R79	*Athabaskan*	15.5.44	12.1.48	21.4.66	BU 7.69. Refit for training 15.9.49–13.3.50 (2 Squids replaced Y mount); mod 12.53–10.54
Halifax		4.5.46			
R04	*Cayuga*	7.10.43	20.10.47	27.2.64	BU 6.10.64. Refit with 2 Squid added, 12.48–9.49; mod 7.52–3.53.
Halifax		28.7.45			

'J'/'K' Class
Ordered 25.3.37

No./Builder	Name				Notes
F00	*Jervis***	26.8.37	12.5.39	28.8.46	BU 3.1.49.
Hawthorn		9.9.38			
F22	*Jackal*	24.9.37	31.3.39		WL(B) 12.5.42.
John Brown		25.10.38			
F34	*Jaguar*	25.11.37	12.9.39		WL(T) 26.3.42.
Denny		22.11.38			
F46	*Juno*	5.10.37	25.8.39		Ordered as *Jamaica*, ren 38, WL(B) 21.5.41
Fairfield		8.12.38			
F51	*Janus*	29.9.37	5.8.39		WL(T) 23.1.44.
Swan Hunter		20.11.38			
F61	*Javelin*	11.10.37	10.6.39	31.7.46	Ordered as *Kashmir*, BU 11.49. Allocated to STT 21.2.48.
John Brown		21.12.38			
F72	*Jersey*	20.9.37	28.4.39		WL(M) 5.4.41.
White		26.9.38			
F84	*Jupiter*	28.9.37	25.6.39		WL(T) 28.2.42.
Yarrow		27.10.38			
—	*Jubilant*				Canc 12.36
F01	*Kelly***	26.8.37	23.8.39		WL(B) 23.5.41.
Hawthorn		25.10.38			
F28	*Kandahar*	18.1.38	10.10.39		WL(M) 20.12.41.
Denny		21.3.39			
F12	*Kashmir*	18.11.37	26.10.39		Ex-*Javelin*. WL(B) 23.5.41.
Thornycroft		4.4.39			
F37	*Kelvin*	5.10.37	27.11.39	21.9.45	BU 6.4.49. Allocated for STT 21.2.48.
Fairfield		19.1.39			
F45	*Khartoum*	27.10.37	6.11.39		CTL explosion 23.6.40.
Swan Hunter		6.2.39			
F50	*Kimberley*	17.1.38	21.2.40	21.9.45	BU 6.49. Allocated for STT but replaced by ex-German *Nonsuch*.
Thornycroft		1.6.39			
F64	*Kingston*	6.10.37	14.9.39		CTL(B) 11.4.42, used as as blockship Malta.
White		9.1.39			
F91	*Kipling*	26.10.37	22.12.39		WL(B) 11.5.42.
Yarrow		19.1.39			

'L'/'M' Class
Ordered 31.3.38

No./Builder	Name				Notes
F99	*Laforey***	1.3.39	26.8.41		WL(T) 30.3.44.
Yarrow		15.2.41			
F63	*Ghurka*	18.10.38	18.2.41		Ex-*Larne*; WL(T) 17.1.42.
Cammell		8.7.40			
F87	*Lance*	1.3.39	13.5.41		CTL after bombing 5,9.4.42, and BU 6.44.
Yarrow		28.11.40			
F74	*Legion*	1.11.38	19.12.40		CTL(B) 23.3.42, again bombed and BU *in situ* 1944.
Hawthorn		26.12.39			
F55	*Lightning*	15.11.38	28.5.41		WL(T) 12.3.43.
Hawthorn		22.4.40			
F40	*Lively*	20.12.38	20.7.41		WL(B) 11.5.42.
Cammell		28.1.40			
F32	*Lookout*	23.11.38	30.1.42	18.12.45	BU 29.2.48
Scotts		4.11.40			
F15	*Loyal*	23.11.38	31.10.42		CTL(M) 12.10.44, BU 5.8.48.
Scotts		8.10.41			

Ordered 7.7.39

No./Builder	Name				Notes
G14	*Milne***	24.1.40	6.8.42	16.8.46	Turkish *Alp Arslan* 1959.
Scotts		31.12.41			
G23	*Mahratta*	18.8.41	8.8.43		Ex-*Marksman*; WL(T) 25.2.44.
Scotts		28.7.42			
G35	*Marne*	23.10.39	2.12.41	29.6.46	Turkish *Maresal Fevsi Cakmak* 1959. Type 62 conversion canc 15.5.54.
VA Walker		30.10.40			
G44	*Martin*	23.10.39	4.4.42		WL(T) 10.11.42.
VA Walker		12.12.40			
G52	*Matchless*	14.9.40	26.2.42	25.6.46	Turkish *Kilic Ali Pasha* 1959.
Stephen		4.9.41			
G73	*Meteor*	14.9.40	12.8.42	31.1.46	Turkish *Piyale Pasha* 1959. Planned 2 Type 62 conversion canc 15.5.54. substituted 11.3.54.
Stephen		3.11.41			
G86	*Musketeer*	7.12.39	18.9.42	16.8.46	BU 3.9.55.
Fairfield		2.12.41			
G90	*Myrmidon*	7.12.39	5.12.42		ORP *Orkan*, WL(T) 8.10.43.
Fairfield		2.3.42			

'N' Class
Ordered 15.4.39

No./Builder	Name				Notes
G97	*Napier***	26.7.39	11.12.40	7.3.46	RAN 1940–5, BU 17.1.56. Provisionally chosen for Type 16 conversion 6.2.51, but not carried out.
Fairfield		22.5.40			
G25	*Nepal*	9.9.39	29.5.42	20.3.51	Ex-*Norseman*. Minesweeping trials ship 12.46–10.47, then trials ship at Rosyth 1947–50 and flag duties. Planned Type 15 reb canc 5.54. BU 16.1.56.
Thornycroft		4.12.41			

G65 *Nerissa* — 26.7.39 12.2.41 — 28.9.46 — ORP *Piorun* 1940–6. Ren *Noble* on
John Brown — 7.5.40 — return to RN, as previous name had been allocated to an *Algerine* class sweeper. Planned Type 16 reb not undertaken. BU 2.12.55.

G02 *Nestor* — 26.7.39 12.2.41 — RAN 1941, WL(B) 15.6.42.
Fairfield — 9.7.40

G38 *Nizam* — 27.7.39 19.12.40 — 11.1.46 — RAN 1941–5. Planned Type 16 reb
not
John Brown — 4.7.40 — undertaken. BU 16.11.55.

G84 *Noble* — 10.7.39 20.2.42 — RNLN *Van Galen* 1942
Denny — 17.4.41

G16 *Nonpareil* — 22.5.40 30.10.42 — RNLN *Tjerk Hiddes* 1942.
Denny — 25.6.41

G49 *Norman* — 27.7.39 29.9.41 — 6.3.46 — RAN 1941–5. BU 1.4.58. Planned
Thornycroft — 30.10.40 — Type 16 reb not undertaken. Was considered for use as RNVR drillship 18.2.56.

'O'/'P' Classes (1st/2nd War Emergency Flotillas)
Ordered 4.9.39

G17 *Onslow*** — 1.7.40 8.10.41 — 10.47 — Ex-*Packenham*, PN *Tippu Sultan* 1949.
John Brown — 31.3.41 — Had been in reserve 1946–7, 8.47 submarine trials and A/S experimental ship Portsmouth. 1945 was HQ ship for scuttling of U-boats (Operation Deadlight).

G39 *Obdurate* — 25.4.40 3.9.42 — 2.48 — BU 30.11.64.
Denny — 19.2.42

G48 *Obedient* — 22.5.40 30.10.42 — 8.47 — BU 19.10.62.
Denny — 30.4.42

G29 *Offa* — 15.1.40 20.9.41 — 2.48 — PN *Tariq* 1949.
Fairfield — 11.3.41

G04 *Onslaught* — 14.1.41 19.6.42 — Ex-*Pathfinder*, PN *Tughril* 1951. Submarine tender at Portsmouth 1.46, submarine target ship 1947.
Fairfield — 9.10.41

G80 *Opportune* — 28.3.40 14.8.42 — 9.53 — BU 25.11.55. Submarine target ship 1.46. 2.50 Air Target Ship.
Thornycroft — 21.2.42

G66 *Oribi* — 15.1.40 5.7.41 — Ex-*Observer*; Turkish *Gayret* 1946.
Fairfield — 14.1.41

G98 *Orwell* — 20.5.40 17.10.42 — 1947 — BU 28.6.65. Reb as Type 16 frigate 1952, reserve 1960. F98 as frigate, D198 as destroyer.
Thornycroft — 2.4.42

Ordered 2.10.39

G06 *Packenham*** — 6.2.40 4.2.42 — Ex-*Onslow*, WL(T) 16.4.43.
Hawthorn — 28.1.41

G69 *Paladin* — 22.7.40 12.12.41 — 1948 — Reb as Type 16, 1952–4, in reserve 3.54, recomm 1.58, reserve 4.61, BU25.10.62. F169 as frigate, D69 as destroyer.
John Brown — 11.6.41

G41 *Panther* — 15.7.40 12.12.41 — WL(B) 9.10.43.
Fairfield — 28.5.41

G30 *Partridge* — 3.6.40 22.2.42 — WL(T) 18.12.42.
Fairfield — 5.8.41

G10 *Pathfinder* — 5.3.40 13.4.42 — Ex-*Onslaught*; bombed 11.2.45, air target, BU 17.11.48.
Hawthorn — 10.4.41

G77 *Penn* — 26.12.39 10.2.42 — 2.48 — STT 4.49, BU 31.1.50.
VA Walker — 12.2.41

G56 *Petard* — 26.12.39 15.6.42 — 9.46 — Ex-*Persistent*, ren 41, BU 6.67. Reb as Type 16 5.53–12.55; reserve 11.56–1960, then reserve again 4.61, active 9.61–6.62 F26 as frigate, D56 as destroyer. Minelayer as Type 16.
VA Walker — 27.3.41

G93 *Porcupine* — 26.12.39 31.8.42 — CTL(T) 9.12.42, towed in halves (*Pork* and *Pine*) to UK, BU 5.47.
VA Walker — 10.6.41

'Q'/'R' Classes (3rd and 4th Emergency Flotillas)
Ordered 2.4.40

G70 *Queenborough* — 6.11.40 10.12.42 — RAN 1945.
Swan Hunter — 16.1.42

G11 *Quadrant* — 24.9.40 28.11.41 — RAN 1945.
Hawthorn — 28.2.42

G45 *Quail* — 30.9.40 7.1.43 — Mined 15.11.43, foundered in tow 18.6.44.
Hawthorn — 1.6.42

G62 *Quality* — 10.10.40 7.9.42 — RAN 1942
Swan Hunter — 6.10.41

G78 *Quentin* — 25.9.40 15.4.42 — WL(T) 2.12.42.
White — 5.11.41

G81 *Quiberon* — 14.10.40 22.7.42 — RAN 1942.
White — 31.1.42

G92 *Quickmatch* — 6.2.41 30.9.42 — RAN 1942.
White — 11.4.42

G09 *Quilliam*** — 19.8.40 22.10.41 — RNLN *Banckert*.
Hawthorn — 29.11.42 1945

H09 *Rotherham*** — 10.4.41 27.8.42 — 1.46 — IN *Rajput* 1949.
John Brown — 21.3.42

H11 *Racehorse* — 25.6.41 30.10.42 — 1.46 — BU 8.12.49. STT 10.49.
John Brown — 1.6.42

H15 *Raider* — 16.4.41 16.11.42 — 1.46 — IN *Rana* 1949. Had been commissioned as tender to aircraft carriers in Mediterranean 6.5.46–8.47.
Cammell — 1.4.42

H32 *Rapid* — 16.6.41 20.2.43 — 1.6.54 — S(T) 3.9.81. Air Training Target Ship and Attendant Destroyer to Carriers 11.4.46. Reb as Type 15 6.51–10.53, reserve from 1954. F138 as Type 15.
Cammell — 16.7.42

H41 *Redoubt* — 19.6.41 1.10.42 — 1.46 — IN *Ranjit* 1949.
John Brown — 2.5.42

H85 *Relentless* — 20.6.41 30.11.42 — 1.46 — Reb as Type 15, 1949–51. Reserve 10.56, recomm 27.6.64, on disposal list 8.65. BU 6.71. F185 as Type 15.
John Brown — 15.7.42

H92 *Rocket* — 14.3.41 4.8.43 — 5.49 — BU 3.67. Reb as prototype Type 15 frigate 7.49–1951, comm 18.5.51; reserve 11.56. Recomm 28.10.60–11.5.62. F193 as Type 15; had been D192. Pennant also given as F191.
Scotts — 28.10.42

H95 *Roebuck* — 19.6.41 10.6.43 — 1.46 — BU 8.8.68. Active 6.49. Reb as Type 15 frigate 1951–3. Reserve 7.56, then refitted as TS to replace *Carron* 11.57. Operational as frigate 5.60–10.62. Underwater explosion trials 1968. F195 as Type 15.
Scotts — 10.12.42

'S'/'T'/'U'/'V' Classes (5th, 6th, 7th, 8th Emergency Flotillas)
Ordered 9.1.41

G12 *Saumarez*** — 8.9.41 1.7.43 — BU 10.50. Mined in Corfu Channel 22.10.46; CTL. BU approved 2.48.
Hawthorn — 20.11.42

G20 *Savage* — 7.12.41 8.6.43 — 2.48 — BU 11.4.62. Propeller silencing trials 1950. Mod 7.54, but not recomm.
Hawthorn — 24.9.42

G07 *Scorpion* — 19.6.41 11.5.43 — Ex-*Sentinel*, RNLN *Kortenaer* 1945.
Cammell — 26.8.42

G01 *Scourge* — 26.6.41 14.7.43 — RNLN *Evertsen* 1945.
Cammell — 8.12.43

G94 *Serapis* — 14.8.41 23.12.43 — RNLN *Piet Hein* 1945.
Scotts — 25.3.43

G03 *Shark* — 5.11.41 11.3.44 — RNN *Svenner* 1944, WL(T) 6.6.44.
Scotts — 1.6.43

G26 *Success* — 25.2.42 6.9.43 — RNN *Stord* 1944.
White — 3.4.43

G46 *Swift* — 12.6.42 6.12.43 — WL(M) 24.6.44.
White — 15.6.43

Ordered 14.3.41

R00 *Troubridge*** — 10.11.41 8.3.43 — 15.8.49 — BU 5.5.70. Reb as Type 15 frigate 1955–7, recomm 12.57, reserve 27.3.69. F09 as Type 15 (D40 as destroyer).
John Brown — 23.9.42

R23 *Teazer* — 20.10.41 13.9.43 — 1946 — BU 7.8.65. Reb as Type 16 frigate, 1953–4. Decomm to disposal list 9.61. F23 as frigate.
Cammell — 7.1.43

R45 *Tenacious* — 3.12.41 30.10.43 — 1946 — BU 29.6.65. Recomm as submarine target ship 11.49, reb as Type 16 frigate 1.51–52, reserve 8.54. F44 as frigate, D45 as destroyer.
Cammell — 24.3.43

R89 *Termagant* — 25.11.41 18.10.43 — 1946 — BU 5.11.65. Reb as Type 16 frigate 1952–3, submarine target ship 16.5.53, reserve 8.57, recomm for trials 10.58, in reserve 1960. F189 as frigate, D189 as destroyer.
Denny — 22.3.43

R33 *Terpsichore* — 25.11.41 20.1.44 — 1946 — BU 17.5.66. Reb as Type 16 frigate 1953–4, reserve 1955. F19 as frigate, D33 as destroyer.
Denny — 17.6.43

R11 *Tumult* — 16.11.41 2.4.43 — 1946 — BU 25.20.65. Reb as Type 16 frigate 1953–4, reserve 12.57. F121 as frigate, D121 as destroyer.
John Brown — 9.11.42

R56 *Tuscan* — 6.9.41 11.3.43 — 1946 — BU 25.6.66. Reb as Type 16 frigate 5.52–9.53 but remained in reserve. F156 as frigate (D156 as destroyer).
Swan Hunter — 28.3.42

No.	Name / Builder	Laid / Launched	Completed	Sold	Fate
R67	*Tyrian*	15.10.41	8.4.43	1946	BU 9.3.65. Reb as Type 16 frigate 1951–2. Recomm 8.52, reserve 11.56. F67 as frigate.
	Swan Hunter	27.7.42			
Ordered 12.6.41					
R97	*Grenville***	1.11.41	27.5.43	1946	BU 1983. Active by 1951, reb as Type 15 frigate 1953–4. Used for helicopter trials 1957. Reserve 1960. Refit as ASWE (radar) trials ship 1969. Recomm 10.69. Tested SCOT satellite terminal 1970. Sale list 1974.
	Swan Hunter	12.10.42			
R83	*Ulster*	12.11.41	30.6.43	12.52	BU 2.11.80. Reb as Type 15 frigate 1954–6. Navigation training ship 1967, Plymouth harbour TS 1977. F83 as Type 15.
	Swan Hunter	9.11.42			
R69	*Ulysses*	14.3.42	23.12.43	1946	BU 1969. Recomm 12.51–1953, reb as Type 15 frigate 1954–5, 1960 TS, reserve 12.60. F17 as Type 15 (D169 as destroyer).
	Cammell	22.4.43			
R53	*Undaunted*	8.9.42	3.3.44	3.46	S(T) 11.78. Reb as Type 15 frigate 1951–4. Helicopter trials (Wasp) 1959. Paid off for disposal 3.73. F53 as Type 15.
	Cammell	19.7.43			
R42	*Undine*	18.3.42	23.12.43	5.46	BU 15.11.65. Reb as Type 15 frigate 1952–4. Reserve 1960. F141 as Type 15 (D141 as destroyer).
	Thornycroft	1.6.43			
R08	*Urania*	18.6.42	18.1.44	1947	BU 2.2.71. Reb as Type 15 frigate 1953–5, reserve 1959. F08 as Type 15.
	VA Barrow	19.5.43			
R99	*Urchin*	28.3.42	24.9.43	1947	BU 6.8.67. Reb as Type 15 frigate 1952–4, reserve 11.56, then refitted as TS 12.57 (commissioned 8.59), reserve 1964. Stern used to repair *Ulster* 1966. F196 as Type 15 (D199 as destroyer).
	VA Barrow	8.3.43			
R22	*Ursa*	2.5.42	1.3.44	1946	BU 25.9.67. Reb as Type 15 frigate 1952–4, reserve 11.56, then refitted as TS 28.10.66. F200 as Type 15 (D222 as destroyer).
	Thornycroft	22.7.43			
Ordered 1.9.41					
R08	*Hardy***	14.5.42	14.8.43		WL(T) 30.1.44.
	John Brown	18.3.43			
R17	*Valentine*	8.10.42	28.2.44		RCN *Algonquin* 1944.
	John Brown	2.9.43			
R50	*Venus***	12.1.42	28.8.43	1949	BU 20.12.72. Reb as Type 15 frigate 1952–4, refitted as TS 1955, reserve 1964. Target ship for Sea Dart in SSM role 10.69. F50 as Type 15.
	Fairfield	23.2.43			
R28	*Verulam*	26.1.42	10.12.43	1949	BU 23.10.72. Reb as Type 15 frigate 1951–2, reserve 9.54. ASWE (radar) trials ship 1958–61, UWDE trials ship 1961, paid off for disposal 21.12.70. F29 as Type 15 (D28 as destroyer).
	Fairfield	22.4.43			
R93	*Vigilant*	31.1.42	10.9.43	1947	BU 4.6.65. Reb as Type 15 frigate 1951–2; training frigate 11.56, to reserve 11.63. F93 as Type 15.
	Swan Hunter	22.12.42			
R75	*Virago*	16.2.42	5.11.43	1949	BU 4.6.65. Reb as Type 15 frigate 1952–3. Reserve 1955, active 1962–3. F76 as Type 15 (D75 as destroyer).
	Swan Hunter	4.2.43			
R64	*Vixen*	31.10.42	5.3.44		RCN *Sioux* 1944.
	White	14.9.43			
R41	*Volage*	31.12.42	26.5.44	1949	BU 1972. Mined in Corfu Channel 22.10.46. Reb as Type 15 frigate 1952–4, reserve 1956; harbour TS Portsmouth (Royal Marines) 1964–6, then laid up. F41 as Type 15.
	White	15.12.43			

'W'/'Z' Classes (9th and 10th Emergency Flotillas)

No.	Name / Builder	Laid / Launched	Completed	Sold	Fate
Ordered 3.12.41					
R01	*Kempenfelt***	24.6.42	25.10.43	1946	Ex-*Valentine*; Yugoslav *Kotor* 1956. Was in Portsmouth Reserve 1946–7, then in Simonstown (South Africa) Reserve 1948–53, then back in Portsmouth before sale.
	John Brown	8.5.43			
R98	*Wager*	20.11.42	14.4.44	1.46	Yugoslav *Pula* 1956. Simonstown Reserve 1948–50.
	John Brown	1.11.43			
R59	*Wakeful***	3.6.42	17.2.44		Ex-*Zebra*. BU 5.7.71. Active post-war. Reb as Type 15 frigate 4.51–53. Began conversion to radar/nav TS 1957, replaced *Starling* 11.59, experimental satellite terminal fitted 1966–7. Left Portsmouth for de-equipping 26.2.70. F159 as Type 15; D159 as destroyer.
	Fairfield	30.6.43			
R78	*Wessex*	20.10.42	11.5.44	1.46	SAN *Jan Van Riebeck* 1950. Left Devonport Reserve for Simonstown Reserve 1948.
	Fairfield	2.9.43			
R37	*Whelp*	1.5.42	26.4.44	1946	SAN *Simon van der Stel* 1952. Had left for Simonstown Reserve 28.11.47.
	Hawthorn	3.6.43			
R87	*Whirlwind*	31.7.42	20.7.44		S(T) 29.10.74. Reb as Type 15 1952–3. Approved for BU 1966. F187 as Type 15; D187 as destroyer.
	Hawthorn	30.8.43			
R72	*Wizard*	14.9.42	30.3.44	1966	BU 7.3.67. Active post-war. Reb as Type 15 frigate 1953–4. F72 as Type 15.
	VA Barrow	29.9.43			
R48	*Wrangler*	23.9.42	14.7.44		SAN *Vrystaat* 1956. Reb as Type 15 1951–3, in Mediterranean 1953–5. Not decomm post-war. F157 as Type 15 (D158 as destroyer).
	VA Barrow	30.12.43			
Ordered 10.2.42					
R06	*Myngs***	27.5.42	23.6.44	9.54	Egyptian *El Qaher* 1955. Had been placed in reserve pending frigate conversion.
	VA Walker	31.5.43			
R66	*Zambesi*	21.12.42	18.7.44	1946	BU 12.2.59.
	Cammell	21.11.43	1950	1954	
R39	*Zealous*	5.5.43	9.10.44	1947	Israeli *Elath* 1955, first warship sunk by ship-to-ship missiles, 21.10.67.
	Cammell	28.2.44			
R81	*Zebra*	14.5.42	13.10.44	1947	BU 12.2.59. For projected Type 15 conversion rem main armament 1954–5, but discarded instead.
	Denny	8.3.44			
R95	*Zenith*	19.5.42	22.12.44	1947	Egyptian *El Fateh* 1955.
	Denny	5.6.44			
R19	*Zephyr***	13.7.42	6.9.44		BU 2.7.58.
	VA Walker	15.7.43			
R02	*Zest*	21.7.42	20.7.44	9.52	BU 18.8.70. Had been in reserve 2.47–7.47. Reb as Type 15 frigate 2.54–3.56, reserve 7.68. F102 as Type 15 (D02 as destroyer).
	Thornycroft	14.10.43			
R54	*Zodiac*	7.11.42	23.10.44	1947	Israeli *Yaffa* 1955.
	Thornycroft	11.3.44	1949	1952	

'Ca' Class (11th Emergency Flotilla)

No.	Name / Builder	Laid / Launched	Completed	Sold	Fate
Ordered 16.2.42					
R01	*Caprice*	28.9.42	5.4.44	1946	Ex-*Swallow*; BU 5.10.73. Mod 1959, res 2.69, TS for Engineer Officers 1971–3, paid off for disposal 3.73.
	Yarrow	16.9.43			
R62	*Cassandra*	30.1.43	28.7.44	1946	BU 28.4.67 Mod in 1959, paid off 1.66.
	Yarrow	29.11.43			
Ordered 24.3.42					
R07	*Caesar***	3.4.43	5.10.44	1946	BU 6.1.67. Mod in 1957–60, paid off 6.65.
	John Brown	14.2.44			
R85	*Cambrian*	14.8.42	17.7.44	1946	BU 3.9.71. Mod ?, comm 1.63 (after refit?), paid off 12.68.
	Scotts	10.12.43			
R30	*Carron*	26.11.42	6.11.44	1946	BU 4.4.67. Mod completed 8.55 as TS (deckhouse vice B gun), rest of armament off 10.57. 7.60 Navigation TS. Paid off 3.63.
	Scotts	28.3.44			
R15	*Cavendish***	19.5.43	13.12.44	1946	BU 7.8.67. Mod 1956, laid up 1964.
	John Brown	12.4.44			
Ordered Cammell 24.3.42, re-ordered 11.42					
R25	*Carysfort*	12.5.43	20.2.45	1946	BU 13.11.70. Mod 1956, paid off 2.69.
	White	25.7.44			
R71	*Cavalier*	28.2.43	22.11.44	1946	Museum ship 1977. Mod 1957, res 7.63, refit 8.64–1.66 when Seacat fitted, paid off 7.72.
	White	7.4.44			

'Ch', 'Co', 'Cr' Classes (12th through 14th Emergency Flotillas)

No.	Name / Builder	Laid / Launched	Completed	Sold	Fate
Ordered 24.7.42					
R52	*Chaplet*	29.4.43	24.8.45	1951	BU 6.11.65. Refitted as minelayer as 9.61 mod.
	Thornycroft	18.7.44	1953		
R29	*Charity*	9.7.43	19.11.45	1955	PN *Shah Jehan*, 1959.
	Thornycroft	30.11.44			
R61	*Chequers***	4.5.43	28.9.45	11.64	BU 23.7.66.
	Scotts	30.10.44			
R90	*Cheviot*	27.4.43	11.12.45		BU 22.10.62. Became TS Rosyth 3.60.
	Stephen**	2.5.44			
R51	*Chevron*	18.3.43	23.8.45	1957	BU 12.69.
	Stephen	23.2.44			

[Destroyers, continued]

Pennant	Name / Builder	Laid down	Launched	Completed	Other	Notes
R36	*Chieftain*, Scotts	27.6.43	26.2.45	7.3.46		1953 BU 20.3.61. Refitted as minelayer as mod.
	Ordered 30.7.42					
R91	*Childers**, Denny	27.11.43	27.2.45	19.12.45		1951 BU 22.9.63.
R21	*Chivalrous*, Denny	27.11.43	22.6.45	13.5.46		PN *Taimur* 1954.
	Ordered 7.8.42					
R43	*Comus*, Thornycroft	21.8.43	14.3.45	8.7.46		BU 12.11.58. Proposed sale to Peru abandoned.
R63	*Concord*, Thornycroft	18.11.43	14.5.45	20.12.46		1957 Ex-*Corso*; BU 22.10.62. HTS 1957 Rosyth.
	Ordered 12.8.42					
R12	*Contest*, White	1.11.43	16.12.44	9.11.45		1959 BU 2.2.60. Refitted as minelayer as mod.
	Ordered 14.8.42					
R76	*Consort*, Stephen	26.5.43	19.10.44	19.3.46		1957 BU 15.5.61.
	Ordered 12.9.42					
R34	*Cockade*, Yarrow	11.3.43	7.3.44	29.9.45		1958 BU 23.7.64.
R26	*Comet*, Yarrow	14.6.43	22.6.44	6.6.45	1953	1948 BU 23.10.62. Refitted as minelayer. 2.58.
R71	*Constance**, VA Walker	18.3.43	22.8.44	31.12.45		BU 8.3.56.
R57	*Cossack**, VA Walker	18.3.43	10.5.44	4.9.45		12.59 BU 1.3.61.
R68	*Crispin*, White	1.2.44	23.6.45	10.7.46		1954 Ex-*Craccher*; PN *Jahangir* 1958.
R82	*Creole*, White	3.8.44	22.11.45	14.10.46		1953 PN *Alamgir* 1958.
R16	*Crescent**, John Brown	16.9.43	20.7.44	21.9.45		RCN 1945.
R35	*Cromwell*, Scotts	24.11.43	6.8.45	6.9.46		Ex-*Cretan*; RNN *Bergen* 1946.
R46	*Crown*, Scotts	16.1.44	19.12.45	17.4.47		RNN *Oslo* 1946.
R27	*Crozier*, Yarrow	26.10.43	19.9.44	30.11.45		RNN *Trondheim* 1946.
R20	*Crusader**, John Brown	15.11.43	5.10.44	26.11.45		RCN 1945.
R38	*Crystal*, Yarrow	13.1.44	12.2.45	9.2.46		RNN *Stavanger* 1946.

1942 'Battle' Class
Ordered 27.4.42

Pennant	Name / Builder	Laid down	Launched	Completed	Other	Notes
R14	*Armada*, Hawthorn	29.12.42	9.12.43	2.7.45	1949	1947 BU 18.12.65. Paid off spring 1960.
R80	*Barfleur*, Swan Hunter	28.10.42	1.11.43	14.9.44		BU 29.9.66. Paid off 1958.
R32	*Camperdown*, Fairfield	30.10.42	8.2.44	18.6.45	1957	1947 BU 24.9.70. To reserve 4.62.
R55	*Finisterre*, Fairfield	8.12.42	22.6.44	11.9.45		1947 BU 12.6.67. Active by 1953. To reserve 4.62.
R74	*Hogue*, Cammell	6.1.43	1.4.44	24.7.45	1957	1947 BU 1962.
R44	*Lagos*, Cammell	8.4.43	4.8.44	2.11.45	1957	1947 BU 6.67. Paid off about 5.60.
R18	*St. Kitts*, Swan Hunter	8.9.43	4.10.44	21.1.46		1953 BU 19.2.62.
R84	*Saintes*, Hawthorn	8.6.43	19.7.44	27.9.46		BU 1.9.72. To reserve 4.62.
R70	*Solebay*, Hawthorn	3.2.43	22.2.44	11.10.45	5.57	1947 BU 11.8.67; HTS Portsmouth 1962. 7.53 Paid off 4.62.
R77	*Trafalgar*, Swan Hunter	15.2.43	12.1.44	23.7.45	1957	1947 BU 1970. Paid off 5.63.

Ordered 12.8.42

Pennant	Name / Builder	Laid down	Launched	Completed	Other	Notes
R09	*Cadiz*, Fairfield	10.5.43	16.9.44	12.4.46		1953 PN *Khaibar* 1956.
R47	*Gabbard*, Swan Hunter	2.2.44	16.3.45	10.12.46		1953 PN *Badr* 1956.
R24	*Gravelines*, Cammell	10.8.43	30.11.44	14.6.46		BU 4.4.61. In reserve upon completion, but active by 7.49. Major refit abandoned 11.58.
R65	*St. James*, Fairfield	20.5.43	7.6.45	12.7.46		1953 BU 19.3.61. Major refit abandoned 11.58.
R60	*Sluys*, Cammell	24.11.43	28.2.45	30.9.46		1953 Iranian *Artemiz* 1967.
R31	*Vigo*, Fairfield	11.9.43	27.9.45	9.12.46		BU 6.12.64. In reserve upon completion, active 7.49.

1943 'Battle' Class
Ordered 10.3.43

Pennant	Name / Builder	Laid down	Launched	Completed	Other	Notes
I.06	*Agincourt*, Hawthorn	12.12.43	29.1.45	25.6.47		BU 27.10.74. Conversion to radar picket completed 5.62. Reserve 10.66.
I.22	*Aisne*, VA Walker	26.8.43	12.5.45	29.3.47		BU 27.6.70. Conversion to radar picket completed 2.62. Reserve 8.68.
I.17	*Alamein*, Hawthorn	1.3.44	28.5.45	21.5.48	3.50	BU 1.12.64. Returned to service by 5.58.
I.51	*Albuera*, VA Walker	16.9.43	28.8.45	—		Canc 23.10.45 but hull retained; BU 21.11.50.
I.68	*Barrosa*, John Brown	28.12.43	17.1.45	14.2.47	3.50	BU 12.78. Conversion to radar picket completed 4.62. Reserve 12.68.
I.43	*Matapan*, John Brown	11.3.44	30.4.45	5.9.47	1978	BU 8.79. Laid up after trials, converted into sonar test ship 2.71–1973.

Ordered 23.4.43

Pennant	Name / Builder	Laid down	Launched	Completed	Other	Notes
I.88	*Belleisle*, Fairfield	10.11.43	7.2.46	—		Canc 23.10.45, BU 5.46.
I.97	*Corunna*, Swan Hunter	12.4.44	29.5.45	6.6.47		BU 23.11.74. Conv to radar picket completed 2.62. Reserve 4.67.
I.16	*Jutland*, Hawthorn	14.8.44	2.11.45	—		Canc 23.10.45 but retained; hull used for experiments at Rosyth; sold 17.10.57, BU 10.57.
I.53	*Mons*, Hawthorn	29.6.45	—	—		Canc 23.10.45, BU on slip.
I.58	*Namur*, Cammell	29.4.44	12.6.45	—		Canc 23.10.45 but hull retained, BU 2.51.
I.82	*Navarino*, Cammell	22.5.44	21.9.45	—		Canc 23.10.45, BU 4.46.
I.98	*Omdurman*, Fairfield	8.3.44	—	—		Canc 23.10.45 but hull retained, used for experiments at Rosyth, BU 12.57.
I.02	*Oudenarde*, Swan Hunter	12.10.44	12.10.44	—		Canc 23.10.45, BU 29.4.46.
I.10	*Poitiers*, hawthorn	9.2.45	4.1.46	—		Canc 23.10.45, BU on slip.
I.83	*River Plate*, Swan Hunter	11.4.45	—	—		Canc 23.10.45, BU on slip.
I.42	*St. Lucia*, Stephen	19.1.45	—	—		Canc 23.10.45, BU on slip.
I.37	*San Domingo*, Cammell	9.12.44	—	—		Canc 23.10.45, BU on slip.
I.31	*Somme*, Cammell	24.2.45	—	—		Canc 23.10.45, BU on slip.

Ordered 24.4.43

Pennant	Name / Builder	Laid down	Launched	Completed	Other	Notes
I.09	*Dunkirk*, Stephen	19.7.44	27.8.45	27.11.46	3.50	BU 22.11.65. In service by 5.58. Paid off 5.63, last unconverted 1943 'Battle' in service.
I.62	*Jutland*, Stephen	27.11.44	20.2.46	30.4.47		Ex-*Malplaquet*; BU 14.5.65.

Ordered 5.6.43

Pennant	Name / Builder	Laid down	Launched	Completed	Other	Notes
I.72	*Talavera*, John Brown	4.9.44	27.8.45	—		Canc 23.10.45, BU 4.46.
I.59	*Trincomalee*, John Brown	27.2.45	8.1.46	—		Canc 23.10.45, BU 2.46.
I.07	*Waterloo*, Fairfield	14.6.45	—	—		Ex-*Vimiera*; canc 23.10.45, BU on slip.

RAN Ships: ordered 7.10.44

Pennant	Name / Builder	Laid down	Launched	Completed	Other	Notes
D59	*Anzac*, Williamstown	23.9.46	20.8.48	22.3.51		TS 3.61. BU 1.76.
D37	*Tobruk*, Cockatoo	5.8.46	20.12.47	17.5.50	29.10.60	Sold 15.2.72, BU. Briefly commissioned 11.61.

1943 Intermediate Destroyers ('Weapon' Class)
Ordered 3.2.43

Pennant	Name / Builder	Laid down	Launched	Completed	Other	Notes
G85	*Sword*, White	17.9.45	—	—		Susp 17.10.45, BU on slip. Ex-*Celt*.
G64	*Scorpion*, White	16.2.44	15.8.46	17.9.47		Ex-*Centaur*, Ex-*Tomahawk*. BU 17.6.71. Mod completed ?, reserve April 1963. STT. Tested new A gun mount 1955.

Ordered 2.4.43

Pennant	Name / Builder	Laid down	Launched	Completed	Other	Notes
G18	*Battleaxe*, Yarrow	22.4.44	12.6.45	23.10.47		BU 20.10.64. Mod completed 2.59, CTL (collision) 1.8.62.
G31	*Broadsword*, Yarrow	20.7.44	5.2.46	4.10.48		BU 8.10.68. Mod completed 10.58, reserve 1.63. STT 1968.
G96	*Crossbow*, Thornycroft	26.8.44	20.12.45	4.3.48		BU 27.1.72. Mod completed 4.59, reserve 1.63 (left in tow 11.12.63). TS for HMS *Sultan* 1966.
G28	*Culverin*, Thornycroft	27.4.44	3.46	—		Canc 5.10.45, BU 3.46.

'G' Class (continued)

Ordered 7.4.43

G82 *Carronade*	26.4.44	—	Canc 5.1.46, BU 5.4.56.	
Scotts	4.4.46			
G34 *Claymore*	—	—	Canc 26.10.45.	
Scotts	—			

Ordered 24.4.43

G74 *Cutlass*	28.9.44	—	Canc 5.1.46, BU 20.3.46.
Yarrow	20.3.46		
G23 *Dagger*	7.3.45	—	Canc 2.11.45, BU on slip.
Yarrow	—		
G44 *Howitzer*	26.2.45	—	Canc 5.10.45, BU on slip.
Thornycroft	—		
G78 *Musket*	—	—	Susp 17.10.45.
Thornycroft	—		

Ordered 29.4.43

G02 *Dirk*	—	Canc 26.10.45.
Scotts	—	
G53 *Grenade*	—	Canc 23.12.44.
Scotts	—	
G99 *Halberd*	—	Canc 23.12.44.
Scotts		

Ordered 23.5.43

G21 *Rifle*	30.6.44	Canc 27.12.45, BU on slip.
Denny	—	
G30 *Spear*	29.9.44	Canc 27.12.45, BU on slip.
Denny	—	

Ordered 27.5.43

G55 *Longbow*	11.4.45	Canc 5.10.45, BU on slip.
Thornycroft	—	
G06 *Poniard*	—	Canc 23.12.45.
Scotts		

Daring Class (1944 'Battle' Class)

Ordered 5/6/43

I.05 *Danae*				Not laid down Ex-*Vimiera*, canc
Cammell	18.12.45.			
I.06 *Delight*	5.9.46	9.10.53	1.61	Ex-*Ypres* (45), (46);
Fairfield	21.12.50	7.65	9.67	Ex-*Disdain*, BU 12.70

Ordered 24.1.45

I.52 *Dainty*	17.12.45	26.2.53	1.61	BU 1971.
White	16.8.50	4.65	31.7.69	
I.15 *Daring*	29.9.43	8.3.52	1.61	BU 15.6.71.
Swan Hunter	10.8.49	12.66	12.68	
I.40 *Decoy*	—			Canc 18.12.45.
VA Walker				
I.45 *Delight*	—			Canc 18.12.45.
VA Walker				
I.35 *Demon*	—			Canc 18.12.45.
Swan Hunter				
I.73 *Dervish*	—			Canc 18.12.45.
White				
I.87 *Desperate*	—			Canc 27.12.45.
John Brown				
I.81 *Diamond*	15.3.49	21.2.52	12.69	BU 12.11.81. Reserve 1965–7. HTS for *Collingwood*/*Sultan* from 1970.
John Brown	14.6.50			

Ordered 16.2.45

I.19 *Desire*	—			Canc 18.12.45.
Hawthorn				
I.56 *Decoy*	22.9.46	28.4.53	8.69	Ex-*Dragon*; Peruvian *Ferre* 1969. Seacat trials ship 7.60 to 10.62. Reserve 3.65–8.67.
Yarrow	29.3.49			
I.47 *Defender*	22.3.49	5.12.52	1.61	Ex-*Dogstar*; BU 1972.
Stephen	27.7.50	1965	9.69	
I.77 *Diana*	—			Canc 18.12.45.
Hawthorn				
I.26 *Diana*	3.4.47	19.3.53	10.69	Ex-*Druid*; Peruvian *Palacios* 1969.
Yarrow	8.5.52			
I.94 *Duchess*	2.7.48	23.10.52		RAN 1964 to replace *Voyager*; loan converted to purchase 1972.
Thornycroft	9.4.51			

RAN ships ordered 3.12.46.

D11 *Vampire*	1.7.52	23.6.59		TS 1980; Museum Ship.
Cockatoo	27.10.56	1988.		
D08 *Vendetta*	1.7.49	26.11.58	10.10.79	BU 1987.
Williamstown	3.5.54			
D04 *Voyager*	1.10.49	12.2.57		C 11.2.64
Cockatoo	1.3.52			
— *Waterhen*	2.52	—		
Williamstown				

'G' Class (1944 Intermediate Destroyers)

Note none was laid down.

Ordered 12.7.44

G19 *Guernsey*	Canc 12.12.45.
Denny	
G40 *Glowworm*	Renamed *Guinevere*, then *Gift*; canc 12.12.45.
Denny	

Ordered 30.8.44

G07 *Gael*	Canc 18.12.45.
Yarrow	
G03 *Gallant*	Canc 18.12.45.
Yarrow	
G59 *Gauntlet*	Canc 18.12.45.
Thornycroft	
G67 *Gift*	Renamed *Glowworm* (G45), canc 18.12.45.
Thornycroft	
G76 *Grafton*	Canc 12.12.45.
White	
G88 *Greyhound*	Canc 12.12.45.
White	

'County' Class

First Series

D02 *Devonshire*	9.3.59	15.11.62	28.7.78	DLG 01. S(T) 17.7.84. Sale to Egypt as minelayer (on which work had been done) was cancelled 1979.
Cammell	10.6.60			
D06 *Hampshire*	26.3.59	15.3.63	4.76	DLG 02. BU 1979.
John Brown	16.3.61			
D12 *Kent*	1.3.60	15.8.63		DLG 03. HTS 7.80 instead of *Fife*.
H&W	27.9.61			
D16 *London*	26.2.60	14.11.63	12.81	DLG 04.
Swan Hunter	7.12.61			

Second Series

D19 *Glamorgan*	13.9.62	13.10.66		DLG 05. To Chile as *Almirante Latorre* 1986.
VA Tyne	9.7.64			
D21 *Norfolk*	15.3.66	7.3.70		DLG 06. To Chile as *Capitan Prat* 2.82.
Swan Hunter	16.11.67			
D18 *Antrim*	20.1.66	14.7.70		DLG 07. To Chile as *Almirante Cochrane* 6.84.
Fairfield	19.10.67			
D20 *Fife*	31.5.62	21.6.66		DLG 08. To Chile as *Almirante Blanco Encalada* 8.87.
Fairfield	9.7.64			

Type 82

D23 *Bristol*	15.11.67	31.3.73	HTS 1991.
Swan Hunter	30.6.69		

Type 42 (DDG series)

Batch I

D80 *Sheffield*	15.1.70	16.2.75		DDG 01. WL (missile) 10.5.82.
VA Barrow	10.6.71			
D86 *Birmingham*	28.3.72	3.12.76	12.11.99	Towed for BU 20.10.00.
Cammell	30.7.73			
D108 *Cardiff*	6.11.72	24.9.79		
VA Barrow	22.2.74			
D118 *Coventry*	29.1.73	20.10.78		WL(B) 26.5.82.
Cammell	21.6.74			
D87 *Newcastle*	21.2.73	23.3.78	11.04	
Swan Hunter	24.4.75			
D88 *Glasgow*	16.4.74	24.5.79	11.04	
Swan Hunter	14.4.76			

Batch II

D89 *Exeter*	22.7.76	19.9.80	
Swan Hunter	25.4.78		
D90 *Southampton*	21.10.76	31.10.81	
VT	29.1.79		
D91 *Nottingham*	6.2.78	14.4.83	
VT	18.2.80		
D92 *Liverpool*	5.7.78	9.7.82	
Cammell	25.9.80		

Batch III (DDG 11–14)

Ordered 10.11.78

D95 *Manchester*	19.5.78	16.12.82
VA Barrow	27.11.80	

Ordered 27.3.79

D96 *Gloucester*	25.10.79	11.9.85
VT	2.11.82	

Ordered 25.4.79

D97 *Edinburgh*	8.9.80	17.12.85
Cammell	14.4.83	

D98	*York*	18.1.80	9.8.85		
	Swan Hunter	21.6.82			

II. ESCORT DESTROYERS ('HUNT' CLASS)

Type I/II (stars indicate Type II)

Ordered 21.3.39

L05	*Atherstone*	8.6.39	23.3.40	10.45	BU 25.11.57.
	Cammell	12.12.39			
L17	*Berkeley*	8.6.39	6.6.40		WL(B) 19.8.42.
	Cammell	29.1.40			
L35	*Cattistock*	9.6.39	22.7.40	26.3.46	BU 2.7.57.
	Yarrow	22.2.40			
L46	*Cleveland*	7.7.39	18.9.40	9.45	Sold for BU, wrecked.
	Yarrow	24.4.40	28.6.57		
L87	*Eglinton*	8.6.39	28.8.40	1945	BU 28.5.56. Briefly reactivated from reserve 6.55 in Exercise Sleeping Beauty (test of Reserve Fleet activation).
	VA Walker	28.12.39			
L08	*Exmoor*	8.6.39	1.11.40		WL(T or M) 25.2.41.
	VA Walker	25.1.40			
L11	*Fernie*	8.6.39	29.5.40	1947	BU 7.11.56. Aircraft target ship 8.45–1947.
	John Brown	9.1.40			
L20	*Garth*	8.6.39	1.7.40	12.45	BU 15.8.58.
	John Brown	14.2.40			
L37	*Hambleton*	8.6.39	8.6.40	12.45	BU 4.2.58.
	Swan Hunter	12.12.39			
L48	*Holderness*	29.6.39	10.8.40	20.5.46	BU 20.11.56.
	Swan Hunter	8.2.40			

Ordered 11.4.39

L54	*Cotswold*	11.10.39	16.11.40	29.6.46	BU 11.9.57.
	Yarrow	18.7.40			
L78	*Cottesmore*	12.12.39	29.12.40	28.2.46	Egyptian *Ibrahim el Awal* 1950.
	Yarrow	5.9.40			
L60	*Mendip*	10.8.39	12.10.40	20.5.45	ROCN *Lin Fu* 1947, ret 1949, Egyptian *Mohammed Ali El Kebir* 1949, captured by Israelis 31.10.56, became *Haifa*.
	Swan Hunter	9.4.40			
L82	*Meynell*	10.8.39	30.12.40	12.46	Ecuadorian *Presidente Vlasco Ibarra* 1954. Aircraft target ship 11.9.45–12.46.
	Swan Hunter	7.6.40			
L92	*Pytchley*	26.7.39	23.10.40	8.46	BU 1.12.56.
	Scotts	13.2.40			
L58	*Quantock*	26.7.39	6.2.41	12.45	Ecuadorian *Presidente Alfaro* 1954. Had been converted to Air Target Ship. WL 3.8.44 German explosive motorboat.
	Scotts	22.4.40			
L66	*Quorn*	26.7.39	21.9.40		
	White	27.3.40			
L25	*Southdown*	22.8.39	8.11.40	22.5.46	Air Target Ship 8.9.45, BU 1.11.56.
	White	5.7.40			
L96	*Tynedale*	27.7.39	2.12.40		WL(T) 12.12.43.
	Stephen	5.6.40			
L45	*Whaddon*	27.7.39	28.2.41	10.45	BU 5.4.59.
	Stephen	16.7.40			

Ordered 4.9.39

L06	*Avon Vale**	12.2.40	17.2.41	9.12.45	RHN *Aegaion* 3.44, but not transferred due to mutinous condition of RHN; BU 15.5.58.
	John Brown	23.10.40			
L30	*Blankney*	17.5.40	11.4.41	14.5.46	BU 7.3.59.
	John Brown	19.12.40			
L24	*Blencathra*	18.11.39	14.12.40	19.7.48	Conv to aircraft target ship 16 21.10.45. She and *Cattistock* were offered to Norway 16.1.50, but two Type II were substituted 15.4.50. BU 2.1.57.
	Cammell	6.8.40			
L42	*Brocklesby*	18.11.39	9.4.41	1.5.46	Refitted 1951/2 as experimental ship, ran VDS (Type 192) trials until 1960, then training and experimental vessel until paid off 22.6.63. Last 'Hunt' in RN service. BU 28.10.68.
	Cammell	30.9.40			
L31	*Chiddingfold**	1.3.40	16.10.41	25.3.46	IN *Ganga* 1953.
	Scott	10.3.41			
L52	*Cowdray**	30.4.40	29.7.42	30.1.50	Bombed and beached 11.8.42, salved, BU 3.9.59.
	Scott	22.7.41			
L62	*Croome**	7.6.40	29.6.41	10.45	BU 13.8.57.
	Stephen	30.1.41			
L63	*Dulverton**	16.7.40	27.9.41		WL(B) 13.11.43.
	Stephen	1.4.41			
L68	*Eridge**	21.11.39	28.2.41		CTL(T) 29.8.42, BU 10.46.
	Swan Hunter	20.8.40			
L70	*Farndale**	21.11.39	27.4.41	1951	BU 29.11.62.
	Swan Hunter	30.9.40			
L85	*Heythrop**	18.12.39	21.6.41		WL(T) 20.3.42.
	Swan Hunter	20.10.40			
L88	*Lamerton**	10.4.40	16.8.41	20.3.46	IN *Gomati* 1953.
	Swan Hunter	14.12.40			
L100	*Liddesdale*	22.11.39	3.3.41	11.12.45	BU 1948.
	VA Walker	19.8.40			
L72	*Oakley**	22.11.39	17.6.41		ORP *Kujawiak* 1941, WL(M) 16.6.42.
	VA Walker	13.10.40			
L108	*Puckeridge**	1.1.40	30.7.41		WL(T) 6.9.43.
	White	6.3.41			
L115	*Silverton**	5.12.39	28.5.41	8.9.46	ORP *Krakowiak* 1941–6, BU 11.3.59.
	White	4.12.40			
L122	*Wheatland**	30.5.40	3.11.41	9.45	Part of artificial harbour at Harwich 8.55, BU 20.9.57.
	Yarrow	7.6.41			
L128	*Wilton**	7.6.40	18.2.42	2.46	Part of Training Squadron at Rosyth 1.50–1952, including use as Air Target. BU 4.12.59.
	Yarrow	17.10.41			

Ordered 5.9.39

L95	*Lauderdale**	21.12.39	24.12.41		RHN *Aigaion* 1946. Only 'Hunt' to cross the Atlantic, for trials with RCN, 2–3.42.
	Thornycroft	5.8.41			
L90	*Ledbury**	24.1.40	11.2.42	3.46	BU 7.58.
	Thornycroft	27.9.41			

Ordered 20.12.39

L03	*Badsworth**	15.5.40	18.8.41		RNN *Arendal* 1944.
	Cammell	17.3.41			
L14	*Beaufort**	17.7.40	3.11.41	8.12.45	RNN *Haugesund* 1952.
	Cammell	9.6.41			
L26	*Bedale**	25.5.40	9.5.42	23.7.46	ORP *Slazak* 1941–5, IN *Godavari* 1952.
	Hawthorn	23.7.41			
L84	*Bicester**	29.5.40	18.6.42	1.50	Coronation review 1953 as part of Reserve Fleet. BU 23.8.56.
	Hawthorn	5.9.41			
L43	*Blackmore**	10.2.41	14.4.42	12.45	RDN *Esbern Snare*, 1952.
	Stephen	2.12.41			
L51	*Bramham**	7.4.41	16.6.42		RHN *Themistokles*, 1943.
	Stephen	29.1.42			
L71	*Calpe**	12.6.40	11.12.41	17.1.46	RDN *Rolf Krake* 1952.
	Swan Hunter	28.4.41	1952.		
L08	*Exmoor**	7.6.40	18.10.41	10.11.45	*Ex-Burton*; RDN *Valdemar Sejr* 1952.
	Swan Hunter	12.3.41			
L77	*Grove**	28.8.40	5.2.42		WL(T) 12.6.42.
	Swan Hunter	29.5.41			
L84	*Hursley**	21.12.40	2.4.42		RHN *Kriti* 1943.
	Swan Hunter	25.7.41			
L28	*Hurworth**	10.4.40	5.10.41		WL(M) 20.10.43.
	VA Walker	16.4.41			
L74	*Middleton**	10.4.40	10.1.42	1.46	BU 4.10.57.
	VA Walker	12.5.41			
L98	*Oakley**	19.8.40	7.5.42	12.45	Ex-*Tickham*; FRGN *Gneisenau* 1958.
	Yarrow	15.1.42			
L10	*Southwold**	18.6.40	9.10.41		WL(M) 24.3.42.
	White	29.5.41			
L90	*Tetcott**	29.7.40	11.12.41	17.1.46	BU 24.9.55.
	White	12.8.41			
L59	*Zetland**	2.10.40	27.6.42	20.4.46	RNN *Tromso* 1952.
	Yarrow	6.3.42			

Type III

Ordered 4.7.40

L07	*Airedale*	20.11.40	8.1.42		WL(B) 15.6.42.
	John Brown	12.8.41			
L12	*Albrighton*	30.12.40	22.2.42	8.1.46	FRGN *Raule* 1957.
	John Brown	11.10.41			
L22	*Aldenham*	22.8.40	5.2.42		WL(M) 14.12.44.
	Yarrow	27.8.41			
L32	*Belvoir*	14.10.40	29.3.42	7.45	Offered to FFN 15.6.44, not accepted. BU 21.10.57.
	Yarrow	18.11.41			
L81	*Catterick*	1.3.41	12.6.42		RHN *Admiral Hastings* 1946.
	VA Barrow	22.11.41			
L83	*Derwent*	29.12.40	24.4.42	20.7.45	Had been severely damaged 3.43; repair work stopped 1.45. On reduction to reserve machinery was removed for training at HMS *Manadon*. Hulk BU 21.2.47.
	VA Barrow	22.8.41			

Ordered 19.7.40

L50	*Bleasdale*	31.10.40	16.4.42	26.11.45		Radio firing ship for destruction of
	VA Walker	23.7.41	2.46	21.4.52		Heligoland fortifications, 18.4.47. BU 14.9.56.

Ordered 28.7.40

No.	Name / Builder				Notes
L47	*Blean*	22.2.41	23.8.42		WL(T) 11.12.42.
	Hawthorn	15.1.42			
L65	*Bolebroke*	3.4.41	27.6.42		RHN *Pindos* 1942.
	Swan Hunter	5.11.41			
L67	*Border*	1.5.41	5.8.42		RHN *Adrias* 1942, CTL(M) 22.10.43, BU 20.11.45.
	Swan Hunter	3.2.42			
L09	*Easton*	25.3.41	7.12.42	29.10.45	Never fully repaired from damage due to ramming a U-boat, 22.8.43, hence prematurely BU, 1.53.
	White	11.7.42			
L15	*Eggesford*	23.6.41	21.1.43	25.11.46	FRGN *Brommy* 1959.
	White	12.9.42			
L36	*Eskdale*	18.1.41	31.7.42		RNN 1942, WL(T)
	Cammell	16.3.42	14.4.43.		
L44	*Glaisdale*	4.2.41	12.6.42	2.8.44	RNN 1942; RNN *Narvik* 1946. Had been returned to RN after serious mine damage 23.6.44, then in reserve, repaired for transfer.
	Cammell	5.1.42			
L27	*Goathland*	30.1.41	6.11.42	10.44	CTL(M) 24.7.44, BU 2.46. HQ ship at Normandy.
	Fairfield	3.2.42			
L19	*Haldon*	16.1.41	30.12.42		FFN *La Combattante*, WL(M) 23.2.45.
	Fairfield	27.4.42			
L53	*Hatherleigh*	12.12.40	10.8.42		RHN *Kanaris* 1942.
	VA Walker	18.12.41			
L75	*Haydon*	1.5.41	24.10.42	10.47	BU 18.5.58.
	VA Walker	2.4.42			
L56	*Holcombe*	3.4.41	16.9.42		WL(T) 12.12.43.
	Stephen	14.4.42			
L57	*Limbourne*	8.4.41	24.10.42		WL(T) 23.10.43.
	Stephen	12.5.42			
L73	*Melbreak*	23.6.41	10.10.42	8.45	Never recomm after repairs for damage incurred 5.5.45, completed 11.8.45. At Coronation Review 6.53, BU 22.11.56.
	Swan Hunter	5.3.42			
L91	*Modbury*	5.8.41	25.11.42		RHN *Miaoulis* 1942.
	Swan Hunter	13.4.42			
L89	*Penylan*	4.6.41	31.8.42		WL(T) 3.12.42.
	VA Barrow	17.3.42			
L39	*Rockwood*	29.8.41	4.11.42		CTL(B) 11.11.43, BU 8.46.
	VA Barrow	13.6.42			
L16	*Stevenstone*	2.9.41	18.3.43	31.12.47	BU 9.59.
	White	23.11.42			
L18	*Talybont*	28.11.41	19.5.43	31.12.47	BU 14.2.61.
	White	3.2.43			
L69	*Tanatside*	23.6.41	4.9.42		RHN *Adrias* 1946. Began Far East refit Taranto 16.7.45, not completed, and under care and maintenance 11.45; then offered to RHN.
	Yarrow	30.4.42			
L86	*Wensleydale*	28.7.41	30.10.42		CTL(C) 21.11.44, BU 25.2.47.
	Yarrow	20.6.42			

Type IV

Ordered 28.7.40

No.	Name / Builder				Notes
L76	*Brecon*	27.2.41	18.12.42	4.12.45	BU 17.9.62.
	Thornycroft	27.6.42			
L79	*Brissenden*	28.2.41	12.2.43	19.6.48	Proposed conversion as Kuwaiti royal yacht (1958) did not materialise. BU 3.3.65.
	Thornycroft	15.9.42			

III. SLOOPS

Grimsby Class

Ordered 1.11.32

No.	Name / Builder				Notes
L16	*Grimsby*	23.1.33	17.5.34		WL(B) 25.5.41.
	Devonport	19.7.33			
L36	*Leith*	6.2.33	12.7.34	6.45	Merch 1946.
	Devonport	9.9.33			

Ordered 1.5.33

L59	*Lowestoft*	21.8.33	22.11.34	6.45	Merch 1946.
	Devonport	11.4.34			
L65	*Wellington*	25.9.33	24.1.35	6.8.45	Became home ship of Worshipful Company of Master Mariners, London 1947; still exists.
	Devonport	29.5.34			

Ordered 14.8.33

L67	*Indus*	8.12.33	15.3.35		RIN; WL(B) 6.4.42.
	Hawthorn	24.8.34			

Ordered 10.1.34

L53	*Deptford*	30.4.34	20.8.35	3.7.45	BU 11.5.48.
	Chatham	5.2.35			

Ordered 1.3.34

No.	Name / Builder				Notes
L76	*Londonderry*	11.6.34	20.9.35	22.5.45	BU 8.6.48.
	Devonport	16.1.35			

Ordered 1.3.35

L97	*Aberdeen*	12.6.35	17.9.36	8.45	BU 16.12.48.
	Devonport	22.1.36			
L47	*Fleetwood*	14.8.35	19.11.36	4.8.45	BU 10.10.59. Reactivated (disarmed) beginning 2.46 as radar training ship, active to 1959.
	Devonport	24.3.36			

RAN ships:

Ordered 22.12.33

L77	*Yarra*	24.5.34	19.12.35		WL(G) 4.3.42.
	Cockatoo	28.3.35			

Ordered 2.1.35

L74	*Swan*	1.5.35	10.12.36	18.8.48	TS 1956–64; BU 1965. Conversion to
	Cockatoo	28.3.36	1956	21.9.64	TS began 10.54.

Ordered 1938

L44	*Parramatta*	9.11.38	8.4.40		WL(T) 27.11.41.
	Cockatoo	18.6.39			
L71	*Warrego*	10.5.39	21.8.40	8.8.63	Survey ship 1945–63, BU 1965.
	Cockatoo	10.2.40			

Bittern Class

Ordered 5.10.33

L56	*Enchantress*	9.3.34	4.4.35	3.46	Ex-*Bittern*; merch 1946.
	John Brown	21.12.34			

Ordered 1.5.35

L81	*Stork*	19.6.35	10.9.36	17.9.45	BU 3.6.58.
	Denny	21.4.36			

Ordered 26.5.36

L07	*Bittern*	27.8.36	15.3.38		WL(B) 30.4.40.
	White	27.8.36			

Royal Indian Navy version:

Ordered 8.9.39

U21	*Jumna*	24.2.40	13.8.41	31.12.80	BU.
	Denny	16.11.40			
U95	*Sutlej*	4.1.40	23.4.41	31.12.79	BU.
	Denny	1.10.40			

Ordered 29.8.40

U52	*Godavari*	30.10.41	28.6.43		PN *Sind* 1947.
	Thornycroft	21.1.43			
U40	*Narbada*	30.8.41	29.4.43		PN *Jhellum* 1947.
	Thornycroft	21.11.42			

Egret Class

Ordered 5.3.37

L61	*Auckland*	16.3.37	16.11.38		Ex-*Heron*; WL(B) 24.6.41.
	Denny				
L75	*Egret*	21.7.37	10.11.38		WL(B) 27.8.43.
	White	31.5.38			

Ordered 19.3.37

L86	*Pelican*	7.9.37	2.3.39	6.51	BU 29.11.58.
	Thornycroft	12.9.38	8.54	13.2.57	

Black Swan Class and Modified Version

Ordered 1.1.38

L57	*Black Swan*	20.6.38	27.1.40	5.52	BU 13.9.56.
	Yarrow	7.7.39			
L18	*Flamingo*	26.5.38	3.11.39	1948	FRGN *Graf Spee*
	Yarrow	18.4.39	1.49	12.55	1957.

Ordered 21.6.39

L01	*Erne*	22.9.39	26.4.41	19.2.46	RNVR TS *Wessex* 1949, BU 1965.
	Furness	5.8.40			
U99	*Ibis*	22.9.39	30.8.41		WL(T) 10.11.42.
	Furness	28.11.40			

Ordered 13.4.40

U29	*Whimbrel*	31.10.41	13.1.43	6.49	Egyptian *El Malek Farouk* 1949, *Tariq* 1954, may become British museum ship 2006.
	Yarrow	25.8.42			
U45	*Wild Goose*	28.1.42	11.3.43	1955	BU 27.2.56.
	Yarrow	14.10.42			
U08	*Woodpecker*	23.2.41	14.12.42		WL(T) 20.2.44 (foundered in tow 27.10.44).
	Denny	29.6.42			
U28	*Wren*	27.2.41	4.2.43	1955	BU 2.2.56.
	Denny	11.8.42			

Ordered 9.1.41

U05	*Chanticleer*	6.6.41	29.3.43		CTL(T) 18.11.43, BU 1946.
	Denny	24.9.42			

U23	*Crane*	13.6.41	10.5.43	1947	BU 3.65.
	Denny	9.11.42	late 1951	1962	
Ordered 27.3.41					
U38	*Cygnet*	30.8.41	1.12.42	1955	BU 16.3.56.
	Cammell	28.7.42			
U87	*Kite*	25.9.41	1.3.43		WL(T) 21.8.44.
	Cammell	13.10.42			
U62	*Lapwing*	17.12.41	21.3.44		WL(T) 20.3.45.
	Scotts	16.7.43			
U11	*Lark*	5.5.42	10.4.44		CLT(T) 17.2.45, beached, abandoned
	Scotts	28.8.43			13.6.45.
U82	*Magpie*	30.12.41	30.8.43	End 1956	BU 12.7.59.
	Thornycroft	24.3.42			
U96	*Peacock*	20.11.42	10.5.44	Mid1954	BU 7.3.58.
	Thornycroft	11.12.43			
U49	*Pheasant*	17.3.42	12.5.43	1947	BU 15.1.63.
	Yarrow	21.12.42			
U69	*Redpole*	18.5.42	24.6.43	1947	BU 20.11.60. Disarmed Navigation TS
	Yarrow	25.2.43	1949	1960	1949–60.
Ordered 18.7.41					
U66	*Starling*	21.10.41	1.4.43	1959	BU 6.7.65. Navigation
	Fairfield	14.10.42			TS 3.46–1959.
U90	*Woodcock*	21.10.41	29.5.43	10.12.46	BU 28.11.55.
	Fairfield	26.11.42			
Ordered 3.12.41					
U07	*Actaeon*	15.5.44	24.7.46	12.3.53	FRGN *Hipper* 1957.
	Thornycroft	25.7.45			
Ordered 18.12.41					
U16	*Amethyst*	25.3.42	2.11.43	1953	Made the celebrated dash down the Yangtze River under Communist fire,1949; BU 19.1.57.
	Stephen	7.5.43			
U58	*Hart*	27.3.42	12.12.43	1952	FRGN *Scheer* 1957.
	Stephen	7.7.43			
Ordered 11.2.42					
U39	*Hind*	31.8.42	11.4.44	1951	BU 10.12.58.
	Denny	30.9.43			
U30	*Mermaid*	8.9.42	12.5.44	Late1954	FRGN *Scharnhorst*
	Denny	11.11.43	1957.		
Ordered 12.8.42					
U60	*Alacrity*	5.4.43	13.4.45	Early1952	BU 3.11.56.
	Denny	1.9.44			
U33	*Opossum*	28.7.43	16.6.45	1959	BU 24.6.60.
	Denny	30.11.44			
Ordered 5.10.42					
U42	*Modeste*	15.2.43	3.9.45	9.58	BU 11.3.61.
	Chatham	29.1.44			
U64	*Nereide*	15.2.43	6.5.46	1955	BU 18.5.58.
	Chatham	29.1.44			
Re–ordered 8.12.42					
U20	*Snipe*	21.9.44	9.9.46	5.53	BU 23.8.60.
	Denny	20.12.45			
U71	*Sparrow*	30.11.44	16.12.46	3.56	BU 26.5.58.
	Denny	18.2.46			
Ordered 21.6.43					
U34	*Nonsuch*	26.2.45			Cancelled 10.45, BU.
	Chatham	—			
U84	*Nymphe*	26.2.45			Cancelled 10.45, BU.
	Chatham	—			
Re–ordered 9.10.44					
U37	*Partridge*	—			Cancelled 2.11.45.
	Thornycroft				
U05	*Waterhen*	—			Cancelled 2.11.45.
	Denny				
U31	*Wryneck*	—			Cancelled 2.11.45.
	Denny				

For Royal Indian Navy:

Ordered 10.9.41					
U10	*Cauvery*	28.10.42	21.10.43	30.9.77	*Kavari* 1969.
	Yarrow	15.6.43			
U46	*Kistna*	14.7.42	22.4.43	31.12.80	*Krishna* 1969.
	Yarrow	22.4.43			

IV. FRIGATES

'River' Class

Ordered 11.2.41					
K92	*Exe*	16.5.41	6.8.42	1947	BU 20.9.56.
	Fleming	9.3.42			
K227	*Itchen*	14.7.41	28.12.42		WL(T) 22.9.43.
	Fleming	29.7.42			
K235	*Jed*	27.9.41	30.11.42	19.12.45	BU 25.7.57.
	Hill	30.7.42			
K241	*Kale*	22.9.41	4.12.42	1946	BU 1956.
	Inglis	24.6.42			
K219	*Ness*	22.9.41	22.12.42	1946	BU 1956.
	Robb	30.7.42			
K215	*Nith*	3.9.41	16.2.43	1946	Egyptian *Domiat* 1948.
	Robb	25.9.42			
K251	*Ribble*	5.9.41	25.6.43		RNLN *Johan Maurits van Nassau* 1943.
	Simons	23.4.43			
K224	*Rother*	29.12.41	3.4.42	1945	BU 1959.
	Smiths	20.11.41			
K246	*Spey*	26.6.41	19.5.42	1945	Egyptian *Rashied* 1948.
	Smiths	18.12.41			
K217	*Swale*	18.7.41	24.6.42	1947	BU 26.2.55.
	Smiths	16.1.42			
K232	*Tay*	19.8.41	5.8.42	1947	BU 28.9.56.
	Smiths	18.3.42			
Ordered 15.3.41					
K239	*Test*	15.8.41	12.10.42	1951	RIN *Neza* 1946–47, accomm. ship for Malayan Naval Force 1949–51, BU25.2.55.
	Hall Russell	30.5.42			
Ordered 8.5.41					
K222	*Teviot*	4.10.41	30.1.43	1.47	SAN 1945–6, BU 1955.
	Hall Russell	12.10.42			
K243	*Trent*	31.1.42	27.2.43		RIN *Khukri* 1946.
	Hill	10.10.42			
K248	*Waveney*	8.10.41	16.9.42	1947	BU 9.11.57. Converted to LSH(S).
	Smiths	30.4.42			
K230	*Wear*	16.10.41	24.10.42	1946	BU 29.10.57.
	Smiths	1.6.42			
Ordered 19.5.41					
K21	*Dart*	8.9.41	15.5.43	1947	BU 1957.
	Blyth	10.10.42			
K250	*Tweed*	31.12.41	28.4.43		WL(T) 7.1.44.
	Inglis	24.11.42			
Ordered 1.6.41					
K221	*Chelmer*	29.12.41	29.9.43	1946	BU 8.57.
	John Brown	27.3.43			
K254	*Ettrick*	31.12.41	11.7.43	30.5.45	RCN 29.1.44–45; BU
	Crown	5.2.43	6.53.		
Ordered 20.6.41					
K255	*Balinderry*	6.11.41	2.9.43	1947	BU 7.7.61.
	Blyth	7.12.42			
K256	*Bann*	18.6.42	7.5.43		RIN *Tir* 1945.
	Hill	29.12.42			
K257	*Derg*	16.4.42	10.6.43		RNVR TS *Cambrian 1947, Wessex*
	Robb	7.1.43			1951, BU 9.60.
K258	*Strule*	15.7.42	30.7.43		Ex-*Glenarm*, FFN *Croix de Lorraine*
	Robb	8.3.43			1944.
Ordered 3.7.41					
K259	*Lagan*	7.1.42	2.12.42		CTL(T) 20.9.43, BU
	Smiths	28.7.42	1946.		
K261	*Mourne*	21.3.42	30.4.43		WL(T) 15.6.44.
	Smiths	24.9.42			
K260	*Moyola*	9.2.42	15.1.43		FFN *Tonkinois* 1944, *La Confiance* 1953.
	Smiths	27.8.42			
Ordered 30.9.41					
K262	*Aire*	13.6.42	28.7.43		*Tamar* 3.46 as Hong Kong base ship, REN *Aire* 12.46, wrecked (CTL) 23.12.46
	Fleming	22.4.43			
Ordered 8.11.41					
K263	*Braid*	1.12.42	21.1.44		FFN *L'Aventure*
	Simons	30.11.43	1944.		
Ordered 13.12.41					
K264	*Cam*	30.6.42	31.4.44		CTL(M) 1944, BU 1945.
	John Brown	31.7.43			
K265	*Deveron*	16.4.42	2.3.43		RIN *Dhanush* 1945, PN *Zulfiquar* 1948.
	Smiths	12.10.42			
K266	*Fal*	20.5.42	2.7.43		Burmese *Mayu* 1947.
	Smiths	9.11.42			
Ordered 19.12.41					
K267	*Frome*	30.5.42	3.3.44		FFN *L'Escaramouche* 1944, *Ailette* 1957.
	Blyth	1.6.43			

Ordered 1.1.42

K252 *Helford*	27.6.42	26.6.43		1946 BU 29.6.56.
Hall Russell	6.2.43			
K253 *Helmsdale*	13.8.42	15.10.43		1953 Post-war sonar trials ship; 1946–/ propeller silencing trials with glass panels inbottom of hull; at Coronation Review 6.53. BU 7.11.57.
Inglis	5.6.43			

Ordered 24.1.42

K523 *Dovey*	23.3.43	25.2.44		1945 Ex-*Lambourne*; BU 2.11.55.
Fleming	14.10.43			
K269 *Meon*	31.12.42	31.12.43	7.7.65	RCN 7.4.44–22.4.45; converted to LSH(S) 1945 later with pennant L269; after completion of conversion laid up 12.45, then living ship for reserve ships at Harwich; recomm 3.4.51, was HQ ship for Gulf amphibious force 1952–60 (flag of LSTs at Suez, 11.56); HQ ship of Amphibious Warfare squadron 1960–5. BU 14.5.66.
Inglis	4.8.43			
K270 *Nene*	20.6.42	8.4.43	11.6.45	RCN 6.4.44; ret 45; BU 21.7.55.
Smiths	9.12.42			
K271 *Plym*	1.8.42	16.5.43		1946 RNVR TS 1948–9, expended in first British atomic bomb test, 3.10.52.
Smiths	4.2.43			

Ordered 26.2.42

K272 *Tavy*	17.10.42	3.7.43		1945 BU 8.7.55.
Hill	3.4.43			

Ordered 14.4.42

K292 *Torridge*	17.10.42	6.6.44		FFN *La Surprise* 1944.
Blyth	16.8.43			
K293 *Tees*	21.10.42	28.8.43		1945 BU 16.7.55.
Hall Russell	20.5.43			

Ordered 20.5.42

K294 *Towy*	3.9.42	10.6.43		1945 BU 27.6.56.
Smiths	4.3.43			
K295 *Usk*	6.10.42	14.7.43		1946 Egyptian *Abikir* 1948.
Smiths	3.4.43			

Ordered 14.6.42

K411 *Ribble*	31.12.42	4.8.44	11.6.45	Ex-*Duddon*; RCN 7.44–5; BU 9.7.57.
Blyth	10.11.43			
K370 *Windrush*	18.11.42	3.11.43		FFN *La Decouverte*
Robb	18.6.43	1944.		
K371 *Wye*	18.11.42	9.2.44		1945 BU 22.2.55.
Robb	16.8.43			

Ordered 15.7.42

K392 *Nadder*	11.3.43	20.1.44		RIN *Shamsher* 1944, PN 1948.
Smiths	15.9.43			
K356 *Odzani*	18.11.42	2.9.43		1946 BU 6.57.
Smiths	19.5.43			
K458 *Teme*	25.5.43	16.3.44		CTL(T), sold for BU 8.12.45, BU 1946.
Smiths	11.11.43			

Ordered 24.7.42

K... *Naver*				Cancelled 1943; reordered as *Loch Achanalt*.
Robb				

Ordered 10.8.42

K97 *Avon*	8.1.43	19.6.43	30.5.46	Portuguese *Nuno Tristao* 1949.
Hill	19.6.43			

Ordered 9.9.42

K365 *Lochy*	23.2.43	8.2.44		1947 BU 29.6.56.
Hall Russell	30.10.43			

Ordered 11.9.42

K367 *Taff*	14.4.43	7.1.44		1947 BU 6.57
Hill	11.9.43			

Ordered 2.10.42

K526 *Awe*	27.5.43	21.1.44		Portuguese *Diogo Gomes* 1949.
Fleming	28.12.43			
K17 *Halladale*	25.6.43	11.5.44		1947 Merch 1949.
Inglis	28.1.44			

RAN Ships

Ordered 16.8.41

K375 *Barcoo*	21.10.42	17.8.44	4.56	BU 3.72. Modernised as frigate but
Cockatoo	26.8.43	1959	14.2.64	employed as survey ship post-war.
K406 *Barwon*	31.5.43	10.12.45	31.3.47	BU 8.62. Note installation of Squid
Cockatoo	3.8.44			4.47, while in reserve.
K376 *Burdekin*	1.7.42	27.6.44		1946 BU 1961.
Walkers	30.6.43			
K377 *Diamantina*	12.4.43	27.4.45	8.46	Oceanographic research ship, then
Walkers	6.4.44	—	2.80	museum ship 1980.
K354 *Gascoyne*	3.7.42	18.11.43	1956	BU 1972. Modernised as frigate but
Morts	20.2.43	1959	2.2.66	employed as survey ship post-war.

K363 *Hawkesbury*	7.8.42	5.7.44	4.46	BU 1962.
Morts	24.7.43	5.52	14.2.55	

Ordered 2.6.42

K408 *Culgoa*	15.7.43	24.12.46	5.4.54	Ex-*Macquarrie*; BU 3.72. Accomm ship 12.62–6.71, sold 2.72. AA version.
Melbourne	22.9.45			
K364 *Lachlan*	23.3.43	12.2.45		RNZN 1949. Survey ship until refit then in reserve until sale.
Morts	25.3.44			
K532 *Macquarrie*	3.12.42	7.12.45	19.12.46	Ex-*Culgoa*; BU 8.62. Recomm 1952–3 as patrol and weather ship for Monte Bello Island nuclear test.
Morts	3.3.45	8.52	19.9.53	
K442 *Murchison*	3.6.43	17.12.45	12.55	BU 1962. A/A version. TS 11.54–12.55.
Evans	31.10.44			
K534 *Murrumbidgee*	28.10.43			Cancelled 4.4.44, BU on slip.
Melbourne				
K535 *Shoalhaven*	1.12.43	1.5.46	1956	BU 1962. A/A version.
Walkers	14.12.44			
K533 *Warburton*	—			Cancelled 4.4.44, not laid down.
Evans				

Ordered 10.12.42

K424 *Campaspe*	—			Cancelled 4.4.44, not laid down.
Cockatoo				
K55 *Naomi*	—			Cancelled 4.4.44, not laid down.
Cockatoo				
K86 *Wimmera*	—			Cancelled 4.4.44, not laid down.
Morts				
K98 *Wollondilly*	—			Cancelled 4.4.44, not laid down.
Morts				

Ordered 11.12.42

J467 *Balmain*	—			Cancelled 4.4.44, not laid down.
Morts				
J468 *Nepean*	—			Cancelled 4.4.44, not laid down.
Morts				
K66 *Williamstown*	—			Cancelled 4.4.44, not laid down.
Melbourne				

Ordered 23.12.42

K09 *Bogan*	17.1.44	—		Cancelled 4.4.44, BU on slip.
NSW				
K698 *Condamine*	30.10.43	22.2.46	2.12.55	BU 1961. AA version.
NSW	4.11.44			

RCN Ships

Ordered 6.10.41 under lend-lease as US Navy PG 101–106, respectively; all but first two to RN. Return dates are return to USN under terms of lend-lease.

K296 *Adur*	10.3.42	1.12.42		RCN *Nadur*, then USN *Asheville* as completed; Argentine *Hercules* 1946.
CanV	22.8.42			
K297 *Annan*	16.3.42	16.12.42		USN *Natchez* as completed; Dominican *Juan Pablo Duarte* 1948.
CanV	12.9.42			
K298 *Barle*	10.6.42	30.4.43		Ret 27.2.46, BU.
CanV	26.9.42			
K299 *Cuckmere*	4.5.42	14.5.43		CTL(T) 11.12.43, ret 6.11.46, BU.
CanV	24.10.42			
K300 *Evenlode*	28.6.42	4.6.43		Ret 5.3.46, BU.
CanV	8.11.42			
K301 *Findhorn*	23.8.42	25.6.43		Ret 20.3.46, BU.
CanV	5.12.42			

Ordered 10.41. Only starred ships were completed with single 4in guns fore and aft.

K407 *Beacon Hill*	16.7.43	16.5.44	6.2.46	BU 1968. Reb 1954–7.
YarrowC	6.11.43	16.6.49	1954	
		21.12.57	15.9.67	
K663 *Cap de la Madeleine*	5.11.43	30.9.44	25.11.45	BU 1966. Disc/reacq, reb.
Morton	13.5.44	7.12.54	15.5.66	
K350 *Cape Breton**	5.5.42	25.10.43	26.1.46	Break 1948.
Morton	24.11.42			
K665 *Eastview*	26.8.43	3.6.44	17.1.46	Break 1948.
CanV	17.11.43			
K318 *Grou*	1.5.43*	4.12.43	25.2.46	BU 1948.
CanV	7.8.43			
K418 *Joliette*	19.7.43	14.6.44	19.11.45	Chilean *Iquique* 1946.
Morton	12.11.43			
K419 *Kokanee*	25.8.43	6.6.44	21.12.45	Indian pilot vessel *Bengal*.
YarrowC	27.11.43			
K668 *La Hulloise*	10.8.43	20.5.44	6.12.45	BU 1966.
CanV	29.10.43	24.6.49		
	9.10.57	16.7.65		
K672 *Longueuil*	17.7.43	18.5.44	31.12.45	Break 1948.
CanV	30.10.43			
K673 *Magog*	16.6.43	7.5.44		CTL(T) 14.10.44, BU 1947.
CanV	22.9.43			

K444 *Matane**   23.12.43 23.10.43 11.2.46   ex-*Stormont*; break 1948.
CanV   29.5.43

K319 *Montreal**   23.12.43 12.11.43 15.10.45   BU 1947.
CanV   12.6.43

K322 *Outremont**   18.11.43 27.11.43 5.11.45   BU 1966. Disc/reacq, reb.
Morton   3.7.43 2.9.55 7.6.65

K324 *Prince Rupert*   6.8.42 20.8.43 16.1.46   Break 1948.
YarrowC   3.2.43 16.1.46

K325 *St Catherines**   2.5.42 31.7.43 8.11.45   Merch 1950; weather ship in North
YarrowC   6.12.42   Pacific 1952–7.

K456 *St John**   28.5.42 14.12.43 2.11.45   BU 1947.
CanV   25.8.43

K681 *Stettler*   31.5.43 7.5.44 9.11.45   BU 1967. Disc/reacq.
CanV   10.9.43 27.2.54 31.8.66

K327 *Stormont**   6.5.43 28.11.43 9.11.45   Ex-*Matane*; sold 1947; rebuilt 1951 as
CanV   14.7.43   Onassis yacht *Christina*.

K328 *Swansea**   15.7.42 4.10.43 2.11.45   BU 1967. TS 1948–53, reb 1953–7,
YarrowC   19.12.42   paid off 14.10.66. Only RCN frigate at 1953 Coronation Review.

K459 *Thetford Mines*   7.7.43 30.10.43 18.11.45   Merch 1946.
Morton

K329 *Valleyfield**   30.11.42 7.12.43   WL(T) 7.5.44.
Morton   17.7.43

K03 *Verdun**   5.5.42 11.9.43 23.1.46   *Verdun of Canada* 1942, REN *Dunver*
Morton   10.11.42   1944, break 1948.

K330 *Waskesiu**   2.5.42 17.6.43 29.11.46   Indian pilot ship *Hooghly* 1947.
YarrowC   6.12.42

Ordered 9.12.41 under Lend-Lease as USN PG 107–110, respectively; to Royal Navy and returned 1946.

K302 *Inver*   17.9.42 19.7.43   Ret 4.3.46, BU.
CanV   12.12.42

K303 *Lossie*   1.10.42 14.8.43   Ret 26.1.46, merch.
CanV   30.4.43

K304 *Parret*   31.10.42 31.8.43   Ret 5.2.46, BU.
CanV   30.4.43

K305 *Shiel*   8.11.42 30.9.43   Ret 4.3.46, BU.
CanV   26.5.43

Ordered 4.42

K320 *New Glasgow**   4.1.43 23.12.43 5.11.45   BU 1967. Disc/reacq, reb.
YarrowC   5.5.43 30.1.54 30.1.67

K326 *Port Colborne**   16.12.42 15.11.43 7.11.45   BU 1947.
YarrowC   21.4.43

K331 *Wentworth*   11.11.42 7.12.43 10.10.45   BU 1947.
YarrowC   6.3.43

Ordered 6.42

K244 *Charlottetown*   26.1.43 28.4.44 25.3.47   Break 1948.
Davie   16.9.43

K317 *Chebogue*   19.3.43 22.2.44   CTL(T) 4.10.44, wrecked 11.10.44,
YarrowC   sold for BU 13.12.47, but wrecked.

K670 *Fort Erie*   3.11.43 27.10.44 22.11.45   Ex-*La Tuque*; BU 26.3.65 22.5.66.
Davie   27.5.44   Disc/reacq, reb; TS 17.4.56.

K414 *Glace Bay*   23.9.43 2.9.44 17.11.45   Ex-*Lauzon*; Chilean *Esmeralda* 1946.
Davie   26.4.44

K318 *Jonquiere*   26.1.43 10.5.44 4.12.45   BU 1967; reb.
Davie   28.10.43 20.9.54 12.9.66

K337 *Kirkland Lake*   16.11.43 21.8.44 14.12.45   Ex-*St. Jerome*; BU 1947.
Morton   27.4.44

K669 *Lanark*   27.11.43 6.7.44 24.10.45   BU 22.5.66. Disc/reacq, reb.
CanV   10.12.43 26.4.56 16.3.65

K671 *Lauzon*   1.7.43 30.8.44 7.11.45   Ex-*Glace Bay*; BU
Davie   10.6.44 12.12.53 24.5.63   1964. Disc/reacq, reb.

K400 *Levis*   23.3.43 21.7.44 30.1.46   Break 1948.
Davie   26.11.43

K321 *New Waterford*   17.2.43 21.1.44   BU 1967.
YarrowC   3.7.43

K448 *Orkney*   19.5.43 18.4.44 22.1.46   Israeli immigrant ship *Valetta*, then
YarrowC   18.9.43   Israel Navy *Mivtakh* 1950.

K676 *Penetang*   22.9.43 19.10.44 10.11.45   Ex-*Rouyn*; RNN *Draug*
Davie   6.7.44 1.6.54   1956. Disc/reacq, reb.

K678 *Runnymede*   11.9.43 14.6.44 19.1.46   Break 1948.
CanV   27.11.43

K323 *Springhill*   3.5.43 21.3.44 1.12.45   BU 1947.
YarrowC   7.9.43

Ordered 1–2.43

Note: one source lists *Fort Etic* (Quebec) cancelled 12.43.
Cancellations of unnamed ships: nine from CanV, ten from Davie, eight from YarrowC, and two from Quebec.

K... *Alexandria*   —   Cancelled 12.43.
Montreal

K... *Alvington*   —   Cancelled 12.43.
CanV

K661 *Antigonish*   2.10.43 4.7.44 5.2.46   BU 1968. Reb 1956–7.
YarrowC   10.2.44 30.11.66

K685 *Buckingham*   11.10.43 2.11.44 16.11.45   Ex-*Royalmount*; BU 1966. Disc/reacq,
Davie   28.8.44 25.6.54 23.3.65   reb 1953–4. Used for helicopter trials 1956.

K409 *Capilano*   18.11.43 25.8.44 24.11.45   Merch 1947.
YarrowC   8.4.44

K664 *Carlplace*   30.11.43 13.12.44 13.11.45   Dominican Navy *Presidente Trujillo*
Davie   6.7.44   1946.

K410 *Coaticook*   14.6.43 25.7.44 29.11.44   Break 1949.
Davie   25.11.43

K... *Fort Erie* — (Quebec)   Cancelled 12.43.

K... *Foster*   Cancelled 12.43.
Davie

K684 *Granby*   26.11.43 11.11.44   Ex-*Victoriaville*; BU 1974.
Davie   23.6.44

K66 *Hallowell*   22.11.43 8.8.44 7.11.45   Israeli immigrant ship *Sharon* 1949,
CanV   28.3.44   Israel Navy *Misnak* 1952.

K... *Hardrock*   Cancelled 12.43
CanV

K... *Henryville*   Cancelled 12.43
CanV

K667 *Incharran*   25.10.43 18.11.44   Conv to museum ship abandoned,
Davie   6.6.44   BU 1970.

K... *Le Havre* — (Montreal)   Cancelled 12.43

K519 *Lasalle*   4.6.43 29.6.44   Break 1948.
Davie   12.11.43

K... *Lingabar*   Cancelled 12.43.
Davie

K344 *Sea Cliff*   20.7.43 26.9.44   Ex-*Megantic*; Chilean Navy
Davie   8.7.44   *Cavadonga* 1946.

K... *Megantic*   Cancelled 12.43.
Davie

K... *Merrittonia*   Cancelled 12.43.
Davie

K... *Northumberland*   Cancelled 12.43.
YarrowC

K... *Peasaquid*   Cancelled 12.43.
YarrowC

K... *Plessville*   Cancelled 12.43.
Davie

K675 *Poundmaker*   29.1.44 17.9.44 25.11.45   Peruvian Navy *Teniente Ferre* 1947.
CanV   21.4.44

K662 *Prestonian*   20.7.43 13.9.44 9.11.45   Ex-*Beauharnois*; RNN *Troll* 1956.
Davie   22.6.44 22.8.53 24.4.56   Disc, reacq, reb.

K... *Ranney Falls*   Cancelled 12.43.
Davie

K... *Rouyn*   Cancelled 12.43.
Davie

K677 *Royalmount*   17.1.44 25.8.44 17.11.45   Ex-*Alvington*, BU 1948.
CanV   15.4.44

K... *Ste Agathe*   Cancelled 12.43.
Davie

K... *St Edouard*   Cancelled 12.43.
Davie

K680 *St Pierre*   30.6.43 22.8.44 22.11.45   Peruvian Navy *Teniente Palacios* 1947.
Davie   1.12.43

K... *St Romauld*   Cancelled 12.43.
Davie

K454 *St Stephen*   5.10.43 28.7.44 22.11.45   Weather ship post-war.
YarrowC   6.2.44

K366 *Ste Therese*   18.5.43 28.5.44 22.11.45   BU 1967. Disc/reacq, reb.
Davie   16.10.43 22.1.55 30.1.67

K... *Shipton*   Cancelled 12.43.
Davie

K531 *Stone Town*   17.11.43 27.7.44 13.11.45   Briefly to have been renamed
CanV   28.3.44   *Glengarry* (1943); weather ship 1950.

K682 *Strathadam*   6.12.43 29.9.44 7.11.45   Merch conversion abandoned; Israeli
YarrowC   20.3.44   Navy *Misgav* 1950.

K683 *Sussexvale*   15.11.43 29.11.44 16.11.45   Ex-*Valdorian*; BU 1967.Disc/reacq,
Davie   12.7.44 18.3.55 30.11.66   reb.

K... *Sussexvale*   Cancelled 12.43.
Davie

K... *Tisdale*   Cancelled 12.43.
CanV

K538	*Toronto*	10.5.43	6.5.44	27.11.45	Ex-*Giffard*; RNN *Garm* 1956. Reb, not
	Davie	18.9.43	26.3.53		disc. Post-war.
K...	*Westbury*				Cancelled 12.43.
	Davie				
K...	*Westville*				Cancelled 12.43.
	Davie				
K...	*Wulastock*				Cancelled 12.43.
	YarrowC				

'Loch' Class

Starred ships had geared turbines instead of reciprocating engines.

Ordered 24.7.42					
K424	*Loch Achanalt*	14.9.43	11.8.44	6.45	RCN 1944; RNZN *Pukaki* 1948.
	Robb	23.3.44			
Ordered 28.12.42					
K432	*Loch Boisdale*	8.11.43	1.12.44		SAN *Good Hope* 1944.
	Blyth	5.7.44			
Ordered 19.1.43					
K425	*Loch Dunvegan*	29.9.43	30.6.44	21.3.47	BU 25.8.60.
	Hill	25.3.44	6.50	1952	
Ordered 25.1.43					
K426	*Loch Achray*	13.12.43	1.2.45	1947	RNZN *Kaniere* 1948.
	Smiths	7.7.44			
K601	*Loch Affric*				Cancelled 31.10.43.
	Ailsa				
K607	*Loch Clunie*				Cancelled 31.10.43.
	Ailsa				
K422	*Loch Eck*	25.10.43	7.11.44	1947	RNZN *Hawea* 1948.
	Smiths	25.4.44			
K612	*Loch Ericht*				Cancelled 31.10.43.
	Ailsa				
K390	*Loch Fada*	8.6.43	10.4.44	10.67	BU 1968.
	John Brown	14.12.43			
K617	*Loch Garve*				Cancelled 31.10.43.
	Hall Russell				
K618	*Loch Glashan*				Cancelled 31.10.43.
	Smiths				
K623	*Loch Harray*				Cancelled 31.10.43.
	Smiths				
K433	*Loch Insh*	17.11.43	30.10.44		Malaysian *Hang Tuah* 1964; mod
	Robb	10.5.44			1952–4.
K625	*Loch Katrine*	31.12.43	29.12.44	5.7.46	RNZN *Rotoiti* 1949.
	Robb	21.8.44			
K626	*Loch Ken*				Cancelled 31.10.43.
	Smiths				
K631	*Loch Linfern*				Cancelled 31.10.43.
	Smiths				
K637	*Loch Minnick*				Cancelled 31.10.43.
	Smiths				
K434	*Loch Quoich*	3.12.43	11.1.45	6.54	BU 13.11.57.
	Blyth	2.9.44			
K641	*Loch Nell*				Cancelled 31.10.43.
	Robb				
K642	*Loch Odairn*				Cancelled 31.10.43.
	Robb				
K643	*Loch Ossian*				Cancelled 31.10.43.
	Smiths				
K645	*Loch Ruthven*	4.1.44	8.10.44	24.6.46	BU 1966. Mod 1952–7.53.
	Hill	3.6.44	1953	1963	
K646	*Loch Ryan*				Cancelled 31.10.43.
	Pickersgill				
K648	*Loch Scavaig*	31.3.44	22.12.44	17.12.46	BU 5.9.59. Mod 1952.
	Hill	9.9.44	6.50	9.52	
K649	*Loch Scridain*				Cancelled 31.10.43.
	Pickersgill				
K652	*Loch Tanna*				Cancelled 31.10.43.
	Blyth				
K431	*Loch Tarbert*	30.11.43	22.2.45	5.7.46	BU 18.9.59.
	Ailsa	19.10.44			
K653	*Loch Tilt*				Cancelled 31.10.43.
	Pickersgill				
K656	*Loch Urigill*				Cancelled 31.10.43.
	Blyth				
K657	*Loch Vennacher*				Cancelled 31.10.43.
	Blyth				
K658	*Loch Veyatie*	30.4.44	13.7.46	1956	BU 12.8.65.
	Ailsa	8.10.45			
K659	*Loch Watten*				Cancelled 31.10.43.
	Blyth				

Ordered 2.2.43					
K478	*Loch Alvie*	31.8.43	21.8.44	1946	RCN 1944, ret; BU 1965. Mod
	Barclay	14.4.44	4.50	11.63	10.52–3.54
K693	*Loch Arkaig**	1.11.44	17.11.45	1952	BU 28.1.60.
	Caledon	7.6.45			
K...	*Loch Coulside*				Cancelled 31.10.43.
	Barclay				
K609	*Loch Craggie*	28.12.43	23.10.44	26.10.46	BU 25.10.63. Offered to New Zealand
	H&W	23.5.44	4.50	1953	and Portugal.
K613	*Loch Erisort*				Cancelled 31.10.43.
	Barclay				
K429	*Loch Fyne*	8.12.43	9.11.44	6.46	BU 6.8.70. Mod 1952–4. Reserve 1955,
	Burntisland	24.5.44	10.50	6.5.63	tropicalised for Gulf service 1956.
K619	*Loch Glendhu*	29.5.44	23.2.45	1954	BU 14.11.57.
	Burntisland	18.10.44			
K620	*Loch Gorm*	28.12.43	18.12.44	12.9.46	Merch 1961. Had been offered to
	H&W	8.6.44			Portugal.
K628	*Loch Killisport*	28.12.43	9.7.45	11.47	BU 3.70; mod 1953–4.
	H&W	6.7.44	4.50	4.8.65	
K437	*Loch Lomond*	7.12.43	16.11.44	1947	BU 7.10.68. Mod 1953–4.
	Caledon	19.6.44	4.50	14.12.64	
K639	*Loch More*	16.3.44	24.2.45		BU 27.8.63.
	Caledon	3.10.44			
K...	*Loch Seaforth*				Cancelled 31.10.43.
	Caledon				
K655	*Loch Tralaig**	26.6.44	4.7.45	2.53	BU 24.8.63.
	Caledon	12.2.45			
Ordered 13.2.43					
K438	*Loch Assynt*	11.2.44	2.8.45		Completed as depot ship *Derby Haven*;
	Swan Hunter	14.12.44			Iranian *Badr* 1949.
K430	*Loch Cree*	18.10.43	8.3.45		SAN *Natal* 1944.
	Swan Hunter	19.6.44			
K621	*Loch Griam*	—			Cancelled 31.10.43.
	Swan Hunter				
K629	*Loch Kirbister*	—			Cancelled 31.10.43.
	Swan Hunter				
K635	*Loch Lyon*	—			Cancelled 31.10.43.
	Swan Hunter				
K517	*Loch Morlich*	15.7.43	2.8.44		RCN 1944, ret; RNZN *Tutira* 1949.
	Swan Hunter	30.1.44			
K421	*Loch Shin*	6.9.43	10.10.44	13.9.48	RNZN *Taupo* 1948.
	Swan Hunter	23.2.44			
K654	*Loch Torridon*	2.5.44	19.10.45		Completed as sub depot ship *Woodbridge Haven* (P58); HQ 2nd M/S Sqdn in Med 1955; Minesweeper Support Ship 1960, replaced by HMS *Abdiel*; ret home 11.7.63. BU 8.65.
	Swan Hunter	13.1.45			
Ordered 6.3.43					
K391	*Loch Killin*	22.6.43	12.4.44	22.9.45	BU 24.8.60.
	Burntisland	29.11.43			
Ordered 2.5.43					
K602	*Loch Ard*	20.1.44	21.5.45		SAN *Transvaal* 1944.
	H&W	2.8.44			
K...	*Loch Awe*				Cancelled 31.10.43.
	H&W				
K...	*Loch Badcall*				Cancelled 31.10.43.
	Pickersgill				
K...	*Loch Caroy*				Cancelled 31.10.43.
	Pickersgill				
K...	*Loch Creran*				Cancelled 31.10.43.
	Smiths				
K...	*Loch Doine*				Cancelled 31.10.43.
	Smiths				
K...	*Loch Earn*				Cancelled 31.10.43.
	Hill				
K...	*Loch Enoch*				Cancelled 31.10.43.
	H&W				
K...	*Loch Eye*				Cancelled 31.10.43.
	H&W				
K...	*Loch Eynort*				Cancelled 31.10.43.
	H&W				
K...	*Loch Goil*				Cancelled 31.10.43.
	H&W				
K...	*Loch Harport*				Cancelled 31.10.43.
	Hall Russell				
K...	*Loch Hourne*				Cancelled 31.10.43.
	H&W				
K...	*Loch Inchard*				Cancelled 31.10.43.
	H&W				

Cancelled 'Loch' Class

Pennant	Name	Builder	Notes
K...	*Loch Kirkaig*	H&W	Cancelled 31.10.43.
K...	*Loch Kishorn*	Robb	Cancelled 31.10.43.
K...	*Loch Knockie*	Pickersgill	Cancelled 31.10.43.
K...	*Loch Laro*	H&W	Cancelled 31.10.43.
K...	*Loch Lurgain*	H&W	Cancelled 31.10.43.
K...	*Loch Ronald*	H&W	Cancelled 31.10.43.
K...	*Loch Sheallag*	H&W	Cancelled 31.10.43.
K...	*Loch Shiel*	H&W	Cancelled 31.10.43
K...	*Loch Skaig*	Smiths	Cancelled 31.10.43.
K...	*Loch Skerrow*	Hill	Cancelled 31.10.43.
K...	*Loch Stemster*	H&W	Cancelled 31.10.43.
K...	*Loch Stennes*	Smiths	Cancelled 31.10.43.
K...	*Loch Striven*	H&W	Cancelled 31.10.43.
K...	*Loch Sunart*	H&W	Cancelled 31.10.43.
K...	*Loch Swin*	H&W	Cancelled 31.10.43.
K...	*Loch Tummell*	H&W	Cancelled 31.10.43.
K...	*Loch Vanavie*	H&W	Cancelled 31.10.43.

Ordered 10.7.43

Pennant	Name	Builder	Notes
K...	*Loch Maberry*	Hall Russell	Cancelled 31.10.43.

'Bay' Class

Ordered 19.1.43

Pennant	Name	Builder	Dates	Completed	Disposal	Notes
K606	*Bigbury Bay*	Hall Russell	30.5.44 / 16.11.44	10.7.45	25.11.58	Ex-*Loch Carloway*; Portuguese Navy *Pacheco Pereira* 1959. F06 after 1949.

Ordered 25.1.43

Pennant	Name	Builder	Dates	Completed	Disposal	Notes
K630	*Cardigan Bay*	Robb	14.4.44 / 28.12.44	25.6.45	1.62	Ex-*Loch Laxford*; BU 5.3.62
K636	*Carnarvon Bay*	Robb	8.6.44 / 15.3.45	20.9.45	1.47 / 28.8.59.	Ex-*Loch Maddy*; BU
K644	*Cawsand Bay*	Blyth	24.4.44 / 26.2.45	13.11.45		Ex-*Loch Roan*; BU 5.9.59. Had never commissioned.
K435	*Enard Bay*	Smiths	27.5.44 / 31.10.44	4.1.46 / 12.51	1946 / 1954	Ex-*Loch Bracadale* BU 15.11.57
K611	*Herne Bay*	Smiths	7.8.44 / 15.5.45	6.6.48		Ex-*Loch Eil*; completed as surveying ship *Dampier*.
K614	*Hollesley Bay*	Smiths	27.11.44	—		Ex-*Loch Fannich*; cancelled 1945.
K423	*Largo Bay*	Pickersgill	8.2.44 / 3.10.44	26.1.46 / 2.52	1946 / 1954	Ex-*Loch Foin*; BU 11.7.58. Had been earmarked for transfer to RCN.
K427	*Luce Bay*	Pickersgill	29.4.44 / 12.4.45	10.2.49		Ex-*Loch Glass*; completed as survey ship *Dalrymple*, to Portugal as *Alfonso de Albuquerque* 1966.
K624	*Morecambe Bay*	Pickersgill	30.4.44 / 1.11.44	22.2.49	1956	Ex-*Loch Heilin*; to Portugal as *Dom Francesco de Almeida* 1961.
K627	*Mounts Bay*	Pickersgill	23.10.44 / 8.6.45	11.8.49		Ex-*Loch Kilburnie*; to Portugal as *Vasco da Gama* 1961.
K638	*Pegwell Bay*	Pickersgill	30.11.44 / 1.9.44	20.7.50		Ex-*Loch Mochrum*; completed as survey ship *Cook*.

Ordered 2.2.43

Pennant	Name	Builder	Dates	Completed	Disposal	Notes
K634	*St Austell Bay*	H&W	30.5.44 / 8.11.44	29.5.45	1957	Ex-*Loch Lyddoch*; BU 4.7.59.

Ordered 13.2.43

Pennant	Name	Builder	Dates	Completed	Disposal	Notes
K600	*St Bride's Bay*	H&W	30.5.44 / 16.1.45	15.6.45	14.12.61	Ex-*Loch Achility*; BU 3.9.62.
K604	*Start Bay*	H&W	31.8.44 / 15.2.45	15.2.45		Ex-*Loch Arklet*; BU 7.58. Had never commissioned.
K605	*Tremadoc Bay*	H&W	31.8.44 / 29.3.45	11.10.45	1951	Ex-*Loch Arnish*; BU 18.9.59.

Ordered 2.5.43

Pennant	Name	Builder	Dates	Completed	Disposal	Notes
K640	*Thurso Bay*	Hall Russell	30.9.44 / 19.10.45	23.9.49		Ex-*Loch Muick*; completed as survey ship *Owen*; BU 15.7.70.
K...	*Veryan Bay*	Hill	8.6.44 / 11.11.44	13.5.45	3.57	Ex-*Loch Swannay*; BU 1.7.59.
K633	*Whitesand Bay*	H&W	8.8.44 / 16.12.44	30.7.45	9.54 / 13.2.56.	Ex-*Loch Lubnaig*; BU
K615	*Widemouth Bay*	H&W	26.4.44 / 19.10.44	13.4.45 / 6.51	1950 / 1954	Ex-*Loch Frisa*; BU 3.11.57
K616	*Wigtown Bay*	H&W	24.10.44 / 26.4.45	19.1.46		Ex-*Loch Garasdale*; BU 4.59. Had never commissioned.

Ordered 27.12.43

Pennant	Name	Builder	Dates	Completed	Disposal	Notes
K622	*Burghead Bay*	Hill	21.9.44 / 3.3.45	20.9.45	6.8.58	Ex-*Loch Harport*; Portuguese *Alvaro Cabral* 1959.
K650	*Porlock Bay*	Hill	22.11.44 / 14.6.45	8.3.46	1949	Ex-*Loch Muick*; Finnish *Matti Kurki* 1962.

Ordered 19.1.44

Pennant	Name	Builder	Dates	Completed	Disposal	Notes
K608	*Padstow Bay*	Robb	25.9.44 / 24.8.45	11.3.46	1949	Ex-*Loch Coulside*; BU 11.8.59

Despatch Vessels (converted from 'Bay' Class)

Ordered 25.1.43

Pennant	Name	Builder	Dates	Completed	Disposal	Notes
K647	*Alert*	Blyth	28.7.44 / 10.7.45	24.10.46	18.5.64	Ex-*Dundrum Bay*; ex-*Loch Scamadale*; BU 11.71
K346	*Surprise*	Smiths	21.4.44 / 14.3.45	9.9.46	14.12.64	Ex-*Loch Carron*, ex-*Gerrans Bay*; BU 29.6.65

Type 12

Pennant	Name	Builder	Dates	Completed	Disposal	Notes
F36	*Whitby*	Cammell	30.9.52 / 2.7.54	10.7.56	12.74	FSA 01. Str 1975, BU 1979.
F63	*Scarborough*	VA Tyne	11.9.53 / 4.4.55	10.5.57	Aut1972	FSA 02. Proposed 1974 sale to Pakistan canc. BU 8.77.
F65	*Tenby*	Cammell	23.6.53 / 4.10.55	18.12.57	8.12.72	FSA 03. Proposed 1974 sale to Pakistan canc. BU 1977.
F73	*Eastbourne*	VA Tyne	13.1.54 / 29.12.55	9.1.58		FSA 04. TS 1973 (disarmed), HTS 1979, BU 7.3.85.
F43	*Torquay*	H&W	11.3.53 / 1.7.54	10.5.56	3.85	FSA 05. TS 1966–1974, then CAAIS test ship (large deckhouse aft). BU 1987.
F77	*Blackpool*	H&W	20.12.54 / 14.2.57	14.8.58		FSA 06. Lent to RNZN 16.6.66–6.71, for disposal on return. BU 5.78.

Built to Indian account:

Pennant	Name	Builder	Dates	Completed	Notes
F40	*Talwar*	Cammell	7.6.57 / 18.7.58	26.4.59	BU 1992.
F43	*Trishul*	H&W	19.2.57 / 18.6.58	13.1.60	Retired 1992.

Improved Type 12 (*Rothesay*) class

Pennant	Name	Builder	Dates	Completed	Disposal	Notes
F107	*Rothesay*	Yarrow	6.11.56 / 9.12.57	23.4.60	30.3.88	FSA 07. BU 1988.
F108	*Londonderry*	White	15.11.56 / 20.5.58	18.10.61	29.3.84	FSA 08. Converted to trials ship 1975–10.79; tests included pump jet propulsion Static TS 1984, S(T) 15.6.89.
F101	*Yarmouth*	John Brown	29.11.57 / 23.3.59	26.3.60		FSA 09. S(T) 7.87.
F103	*Lowestoft*	Stephen	19.6.58 / 23.6.60	26.9.61	1985	S(T) 16.6.86.
F111	*Otago*	Thornycroft	5.9.57 / 11.12.58	22.6.60		FSA 11; hull number indicates this ship was ordered for RN. Pennant is that used by RNZN. Stricken 1982.
F106	*Brighton*	Yarrow	23.7.57 / 30.10.59	28.9.61		FSA 12. BU 16.9.85.
F113	*Falmouth*	Swan Hunter	23.11.57 / 15.12.59	25.7.61	7.80	FSA 13. BU 1989.
F115	*Berwick*	H&W	16.6.58 / 15.12.59	1.6.61	1985	FSA 15. S(T) 9.86.
F129	*Rhyl*	Portsmouth	29.1.58 / 23.4.59	31.10.60	1983	FSA 17. S(T) 9.85.
F126	*Plymouth*	Devonport	1.7.58 / 20.7.59	11.5.61	26.4.88	FSA 18. Falklands War. Museum ship 1988.

Rothesay Class for New Zealand (ordered for New Zealand):

Pennant	Name	Builder	Dates	Completed	Notes
F148	*Taranaki*	White	27.6.58 / 19.8.59	28.3.61	Discarded 1982.

Rothesay Class for South Africa:

Pennant	Name	Builder	Dates	Completed	Notes
F145	*President Kruger*	Yarrow	6.4.60 / 21.10.60	1.10.62	C 18.2.82.
F147	*President Pretorius*	Yarrow	21.11.60 / 28.9.62	4.3.64	BU 1990.
F150	*President Steyn*	Stephen	20.5.60 / 23.11.61	26.4.63	BU 1990.

Australian Type 12 (one unnamed ship each at Cockatoo and Williamstown cancelled 1956)

F45	*Yarra*	9.4.57	27.1.61	22.11.85	BU 1985.
	Williamstown	30.9.58			
F46	*Paramatta*	3.1.57	31.1.59		BU 1991.
	Cockatoo	31.1.59			
F48	*Stuart*	20.3.59	27.6.63		BU 1991.
	Cockatoo	8.4.61			
F49	*Derwent*	16.6.59	30.4.64		Scuttled 21.12.94.
	Williamstown	17.6.61			

Leander Class
Batch I

F114	*Ajax*	12.10.59	10.12.63	31.5.85	FSA 14, ex-*Fowey*. BU 19.2.88.
	Cammell	16.8.62			
F109	*Leander*	10.4.59	27.3.63	1.8.86	FSA 16, ex-*Weymouth*. S(T) 9.89.
	H&W	28.6.61			
F104	*Dido*	2.12.59	18.9.63		FSA 19, ex-*Hastings*. RNZN *Southland*
	Yarrow	22.12.61			1983.
F127	*Penelope*	14.3.61	31.10.63	31.3.91	FSA 20, ex-*Coventry*. To Ecuador as
	VA Tyne	17.8.62			*Presidente Eloy Alfaro* 1991
F10	*Aurora*	1.6.61	9.4.64	30.4.87	FSA 21. Bought for refurbishment for
	John Brown	28.11.62			foreign sale. BU 1990.
F15	*Euryalus*	2.11.61	16.9.64	4.4.89	FSA 22. BU 1993.
	Scotts	6.6.63			
F18	*Galatea*	29.12.61	25.4.64	30.7.86	FSA 23. S(T) 21.7.88.
	Swan Hunter	23.5.63			
F28	*Cleopatra*	19.6.63	4.1.66		FSA 24, ex-*Sirius*. BU 1994.
	Devonport	25.3.64			
F38	*Arethusa*	7.9.62	24.11.65	4.4.89	FSA 25. S(T) 1991.
	White	5.11.63			
F39	*Naiad*	30.10.62	15.3.65	29.4.87	FSA 26. Explosive trials under name
	Yarrow	4.11.63			*Hultec*. S(T) 24.9.90.

Batch II

F40	*Sirius*	9.8.63	15.6.66	12.2.93	FSA 27. Str 28.2.93.
	Portsmouth	22.9.64			
F42	*Phoebe*	25.7.63	14.5.66		FSA 28. BU 1992.
	VA Tyne	19.12.64			
F45	*Minerva*	3.6.63	15.4.66	12.3.92	FSA 29. BU 1994.
	Stephens	8.7.64			
F47	*Danae*	16.12.64	7.9.67	7.91	FSA 30. To Ecuador as *Moran*
	Devonport	31.10.65			*Valverde* 1991.
F52	*Juno*	16.7.63	18.7.67		FSA 31. TS 1985, str 4.12.92. BU 1995.
	Thornycroft	24.11.65			
F56	*Argonaut*	27.11.64	17.8.67	31.3.93	FSA 32. BU.
	Hawthorn Leslie	8.2.66			

Batch III (broad-beam)

F57	*Andromeda*	25.5.66	2.12.68	7.4.93	FSA 33. Indian *Krishna* 1995.
	Portsmouth	24.5.67			
F58	*Hermione*	6.12.65	11.7.69		FSA 34. Str 26.6.92.
	Stephens	26.4.67			
F60	*Jupiter*	3.10.66	9.8.69		FSA 35. Str 30.4.92.
	Yarrow	4.9.67			
F69	*Bacchante*	27.10.66	17.10.69		FSA 36. RNZN *Wellington* 1982.
	VA Tyne	29.2.68			
F71	*Scylla*	17.5.67	12.2.70	3.12.93	FSA 37. Str 14.12.93.
	Devonport	8.8.68			
F75	*Charybdis*	27.1.67	2.6.69		FSA 38. S(T) 6.93. Str 10.91.
	H&W	28.2.68			
F12	*Achilles*	1.12.67	9.7.70	1989	FSA 39. Chilean *Ministro Zenteno* 1990.
	Yarrow	21.11.68			
F16	*Diomede*	30.1.68	2.4.71	7.7.88	FSA 40. PN *Hamsher* 1988.
	Yarrow	15.4.69			
F70	*Apollo*	1.5.69	28.5.72	8.88	FSA 41. PN *Zulfiquar* 1988 *Bravo*.
	Yarrow	15.10.70			
F72	*Ariadne*	1.11.69	10.2.72	1989	FSA 42. Chilean *General Baquedano*
	Yarrow	10.9.71			1992.

Indian Construction:
Broad-beam *Leander* (modified electronics in most ships)

F33	*Nilgiri*	10.66	3.6.72		Stricken 31.5.96.
	Mazagon	12.10.68			
F34	*Himgiri*	4.11.68	23.11.74		Stricken 6.5.05.
	Mazagon	6.5.70			
F36	*Dunagiri*	25.1.73	5.5.77		
	Mazagon	9.3.74			
F35	*Udaygiri*	14.9.70	18.2.76		
	Mazagon	24.10.72			
F37	*Taragiri*	15.10.75	16.5.80		Modified version (enlarged
	Mazagon	25.10.76			telescoping hangar).
F38	*Vindhyagiri*	5.11.76	8.7.81		Modified version (enlarged
	Mazagon	12.11.77			telescoping hangar).

Modified *Leander* (Project 16: Soviet weapons and electronics)

F20	*Godavari*	2.6.78	10.12.82	
	Mazagon	15.5.80		
F21	*Gomati*	17.8.82	10.12.85	
	Mazagon	20.3.84		
F22	*Ganga*	3.6.80	16.4.88	
	Mazagon	21.10.81		

Further modified *Leander* (Project 16A)

F31	*Bramaputra*	1989	14.4.00	
	Mazagon	29.1.94		
F37	*Betwa*	22.8.94	7.7.04	
	Mazagon	26.2.98		
F39	*Beas*	3.98	11.7.05	
	Mazagon	2002		

Leander class for New Zealand:

F55	*Waikato*	10.1.64	16.9.66	
	H&W	18.2.65		
F148	*Canterbury*	12.4.69	22.10.71	
	Yarrow	6.5.70		

Type 41

F14	*Leopard*	25.3.53	30.9.58	12.12.75	FA 01. BU 1977.
	Portsmouth	23.5.55			
F27	*Lynx*	13.8.53	14.3.57		FA 02. Bangladesh *Abu Bakr* 1982
	John Brown	12.1.55			
F31	*Panther*	20.10.55	31.3.58		FA 03. Completed for India as
	John Brown	20.10.55			*Brahmaputra*. Stricken 30.6.86.
F34	*Puma*	16.11.53	27.4.57	6.72	FA 04. BU 12.76.
	Scotts	16.11.53			
F37	*Jaguar*	2.11.53	12.12.59		FA 05. Bangladesh *Ali Haider* 1978.
	Denny	20.7.57			

Built to Indian account:

F37	*Beas*	29.11.56	24.5.60		Stricken 12.92.
	VA Tyne	9.10.58			
F38	*Betwa*	29.5.57	8.12.60		Stricken 31.12.91.
	VA Tyne	15.9.59			

Type 61

F32	*Salisbury*	23.1.52	27.2.57		FD 01. Sale to Egypt canc 1978 while
	Devonport	25.6.53			on delivery trip. 5.80 HTS Devonport.
					S(T) 9.85.
F59	*Chichester*	26.6.53	16.5.58	23.7.76	FD 02. BU 17.3.81. Converted to
	Fairfield	21.4.55			Hong Kong guardship 1973.
F99	*Lincoln*	1.6.55	7.7.60	11.76	FD 03. Sale to Egypt canc 1978. 8.79
	Fairfield	6.4.59			recomm briefly as submarine target.
					BU 1983.
F61	*Llandaff*	27.8.53	11.4.58		FD 04. Bangladesh *Omar Farooq*
	Hawthorn Leslie	30.11.55			1976. BU 4.83.

HMS *Mermaid*

F76	*Mermaid*	28.10.65	6.68	1977	Comm into RN 16.5.73, Malayan
	Yarrow	29.12.66			*Hang Tuah* 1977.

Type 81

F117	*Ashanti*	15.1.58	23.11.61	3.77	FGP 01. Fitted with VDS 1968. S(T)
	Yarrow	9.3.59			9.88
F119	*Eskimo*	22.10.58	21.2.63	1979	FGP 02. S(T) 1.86.
	White	20.3.60			
F122	*Ghurka*	3.11.58	13.2.63	28.7.80	FGP 03. Fitted with VDS 1968.
	Thornycroft	11.7.60			Recomm 24.7.82. Indonesian
					Wilhelmus Zakarias Yohannes 1984.
F124	*Zulu*	13.12.60	17.4.64	8.79	FGP 04. Recomm 9.8.82. Indonesian
	Stephens	3.7.62			*Martha Kristina Tiyahahu* 1984.
F125	*Mohawk*	23.12.60	29.11.63	15.10.79	FGP 05. BU 12.82.
	VA Barrow	5.4.62			
F131	*Nubian*	7.9.59	9.10.62	1979	FGP 06. S(T) 1987.
	Portsmouth	6.9.60			
F133	*Tartar*	22.10.59	26.2.62	12.80	FGP 07. Recomm 17.7.82. Last to
	Devonport	19.9.60			decomm originally. Decomm again
					29.3.84. Indonesian *Hasanuddin* 1984.

Type 21

F169	*Amazon*	6.11.69	11.5.74	30.9.93	PN *Babur* 1993.
	VT	26.4.71			
F170	*Antelope*	23.3.71	19.7.75		WL(B) 24.5.82.
	VT	16.3.72			
F171	*Active*	23.7.71	17.6.77		PN *Tippu Sultan*
	VT	23.11.72	1994.		
F172	*Ambuscade*	1.9.71	5.9.75	28.5.93	PN *Tariq* 1993.
	Yarrow	18.1.73			

F173	*Arrow*	28.9.72	29.7.76	2.12.93	PN *Khyber* 1993.
	Yarrow	5.2.74			
F174	*Alacrity*	5.3.73	2.7.77	9.12.93	PN *Badr* 1994.
	Yarrow	18.9.74			
F184	*Ardent*	26.2.74	13.10.77		WL(air attack) 21.5.82.
	Yarrow	9.5.75			
F185	*Avenger*	30.10.74	15.4.78		PN *Shahjahan* 1994
	Yarrow	20.11.75			

Type 22

Batch I

Ordered 8.2.74					
F88	*Broadsword*	7.2.75	3.5.79		Brazilian *Greenhalgh* 1995.
	Yarrow				
Ordered 4.9.75					
F89	*Battleaxe*	4.2.76	28.3.80		Brazilian *Dodsworth* 1996.
	Yarrow	12.5.77			
Ordered 7.9.76					
F90	*Brilliant*	25.3.77	15.5.81		Brazilian *Bosisio* 1996.
	Yarrow	15.12.78			
Ordered 21.10.77					
F91	*Brazen*	18.8.78	2.7.82		Brazilian *Rademaker* 1997.
	Yarrow	4.3.80			

Batch II

Ordered 25.4.79					
F92	*Boxer*	1.11.79	14.1.84	22.3.99	Decomm and struck 4.8.99.
	Yarrow	17.6.81			S(T) 9.04
F93	*Beaver*	20.6.80	18.12.84	5.2.99	BU; began tow to Turkey 21.2.01.
	Yarrow	8.5.82			
Ordered 27.8.81					
F94	*Brave*	5.4.82	4.7.86	1.4.99	S(T) 9.04
	Yarrow	19.11.83			
Ordered 23.2.82					
F95	*London*	7.2.83	5.6.87	11.6.99	Ex-*Bloodhound*; to Romania 2003 as
	Yarrow	27.10.84			*Regina Maria*.
Ordered 14.12.83					
F96	*Sheffield*	29.3.84	26.7.88	14.11.02	To Chile 2003 as *Almirante Williams*.
	Swan Hunter	26.3.86			
F98	*Coventry*	29.3.84	14.10.88	26.11.01	Decomm 28.2.02; to Romania 2003 as
	Swan Hunter	8.4.86			*Regele Ferdinand*.

Batch III

Ordered 14.12.83					
F99	*Cornwall*	14.12.83	23.4.88		
	Yarrow	14.10.85			
F85	*Cumberland*	12.10.84	10.6.89		
	Yarrow	21.6.86			
Ordered 28.1.85					
F86	*Campbeltown*	4.12.85	27.5.89		
	Cammell	7.10.87			
F87	*Chatham*	12.5.86	4.5.90		
	Swan Hunter	20.1.88			

Type 23

Ordered 29.10.84					
F230	*Norfolk*	19.12.85	1.6.90		To Chile 2005, delivery 2008.
	Yarrow	10.7.87			
Ordered 15.7.86					
F231	*Argyll*	20.3.87	31.5.91		
	Yarrow	8.4.89			
F229	*Lancaster*	18.12.87	9.11.91		
	Yarrow	24.5.90			
F233	*Marlborough*	22.10.87	14.6.91		To Chile 2005, delivery 2008.
	Swan Hunter	21.1.89			
Ordered 11.7.88					
F234	*Iron Duke*	12.12.88	20.5.93		
	Yarrow	2.3.91			
F235	*Monmouth*	1.6.89	24.9.93		
	Yarrow	23.11.91			
F236	*Montrose*	1.11.89	2.6.94		
	Yarrow	31.7.92			
Ordered 19.12.89					
F237	*Westminster*	18.1.91	13.5.94		
	Swan Hunter	4.4.92			
F238	*Northumberland*	4.4.91	29.11.94		
	Swan Hunter	4.4.92			
F239	*Richmond*	18.2.92	8.11.94		
	Swan Hunter	6.4.93			
Ordered 23.1.92					
F82	*Somerset*	12.10.92	20.9.96		
	Yarrow	25.6.94			
F80	*Grafton*	13.5.93	29.5.97		To Chile 2005, delivery 2008.
	Yarrow	3.12.94			
F81	*Sutherland*	14.10.93	4.7.97		
	Yarrow	9.3.96			
Ordered 28.2.96					
F78	*Kent*	16.4.97	8.6.00		
	Yarrow	27.5.98			
F79	*Portland*	14.1.98	3.5.01		
	Yarrow	15.5.99			
F83	*St Albans*	5.3.99	27.10.01		
	Yarrow	6.5.00			

Type 14

F78	*Blackwood*	14.9.53	22.8.57	1967	FSB 01. BU 1976.
	Thornycroft	4.10.55			
F80	*Duncan*	17.12.53	21.10.58		FSB 02. HTS 1971, BU 1985.
	Thornycroft	30.5.57			
F48	*Dundas*	17.10.52	9.3.56	2.78	FSB 03. BU 1983.
	White	25.9.53			
F84	*Exmouth*	24.3.54	20.12.57	2.76	FSB 04. BU 1979.
	White	16.11.55			
F51	*Grafton*	25.2.53	11.1.57	10.4.69	FSB 05. BU 14.12.71.
	White	13.9.54			
F54	*Hardy*	4.2.53	15.12.55	28.4.78	FSB 06. S(T) 7.83.
	Yarrow	25.11.53			
F85	*Keppel*	27.3.53	6.7.56	1977	FSB 07. BU 1979.
	Yarrow	31.8.54			
F88	*Malcolm*	1.2.54	12.12.57	5.71	FSB 08. BU 1973.
	Yarrow	18.10.55			
F91	*Murray*	30.11.53	5.6.56		FSB 09. BU 9.70.
	Stephens	25.2.55			
F94	*Palliser*	15.3.55	13.12.57	5.73	FSB 10. BU 27.3.83.
	Stephens	10.5.56			
F62	*Pellew*	5.11.53	26.7.56	1.4.69	FSB 11. BU 17.5.71.
	Swan Hunter	29.9.54			
F97	*Russell*	11.11.53	7.2.57		FSB 12. BU 1985.
	Swan Hunter	10.12.54			
Indian Type 14 frigates (built to Indian account):					
F49	*Khukri*	19.12.55	15.7.58		WL(T) 9.12.71.
	White	20.11.56			
F44	*Kirpan*	5.11.56	7.59		Coast Guard 1978.
	Stephen	19.8.58			
F46	*Kuthar*	19.9.57	11.59		Coast Guard 1978.
	White	14.10.58			

V. COASTAL SLOOPS

Ordered 15.12.33					
L70	*Kingfisher*	1.6.34	18.6.35		BU 1947.
	Fairfield	14.2.35			
Ordered 21.3.35					
L42	*Mallard*	12.6.35	15.7.36		BU 1947.
	Stephen	26.3.36			
L52	*Puffin*	12.6.35	26.8.36		CTL 26.3.45, BU 1947.
	Stephen	5.5.36			
Ordered 21.1.36					
L30	*Kittiwake*	7.4.36	29.4.37		Merch 1947.
	Thornycroft	30.11.36			
L06	*Sheldrake*	21.4.36	1.7.37		Merch 1946.
	Thornycroft	28.1.37			
Ordered 13.1.37					
L62	*Widgeon*	8.3.37	16.6.38		BU 25.9.47.
	Yarrow	2.2.38			
Ordered 6.4.38					
L89	*Guillemot*	22.8.38	28.10.39		BU 11.50.
	White	6.7.39			
L21	*Pintail*	22.8.38	28.11.39		WL 10.6.41.
	White	18.8.39			
L39	*Shearwater*	15.8.38	7.9.39		BU 1947.
	Denny	18.4.39			

VI. CORVETTES

'Flower' Class

Ordered 25.7.39					
M48	*Anemone*	26.10.39	12.8.40		Merch 1949.
	Blyth	22.4.40			
M86	*Arbutus*	30.11.39	12.10.40		WL(T) 5.2.42.
	Blyth	5.6.40			
M36	*Asphodel*	20.10.39	11.9.40		WL(T) 9.4.44.
	Brown	25.5.40			

Pennant	Name	Builder			Fate
M96	*Aubrieta*	Brown	27.10.39 23.12.40	5.9.40	Merch 1948.
M12	*Auricula*	Brown	25.11.39 5.3.41	14.11.40	WL(M) 6.5.42.
M25	*Azalea*	Cook	15.11.39 19.7.40	8.7.40	Merch 1946.
M66	*Begonia*	Cook	13.3.40 6.9.40	18.9.40	USN *Impulse* 1942–5.
M80	*Bluebell*	Fleming	25.10.39 16.10.40	24.4.40	WL(T) 17.2.45.
M18	*Campanula*	Fleming	26.10.39 6.9.40	23.5.40	BU 21.8.47.
M09	*Candytuft*	Grangemouth	31.10.39 16.10.40	8.7.40	USN *Tenacity* 1942–5.
M00	*Carnation*	Grangemouth	26.2.40 22.2.41	3.9.40	RNLN *Frisio* 1943–5.
M75	*Celandine*	Grangemouth	30.4.40 30.4.41	28.12.40	BU 10.48.
M36	*Clematis*	Hill	11.10.39 27.7.40	22.4.40	BU 9.49.
M94	*Columbine*	Hill	2.11.39 9.11.40	13.8.40	Merch 1949.
M45	*Convolvulus*	Hill	17.1.40 26.2.41	22.9.40	BU 5.10.47.
M32	*Coreopsis*	Inglis	19.9.39 17.8.40	23.5.40	RHN *Kreizis* 1943.
M49	*Crocus*	Inglis	26.10.39 20.10.40	26.6.40	Merch 1946.
M82	*Cyclamen*	Lewis	30.11.39 30.9.40	20.6.40	Merch 1948.
M59	*Dahlia*	Lewis	28.2.40 21.3.41	31.10.40	BU 20.10.48.
M77	*Delphinium*	Robb	31.10.39 15.11.40	6.6.40	BU 1949.
M07	*Dianella*	Lewis	8.12.39 6.1.41	3.9.40 24.6.47.	Ex-*Daffodil*; BU
M95	*Dianthus*	Robb	31.10.39 17.3.41	9.7.40	Merch 1949.
M99	*Gardenia*	Simons	20.9.39 24.5.40	10.4.40	C 9.11.42.
M16	*Geranium*	Simons	21.9.39 24.6.40	23.4.40	RDN *Thetis* 1945.
M34	*Gladiolus*	Smiths	19.10.39 6.4.40	24.1.40	WL(T) 16.10.41.
M72	*Godetia*	Smiths	4.1.40 15.7.40	8.5.40	C 6.9.40.
—	*La Bastiase*	Smiths	18.11.39 22.6.40	8.4.40	WL(M) trials 22.6.40; FN order.

Ex-French Ships:

Pennant	Name	Builder			Fate
K122	*Fleur de Lys*	Smiths	30.1.40 26.8.40	21.6.40	Ex-FN *La Dieppoise*; WL(T) 14.10.41.
K46	*La Malouine*	Smiths	13.11.39 29.7.40	21.3.40	BU 22.5.47.
K107	*Nasturtium*	Smiths	23.3.40 26.9.40	4.7.40	Ex-FN *La Paimpolaise*; merch 1948, RHN *St Lykoudis* 1950.

Ordered 31.8.39

Pennant	Name	Builder			Fate
K03	*Heliotrope*	Crown	23.10.39 12.9.40	5.6.40	USN *Surprise* 1942.
K64	*Hollyhock*	Crown	27.11.39 19.11.40	19.8.40	WL(B) 9.4.42.
K27	*Honeysuckle*	Ferguson	26.10.39 14.9.40	22.4.40	BU 11.50.
K39	*Hydrangea*	Ferguson	22.11.39 3.1.41	4.9.40	Merch 1948.
K23	*Jasmine*	Ferguson	23.12.39 16.5.41	14.1.41	Sold 11.9.48 to France.
K69	*Jonquil*	Fleming	27.12.39 21.10.40	9.7.40	Merch 1948.
K82	*Larkspur*	Fleming	26.3.40 4.1.41	5.9.40	USN *Fury* 1942.
K60	*Lavender*	Hall	30.4.40 16.5.41	27.11.40	Merch 1948.
K05	*Lobelia*	Hall Russell	27.6.40 16.7.41	15.2.41	FFN 1941–7.
K54	*Marguerite*	Hall Russell	30.12.39 20.11.40	8.7.40	Weather ship *Weather Observer* 1947.
K87	*Marigold*	Hall Russell	26.1.40 28.2.41	4.9.40	WL(T) 9.12.42.
K38	*Mignonette*	Hall Russell	15.7.40 7.5.41	28.1.41	Merch 1946.

Pennant	Name	Builder			Fate
K11	*Mimosa*	Hill	22.4.40 11.5.41	18.1.41	FFN 1941; WL(T) 9.6.42.
K65	*Myosotis*	Lewis	21.6.40 30.5.41	28.1.41	Merch 1946.
K74	*Narcissus*	Lewis	9.9.40 17.7.41	29.3.41	Merch 1946.
K19	*Nigella*	Philip	28.11.39 25.2.41	21.9.40	Merch 1947.
K61	*Penstemon*	Philip	28.11.39 31.7.41	18.1.41	Merch 1947.
K79	*Pentunia*	Robb	4.12.39 13.1.41	19.9.40	ROCN *Fu Po* 1946.
K47	*Polyanthius*	Robb	19.3.40 23.4.41	30.11.40	WL(T) 21.9.43.
K91	*Primrose*	Simons	22.9.39 15.7.40	8.5.40	Merch 1949.
K14	*Primula*	Simons	23.9.39 27.8.40	22.6.40	Merch 1946.
K97	*Salvia*	Simons	26.9.39 20.9.40	6.8.40	WL(T) 24.12.41.
K10	*Snapdragon*	Simons	27.9.39 28.10.40	3.9.40	WL(B) 19.12.42.
K41	*Sunflower*	Smiths	24.5.39 25.1.41	19.8.40	BU 8.47.

Ordered for French Navy, taken over:

Pennant	Name	Builder			Fate
K67	*Snowdrop*	Smiths	4.2.41 30.7.41	12.5.41	Merch conv abandoned 1949, BU 9.49.
K29	*Tulip*	Smiths	30.5.40 18.11.40	4.9.40	Merch 1950.
K85	*Verbena*	Smiths	29.6.40 19.12.40	1.10.40	Merch conv abandoned 1948, BU 1.10.51.
K37	*Veronica*	Smiths	9.7.40 18.2.41	17.10.40	USN *Temptress* 1942–5.
K44	*Wallflower*	Smiths	23.7.40 7.3.41	14.11.40	Merch 1949.
K98	*Zinnia*	Smiths	20.8.40 30.3.41	28.11.40	WL(T) 23.8.41.

Ordered 19.9.39

Pennant	Name	Builder			Fate
K73	*Arabis*	H&W	30.10.39 5.4.40	14.2.40	USN *Saucy* 1942, ret RN as *Snapdragon* 1945.
K28	*Calendula*	H&W	30.10.39 6.5.40	21.3.40	USN *Ready* 1942–5.
K31	*Camellia*	H&W	14.11.39 18.6.40	4.5.40	Merch 1948.
K88	*Clarkia*	H&W	30.10.39 22.4.40	7.3.40	BU 1947.
K50	*Erica*	H&W	22.2.40 9.8.40	18.6.40	WL(M) 9.2.43.
K43	*Freesia*	H&W	18.6.40 19.11.40	3.10.40	Merch 1946, wrecked 1.4.47.
K90	*Gentian*	H&W	20.4.40 20.9.40	6.8.40	BU 1947.
K22	*Gloxinia*	H&W	21.3.40 22.8.40	2.7.40	BU 15.7.47.
K15	*Heartsease*	H&W	14.11.39 4.6.40	20.4.40	Ex-*Pansy*; USN *Courage* 1942–5.
K69	*Heather*	H&W	22.5.40 1.11.40	17.9.40	BU 1947.
K24	*Hibiscus*	H&W	14.11.39 21.5.40	6.4.40	USN *Spry* 1942–5.
K84	*Hyacinth*	H&W	20.4.40 3.10.40	19.8.40	RHN *Apostolis* 1943.
K33	*Kingcup*	H&W	19.7.40 30.12.40	31.10.40	Merch 1946.
K81	*Mallow*	H&W	14.11.39 2.7.40	22.5.40	Yugoslav *Nada* 1944, REN *Partizanka* 1945, to Egypt as *El Sudan* 1948.
K76	*Orchis*	H&W	18.6.40 29.11.40	15.10.40	CTL(M) 21.8.44.
K40	*Peony*	H&W	24.2.40 2.8.40	4.6.40 1943.	RHN *Sakhtouris*
K55	*Periwinkle*	H&W	30.10.39 8.4.40	24.2.40	USN *Restless* 1942–5.
K63	*Picotee*	H&W	21.3.40 5.9.40	19.7.40	WL(T) 12.8.41.
K71	*Pimpernel*	H&W	19.7.40 30.12.40	16.11.40	BU 10.48.
K78	*Rhododendron*	H&W	22.5.40 18.10.40	2.9.40	Merch 1950.

Ordered 21.9.39

K01	*Acanthus*	21.12.39	1.10.41		RNN *Andenes* 1941–6.
	Ailsa	26.5.41			
K58	*Aconite*	25.3.40	23.7.41		FFN *Aconit* 1941–7.
	Ailsa	31.3.41			
K17	*Amaranthus*	4.5.40	12.2.41		Merch 1946.
	Fleming	17.10.40			
K51	*Rockrose*	28.10.40	4.11.41		SAN *Protea* 1947.
	Hill	26.7.41			
K04	*Saxifrage*	1.2.41	6.2.42		Merch 1947.
	Hill	24.10.41			
K08	*Spiraea*	31.5.40	22.2.41		Merch 1948.
	Inglis	31.10.40			
K20	*Starwort*	11.6.40	26.4.41		Merch 1948.
	Inglis	12.2.41			
K57	*Sundew*	4.11.40	19.9.41		FFN *Roselys* 1942–7.
	Lewis	28.5.41			
K35	*Violet*	21.3.40	3.2.41		Merch 1947.
	Simons	30.12.40			
K53	*Woodruff*	29.4.40	7.4.41		Merch 1948.
	Simons	28.2.41			

Ordered 12.12.39

K100	*Alyssum*	24.6.40	17.6.41		FFN *Alysse* 1941, WL(T) 8.2.42.
	Brown	3.3.41			
K114	*Bellwort*	17.9.40	20.11.41		Irish *Cliona* 1946.
	Brown	11.8.41			
K120	*Borage*	27.11.40	29.4.42		Irish *Macha* 1946.
	Brown	22.11.41			
K134	*Clover*	29.7.40	13.5.41		Merch 1947.
	Fleming	30.1.41			
K140	*Coltsfoot*	4.9.40	1.11.41		Merch 1947.
	Hall	12.5.41			
K183	*Coriander*	19.9.40	16.9.41		Ex-*Iris*; FFN *Commandante Detroyat* 1941.
	Hall Russell	9.6.41			
K105	*Loosestrife*	9.12.40	25.11.41		Merch 1947.
	Hall Russell	25.8.41			
K93	*Lotus*	26.5.41	23.5.42		FFN *Commandante d'Estienne d'Orves* 1942–7.
	Hill	17.1.42			
K144	*Meadowsweet*	12.8.41	8.7.42		Merch 1951.
	Hill	28.3.42			
K123	*Oxlip*	9.12.40	28.12.41		Irish *Maev* 1946.
	Inglis	28.8.41			

Ordered 15.12.39

K126	*Burdock*	13.6.40	27.3.41		BU 6.47.
	Crown	14.12.40			
K108	*Campion*	16.9.40	7.7.41		BU 20.4.47.
	Crown	20.6.41			
K130	*Lotus*	26.3.41	9.5.42		Ex-*Phlox*; merch 1947.
	Robb	16.1.42			
K111	*Pennywort*	11.3.41	5.3.42		BU 2.49.
	Inglis	18.10.41			
K137	*Pink*	20.5.41	2.7.42		CTL(T) 27.6.44, BU 1947.
	Robb	16.2.42			
K117	*Ranunculus*	10.7.40	28.7.41		FFN *Renoncule* 1941–6.
	Simons	25.6.41			
K102	*Rose*	3.9.40	31.10.41		RNN; C 26.10.44.
	Simons	22.9.41			
K128	*Samphire*	4.12.40	30.6.41		WL(T) 30.1.43.
	Smiths	14.4.41			
K142	*Stonecrop*	4.2.41	30.7.41		Merch 1947.
	Smiths	12.5.41			
K132	*Vetch*	15.3.41	11.8.41		Merch 1948.
	Smiths	27.5.41			

Ordered 8/4/40

French ships taken over by RN:

K184	*Abelia*	19.8.40	3.2.41		Merch 1948.
	H&W	28.11.40			
K185	*Alisma*	19.8.40	13.2.41		Merch 1948.
	H&W	17.12.40			
K186	*Anchusa*	17.9.40	1.3.41		Merch 1946.
	H&W	15.1.41			
K187	*Armeria*	17.9.40	28.3.41		Merch 1948.
	H&W	16.1.41			
K188	*Aster*	15.10.40	9.4.41		BU 1946.
	H&W	12.2.41			
K189	*Bergamot*	15.10.40	12.5.41		Merch 1947.
	H&W	15.2.41			

RN orders:

K192	*Bryony*	16.11.40	16.6.41		Merch 1947.
	H&W	15.3.41			
K193	*Buttercup*	17.12.40	24.4.42		RNN *Nordkyn* 1942.
	H&W	10.4.41			
K195	*Chrysanthemum*	17.12.40	26.1.42		FFN *Commandante Drogou* 1942–7.
	H&W	11.4.41			
K196	*Cowslip*	16.1.41	9.8.41		Merch conversion abandoned 1948, BU 4.49.
	H&W	28.5.41			
K197	*Egalantine*	16.1.41	27.8.41		RNN *Soroy* 1941.
	H&W	11.6.41			
K199	*Fritillary*	15.2.41	1.11.41		Merch 1947.
	H&W	22.7.41			
K200	*Genista*	15.2.41	8.12.41		Weather ship *Weather Recorder* 1947.
	H&W	24.7.41			
K190	*Vervain*	16.11.40	9.6.41		Ex-*Broom*; WL(T) 20.2.45.
	H&W	12.3.41			
K201	*Gloriosa*				Cancelled 23.1.41.
	H&W				
K202	*Harebell*				Cancelled 23.1.41.
	H&W				
K203	*Hemlock*				Cancelled 23.1.41.
	H&W				
K204	*Ivy*				Cancelled 23.1.41.
	H&W				
K205	*Ling*				Cancelled 23.1.41.
	H&W				
K206	*Marjoram*				Cancelled 23.1.41.
	H&W				

Ordered 28.6.40

K207	*Monkshood*	1.10.41	31.7.41		Merch 1948.
	Fleming	17.4.41			
K208	*Montbretia*	16.11.40	29.9.41		RNN 1941; WL(T) 18.11.42.
	Fleming	27.5.41			

Ordered 3.8.40

K212	*Hyderabad*	24.12.40	23.2.42		Ex-*Nettle*; BU 10.48.
	Hall	23.9.41			
K213	*Poppy*	6.3.41	12.5.42		Merch 1946.
	Hall	20.11.41			
K214	*Potentilla*	28.2.41	5.2.42		RNN 1942–4; BU 1946.
	Simons	18.12.41			
K211	*Snowflake*	19.5.41	2.11.41		Ex-*Zenobia*; weather ship *Weather Watcher* 1946.
	Smiths	22.8.41			
K209	*Sweetbriar*	4.4.41	8.9.41		Merch 1949.
	Smiths	30.4.41			
K210	*Thyme*	30.4.41	23.10.41		Weather ship *Weather Reporter* 1946.
	Smiths	25.7.41			

Ordered 24.8.40

K226	*Godetia*	15.1.41	26.12.41		Ex-*Dart*; BU 1947
	Crown	24.9.41			

Ordered 24.10.40

K216	*Tamarisk*	10.2.41	26.12.41		Ex *Ettrick*; RIIN *Tombazis* 1941–52.
	Fleming	28.7.41			

Ordered 29.10.40

K72	*Balsam*	16.4.41	28.11.42		Ex-*Chelmer*; BU 20.4.47.
	Brown	30.5.42			

Ordered 24.10.41

——	*Amaryllis*				Re-ordered 9.12.42 as *Allington Castle*.
	Fleming				

Ordered 8.12.41

K274	*Betony*	26.9.42	31.8.43		RIN *Sind* 1945, Thai *Prasae* 1947.
	Hall	22.4.43			

Ordered 26.2.42

K275	*Buddleia*	30.11.43	10.11.43	5.7.45	RCN *Giffard* (K402) as completed, sold 10.52 for BU.
	Hall	19.6.43			

Ordered 15.5.42

K306	*Bugloss*	26.11.42	8.11.43		RIN *Assam* 1945–8.
	Crown	21.6.43			
K307	*Bulrush*	22.2.43	8.2.44	18.7.45	RCN *Mimico* (K485) as completed, merch 1950.
	Crown	11.10.43			

Ordered 22.7.42

K385	*Arabis*	26.2.43	16.3.44		RNZN 1944–8, BU 8.51.
	Brown	28.10.43			
K348	*Burnet*	2.11.42	23.9.43		RIN *Gondwana* 1945, Thai *Bangpakong* 1947.
	Ferguson	31.5.43			
K360	*Ceanothus*	5.2.43	1.12.43	9.7.45	RCN *Forest Hill* (K486) as completed, BU 1947.
	Ferguson	30.8.43			

Ordered 25.7.42

K382	*Candytuft*	27.2.43	5.1.44	17.6.45	RCN *Longbranch* (K487) as completed, merch 1947.
	Inglis	28.9.43			
K395	*Charlock*	6.4.43	10.3.44		RIN *Mahratta* 1946.
	Ferguson	16.11.43			

In this list, reb refers to reconstruction with long forecastle etc.
Ordered 1.40 (Canadian production, initially for RN). All given to RCN.

K145 *Arrowhead*	11.4.40	15.5.41		Merch 1947.
Marine	8.8.40			
K182 *Bittersweet*	17.4.40	15.5.41		BU 11.50.
Marine	12.9.40			
K150 *Eyebright*	20.2.40	15.5.41	17.6.45	Mod 1942. Merch 1950.
CanV	22.7.40			
K194 *Fennel*	29.3.40	15.5.41	12.6.45	Mod 1942.
Marine	20.8.40			
K159 *Hepatica*	24.2.40	15.5.41	27.6.45	Mod 1943. BU 1948.
Davie	6.7.40			
K191 *Mayflower*	20.2.40	15.5.41	15.5.45	Mod 1942. BU 1949.
CanV	3.7.40			
K166 *Snowberry*	24.2.40	15.5.41	8.6.45	Mod 1942. BU 8.47.
Davie	8.8.40			
K198 *Spikenard*	24.2.40	15.5.41		WL(T) 11.2.42. Not mod.
Davie	10.8.40			
K172 *Trillium*	20.2.40	15.5.41	27.6.45	Mod 1942. Merch 1950.
CanV	26.6.40			
K155 *Windflower*	24.2.40	15.5.41		C 7.12.41. Not mod.
Davie	4.7.40			

RCN orders: Ordered 1–2.40

K129 *Agassiz*	29.4.40	23.1.41	14.6.45	BU 1946. Mod 1944.
Burrard	15.8.40			
K103 *Alberni*	19.4.40	4.2.41		WL(T) 21.8.44. No mod.
YarrowC	22.8.40			
K127 *Algoma*	18.6.40	11.7.41	6.7.45	Mod 1944. Venezuela *Constitucion*
Port Arthur	17.12.40			1946.
K148 *Amherst*	23.5.40	5.8.41	11.7.45	Mod 1943. Venezuela *Federacion* 1946.
St. John	4.12.40			
K113 *Arvida*	28.2.40	22.5.41	14.6.45	Mod 1944. Merch 1950.
Morton	21.9.40			
K147 *Baddeck*	14.8.40	18.5.41	4.7.45	Mod 1943. Merch 1946.
Davie	20.11.40			
K138 *Barrie*	4.4.40	12.5.41	26.6.45	Mod 1944. Merch 1947; Argentine
Collingwood	23.11.40			Navy *Capitan Canepa* 1957.
K165 *Battleford*	30.9.40	31.7.41	18.7.45	Mod 1944. Venezuela *Libertad* 1946.
Collingwood	15.4.41			
K149 *Brandon*	10.10.40	22.7.41	22.6.45	Mod 1942. BU 1945
Davie	29.4.41.			
K179 *Buctouche*	14.8.40	5.6.41	15.6.45	Mod 1944. BU 1949 (sold 1945).
Davie	20.11.40			
K154 *Camrose*	17.9.4	30.6.41	18.7.45	Mod 1943. BU 1947.
Marine	16.11.40			
K116 *Chambly*	20.2.40	18.12.40	20.6.45	Mod 1944. Merch 1952.
CanV	29.7.40			
K156 *Chicoutimi*	5.7.40	12.5.41	16.6.45	Not mod. BU 1946.
CanV	16.10.40			
K131 *Chilliwack*	3.7.40	8.4.41	14.7.45	Mod 1943. BU 1946.
Burrard	14.9.40			
K124 *Cobalt*	1.4.40	25.11.40	17.6.45	Mod 1944. Merch 1953.
Port Arthur	17.8.40			
K180 *Collingwood*	2.3.40	9.11.40	23.7.45	Mod 1943. BU 1950.
Collingwood	27.7.40			
K157 *Dauphin*	6.7.40	17.5.41	20.6.45	Mod 1943. Merch 1949.
CanV	24.10.40			
K104 *Dawson*	7.9.40	6.10.41	19.6.45	Mod 1944. BU 22.3.46.
Victoria	8.2.41			
K167 *Drumheller*	4.12.40	13.9.41	11.7.45	Mod 1943. BU 1949 (sold 1946).
Collingwood	5.7.41			
K177 *Dunvegan*	30.8.40	9.9.41	3.7.45	Mod 1943. Venezuela *Independencia*
Marine	11.12.40			1946.
K106 *Edmundson*	23.8.40	12.10.41	16.6.45	Mod 1943. Merch 1946.
YarrowC	22.2.41			
K163 *Galt*	27.5.40	15.5.41	21.6.45	Mod 1944. BU 1946.
Collingwood	28.12.40			
K176 *Kamloops*	29.4.40	17.3.41	27.6.45	Mod 1944. Ex-*Jasper*; BU 1945.
Victoria	7.8.40			
K171 *Kamsack*	20.11.40	4.10.41	22.7.45	Mod 1944. Ex-*Carleton*; Venezuela
Port Arthur	5.5.41			*Carabobo* 1945.
K125 *Kenogami*	20.4.40	29.6.41	9.7.45	Mod 1944. BU 1950 (sold 1.50).
Port Arthur	5.9.40			
K160 *Lethbridge*	5.8.40	25.6.41	23.7.45	Mod 1944. Merch 1952.
CanV	21.11.40			
K115 *Levis*	11.3.40	16.5.41		WL(T) 20.9.41. Not mod.
Davie	4.9.40			
K134 *Louisburg*	4.10.40	2.10.41		WL(T) 6.2.43. Not mod.
Morton	27.5.41			

K151 *Lunenburg*	28.9.40	4.12.41	23.7.45	Mod 1943. BU 1946.
	10.7.41			
K112 *Matapedia*	2.2.40	9.5.41	16.6.45	Mod 1944. BU 1950 (sold 12.50).
Morton	14.9.40			
K139 *Moncton*	17.12.40	24.4.42	12.12.45	Mod 1944. Merch 1953.
St John	11.8.41			
K164 *Moose Jaw*	12.8.40	19.6.41	8.7.45	Mod 1944. BU 1949 (sold 9.49).
Collingwood	9.4.41			
K170 *Morden*	25.10.40	6.9.41	29.6.45	Mod 1944. BU 1950 (sold 11.50).
Port Arthur	5.5.41			
K101 *Nanaimo*	27.4.40	26.4.41	28.9.45	Not mod. Merch 1953.
YarrowC	30.10.40			
K118 *Napanee*	30.3.40	12.5.41	12.7.45	Mod 1943. BU 1946.
Kingston	31.8.40			
K178 *Oakville*	21.12.40	18.11.41	2.7.48	Mod 1944. Venezuela *Patria* 1946.
Port Arthur	21.6.41			
K119 *Orillia*	4.3.40	25.11.40	2.7.45	Mod 1944. BU 1951 (sold 1.51).
Collingwood	15.9.40			
K146 *Pictou*	12.7.40	29.4.41	17.7.45	Mod 1944. Merch 1946.
Davie	5.10.41			
K161 *Prestcott*	31.8.40	26.6.41	20.7.45	Mod 1943. BU 1946.
Kingston	7.1.41			
K133 *Quesnel*	9.5.40	23.5.41	3.7.45	Mod 1943. BU 1945,
Victoria	12.11.40			
K121 *Rimouski*	12.7.40	26.4.41	24.7.45	Mod 1943. BU 12.50 (sold 12.50).
Davie	3.10.41			
K169 *Rosthern*	18.6.40	17.6.41	19.7.45	Not mod. BU 1946.
Port Arthur	30.11.40			
K181 *Sackville*	28.5.40	30.12.41	8.7.46	Mod 1944. Survey ship 1953, museum
St John	15.5.41	4.8.50		ship 1990.
K158 *Saskatoon*	9.8.40	9.6.41	25.6.45	Mod 1944. BU 1946.
CanV	6.11.40			
K13 *Shawinigan*	4.6.40	19.9.41		WL(T) 24.11.44. Mod 1944.
Davie	16.5.41			
K110 *Shediac*	5.10.40	8.7.41	28.8.45	Mod 1944. Merch 1954.
Davie	29.4.41			
K152 *Sherbrooke*	5.8.40	5.6.41	28.6.45	Mod 1944. BU 1947.
Marine	25.10.40			
K153 *Sorel*	24.8.40	19.8.41	8.6.45	Mod 1942. BU 1946.
Marine	16.11.40			
K162 *Sudbury*	25.1.41	15.10.41	28.8.45	Mod 1944. Merch 1949.
Kingston	31.5.41			
K141 *Summerside*	4.10.40	11.9.41	6.7.45	Mod 1944. BU 1946.
Morton	17.5.41			
K168 *The Pas*	7.1.41	21.10.41	24.7.45	Not mod. BU 1945.
Collingwood	16.8.41			
K174 *Trail*	20.7.40	30.4.41	17.7.45	Mod 1944. BU 1950 (sold 8.50).
Burrard	17.10.40			
K175 *Wetaskiwin*	11.4.40	17.12.40	19.6.45	Mod 1944. Ex-*Banff*; Venezuela
Burrard	18.7.40			*Victoria* 1946.
K173 *Weyburn*	21.12.40	26.11.41		WL(M) 22.2.43. Not mod.
Burrard	26.7.41			

Ordered 3.12.40

K218 *Brantford*	24.2.41	15.5.42	17.8.45	Not mod. Merch 1950.
Midland	6.9.41			
K229 *Dundas*	19.3.41	1.4.42	17.7.45	Mod 1943. BU 1945.
Victoria	23.7.41			
K220 *Midland*	24.2.41	17.11.41	1.7.45	Mod 1944. Sold 11.45 (merch?).
Midland	25.6.41			
K228 *New Westminster*	4.2.41	31.1.42	21.6.45	Mod 1943. Merch 1950.
Victoria	14.5.41			
K223 *Timmins*	14.12.40	10.2.42	15.7.45	Mod 1944. Merch 1949.
YarrowC	26.6.41			
K240 *Vancouver*	16.6.41	20.3.42	26.6.45	Mod 1943. Ex-*Kitchener*; BU 1945.
YarrowC	26.8.41			

Ordered 3.41: Long-forecastle type

K231 *Calgary*	22.3.41	16.12.41	19.6.45	BU 1946.
Marine	23.8.41			
K244 *Charlottetown*	7.6.41	13.12.41		WL(T) 11.9.42.
Kingston	10.9.41			
K245 *Fredericton*	22.3.41	8.12.41	14.7.45	Merch 1946.
Marine	2.9.41			
K237 *Halifax*	26.4.41	26.11.41	17.7.45	Merch 1945.
Halifax	4.10.41			
K225 *Kitchener*	28.8.41	28.6.42	12.7.45	Ex-*Vancouver*; BU 1949 (sold 4.49).
Marine	18.11.41			
K273 *La Malbaie*	22.3.41	28.4.42	28.6.45	Ex-*Fort William*; BU 1946.
Marine	25.10.41			
K233 *Port Arthur*	28.4.41	26.5.42	11.7.45	Ex-*Fredericton*; BU 1945.
Port Arthur	18.9.41			

No.	Name / Builder	Laid down / Launched / Completed	Fate
K234	Regina	22.3.41 22.1.42	WL(T) 8.8.44.
	Marine	14.10.41	
K242	Ville de Quebec	7.6.41 24.5.42 6.7.45	Ex-Quebec; merch 1946.
	Morton	12.11.41	
K238	Woodstock	23.5.41 1.5.42 27.1.45	Merch 1951.
	Collingwood	10.12.41	

Ordered 6.10.41 (Lend-Lease order taken over by USN)

No.	Name / Builder	Dates	Fate
K277	Comfrey	6.1.42 21.11.42	USN Action 1942.
	Collingwood	28.7.42	
K278	Cornel	6.1.42 10.12.42	USN Alacrity 1942.
	Collingwood	4.9.42	
K279	Dittany	1942 31.5.43	USN Beacon 1942.
	Collingwood	31.10.42	
K284	Flax	28.2.42 8.12.42	USN Brisk 1942.
	Kingston	15.6.42	
K285	Honesty	1942 18.5.43	USN Caprice 1942.
	Kingston	28.9.42	
K282	Linaria	1942 22.6.43	USN Clash 1942.
	Midland	18.11.42	
K287	Mandrake	11.41 6.4.43	USN Haste 1942.
	Morton	22.8.42	
K288	Milfoil	11.41 31.3.43	USN Intensity 1942.
	Morton	5.8.42	
K289	Musk	23.11.41 22.12.42	USN Might 1942.
	Morton	15.7.42	
K290	Nepeta	23.7.42 20.7.43	USN Pert 1942.
	Morton	29.11.42	
K291	Privet	14.8.42 16.8.43	USN Prudent 1942.
	Morton	4.12.42	

Ordered 6.12.41 (Lend-Lease order taken over by USN, then cancelled; served with RN)

No.	Name / Builder	Dates	Fate
K286	Rosebay	1.10.42 28.7.43	USN Splendor; canc, to RN, merch 1947.
	Kingston	11.2.43	
K280	Smilax	1942 21.6.43	USN Tact; canc; Argentine Republica 1949.
	Collingwood	24.12.42	
K281	Statice	1942 20.9.43	USN Vim; canc, merch conv canc 1951, BU.
	Collingwood	10.4.43	
K285	Willowherb	1942 1943	
	Midland	24.3.43	

Ordered 2.42

No.	Name / Builder	Dates	Fate
K15	Atholl	15.8.42 14.10.43 17.7.45	BU 1952 (sold 10.52).
	Morton	4.4.43	
K686	Fergus	10.12.43 18.11.44 14.7.45	Merch 1945.
	Collingwood	30.8.44	
K338	Lindsay	30.9.42 15.11.43 18.7.45	Merch 1946.
	Midland	4.6.43	
K401	Louisburg	11.1.43 13.12.43 25.6.45	Dominican Navy Juan Alejandro Acosta 1947.
	Morton	13.7.43	
K520	Norsyd	14.1.43 22.12.43 25.6.45	Merch 1945, Israel Navy Haganah 1950.
	Morton	31.7.43	
K339	North Bay	24.9.42 25.10.43 1.7.45	Merch 1946.
	Collingwood	27.4.43	
K340	Owen Sound	11.11.42 17.11.43 19.7.45	Merch 1946.
	Collingwood	15.6.43	
K537	Riviere du Loup	5.1.43 21.11.43 2.7.45	Dominican Juan Bautista Maggiolo 1947.
	Morton	2.7.43	

Ordered 4.42

No.	Name / Builder	Dates	Fate
K333	Cobourg	25.11.42 11.5.44 15.6.45	Merch 1945.
	Midland	14.7.43	
K335	Frontenac	25.11.42 26.10.43 22.7.45	Sold for merch 10.45.
	Kingston	2.6.43	
K687	Guelph	29.5.43 9.5.44 27.6.45	Ex-Sea Cliff; merch 1945.
	Collingwood	20.12.43	
K415	Hawkesbury	20.7.43 14.6.44 10.7.45	Merch 1950.
	Morton	16.11.43	
—	Ingersoll		Cancelled 12.43.
	Morton		
K343	St. Lambert	8.7.43 27.5.44 20.7.45	Merch 1950.
	Morton	6.11.43	
K368	Trentonian	19.2.43 1.12.43 22.2.45	WL(T) 22.2.45.
	Kingston	1.9.43	
K346	Whitby	1.4.43 6.6.44 16.7.45	Merch 1946
	Marine	18.9.43	

Ordered 6.42

No.	Name / Builder	Dates	Fate
K358	Asbestos	20.7.43 16.6.44 9/7/45	Sold to Dominican Navy 1948 but wrecked off Cuba; CTL.
	Morton	22.11.43	
K540	Beauharnois	8.11.43 25.9.44 12.7.45	Ex-Buckingham; merch 1946, Israeli Wedgewood 1950.
	Morton	11.5.44	
K332	Belleville	21.1.44 19.10.44 5.7.45	Dominican Juan Bautista Cambiaso 1947.
	Kingston	17.6.44	

No.	Name / Builder	Dates	Fate
—	Brampton		Cancelled 12.43.
	Kingston		
K440	Lachute	24.11.43 26.10.44 10.7.45	Dominican Navy Cristobal Colon 1947.
	Morton	9.6.44	
—	Listowel		Cancelled 12.43.
	—		
—	Meaford		Cancelled 12.43.
	—		
K688	Merrittonia	23.11.43 0.11.44 11.7.45	Ex-Pointe Claire; sold 16.11.45, wrecked 30.11.45.
	Morton	24.6.44	
K341	Parry Sound	11.6.43 30.8.44 10.7.45	Merch 1950.
	Marine	13.11.44	
K342	Peterborough	14.9.43 1.6.44 19.7.45	Dominican Gerardo Jansen 1947.
	Kingston	15.1.44	
—	Renfrew		Cancelled 12.43.
	—		
—	Simcoe		Cancelled 12.43.
	—		
K345	Smiths Falls	21.1.44 28.11.44 8.7.45	Merch 1945.
	Kingston	19.8.44	
K457	Stellarton	16.11.43 29.9.44 1.7.45	Chile Casma 1946.
	Morton	27.4.44	
K455	Strathroy	18.11.43 20.11.44 12.7.45	Chile Chipana 1946.
	Marine	15.6.44	
K394	Thorlock	25.9.43 13.11.44 15.7.45	Chile Papudo 1946.
	Marine	15.5.44	
K369	West York	23.7.43 6.10.44 9.7.45	Merch 1946.
	Marine	25.1.44	

Ordered 6.43: five ships, all cancelled 12.43 (not named)

'Castle' Class

Ordered 9.12.42

No.	Name / Builder	Dates	Fate
K689	Allington Castle	22.7.43 19.6.44 1947	BU 20.12.58.
	Fleming	29.2.44	

Ordered 19.12.42

No.	Name / Builder	Dates	Fate
K412	Bamborough Castle	1.7.43 30.5.44 1950	BU 22.5.59.
	Lewis	11.1.44	
K379	Caister Castle	26.8.43 29.9.44 1947	BU 3.56.
	Lewis	22.5.44 2.53 1955	
K696	Denbigh Castle	30.9.43 30.12.44	CTL(M) 13.2.45.
	Lewis	5.8.44	
K413	Farnham Castle	25.6.43 31.1.45 1947	BU 31.10.64. Had been offered to Norway.
	Crown	25.4.44	
K355	Hadleigh Castle	4.4.43 18.9.43 8.46	BU 1.59.
	Smiths	21.6.43	
K529	Hedingham Castle	2.11.43 12.5.45 8.45	Ex-Gorey Castle; BU 4.58.
	Crown	30.10.44 1946 1956	
K420	Kenilworth Castle	7.5.43 22.11.43 1948	BU 20.6.59.
	Smiths	17.8.43	
K691	Lancaster Castle	10.9.43 15.9.44 1947	BU 6.9.60. Had been offered to Norway.
	Fleming	14.4.44	
K443	Maiden Castle	43 11.44	Completed as rescue Empire Lifeguard.
	Fleming	8.6.44	
K530	Oakham Castle	30.11.43 10.12.44 12.50	Weather ship Weather Reporter 1957.
	Inglis	20.7.44	
K450	Pembroke Castle	3.6.43 29.6.44 15.2.46	RCN Tillsonburg (K496) 1944; merch 1947; ROCN Kao An 1952.
	Ferguson	12.2.44	
K695	Rayleigh Castle	1943 10.44	Completed as rescue ship Empire Rest.
	Ferguson	19.6.44	
K447	Norwich Castle	30.8.43 6.9.44 17.11.45	Ex-Totnes Castle; RCN Humberstone (K497) 1944; merch 1947.
	Inglis	12.4.44	

Ordered 19.1.43

No.	Name / Builder	Dates	Fate
K405	Alnwick Castle	12.6.43 11.11.43 1957	BU 12.58
	Brown	23.5.44	
K694	Barnard Castle	1943 1945	Completed as rescue ship Empire Shelter.
	Brown	3.10.44	
K...	Caldicot Castle		Cancelled 31.10.43.
	Brown		
K...	Dover Castle		Cancelled 31.10.43.
	Inglis		
K...	Dudley Castle		Cancelled 31.10.43.
	Inglis		
K383	Flint Castle	20.4.43 31.12.43 3.56	BU 10.7.58.
	Robb	1.9.43	
K378	Guildford Castle	25.5.43 11.3.43 15.11.45	RCN Hespeler (K489), merch 1946.
	Robb	13.11.43	
K396	Hedingham Castle	23.7.43 10.5.44 12.4.46	RCN Orangeville (K491), merch 1947, ROCN Te An 1951.
	Robb	26.1.44	
K389	Knaresborough Castle	22.4.43 5.4.44 1947	BU 16.3.56.
	Blyth	22.4.43 1952 1955	

K397	*Launceston Castle* Blyth	27.5.43 27.11.45	20.6.44 10.51	1947 11.56	BU 3.8.59.
K373	*Sandgate Castle* Smith	23.6.43 28.12.43	18.5.44	22.11.45	RCN *St Thomas* (K488), merch 1946.
K393	*Tamworth Castle* Smith	25.8.43 26.1.44	3.7.44	17.2.46	RCN *Kincardine* (K490), merch 1946.
K460	*Walmer Castle* Smith	23.9.43 10.3.44	5.9.44	16.11.45	RCN *Leaside* (K492), merch 1946.
K537	*York Castle* Ferguson	1944 20.9.44	2.45		Completed as rescue ship *Empire Comfort*.

Ordered 23.1.43

K...	*Bere Castle* Brown				Cancelled 31.10.43.
K...	*Calshot Castle* Brown				Cancelled 31.10.43.
K521	*Hever Castle* Blyth	29.6.43 24.2.44	15.8.44	21.11.45	RCN *Copper Cliff* (K495), merch 1947, PLAN 1949.
K384	*Leeds Castle* Pickersgill	22.4.43 12.10.43	15.2.44	11.56	BU 5.6.58.
K...	*Monmouth Castle* Lewis				Ex-*Peel Castle*; cancelled 31.10.43.
K693	*Morpeth Castle* Pickersgill	23.6.43 26.11.43	13.7.43	1946	BU 9.8.60.
K446	*Nunnery Castle* Pickersgill	12.8.43 26.1.44	8.10.44	15.2.46	RCN *Bowmanville* (K493), merch 1946, PLAN *Kuang Chou* 1949.
K692	*Oxford Castle* H&W	21.6.43 11.12.43	10.3.44	1946	BU 6.9.60.
K449	*Pevensey Castle* H&W	21.6.43 11.1.44	10.6.44	2.46	Weather ship *Weather Monitor* 1959.
K...	*Rhuddlan Castle* Crown				Cancelled 31.10.43.
K398	*Rising Castle* H&W	21.6.43 8.2.44	26.6.44	14.3.46	RCN *Arnprior* (K494), to Uruguay as *Montevideo* 1946.
K536	*Scarborough Castle* Fleming	1944 8.9.44	1.45		Completed as rescue ship *Empire Peacemaker*.
K453	*Sherbrooke Castle* H&W	21.6.43 24.2.44	14.7.44	8.3.46	RCN *Petrolia* (K498), merch 1946.
K...	*Thornbury Castle* Ferguson				Cancelled 31.10.43.
K399	*Tintagel Castle* Ailsa	29.4.43 13.12.43	7.4.44	8.56	BU 6.58.
K461	*Wolvesey Castle* Ailsa	1.6.43 24.2.44	15.6.44	15.2.46	RCN *Huntsville* (K499), merch 1947.

Ordered 2.2.43

K386	*Amberley Castle* Austin	31.5.43 27.11.43	24.11.43	1947	Weather ship *Weather Adviser* 1960.
K387	*Berkeley Castle* Barclay	23.4.43 19.8.43	18.11.44	1947	BU 24.2.56.
K379	*Carisbrooke Castle* Caledon	12.3.43 31.7.43	17.11.43 5.52	1947 11.56	BU 14.6.58.
K388	*Dumbarton Castle* Caledon	6.5.43 28.9.43	25.2.44	1947	BU 3.61.
K416	*Hurst Castle* Caledon	6.8.43 23.2.44	9.6.44		WL(T) 1.9.44.

Ordered 6.2.43

K362	*Portchester Castle* Swan Hunter	17.3.43 21.6.43	8.11.43 5.51	1947 11.56	BU 14.5.58.
K372	*Rushen Castle* Swan Hunter	8.4.43 16.7.43	24.2.44	7.46	Weather ship *Weather Surveyor* 1960
K374	*Shrewsbury Castle* Swan Hunter	5.5.43 16.8.44	29.4.44		RNN *Tunnsberg Castle* 1944, WL(M) 12.12.44.

Ordered 3.3.43

K...	*Appleby Castle* Austin				Cancelled 31.10.43.
K...	*Tonbridge Castle* Austin				Cancelled 31.10.43. Was to have been transferred to RCN.

Ordered 15.3.43 (construction in Canada for RN)

K...	*Avedon Castle* Kingston				Cancelled 12.43.
K...	*Barnwell Castle* Kingston				Cancelled 12.43.
K...	*Beeston Castle* Kingston				Cancelled 12.43.
K...	*Bodiam Castle* Collingwood				Cancelled 12.43.
K...	*Bolton Castle* Collingwood				Cancelled 12.43.
K...	*Bowes Castle* Kingston				Cancelled 12.43.

K...	*Bramber Castle* Collingwood				Cancelled 12.43.
K...	*Bridgnorth Castle* Collingwood				Cancelled 12.43.
K...	*Brough Castle* Collingwood				Cancelled 12.43.
K...	*Canterbury Castle* Midland				Cancelled 12.43.
K...	*Carew Castle* Collingwood				Cancelled 12.43.
K...	*Chepstow Castle* Collingwood				Cancelled 12.43.
K...	*Chester Castle* Collingwood				Cancelled 12.43.
K...	*Christchurch Castle* Midland				Cancelled 12.43.
K...	*Clare Castle* Collingwood				Cancelled 12.43.
K...	*Clavering Castle* Collingwood				Cancelled 12.43.
K...	*Clitheroe Castle* Collingwood				Cancelled 12.43.
K...	*Clun Castle* Midland				Cancelled 12.43.
K...	*Colchester Castle* Midland				Cancelled 12.43.
K527	*Coree Castle* Collingwood				Cancelled 12.43.
K528	*Cornet Castle* Collingwood				Cancelled 12.43.
K...	*Cowes Castle* Collingwood				Cancelled 12.43.
K...	*Cowling Castle* Midland				Cancelled 12.43.
K...	*Criccieth Castle* Morton				Cancelled 12.43.
K...	*Cromer Castle* Morton				Cancelled 12.43.
K...	*Devizes Castle* Kingston				Cancelled 12.43.
K...	*Dhyfe Castle* Collingwood				Cancelled 12.43.
K...	*Dunster Castle* Midland				Cancelled 12.43.
K...	*Egremont Castle* Kingston				Cancelled 12.43.
K...	*Fotheringay Castle* Morton				Cancelled 12.43.
K...	*Helmsley Castle* Morton				Cancelled 12.43.
K...	*Malling Castle* Morton				Cancelled 12.43.
K...	*Malmesbury Castle* Morton				Cancelled 12.43.
K...	*Raby Castle* Morton				Cancelled 12.43.
K...	*Trematon Castle* Morton				Cancelled 12.43.
K...	*Tutbury Castle* Morton				Cancelled 12.43.
K...	*Wigmore Castle* Midland				Cancelled 12.43.

Ordered 4.5.43.

K...	*Norwich Castle* Brown				Cancelled 31.10.43.
K...	*Oswestry Castle* Crown				Cancelled 31.10.43.
K...	*Pendennis Castle* Crown				Cancelled 31.10.43.

Ordered 10.7.43.

K...	*Alton Castle* Fleming				Cancelled 31.10.43.
K...	*Warkworth Castle* Fleming				Cancelled 31.10.43.

Index

Page references in *italics* refer to illustration captions. Ships are British unless otherwise specified.